Volume 2

THE HUMAN MOTOR

THE HUMAN MOTOR
Or the Scientific Foundations of Labour and Industry

JULES AMAR

Routledge
Taylor & Francis Group

LONDON AND NEW YORK

First published in 1920 by George Routledge & Sons, Ltd.

This edition first published in 2019
by Routledge
2 Park Square, Milton Park, Abingdon, Oxon OX14 4RN

and by Routledge
52 Vanderbilt Avenue, New York, NY 10017

Routledge is an imprint of the Taylor & Francis Group, an informa business

© 1920 Jules Amar

British Library Cataloguing in Publication Data
A catalogue record for this book is available from the British Library

ISBN: 978-0-367-02458-1 (Set)
ISBN: 978-0-429-02526-6 (Set) (ebk)
ISBN: 978-0-367-02461-1 (Volume 2) (hbk)
ISBN: 978-0-367-02462-8 (Volume 2) (pbk)
ISBN: 978-0-429-39945-9 (Volume 2) (ebk)

Publisher's Note
The publisher has gone to great lengths to ensure the quality of this reprint but points out that some imperfections in the original copies may be apparent.

Disclaimer
The publisher has made every effort to trace copyright holders and would welcome correspondence from those they have been unable to trace.

THE
HUMAN MOTOR

OR

THE SCIENTIFIC FOUNDATIONS OF LABOUR
AND INDUSTRY

BY

JULES AMAR, D.Sc.,

WITH 309 ILLUSTRATIONS AND NUMEROUS TABLES

LONDON :
GEORGE ROUTLEDGE & SONS, LTD.,
NEW YORK: E. P. DUTTON & CO.,
1920

Translated by,
Elsie P. Butterworth
and
George E. Wright

AUTHOR'S PREFACE

RECENT investigations in the comparatively new science of industrial work, and recent advances in its applications to the economic life of the community render the issue of the present work apposite.

The work of Chauveau and Taylor has awakened widespread interest. It is hoped that this volume may serve both, to guide the practical application of their researches, and also to stimulate further progress in the same field. It may also remind the student of the fact—often forgotten—that the study of human labour, and its mechanical and physiological conditions, originated in France, for as far back as the year 1785 Coulomb made the first steps by co-ordinating the physical and biological sciences.

The author has thought it well to commence this volume with a short and simple resumé of the general principles of Theoretical Mechanics which will be applied in the study of the Human Motor. Also to devote some space to the explanation of the laws of thermo-dynamics and of the Conservation of Energy. These provide us with the means by which muscular work and fatigue can be measured with an accuracy not to be found in the results obtained by the American scientists. Full and accurate references to the bibliography of the subject will also be found.

It has been, in short, the author's desire to bring together in one volume all the physical and physiological elements of industrial work. The task of presenting, in a form suitable for general reading, a subject of which the material is so scattered and complex is indeed difficult. Success would have been impossible unless due regard were given to the mechanical laws governing the movements of the human body. The nature of the living motor cannot be fully understood unless the physiological limits of normal activity are appreciated.

From these points of view, Taylor's system, which has produced so profound an effect in industry has been carefully examined.

The problem of obtaining from the workman an increased output is intimately bound up with the question of the relations of work and wages. Apart from some incidental observations this latter problem will not be dealt with herein, although, it is hoped, that sufficient evidence will be given to show both employers and employed that the scientific organisation of labour is advantageous to their joint and several interests and entails no material sacrifices or moral concessions.

The writer is well aware that there are numerous gaps in his treatment of the subject. He hopes that these lacunae may stimulate others to a more complete treatment of the subject, and he trusts that his imperfect work may receive the approbation and assistance of the leaders of scientific thought.

J. AMAR.

PUBLISHER'S PREFACE

ALTHOUGH the present work was published in France in the year 1914 it has not been possible, owing to war conditions, to present an English translation thereof until the present date.

Owing, however, to the general suspension of such experimental research as this during the war (except in regard to the application of these principles to the re-education of the disabled), the English reader will not find that the value of the book has been in any way affected by the time which has transpired between its first production and its translation.

As will be seen from his preface, M. Amar has laid special emphasis on the need for the application to the study of the Human Motor of the general principles of Mechanics. He has therefore devoted Book I. to a general exposition thereof.

The reader who is familiar with the general principles of Mechanics and Thermo-dynamics may therefore be advised to commence his reading at Book II.

It has not been thought necessary to convert metric measures into their English equivalents, since it is probable that most English workers in this field would themselves employ the C.G.S. System. Full and convenient tables of equivalents and conversion factors are, however, here provided.

G. R. & S., LTD.

TABLES FOR CONVERTING METRIC
TO ENGLISH WEIGHTS AND MEASURES

1 Millimetre = ·039 (about 1/25th) Inches.									
Millimetres ...	1	2	3	4	5	6	7	8	9
Inches	·039	·079	·118	·157	·197	·236	·278	·315	·354

1 Centimetre = ·394 (about 2/5ths) Inches.									
Centimetres ...	1	2	3	4	5	6	7	8	9
Inches	·394	·787	1·18	1·575	1·97	2·36	2·78	3·15	3·54

1 Metre = 3·281 (3 Feet 3⅜ Ins.) Feet.									
Metres	1	2	3	4	5	6	7	8	9
Feet	3·28	6·56	9·84	13·12	16·41	19·69	22·97	26·25	29·53

1 Metre = 1·094 (about 1 1/11th) Yards.									
Metres	1	2	3	4	5	6	7	8	9
Yards	1·09	2·19	3·28	4·38	5·47	6·56	7·66	8·7 5	9·84

1 Kilometre = ·6214 (about ⅝) Miles.									
Kilometres	1	2	3	4	5	6	7	8	9
Miles	·62	1·24	1·86	2·49	3·11	3·73	4·35	4·97	5·59

Table for converting Metric to English Weights and Measures

(Continued)

1 SQUARE CENTIMETRE = ·155 SQUARE INCHES.

Square Centimetres	1	2	3	4	5	6	7	8	9
Square Inches ...	·16	·31	·46	·62	·78	·93	1·08	1·24	1·39

1 SQUARE METRE = 1·196 (ABOUT 1 1/5TH) SQUARE YARDS OR 10¾ SQUARE FEET.

Square Metres...	1	2	3	4	5	6	7	8	9
Square Feet ...	10·75	21·5	32·3	43·0	63·75	64·5	75·3	86·0	96·8
Square Yards...	1·2	2·4	3·59	4·78	5·98	7·18	8·37	9·57	10·75

1 CUBIC CENTIMETRE = ·061 CUBIC INCH.

Cubic Centimetres	1	2	3	4	5	6	7	8	9
Cubic Inches ...	·061	·122	·183	·244	·305	·366	·427	·488	·549

1 CUBIC METRE = 1·31 (ABOUT 1 1/3RD) CUBIC YDS, OR 35·3 CUBIC FT.

Cubic Metres ...	1	2	3	4	5	6	7	8	9
Cubic Feet ...	35·3	70·6	105·9	141·3	176·6	211·9	247·2	282·5	317·8
Cubic Yards	1·31	2·62	3·92	5·23	6·54	7·85	9·16	10·46	11·77

1 LITRE = ·22 GALLONS.

Litres	1	2	3	4	5	6	7	8	9
Gallons	·22	·44	·66	·88	1·10	1·32	1·54	1·76	1·98

Table for converting Metric to English Weights and Measures

(Continued)

1 GRAMME = ·035 OZ.									
Grammes	1	2	3	4	5	6	7	8	9
Ounces	·035	·07	·105	·14	·175	·21	·245	·28	·32

1 KILOGRAMME = 2·205 LBS.									
Kilogrammes ...	1	2	3	4	5	6	7	8	9
Pounds	2·205	4·41	6·61	8·82	11·02	13·23	15·43	17·64	19·84

1 KILOGRAMME-METRE = 7·233 FOOT POUNDS.									
KILOGRAMMETRES	1	2	3	4	5	6	7	8	9
Foot lbs.	7·23	14·47	21·69	28·93	36·17	43·4	50·63	57·86	65·1

1 METRIC HORSE POWER (32·550 FT. LB. MIN.) = ·9863 BRITISH HORSE POWER (33·000 FT. LB. MIN.)									
Metric H.P. ...	1	2	3	4	5	6	7	8	9
British H.P. ...	·986	1·972	2·958	3·944	4·93	5·916	6·90	7·888	8·874

1 GREAT CALORIE = 3·97 BRITISH THERMAL UNITS.									
Calories	1	2	3	4	5	6	7	8	9
B. Th. U.	3·97	7·94	11·9	15·88	19·85	23·82	27·79	31·76	35·73

Table for converting Metric to English Weights and Measures
(Continued).

1 KILOGRAMME PER SQUARE CENTIMETRE = ·071 LBS. PER SQ. INCH.

Kg. per Sq. Inch	1	2	3	4	5	6	7	8	9
Lbs. per Sq. In.	·071	·142	·213	·284	·355	·426	·497	·568	·639

1 METRE PER SECOND = 2·237 MILES PER HOUR.

Metres per Sec.	1	2	3	4	5	6	7	8	9
Miles per Hour	2·24	4·48	6·72	8·96	11·2	13·44	15·68	17·92	20·16

COMPARISON OF THERMOMETERS.

C.	F.	C.	F.	C.	F.	C.	F.
100	212	69	156·2	38	100·4	7	44·6
99	210·2	68	154·4	37	98·6	6	42·8
98	208·4	67	152·6	36	96·8	5	41
97	206·5	66	150·8	35	95·	4	39·2
96	204·8	65	149	34	93·2	3	37·4
95	203	64	147·2	33	91·4	2	35·6
94	201·2	63	145·4	32	89·6	1	33·8
93	199·4	62	143·6	31	87·8	0	32
92	197·6	61	141·8	30	86		
91	195·8	60	140·	29	84·2		
90	194·	59	138·2	28	82·4	— 1	30·2
89	192·2	58	136·4	27	80·6	— 2	28·4
88	190·4	57	134·6	26	78·8	— 3	26·6
87	188·6	56	132·8	25	77	— 4	24·6
86	186·8	55	131	24	75·2	— 5	23
85	185	54	129·2	23	73·4	— 6	21·2
84	183·2	53	127·4	22	71·6	— 7	19·4
83	181·4	52	125·6	21	69·8	— 8	17·6
82	179·6	51	123·8	20	68	— 9	15·8
81	177·8	50	122	19	66·2	— 10	14
80	176	49	120·2	18	64·4	— 11	12·2
79	174·2	48	118·4	17	62·6	— 12	10·4
78	172·4	47	116·6	16	60·8	— 13	8·6
77	170·6	46	114·8	15	59	— 14	6·8
76	168·8	45	113	14	57·2	— 15	5
75	167	44	111·2	13	55·4	— 16	3·2
74	165·2	43	109·4	12	53·6	— 17	1·4
73	163·4	42	107·6	11	51·8	— 18	·4
72	161·6	41	105·8	10	50	— 19	2·2
71	159·8	40	104·	9	48·2	— 20	4
70	158	39	102·2	8	46·4		

CONTENTS

CHAP.   PAGES

BOOK I

The General Principles of Mechanics

I. STATICS AND KINETICS   –   –   –   –   1–30

II. DYNAMICS AND ENERGETICS   –   –   –   –   31–59

III. RESISTANCE OF MATERIALS—ELASTICITY—
MACHINES –   –   –   –   –   –   –   60–84

BOOK II

The Human Machine

I. THE HUMAN STRUCTURE   –   –   –   –   85–116

II. THE MUSCULAR MOTOR AND ALIMENTATION   –   117–138

III. ALIMENTATION AND THE EXPENDITURE OF
ENERGY –   –   –   –   –   –   –   139–164

BOOK III

Human Energy

I. THE LAWS OF ENERGETIC EXPENDITURE   –   165–186

II. THE YIELD OF THE HUMAN MACHINE   –   –   186–198

III. THE PHYSIOLOGICAL EFFECTS OF LABOUR-FATIGUE   199–214

BOOK IV

Man and His Environment

I. THE INTERNAL ENVIRONMENT –   –   –   –   215–226

II. THE EXTERNAL ENVIRONMENT   –   –   –   227–236

III. THE EXTERNAL ENVIRONMENT (continued)   –   237–249

IV. THE EXTERNAL ENVIRONMENT (continued)   –   250–260

CONTENTS

CHAP.   PAGES

BOOK V

Experimental Methods

I.   MEASUREMENTS AND INSTRUMENTS –   –   –   261–288

II.   MEASUREMENTS—THE DYNAMIC ELEMENTS OF
THE HUMAN MACHINE   –   –   –   –   289–307

III.   THE MEASUREMENT OF ENERGY   –   –   –   308–332

BOOK VI

Industrial Labour

I.   THE HUMAN BODY IN EQUILIBRIUM AND MOVE-
MENT—LOCOMOTION   –   –   –   –   –   333–358

II.   INDUSTRIAL LABOUR AND LOCOMOTION (*continued*)   359–391

III.   INDUSTRIAL LABOUR—TOOLS –   –   –   –   392–426

IV.   INDUSTRIAL WORK (*continued*)   –   –   –   427–461

      GENERAL CONCLUSIONS –   –   –   –   –   462–466

THE HUMAN MOTOR.

BOOK I.

GENERAL PRINCIPLES OF MECHANICS.

CHAPTER I.

1. General.—A consideration of the general laws of mechanics is an indispensable preliminary to the study of any machine (animate or inanimate). It is only thus that the problems involved in equilibrium and movement can be properly appreciated.

The subject of mechanics is generally divided under three heads :—

1. Kinetics. (The study of movement in itself).

2. Statics. (The study of the equilibrium of forces).

3. Dynamics. (The study of force in action).

Such subdivision is both simple and logical. It does not exclude consideration of all the physical properties of the bodies under study. Mechanics in the practical department, to which the term " Applied Mechanics " is given, specifically takes account of all such properties, and especially of the deformation caused by the application of forces. It further deals with the strength of materials and the limiting stresses which solid bodies can sustain.

A clear understanding of the mechanism of human activity is not possible without some general knowledge of the above laws. The writer has therefore thought it necessary to devote the earlier pages of this work to the subject of mechanics in general, both in order to give completeness to the discussion and also to save the reader the inconvenience of having frequently to refer to text-books and other works of reference.

2. (1). Kinetics.—When we see a body change its place, we say that it is moving and we imply that it has been stationary. In reality, all movement is relative and is reckoned by comparison of the body which moves, with another body, which serves as a datum.   A man walking moves, relatively to the earth surface, the earth itself being in motion.   The earth is moving relatively to the sun, while the sun also moves in space.

Let the moving body be considered as a point.   In moving, the point traces out a path which may be straight or curved. Its motion is either uniform or variable according as to whether the space passed over in equal intervals of time is the same or differs from time to time in its progress.

The unit of time being the " second," the speed in the case of uniform motion is the space traversed in one second.   Denote the speed by " v."   At the end of " t " seconds the body will have passed through a space given by the equation.

$$s = vt.$$

This is the fundamental equation for a body moving at a constant speed.

If the motion is variable the speed must increase or decrease from one moment to another.

This increase of speed is called " acceleration " and is denoted by the symbol " f."   The acceleration is the rate of change of velocity.   It may be positive if the speed increases, or negative if it decreases.

If we want to find the true speed of a moving body at any given instant we must take an infinitely short period of time and find the space traversed in this period.   Using the notation of the differential calculus, we write that the speed v.

$$v = \frac{ds}{dt}$$

i.e., the speed is the differential of space with regard to time.

In the same way the acceleration " f ", which is the *rate of change of velocity*, can be represented by the equation.

$$f = \frac{dv}{dt}$$

A simple and common case is that of uniform acceleration ; the speed increases or decreases in equal quantities in equal times.   If a body is allowed to fall, the speed is zero at the moment of release, f at the end of 1 second, and ft at the end of t seconds. The average speed then is :

$$v_m = \frac{0 + ft}{2} = \tfrac{1}{2} ft.$$

Everything happens exactly as if the body fell with a uniform movement—not varied—and at the speed v_m.   The space covered $s = v_m \times t$ will be

$$s = \tfrac{1}{2} ft \times t = \tfrac{1}{2} ft^2,$$

This formula expresses the well known law of the fall of bodies, the spaces covered being proportional to the squares of the time taken to traverse them.

So far we have been considering motion in a straight line. Similar considerations apply to motion along a curved path.

The most common example of curvilinear motion is that in which the path is the circumference of a circle. The elements of many machines, such as the arms of a windmill, waterwheels, the flywheels of engines, and the like, have this circular movement which is generally uniform.

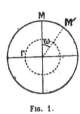

Fig. 1.

The speed of the moving body M (fig. 1), in a uniform circular motion, is the arc described in a second. If it described the whole circumference $2\pi r$ in t seconds, the speed would be $v = \dfrac{2\pi r}{t}$. If in a second it goes from M to M' the arc MM' will be $\omega r = v$. The angle ω (omega) is called the angular speed of the moving body. From the two expressions, $\dfrac{2\pi r}{t}$ and ωr, for v we deduce

$$\omega = \frac{2\pi}{t}$$

In the case of high velocity, we consider the number of revolutions per second, n times $2\pi r$.

To define the unit of speed assume a circle with a radius equal to 1, shown dotted in fig. 1. If the radius is taken as the unit of arc, it is contained 2π times in the circumference; the arc equal to the radius is called a radian and corresponds to an angle of about 57° 18′ because 180° (2 right angles) corresponds to π radians.

$$\frac{180°}{\pi} = \frac{180°}{3\cdot1416} = 57°18'.$$

Hence, given an angular speed ω (in degrees) it would be expressed in radians by the formula

$$\omega \div \frac{180}{\pi} = \frac{\omega\pi}{180}$$

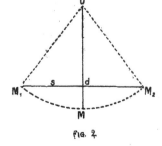

fig. 2.

Another familiar and important kind of motion is that exhibited by a pendulum or the piston of a steam engine or a tuning fork. It is called *Harmonic Motion*. In fig. 2 let OM represent a pendulum, the point of suspension being at O and the " bob " at M. If the pendulum swings to the position M, the distance $M_1d = s$, and is called the *displacement*.

A *complete oscillation* or *cycle* is performed when the pendulum has swung to an equal distance in the opposite direction to M_2 and has returned to the starting point at M. The time taken for the complete cycle is known as the period denoted " T." The *frequency* is the number of such cycles per second denoted " N."

In fig. 3 we see that the displacement $s = OM_1 \times \sin MOM_1$. Denote the length of the pendulum, which is the radius of the arc of the circle described thereby as " a." We have then :—

$$s = a \sin MOM_1 \text{ (fig. 3)}.$$

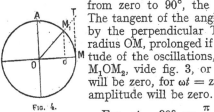

Fig. 3.

Taking ω as the angular speed of the oscillating point, the angle MOM_1 will be equal to ωt at the end of the time t.

Then :— $s = a \sin \omega t.$

Assume the circle in fig. 4 to have unit radius, then the sine of an angle MOM_1 is the perpendicular M_1d, its cosine is Od; and we see that the sine takes values from O to 1, as the angle varies from zero to 90°, the cosine varies inversely. The tangent of the angle MOM_1 is represented by the perpendicular TM on OM, which cuts radius OM, prolonged if necessary. The amplitude of the oscillations, as shown by the angle M_1OM_2, vide fig. 3, or the demi-amplitude ωt will be zero, for ωt = zero, sin $\omega t = o$, and the amplitude will be zero.

Fig. 4.

For $\omega t = 90°$ or $\dfrac{\pi}{2}$ we have sin $\omega t = 1$; therefore $s = a$. It is to be noticed that at the end of the period, T, the moving body has come back to its original position, having traversed 360° or 2π ; therefore $\omega t = 2\pi$, or $t = \dfrac{2\pi}{\omega}$; the duration of t is thus equal to T ; therefore $T = \dfrac{2\pi}{\omega}$. There are also N double oscillations or N periods per second ; thus $N \times T = 1$, or $N = \dfrac{1}{T} = \dfrac{\omega}{2\pi}$, or again $\omega = \dfrac{2\pi}{T}$. These simple calculations show that, finally, the value ωt is expressed by : $\omega t = \dfrac{2\pi t}{T}$; so that the law of a harmonic motion becomes :—

$$s = a \sin \frac{2\pi t}{T}$$

The instantaneous velocity attains its greatest value at the moment of departure and diminishes to the end of the swing ; from M_1 to M it accelerates gradually and decreases progressively from M to M_2. It follows that the acceleration always tends to bring the moving body back to its initial position M at the centre of the oscillation.

Using the expression $\dfrac{ds}{dt}$, for the instantaneous velocity v we have :—

$$v = \frac{2\pi a}{T} \cos 2\pi \frac{t}{T}$$

its value at departure is the maximum, because $\omega t = 0$, $\cos 2\pi \dfrac{t}{T} = 1$; therefore $v = \dfrac{2\pi a}{T}$

The expression $\dfrac{dv}{dt}$ gives for the acceleration, the formula

$$f = - \frac{4\pi^2 a}{T^2} \sin 2\pi \frac{t}{T}$$

Familiar examples of these periodic movements are afforded by the moving elements of the plane, the saw, the piston, etc. Thus with the sawyer and the filer, the speed of the tool falls to zero at the end of each stroke. Whatever may be the movement, it obeys a more or less complex law connecting space and time, the only elements considered in kinetics. In short, every movement can be expressed by an equation.

3. Representation and Registration of Movement.—Given the path of a moving point, we know that it can be either rectilineal or curvilinear (R or C). In the former case, the straight line represents a path of movement, XX', the motive power being able to cause movement either in the direction XX' or in the opposite direction X'X. A rectilineal trajectory has therefore a path and two opposite directions of movement (fig. 5).

FIG. 5.

If the speed is MM' in a second it can be represented by the straight line MM', provided that the point has moved from M to M' with a uniform speed.

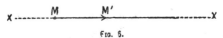

Fig. 6.

The line MM' is called a " vector " ; M is its origin, M' its extremity (it is marked with an arrow). Hence the vector MM' (from the Latin : *vehere*, to carry) represents in magnitude,. direction, and sense the speed of the moving point. If the speed is reversed in direction, the vector will have its origin at M', and its extremity at M.

In the case of a curvilinear movement, fig. 7, the moving point passes from M to M' in the time *t*. The speed of the point when in the position M may thus be regarded as its speed when moving along an extremely short chord (shown in dotted lines). This chord, when produced is, in fact, the tangent to the curved path at the position M and the vector representing the velocity at this position will be the tangent MV.

Similarly the velocity at another position, M", will be represented by a vector M"V", which is a tangent to the path of the moving point at the position M".

If the motion of the point is at uniform velocity,

Vector MV = vector M"V".

In the case of variable velocity the vectors MV and M"V" will be of different lengths proportional to the velocities of the point at M and M" respectively. When a point or body is moving along a curvilinear path the vectors representing its velocity at different stages of its movement are always tangential to the path and the actual instantaneous velocities of the point are also along tangents, as will be seen when a stone describing a circular path in a sling is released, the stone flying off at a tangent to the path.

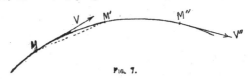

Fig. 7.

In the same way, acceleration can be represented as a vector; we shall come across other examples later. The advantage of this method of representation is, that it is capable of the widest application. Suppose a moving point takes a direction AB in relation to a line XX'. If it remains in the same plane as the two lines, its speed for example, will be MV along one of them, but in relation to the other it will be the projection MV of MV. It will be understood, without further explanation that the projection can be made by dropping a line through V perpendicular to XX' (fig. 8).

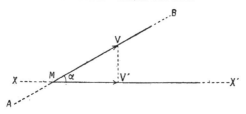

FIG. 8.

Calling the angle between the two directions α, we have

$$MV' = MV \cos \alpha \; ;$$

this angle is said to be a directing cosine of MV.

More generally, the moving point goes from M to M′ following the diagonal of a cube or parallelopiped (fig. 9) ; we want to know its speed in relation to the three dimensions of the figure, OX, OY, OZ. For this it is necessary to project MM′ by two lines parallel to OZY, which will give mm' and by two lines parallel to ZBC which will give $m_1m'_1$, and lastly by two lines parallel to BYD, which gives $m_2m'_2$. If, therefore, the speed of the given vector is MM′, we can easily calculate the resolved speed along the three rectangular axes. If we call the directing cosines of the vector MM^1 α, β, γ we shall have $mm' = MM' \cos \alpha$, $m_1m'_1 = MM' \cos \beta$, $m_2m'_2 = MM' \cos \gamma$.

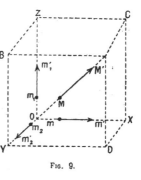

FIG. 9.

4. Equations and Diagrams.—Any movement can be defined by an equation ; thus a simple harmonic motion is :—

$$s = a . \sin 2\pi \frac{t}{T} ,$$

A rectilineal movement with uniform acceleration is :—

$$s = \tfrac{1}{2} ft^2,$$

or movement at constant velocity is :

$$s = vt.$$

Motion can also be shown by a diagram or graph. Let there be two lines, OX and OY, at right angles to one another, the line OX is termed the abscissa and the line OY the ordinate ; they are both called axes of co-ordinates and the point O is their origin (fig. 10). If we plot time as abscissæ, that is to say, the values of t from zero to T (which is the period), and the corresponding values of the displacement as ordinates, we shall have the curve OT. If $t = 0$, then $s = 0$.

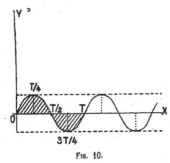

T/4
T/2 T
3T/4

Fig. 10.

If $t = \dfrac{T}{4}$, we shall have $s = a$;

if $t = \tfrac{1}{2}\,T$, $s = 0$, and so on. The curve is repeated periodically like the movement, and is called "sinusoidal." Thus the movemen that has for its equation

$s = a \sin 2\pi \dfrac{t}{T}$ is shown by the

diagram above ; there we see clearly the amplitude and the period of the movement, and we can ascertain the character of the oscillations.

Let us take a simple rule, that of the movement

$$s = vt.$$

The moving point occupies the two positions M and M' in the time t and t'. Take the lengths OP and OP' proportional to the

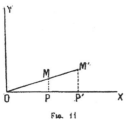

Fig. 11

time on the line of the abscissæ, and the lengths PM and P'M' (fig. 11). proportional to the spaces traversed, on the axes of the ordinates. The line OMM' will give the diagram or the curve of the movement. Knowing the equation of a movement it will always be possible to represent it by a graph. For this squared paper should be used. Generally, in equations analogous to $s = vt$, there are two variables, s and t, space and time, that is to say, y and x. Their relation constitutes the law of the phenomenon considered. Thus the height p of a barometer diminishes in proportion as a mountain is climbed. The variation of one of the heights determines that of the other ; from this is derived the term "variable." Therefore, if one of the variables is known, owing to their relation, the value of the other can be calculated. The known quantity is described as the independent variable and a function f obtained therefrom. There can be several independent variables. For example, the barometric height is a function of the height of the ascent h, and of the temperature T of the air, etc.

We write :— $s = f\,(t)$,
$p = f\,(h,\ T)\ \dots,$

to designate the above-mentioned functions.

But when there are two independent variables, we take three axes of rectangular co-ordinates to represent the variation of the function. We shall not insist upon this complex method, but shall say that, to find the law of a phenomenon, we must deduce, if possible, a formula, which will satisfy all the values of the independent variable x and its function y, obtained by experiment.

Thus, let us write $y = f(x)$ as the law of the propagation of light, x being the distance and y the quantity of light r~~~~~~~ on a plane surface. Experience gives

At a distance 1, a quantity of light ... 1

,, ,, 2, ,, ,, ... $\frac{1}{4} = \left(\frac{1}{2}\right)^2$

,, ,, 3, ,, ,, ... $\frac{1}{9} = \left(\frac{1}{3}\right)^2$

. . . . . .

There is no doubt, therefore, that y is the inverse of the square

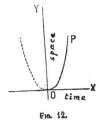

Fig. 12.

of x, or that $y = \dfrac{1}{x^2}$

$\dfrac{1}{x^2}$ is the form of the function desired.

In the same way, in the case of falling bodies, $y = \frac{1}{2}ft^2$. The diagram given by this equation is an arc of parabola OP passing through the origin (fig. 12), which demonstrates to the eye the more rapid increase of space than of time.

5. Graphic Method.—Instead of making graphs from the results of experiments, a method has been devised by which they are directly traced by the moving point. Let us take again as an example the fall of a body, and take a registering point to which is attached a piece of lead, which hangs in front of a cylinder covered with paper. The cylinder can turn on its own axis. Let us suppose it stationary, and let the tracing point fall from M to M′; we note the duration t, and the space traversed s = MM′; which tells us nothing of the variation of space in relation to time (fig. 13); but let us turn the cylinder on its axis by a clockwork movement at a known and steady speed; we shall have, in developing the graph on paper (fig. 14) the spaces traversed in equal times. In short, the times, 1, 2, 3 ... seconds will be abscissæ, the

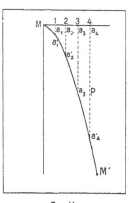

Fig. 14

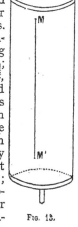

Fig. 13.

spaces a_1 a'_1, a_2a' will be ordinates ; and we shall find that
the spaces have increased as the square of the time. The curve
described will be an arc of parabola MM′.   In the same way if
we attach a style to a vibrating tuning-fork, the point will trace
a sinusoidal curve (fig. 15) on a plate covered with soot.

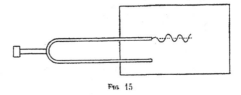

Fɪɢ 15

Such is the principle of the graphic method of direct representation used for the first time by General Morin at the suggestion
of Poncelet, and carried to its highest degree of perfection by
Marey.

The physiologist Marey (1830–1904) gave it a more practicable
form, utilizing transmission by air ; he invented for this purpose
the "tambour" which bears his name ; it is a metallic vessel

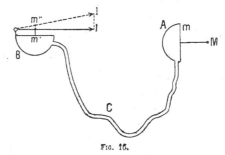

Fɪɢ. 16.

closed by a membrane of indiarubber m.   The moving body M
is joined to the centre of that membrane, which it either pushes
or pulls according to the direction of its movement ; the compressions and expansions of air produced in the vessel A (fig. 16)
are transmitted by an indiarubber tube to another tambour B,
to which a style is attached at the middle of the diaphragm m'.
Thus all the movements of the point M are transmitted to the
point l, and can be recorded on a cylinder or a revolving slab.

The receiving tambour B can always be employed in conjunction with a transmitting tambour A adapted to the nature of
the movement.   Also, by modifying the length of the style,
slight movements can be magnified.   It is easily seen that a
small displacement at m' would be expressed by the length 1,1′
(see *Methods*, Book v., § 195).

6. Photography has resolved in a most striking and beautiful way the problems of kinetics. The instantaneous photograph has already made it possible to take and fix on the sensitive film the positions of a moving point or body from one moment to another. Even this is too slow, however ; Muybridge and Marey had recourse therefore to chronophotography ; its actual principle being that the sensitive film unrolls itself at a known speed and by an arrangement of shutters, which mask and un-mask the object rapidly, a series of exposures at very close intervals can be taken. The instantaneous shutters only allow, therefore, a photo-chemical action of a very short duration, for the sensitiveness of gelatine-bromide is such that an exposure of $\frac{1}{100000}$ of a second suffices in sunlight.

In practice $\frac{1}{500}$ of a second exposure is not exceeded. The film advances at each closing of the shutter, and thus we get a large number of images in series at equal intervals.

Marey, with his chronophotograph, obtained pictures 9 centi-metres square. To-day 200 photographs can be taken in a second. If a moving body is to be photographed, the initial position of it is fixed in relation to a datum line, and we place on the same diagram copies of the various photo-graphs joined together to form a series. The various positions of the same part of a body in relation to time can then be followed.

Instead of the moving film, Marey, following Janssen, employed the fixed plate ; in those circumstances, he could only take a few pictures, and the body could not have a large surface in order to avoid super-position When the object is large (a galloping horse or a man jumping) certain points or lines are emphasised by making them brilliant, the subject being black or draped in black velvet and moving in front of a black background.

For examples white sticks or stripes (fig. 17) will indicate the spine, the line that joins the shoulders and that which joins the hips. In the Prince's Park, where Marey in-stalled a laboratory, the subjects passed, on a track of blackened stones, before the opening of a shed of which the walls and floor were

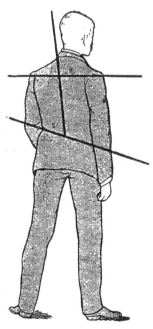

Fig. 17.

also blackened, and of which the the background was hung with black velvet. L. Soret placed little incandescent lamps on the head and feet and photographed by these means the chorographic movements. The American, Fred Colvin, attached a ring with an electric torch to the index finger of a workman. The trajectory of a moving body may thus be obtained and a general view of the movement realized.

This method of points and lines constitutes geometrical chronophotography. It has been employed in the analytical study of animal locomotion, the movement of projectiles, etc. The employment of films permits the exhibition of various pictures at a speed which, if they are projected, synthetises them to the eye, provided that the retained impression lasts $\frac{1}{20}$ of a second : this is the principle of cinematography ([1])

7. Movements of Bodies.—Natural bodies are systems not material points ; they are assumed, for simplification, to be indeformable, and their dimensions to remain invariable ; in reality, perfect solids do not exist, as they become more or less self-deformed. However, the movements of a solid body are as follows :—

1. MOVEMENTS OF TRANSLATION.—The body is moved without turning, each of the straight lines thereof remaining parallel. Such a movement is generally attained by the use of guides.

2. MOVEMENTS OF ROTATION.—Here the body revolves on a straight line, called the axis of rotation, and each point of the body has the same angular speed of rotation. The movements of rotation take place around horizontal or vertical axes supported by pivots or bearings ; if a complete revolution is not required, hinges are used as with doors, lids of boxes, etc.

3. HELICOIDAL MOVEMENTS.—In this case the body turns round the axis, at the same time being displaced along the length of the axis ; there is rotation and translation. The rotation may be in either direction (*vide* fig. 18). Either from left to right (*dextrorsum helix*) or from right to left (*sinistrorsum helix*).

The first type of helix, the right-handed, is the more common. The vertical distance *ab* between two revolutions of a helix is called the pitch.

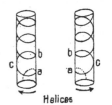

Helices

dextrorsum   sinistrorsum

Fig. 18.

([1]) See J. L. Breton, *La Chronophotographie* (in *Rev. Scient. et Indust.*, 1897, p. 179) ; Marey, *La Chronophotographie*, 1899 ; Karl Marbe, *Theorie der Kinematographischen Projectionen*, Leipzig, 1910.

8. Composition of Movements.—A point, or a material system, can have various movements : in that case it is possible to compose them on the principle of a parallelogram. Thus if a piece of metal is let fall from a boat it will fall vertically from M to M' ; if the boat is moving so that it reaches first the point M_1 in the same time, the piece of metal will reach the point M'_1, having followed the diagonal of the parallelogram $MM_1 M'M'_1$ (fig. 19). From this can be determined the resultant of any two vectors expressing speed, acceleration, etc.

Fig. 19.

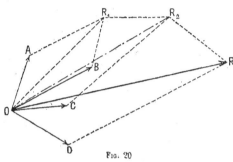

Fig. 20

We may have 3, 4 or more movements or vectors to deal with. It is just as simple to get the resultant of the first two with the third, this new resultant with the fourth, and so on until the final resultant OR is obtained (fig. 20).

Conversely, two directions OX and OY being given, a movement or a vector can be resolved in either of these two directions as shown in fig. 21.

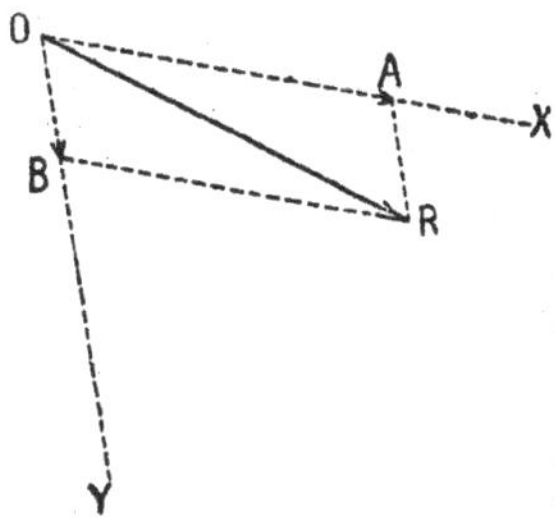

Generally a given vector can be resolved in the three dimensions of space (see § 3).

Thus vectors of speeds and accelerations are composed and resolved in the same way as movements.

The vectors representing movements of rotation are composed in the same way. We have seen that a uniform rotation and translation combined produces helicoidal movement (§ 7). If, however, the motion is compounded of rotation around an axis and translation in a direction at right angles to that axis, as in fig. 22, where the circle O rolls

Fig. 21.

along the straight line X X′, any point M in the circumference of that circle traces out a curve ABD, which is called a cycloid. Any point on the wheel of a vehicle running on a level surface describes this curve.

The line X X′ on which O rolls is called the base.

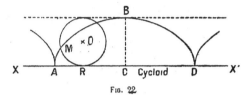

FIG. 22.

The curve is repeated after the circle has made a complete revolution as shown at A and D.

If, instead of the base being a straight line, it is itself the circ-ference of a circle, two other varieties of the cycloid are produced. These are called the Epicycloid or the Hypocycloid according as the generating circle O rolls outside or inside the base circle. These two curves are shown in figs. 23 and 24 respectively.

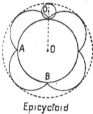

Epicycloid

FIG 23.

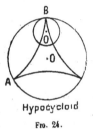

Hypocycloid

FIG. 24.

It is to be noted also that in a cycloid the position of the point M is given by the tangent of the curve at that point, MT ; the normal MR of that tangent will cut the diameter RR′, pendicular to the base, at a point R, which is the point of contact, between the circle and the base. In short, the different positions of M might be considered as the result of the rotations round the points R_1, R_2 . . . thus determined, these points being called instantaneous centres of rotation (fig. 25).

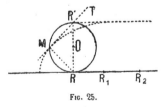

FIG. 25.

Generally speaking, every figure moving in its plane can pass from a position (1) to a position (2) by means of a rotation round an instantaneous centre. The intersection of the perpendiculars to the paths traversed furnish that centre. Let the straight line, AB, move to A'B' (fig. 26). The paths are AA' and BB', and the perpendiculars drawn from their centres intersect at the centre of rotation R. If the final position (2) is such that A'B' is parallel to AB, the perpendiculars of the trajectories will also be parallel ; and the centre of rotation will be at infinity ; so that a rotation in these conditions is equivalent a translation from AB to A'B' (fig. 27).

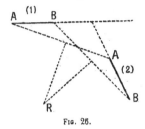 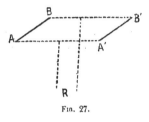

Fig. 26.   Fig. 27.

The example of the cycloid, in which continuous displacement brings into existence successive centres of rotation, justifies the name of instantaneous centre.

Finally, if one considers a solid as a pile of plane figures, it will be understood that by a similar rotation, the whole solid can pass from one position to another, all the centres of rotation being on the same line called the instantaneous axis of rotation. As is evident, that instantaneous axis may be at infinity, in which case there is a translation of the solid. In general it may be said that any movement of a solid in space can always be effected by translation, followed by a rotation ; as in the case of a helicoidal movement (§ 7) such as a screw being turned in its nut.

9. Jointed Systems.—To transform a movement of one nature into another, we have recourse to jointed systems. It is sufficient to mention the example of the crank which transforms a reciprocating rectilineal movement into a continuous circular movement, and *vice versa*. The rotation is produced round the axis O (fig. 28) by the crank OM jointed to the connecting rod MC, which gives a reciprocating movement to the body CD. It is easily seen that the normals at M and C give the position R of the instantaneous centre of the

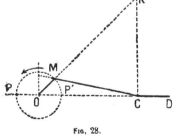

Fig. 28.

rotation ; also, if CD transmits the movement to OM, the point M at P or P′ will be in the same straight line with CD and could not pass those two positions, called dead points, except by virtue of an acquired speed because at these points, the speed would otherwise be non-existant.

10. Time.—We have said that kinetics is the study of movement, that is to say, of space and time, from which results the idea of speed. The unit of time, the second, is too long a period for the analytic study of movement. Therefore both cinematography and physiology have to employ means to register intervals of time of $\frac{1}{1000}$ of a second and sometimes—but rarely—of $\frac{1}{10000}$ of a second. These will be described later on (*Methods*, Book v., § 198).

11. The Study of Forces.—Movement is the only phenomenon which can be understood by observation ; it can be studied, and its laws determined without having recourse to any other hypothesis. As for the fundamental cause of movement, it appears to be a question of metaphysics, rather than of science. When, however, we are dealing with a point or a material system, the immediate cause which produces the movement is called force ; and when the movement is uniform it is again force which can modify the motion. In fact, the given body would remain stationary, or in its uniform movement, if it were not subjected to some other exterior action or force. It would persist in inaction through what is called inertia.

Therefore the principle of inertia introduces—but not necessarily—the idea of force.

We say : not necessarily, because eminent mathematicians have been able to dispense with it in all the developments of mechanical laws. For instance, Kirchhoff in 1877, and Hertz, in 1894. Carnot wrote even in 1803, " What can be understood, in the precise language of mathematics by a force, that is to say, by a cause double or triple of another ? . . . . Are the causes, the will or the physical constitution of a man or an animal, which by its action, gives birth to movement ?—But what is a will double or triple of another will ? " [1]

An ever-present example of force is given by the action of the earth on the bodies on its surface, the force of gravity ; bodies are drawn by the earth and fall towards it vertically by a uniformly accelerated movement, by virtue of a special force ; their acceleration is constant in the same place ; it is represented by the letter g, and it is about equivalent to 9.81_m, that is to say, the acceleration of a falling body is 9.81_m at the end of a second.

[1] Lazare Carnot, *Principes Fondamentaux de l'Equilibre et du Mouvement*, 1803 ; Preface, p. x.

Instead of $s = \frac{1}{2}ft^2$, we write $s = \frac{1}{2}gt^2$. A body placed on a table exerts pressure by reason of gravity ; a hand that pushes an obstacle exerts pressure, or, rather, effort. It would seem that the idea of force is derived unconsciously from the sensation of muscular effort, whether in the case of traction of pressure, of the extension of a piece of elastic, of the flexion of a stick, in short, of all sorts of deformations. Force and deformation are really cause and effect, and one serves as a measure of the other ; the measurement of forces or dynamometry is founded on the deformation of springs (see *Methods*, § 205).

The force of gravity exists between the stars in the universe and has received the name of universal attraction or gravitation on the earth. The value of the acceleration g diminishes with altitude and increases in the opposite direction ; but these variations are of practically no account in the cases we are considering. As for the origin of universal force, there are speculations which favour a theory of electric attraction ; perhaps the attraction called chemical affinity may be referred to the same theory. We shall see elsewhere to what hypothesis the origin of muscular force is attributed (§ 345).

Force is a calculable quantity, a vector ; it possesses sense, direction, and magnitude, besides having a point of application on the body on which it acts. All that has been said on the subject of vectors applies strictly to forces.

12. Composition & Resolution of Forces.— Two forces F_1 and F_2, are composed on the principle of a parallelogram (§ 8), and have a resultant R (fig. 29) ; the vectors F_1, F_2 and R measure the composing and resultant intensities. There is an example of that composition in the tow rope on the bow of a boat, a horse being on either bank and the boat advancing in the direction of the stream.

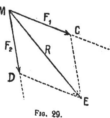

Fig. 29.

The magnitude or intensity of R is easily calculated. In the triangle MCE, $CE = F_2$ and $R^2 = F_1^2 + F_2^2 - 2F_1F_2 \cos \overset{\wedge}{MCE}$.

Therefore the angles at C and M are supplementary (making together 180°), from which it follows that the positive cosine of one is equal to the negative cosine of the other.

Thus $- \cos \overset{\wedge}{MCE} = + \cos \overset{\frown}{CMD} = + \cos \overset{\frown}{F_1, F_2}$. from which we get finally

$$R^2 = F_1^2 + F_2^2 + 2F_1F_2 \cos \overset{\frown}{F_1, F_2}.$$

So that, knowing the two forces and the angle which they form, one can deduce the intensity of the resultant.

When these forces are at right angles

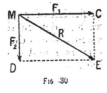

F₁G. 30

$\cos F_1, F_2 = \cos 90° = 0$;
and it follows that
$R^2 = F_1^2 + F_2^2$; vide fig. 30.

In the same way three or more forces can be composed and their resultant calculated.

Conversely, a force, R, being given, it can be resolved into two, or more forces. Two, on the principle of the parallelogram Three, on that of a parallelopiped (§ 8); if there are more than three directions, the problem is indeterminate. Generally, the method of decomposition is that of three rectangular axes. Let F_1, F_2, F_3, be the three forces to be determined along the axes X, Y, and Z, and R the known force (fig. 31).

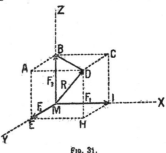

F₁G. 31.

By means of projecting planes, we form the parallelopiped of ABCDEMHI, which will give the desired forces the intensities F_1, F_2, F_3.

Notice that in the right angled triangle BMD :—
$$\overline{MD^2} = \overline{BM^2} + \overline{BD^2};$$
and in the right angled triangle BDC, we have ·
$$\overline{BD^2} = \overline{BC^2} + \overline{CD^2}.$$
Therefore
$$\overline{MD^2} = \overline{BM^2} + \overline{BC^2} + \overline{CD^2},$$
that is to say, that the square of the resultant is equal to the sum of the squares of the components : thus :
$$R^2 = F_1^2 + F_2^2 + F_3^2,$$
or more generally
$$R^2 = X^2 + Y^2 + Z^2.$$
We also know that the directing cosines (§ 3) can be written $F_1 = R \cos \alpha$, $F_2 = R \cos \beta$, and $F_3 = R \cos \gamma$.

If inversely the three forces were known it would be easy to find their resultant, and by means of the directing cosines, to find their direction. It is unnecessary to add that if the resultant R and one of the two rectangular forces F_1, are given, the other F_2 (fig. 32) can be deduced from it.

$$F_2^2 = R^2 - F_1^2$$

Forces, therefore, always act upon a point or a material body as if they were independent. Their resultant effect is their algebraic sum.

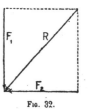

Fig. 32.

Thus the resultant of the forces which act upon M is the sum $(F_1 + F_2)$ (fig. 33). That on the point M' will be the difference $(F_3 - F_1)$.

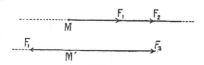

Fig. 33.

13. Equilibrium of Force: Statics.

Two opposite and equal forces of the same intensity, acting on one point cause no displacement. It is said that they are in equilibrium, their resultant being obviously zero. If two or three forces act on the same point, for that point to be in equilibrium, their resultant must be zero, or what comes to the same thing, the components following the three rectangular axes are zero. It may be remarked that by equilibrium it is to be understood that the point M will remain stationary if it was stationary before the application of forces, or it will keep its uniform movement if it were then moving; in short, the point will be as free after as before.

It must be remembered that forces produce deformations, very visible, for example, in a piece of elastic, less so on a piece of metal, but always there; each deformation creating a force in the opposite direction to that which produced it, this being the principle of equal action and reaction. Thus a spring is deformed when it is pulled out, and it develops a reaction which brings it back to its initial state when the pull ceases.

We must therefore distinguish between theoretical equilibrium in which no reaction exists, and natural equilibrium, which is essentially a constrained equilibrium. The theoretical statics of a solid body deliberately neglect the deformations which it suffers, or the resistance of the matter which constitutes it.

14. Restraint and Friction.

No point or material system is absolutely free; thus the extremity of a pendulum can be represented by a point, but in all its displacements that point is limited by the length of the rod. In the same way a point can be considered as moving on a surface, like a rolling ball; a solid can also be so fixed that it can only turn round an axis or slide along that axis.

Restraints can be replaced by forçes, because the surface which everywhere opposes its reaction to the ball and obliges it to move thereupon can be replaced by a force equal to that reaction. The tension of a string ABC can be replaced by

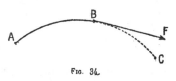

a force BF, if the string were cut at B and its restraint thus removed (fig. 34). The surface of liquids take the shape of a membrane held by tangential forces F_1, F_2. . . . equivalent to the restraining effects of the walls of the vessel. This is what is called the surface tension of liquids (fig. 35). Such restraints can be without friction or with

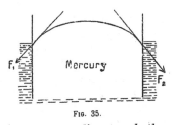

Fɪɢ. 35.

friction according to whether or not the surface offers a resistance to the displacement of the material point; that resistance will be examined later (§ 39). It is important, in all cases, not to make abstractions and to be sure that the frictions are forces. Let there be a force F applied to the moving point M, which moves along the curve S (fig. 36); F can be resolved into a perpendicular component MN, which exerts a pressure on

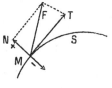

Fɪɢ. 36.

the surface and is neutralised by the reaction of this latter; and a tangential component MT will produce the movement of the point M. Experiment shows that up to a certain value of MT, movement is not produced, this value being that of the friction on the surface. Therefore it is a force, a resistance to movement. In fact, the various points of a solid are subject to restraint and to friction, and as a solid is always deformable it is subject to connexions modified by internal forces, by opposition to external forces. The condition of equilibrium demands that the resultant of all these forces shall be zero. This condition is necessary; otherwise exterior forces with a zero resultant could break a body of which the internal forces had not also a zero resultant.

15. Reduction of a System of Forces.—The number of forces applied to a solid can be reduced because the intensity of a force is not changed if it is produced in the same straight line from one point in a solid to another, from A to B, for example (fig. 37), and it is possible to transfer several concurrent forces to a point where they can be replaced by a single resultant OR

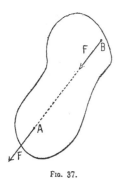

FIG. 37.

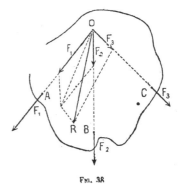

FIG. 38.

(fig. 38). That resultant must be zero in the case of equilibrium, that is to say, their rectangular components, X, Y, Z, must satisfy the condition that $X = 0$, $Y = 0$, $Z = 0$. But a system of forces may not be concurrent. The directions of some may meet at the point 0, whilst others do not ; in this case equal and parallel forces are directed to the point 0, and the forces which do not meet at 0 are produced in like manner. The new system will have a general resultant in relation to the point 0 ; at the same time, the forces which do not meet at 0, such as F_4 and F_5 tend to produce movement of the solid round the point 0 ; they have a moment (from *movimentum*) in relation to 0. There is, therefore, as well as the general resultant, a moment of each of these forces, or a resultant moment of all these forces if they are united. The moment of a force, such as F_4, in relation to the point 0, is the product of that force by its distance from that point (vide fig. 39).

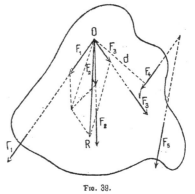

FIG. 39.

We see that by its moment a force tends to turn the body round the point 0, or an axis which would pass through it, with a radius or leverage equal to d. In resolving the resultant moment along the three rectangular axes, the condition of equilibrium demands that the three components L, M and N of the moment should be zero, *i.e.* :—

$$L = 0, \qquad M = 0, \qquad N = 0.$$

The reduction of a system of forces to a general resultant and a resultant moment, shows that the equilibrium of a solid demands six conditions and six equations.

16. Parallel Forces.—If two divergent forces, F_1 and F_2, change their direction and become parallel (fig. 40), the point of convergence is infinity and the resultant will be at a point

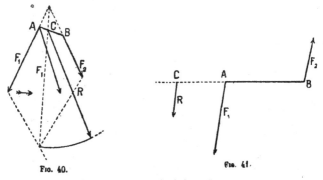

Fig. 40.

Fig. 41.

in the straight line AB, which joins the points of application of F_1 and F_2. This resultant will be equal to the sum of the two forces if they have the same direction, to their difference if they are unequal and in opposite directions (fig. 41). It will have a direction parallel to them, and it will divide the line AB into segments, inversely proportional to these forces. Thus—

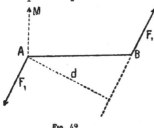

Fig. 42.

$$\frac{F_1}{F_2} = \frac{CB}{CA}.$$

The point C is said to be the centre of parallel forces.

If the two forces are equal and in a contrary direction, their resultant is zero : $F_1 = F_1'$ and $F_1 - F_1' = 0$ (fig. 42) ; they are said to form a couple. The couple tends to produce a movement of rotation ; it possesses a moment, and it is easily seen that the moment of F_1' in relation to the point A is—

$$F_1' \times d$$

That of F_1 in relation to the same point A is zero : so that the moment of the couple is the product of one of the two forces by the distance d. This moment is shown, for example, when two horses are harnessed to a cart : also in an auger and a corkscrew. The moment is represented by a vector AM perpendicular to the plane of the couple ; thus AM $= F_1'' \times d$; this being the axis of the couple.

The resolution of a force into two parallel forces and the composition of three or more forces are very simple propositions ; they are explained by the above.

As the forces applied to a solid have a general resultant R and a resultant moment, M, and as that moment becomes a couple, it follows that :

The forces of a system unite into a single force and into a couple, or into a force and a moment.

In taking into consideration the displacements compatible with the restraints of a solid, it also follows that there must be six equations to express the equilibrium of a solid, namely the components of its translation (X, Y, and Z), and those of its moment or of its rotation (L, M and N) which must be separately zero. In effect, an entirely free solid body has six degrees of liberty. Thus, a moving point on a surface can only move in the direction of X and Y, that is, two degrees of liberty ; a bicycle has three degrees of liberty.

17. Applications (1) RESOLUTION OF FORCES.—Given a vertical force, F, that of gravity, for example, it can be subdivided into two equal forces applied to the points A and B, and the points A and B must be equi-distant from M (see § 20) (fig. 43). If a

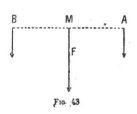

Fig. 43

force F is subdivided between three points, A, B, and C, a triangle ABC is constructed, and, joining AM, F is first resolved into F_1 and F_2 ; and then F_2 into F_3 and F_4, thus giving a final subdivision into three forces, F_1, F_3, F_4 (fig. 44). Those three forces will be equal if the triangle ABC is equilateral. The first case is that of a bicycle, for example ; the second that of the majority of three-legged supports for physical instruments.

The subdivision into four points—like the four legs of a table—is theoretically unstable, seeing that, on ground where the resistance varies from one point to another, two legs would alone support all the weight. In practice, the legs and the ground give somewhat, which results in stability being reached.

2. DEGREES OF LIBERTY.—The restraints of solid bodies or their degree of liberty, enable their movements to be recorded. Numerous examples of this

Fig. 44.

will be found when considering the articulations of the human body.

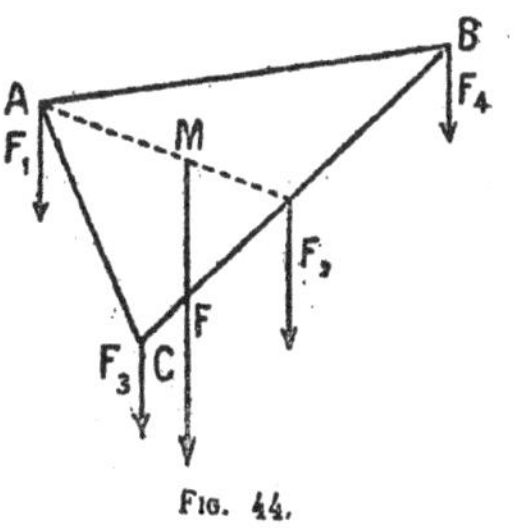

18. Mass.—It is said that two bodies have the same mass when, under the action of equal forces, they take the same acceleration. If their acceleration is different, the masses of the bodies are correspondingly different; in general terms the mass is proportional to the acceleration, and—

$$\frac{F}{m} = f, \quad \frac{F}{m'} = f', \quad \frac{F}{m''} = f'', \quad \ldots,$$

or

$$\frac{m}{m'} = \frac{f'}{f}; \quad \frac{m'}{m''} = \frac{f''}{f'}; \quad \ldots;$$

and also for the forces F and F′ producing the same acceleration f on the masses m and m':

$$\frac{F}{m} = f; \quad \frac{F'}{m'} = f; \quad \text{from which } \frac{F}{F'} = \frac{m'}{m} \text{ etc.}$$

It follows that $F = mf$, that is to say: The force is the product of the mass and the acceleration; and can be measured by the product.

The intensity of gravity, which is also a force, will be $P = mg$, where P is the weight of a body. In the same manner the acceleration of gravity being constant, $P' = m'g$, $P'' = m''g$.

Thus the weights of bodies are in proportion to the masses.

$$\frac{P}{P'} = \frac{m}{m'}, \quad \ldots$$

In the formula $P = mg$, if the unit of mass $m = 1$, then $P = g$, and the intensity of gravity will be that of the acceleration, g due to gravity. At Paris, $g = 9\cdot80978$ metres, or approximately $9\cdot81$ metres per second. In the C.G.S. system the unit of mass is defined as the mass of a cubic centimetre of water at a temperature of 4° centigrade, which is called the gramme. The unit of length is the centimetre.

It follows that the force of the weight: $p = mg$, will be: $p = 1^{gr} \times 980\cdot97$ centimetres $= 980\cdot97$ gramme centimetres.

The unit of force in the C.G.S. System is, therefore the gramme-centimetre, or the dyne; it is the fraction $\frac{1}{g}$ or $\frac{1}{981}$ of a gramme. The value of g being constant, the gramme becomes the unit of force or weight. The unit of time being the second, we have the C.G.S. system, which is almost universal for scientific measurements.

The definition $F = mg$ or Mf, that has been given for any force, can be compared with that given above (§ 11); one is dynamic, the other static. As for the word mass, it does not connote either physics or metaphysics. If mass is defined as the quantity of matter, it remains to be proved that the nature of that matter does not modify the value of the mass.

When speed and acceleration are communicated to bodies in a brief interval of time the effects of inertia can be appreciated. A traveller who gets out of a carriage in motion may fall because his body has retained the movement of the carriage. The same effect is utilised by the workman who hits the back of a plane to release the iron ; the blade has resisted by its inertia. In the same way the head of a hammer is driven into its handle by striking the end of the handle on the bench. Instantaneous speed and force do not exist, but a force can act in a very short space of time, causing shock (§ 41).

19. The smallest mass of a body that has the properties of matter is the mass of the molecule. A molecule is not necessarily indivisible ; it can be composed of atoms which are themselves theoretically indivisible. The properties of matter are generally considered in relation to the molecule.

Analysing the constitution of the molecule, chemistry has established that it is composed of a single atom in the case of mercury, of two in that of oxygen, etc. The signs are Hg for the one, O_2 for the other. The molecules can be condensed and pass from the gaseous to the liquid or solid states.

Composite bodies, acids, bases, salts, etc., have polyatomic molecules. The most complex molecular constructions are found in organic substances such as in albumen (white of egg). The weight of a molecule is the sum of the weight of the atoms of which it is composed assuming $H = 1$ gramme as the atomic weight of hydrogen, the atomic weight of all elements has been determined. For example :—

$H = 1$ (hydrogen)	$S = 32$ (sulphur)
$O = 16$ (oxygen)	$C = 12$ (carbon)
$N = 14$ (nitrogen)	$P = 31$ (phosphorus)

Consider a molecule of glucose. It contains 6 atoms of carbon, 6 of oxygen, and 12 of hydrogen. It is represented thus : Glucose $= C_6H_{12}O_6$

The molecular weight is—

$$(12 \times 6) + (1 \times 12) + (16 \times 6) = 180 \text{ grammes.}$$

The molecule of water is $H_2O = 18$ grammes, and so on.

It is a remarkable thing that the biological properties of a molecule depend not only on its nature, but also its form. Thus a certain microbe will ferment a sugar of which the atoms have a certain arrangement, but it will not ferment another of the same composition and the same molecular weight, if the atoms are differently arranged.

The influence of molecular structure (stereochemistry) on physiological operations is still an obscure problem. As for the reality of the molecule, recent works show that it does not admit of a doubt. By the calculations of M. Jean Perrin [1] it is known that 1 gramme of glucose contains 100 milliards of milliards (10^{20}) of real molecules.

20. Centre of Mass or Gravity.—By centre of mass is understood that point in a body through which the resultant of all the weights of its parts passes, in every position the body can

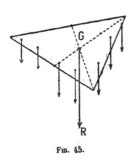

assume. More precisely, if all the forces, which represent the effects of gravity on the molecules of the body, are composed, their resultant G R, is at the centre of its bulk, which is the centre of gravity, G (fig. 45). The position of the centre of gravity only depends on the form of the body and the distribution of its matter at a given moment ; it depends on the form alone if the body is homogeneous, that is to say, of similar structure in all its parts. But that is a comparatively rare case, and in heterogeneous bodies, the centre of gravity must be determined experimentally.

Fɪɢ. 45.

The vertical line which traverses a body at its centre of gravity ; such an axis has special properties (§ 41).

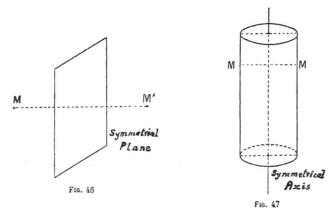

Symmetrial Plane

Fɪɢ. 46

Symmetrical Axis

Fɪɢ. 47

---

[1] Jean Perrin (*Journal de Physique*, 1910, p. 10 ; *Revue Scientifique*, 1911, p. 774) ; *Les Atomes* (Paris, 1913).

The centre of gravity of homogeneous bodies is the centre of their shape ; that of a surface (parallelogram, rectangle) is the point where the diagonals intersect ; that of triangles (fig. 45 above) is at the intersection of their diagonals ; that of a circle is its centre, and, in general, if any surface can be cut into traingles, the centre of gravity of the surface will be the resultant of those of all the triangles.

Solids, having the preceding surfaces for sections, have similar axes of gravity, on which at equal distances, from the two faces, the centres of gravity lie.

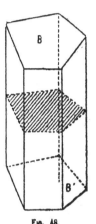

F$_{IG}$. 48.

If an iron triangle weighing 60 kilogrammes, is held by three workmen at the corners, each would support 20 kilogrammes.

The position of the centre of gravity can be found on the plan, or on the axis of symmetry of a body, when there is one, as is the case when two equi-distant points of the body are are found in the perpendicular to that plan or axis (figs. 46 and 47). But the centre of gravity can be found on a plane called the diametrical plane whenever this plane divides all the surfaces which cross it into two equal parts. Thus in a prism the plane which bisects the sides is the diametrical plane (fig. 48).

It is shewn in treatises on geometry or statics that :

1. The centre of gravity of a prism is in the middle of the straight line which joins the centres of gravity of its two bases B and B¹, and this rule applies also to a cylinder.

2. The centre of gravity of a pyramid is at a quarter of the distance from the base on the straight line which joins the apex to the centre of gravity of the base, and the same applies to a cone.

All that has just been said concerns homogeneous bodies. The experimental determination of the centre of gravity of any body can be made in the following way :—

1. The body is suspended by two of its points successively. The two directions of the suspension intersect at the centre of gravity.

2. The body is placed on a knife edge, so that it balances, that is to say, it is in equilibrium.

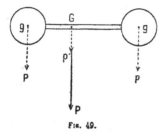

Fig. 49.

3. If a composite body is under consideration, the centre of gravity of each part can be found, and the forces of gravity composed from these. Thus, for a dumb-bell with equal spheres, p, p and p' would be resolved into a force P acting at the centre of the bar if it is homogeneous, or at another point if it is heterogeneous (fig. 49); the point G is obtained by the ordinary method for the composition of parallel forces.

For a system of weights P_1, P_2, P_3, P_4, joined together by rigid bars (the weights of which can be neglected) the result will be:—The weights of 1 and 3 kilo-grammes (fig. 50) have a re-sultant at a quarter of the distance OO' at g; this result-ant (of 4 kilogrammes) and the weight of 2 kilogrammes have resultant of 6 kilo-

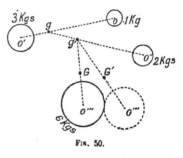

Fig. 50.

grammes placed at a third of the distance gO'' at g'; finally this resultant of 6 kilogrammes is composed with the 6 kilogrammes of the fourth weight and the final resultant will be at G in the middle of O'O''', and will be equivalent to 12 kilogrammes.

The system of the weights must not, if articulated at the points O, O', O'', O''', change its formation during the above determina-tion, the general centre of gravity being relative to an invariable position of the weights, of which the individual centres of gravity have been found. In fact, if the body O''' (dotted line) is dis-placed, the centre G in its turn will be displaced in space to G'.

21. Stability of Equilibrium.—The conditions of equilibrium of a body depends on the effects of gravity and the reaction on the body of its support.

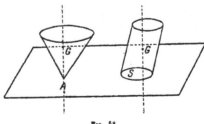

Fig. 51

To produce a state of equilibrium, a body placed on a surface must have its axis of gravity passing through the point on which it rests, A, or within the base on which it rests, S (fig. 51).

That base is called the base of support. If a body is inclined, and still remains, in contact with its base of support, its centre of gravity will be displaced. It can either be raised or lowered, and it is easy to see (fig. 52) that the equilibrium is most stable when the centre of gravity is as low as possible and unstable (G_1) when the centre is as high as possible. But a sphere which rolls on a horizontal surface possesses a centre of gravity always

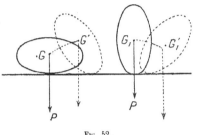

Fig. 52.

at the same distance from that surface, the equilibrium, in this case being said to be indifferent. It is not enough that the axis of gravity should fall within the base of support for the equilibrium to be the most stable ; the centre of gravity must be at the minimum distance from that base. But it is clear that in all cases it is a necessary condition of equilibrium that the axis of gravity should fall within the surface of support (fig. 53).

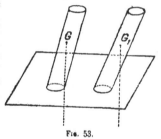

Fig. 53.

22. The stability of a material edifice depends both on the size of its base of support and on the small height of its centre of gravity. Subject to a lateral force which tends to overturn it, it resists by virtue of its thickness in the direction of that force, and its weight. Take a vertical wall of thickness E in the direction of the horizontal force, H, tending to overturn it on its edge, AA' (fig. 54). The moment, **M**, of that force in relation to the point B, is the product :

$$\mathbf{M} = \mathrm{H} \times \mathrm{BC} \text{ (see § 16).}$$

Let the section BCDE (fig. 55) be examined as if it represented the projection of the whole wall (the wall seen in profile). Then—

$$\mathbf{M} = \mathrm{H} \times \mathrm{EI}.$$

Now the force H and the weight P of the wall have a resultant in the direction of RK, and the reaction of the ground is equal and opposite in the direction KR'. This reaction, applied to the

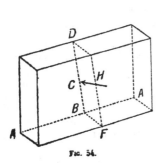

Fig. 54.

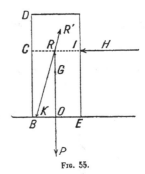

Fig. 55.

point K has a zero moment in relation to that point. But H and P have the following moments :—

$$\text{moment of } H = H \times EI.$$
$$\text{,,} \quad \text{,,} \quad P = P \times KO.$$

In order that those two moments may be equal it is necessary that—

$$H \times EI = P \times KO, \text{ or } KO = EI \times \frac{H}{P}$$

In proportion as the horizontal force H increases, KO must increase, the limit being when KO = OB, half the thickness of the wall ; then

$$OB = EI \times \frac{H'}{P} ;$$

the maximum horizontal effort H' will be

$$H' = P \times \frac{OB}{EI}$$

The maximum moment, $\mathbf{M} = H' \times EI$, is the moment of stability of the wall. It will be seen that

$$\mathbf{M} = P \times OB \text{ or } \frac{P \times e}{2}$$

that is to say, the product of the weight by the semi-thickness of the wall, or the product of the weight by the distance from the side to the axis of gravity.

CHAPTER II.

GENERAL PRINCIPLES OF MECHANICS (*Continued*).

STUDY OF FORCES—DYNAMICS.

23. Definition.—Dynamics is the study of the movements produced by given forces, and conversely the forces that must be brought into play to produce a certain movement.

If a material point is considered the forces acting on it can be reduced to a single resultant, and in the practical case of material systems the whole mass can be assumed as concentrated at the centre of gravity and the forces or their resultant as acting at that centre. To simplify calculations, friction, and, in particular, the resistance which air opposes to the movement of bodies (see § 42) are neglected.

24. Movement of a Point. Projectiles.—When a force, constant in strength and direction, acts on a point M, the movement is (§ 2) :

$$s = \tfrac{1}{2} ft^2, \text{ and the speed } v = ft.$$

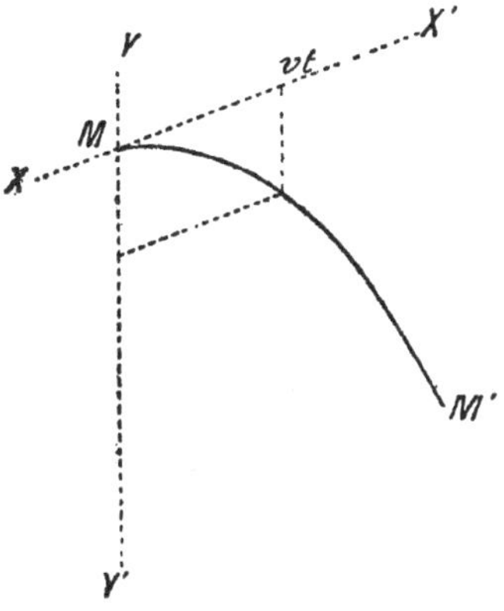

FIG. 56.

In the case of a body which was in repose and which would fall by the action of gravity it follows that

$$s = \tfrac{1}{2} gt^2 \text{ and } v = gt.$$

From which is deduced

$$v^2 = g^2t^2 = 2g \times \tfrac{1}{2} gt^2 = 2gs.$$

Then :

$$v = \sqrt{2gs}.$$

The height of the fall s is usually designated by h, and then

$$s = \sqrt{2gh}.$$

Also :

$$h = \frac{v^2}{2g}$$

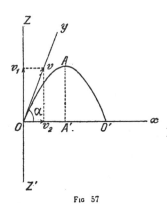

Fig 57

But if the point already has a uniform movement, there will be a resultant movement. It is what is found, for example, in the fall of a body moving in a horizontal direction, this being the movement of projectiles. Let a point, M, having a speed v, in the direction XX', be attracted by gravity in the direction YY' (fig. 56); then it will describe a parabola (§ 5). In time t, the space traversed will be vt on XX', $\frac{1}{2} gt^2$ on YY'; the parallelogram of these movements will give the required trajectory.

Suppose a projectile to be thrown from a point O with a speed v and at an angle of inclination α (fig. 57); it will eventually reach the horizontal ox (the ground) by reason of gravity. But the speed v has a vertical component $v_1 = v \sin \alpha$, which would be added algebraically to the speed of the fall in the direction ZZ', and a horizontal speed $v_2 = v \cos \alpha$. Therefore the vertical speed will be $V = v \sin \alpha - gt$ at the instant t, and the space traversed will be

$$Z = (v \sin \alpha)\, t - \tfrac{1}{2}gt^2.$$

And in the direction Ox the speed and the space traversed will be

$$v_2 = v \cos \alpha, \text{ and } x = (v \cos \alpha)\, t.$$

Thus—

$$Z = x \tan \alpha - \frac{g}{2v^2 \cos^2 \alpha}\, x^2.$$

This is the equation of a parabola having a vertical axis AA'. When the projectile is at the point A, its speed $V = v \sin \alpha - gt$, which is equal to zero, and therefore

$$v \sin \alpha - gt = 0, \text{ and } t = \frac{v \sin \alpha}{g}$$

Thus the duration t of the ascension is found; it must be the same for the descent, so that the total duration is $\dfrac{2v \sin \alpha}{g}$ and corresponds to the range OO' of the projectile or to the amplitude of the throw. The equation of the range OO' will be therefore :

$$v_2 \times 2t \text{ or } v \cos \alpha \times \frac{2v \sin \alpha}{g} = \frac{2v^2 \sin \alpha \cos \alpha}{g} = \frac{v^2 \sin 2\alpha}{g}$$

The greatest range or the maximum amplitude is when sin 2α = 1, or 2α = 90°, and α = 45° It is necessary, therefore, to project at an angle of less than 45° In the general equation of Z, given x (the point it is desired the projectile should reach) and the oblique speed v, the angle can be calculated at which the projectile must be projected.

It is not necessary here to follow further the question of projectiles, but it may be noted that the trajectory is modified by the resistance of the air, and that this diminishes the range (see also § 263).

25. Central Force.—Gravity is an example of what are called central forces, because the earth draws bodies as though to a central point, and in turn is drawn by the sun, the centre of our planetary system. The direction of a central force always passes through the centre, but the force can be attractive or repellant, and act according to the distance of the moving body or the square of that distance. Universal gravity causes a movement of the stars in ellipses, but within the limits under study, that attraction is perceptibly vertical to the earth and is apparently a parabola.

Conversely, the movement or the trajectory being known, the force can be determined. Take the case of a moving body constrained to describe a circle with a centre O (fig. 58) and find the central force. Suppose the angular speed ω to be constant. Then, the required force must be $F = mf$, and the acceleration f is here constant. It must also be noticed that, in a varying curvilinear movement, the acceleration has two components. In fact, when the moving body goes from M to M′, the speed changes from v to $v + dv$, dv being the acceleration in an infinitely small space of time, dt, and the angle MOM′ will be $d\alpha$. Draw M′A equal and parallel to v. The acceleration is shown by $\dfrac{AB}{dt}$.

As AB is the resultant of the rectangular vectors BC and AC, the acceleration $\dfrac{AB}{dt}$ is the sum of a tangential acceleration $\dfrac{BC}{dt}$, and of a centripetal acceleration $\dfrac{AC}{dt}$. And there is no difficulty

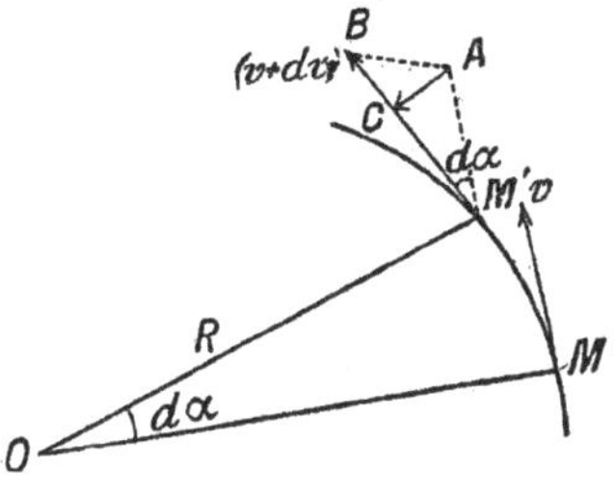

Fig. 58.

in seeing that the former is equal to $\dfrac{dv}{dt}$ as has been already shown (§2), whilst the latter is $\dfrac{v^2}{R}$, R being the radius of the curvature at M′ ; because

$$AC = v\,d\alpha, \text{ and } \frac{AC}{dt} = v\,\frac{d\alpha}{dt}$$

on the other hand $\frac{d\alpha}{dt} = \frac{v}{R}$; therefore : $\frac{AC}{dt} = \frac{v^2}{R}$ (fig. 58).

When the moving body has to describe a circle with a uniform movement, the tangential acceleration is zero, and only the centripetal acceleration need be considered

$$f = \frac{v^2}{R};$$

The centripetal force will be :

$$F = mf = m\,\frac{v^2}{R}$$

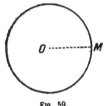

In fact, that force is a reaction. In considering an example such as a stone in a sling, it will be seen that it exerts a pull on the string along the radius OM and creates there a reaction (tension) ; this is the centrifugal force equal to the centripetal force (fig. 59). Centrifugal force appears in rapid movements of rotation, causing the rupture of fly-wheels and of millstones ; it obliges the circus rider to lean towards the inside of the track, rails to be raised on the outer sides of curves (superelevation of the permanent way) ; it explains the operation of centrifugal drying machines and the performance of certain acrobatic feats, such as the so-called looping the loop by a cyclist.

Fig. 59.

26. Pendulum.—The pendulum is a material point which swings at the end of an inextensible wire fixed at the opposite end. This movement is circular, but on an arc of a circle only (fig. 60).

The pendulum having been taken to M_1, is released and will oscillate from M_1 to M_2, the duration of this single oscillation being

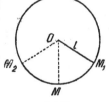

$$t = \pi\,\sqrt{\frac{l}{g}};$$

l represents the length of the pendulum and the oscillations are presumed to be small.

Fig. 60.

The theory of the pendulum makes it necessary to resort to the integral and differential calculus which should not be employed in an elementary treatise. But it must be shown that the intensity of gravity in the formula can, inversely, be deduced from the duration t, for a length l of the pendulum. In Paris, if $l = 99.39$ c.m., the value of $g = 9.81$ m. Thus in Paris the length of a seconds pendulum is about 0.994 m.

In fairly deep mines, t diminishes, therefore g increases, but the most practically realisable pendulum is a heavy body attached to a wire, fixed on a horizontal axis. It is what is called a compound pendulum, the duration of its single oscillation being given by the formula :—

$$t' = \pi \sqrt{\frac{I}{Mgl'}} \; ;$$

M being the mass of the pendulum, I its moment of inertia (see § 31), and l' the distance from the axis of suspension to the centre of gravity. To find the equivalent simple pendulum we solve the equation.

$$\sqrt{\frac{I}{Mgl'}} = \sqrt{\frac{l}{g}} \; ;$$

from which, evidently, $t' = t$ and $l = \frac{I}{Ml'}$. The musical metronome (§ 197) is a pendulum which has two divisions ; a heavy weight, attached to the lower half, performs the movement, a smaller weight, movable on the stem, permits of its regulation by modifying the moment of inertia as will be considered later.

The movements of a child playing in a swing are similar to the movements of the pendulum.

27. Movement of a Material System.—In the movement of a material system, the acting forces are either external forces (gravity, reaction, pressure of air, etc.) or internal forces, equal and opposite, acting between various points of the system. These latter have a zero resultant, and if it is assumed—which is permissible—that the mass of the system is concentrated at the centre of gravity G, the movement will be that of the point G, under the action of the external forces only to the exclusion of the others. This is the theorem of movement of the centre of gravity. A body will therefore describe a parabola in space, under the influence of its initial speed and the force of gravity. In reality, it is the centre of gravity of that body which will describe that parabola. An exploding bomb would be in this category, the general centre of gravity describing a parabola, whilst the fragments would have indeterminate movements.

In the movement of a system it is useful to consider the product mv of the mass by the velocity, a product which is called the momentum. The force giving to the mass a speed dv in the infinitely short space of time dt gives

$$F = m \frac{dv}{dt}$$

which means $F = mf$ for the duration of a second. In the element of time dt, the force has an impulse" $F \times dt$, equivalent to the product $M \times dv$. From the instant zero to the instant t, the equation $Fdt = mdv$, will be the sum of several similar products. This sum has as its sign, in the integral calculus,

$$\int_0^{} Fdt = MV - MV_0.$$

This equation expresses that, in a rectilineal movement, the "impulse" Ft develops a momentum mv. Therefore, to stop a wagon of 60 kilogrammes, travelling at a speed of 5 metres, in the space of 3 seconds, a force of 10·2 Kg is necessary because :

$$F = \frac{MV}{3} = \frac{60}{9 \cdot 81} \times \frac{5}{3} = 10 \cdot 2\,\text{kg}.$$

In a curvilinear movement the equation still holds but F will only designate the tangential force.

Consider now the projection of a point belonging to a material system on a plane perpendicular to the axis OZ. If the direction of the force which acts on that point passes through a similar point during the movement, for example, through the point O, the moment of the force will be zero, at any time. In short,

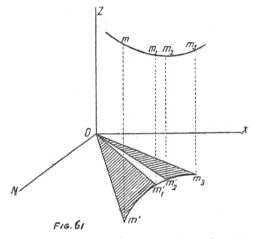

FIG. 61

the sum of the moments of the impulse Fdt, in relation to the fixed axis, will always be zero, and in consequence the sum of the moments of the momentums of a system will not be modified and will not be increased. This sum is constant. It can be seen (fig. 61) that the masses sweep out, with the radii Om', Om_1 . . . areas proportional to the time, and that the sum of the products of the masses forming the system, into the areas remains constant. This is the theorem of areas, only applicable to the case of external forces with zero moment. If, however, there was no external force, the sum of the areas would be zero. This is the case if a man is standing upright on a perfectly smooth surface ; if he wants to turn his body, one part will not turn in one direction without the other turning in the opposite direction, so that the sum of the described areas will be zero. If he slides one leg forward, the other will slip back and he will fall (see further on, § 263)

28. Work.—When a force acts either to produce or retard the displacement of a body (a point or a system of points) we say that it performs work. Work is the product of force by the displacement l in its own direction giving

$$\mathbf{T} = F \times l.$$

A force of 1 kilogramme, displacing a body 1 metre on a path in its direction, performs work equal to 1 kilogrammetre (sign : kgm.).

In the C.G.S. system the unit is the work done by 1 dyne for 1 centimetre of displacement, this unit being the *erg* (from εργον, work).

The dyne is $\dfrac{1^{gr}}{981}$, the erg will be $\dfrac{1}{981} \times 1^{cm.}$ or

$$\frac{\cdot001 \text{ kg.}}{981} \times \cdot01\text{m} = \frac{1}{981 \times 10^5} \text{ of a kilogrammetre,}$$

that is to say, a kilogrammetre equals $9 \cdot 81 \times 10^7$ ergs, nearly 100 million ergs.

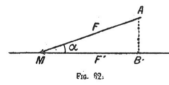

Fig. 62.

According to whether a force acts in the direction of the displacement or in the opposite, it produces either motive or resistant work. As an example of resistant work may be mentioned the sliding down of a barrel on an inclined surface, its fall being restrained by means of a rope. This resistant work is also called negative work, the other being said to be positive work.

The force can have an oblique direction in relation to the displacement. This is the case when a rope is pulling a wagon on rails at an angle therewith. Then the only useful component of the force is the projection of F on the line of the displacement, and then

$$F' = F \cos \alpha,$$

because MB $=$ MA cos α
(fig. 62).

For a displacement l
the work will be :

$$\mathbf{T} = \mathrm{F}\,l\,\cos\,α.$$

Consider a curvilineal
displacement MM′ (fig.
63), the force having the
direction mm' ; the work
will be the same as if the
force had displaced the

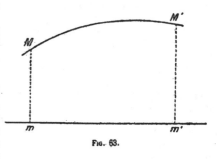

Fig. 63.

projection of the point M in the direction mm' from m to m'.

Then

$$\mathbf{T} = \mathrm{F} \times mm'.$$

Therefore the work done by a force that is constant in magnitude and direction, depends only on the initial and final position of the moving body. If the force is tangential at each point of the curve, the work done will be

Fig. 64

$$\mathbf{T} = \mathrm{F} \times \mathrm{MM}'.$$

If not, it will form an angle α with the tangent at each point of the curve (fig. 64) ; if the element of length traversed is denoted, dl, the work done is F dl cos α for such element of length. The sum of the work done is the integral

$$\mathbf{T} = \int_{0}^{l} \mathrm{F}dl\,\cos\,α.$$

This general expression of work done applies equally to forces of constant and variable intensity.

If we plot the values of F cos α as ordinates and the lengths dl as abscissæ, we obtain the curve AB. The area ABOl is the value of the total work as represented by the above integral (fig. 65) Such areas as the above, which are bounded by a curve, can be measured by means of a planimeter or by the method of quadrature (§ 218).

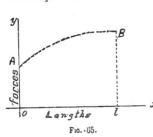

Fig. 65.

It is essential to remember that work does not consist of force alone. If, for example, water is drawn out of a well, the effort put forth is in proportion to the weight to be lifted, but that weight has to traverse the whole depth of the well. The work done is the product of the two factors; force and displacement. In the same way, it is not enough to press a file heavily on a piece of metal, as it is in displacing the file under a certain pressure that it will produce work the really useful effect. All industrial machinery illustrates the work done by forces. It is not however, necessarily correct to estimate the energy expended by the quantity of work accomplished, because the former depends. in addition to the force and displacement, on various factors. Thus, if two labourers are each digging over 100 square metres, the one who has the hardest ground and the worst tools will do more work in the mechanical sense, although the result is the same.

Before Poncelet (1826) and Coriolis (1829), the word force was used in the sense of work, that incorrect use has disappeared to-day. The great natural philosophers of the XVIIth and XVIIIth Centuries (Huyghens, Bernoulli, De La Hire, Lavoisier, Carnot) and even Helmholtz, as late as 1848, did not use the term force except as the expression of the product of a weight by a distance.

29. Work of a Deformable System.—A system subjected to external forces and deformable by their action is at the same time constrained by internal forces, each of its points is therefore displaced internally and externally, producing external work and internal work. Let A and B be two points of the system, the action of the one equalling the reaction of the other. This will be a force F (fig. 66). If the deformation of the body separates A from B by a very small quantity dr, the work done will be $+ (F \times dr)$. If, on the contrary, it draws them together, the work done will be negative and equal to $- (F \times dr)$.

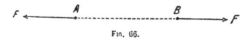

Fig. 66.

The total internal work will be the sum, positive or negative, of the elements of work Fdr. It is designated by T_i. In a perfect undeformable solid, $T_i = O_z$, the work of the internal forces being zero, and the work of the external forces T_e only being considered.

The internal work is of a molecular order; thus the molecules of a gas, set in motion in every direction by a variation of temperature, produce work T_i, which is not necessarily zero. Obviously internal agitation exists in the muscles which sustain an effort of some duration, a static effort, and those molecular vibrations constitute work; certain learned scholars have created, to express this, the term static work (Heidenhain, Haughton,

Chauveau) ; the idea, although correct, is a contradiction of terms : work, pre-supposing movement, and statics implying absence of movement.

30. Principle of Vis Viva.—Let there be a body with a weight P falling from a height h. The weight will perform work $T = P \times h$. It is known that $P = mg$ and that $h = \frac{1}{2} gt^2$; there fore it follows that :

$$T = \tfrac{1}{2} mg^2 t^2.$$

At the time t, the speed is $v = gt$, therefore

$$g^2 t^2 = v^2,$$

and finally

$$T = Ph = \tfrac{1}{2} mv^2.$$

Whether it is question of a point or of a material system, the equation $T = \frac{1}{2} mv^2$ applies if in the working of the system the sum $T_e + T_i$, of external and internal work is not equal to zero.

The product mv^2 has been named "vis viva" (Leibnitz), or energy of motion, and the semi-product $\frac{1}{2} mv^2$ " live power " (Belanger) or actual energy. Thus the work done in a material system endows it with a certain actual energy or " live power " which becomes, in a way, potential work in the system. If, for example, a spring is coiled by depressing it with a weight P, the weight will perform work $P \times r$, by a contraction r of the spring, and if the weight is removed, the spring will expand performing work

$$\tfrac{1}{2} mv^2 = Pr.$$

The stored-up, latent, or potential energy does work in becoming actual or kinetic energy. [1]

If a fly-wheel in motion receives energy, its speed will change from v to v' and its actual or kinetic energy from $\frac{1}{2} mv^2$ to $\frac{1}{2} mv'^2$. Thus the work developed is found in the increase of energy. It is written :

$$T = \tfrac{1}{2} mv'^2 - \tfrac{1}{2} mv^2 = \tfrac{1}{2} m (v'^2 - v^2).$$

31. Given that the speed of a body rotating round a fixed axis is ωr (§ 2), its " vis viva " will be $m\omega^2 r^2$, and its energy $\frac{1}{2} m\omega^2 r^2$. The radius r varies according to the position of each point in relation to the axis. A value of r designated by ρ is calculated for the given body. The whole of the bulk in rotation is imagined as concentrated at a circumference having the radius ρ, and then $\frac{1}{2}\omega^2 M\rho^2$, M being the total mass, ρ is called the radius of gyration of the body and $M\rho^2$ its moment of inertia. Thus the energy of a rotating body is the semi-product of the square of the angular speed by the moment of inertia.

---

[1] Expression already used by Lazare Carnot (*loc. cit.*, p. 247).

Knowing the mass M and the angular speed, we obtain the radius of gyration for various bodies. For example :—

1°. For a thin rectilineal rod, having the axis of rotation perpendicular to its length l :

$$\rho^2 = \frac{l^2}{3}$$

2°. For a cylinder of radius r, turning round its axis :

$$\rho^2 = \frac{r^2}{2}.$$

If turning round a diameter of the base, the height being h :

$$\rho^2 = \frac{3r^2 + 4h^2}{12}.$$

3°. For the rim of a wheel of rectangular section, of which the external and internal radii are r and r' :

$$\rho^2 = \frac{r^2 + r'^2}{2}.$$

4°. For the frustrum of a solid cone, with radii r and r' and height h, having for axis a straight line situated in one of the base and at the centre of the figure, and :

$$\rho^2 = \frac{h^2}{9}\left(1 + \frac{d}{r + r'}\right) + \frac{(r+r')^2 - 2d^2}{16},$$

d being the difference $r—r'$.

5°. For a Rectangular parallelopiped having as sides a, b, c, and turning round an axis drawn through the middle of the side b parallel to a :

$$\rho^2 = \frac{1}{3}\left(c^2 + \frac{1}{4}b^2\right) \text{ (fig. 67).}$$

The preceding values of the moment of inertia, or, more exactly, of the radius of gyration, are for homogeneous bodies. They do not apply, strictly speaking, in the case of non-homogeneous parts, such as the parts composing the animal locomotive apparatus.

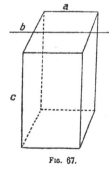

Fig. 67.

32. Energy.—The fact that live power comes from stored-up work, and can be restored, has led the natural philosophers to identify that live power $\frac{1}{2}mv^2$ with a sort of immaterial substance capable of concealing itself and of appearing in the body ; it has been called energy. Energy is therefore the capacity for work; it can be in reserve, that is, potential, or it can translate itself into work and become kinetic.

The kinetic energy of a spring when it expands is the restoration of the potential energy which it accumulated when it was compressed.

Every body has a reserve of energy, either potential or kinetic, stored within it. A body placed at a given height possesses the power of performing, in falling, a certain quantity of work. This work is a measure of the kinetic energy which is equal to the potential energy. In all this something is preserved and has merely changed its form....It is also interesting to note, regarding energy, that it explains the production of heat by friction. Rumford, Davy and others showed that friction—real mechanical energy—was transformed into heat. It was suspected also that light was transformed into heat, and that the latter provided the force of machines and of animals.[1] A poor German doctor, of Heilbronn, Robert-Jules Mayer (1814–1878) attempted to prove this.

The history of the birth of " energetics " is very curious. The word " energy," in the sense of work was employed by Bernoulli in a letter to Varignon ([2]), dated 1717, and by Couplet ([3]) in 1726. Young ([4]) used it in 1807, but its adoption exclusively in physics took place, thanks to Rankine and William Thomson (later Lord Kelvin) between 1850 and 1870. At the same time a number of natural philosophers, from Huyghens (1680), Leibnitz (1696) and Lazare Carnot (1803) until Helmholtz (1847) made use of the expression " live force " to designate work, or, more briefly, of the word force ([5]).

These early philosophers were puzzled by the fact that " force " could apparently be destroyed. But Leibnitz solved the difficulty by explaining that in impact and in friction the " live force " lost gave birth to heat by the agitation of the particles of the body acted upon. " The forces," he said, " are not destroyed, but dissipated amongst the component parts of the body. They are not lost ; it is like changing sovereigns into silver ([6])." Thus heat was regarded as the movement of invisible parts of bodies, " diversified and very rapid movement," according to Robert Boyle,([7]) Rumford,([8]) Young (already quoted), Davy,([9]) Am-

---

[1] Herschell, *Outline of Astronomy*, 1833.
[2] Varignon, *Nouvelle Méchanique*, 2 vols., 1725.
[3] Couplet, *Mémoires de l'Acad. Roy. des Sciences*, 1726, p. 119.
[4] Thomas Young, *Lectures on Natural Philosophy*, viii., 1807.
[5] For instance, the famous *Mémoire sur la Conservation de la Force* of Helmholtz (1847), French translation by Pérard (1869). This publication, which caused a sensation at the time, to-day appears to us as of very mediocre interest.
[6] Leibnitz *Mém. Acad. Sciences*, 1728.
[7] Robert Boyle, *Works*, iii., 1744.
[8] Rumford, from 1798 ; see *Mémoir de l'Institute*, 1804, and *Essays*.
[9] Davy, *Elem. Philos. Chim.*, translated by Van Mons, 2 vols., 1813–14, vol. i., p. 53.

pere.[1] and Fresnel.[2] The latter natural philosopher declared
in very clear terms that heat is a vibration. And until that date
(1822) the relation between work and heat in such transformations
was only considered to be *qualitative*. The possibility of a
quantitative relation was not then foreseen.

In 1824 Sadi-Carnot [3] investigated the production of work
at the expense of heat in the steam engine. Comparing thermal
engines with hydraulic engines, he recognised that the power
of a steam engine depends on the difference of temperature
between the boiler and the condenser, in the same way that the
power of a water wheel depends on the difference of the level of
the mill-race above and below. In some posthumous notes, only
published in 1878 (forty-six years after his death) Carnot admitted a destruction of heat in its transformation into work.
He had therefore arrived at the law of the " equivalence " of heat
and work. But his thought was specially arrested by the fact
that without a fall of temperature, without a rupture of thermal
equilibrium there was no possibility of motive power being produced. The maximum power, in other words, the greatest
quantity of work of a thermal engine, is fixed by that difference
of temperature. Already Pictet [4] had attributed a " tension "
to heat and Berthollet wrote these curious lines : " We can compare this tension to the effort of an elastic substance which puts
itself in equilibrium of elasticity with other similar substances
which react upon it ; its effect is all the greater the more difference there is between their temperatures ; from which we can
draw the conclusion that the caloric acts with more energy on
bodies of which the temperature is different, and the tension is
greater.[5]" This principle, affirmed by Berthollet in 1803,
appears to us to have inspired all the authors, after Carnot.
" We can say," taught Poncelet in 1826, " that a certain
quantity of heat must develop, against the resistances directly
opposed to its action, quantities of absolute work, which are
always the same or independent of the method of that action
and the nature of the bodies. This principle is somewhat
analogous to that put forward by M. Sadi-Carnot, an old
pupil of the Ecole Polytechnique, in a little work called
Réflexions. . . . [6] "

---

[1] Ampère *Ann. phys. et Chimie*, 1821, vol. LVIII, p. 432.
[2] Fresnel, *De la Lumière* : addition to the *Chemistry* of Thompson, 1822.
[3] S.-Carnot, *Réflexions sur la Puissance Motrice du Feu* (1824) : new editions 1887 and 1903 (Hermann).
[4] Pictet, *Essais de Physique*.
[5] Berthollet, *Essai de Statique Chimique*, vol. I. p. 155 ; (1803).
[6] Poncelet, *Mécanique Industrielle*, p. 216 (note).

But Coriolis contented himself with writing in 1829 : " It would seem that the maximum work of a steam engine depends on the temperature at which the steam is formed (^{1})."

Thus the principle of Carnot, only awakened rare echoes at that period.

On the other hand, Mohr,(^{2}) Seguin Senior (^{3}) affirmed the " equivalence " of the work produced and of the heat which was its origin. And their affirmations were like the reflections of the " dream "—this was the word—cherished by Hans Oerstedt of the universality of the transformations of the forces of nature.(^{4})

The doctrine of the Equivalence of work and of heat and of all the terrestial energy, was definitely confirmed by Robert Mayer (^{5}) in 1842, and further developed as to " the energies of life " in 1845.

33. Principle of Mayer or of Equivalence.—Heat is transformed into work, and work into heat, at an absolutely invariable rate, or in other words : A constant relation of equivalence exists between work and heat.

The quantity of heat necessary to raise 1 kilogramme of water from 0° to 1° centigrade is called a "Grande Calorie " or kilo calorie (C).

The experiments of Joule, of Hirn, of Edlund, and many other physicists, have proved that : an amount of work of 426·4 kgm., or, approximately 425 kilogrammetres, is equal to one "great calorie " (C). Inversely a kilogrammetre is equal to $\frac{1}{425}$of a great calorie. 425 kilogrammetres thus defines the mechanical equivalent of Heat (^{6}).

$$\frac{\text{Work}}{\text{Heat}} = 425 = \text{E}.$$

E is the mechanical equivalent of heat. In 1843 the English physicist Joule proved that the work accomplished by an electric motor had its source in the chemical reactions between the acids and the metal of the battery supplying energy to drive it, that is to say, in the oxidation of the zinc. He claimed that the chemical

(^{1}) Coriolis, *Traité de la Mécanique des Corps Solides et du Calcul de l'effet des Machines*, 2nd ed., 1844, p. 282 (1st ed., 1829).

(^{2}) Mohr, *Liebig's Ann.*, vol. XXIV, (1837).

(^{3}) Seguin senior, *Comptes Rendus Acad. Sc.*, 1839, vol. XXV. (p. 420).

(^{4}) Oerstedt, *La Dynamologie (Ansicht der Chemischen Naturgesetze)*, Berlin, 1812.

(^{5}) Jules-Robert Mayer was born at Heilbronn in 1814 ; son of a chemist, he became a doctor of medicine and travelled to Munich, Paris, etc. His first memoire, of a few pages only, appeared in *Annalen der Pharm. und Chemie*, of Liebig, vol. XLII ; 1842.

(^{6}) So named by Robert Mayer himself.

force can become the calorific force and the latter work. In animals, he added, the production of work is due to the chemical operations of the organism which develop heat, so that the reactions being constant; the ascent of a mountain will tend to cool the body. [1]

Robert Mayer, more of a physiologist than Joule, examined this last problem in an admirable paper,[2] which appeared in 1845, He said : " The chemical energy contained in the food consumed and the oxygen breathed, is the source of two kinds of forces : movement and heat ; and the sum of the physical forces produced by an animal is the equivalent of the total sum produced by the chemical process which has taken place at the same time. If all the mechanical work performed by a horse during a certain time after being converted into heat is added to the heat produced simultaneously in its body, the sum will be equal to the quantity of heat evolved in the corresponding chemical reaction."

Helmholtz (1847) generalised the doctrine of equivalence, and from that time, adopting the term Energy, all the natural philosophers were agreed that Energy is that which is conserved in the following transformations : work, heat, light, electricity, etc. There is undoubtedly a relation between work and heat ; but chemical energy is first converted into heat energy and then into work. The same applies to luminous or electric energy, etc. There is no doubt about the truth of the principle of equivalence or of the conservation of energy.

A body, therefore, possesses the power to furnish a determined quantity of energy, in one of the preceding forms, that power being analogous to the fortune of a man, a fortune of which the precise nature is not specified. Energy is thus manifested as an invisible and universal entity capable of changing its aspect without change of magnitude. It is an invariant, as the geometricians say.

34. Interpretation and Application of the Principle of Equivalence.—The principle of equivalence, in relation to mechanical and thermal energy only, is shown by the relation :—

$$T = EQ,$$

in mechanical units (kilogrammetres) or

$$\frac{T}{E} = Q$$

in calories.

---

[1] Joule, *Philos. Mag.*, 1843, ser. III., vol. xxiii.
[2] Jules-Robert Mayer, *Die Organische Bewegung in ihrem Zusammenhang mit dem Stoffwechsel*, 1845 (trans. by Perard in 1872 ; *sub. tit. Du Mouvement Organique*).

In another form it can be written

$$T - EQ = O_o,$$

and signifies that the internal energy of a body in which heat is transformed into work has not varied. In a steam engine a body of water is converted into steam, which moves a piston, after which the water is brought back to its initial temperature, the piston also returning to its original position, the cycle of the operation being completed. The principle of Equivalence, in virtue of which

$$T = EQ$$

presumes therefore a completed cycle of operations.

The authoritative demonstration of this fact is due to an experiment by Edlund ; work T is expended in pulling a metal wire by means of a weight P. The wire evolves heat to the amount of q calories. Allow it to return to its original length by removing the weight and it will evolve q' calories ; and we see that :—

$$q' - q = \frac{T}{E} \text{ or } \frac{T}{425}.$$

A return to the initial state, and an absence of variation of the internal energy is therefore necessary.

But if the cycle is not completed, if the body does not go back to its initial state, its internal energy will have undergone a variation U. Then the equivalence between the variation U and the work T on the one side and the heat Q on the other will be

$$\frac{T + U}{425} = Q \text{ (in calories).}$$

In the experiment of Edlund it was

$$q + \frac{T}{425} = q'.$$

If, by the aid of chemical reactions, a body could produce heat and work there would be an equivalence between the variation of its internal energy U and the external mechanical and thermal phenomena, the heat being either evolved or absorbed. From which :—

$$U = T \pm EQ.$$

Chemists have made an interesting application of this law of equivalence : they burn an organic substance in a closed and perfectly rigid vessel and the gases due to the combustion not being able to expand, there will be no work :

$$T = o.$$

Therefore :

$$U = EQ :$$

all the chemical energy will then be transformed into heat. Such is the principle of thermochemistry or the art of measuring the heats of combustion of substances. For this the "bomb" calorimeter of Berthelot is generally used, modified by Mahler and subsequently by Donkin. In the chamber of that calorimeter the substance is burnt in contact with compressed oxygen at a pressure of 25 atmospheres. The heat can be measured by correct and proved methods for which reference must be made to special treatises. Simpler calorimeters are also used, such as that of Bunsen, or that of Fery.([1])

But the general case is that in which

$$U = T \pm EQ.$$

Let there be an electric battery driving a motor. Work T is done and q calories of heat are evolved, but if the unused chemical reaction of the battery be neglected, the calorimeter will indicate q' calories. This experiment shows, in accordance with the principle of equivalence that

$$\frac{T}{E} + q = q'.$$

In the first case :—

$$U = \frac{T}{E} + q;$$

In the second case :—

$$U = q'; \text{ from which } q' = \frac{T}{E} + q.$$

This is the case with living beings. Animals and vegetables burn food internally, and in repose they produce heat exclusively. But mechanical work, of which animals only are capable, leads to the general relation :

$$U = T + EQ.$$

(see § 103).

Lastly, as will be examined later in detail, the work can be motive, or resistant, that is to say, positive or negative (§ 28). If it is negative,

$$U = EQ - T:$$

the modification of internal energy will not be as great as if the work were positive, which amounts to saying that negative work, far from making demands on that internal energy, on the contrary tends to economise it.

35. Principle of Carnot.—Sadi-Carnot established a principle of great importance to express the relation of work and heat,

---

([1]) Fery, *Journal de Physique*, 1912, p. 550.

in the dynamic sense of that form of energy. Henry Le Chatelier has given it concrete expression in the law of the displacement of equilibrium or Le Chatelier's law : "Any system producing work is the seat of a disturbance of equilibrium. Conversely, wherever there can be re-establishment of that equilibrium, there can be production of work." [1] Carnot had shown the disturbance of thermal equilibrium in the difference of temperature between the steam coming out of the boiler and the water going into the condenser, a difference analogous, in the fall of water, to the vertical distance between the head and tail race, by virtue of which the water does work. There are two components of each kind of energy, thus :—Mechanical energy = force (or weight) × the distance traversed ; heat energy = entropy [2] × difference of temperature.

Entropy is a quantity which varies with the absolute temperature as gravity varies on the surface of the earth with the distance from the centre. When a substance takes in or gives out heat it is said to change its entropy.

Electric energy = quantity of electricity × difference of the potential [3]

Chemical energy = mass × chemical potential.

The chemical potential expresses what is also understood by the term " affinity," now obsolete.

To return to calorific energy : it has been said that it is proportional to the change of temperature. If, therefore, it is transformed into mechanical energy, this in its turn will be proportional to the same change of temperature. Now, steam increases in pressure with the temperature by $\frac{1}{273}$ of its value for 1 degree C ; if in a heat engine, the temperature of the condenser is reduced by 1, 2, 3 . . . degrees, the work will increase by

$$\frac{1}{273}, \quad \frac{2}{273}, \quad \frac{3}{273} \cdots$$

of its value. In cooling to 273°, all the heat will be transformed into work. A condenser at — 273°C would be at absolute zero ; a fictitious temperature serving as the basis of an absolute scale. Thus 15° centigrade represents an absolute temperature of

$$288° = 273 + 15.$$

---

[1] Henry Le Chateliu, *Lecons sur le Carbone.* We have drawn largely on the ideas set forth in this authoritative work.

[2] The conception of entropy is due to a learned German physicist, Clausius (1857).

[3] We say briefly : intensity × potential, or if we use the corresponding electrical units : amperes—volts.

A quantity of steam having a quantity of heat Q is taken from a boiler and supplied to an engine at an absolute temperature T. It produces work, and the remainder having heat Q' goes to the condenser at a temperature T'. But it is known that $\frac{Q}{T}$ or $\frac{Q'}{T'}$ expresses the entropy $= \dfrac{\text{heat energy}}{\text{temperature difference.}}$ Consequently the engine receives a quantity of entropy $\frac{Q}{T}$ and gives up another $\frac{Q'}{T'}$. The quantity of heat transformed into work $Q - Q'$ is a fraction $\dfrac{Q - Q'}{Q}$ of the total quantity furnished by the source of heat.

In order that the above fraction may be a maximum, it is necessary that during the transformation no loss of heat (by radiation or conduction) should take place, and also that the fall of temperature should take place gradually from T to T', and that the water should be brought gradually from T' to T.—In other words, the water must accomplish a complete cycle which will bring it back to its initial state. The change of temperature is, necessarily, very slow, so that the machine may be at any moment nearly in equilibrium and be able to function in either direction, thus being reversible.

To effect the maximum work, a heat engine must perform a complete and reversible cycle, this being known as the Carnot Cycle. Throughout the cycle Q and T vary in such a way that the entropy $\frac{Q}{T}$ does not change in becoming $\frac{Q'}{T'}$, as it is conserved. The principle of Carnot is also called the principle of the conservation of Entropy :

$$\frac{Q}{T} = \frac{Q'}{T'} ; \text{ therefore } Q' = Q \times \frac{T'}{T}.$$

And the fraction transformed into work $\dfrac{Q - Q'}{Q}$ will have as its expression

$$\frac{Q - Q'}{Q} = 1 - \frac{T'}{T} \text{ or } \frac{T - T'}{T}.$$

But if, somewhere, there is loss of heat, the entropy is not conserved, it tends to diminish.

36. Thermodynamics : Energetics.—The two principles which register the relations of heat and of work constitute thermodynamics. In extending them to all the forms of energy, a complete science has been constituted called energetics. And it is seen that, every time a cycle of operations is completed the law of equivalence applies, and whenever a completed cycle is reversible, the principle of Carnot operates. Nevertheless, use is made of the law of equivalence even when a complete cycle is not performed, we say:

$$U = T \pm Q.$$

Experiment justifies this equation. In addition it is used in irreversible transformations. Nature evolves in an irreversible manner. She follows one direction and does not reverse her progress. Life develops in the direction of age, but never in that of rejuvenation.

37. Comparison of the Forms of Energy.—To compare energies quantitatively there must be common measure. It has been agreed to adopt the calorie. Mechanical energy is measured at 425 kilogrammetres per great calorie. Solar energy, received by a thermo-pile, is measured in calories. Similarly electric energy can be transformed into heat. The common unit is therefore the calorie, but it does not follow that the nature of energy is the same in all its aspects and that it can always be converted into heat. From the qualitative point of view, the various forms of energy form a hierarchy. Some (mechanical, elastic, electric) are interchangeable without taking a calorific path in that exchange. That is an advantage, because heat is never an efficient intermediary ; it causes a depreciation or degradation of the energies mentioned.

Radiant energy, however, in its various forms, is always transformed into heat ; it degrades to exhaustion. A steam engine only performs work by degrading a quantity of heat, rejected unprofitably to the condenser. It is an important fact in the doctrine of energetics that the energies have a natural tendency to degrade into heat, an inevitable tendency in some, but able in others, to be moderated. As for chemical energy, it only degrades in part in its transformations into work or into electric current. It would degrade entirely if facilities were not offered to it by which it could change into work or electricity. That is why it is convenient to consider both " free " energy, capable of useful transformation and " bound " energy [1] of degradation (heat). All spontaneous chemical reaction will plainly tend to produce the maximum of heat (principle of maximum energy, of Berthelot) [2].

---

[1] The distinction between free and bound energy belongs to Helmholtz *Journal de Physique*, 1884, p. 408 *seq*.
[2] It is improperly called the principle of maximum work.

Speaking broadly, we might say that the molecular energy of matter has two alternative destinations. On the one hand, if directed and controlled, it can do useful work. On the other hand, if left to itself without such direction and control, it inevitably tends to be dissipated in heat.

Helmholtz described these two conditions as those of molecular order and disorder respectively. An analogy might be found in the case of a body of troops marching. If, acting under orders, their progress will be orderly and regular ; if left to themselves, disorder and confusion will result.

Disorder more easily than order can occur in molecular movements as among troops ; the state of degradation being the more probable one.

Not less curious is the fact that chemical energy can transform itself into all the other forms, without any one of the latter being able in their turn to transform themselves into chemical energy.

Nevertheless, solar radiation, or even a source of artificial light acting on the green leaves of plants, has an effect on living matter. The chlorophyll of vegetables is indispensable to that work of synthesis. Chemical energy thus accumulates little by little, in vegetable bodies, from every diminution.

It must be recognised that solar radiation is the origin of all the energy in the world, whilst the two poles of energetic transformation are chemical energy and heat energy.

38. Vital Energy.—The teachings of energetics are just as true in regard to the animate world as the inanimate world. Thus the number of calories given to an organism by a given quantity of food is found to correspond exactly with the calories radiated from that organism. If work is done the number of calories required by the law of equivalence will be absorbed, the rest being equally radiated to the exterior. Therefore vital energy represents nothing quantitatively, and there is no place for it in the cycle of energy (see § 103). Does an intellectual energy absorbed by all the manifestations of thought exist ? Apparently not, because experiment has shown that the balance of the energies is always exact and always the same whether a man takes up or does not take up intellectual occupations (see § 149). Finally, among the elements of cerebral nervous matter, does there exist a source of intellectual energy which may not be perceptible by our methods of measurement and which cannot be expressed in calorific values ? There is no absurdity in such a question, but so far no experimental result has established the presence of a source of energy in man of a totally different nature from the known energies. Science, therefore, cannot take this speculation into account for the present,

The problem of mysterious energies of the organism leads to that of inter-cellular reactions of these varieties and of the obscure laws by which they are regulated. The resistance of living animals to depressing, pathogenic and toxic conditions induced the earlier physicians to hypothecate the existence of a "vital force" either in the blood or in the nervous system. A little of this doctrine, and a little of the belief in the soul combined to decide certain minds in favour of a special energy in the human being which they termed a survival of the divine breath.

To-day those gratuitous hypotheses are superseded by the theory of radioactivity, which manifests itself in solid, liquid or gaseous matter. The fact that a single trace of radioactive substance emits, almost indefinitely, luminous, thermal or electric energy, leaves the door open to a radioactive theory of thought according to which the nervous matter dissociates or disengages itself in such a manner as to develop intellectual energy.

Positive science cannot embrace such suppositions. Without doubt it has been found (¹) that the tissues of man are radioactive, that the brain exhibits even special activity. But the phenomenon is connected with nutrition, which enriches the organism with radioactive elements. Also it is said that old subjects have a superior intensity to that observed in the young. Death does not end that radioactivity, although all thought has disappeared. Therefore it is as well to reserve one's opinion on these difficult and uncertain problems. Lastly, in regard to the action of nervous organs, one is constrained to admit that an unknown form of energy emanates from them, which cannot be measured in calories and which, in consequence, escapes us. Nervous energies, which were once upon a time called "nervous fluids," after having been the "animal spirits" of the Cartesian school, act in the functions of the animal like the priming of a gun. They release the machinery whose work is incommeasureable by any calorimetric valuations.

39. Loss of Energy, Passive Resistance.—Natural phenomena all tend to transform the energies into one of their single forms, namely, heat, which it is a destructive change. Thus animal organism loses all its chemical energy as heat, if it is in repose, but if it produces mechanical work, this will be taken from free energy, everything else being lost as heat.

In the movement of solid bodies, a similar loss, more or less violent, always takes place, seeing that indeformable and perfect solids do not exist. The parts of machines being deformed a little at points of contact, there is as a result external friction of a vibratory nature, in consequence of which there is a dissipation

---

(¹) R. Werner, *Münch. Med. Wochenschrift*, No. 1 (1906) ; A. Caan, *Sitzungsber d. Heidelb. Akad d Wissensch. Mém.* v. (1911).

of energy. These frictions or passive resistances can either be due to a continuous sliding or rolling contact, (§ 14) or else to a contact of very short duration, as in impact, or, lastly, to friction against a magnetic field. Thus the work done by a copper disc, which turns between the poles of an electro-magnet is transformed into heat (Foucault's currents). The friction produced by sliding and rolling shows that the surfaces of bodies are never perfectly polished ; they present roughnesses, from which ensues a veritable adhesion of the molecules in contact, causing a resistance called the force of friction capable of opposing movement. When a surface slides or a cylinder rolls on another surface, which is horizontal, the friction will be proportional to the pressure of the body and will vary according to the substances employed. Let Φ (phi, Greek letter) be the friction of sliding of a body whose weight is P ; the friction per kilogramme will be :

$$f = \frac{\Phi}{P};$$

this is the unit or the co-efficient of friction of sliding bodies. Let Φ', in the same way, be the friction of a rolling cylinder of weight P ; then :

$$\varphi = \frac{\Phi'}{P}$$

this is the unit or the co-efficient of friction of rolling bodies. For instance :

	Co-efficients of	
	sliding.	rolling.
Wood on wood (dry) . . . . $f = 0\cdot40$	$\varphi = 0\cdot002$
Metals on metals . . . . $= 0\cdot19$	$= 0\cdot002$

It is clear that the effort necessary to overcome the friction is larger in sliding than in rolling. Also, φ diminishes in proportion as the radius of the rolling body increases. For a displacement l, the work done in sliding or rolling will be :

$$\Phi \times l = f \times P \times l \quad \text{or} \quad \Phi' \times l = \Phi \times P \times l.$$

These are the values of vibratory energy changed into heat (§ 32). If there is sufficient friction between a moving surface and a fixed surface it will not only retard but stop the movement.

Such is the case of the slipper or shoe which is applied to the rim of a wheel and serves as a brake, and it is also the case of brakes in general, of which the classic type is Prony's brake. In this friction is produced on the shaft A of an engine (fig. 68) by a brake band C provided with blocks of wood and terminated by lever of a length L. In practice the belt encircles a pulley keyed on the shaft, and in tightening the screws e, e, the brake band C is forced

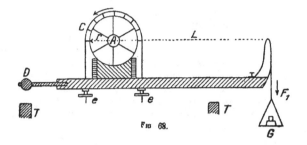

Fig 68.

into frictional engagement with the pulley so that the engine assumes a steady speed equal to that which it would have if it did a definite work, against the resistances which oppose it. Therefore the work done by an engine in overcoming the friction equals the ordinary capacity of the engine for doing work. In order that the lever L shall not be dragged round by the rotation of the brake-band, weights F_1 are placed in the scale G, which hold it horizontal, but allow slight oscillations. The counter weight D allows the lever and the scale pan to be in equilibrium before each experiment, the movements being limited by the stops T and T'. Thus, in equilibrium, the force of friction which acts at the extremity of the radius r of the pulley, will have the same moment as the force F, acting at the extremity of the lever L, from which :

$$\Phi \times r = F_1 \times L.$$

The work done by friction $2 \pi r \times \Phi$ per revolution will be the expression $2 \pi F_1 L$. The work done $2 \pi F_1 L \times n$, per n revolutions, can be estimated from the values of F found by experiment. It is well to remember, on the one hand, that a Prony brake gives the work done by an engine making n revolutions in a known time ; whilst, on the other hand, that the friction has allowed the production of a static effort (raising of a loaded scale) at the expense of mechanical energy.

Sliding friction has many practical applications, whether it be to maintain a ladder in position when leaning against a wall with its base on the ground, to retain the work in a joiner's vice, or to rotate pulleys by means of belts. It can be rectilineal in the case of sledges, concentric to an axis as in a pivot, or circular as in a spindle.

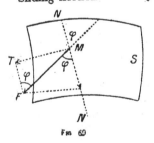

Fig 69.

When a point M slides with friction on a surface the force F, which pulls it along, has a component N which produces the friction $\Phi = f \times N$, and a tangential component T which tends to overcome that friction (fig. 69). Equilibrium is not reached until

$$T = \Phi = f \times N,$$

that is to say, at that moment

$$\frac{T}{N} = f.$$

And as $T = F \sin \varphi$, $N = F \cos \varphi$.

$$\frac{T}{N} \text{ or } f = \frac{\sin \varphi}{\cos \varphi} = \text{tang } \varphi.$$

This is the angle of friction or the greatest inclination that the direction of the force can make with the vertical and sliding continue.

If the force is that of gravity G (fig. 70), by gradually increasing the inclination of the surface S to the horizontal, it will be found that the angle of friction is equal to the angle of inclination—but only in equilibrium.

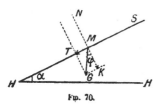

Fig. 70.

Rolling friction is exhibited in the haulage of carriages. The larger the radius of the wheel the smaller the friction, the haulage being produced tangentially. By dividing the effort of traction of a vehicle by its weight, the co-efficient of traction is obtained. This co-efficient is 0·005 on railways, that is to say, for a wagon of 10,000 kilogrammes (10 metric tons) there must be a tractive effort of

$$10{,}000 \times 0{\cdot}005 = 50 \text{ kilogrammes.}$$

In railways the tractive effort per metric ton is adopted (§ 256).

40. Impact.—An emission of energy also takes place when a body in movement encounters suddenly a body in repose or moving at a lesser speed. The impact has a very short duration. If a body of mass M and speed V meets a body of a mass m and speed v; the latter experiences percussion at the point of contact (fig. 71). If the movement takes place in the same direction, M is added to m and the new speed will be u. As far as movement is concerned we have :

M m

Fig. 71.

$$MV + mv = (M + m)\,u \; ; \text{ hence } u = \frac{MV + mv}{M + m}$$

Impact deforms bodies at the point of contact and this deformation can be permanent as in the contact of two plastic bodies such as two balls of lead. In this case, a diminution of energy is produced, because after the shock :

$$\frac{MV^2}{2} + \frac{mv^2}{2};\ \text{is changed to}\ \frac{(M+m)\ u^2}{2};\ \text{the}$$

difference, or the loss of energy, being :

$$\tfrac{1}{2}\ (MV^2 + mv^2 - (M+m)\ u^2).$$

Replace u by the above value. The loss of energy

$$= \tfrac{1}{2}\frac{Mm}{M+m}(V-v)^2.$$

This is equal to the energy of a mass $\dfrac{Mm}{M+m}$ moving with a speed equal to the difference of the speeds of the two bodies prior to the impact. If the two bodies are of the same mass, $M = m$; then the loss of energy

$$= \tfrac{1}{2}\frac{M^2}{2M}\ (V-v)^2\ \text{ or }\ \tfrac{1}{4}M\ (V-v)^2.$$

If one of the bodies is at rest, *i.e.*, $v = O$; then the loss will be : $\tfrac{1}{4}MV^2$, and the moving body will lose half its energy. It was a propos of " live " force thus transformed into vibratory energy, and then into heat, that Leibnitz made the comparison of sovereigns which could be changed into silver (§ 32).

Consider two bodies, which, after the deformation due to impact, return to their initial form, owing to their elasticity. For example, two ivory balls. At the moment of contact the mass M loses a speed V — u, and the elasticity of m causes it to lose the same, in all, 2V — 2u, which reduces V to the final value :

$$V_1 = V - (2V - 2u) = 2u - V.$$

The mass m had gained $(u - v)$, and by the reaction caused by its elasticity it will gain as much again, that is, in all 2 V — 2u, its final speed being therefore :—

$$(2u - 2v) + v,\ \text{or}\ v_1 = 2u - v.$$

And the two elastic bodies will part, the reaction being of as short duration as the action.

Replace u by its value, as before, the speeds V and v_1 are obtained as functions of V, v, M and m, and it will be seen that

$$\tfrac{1}{2}MV_1^2 + \tfrac{1}{2}mv_1^2 = \tfrac{1}{2}MV^2 + \tfrac{1}{2}mv^2,$$

in other words, in the impact of perfectly elastic bodies, the sum of the energies is conserved, being the same after as before the impact, In practice, the restored energy is less than the original energy, and there is often a very slight dissipation into heat, a dissipation which increases if the bodies are good conductors of heat and if the impact is of relatively long duration.

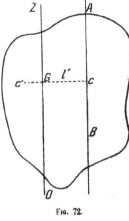

Fig. 72.

41. In impact the forces are of such a brief duration that they have been wrongly called instantaneous forces which would presume infinitely hard bodies. Hertz has shown that with spheres of the same radius the duration of the impact depends on the relative speed and the elastic properties of the substances. Between two cylinders of steel Hamburger obtained an average duration of $\frac{8}{10000}$ of a second, and Hopkinson obtained the same result.

Mention must be made of the part played by the axis of gravity (§ 20) as an axis of rotation of a body subjected to impact. If I_g is the moment of inertia of a body round its axis of gravity OZ (fig. 72), the moment in relation to a parallel axis AB will be $I_g + Ml'^2$, M being the mass of the body, and l', the distance between the two axes. As $I = M\rho^2$, therefore :

$$I = M\rho^2 = M\rho'^2 + Ml'^2,$$

and finally,

$$l = M (\rho'^2 + l'^2).$$

If the axis of rotation coincides with the axis of gravity, it is clear that the moment of inertia will be the minimum.

On the other hand, presuming that the body oscillates in relation to the axis AB like a pendulum of a length l', then

$$l = \frac{I}{Ml'},$$

l being the length of the equivalent simple pendulum. And in consequence :

$$l = M (\rho'^2 + l'^2) : \quad Ml' = \frac{\rho'^2 + l'^2}{l'} = l' + \frac{\rho'^2}{l'} \ (\text{§ 26}).$$

Let the length $CC' = l$, the point C' will oscillate like a simple pendulum attached to the fixed point C. The point C' is the centre of percussion. And so that there may not be percussion on the axis of rotation AB, that percussion.

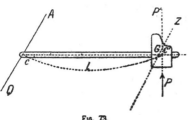

must be perpendicular to the plane ABG. It is in this way that, in a hammer, vide fig. 73, the percussion takes place in the direction PP′ and $CC' = l' + \frac{\rho'^2}{l'}$; the head of the hammer throws the centre of gravity back between C and C′. In these conditions the percussion is nought on the axis QA, that is to say, at the hand.

The quantity $C'G = \frac{\rho'^2}{l'}$ is always small.

A knowledge of the laws of impact is important in the study of machines, and finds an interesting application in the game of billiards, and a useful application in the driving in of stakes or piles for foundations.

The effect of impact, as expressed by the resultant movement, depends as much on the speed as on the mass of the body. Thus a stone thrown by hand against a door would make it turn on its hinges, whereas a shot from a cannon passes through the door without displacing it, the movement not having had time to spread around the part struck. A jet of sand projected at a high speed is employed to grind glass, metals are cut by means of circular saws without teeth moving at a great speed, and high speeds are usefully applied in other interesting ways. The effect of mass is no less obvious : a nail does not penetrate a plank unless the latter is supported on something ; it is better to use a fairly heavy hammer to knock in nails than a light one, because M and m being the mass of the hammer and of the nail respectively, the loss of energy due to the impact is :—

$$\frac{Mm}{M + m}(V - v)^2.$$

The relation of that loss to the energy $\frac{1}{2}MV^2$ of the hammer is

$$\frac{m}{M + m}\left(1 = \frac{v}{V}\right)^2.$$

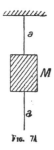

that is to say that the relative loss will be less in proportion as the mass M of the hammer is greater and its speed V slower. Thus shoemakers use a stone to receive the blow of the hammer, and that large anvils do not spoil bars. Lastly, take a mass M suspended by a string a, and carrying an identical string a'. If a' is pulled sharply it is broken, but if pulled steadily the upper string a is broken, because, in the first case, the rapid impulse has not allowed the pull to be transmitted, whereas in the second case the mass M has added its effect to that of the pull (fig. 74).

42. Certain other passive resistances intervene in movement and oblige the motive power to be increased. First of all the resistance of fluids must be considered. According to whether the movement takes place in the air or in water, there results a resistance proportional to the square of the speed of the current flowing at the surface perpendicularly opposed to the current, and to the density of the fluid.

Then :

$$R = K \times S \times V^2 \times d.$$

In taking the density of water in relation to that of air,

$$R = KSV^2$$

for the resistance in air. The co-efficient K is approximately $\frac{1}{13}$; and S and V are expressed in metres and R in kilogrammes. For water it will be K'.

The co-efficients K and K' vary with the form of the body in movement.

The stiffness of a cord or belt causes it to resist bending around a pulley, a resistance which requires the expenditure of a certain force at a dead loss to get a useful result. This inflexibility is expressed by the force f and it is shown approximately that :

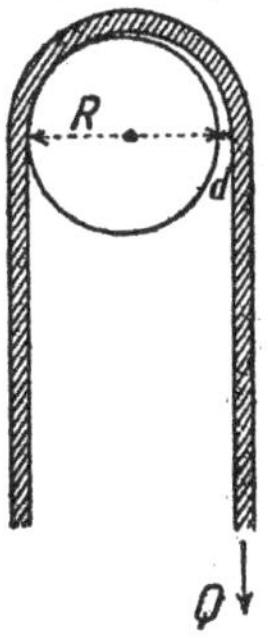

$$f = \frac{d \times Q}{R + r} ;$$

It increases with the distance Q to be displaced, and the distance d (co-efficiency of inflexibility) ; and it diminishes when the radii of the pulley and of the belt increase (fig. 75). The inflexibility is, however, never a negligible quantity.

Fig. 75.

CHAPTER III.

PRINCIPLES OF GENERAL MECHANICS (*Continued*).

Resistance of Materials.—Machines.

43. Deformation of Bodies : Elasticity.—In the foregoing study of equilibrium and the movement of bodies, it has been assumed that they remained indeformable under the actions of forces. But this is a false assumption, and we can, in practice, only study constrained equilibrium (§ 13) such as is brought into play by the internal forces of a body. It is therefore necessary briefly to consider the value taken by these tensions under the action of external forces, and to ascertain to what degree the latter can act without entirely overcoming the internal tensions, *i.e.*, without breaking the body. The study of the deformation and resistance of materials is the necessary complement of the science of work. Under the action of forces, matter is extended, compressed, sheared, bent and twisted, and its molecules, in each of these cases, are displaced. If when the effort has ceased, the molecules re-establish themselves in their original positions, it is said that the material is perfectly elastic. If, on the other hand, they re-establish themselves slowly or incompletely, the elasticity is imperfect. The definition of elasticity, therefore, is as follows : —The power to return to the initial form after a deforming force has ceased to act. It is evident that the deformation is proportional to the effort, as long as the magnitude of that effort has not exceeded a certain value, at which return to the initial state becomes impossible. This value is called the limit of elasticity.

If the force applied is such as to stress the material beyond the elastic limit, the deformation becomes permanent. The material is said to have received a permanent set. If the force is still further increased rupture of the material will eventually occur.

A knowledge of the elastic limit of various materials is of prime importance in the study of energetics. For example, the energy stored in a clock spring by the act of winding up will be restored with the greater completeness, in its unwinding, the more that the material of the spring approximates to a, (theoretically), perfect elastic material.

In the majority of substances, however, the elasticity is imperfect; the return to the initial state is incomplete owing to internal friction, which dissipates a part of the energy (*Elastiche Nacdwirkung*, Weber). Furthermore, the elasticity, even of metals such as platinum or steel, is subject to fatigue and diminishes. Workmen know that the best springs end by being worn out.

Furthermore, the internal " viscosity " of materials causes a certain retention or accumulation of the effects of repeated stresses and thereby the elasticity of those materials is modified.

44. Tension and Compression.—The simplest of the deformations is that which is produced by a stress F acting in the direction of the axis of a rod of the substance considered, shortening it (compression) or elongating it (tension). It is evident that, for a given stress F, the deformation l will be proportional to the length L of the rod and to a co-efficient α which is a measure of the " souplesse " of the material,[1] that is to say, to the product $L \times \alpha \times F$, but it will be smaller in proportion as the section S of the rod is larger; therefore

$$\pm l = \frac{L \times \alpha \times F}{S},$$

the sign $+$ marks the elongation, the sign $-$ the contraction. The lengths l, L are expressed in millimetres, the section S in square millimetres; the effort F in kilogrammes. Thus the higher the co-efficient of flexibility α, the greater the deformation will be.

It is convenient, however, to characterise bodies by their resistance to deformation, their rigidity, or their elastic force being exactly the reverse of the co-efficient α. Then $\frac{1}{\alpha} = E$, E being the " modulus of elasticity " or "Youngs" modulus. Therefore :

(1) $$\pm l = \frac{L \times F}{S \times E}$$

" Souplesse " and elastic force are often confused, but it will be remembered that indiarubber has a large co-efficient of " souplesse " and inversely a small " modulus of elasticity."

The relation (1) allows the value of the modulus E to be calculated.

---

[1] It is a co-efficient analogous to that of the dilatation of bodies by heat.

$$\text{Thus} \quad E = \frac{L \times F}{S \times l}.$$

Letting $L = l$ and $S = 1$ square millimetre, $E = F$, that is to say that Young's Modulus expresses an effort capable of doubling the length of a rod of 1 square millimetre. In practice, this hypothesis is never true, because the matter cannot be deformed to that point, but breaks when its tenacity, which is the cohesion between its molecules is overcome. The formula (1) is only true for efforts not overstepping the limit of elasticity. It is only within the limit that we can apply Robert Hook's (¹) law : ut tensio, sic vis (similar deformation for similar effort.)

When the stress has reached an amount sufficient to overcome the cohesion of the material, the limit of elasticity is exceeded and the body breaks. This point, the breaking stress, whether it be due to break by tension or compression (crushing) is found by experiment, and depends in an irregular way on the dimensions of the body. Thus Rondelet and Hodgkinson found, for different woods, that it increases as the square of the section, and inversely, that it diminishes as the square of the length. Then—

$$R = K \frac{s^2}{h^2}$$

the section being squared, and the length equal at the most to 15 times the side of the section, the co-efficient $K = 2.565$ is expressed in kilogrammes, S in square centimetres and h in decimetres.

It has been found that circular sections resist the most, hence the advantages of round bodies. Cubic bodies are also very resistant. Finally, the modulus E and the resistance R diminish as the matter becomes fatigued, but increase, in woods, according to density, age, and dryness.

The following figures illustrate this point :—

	Young's Modulus.	R (resistance to rupture.)
Steel	$E = 20,000 \dfrac{kg}{mm^2}$	$83 \dfrac{kg}{mm^2}$
Pine wood (in axial direction)	$E = 1,100 \dfrac{kg}{mm^2}$	$8 \dfrac{kg}{mm^2}$

(¹) Robert Hooke, an English natural philosopher (1635-1703),

45. Flexure or Bending.—When a prismatic rod is fixed at one end and subjected to a stress at the other, it is bent. The top surface will be elongated (convex) the lower shortened (concave) and in the intervening space there will be a plane the length of which is not altered, called the "invariable fibre" or neutral axis. The deflection y is, all things being equal, proportional to the stress F (fig. 76).

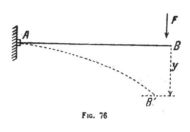

Fig. 76

It can be proved that y varies directly as the cube of the length L of the rod, and inversely as the area a of the section [1] as well as of the cube of the depth e (fig. 77). Then :—

$$(2) \qquad y = \frac{4FL^3}{Eae^3}$$

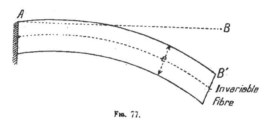

Fig. 77.

If the section is circular, of radius r, the formula will become

$$(2\ a) \qquad y = \frac{4FL^3}{3E\,\pi r^4}.$$

It will be seen how useful it is to have parts of a large section, and substances of a large modulus of elasticity. It is important to note that the deformation does not extend to the centre. There is, therefore, economy of material in using hollow rods. A hollow rod or tube has a far greater resistance to bending than a solid rod having the same amount of material in its cross section.

Nature exhibits this economy of material in the tubular structure of the stalks of vegetables, the quills of birds, and in many bones.[2]

---

[1] The area a is perpendicular to the direction of the stress ; the depth e is parallel to this direction.

[2] The observation is that of Galileo (*Discorsi e. Dimostrazioni* ; see *Opere*, vols. viii. and ix. Milan edition, 1811).

Example :—Take a hollow rod, of which the external radius is R, the internal radius is R' ; the full section is : $\pi R^2 - \pi R'^2 = \pi (R^2 - R'^2)$; a solid rod of equal cross section must have a radius r, so that :

$\pi r^2 = (R^2 - R'^2)$ (fig. 78).

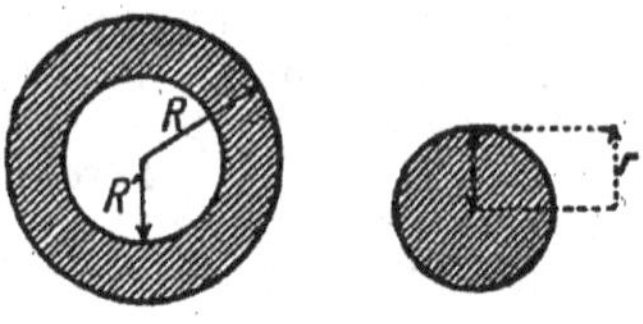

Apply the formula (2*a*) and

Fig. 78.

$$y = \frac{4FL^3}{3E\pi(R^4 - R'^4)} \text{ in one case.}$$

$$y' = \frac{4FL^3}{3E\pi r^4} \text{ in the other.}$$

Suppose that R $=$ 2 R' ; then

$$\pi r^2 = \pi\left(R^2 - \frac{R^2}{4}\right) \text{ or } r^2 = \tfrac{3}{4} R^2.$$

Consequently

$$y = \frac{4FL^3}{3E\pi\left(R^4 - \dfrac{R^4}{16}\right)} = \frac{64FL^3}{45E\pi R^3}, \text{ and } y' = \frac{4FL^3}{3E\pi\dfrac{9}{16}R^4} = \frac{64FL^3}{27E\pi R^4}$$

The two deflections are therefore to each other as 27 and 45.

$$\frac{y}{y'} = \frac{1}{45} : \frac{1}{27} = \frac{27}{45} = \frac{3}{5}.$$

In other terms, the resistance of the solid rod is $\tfrac{3}{5}$ of that of a hollow rod of the same sectional area of which the external radius is double the internal radius.

The ratio will be slightly less than 1 to 4 if R' $= \tfrac{4}{5}$ R.   In the long bones of man (§ 66), R' generally falls between $\tfrac{1}{2}$ R and $\tfrac{3}{5}$ R : Usually R' $= \tfrac{1}{2}$ R for the thigh bone or femur.

According as a beam is simply supported (fig. 79), or is fixed (fig. 80) at its two extremities, the deflections are, respectively :

$$y' = \frac{FL^3}{4\,Eac^3} \text{ and } y'' = \frac{FL^3}{16Eac^3},$$

that is to say, 16 and 64 times less.

Fig 79   **Fig. 80.**

Calculation also shows that the cross section of a rod fixed at one end can be progressively reduced towards the outer, and unsupported end, while maintaining the same resistance to bending, as if the cross section had been uniform throughout the length of the beam. The resultant profile is parabolic. The beams of old-fashioned steam engines have this contour. Such designs are examples of the economical use of material.

In the structure of the stalks of vegetables and the wings of birds we similarly find that the substance of such members is disposed to the best advantage for sustaining the various stresses to which they are subjected.

46. Torsion.—A third method of deformation takes place when a tangential effort, a " couple " of forces, act on a cylinder and make the layers of matter slide one upon another. The sliding does not reach to the centre, which constitutes the neutral axis. For an angle of torsion θ, a layer $OO'AB$ will be brought to

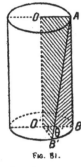

$OO'AB'$ (fig. 81) presuming the base OA to be fixed, and the couple applied perpendicularly to the axis, at $O'B$. The angle of torsion is proportional to the twisting moment M and to the length L of the axis, but inversely proportional to the 4th power of the radius, and to a coefficient G, called the modulus of torsion or of rigidity. Then

$$(3) \qquad \theta = \frac{2ML}{\pi r^4 G}.$$

In the case of a hollow cylinder, of which the radii are r_1 and r'_1

$$\theta = \frac{2ML}{\pi G \left(r_1^4 - r_1'^4 \right)}.$$

Fig. 81.

Torsion of a Cylinder.

It is evident that with equal quantities of material r_1 and r'_1 have such values that :

$$r_1^4 - r_1'^4 > r^4 ;$$

which increases the resistance to torsion of the cylinder considered.

It is usual, in practice, to substitute the diameter d for the radius r and to write

$$r^4 = \frac{d^4}{16}, \text{ whence } \theta = \frac{32ML}{\pi d^4 G};$$

The expression $\dfrac{\pi G}{32}$ is denoted by the symbol γ, known as the co-efficient of Coulomb,

$$\theta = \frac{ML}{\gamma d^4} ;$$

whence the moment :

$$M = \gamma \frac{d^4 \theta}{L}.$$

The moment of torsion M is expressed by the product of the stress F into the diameter d, because the couple acts on the axis. The industrial units were the kilogramme and the millimetre, but to-day the gramme and the centimetre are adopted a unit of moment 100 times less, so that, for the same angle of torsion, the value in grammes-centimetres is 100 times bigger than in kilogrammes-millimetres. Thus G is equal to 8,000 kilogrammes for steel, 400 for oak, etc. Corresponding values 785 and 39 have been arrived at for γ, or grammes-centimetres $78{\cdot}5 \times 10^3$ and $3{\cdot}9 \times 10^3$.

To twist an oak stick of 6 centimetres in diameter and 25 centimetres long through one radian (57°, 18° approximately) there must be a couple :

$$M = 3{\cdot}9 \times 10^3 \cdot \frac{60^4 \times 1}{250} = 20 \times 10^7 \text{ grammes-centimetres.}$$

Between Young's modulus E and the modulus of rigidity G there is the relation :

$$R = \frac{E}{2\,(1+\sigma)}.$$

the co-efficient σ indicating the relation of the transversal contraction to the elongation of the stick. This (Poisson's) co-efficient σ is $\frac{1}{2}$ for indiarubber according to the most correct estimates, but it generally varies for different substances between $\frac{1}{4}$ and $\frac{2}{3}$. In bodies called anisotropic ([1]) it is greater than unity; it is $\sigma = 1{\cdot}47$ to $1{\cdot}65$ for cocoon silk. The modulus of rigidity thus lies between

$$\frac{E}{2\left(1 + \frac{1}{4}\right)} \text{ and } \frac{E}{2\left(1 + \frac{3}{5}\right)}$$

that is between $\frac{2}{5}$ E and $\frac{5E}{16}$.

The system of $\frac{kg.}{mm^2}$, used to estimate E, does equally for G ; but the kilogramme being expressed by $981 \times 1,000$ dynes, or $0{\cdot}981 \times 10^6$ in the C.G.S. System, and the square millimetre being 100 times smaller than the square centimetre, this system is $0{\cdot}981 \times 10^8$ times less than the C.G.S. system.

It follows therefore that :—

$$\gamma = \frac{\pi G}{32} = \frac{\pi \times 0{\cdot}981 \times 10^8}{32} = 0{\cdot}9631 \times 10^7,$$

([1]) When the elements of the volume of a substance vary in property according to their " orientation," that substance is homogeneous and " anisotropic " : otherwise it is " isotropic."

and that the values of γ in the latter system are deduced from G by the equation :

$$\gamma = G \times 0.963 \times 10^7.$$

The application of these three laws of torsion lead to the use of hollow shafts in machinery, by which weight is reduced and material economised without prejudice to strength.

47. Shearing.—The name of shearing is given to the action produced when a body is broken at any section by causing the two portions of the body to slide past one another. It is seen in the effect of shears cutting a bar, the two parts separating by sliding transversely. The effort of shearing is called the shear stress. The shearing due to the action of a punch, or a fly-press, can also be cited. There is therefore a transverse resistance of the matter, laterally and tangentially, which opposes the sliding. It is that which prevents the threads of screws from breaking. The deformation by torsion is a shear strain. The shear stress which will produce fracture in pinewood is estimated at 23 kilogrammes per square centimetre.

48. Alterations of Elasticity.—The fatigue already discussed in connection with elasticity is the result of various causes :

1. The former state of the substance, the work that it has had to perform, the duration of the action of the stresses endured, and the age of the substance.

2. The real nature of the material, whether the deformation causes temporary or permanent internal frictions, or whether there is viscosity, as in the case of the majority of organic substances.

3. Sharp variations of temperature.

4. Shocks and vibrations whose effects are cumulative and frequently cause its rupture.

49. Role of Elasticity and Work or Elastic Energy.—A fundamental property of the elasticity of bodies is to store and accumulate in them short impulses, those of shock and vibration : a few small items of energy will add together and form a very appreciable quantity of energy. First of all, the work of deformation or elastic energy, that is to say, the product of stress and deformation must be estimated. These are :

1. Work of traction or of compression :

$$T = \tfrac{1}{2} F \times l = \tfrac{1}{2} \frac{F^2 L}{ES} = \frac{SEl^2}{2L}$$

(equations that are deducted from the formula of elongations (1) and easily established directly).

2. Work of flexure :

$$T = \tfrac{1}{2} F \times y = \frac{2}{3} \frac{F^2 L^3}{\pi r^4 E} \text{ (for a cylindrical rod).}$$

3. Work of torsion :

$$T = \tfrac{1}{2} M \times \theta = \frac{M^2 L}{\pi r^4 G} \text{ (for a cylindrical rod).}$$

Thus elastic energy is a form of energy (§ 37) equivalent to the others. A shock imparts to an elastic body a certain quantity of energy, the body taking a deformation determined by its section, its length and its " Young's modulus." That energy is transmitted, more or less completely, by the elastic body, and specially, more or less slowly, so that if several shocks succeed

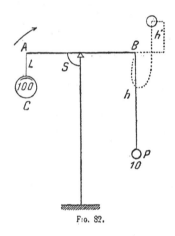

Fig. 82.

each other rapidly, they will be transformed into a continuous action. Thus Marey showed that the application of rubber ropes to the drawing of hand carriages effected an economy of 26 per cent. of the work done, the shocks not being transmitted to the shoulders of the man, excessive effort and discomfort were avoided. The motive power of the heart is, in the same way, rendered regular and economical. Such is also the law of the respiration, etc. An interesting experiment of Marey's is worthy of mention; AB is the beam of a balance (fig. 82). A ball G weighing 100 grammes is attached to A, and to B a ball p weighing 10 grammes, by a string whose length is h. The beam is held horizontal by resting on a special stop S, so that it can only move in the direction of the arrow. The raising and letting fall from a height h' of the little ball p will not cause any movement of the beam.

Replace the string of the ball G by an elastic thread and the beam will be displaced if the little ball is repeatedly dropped. This is a clear example of the transmission and accumulation of the work of shocks, so rapid that in some way they produce a tensile stress, capable of overcoming the weight of the larger ball, and causes a certain displacement of it.

The tension thus produced is the result of the elastic work of the string. The work done in falling by the ball p is p ($h' + h + l$), l being the elongation of the string L ; and the elastic work is $\dfrac{SEl^2}{2L}$, L, L being the length of the elastic string.

From the equation :

$$p\,(h' + h + l) = \frac{SEl^2}{2L},$$

we get :

$$l = \frac{Lp}{SE} + \sqrt{\frac{L^2p^2}{S^2E^2} + \frac{2Lp(h' + h)}{SE}} \; ;$$

and as from the formula $l = \dfrac{FL}{SE}$, we find the value of the tension F.

$F = \dfrac{lSE}{L}$, therefore by substitution :

$$F = p + \sqrt{p^2 + 2p\,\frac{ES\,(h' + h)}{L}}.$$

This result shows, on the one hand, that the height of the fall can be increased in such a manner that F can overcome the weight of the larger ball, and on the other hand, that the tension F depends on the modulus of elasticity E, that is to say, on the nature of the string. If we select a string of small modulus, the deformation operates in a very short time, the tension, being the same throughout the length of the string, will raise the larger ball. If the string were non-elastic and inextensible, the shock would break it, or make ineffectual vibrations.

It can be verified, for instance, that an indiarubber string of 10 centimetres in length and 5 square millimetres in section, would have a tension of 102 gr. approximately, if the shock were produced by a weight of 50 gr. only, falling from a total height of 50 centimetres.

The elastic vibrations sometimes attain to a magnitude which makes them dangerous. From the formula above it is evident that the internal tensions increase in proportion to the hardness of materials with a consequent increase in the value of E. It will also be seen that a body has a natural period of vibration. If the external impulses which it receives are of the same, or even approximately, the same period. "Resonance" is produced, with the result that the elasticity of the body may be overcome and fracture may result.

It is on the above account that bodies of troops break step when crossing a bridge, and there are numerous other applications of the preceding laws in relation to both the utilisation of the accumulation of impulses and also the avoidance of dangerous consequences therefrom.

50. Machines.—A machine is a system employed, either to maintain in equilibrium resistant forces, or to overcome such resistant forces, by other forces, known as moving forces, or powers.

In the static state, the power is equal to the resistance. In the dynamic state power overcomes resistance. A machine is said to be simple when it comprises a single element, with certain connexions whilst it is called composite—like most industrial machines—when it is composed of several simple machines working in conjunction.

The parts of a machine generally have connexions, which limit each part to only one possible movement, which may be defined by a single equation. If, for example, it only turns round an axis, or slides along the length of that axis, the angle of rotation or the value of the translation defines the movement. One or the other of these values is the " parameter " or constant that it is both necessary and sufficient to know.

Machines are therefore systems with complete connexions, that is to say such, that all their points are determined by a single parameter.

51. Simple Machines.—This name is given to the lever (fig. 84) ; to the inclined plane (fig. 88) ; to the pulley (fig. 92) ; to the hand winch (fig. 91) ; to the wedge (fig. 93), and the screw. The conditions of equilibrium of · these machines, under the forces which are applied to them, external forces and forces of restraint (§ 14), are given by an important theorem, that of Alembert relating to virtual work. If any point M of a system is displaced to M′ it is stated to produce work described as " virtual " to distinguish it from the real work that the forces could cause it to accomplish, for instance, in the direction MM′ (fig. 83).

Fig. 83.

The theorem of Alembert says :

" The necessary and sufficient condition for the equilibrium of a system is that for every virtual displacement of the system compatible with its connexions, the sum of the virtual work of the given forces shall be "zero." But the work of the connexions, in the absence of any friction, is zero. Thus a point moving on a plane is subject to a reaction which, being perpendicular to the displacement, produces no work (§ 28). Therefore, it only remains to consider the work of the external forces which must also be zero, according to the theorem of Alembert. In fact, in an equilibrate system with connexions, it is known that all the forces have two resultants (§ 15), of which the work must be zero, because they are themselves both zero. As the virtual work of the one —that of the connexions—is zero, that of the other—the resultant of the external forces—must equally be zero. We apply this theorem to simple machines.

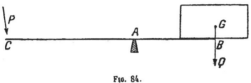

Fig. 84.

(1) *Levers.*—A lever is a rigid bar, movable round a fixed point called the fulcrum (A). The resistance, Q, to be overcome,

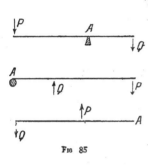

Fig 85

is a force or weight applied at the extremity B of the lever and the power P is applied at the other extremity C (fig. 84). This type of lever is called a lever of the first order. But the resistance can be at the centre of the lever when it is said to be of the second order, or, finally, the power can be applied at the centre when it is said to be of the third order (fig. 85). Scissors, tinman's snips, blacksmiths' tongs, turners' tools, pruning shears, etc., are of the first order. Sheet iron shears, the bakers' knife, nutcrackers, oars or sculls, the handles of pumps, wheelbarrows, pedals of pianos, etc., are of the second order, and spades, coal-tongs, the treadle of the knife-grinder or sewing machine, and the majority of the numerous levers found in the structure of animals are of the third order.

The distances between the fulcrum and the positions of the power and of the resistance constitute the arms of the lever. In the lever CAB (fig. 86), the arms are A*p* and A*r*, and not AC and AB. The resultant R will be applied to the fulcrum, A.

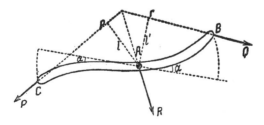

Fig. 86.

As to the condition of equilibrium, the work done by the power for a virtual displacement corresponding to the angle α will be

$$\mathbf{T}_p = \text{moment of P} \times \text{angle } \alpha = \text{P} \times \text{A}p\alpha.$$

The virtual work of the resistance will be :

$$\mathbf{T}_q = \text{moment of Q} \times \alpha = \text{Q} \times \text{A}r\alpha.$$

According to Alembert's theorem.

$$P \times Ap\alpha = Q \times Ar\alpha,$$

or, calling the arms of the lever l and l'

$$Pl = Ql', \text{ or again } \frac{\mathrm{P}}{\mathrm{Q}} = \frac{l'}{l},$$

which is expressed thus : the motor work $Pl\alpha$ is equal to the resistant work $Ql\alpha$, or the moment Pl is equal to the resistant moment Ql, or, finally, the power and the resistance vary in inverse ratio to the arms of the lever. As a result of this last expression, if $l = 10l'$, the power could be 10 times smaller than the resistance and equilibrium would be maintained. The paths traversed vary inversely as the forces, whence the proverb, " What is gained in force is lost in speed " (Galileo). Force is also gained in levers of the second order, because there the power always acts on an arm longer than that of the resistance. But there is a loss of force in

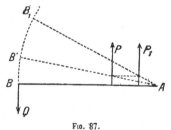

Fig. 87.

levers of the third order where the lengths of the arms are reversed. It will be noted that, in this last case, the machine displaces the resistance with an amplitude which is inversely proportional to the length of the arm to which the power is applied. If the power acts at the position P a displacement BB′ of the resistance results, but if the power acts at the position P_1, the displacement BB_1 will be much greater (fig. 87). It will be understood that to realise this increased amplitude, it will be necessary to lose in force.

52. (2) The Inclined Plane.—This is a rigid plane which is presumed to be perfectly smooth. The load (resistance Q) placed on the plane has a normal component N, and a component parallel to the plane, F. The power P, to balance the load, will be : P = F. It is easy to see that F depends on the angle α, or the inclination of the plane, then

$$F = Q \sin \alpha.$$

If the power acts parallel to the plane, during virtual displacement r,

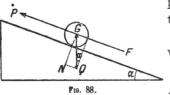

Fig. 88.

then :

$$P \times r = F \times r = Q \times r \sin \alpha,$$

whence :

$$P = Q \sin \alpha \text{ (fig. 88)}.$$

This assumes that P & F are in the same plane. But P can have any direction making an angle φ with the perpendicular, a direction (fig. 89) such that the resultant of P and Q will be perpendicular to the inclined plane and maintain the load there. As Q is already in the plane of that resultant (in AOB) the power must therefore be found in the principal section AOB. As to the value of P, it can easily be obtained by taking GP_1 equal and parallel to P in the same direction, and by projecting P_1 on the direction of the component F of the load. Then $P_2 = P_1 \sin \varphi = P \sin \varphi$ (alternate internal angles) [1]. And as $F = Q \sin \alpha$, the equilibrium is expressed :

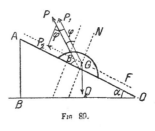

Fig. 89.

$$P \sin \varphi = Q \sin \alpha \; ; \text{ whence } P = Q \, \frac{\sin \alpha}{\sin \varphi}$$

For a given load the power increases as the sine of the angle of inclination of the plane, or as the cosine of its own inclination to that plane, because $\sin \varphi = \cos \beta$. We know that if $\beta = 0$, $\cos \beta = 1$, which will lead to the expression $P = Q \cos \alpha$.

Consider now, the force of sliding friction, Φ, remembering that the co-efficient of friction is $f =$ tang φ (§ 39), φ being the angle of friction, that angle being given by the perpendicular N and the resultant R of the pressure and of the friction. In practice, φ is obtained by inclining the plane until the sliding surface SS^1 just commences to slide. The value of the angle of inclination α will then be the angle of friction φ. Thus if a power P is

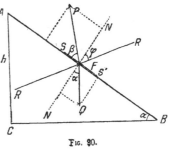

Fig. 90.

---

[1] Instead of sin φ, cos P_1GP_2 or the angle formed by the direction of the power on that of the inclined plane could be taken.

applied to the load imposed on the plane, it can only be pulled by a force superior to $F + \Phi$. The useful component of the tractive force is P cos β, parallel to the plane. The pressure (perpendicular) N is diminished by the perpendicular component of P, which is P sin β. As N = Q cos α, the pressure of the load will be Q cos α — P sin β, and the friction $\Phi = f$ (Q cos α — P sin β).

Finally the tangential component of the resistance is Q sin α = F. Therefore

$$P \cos \beta = Q \sin \alpha + f (Q \cos \alpha - P \sin \beta).$$

From this

$$P = Q \frac{\sin \alpha + f \cos \alpha}{\cos \beta + f \sin \beta} = Q \frac{\sin (a+\varphi)}{\cos (\beta - \varphi)} \text{ (}^1\text{)}$$

P is a minimum for the maximum value of cos (β — φ), or β = φ. Therefore P = Q sin (α + φ) ; it is necessary for the pull to be applied in a direction making the angle β = φ with the inclined plane (fig. 90).

To allow the load simply to slide on the plane by the action of gravity, consider the equilibrium between the component F = Q sin α and the friction $\Phi = fN = fQ \cos \alpha$. The force of sliding friction will be :

$$F - \Phi = Q (\sin \alpha - f \cos \alpha).$$

Replacing f by $\dfrac{\sin \varphi}{\cos \varphi}$, it would be written

$$F - \Phi = Q \frac{\sin \alpha - \varphi}{\cos \varphi}.$$

According to whether α be smaller or greater than φ, the movement would be retarded or accelerated.

The inclined plane is used in small quarry railways, in stations and shops to move packages, and for drays to be loaded with barrels, etc.

The useful power being P cos β and the resistance Q sin α for a virtual displacement of the body, l, the equality of the work depending on motion and resistance respectively is expressed :

$$Pl \cos \beta = Ql \sin \alpha.$$

If l is the total distance covered AB, then

$$AC = AB \sin \alpha = l \sin \alpha = h ;$$

so that :

$$Ql \sin \alpha = Qh,$$

(^{1}) f has been replaced by $\dfrac{\sin \phi}{\cos \phi}$ and simple transformation effected (see any text-book of trigonometry).

and the work will be equal to that of the fall of the weight Q from a height h.

53. (3) **Winch.**—With the aid of handle AB a power P is exerted perpendicularly to the arm BB′, that is to say, tangential to the circumference of the radius BB′ = R. The resistance Q is at the extremity of a rope rolled on the cylinder K, whose radius is r (fig. 91).

For a virtual rotation α of the handle, the work done by the power exerted is PR $\times \alpha$; that of the resistance is — Q$r \times \alpha$ (negative work). The condition of equilibrium is :

$$P r = Q r \text{ whence } P = Q \frac{r}{R}.$$

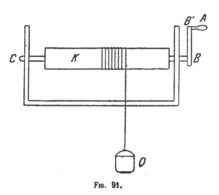

Fig. 91.

A winch has only one degree of liberty, it turns round a fixed axis. Instead of a handle other means may be employed for producing revolutions such as the treadmill and the capstan, both of which are identical in principle with the winch.

54. (4) **The Pulley.**—Consider first the fixed pulley, a wheel turning round an axis 0, which passes through its centre. The axis is supported by an inverted U-shaped hanger, C. The circumference of the wheel is hollowed out to form a groove in which the rope is passed.

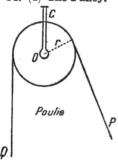

Poulie

Fig. 92.

For a virtual rotation α of the wheel, the work done by the power is P$r\alpha$; that resistance is — Q$r\alpha$; the condition of equilibrium being therefore :

$$P = Q \text{ (fig. 92)}.$$

The power must, therefore, be equal to the resistance.

55. (5) **The Wedge.**—A wedge is a triangular prism which is used to separate two parts of a body from each other; for example, to split logs of wood. The power P is applied to the head AB, whilst the point of the wedge C is driven into the cleft that it is desired to enlarge.

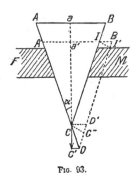

FIG. 93.

Let it be supposed that it is desired to move a part M from a fixed body, F, by driving in the wedge. When the latter advances from A to A′, the resisting surface of the part M has moved through IB′. The power is exerted perpendicularly to AB and the resistance to BC; therefore the former has advanced the distance CC′ = aa′, and the latter the distance II′ = CC″. The principle of virtual work gives

$$P \times CC' = Q \times CC'' \text{ or } \frac{P}{Q} = \frac{CC''}{CC'} \text{ (fig. 93).}$$

In drawing the parallel CD′, it is easy to see that the right angled triangles, CC″D′ and CC′D are similar; whence

$$\frac{CC''}{CC'} = \frac{CD'}{CD}.$$

And in the similar triangles CDD′ and A′DB′,

$$\frac{CD'}{CD} = \frac{A'B'}{A'D} \fallingdotseq \frac{AB}{AC}.$$

consequently :

$$\frac{P}{Q} = \frac{AB}{AC}.$$

The power is to the resistance as the head of the wedge is to its side. Also

$$\frac{AB}{AC} = \frac{2Aa}{AC}, \text{ if the triangle or the prism is isosceles ;}$$

but

$$\frac{Aa}{AC} = \tan \alpha ;$$

therefore

$$\frac{AB}{AC} = 2 \tan \alpha \text{ and } \frac{P}{Q} = 2 \tan \alpha.$$

The smaller the angle α the more efficacious the wedge.

In most of the instruments, based on the wedge, this angle is made smaller the sharper the cutting edge wanted (such as the knife, the razor, the axe, etc.), and the prism is isosceles.

56. (6) **Screws.**—A screw engages in its nut by a rotary movement. It advances through a linear distance equal to the pitch h—for one complete turn $2\pi R$. It will advance by $h \times \dfrac{2\pi R}{\alpha R}$ or $\dfrac{\alpha h}{2\pi}$ for a fraction of a turn αR, corresponding to the angle α so that the work done by the power will be :

$$P \times R \times \alpha$$

if the lever of action is the radius R ; the resistant work will be :

$$- \frac{Q\alpha h}{2\pi}.$$

The condition of equilibrium gives :

$$P\alpha R = Q\alpha \frac{h}{2\pi} \ ; \text{ whence } \ P = Q \frac{h}{2\pi R}.$$

Thus the power needed will be considerably reduced by employing a long lever and a screw with a fine thread.

57. Industrial Machines.—The machinery employed in industry is composed of simple machines. Their aim is the execution of certain work, and they comprise, as a rule, three parts.

(1) The receiver on which the motive force acts. That force is a pressure ; thus the pressure of steam is a motive force, whilst the steam itself, that is to say, the agent, is the motor (latin movere, to move). The motor is, often, a machine called a prime mover put into touch with the receiver or recipient machine. From this is derived the name of motors, given to engines which develop the power or motive force.

According to the form of energy utilised, engines may be classified as heat, hydraulic, pneumatic, electric, elastic or gravitational. Live motors (man and animals) use muscular force, but the nature of the agent which produces this force is not known for certain (see § 345).

(2) The operator, or the tool, is that part of a machine which does the actual work. The tool is directed to the result which it is desired to obtain, its movement being determined by that direction. It is—if it can be said—" blind " compared with the intellectual movements of man and animals.

(3) Mechanism transmits the movement successively, from the receiver to the operator.

58. The principle which regulates the working of machines is that of "vis viva" (§ 30). Let a machine be in movement from the instant t_1 to the instant t_2. In that interval, the powers have done work $\mathbf{T}_m$ and the resistances have done work $\mathbf{T}_r$, and it is known that the machine, which had a "vis viva" $\frac{1}{2}mv_1^2$ has now a "vis viva" $\frac{1}{2}mv_2^2$. The work done is therefore equal to the resistant work and to the increase of vis viva $\frac{1}{2}(mv_2^2 - mv_1^2)$.

The equation is then written :—

$$T_m = T_r + \tfrac{1}{2}(mv_2^2 - mv_1^2).$$

The quantity of energy absorbed in increasing the speed from v_1 to v_2 is $\frac{1}{2}m(v_2^2 - v_1^2)$. When the speed becomes uniform there is no more inertia to be overcome. There is equilibrium between T_m and T_r, whence :

$$\tfrac{1}{2}(mv_2^2 - mv_1^2) = 0, \quad \text{or} \quad v_2 = v_1 ;$$

which is the law of uniform and economical movement, the work done being exactly equal to the resistant work.

When the power is cut off from the machine, T_m becomes zero, and the speed returns to the initial velocity v_1; but the inertia which had absorbed the quantity of energy $\frac{1}{2}m(v_2^2 - v_1^2)$, gives it back as momentum and carries on for some time the work of the machine. It is therefore clear that it is inertia which prevents the speed from passing abruptly from one velocity to another, and momentum which prevents a machine stopping instantaneously.

In practice, the total resistant work T_r includes both the useful work T_u of the machine and the useless work T_i expended in overcoming the forces of friction. The equation is therefore :

$$T_m = T_r = T_u + T_i.$$

The irregularities in the motion of some familiar machines are due to the intermittent or irregular action of the motive force or the resistance (as in the case of pile drivers, hammers, etc.). They are lessened by means of fly wheels and by regulating the admission of steam or combustible gases by the employment of governors. It has been possible to make the action of these regulators or governors extremely sensitive and reliable. Industry has almost satisfied all the exigencies of the dynamic equilibrium of machines.

From the equation

$$T_m = T_u + T_i,$$

can be deduced the relation

$$\frac{T_u}{T_m} = \frac{T_m - T_i}{T_m} = 1 - \frac{T_i}{T_m}.$$

Thus the machine only gives out a part always less than unity of the energy that it receives. That fraction is called its yield, and $\dfrac{T_i}{T_m}$ the co-efficient of loss. Perpetual motion would take place

if $\dfrac{T_u}{T_m} = 1$, which is impossible.

59. Power of Motors.—The power of a motor is the quantity of work or mechanical energy developed in unit time. (It is unfortunate that the term "power" is confused with "force.") Various motors can be compared by the power which they can exert continuously. The practical unit of power is the poncelet, which develops 100 kilogrammetres per second, but the more generally used unit is the horse power "cheval-vapeur" (symbol H.P.) which is 75 kilogrammetres. The watt is also employed for electric motors, the watt being a unit of electric power equalling approximately ·102 kilogrammetres, the kilowatt (1,000 watts) corresponding to a power of 102 kilogrammetres (see units § 63). One horse power equals 735·75 watts.

In live motors, the work is not continuous on account of the phenomena of fatigue (§ 171). It is necessarily intermittent since a day's work is interrupted by a certain number of halts or intervals of repose. Taking the total of the work done, and the total duration of the periods of activity, the quotient of these two quantities gives the useful power of the man or the animal. The power is the rate production of energy.

In industrial practice it is easier to record the quantity of work in a day, halts and repose included.

To increase the power of ordinary motors it is necessary to increase their size. Hence we may consider power per unit of weight. Steam engines develop one horse power per 100 kilogrammes of weight. Internal combustion engines give a horse power per 12, 7, 6 and even 3·500 kilogrammes, and there is included in that weight the cylinders and their accessories (carbureter, oil pump, magneto). These results have been attained mainly by high speeds of rotation.

60. Expenditure of Motors.—The expenditure or input of a motor is its consumption either of fuel in inanimate motors, or of nourishment in animated motors. Every machine or system of machines transforms, but does not create, energy. These transformations may be numerous. Take, for example, the case of electrical supply. The thermal energy of the coal burnt under the boilers is (with considerable loss) converted into mechanical energy in the steam turbine or reciprocating engine. This mechanical energy is converted into electrical energy in the dynamo. This may be again converted into mechanical energy by means of electric motors, into thermal energy in electric radiators or furnaces, into chemical energy in electrolytic processes, and so forth. If we could accurately measure both the outputs of the various pieces of apparatus thus energised, and also all the energy lost in the various conversions and in the various electrical circuits, we should find that this sum was equal to the original input.

The proportion of the total input which is available for useful work depends on the efficiency of the system. In some cases the whole of the output is deliberately wasted as in a Prony brake (§ 39) utilised in testing the mechanical output of an engine where the output is dissipated in friction.

In an inanimate heat engine, the output of work depends on the quanity of heat supplied by the fuel. If no fuel is supplied, no work can be done. The animal motor can, however, do work whether well or ill nourished.

In any motor the total expenditure, or input, of energy may be divided into the static expenditure D_s, needed to overcome the forces of friction, etc., and the dynamic expenditure D_d which corresponds to the useful work done.

In inanimate machines D_s is small compared with D_d. But this is not the case in the animal motor, which is always at pressure, because if it ceased an instant to be in that state, life itself would be arrested. Its static expenditure constantly takes place, and is permanent, because it is determined (it is the essential trait that has already been noted) by physiological necessities. According to Wilhelm Ostwald, " the proper working and healthiness of the organs depends on the constancy of the temperature " (in the higher animals). And as this is a question of internal work (§ 12) all the energy expended statically will be dissipated in heat.

The work done is only a portion, the rest degrades into heat. Thus in very excessive work there may be such a production of heat that the animal might suffer from it. Animals that are forced to race die by excess of " thermogenesis," according to Chauveau.[1]

61. The Yield of Motors.—The relation of useful energy of a motor to the energy that it expends is its yield. In pàra: 58 it was shewn that :

$$\frac{T_u}{T_m} = \frac{T_m - T_i}{T_m} = 1 - \frac{T_i}{T_m}$$

the yield or the co-efficient of useful effect being always less than unity. Motors can therefore be compared with each other, either according to their power or their yield. The useful

---

[1] A Chauveau (special edition of four notes which appeared in *Comptes Rendus Acad. Sciences*, 1907, supplemented by an explanatory note : published by Gauthiers-Villars).

energy is, in practice, that which is actually employed, the sterile energy T_i, comprising all the mechanical and calorific loss which occurs in transmission from the motor to the receiver. From this point of view, the two terms of the yield are T_u and D, D being the total expenditure of the motor, static and dynamic :

This is the gross yield :

$$r = \frac{T_u}{D} = \frac{T_u}{D_s + D_d}.$$

Industry, as a rule, is only concerned with the value r.

But this co-efficient must be analysed. The motor, which has an expenditure D, produces work greater than T_u ; this in a heat engine is called the indicated work.

The machine, owing to internal resistances, has only given a fraction $\frac{T_u}{T_n}$, of the indicated work, this being its yield. The work lost absorbs $(T_n - T_u)$, and the relation of T_n to D will be the co-efficient of transformation of the energy. Also in actual work the motor only expends D_d ; the net yield being the value:

$$R = \frac{T_u}{D_d}.$$

D_s is considerable in the case of animated motors, therefore it must be deducted from the total expenditure D to know the net yield of the muscle, and if, in each method of work, the value of the organic yield is taken, the true co-efficient of the transforma tion of muscular energy $\frac{T_n}{D_d}$ can be deduced from it.

62. The idea of the yield was only recently defined. In 1819 Navier wrote : "A machine is all the more perfect the nearer its useful result (T_u) is to the quantity of the energy[1] that it consumes "[2]. Coriolis is more precise in 1829 : "When one wishes to give an idea of the efficiency of a machine . . . one compares what it yields with what it receives. The fraction that expresses the relation between these two quantities is the measure of the degree of perfection of the machine."[3]

Carnot[4] in 1824, developed the theory of the cycle which bears his name, and showed that the yield, in such a cycle (it is known that thermodynamic operations, in such a case, are closed and reversible (§ 35)) is the maximum. This cycle, which assumes,

---

[1] Quantity of action was then synonymous with work.
[2] Navier, *Notes*, p. 382, in *Architecture Hydraulique*, by Bélidor.
[3] Coriolis, *loc. cit.*, p. 131.
[4] Sadi-Carnot, *Reflexions sur la puissance motrice du feu (l.c.)*.

in a thermal motor, a very slow movement of the pistons, almost in equilibrium (conditions of reversability) and an absence of calorific loss, is purely theoretical, it leads to the expression :—

$$R_{max} = \frac{T - T'}{T} = 1 - \frac{T'}{T}$$

the absolute temperatures T and T' being those of the hot source (the boiler) and the cold (the condenser). The value R_{max} is an ideal, but impossible, value. Carnot only wished to demonstrate that a fraction, always lower than unity, represents the maximum yield in useful work of the expended energy. This disposed the idea of perpetual motion; but his theoretical researches went beyond such a limited object as has been shown (§ 35).

Further, internal combustion engines do not fulfil the condition of reversability, because the gases, having exploded and changed their composition, cannot resume their initial state. It follows that Carnot's question of yield never occurs, and cannot occur, if a change of chemical state or combustion takes place in the cycle and makes it irreversable. This is what takes place in the internal operations of the muscles, as Clausius showed Hirn,[1] at the beginning of his thermodynamic studies.

The gross yield, r, of a thermal engine varies from 7 to 14 per cent. In exceptional circumstances, Dwelshauvers-Déry obtained 23 per cent., with a " superheat " of 430°,

$$T = 430 + 273 = 703°.$$

In internal combustion engines a very high temperature is produced, and by combining the compression of the mixture with a very high temperature, gross yields of 30 to 40 per cent. can be obtained : as in the Diesel engine.

Some trials on a gas engine of 6·73 H.P. have given the following results : [2]

Heat transformed into indicated work ... ... 18·70 per cent.
  ,,   lost by radiation ... ... 7·50 ,,
  ,,   ,, by cooling of the cylinders ... ... 46·00 ,,
  ,,   ,, by the exhaust gases ... ... 27·80 ,,

                                                  100·00 ,,

Organic yield : 73·6% ; from which a gross yield is obtained of

$$r = 18·70 \times \frac{73·7}{100} = 13·76\%.$$

[1] Hirn, *Recherches sur l'équivalent mécanique de la chaleur*, followed by *Rapport* of Clausius, Colmar, 1858, p. 138.
[2] *Génie Civil* of 24th November, 1906.

63. System of Units.—The fundamental units of mechanics are those of time, length and mass.

The unit of time is the second of which there are 60 per minute, and there are 60 minutes in an hour, the hour being the $\frac{1}{24}$ part of the average solar day.

The unit of length is the centimetre (see § 18). The practical unit is the metre = 100 centimetres and the multiples are the kilometre (1,000 metres and the myriametre 10,000 metres). The English mile (1,609·315 metres) and the knot or nautical mile (1,855 metres) are used in England and America.

The unit of mass is the gramme (§ 18), and as multiples are used the kilogramme (1,000 grammes) the metric ton (1,000 kilogrammes), etc.

The centimetre-gramme-second system is called the C G.S. system, and dates from the international congress of electricians in 1881.

In this C.G.S. system, the unit of force is the force which gives the mass of the gramme an acceleration of 1 centimetre. It is called the dyne. As the acceleration of gravity, at Paris, is approximately 9·81 metres = 981 centimetres, the dyne is therefore smaller than the weight of 1 gramme and is $\frac{1}{981}$ gramme or 1 gramme = 981 dynes.

The unit of work or erg is the work of a dyne through a distance of 1 centimetre. As the kilogramme = 981,000 dynes and the metre = 100 centimetres, it will be found that the kilogrammetre, the practical unit, equals :

$$981{,}000 \times 100 = 981 \times 10^5 \text{ ergs.}$$

Use is also made of a unit which equals 10^7 ergs : the joule which corresponds consequently to :

$$\frac{10^7}{981 \times 10^5} = \frac{1}{9 \cdot 1} = \cdot 1019 \text{ kgm. approximately } \cdot 102 \text{ kgm.}$$

The power of a motor is the number of units of work done per second. In practice, the name of watt is given to the unit of power which gives 1 joule per second, or 0·102 kgm. per second. The industrial units such as the poncelet = 100 kilogrammetres, the horse-power = 75 kilogrammetres is equal to :

$$\frac{100}{\cdot 102} = 981 \text{ watts and } \frac{75}{\cdot 102} = 735 \cdot 75 \text{ watts respectively.}$$

As to the equivalence between mechanical and thermal energy, experiment has shown that 426·4 kgm. exactly are transformed into one grand calorie (C) which is the quantity of heat able to raise a kilogramme of water from 0 to 1 degree centigrade.

The grand calorie is therefore equal to :

$$426{\cdot}4 \times 981 \times 10^5 = 418{\cdot}3 \times 10^8 \text{ ergs.}$$

or to 4183 joules. But if one considers the quantity of heat raising a gramme of water from 0 to 1 degree, the unit will be 1,000 times less, and will be the small caloric (c) equivalent to $418{\cdot}3 \times 10^5$ ergs or $4{\cdot}183$ joules.

All the other units are derived from the above.

64. Formulas of Dimensions.—A length l, multiplied by itself, gives an area. A length possesses a single dimension l, whilst an area l^2 possesses two dimensions, a volume l^3 three dimensions.

The speed being the quotient of a length by a time, has as dimension $\dfrac{l}{t}$ or lt^{-1} Acceleration is the quotient of a speed by a time, will therefore have as dimension :

$$\gamma = \frac{lt^{-1}}{t} = lt^{-2}.$$

The force $f = m\gamma$ will have as dimension mlt^{-2}, so in consequence :

$$\text{work} = fl = ml^2 t^{-2}, \text{ etc.}$$

The formulas of dimension which are mentioned here are of fundamental importance. If the results of a series of experiments are expressed by an equation, the terms of that equation must have the same dimensions, otherwise they will contain an error. Thus work done may be expressed by the equation

$$\mathbf{T} = f \times l = \tfrac{1}{2} mv^2 ;$$

m $\tfrac{1}{2} mv^2$, the speed v is that acquired by the moving body, but it must not be multiplied by the time and written $\tfrac{1}{2} mv^2 t$; the formulas of dimension are $ml^2 t^{-2}$ for fl and $ml^2 t^{-2}$ for $\tfrac{1}{2}mv^2$. Therefore, if the time was introduced, the formulas would no longer be homogeneous.

BOOK II.

THE HUMAN MACHINE.

CHAPTER I.

THE HUMAN STRUCTURE.

65. The Materials.—We have first to consider the structure of the matter which constitutes the organs of all living machines. Man and animal do not differ one from the other as to the properties of that matter. But it must be said, first of all, that animated substance or protoplasm does not possess any constant and perfectly defined property; its elementary chemical carbonic, hydrogeneous, oxygeneous, and azotic composition varies very little, its physical characteristics evolve slowly and in a determined direction. As a rule, it hardens with age, it fixes and produces solid elements, minerals, from which it forms new material or tissue.

We shall confine our attention chiefly to the organs of movement and locomotion, that is to say, the bones, muscles, and tendons.

The continuous variation of which the protoplasm is the seat causes it to pass through a succession of different states. This evolution characterises the substances called colloidal or the colloids, the gelatinous silica, for example, so that this silica, left to itself, loses or throws off its aqueous components progressively, and coagulates more and more into the solid state, this being a question of time, or, if it can be said, of age.

Living matter is essentially irritable or excitable. It responds to stimuli, whether of heat, electricity, light, mechanical shock, or chemical action, the reaction being of an obscure nature, but allied to the phenomena of nutrition.[1]

In the animal, this irritability co-ordinates and adjusts itself, all the reactions having a resultant appropriate to this object of defence, it being understood that the word object does not imply a metaphysical finality, but a complex determinism which is becoming clearer every day.

---

[1] Hering *Lotos*, vol. ix., p. 35: 1889.

Sensibility is the superior property which is assured by a special co-ordinating system, the nervous system.

It seems, in consequence, that the nervous tissue centralises the effects of all excitations, and perpetuates them all through life. Hereditary influences, and acquired impressions are perpetuated in this manner. Physically the nervous system maintains the animal substance in a peculiar state, in readiness for reaction. All the protoplasmic molecules are drawn together with a little more force when irritated, and offer a greater resistance to separation. It is obvious that this state will affect the elastic matter of the muscles, and not the rigid substance of the bones.

This internal activity of the protoplasm, this continuous dynamic state, demands four external conditions, four factors, to maintain it :—1. water ; 2. food ; the one for the accomplishment of the chemical reactions, the other to repair organic waste (see § 99) ; 3. oxygen, a gas necessary for cellular combustion and for physiological work (§ 60), and also to repair fatigued matter (§ 147) and replenish the blood, the vehicle which permeates the whole organism of the body ; 4. heat, between certain limits of temperature, the lower kinds of animals living at very variable temperatures and the higher animals living at a temperature said to be constant, or homeothermic. If the variation of temperature is great, death follows, and it seems also that maximum activity is manifested at a constant temperature, which is 37·5° C for man. The reactions of human life are characterised by this "thermic optimum." The variations of intensity of the four preceding factors modify the physical state of living matter, this latter being without physical constancy in the strict sense of the word. Age, sex, and past experience, with their different influences, give different characters to organisms and complicate the problem of the resistance of living materials.

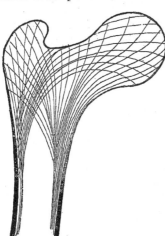

Fig. 94.

Section of femur showing the curves of pressure (after Culmann).

66. The Bones : the Skeleton.—The organs of locomotion are the bones and the muscles ; the former being levers, and the latter being powers. The bony substance is derived from an elementary substance, plastic and gelatinous, which remains unaltered in cartilages, ligaments, and tendons (§ 71). When young, the bones are in the cartilaginous state ; they gradually absorb mineral salts (carbonate and limestone phosphates) and solidify. The composition of bone is very variable ; from 16 to 68% of water, and from 84 to 32% of solid matter, acccording to the nature of the bone. In the solid part there is about 35% of gelatinous organic substance : the " ossein " and 65% of limestone salts ; these increase with age, whilst the amount of water decreases ; in consequence, the density of the bones changes from 1·87 to 2 in the course of the first thirty years.

The skeleton takes its formative elements from the alimentation, through the medium of the blood.

The form of the bones vary, those of the ocomotive limbs being long and hollow tubes, prismatic or practically cylindrical enlarged at the extremities by which they are connected or jointed. These heads (epiphyses) are of a spongy, lamellar substance, the lamella being suitable for sustaining pressure (figs. 94 and 95). They reveal, as Culmann (¹) showed, the curve of pressures in the arches. The mesial part (diaphysis) is a compact tissue, almost homogeneous and very resistant. Besides long bones there are flat bones, such as the frontal bone, which have lamellar matter between two compact blades practically parallel.

There is also a large number of bones of irregular shapes, such as the bones of the " vertebral column," and of the foot and the hand.

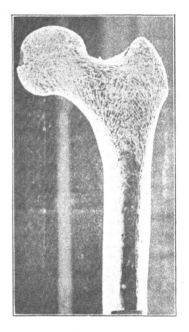

Fig. 95.—Section of a femur (thigh bone).

(¹) Culmann *Anwend d Graph Statik*, vol. i. p. 128 (1888-1900 ; Zurich.)

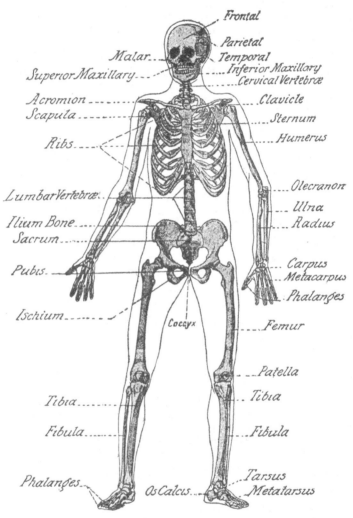

Fig 96 — General Structure of the Skeleton

THE HUMAN SKELETON.

i. THE HEAD.

Cranium.—One frontal bone, two parietal, two temporal, one occipital, behind (not visible in the picture) and two bones (sphenoid and ethmoid) forming the base, the vault of the cranium.

Face.—Two malar bones, two superior maxillaries, and one inferior maxillary : two nasal, two lachrymatory ; the os vomer, and the hyoid bone (which supports the larynx) are not visible in the illustration.

ii. THE TRUNK.

Vertebral Column.—Thirty-three vertebrae, (seven cervical (neck), twelve dorsal, five lumbar, five sacral, and three or four coccygeal). The bones of the sacrum and coccyx in the adult are usually united.

Sternum.—A flat bone.

Ribs.—Twelve pairs, seven " true " ribs joined direct to the sternum ; five " false " ribs joined by one cartilage.

iii. LIMBS.

A. Upper Limbs.

Shoulder.—Scapula, clavicle, the acromion is attached to the scapula and joined to the clavicle.

Arm.—Humerus, whose lower end has two articulating surfaces and a large fossa for the reception of the olecranon.

Forearm.—Ulna, with the olecranon process-radius, with which the bones of the hand articulate.

Hand.—Eight bones of the carpus, five of the metacarpus, three phalanges to each finger, but two to the thumb.

B. Lower Limbs.

Hip.—Pelvis bone, comprising three parts (ilium, ischium, pubis) connected.

Thigh.—Femur, and a free bone : the patella.

Calf.—Tibia, fibula.

Foot.—Seven bones in the tarsus of which the calcaneum (heel) and the astragalus are jointed to the tibia ; five bones in the metatarsus ; three phalanges per toe, except the big toe, which has two.

The table above and the fig. 96 give a general view of the parts of the skeleton and their names.

Fɪɢ. 97.
Front section of the middle
of the head of the humerus.

Fɪɢ 98
Section perpendicular
to the preceding.

The figures 97 to 102 are sections of joint heads by Werner,[1] the sections being " sagittal " (antero-posterior) or " frontal " (perpendicular to the preceding). The reciprocal positions of the principal bones, and the relations between jointed surfaces, will be examined later.

Fɪɢ, 100.

Sagittal section at the middle of the head of the radius

S

Fɪɢ. 99.

Sagittal section of the
ulna with the projec-
tion S of the olecranon.

Fɪɢ. 101.

Section of the middle of the
head of the femur.

[1] Werner, *Die Dicke der menschlichen Gelenkknorpel* (*Inaug Diss.*, Berlin, 1897)

The analogy between the upper and lower limbs must be emphasised. It will only be noted here that the humerus, with the clavicle and the shoulder blade, forms the "scapular belt "; the femur, the longest bone in the body, forms, with the ilium, the " pelvic belt," stronger and less mobile than the other, intimately connected with the vertebral column and offering a great resistance to movement.

Fıa. 102.

67. Resistance of the Skeleton.— The compact part of the bones (of the diaphysis) was studied from the point of view of resistance by Wertheim[1].

Frontal section of the head of the femur 5 millimetres in front of the "neck."

He made use of human bones as fresh as possible : and worked by traction on prisms sufficiently homogeneous ; and he obtained for Young's modulus and the breaking stress R, the following results :—

BONE	SUBJECT	AGE	DENSITY	YOUNG'S MODULUS	BREAKING STRESS PER mm²
Femur	Man ...	30 years	1·984	E = 1,819	10·500 kg.
	—	74 years	1·987	2,638	7·300
	Woman	21 years	1·968	2,181	6·870
	—	60 years	1·849	2,421	6·400
Fibula	Man ...	30 years	1·997	2,059	15·030
	—	74 years	1·947	?	4·335
	Woman	21 years	1·940	2,710	10·260
	—	60 years	0·799	?	3·300

Young's modulus has an average value of 2,300 kilogrammes per square millimetre ; it is double that which has been found for pinewood of which the density is three times less than that of bone (§ 44).

The average resistance to fracture by traction is 12 kilogrammes in the adult and 6 in an old man. Pinewood gives figures a little less (8 kilogrammes). Wertheim's determinations show a decrease in the feminine sex and with age ; which was also observed by Rauber.[2]

---

[1] Wertheim, *Annales de Chimie et de Physique*, 1847, vol. xxi., p. 385.
[2] A. Rauber, *Elasticität und Festigkeit der Knochen*, Leipzig, 1876.

The resistance to fracture by compression is $\frac{1}{4}$ higher than in the case of traction ; it is R $=$ 14 kilogrammes on an average. The values change according to the section and length of the part.

Hodgkinson's formula for wood (§ 44) is applicable here by writing :

$$R = 2{,}700 \times \frac{s^2}{h^2} \cdot$$

But h must not exceed $\frac{1}{2}$ decimetre, and the prisms must approach a cube, cubic forms being very resistant. Under compression :

For a cube of 3 millimetres ... R $=$ 16 kg. per mm^2
    ,,   ,,   5   ,, ... R $=$ 15 ,,

On prisms only 10 to 12 kilogrammes are obtained.([1]).

The rate of application of the compressive stress is of great importance, because the pressure in shock attains a high value.

It will be remembered that the impulse is :

$$Ft = mv ; \quad \text{whence } F = \frac{mv}{t},$$

for a very short duration, tF may reach a very high value, several hundreds of kilogrammes.

68. In " flexion " and " torsion," the resistance of the long bones is increased because they are hollow (§ 45). Lesshaft ([2]) and Otto Messerer.([3]) determined the resistance of bones of normal dimensions. The weight needed to produce initial fracture was :

	Humerus	Radius	Ulna	Femur	Tibia	Fibula
	kg.	kg.	kg.	kg.	kg.	kg.
Man of 31 years ...	850	535	550	1,300	600	300
Woman of 24 years	600	390	310	1,100	650	310

To produce a complete fracture needs 2,900 kilogrammes for the femur, and at least 4,100 for the tibia.

([1]) H. Triepel, *Die Stossfestigkeit des Knochen* (*Arch. f. Anat.*, 1900, p. 229) and *Einführung in die Physikalische Anat.*, Wiesbaden, 1902.

([2]) P. Lesshaft : we quote him according to Triepel.

([3]) O. Messerer, *Ueber Elasticität und Festigkeit der Menschlichen Knochen*, Stuttgart, 1880.

The weights needed to produce rupture by flexion and shearing, were as follows:

| | FLEXION | | SHEARING. | | |
	Maximum	Minimum	Maximum	Minimum	Zone of Rupture
	kg.	kg.	kg.	kg.	
Humerus	300	120	505	250	at the extremities
Radius ...	140	55	334	105	at the middle.
Ulna ...	140	70	235	90	everywhere.
Femur ...	475	230	810	400	at the neck.
Tibia	500	135	1,060	450	lower end.
Fibula ...	55	21	61	20	at the middle.

An effort of torsion acting at the extremity of a lever of 16 centimetres, produces a spiral fracture for efforts of the following values :—

Humerus	Radius	Ulna	Femur	Tibia	Fibula
40 kg.	12 kg.	8 kg.	89 kg.	48 kg.	6 kg.

The modulus of torsion, or rigidity, on compact bone has not been determined. Theoretically Wertheim gave $G = \frac{1}{3} E$ as an average (§ 46). As $E = 2300$, G would equal about 862 ; a value half that of pinewood.

The following values are of interest :

		kg.
Lumbar vertebræ compressed vertically	{ Man of 30 years	1,000
	Woman of 80 years	... 240
Thorax compressed transversely (fracture of the ribs).	{ Man of 30 years	... 200
	Woman of 82 years	... 40
Thorax compressed sagitally.	{ Man of 40 years	... 60
	Woman of 82 years	... 40

Pelvis crushed, one ridge of the ilium to the other ... 180
" Sacrum " crushed sagitally ... ... 170 to 250

To sum up, the resistance of the bones increases with age up to the limits of old age, and is more in man than woman, because the osseus tissue of man is denser and his skeleton more massive. The mode of life and the nature of nutrition modify resistance. This is why the skeleton of a race horse is denser than that of a horse living quietly out at grass. But certain affections attack the bony tissues and decrease their resistance considerably.[1]

---

[1] For the architecture of the skeleton consult H. von Meyer : *Die Statik und Mechanik des Menschlichen Knochen-gerüstes*, Leipzig, 1873. Nevertheless, certain analogies, admitted by the author, are highly doubtful.

69. (11) Muscles and their Resistance.—Muscles are fleshy masses of varying thickness, which are attached to the bones, and partially retain them in their proper relative positions. They are, properly speaking, the agents of movement, as will be explained later.

Muscles are made of extremely thin parallel fibres, in a section 1 centimetre square, there may be nearly 100 millions of them. They are enveloped by a transparent membrane, and terminated by elastic laminæ called " tendons," by which they are connected to the skeleton.

The fibres of the muscles of locomotion have a special construction. Instead of being simple elongated cells, they are striated transversely, presenting the appearance of a pile of discs, some transparent, others opaque. These striated fibres are anistropic and their contents appear to correspond to the structure of colloids, along with some elements called micella, which are more stable than the gelatinous liquid which fills the fibres. The

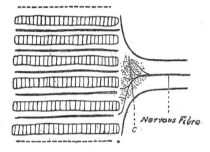

Fig. 103.

Scheme of striated muscular fibre with its nervous connexions.

external aspect of a striated fibre may be compared with that of a spiral spring enclosed in a glass cylinder ; the spirals would project in parallel striæ (fig. 103). Striation is a dynamic state acquired by the protoplasma ([1]).

Nervous filaments of great tenuity approach the muscular fibres and come into contact with them, directly or indirectly— the terminal arborization C distributing itself to the muscular elements and governing them, but it is not known exactly how. The composition of muscles is 74% water, on an average in the adult man : there is more in women and children. Their density exceeds that of water by $\frac{1}{20}$, because the liquid or muscular plasma contains salts and albuminoid bodies, etc. The density is slightly less in the female sex.

It is obvious that the more fibres there are in a muscle, the greater is its resistance ; i.e. the resistance is proportional to the mass of the muscle. It must be remembered that the muscles

([1]) Vlès, *Proprietes optiques des muscles.* These, Paris, 1912.

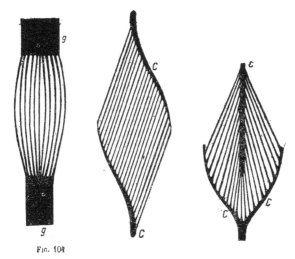

Fig. 104

Functional adaptions of muscular fibres.

are either short and thick, or else long; it is therefore by pressing one against another and by increasing the "mass" of muscles, that the fibres increase their resistance. Thus a great number of fibres are often compressed in a minimum space. The tendons only act as sheaths, g (fig. 104), to receive the extremities of the fibres ; they transform themselves into thin cords, C acting as receivers for the insertion of oblique fibres, in such a manner that these are found in a considerable number in a section perpendicular to their direction. This adaptation, giving a maximum force in a minimun volume, is purely functional (§ 86).

70. The resistance to fracture and the elasticity of the muscles has also been studied by Wertheim, on fresh corpses, hence eliminating any unsuspected nervous influences. For the *sartorious muscle* (of the thigh) he obtained.

SUBJECT	AGE	DENSITY	YOUNG'S MODULUS	R per mm²
Man	1 year	1·071	E = 1·271	0·070 kg.
	30 years	1·058	0·352	0·026
	74 years	1·045	0·261	0·017
Woman	21 years	1·049	0·857	0·040
	60 years	1·040	?	?

From this table it is seen that the muscle of a fresh corpse has a Young's modulus $E = 0.95$, and a resistance to fracture R of 40 grammes per square millimetre. All the values decrease with age. Finally, the resistance to fractures is that of the muscular matter, and its covering and the deformation is not, according to Wertheim, absolutely elastic. It is partially persistent, *i.e.*, return to the original length is retarded (§ 43). The muscle of a corpse has therefore imperfect elasticity.

Determinations made on the living have shown that the muscular elasticity is less imperfect, if not absolutely perfect ; but it is known that, under these conditions, tonicity intervenes, and matter tends to retract itself. The retractibility or the contractability is not the elasticity ; it is the property peculiar to muscle of being able to retract when acted upon by an external stimulus. The contraction is said to be voluntary in the case of the excitation being of direct nervous origin. Mosso ([1]) distinguishes between elasticity and tonicity by means of a special instrument, the myotome, acting on the muscle of the calf. He established, with Benedicenti, that the resistance to deformation is greater—that Young's modulus is higher—in a muscle that is contracted than in one that is in repose. Weiss and Petrèn ([2]) found that this was also the case in the resistance to fracture : for the " force of contraction " adds to the resistance and to the cohesion of the muscular substances. By suppressing the nervous action by means of " curare " (a poison acting on motive nerves) the elasticity of the muscles becomes similar to that of a corpse.([3])

The resistance to torsion, a subject on which there is little information, is less in the contracted muscle than in the relaxed muscle ([4]), this being the opposite of what takes place under traction. But this point needs verification. The muscles have their own resistance, and a resistance due to their tonicity, and by their tendinous insertions on the skeleton, they consolidate it and maintain its parts in relative fixity, thereby giving form and support to the whole structure. It is they, so to speak, which make a safe scaffold for the various parts of the skeleton.

The following table, and fig. 105, show the principal elements of the muscular system.

([1]) A. Mosso et Benedicenti, *Arch. Ital. Biol.*, vol. xxv., p. 379 and 385, 1896 ; vol. xxviii., p. 127.
([2]) Weiss and Carvallo, *Comptes Rendus Biol.*, 1899, p. 122 ; Petrèn, *Skand. Arch. f. Physiol.*, 1899, p. 328, and 1902.
([3]) Spiridon A. Dontas, Ve Congrès de Physiol., à Turin, Sept., 1901. Borelli (*De Motu Animalium*, 1680) had already made this observation.
([4]) Schenck (*Pflueger's Arch.*, vol. lxxix., p. 342 ; lxxxi., p. 583, 1900) ; Kaiser (*Centralblatt f. Physiol.*, vol. xiv., p. 1 and 363, 1900).

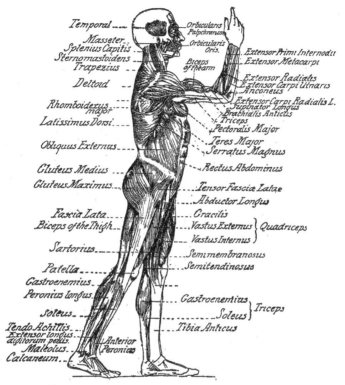

Temporal
Masseter
Splenius Capitis
Sternomastoidens
Trapezius
Deltoid
Rhomboideus major
Latissimus Dorsi
Obliquus Externus
Gluteus Medius
Gluteus Maximus
Fascia Lata
Biceps of the Thigh
Sartorius
Patella
Gastroenemius
Peronius longus
Soleus
Tendo Achillis
Extensor longus digitorum pedis
Malleolus
Calcaneum

Orbicularis Palpebrarum
Orbicularis Oris
Biceps of the arm
Extensor Primi Internodii
Extensor Metacarpi
Extensor Radialis
Extensor Carpi Ulnaris
Anconeus
Extensor Carpi Radialis L.
Supinator Longus
Brathialis Anticus
Triceps
Pectoralis Major
Teres Major
Serratus Magnus
Rectus Abdominus
Tensor Fascia Latae
Abductor Longus
Gracilis
Vastus Externus } Quadriceps
Vastus Internus }
Semi membranosus
Semitendinosus
Gastroenemius
Soleus } Triceps
Tibia Anticus
Anterior Peronia

Fig. 105.—Principal Muscles of the Body.

TABLE OF THE PRINCIPAL MUSCLES.

i. HEAD AND NECK.

Occipito frontalis—corrugator supercilii—orbicularis oris—orbicularis palpebrarum—Levator labii—Depressor labii inferioris angular oris—Buccinator (inside the mouth) Temporal—Masseter — Digastric — Sternohyoid — Splenius capitis— Sternomastoid — Trapezius — Compressor naris — Zygomaticus — Ilio costalis cervicis—Omohyoid.

ii. TRUNK.

Inspiratory and expiratory muscles—Obliquus internus—Latissimus Dorsi—Pectoralis minor—Pectoralis major—Serratus superior—Serratus inferior—Serratus magnus.

iii. Limbs.

A. Upper Limbs.

Deltoid—Biceps of the arm—Brachialis anticus Coracro-brachialis—Triceps—Extensor radialis—Supinator longus—Flexors and extensors of the fingers.

B. Lower Limbs.

Vastus externus and internus—Rectus femoris—Adductor longus and magnus—Sartorius gluteus maximus, medius, and minimus. Obturator externus and internus—Pectineus—Gastrocnemius Semimembranous—Soleus—Tibialis postiens.—Extensors and abductors of the toes.

Most of the muscles that we have studied statically have definite shapes, more or less distinct ; some are short and thick, others long. In complete repose they are " relaxed " and develop their full length. This is, however, infrequent.

71. (iii.) Tendons and Cartilages.—Tendons are organs made of elastic fibre, which are fixed at the extremity of muscles, in continuation of the envelope with which they are covered. They are more compact than muscles, and by adhering to the rugose surfaces of the bones, they serve as solid points of attachment. They are also denser and only contain, on an average, 67% of water. A well-known example of tendons is the " Achilles tendon " which terminates the lower calf muscles, and is fixed to the heel bone (os calcis) (fig. 106). The resistance of tendons was measured by Wertheim, and later by Triepel. The former obtained the following values for the plantar tendon of man :—

Fig. 106.

SUBJECT	AGE	DENSITY	YOUNG'S MODULUS	R PER mm^2
Man ....{	35 years	1·125	E = 139·42	4·910 kg.
	40 years	1·124	134·78	7·100
	74 years	1·105	200·50	5·390
Woman ......{	21 years	1·115	164·71	10·380
	70 years	1·114	169·21	5·610

that is to say, a modulus of 146 and a force of cohesion of 7 kilogrammes on the average. Triepel finds R = about 5, a resistance to traction equal to at least half that of the bones.

The cartilages cover the bony joints and dominate the skeleton of the young. They are more of a cellular than a fibrous nature, and their proportion of water, which varies with age and from one cartilage to another, is very high : 74% approximately in the cartilage of the knee, 68% in the cartilages of the ribs. The mineral salts which they contain, double in quantity between the ages of 20 and 40.

The resistance of cartilages to fracture is greater in compression than in traction ; 1·5 kg. as against 0·18 kg., according to Triepel. Young's modulus is, on the average, 1·50, almost equal to that of the muscles, but it is rarely constant, for it can attain a value of from 16 to 20 in particular cases.

72. (iv). The Nerves.—The nerves are white filaments which, radiating towards all the points of the organism, carry there the " motive excitement " or gather there the sensitive impressions, the " sensation." They emanate from determined centres, these centres being cellular, but the " nervous cell " emits a very long prolongation to the centrifugal function, the cylindric axis, and short appendices, the " dendrites," which connect it with the neighbouring cells. The " spinal cord," which runs through the spinal column, is a very important centre.

Nervous matter contains from 62 to 80% of water, and its density varies from 1·03 to 1·04 and slightly between one sex and the other.[1]

The nervous cell, round or oval, is from $\frac{2}{100}$ to $\frac{9}{100}$ of a millimetre in diameter ; it, and its prolongations, constitute together a " neuron " ; the longest forming a fibre, and a fasciculus or bundle of fibres are found in the single nerve, each having a thickness of from 1 to 20 thousandths of a millimetre.

The nervous cords take the name of the part to which they are connected ; they distribute themselves in an unequal manner and contain an unequal number of fibres. In the motor fibres, for example, there are two or more per long striated muscular fibre, while there is only one in a short fibre. This distribution satisfies the functions of the muscles, which are so diverse and unequal. Krause found 15,000 nervous fibres in the " motor oculis " muscle, the six muscles of the eye together having nearly 18,000, and yet only weighing about 3 grammes. This proportion would lead to 180 million nervous fibres in the whole muscular system (weighing 30 kilogrammes), but according to Stirling there are only 300,000 real motor fibres emanating from the spinal column.

---

[1] Gomperz, *Journal of Physiol.*, vol. xxvii., p. 459 (1901-1902).

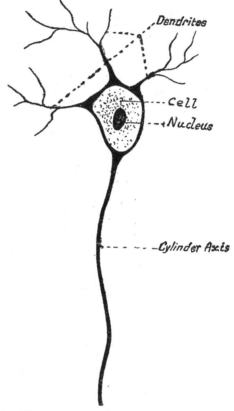

Fig. 107.

Nervous cell with its prolongations (a neuron).

The resistance of nerves is great, needing 25 kilogrammes to break the ulnar, 55 the sciatic nerve ; R = 2 to 3 kilogrammes per square millimetre. The modulus is 10·9 (Wertheim). It is interesting to note that the nerves, of all the organs, are the best conductors of electricity, for in taking 100 as the conductivity K of muscles :

				K.				K.
Muscles	...	...	...	100	Tendons ...	...		30
Nerves	...	...	...	588	Bones	...	...	7

73. Conclusions.—The elastic properties of the organic tissues may be compared with those of other substances such as india-rubber :

SUBSTANCE	DENSITY	YOUNG'S MODULUS	R PER mm^2	AUTHORITIES
Bones	1·95	E = 2,300	12 kg.	various
Tendons	1·12	146	7	various
Muscles	1·05	0·95	0·400	Wertheim
Nerves	1·04	10·9	2·500	various
Indiarubber ...	0·92	variable[1]	0·600	,, [2]
Silk thread	1·33	650	27·500	Frankenheim
Spider's thread	1·58	306	18·350	Benton [3]

It is clear from these figures that the structure of the material has the chief influence on its elastic properties and density.

But it must be noticed that the viscous nature of the muscles and the tendons renders them liable to deformations. Their elasticity, which mitigates the effects of shocks, can be fatigued, for example, by walking or running. Thick organs have only a small retardment of elasticity (elastiche nachwirkung). This has been noticed with thick rods of indiarubber, and is a feature which distinguishes the muscles of athletes.

Elasticity shows itself most in the fundamental organs of life, circulatory and respiratory, and assures efficacious protection and regular working (§ 49).[4] It shows itself less in the skeleton, where its greatest value is found in the ribs. Above all, it is a function of age, its properties in man being at their best between 20 and 40 years of age, though the suppleness of the tissues is much greater at an earlier age. It is utilised during physiological work, and it repairs itself in repose, depending on the method of " alimintation," and on the nature of the activity of the subject. Adaptation and activity, in part, contribute to the elastic accommodation of the muscles. Abnormal efforts, such as rapid movements, tend to deform the tissues permanently, and even to break them when, in old age, their tenacity has weakened. Also, the persistance of the deformation, (such as the contraction of the planar arch of the feet after a fatiguing walk) [5] is accompanied by a diminution, if not a momentary arrest of human activity, and causes acute discomfort.

---

[1] Young's modulus varies with the elognation, from E = 0·07 to E = 15. For ordinary limits of elongation, E = 0·09 (Villari, *Pogg. Ann.*, vol. cxliii., 1871).

[2] Bouasse, Heim, etc. The value R is for vulcanised rubber.

[3] Benton, in *The American Journal of Science*, 1907, p. 75.

[4] Buttersack, *Die Elasticitat, eine Grundfunktion das Lebens*, Stuttgart, 1910.

[5] Dewèvre (*Comptes Rendus Biologie*, 1892 ; *Mémoire*, p. 207).

74. Joints : Degrees of Freedom.—The name of joints is given to the various methods of union between bones, that union being made by the juxtaposition of "jointed surfaces." These surfaces are flat " or curved " (spherical, cylindrical, or oval), their contact necessarily causes friction when the bones are displaced. They are covered with supple, pliable, cartilages of varying thicknesses (fig. 108).

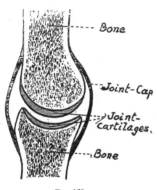

In addition, two joint heads are sometimes enveloped in a fibrous capsule, which is prolonged inwardly by a membrane moistened by an alkaline liquid called "synovia." This synovia gives rise to a cohesion of about 550 grammes per square centimetre ([1]). Finally, ligaments, tendons, and muscles surround the joint and give it a certain fixity, without in any way impeding its movements. Thus every kind of joint has definite connexions varying in number (fig. 109).

Bone
Joint-Cap
Joint-Cartilages,
Bone

Fig. 108.

When the joints are absolutely "fixed," the bones work on each other by fine denticulation, making "sutures" or "synarthrosis" with rigid connexions. When they have a very limited freedom, with a short and large connexion, they are called "amphiarthoroses" or "symphyses" : thus the vertebrae are superimposed with insertions of thick and large cartilaginous masses. The joints, which have ample and diversified movements, are "diarthroses"; for example, the bones of limbs and fingers which act like levers.

The study of Man, as a machine, must be concerned particularly with that of the diarthrosic joints or the moveable connexions of bones and their degree of mobility. The freest movement has six degrees of freedom, three translations, and three rotations (§ 16) : but the shape of jointed surfaces and the connexions are such that they enable joints to be divided into five or six classes, according to the degree of freedom. The surfaces are most often cylindrical, oval or spherical, that is to say, with one, two or three axes, and with one, two or three degrees of freedom. The systems with only one degree of freedom are said to have complete connexions.

([1]) Cohesion is a molecular attraction, it has been measured, as regards synovia, by Bordier, according to a method of Gay-Lussac's.

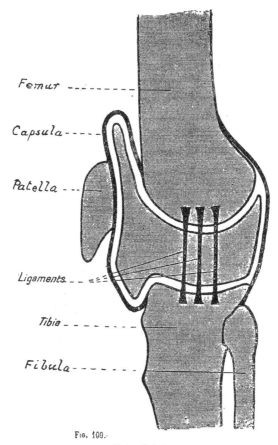

Fig. 109.

Knee Joint.

75. Details of the Types of Joints.—(1) Joints with one axis or only one degree of freedom, are the most numerous. This type is the spherical joint, having a spherical head penetrating into a hemispherical cavity; but it is very rarely found in such a regular shape, for, as a rule, the surface has a groove S,. forming part of the arc of a circle (fig. 110). The movement which results takes place in one plane, and is either a flexion or an extension. The mobile bone turns by means of a hinge, whence the name hinge joints. There are examples of this in

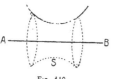

Fig. 110.

the fingers and in the connexion of the astralagus with the tibia (fig. 112).

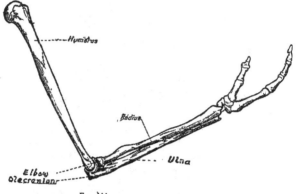

Fig 111.

Elbow Joint.

A pivot joint has also a longitudinal rotation round a single axis, such is the movement of the radius.

If the bone has a helical joint, *i.e.*, when the furrow S is oblique, then the movement is a combined translation and rotation (§ 7), but the rotation is at the most through 180°, and the translation is limited by its connexions. Therefore there are not really two degrees

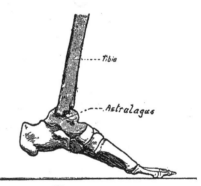

Fig. 112. —

Joints of the Foot.

of freedom, but, practically, only one, the rotation. The elbow offers a clear example of this, where the translation is about 1 millimetre [1] (fig. 111) ; the joint of the astralagus is not far from being a helicoidal joint (fig. 112). When, finally, the section of the head of the joint is a spiral curve (fig. 113) the moving bone goes back, because the distance of the point M to the centre O is not constant, and traction is exerted on the ligaments whose elasticity limits the displacement. This takes place in the knee-joint (fig. 109) or the tibia femur.

[1] W. Hultkranz, *Das Ellenbogengelenk und seine Mechanik*, Jena 1897.

(ii) Movement with two degrees of liberty is shown clearly in " oval joints " with two very unequal axes (ellipsoid joints) or nearly equal axes (spheroid joints) ; the larger axis being perpendicular to the direction of the limb, that is to say, transverse, whereas, if the surfaces fit tightly, the only movement possible will be round the larger axis AB (fig. 114) limited by the contact of the moving bone with the edges of the cavity of the joint.

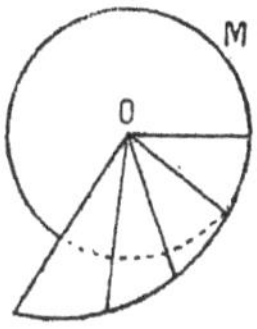

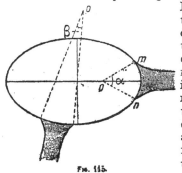

Fig. 113

Such is the case in the joint of the forearm to the wrist (radio carpal) which would only have one degree of liberty, but that, as a rule, movement is equally possible round the small axis CD, and the moving bone can turn on itself ; by which rotation, or torsion with flexion and extension, is produced. It must be added that the oval or ellipse has two different curves, that is to say, two centres of curvature, so that the joint head, in its double movement, does not turn round the same point, for that point changes position. All the intermediate axes can be like AB and CD axes of rotation ; but it can be shown that the movement takes place round the axis, which causes the " minimum " action on the part of the cartilages [1]

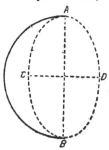

Fig 114
Oval joint.

This was noted by Listing in the movement of the eye-ball. Listing's law establishes that the movement of the eyes entails a very feeble effort by the oculomotor muscles of the eyes. On this subject, we may recall that the moment of inertia of an ellipsoid is a minimum, when the rotation is round the major axis, and the angular displacement is less on that axis than on the minor axis ; for the same displacement mn, the two radii of the minor cur-

Fig. 115.

[1] Fischer, Ueber Gelenke von zwei graden der Freiheit (Arch. f. Anat.), 1897, Suppl., p. 242 ; Otto Fischer, Zur Kinematik des Listingschen Gesetzes (Abhandl. d. Math. Phys. Klasse d. Konigl. Sachs. Gesell, d. Wiss., 1909, vol. xxxi.)

vature ([1]) form an angle β " inferior " to the angle α given by the radii of the major curvature (fig. 115).

The name of a " saddle-joint " is given to the joint where the surface of the fixed bone is analogous to the back of a horse's saddle, the surface of the mobile bone occupying a direction perpendicular thereto. The only clear example is that of the trapezium t (fig. 116) jointed to the metacarpal bone of the thumb ; one saddle covers the other. The movement differs very little from that of the oval joint.

(iii) Three degrees of liberty are observed in the " ball and socket," or three axes joints. Centred one on the other, the joint-head or " ball " and the spheric cavity or cap are such that the former fits into the latter so that the head of the mobile bone touches the sides of the cavity, and the greater the radius of the joint head is than that of the cavity, the greater will be the freedom of movement.

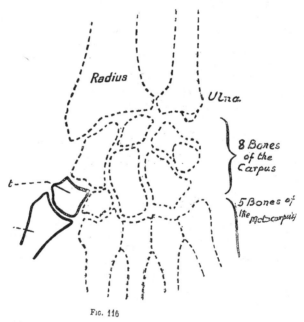

Fig. 116

Joint of the trapezium to the metacarpus (saddle-joint).

([1]) The curvature is small when it forms part of a circumference with a large radius and conversely ; the radius of the curve is therefore the inverse of the curvature.

Three rotations round three rectangular axes are therefore possible, and this is seen in the hip and shoulder joints

These three axes are instantaneous axes, but taking a bone in repose, the thigh, for instance, one can see that the axis of a limb allows of a vertical torsion or rotation ; *i.e.*, there is a frontal axis round which the limb bends, and a sagittal axis for the lateral movements. The amplitude of the lateral movement is about 90° ; that of the shoulder is 150°.

(iv) When two or more joints move together, the degree of freedom increases. This is what occurs in the movements of the hand, mobile from the wrist, which has numerous jointed bones (fig. 116) and in those of the vertebral column, etc.

One cannot here enter into the details of these " combinations " and " compositions " of simple joints ; it will only be pointed out that the greater their freedom of movement the more are the ligaments, tendons and muscles, relieved of an important part of their effort, and this serves to economise force in the human machine.

76. The Human Body. (i) **Shape.**—The various parts which we have examined constitute the organs of locomotion ; but the functions which maintain movement are those of respiration, circulation and innervation of which the seat (except the cerebral centres) is the trunk ; all the digestive apparatus being in the lower part of this trunk. The head contains the directing organs, the senses and the will. And from this complex whole results an admirable harmony. The shape is the least complex ; it approaches that of the " prism." The human body feels the effect of its own weight, and it has been shown that in prismatic or cylindrical shapes the section of the least resistance is about at "the middle of the height." It is there that the weight of the body is felt the most, but it is there also that the body is enlarged, the " pelvis " receiving at that level a veritable reinforcement, and the strength, " according to ancient wisdom, lying in the loins." But an exaggerated development of the iliac bones would inconvenience walking, in producing rotations of the body (see § 270). People who lead normal lives, free from extraordinary exertion of the lower limbs, have a relatively narrow pelvis, in contrast to heavy athletes who have wide and very muscular hips.

Dynamic actions tend to develop or refine the body ; carters, dock labourers, etc., being often massive ; dancers, runners, fencers often being slender. The carrying of loads modifies the shape of the limbs ; for example, walking under a load results in flattening the " foot " and elongating it permanently. It is the same with the hand in the handling of heavy tools (hammer, spade, pick, etc.) ; the axis of the body, the vertebral column tends to become curved in the opposite direction to the load, and under a continuous pressure the column bends and appreciably reduces its length.

Natural aptitude for any trade or occupation is influenced by the proportions of the limbs, long limbs having large but slow movements ; short limbs denote speed. Thus the woodcutter, the blacksmith, the sawyer, etc., can exert the more force or effect the longer the arm at the extremity of which is the tool. The shape of the body is often, on this account, a guide for the choice of workmen suitable to this or that work ; but it is not an absolute guide, because " adaptation " is an extremely important factor ; thus a certain fencer excelled despite his small stature, which put him at a disadvantage and exhausted his forces. As a rule, men are organised and made to work in a certain way, because it is thus that their work is most economical. With regard to age, it is claimed that the strength of the human body is at its maximum between the ages of 25 and 40. In fact, the skeleton does not achieve its consolidation, its ossification, and its welding together until about its twentieth year ; 16 to 18 for the scapula, which in developing presents large surfaces to the muscles for their insertions ; 18 years for the humerus ; 20 to 25 for the ulna, ilium, and femur ; 25 to 30 for the vertebral column. The bones of the hand themselves do not complete their ossification until the age of 12 to 13 years. Hence the importance of not overstraining the young, and not deforming organs, thereby condemning them to develop abnormally. In fact, science should always protest against the practice of making children work before their 15th year, for this causes a misshapen, crippled and stunted humanity. Where are the legislators who have sufficient courage to check this social evil ?

77. (ii) **Stature.**—Stature is the vertical dimension of the body, or the height when a man, standing, is measured by means of an anthropometric measure (see *Technics*, § 201). Often the " height standing " is distinguished from " the height sitting," in the latter case, the subject being seated so as to measure the length of his bust only.

The average height of an adult is 165 centimetres, varying according to the race and the country, its lowest and highest limits being 125 centimetres and 199 centimetres. In France the average stature is 164·6 cms. ; (it was 1·9 cms. more in 1725, and was 166·5 cms. two centuries ago). [1]

That of woman is 10 to 11 centimetres less than that of man, but the difference was only from 5 to 7 centimetres at the

---

[1] L'abbé de Fontenu, *Hist. Acad. Roy. Sc.*, 1725, p. 16.

period just mentioned ([1]) ; thus the stature of woman as well as of man has diminished in the last two hundred years.

The kind of life and the conditions of the surroundings modify the height, workmen being, as a rule, smaller than the general population,([2]) and labourers in workshops and mills smaller than those who live in the open air.([3])   The poor are smaller than the rich in the same country and town.   A comparison was made in various districts in Paris and the difference was quite appreciable in every case.([4])

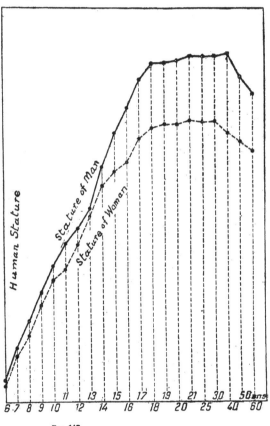

Fig. 117.
Stature of man and woman.

([1]) Voltaire, *Dictionnaire Philos.* (art. *Homme*).
([2]) Beddoe, *The Stature and Bulk of Man in the British Isles*, 1870, p. 148.
([3]) Houzé, *Bull. Soc. Anthrop. de Bruxelles*, 1887.
([4]) Bertillon, L. Manouvrier.

MacAuliffe and Marie found, by a series of measurements, that the Parisian is about 3 centimetres taller than the average Frenchman.[1]

The relation of height to age differs in the two sexes. At birth boys measure 49 9 cms. and girls a little less, 49·2 cms., according to the average of determinations in Paris. The difference grows wider with years. Until 12 years old there is not more than 2·3 centimetres difference. Woman is full-grown at about 18 years of age, but man continues growing and does not stop until between 25 and 30 years of age.

The foregoing curves from results obtained by Quételet [2] give the relative variations of height in both sexes between 6 and 60 years of age (fig. 117).

From fifty onwards the stature undergoes a reduction ; this is senile decay, and reaches 2·5 cms. for man, 2·7 cms. for woman, at about the age of 60. It affects tall people most, and they become bent and shrunken.

In addition to this natural evolution, it is recognised that vertical pressure such as the carrying of weights, slightly reduces the stature and the upright position, when it is continuous and repeated, has the same result. On the contrary, however, a lying or sitting position, such as forced immobility in bed, increases the vertical development of the body. It seems as if people who hold themselves very erect, notably soldiers, increase their stature a little and conserve that increase.

HUMAN STATURE.

AGE	MAN	WOMAN	AGE	MAN	WOMAN
Years.	cms.	cms.	Years.	cms.	cms.
6	104·6	103·2	17	167·0	154·4
7	111·2	109·6	18	170·0	156·2
8	117·0	113·9	19	170·6	157·0
9	122·7	120·0	20	171·1	157·0
10	128·2	124·8	21	172·2	157·7
11	132·7	127·5	25	172·2	157·7
12	135·9	132·7	30	172·2	157·9
13	140·3	138·6	40	171·3	155·5
14	148·7	144·7	50	167·4	153·6
15	155·9	147·5	60	163·9	151·6
16	161·0	150·0			

[1] Marie and MacAuliffe, *Comptes Rend. Acad. Sc.*, 29th May, 1911.
[2] Quételet, *Physique Sociale*, II, ch.ii., iii., and 1869 ; *Anthropométrie*, 1871.

78. Bust and Thoracic Co-efficient.—If we compare different persons, having the same stature, it will be found that the upper half of the body, the bust, varies in size. The dimensions of the bust are of importance on account of the organs it contains. They are estimated by determining : —

1. The thoracic perimeter, taken at the level of the nipples ;

2. The height of the body sitting, which is that of the bust, the head being included ;

3. The span or the horizontal length of the extended arms (see *Technics*, § 203, as to all these measurements). When the bust is normally developed it has been found that the spread exceeds the total height by about 4 centimetres.

On the other hand, the relation of the height of the seated body to the total stature is, on an average, 0·53 ; it is 0·5378 for short people and 0·5285 for tall ones. In the female sex these proportions are slightly less. This relation

$$\frac{\text{Bust}}{\text{Height}} = 0\cdot53$$

is called the " thoracic co-efficient."

From this point of view there are two characteristic types : the people whose lower limbs are too long in comparison with the bust, and those whose lower limbs are too short. M. Louis Manouvrier[1] has called them respectively "macrosoles" and "brachysoles." The development of the thorax is therefore independent of that of the legs.

It can be easily observed in children that their limbs lengthen disproportionately to the bust, which keeps its normal dimensions.

The dimensions of the upper part of the body, measured in a sitting position, are conditioned by the physiological functions of the thorax.[2] The trunk encloses the axis of the body, the vertebral column to which the heart and the lungs are indirectly connected. It is here that all human energy takes its rise. Hence its development is greater in man than in woman. Man's muscular power calls for intense respiratory activity. In woman the digestive functions are predominant.

79. The displacement of air that takes place in the lungs is proportional to the thoracic amplitude. Its greatest value can be determined by making a deep inspiration, followed at once by a forced " expiration," all the air being ejected into a " spirometer." Thus we can measure what Hutchinson called " the vital capa-

---

[1] Louis Manouvrier (*Mémoires de la Soc. d'Anthrop. de Paris*, vol. ii. part 3, 1902).

[2] R. Collignon (*Bull Soc. Anthrop, Paris*, 1883).

city." [1]   For a healthy adult man, the vital capacity is 3·75 litres and 2·75 litres for a woman.[2]   As a rule, from the age of 3 years, when it is 0·400 litres, it has an annual increase of 0·42 litres.   This continues up to the thirtieth year.   It also increases by 0·05 or 0·04 litres per centimetre increase of stature in man and woman respectively [3] from 4 years of age.   In the case of macrosoles, or brachysoles, it depends on the thoracic perimeter.

The vital capacity, as also the thoracic co-efficient, are sensibly larger in persons of medium height, and these often appear more robust and muscular than tall persons.   It would even seem that evolution tends to reduce the stature and give it a more accentuated strength and robustness.[4]   Measurements of vital capacity are therefore very useful (see § 240).

80. (iii) Surface and Volume of the Body.—The relation between the volume, the weight, and the density of a body is:

$$V = \frac{P}{D}.$$

If we know the density D of any body, its volume can be readily deduced from its weight.   D is generally taken as 1·035, which figure is the mean of a large number of measurements made by Mies.[5]

In practice the density is determined from the volume.   The latter can be easily found by placing the subject in a water bath and measuring the volume of water displaced.

The above value for the ratio $\frac{P}{V}$ *i.e.*, 1·035 was the mean of 59 measurements, the subjects having their lungs partially inflated.

The estimation of the measurement of the surface of a body can be made theoretically.   Suppose a " cube " with a volume V ; the side of the cube is $\sqrt[3]{V}$; the total surface, of the six faces of the solid, will be $6 \times (\sqrt[3]{V})^2 = 6\sqrt[3]{V^2}$.   It is obvious that we can substitute the weight for the volume and write S $= K \sqrt[3]{P^2}$.   But the co-efficient K changes according to the shape of the body, which is not really cubic.   For man, it is found that K = 12·312.   The surface is therefore :

$$S = 12\cdot312 \sqrt[3]{P^2},$$

[1] Hutchinson (*Trans. of the Med.-Chir. Soc.*, 1848).
[2] Pagliani, (*Lo Sviluppo Umano per Età*, Milan, 1879).
[3] Arnold, (*Ueber die Athmung des Menschen.*, 1855) ;   Snepf, (*Gazette Médicale*, 1857).
[4] L. Manouvrier, (*loc. cit.*, p. 200).
[5] Mies (*Wirchow's Archiv.*, vol. clvii., p. 90, 1899).

P being expressed in grammes and S in square centimetres. This is " Meeh's relation."[1] Thus the body of an adult weighing 65 kilogrammes has a surface ;

$$S = 12 \cdot 312 \sqrt[3]{65,000^2} = 19,896 \text{ square centimetres or}$$

$1 \cdot 99$ square metres, practically 2 square metres.

If two individuals of different weights are considered (an adult and a child), their surfaces will be to each other as the cube root of the square of their weights ; thus the surface diminishes less rapidly than the weight. We have :

$$\frac{S'}{S} = \frac{12 \cdot 312 \sqrt[3]{P'^2}}{12 \cdot 312 \sqrt[3]{P^2}} = \frac{\sqrt[3]{P'^2}}{\sqrt[3]{P^2}} = \sqrt[3]{\frac{P'^2}{P^2}}.$$

For instance, make $P' = \frac{1}{8} P$, then $\frac{S'}{S} = \frac{1}{4}$. Thus if the weights vary from 8 to 1, the surfaces will only vary from 4 to 1. Therefore children have a larger surface than adults in proportion to their weight. Accurate methods of estimating the surface of bodies are available, but they are generally complex.[2] That of Jules Lefèvre [3] appears to be the simplest : the subject is in a pliable garment moulding itself perfectly to the body. Let P be the weight of the garment, p the weight of a square decimetre of the same stuff ; the relation $\frac{P}{p}$ gives the surface of the body. This procedure is very exact if an accurate balance is employed.

It must be remarked that the surface, volume and density of the human body undergo variations when there is obesity or extreme thinness ; these being causes of which it is difficult to take exact account.

81. (iv) Weight of the Human Body.—The average weight of the human body, with regard to age, for the two sexes has been determined by different authors. The measurements of Quételet, between the limits of 6 and 60 years (*vide* the following table and fig. 118) are as follows:

---

[1] Meeh (*Zeitsch. f. Biol.* vol. xv., p. 440, 1879). The co-efficient K in the formula varies slightly with the state, (thin or fat), of the subject.

[2] We quote, from memory, a geometrical method due to Bouchard (*Comptes Rendus Acad. Sc.*, 1897, vol. lxxiv, p. 844) and another, also geometrical, but more correct, by B. Roussy (*ibid.*, 17th July, 1911, p. 205, and 14th April, 1913, p. 1171). Roussy even takes into account the surface of the ears and the genital parts.

[3] Jules Lefévre, *Bioénergétique*, p. 501 (Masson, Paris, 1911).

WEIGHT OF THE HUMAN BODY.

AGE	MAN	WOMAN	AGE	MAN	WOMAN
Yrs.	kg.	kg.	Yrs.	kg.	kg.
6	18·04	16·74	17	57·40	49·08
7	20·16	18·45	18	61·26	53·10
8	22·26	19·82	19	63·32	54·46
9	24·09	22·44	20	65·00	54·46
10	26·12	24·24	21	65·00	54·46
11	27·85	26·25	25	68·29	55·08
12	31·00	30·54	30	68·90	55·14
13	35·32	34·65	40	68·81	56·65
14	40·50	38·10	50	67·45	58·45
15	46·41	41·30	60	65·50	56·73
16	53·39	44·44			

The average weight of the adult is : 65 kilogrammes for man and 55 kilogrammes for woman, a difference of 10 kilogrammes. And, as in the case of the height, a "senile diminution" is evident at about the fiftieth year.

The differences in weight in different countries are sometimes very great ; thus there are races where man is massive and heavy and some where he is "obese" by development of fats, which is often the result of the diet.

Bouchard denominated the ratio of weight to height as the "segment anthropometrique" denoted by the symbol A.

$$A = \frac{\text{weight in kilogrammes}}{\text{height in decimetres.}}$$

He obtained the following results :—

Normal state ... ... $A = 3·9$ (woman)
$4·0$ (man)
Emaciation ... ... $A = 3·6$
Obesity ... ... $A = 5·4$
Marasmus ... ... $A = 2·9$
Extreme marasmus ... ... $A = 2·0$

(an extremely rare value, even in prolonged inanition).

Thus for an adult, weighing 65 kilogrammes, and whose height is 16·80 decimetres :

$$A = \frac{65}{16·8} = 3·87.$$

The average value of 4 corresponds to a state of normal nutrition.

The weight of the body is an excellent proof of organic development ; it should be particularly studied in infants and

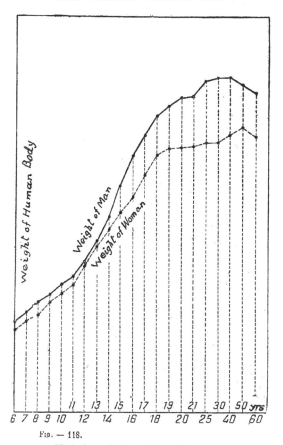

Fig. — 118.

Variation of the weight with age.

children ; (¹) also in the adult its constancy is a guarantee of the adequate reparation of the tissues.

82. "*Inanition*," or a prolonged fast, lowers the weight of the body. A man fasting and only drinking water, lost 300 grammes the first day (Atwater).

After an absolute fast (abstinence from water also) for 36 hours the loss was from 1,600 to 1,700 grammes. Insufficient nourishment caused a loss of weight of 2,350 grammes in thirteen

---

(¹) For children in English schools (Clegg, *British Medical Journal*, No. 17, June, 1911).

days, 180 grammes per day, for a person weighing 55 kilogrammes, or about ·33% in twenty-four hours.[1]

All these diminutions depend on the nature of the nourishment and on the initial condition of the subject.

In professional fasters, such as Succi, for example, physiological inanition lowered the weight of the body in a regular manner. The diagram is an equilateral hyperbola, a curve which approaches the co-ordinates without ever touching them; these axes are the "asymptotes" of the curve; fig. 119 shows three equilateral hyperbola.

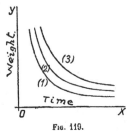

Fig. 119.

The curve of inanition presents, in addition, two irregularities, one at the beginning, marking the appearance of hunger, a phenomenon which soon ceases. At the end of twenty-five to thirty days the crisis is reached. In thirty days Succi lost $\frac{19}{100}$ of his weight, which was about 57 kilogrammes.[2] First the fats, then the muscles of the organism are reduced; the nerves being the last to be affected, and this is the dangerous period.

Inanition attacks the tissues in the order of their importance, reacting less quickly on the motor organs than on those of nutrition. Death is therefore cessation of movement and life is movement. Inanition must be particularly avoided in children, their development suffering from it. Even if followed by abundant nourishment, the normal development of the muscles is affected.[3]

---

[1] Jules Amar, *Le Rendement de la Machine Humaine*, pp. 79-80, Paris, 1910.
[2] Luciani, *Trattato di Fisiologia Umana*, II., pp. 493 and 497, 1910
[3] Hans Aron (*La Nature*. 4 May. 1912).

CHAPTER II.

THE MUSCULAR MOTOR AND ALIMENTATION.

83. (i) **The Muscular Motor.**—The motor, in the human body, is the muscle, and the force is that of contraction.

Nervous excitement, from the motor point of view, is the origin of muscular contraction, and an indefinite relation of cause and effect exists between nervous and muscular movement. The contraction is rapid and sudden, so that the excitement of the nerve is like the priming of an explosive. When the contraction equilibrises a weight without displacing it, (static effort) or moves it (work), the muscle becomes heated, its temperature rising slightly above the normal temperature and a quantity of heat greater than that which is evolved in the state of repose (relaxed muscle) is produced. Thus the muscle functions like a heat engine. Its fuel will be considered later (§ 106).

A sustained muscular contraction is compounded of several impulses. If an extremity of a muscle is fixed at R, and the other end is attached to an indicating style, AO jointed to the point O, and whose point rubs on a moving surface covered with smoke blackened paper, then by an electric stimulus to the nerve N, the trace ACD is produced (fig. 120). The duration of ACD, read on the line T of the time is from 12 to 16 hundredths of a second in adults. It is greater in very young children, and varies according to different circumstances (temperature, nutrition, etc).[1].

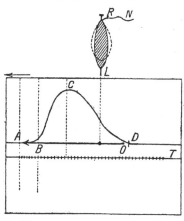

Fıc. 120.

Graph of a muscular jerk.

Now, at the instant A of the excitation, the muscle does not respond; at the end of a time AB the "myographic curve" begins; it therefore includes a "latent period." AB of about $\frac{3}{1000}$ of a second, according to Tiegerstedt and Burdon-

---

[1] Patrizi and Mensi (*Giorn. R. Accad. Med. Torino*, 1894, p. 61).

Sanderson,[1] an "ascendant period" generally longer than the following period which is "descendant." When the excitations succeed each other at average intervals of 15 hundredths of a second a series of impulses resembling fig. 120 is produced.

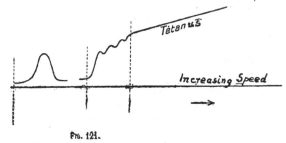

Fig. 121.

Tetanic blending of impulses.

When they follow each other at short intervals they tend to blend themselves into a straight line (fig. 121), which shows a curve for "physiological tetanus."

The number of impulses producing a sustained tetanic contrac-

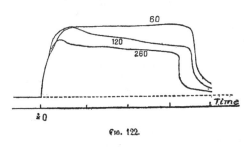

Fig. 122.

tion varies in different muscles according to the age, the temperature, the weight under which the muscle contracts, and its initial state. In man it corresponds to 20 or 30 impulses, that is, 20 or 30 excitations per second. Up to 60 impulses per second the muscle remains tetanised for 4 to 5 minutes, then the curve descends ; there is, from that moment, fatigue ; normal contraction has ceased. Above a frequency of 60, fatigue is more rapid, as is shown in the diagram (fig. 122) from Hofmann.[2] Physiologically, the muscle receives a real nervous or voluntary excitation instead of an electric stimulus, the number of impulses being always sufficient to cause contraction ; this leads directly (fig. 122) to a true state of tetanus. If a contraction takes place voluntarily, experiment shows that the muscle gives a sound corresponding to a determined frequency, which is clearly perceptible

[1] It seems, according to the researches of Piper on the nerve of the biceps of the arm, that the latent period may be a little longer, about $\frac{4}{1000}$ of a second (*Pflüeger's, Archiv.* vol. cxxvii, p. 474, 1909).

[2] F. B. Hofmann (*Pflüegers Archiv.*, vol. xciii., p. 197, 1902).

by means of special apparatus (the myophone). Hence the motor excitantation is periodic, and owing to muscular elasticity, there is in the process a " latent addition " due to the nervous shocks.

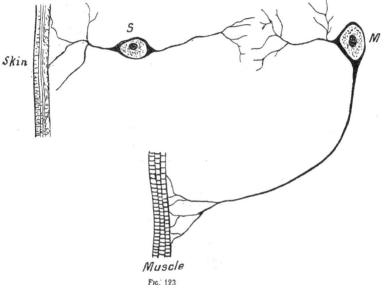

Fig. 123

Reflex sensi-motor arc.

In spite of this fusion of impulses voluntary contraction is more rapid than the contraction due to electric shock, for it can last $\frac{8}{100}$ of a second, with a maximum of 16 contractions per second each corresponding to three impulses (see § 90).

If the excitation is external, as in the case of a person abruptly brought face to face with a danger, or touching, inadvertently, a burning substance, a reflex phenomenon is produced, since the elements of the *sensitive* neuron S, awakened by the burning of the skin (fig. 123) transmit the sensation to the *motor* neuron M, which acts on the muscle and contracts it.

Movement will therefore follow the sensation.

Excitation travels along the nerves at an average speed of **32** metres per second,[1] but the total duration of the reflex action is prolonged because very often several neurons are intercalated in the path.

[1] F. Kiesow (*Arch. Ital. Biol.*, vol. xl., p. 273, 1903). Piper gives 120 metres as the result of his researches on the brachial nerve.

The length of the path is diminished when the nervous centres of the movement are those of the spinal cord ; for example, in simple reflex actions and in "automatic" movements, there being fewer relays.

The duration of the reflex decreases also as the intensity of the excitation increases; it is in fact influenced by the particular state of organisation, acquired, or hereditary, which assists the transmission called the "nervous influx." The time which elapses from the instant of impression, until the instant when movement begins, is the "personal equation"; and it is, obviously, a qualitative element. Numerically it is from $\frac{1}{5}$ to $\frac{1}{10}$ of a second, for various circumstances and individuals.

The following averages are quoted :—

$$
\begin{array}{lll}
\text{Tactile reaction} & \dots \quad \dots \quad \dots & \frac{14}{100} \\
\text{Visual} \quad ,, & \dots \quad \dots \quad \dots & \frac{19}{100} \\
\text{Auditory} \ ,, & \dots \quad \dots \quad \dots & \frac{15}{100}
\end{array}
$$

84. Laws of Muscular Contraction.—Contraction does not necessarily consist in the shortening of the muscle, for if there is sufficient resistance to overcome, the muscle will keep its length ("absolute" static contraction or absolute force) : but, as a rule, it shortens, its width increasing and its length decreasing, hence the volume is not appreciably altered.

The shortening affects all the fibres ; thus the force of contraction is the sum of these elementary contractions. Chauveau [1] has made a minute analysis of the elements which enter into the effort of contraction, as follows :—

According to the law of elasticity, a muscle sustaining a weight P will be lengthened by a quantity $L = \dfrac{PL}{ES}$ (see § 44). If by its contraction it resists this elongation, its internal force will be equal and opposite to P. If it also shortens by a quantity r while sustaining the weight, the internal force will be greater than P by the effort necessary to restore the muscle to its original length ; this supplementary effort will therefore be proportional to the shortening and will be $P \times r$. The force of static contraction, to balance a weight P with a shortening r, will have the total value :

$$F = P + Pr = P\ (1 + r).$$

It is therefore equal to an elastic force F, including the "effective" elastic force P and a "disposable" elastic force Pr, varying with the shortening. It is evident that economy of force is attained by reducing the shortening of the muscle to a mini-

---

[1] A. Chauveau (*Comptes Rendus Sciences*, vol. cxxvii., p. 983, 1898 ; *Journal de Physiologie*, 1899, p. 157).

mum. This law is instinctively observed, thus a workman who pushes a wheelbarrow holds it without bending his arms more than is necessary.

85. Besides the work of the muscle in displacing the weight P, the shortening takes two limiting values, r and r', to which the forces of contraction, F and F' correspond ; so that the force has an average value, $\dfrac{F + F'}{2} = F_m$. Replacing F by P $(1 + r)$ and F' by P $(1 + r')$:

$$F_m = P \left(1 + \frac{r + r'}{2}\right).$$

The dynamic contraction accomplishes work of which the factors are : the average shortening, and the average force F_m. According to whether the work is " positive " or " negative " the average effort increases or diminishes slightly, by a quantity not fixed " a priori." [1] The examination of photographs of active muscles has revealed to Mr. Paul Richer that they are distended to varying degrees according to the motor, or resistant character, of the contraction.

Chauveau verified the laws of elasticity, or rather of muscular contraction, experimentally by causing a man to hold a weight with the forearm bent upon the arm, and by modifying the degree of flexion as well as the value of the weight.[2] The results obtained were satisfactory ; more so than those obtained by Dondus and Van Mansvelt.[3]

It is interesting to recall certain observations made by Winslow [4] in the year 1720. He remarked that the increased distension of the biceps with increase in the flexion of the arm, and the weight supported, could be readily felt. If the arm was bent to a definite degree and then fixed in that position and held so that the flexor muscles were entirely relaxed and exerted no effort, and then an additional stress was applied, the muscles would be proportionately distended, although no movement took place at the elbow joint. The action differed from that of a spring under compression or tension.

The researches of Dondus and of Chauveau were on the preceding lines.

86. According to the laws of elasticity muscular deformation is proportional to the length of the muscle. A bone capable of

---

[1] A. Chaveau (*Journal de Physiologie*, 1900, p. 313.
[2] The apparatus is described by Tissot in the *Journal de Physiologie*, 1899, p. 181.
[3] Dondus and Van Mansvelt, *Over de Elasticitat der Spieren*, Utrecht 1863.
[4] Winslow (*Mem. Acad Roy. d. Sciences*, 1720, p. 87).

considerable movement must be operated by a muscle capable of sustaining considerable deformation ; hence long muscles are best adapted for such movements.

On the contrary, the number of fibres being very great in " short " and " thick" muscles, they can develop considerable efforts. A glance at the muscular system (fig. 105.p,130) shows that not only are muscles short or long, but their shapes are very varied: some being composed of parallel fibres, like the biceps, others of radiating fibres like the temporal. These shapes are rational functional adaptations ; if the muscle is attached to two bones at a distance from each other, susceptible to a small reciprocal displacement, then the fibres are lengthened by thin tendons, there being an economy of muscular substance. Such is the case of the flexors of the fingers. If the muscle has to overcome a powerful resistance, its fibres are " oblique " (see § 69) so as to present a large section ;' and they have the appearance of grains of corn, for a third of their length, the other two-thirds being thin tendons, resulting in a considerable total section, and an economy of matter (fig. 124). This is what takes place in the Masseter, which has short and parallel fibres, and which must be powerful in order to effect mastication.

Fig 124

The adaptation of each muscle to its function has been noted by numerous authors.[1] An observation of Marey's is particularly interesting : the calf of the negro is thin and has long fibres ; that of the white man is fat, short, and prolonged by the long Achilles tendon. Now, in these two cases, the muscle must have the power to lift the weight of the man. Marey found that the calf muscle, being weaker in the negro, is attached to a longer lever, the salient of the os calcis (heel) being 40% further behind the axis of rotation than in the case of the European. This clever physiologist experimented by shortening the os calcis of a rabbit, and at the end of a year he saw the calf increase, that is to say, increase in strength to adapt itself to its function.

Functional variations also are found in the cartilages, which adapt themselves to the work of the locomotor organs.[2]

The motive elements of the body are so arranged as to occupy the minimum of space. This will explain why the muscle is nearly parallel to the bone which it moves instead of approximately

---

[1] Specially W. Roux, Marey, G. Weiss. Also consult W. Roux, *Die Entwickelungs-Mechanik*, Leipzig, 1905 ; *Vortrage u. Aufsatze uber Entwick*, 1905 ; Marey (*Arch. de Physiol*, 1889).
[2] Retterer (*Comptes Rendus Biologie*, 1908, 1909, 1911, *passim*).

perpendicular to it, which latter would, from a mechanical point of view, be the most efficient position. The loss of power is compensated by the resultant economy in space.

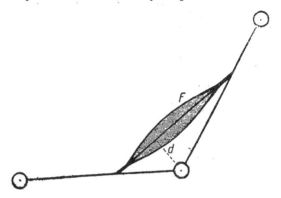

Fig. 125.   Muscular action.

87. The useful action of a muscle is therefore a function of its mass (active fibres), of its degree of contraction, and of the angle which its direction makes with that of the bone to be moved. The muscle has a definite moment of rotation in relation to the axis, for each of its positions. The moment of rotation is the product of the force F of the muscle by the distance d (fig. 125). We have :— $\mathbf{M} = F \times d$.

The contraction modifies F and d. Numerous measurements of the moment of rotation have been made by Braun & Fischer ([1]) on anatomical specimens. F being deduced from the size of the muscular section ; it was found that the moment varied with the angle of flexion up to a certain value. When the arm is fully extended the product of F and d is not zero, as might be expected. It

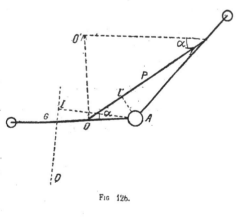

Fig. 126.

([1]) Braune et Fischer (*Abhandl...*, vol. xv., n° 3, p. 247, 1889).

must also be remembered that, in the human body, the muscular power generally acts upon levers of the third order. If a stress is applied at the centre of gravity G of a mobile limb (fig. 126), the useful component of the power will be $OO' = P \sin \alpha$, that is to say, the effort of flexion varies as the sin of the angle of the inclination of the muscle to the mobile limb. The arm of the lever $A1'$ of the power is smaller than that $A1$ of the resistance ; but the amplitude of the movement of this resistance is increased in the relation of $\dfrac{AI}{AI'}$, and produces a large number of useful actions. The motor function of the muscle must be considered in reference to the nature of the movement. "Isolated" muscular action, as Duchenne wrote, "does not exist in nature"[1]; there is co-operation of all the motive forces, often apparently antagonistic ; the "biceps" bends the forearm; the "triceps" produces its "extension"; in fact, they co-ordinate their movement, and combine their efforts so well that the real grouping of the muscles is functional and physiological, and not anatomical. The precise and gradual association of the muscular movements is the work of the nervous system ; it is automatic, the effect of habit, and rapid, because it is in the charge of near centres in the spinal cord ; but normally these centres only begin the movement and the cerebral centres, further away, achieve its perfection.

88. Muscular Force : Absolute Force.—It has been seen that the force of the muscle increases in proportion to its contraction ; if it is loaded so as to prevent its shortening, the "absolute" effort can be measured.[2] On a living subject a particular muscle is chosen with a known section, the kind of lever to which it is attached is noted, and the value of the maximum static effort is calculated. Thus a man of 70 kilogrammes, loaded with a weight of 70 kilogrammes, cannot lift himself when he is seated.[3] The resistance is 140 kilogrammes and

$$P \times Ac = Q \times AB ; \text{ whence } P = Q \frac{AB}{Ac} \text{ (fig. 127)}.$$

Hermann,[4] calculated P by determining exactly the relation $\dfrac{AB}{Ac}$, he obtained a force per square millimetre of the muscles of the calf of as much as 62·4 grammes. For the flexors of the arm,[5]

[1] Duchenne de Boulogne, *Physiologie des Mouvements*, p. 811, Paris, 1867.

[2] So called by E. Weber, author of numerous works on muscular elasticity and with his brother Wilhelm, of a treatise which became famous (?) : *Mécanique de la Locomotion chez l'Homme*, trans. Jourdan, Paris, 1843.

[3] De la Hire (*Mém. Acad. Roy. d. Sciences*, 1699, p. 153).

[4] Hermann (*Arch. f. Physiol.*, vol. lxxiii., p. 429, 1898).

[5] Hencke and Knorz (*Zeitsch. f. Rat. Med.*, vol. xxiv., 1865).

the force is from 50 to 80 grammes. In the masseter muscles ([1]) it rises to 90 to 100 grammes per square millimetre. There are therefore marked differences between various muscles, the average value being 75 grammes per square millimetre of section. In any kind of animal this absolute force is not exceeded.

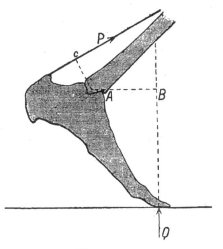

Fig. 127.

Very robust subjects, such as athletes, have large muscles to produce considerable efforts ; for example, in the famous wrestler, Cotch Mehmet, the abdominal muscles were " three " times thicker than that of the average normal man, according to Manouvrier athletes can lift a weight of 350 to 380 kilogrammes, ([2]) and certain labourers (Marseillais, Sicilians, Turks, Tunisians) have great strength,([3])

89. Numerous researches have been made to ascertain the maximum value of the muscular effort that man can develop in his arms, legs, loins and neck. The measurements are neither accurate nor consistent, sometimes " pressures " have been measured, sometimes " tractions," also the "dynamometers" employed were of different types, so that the grip of the hands was not uniform. And finally, the individual differences were very great.

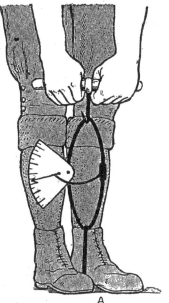

A

Fig. 128.—Test of renal force.

([1]) Rosenthal (*Physik. Med. Soc. in Erlangen*, vol. xxvii, p. 85, 1895).
([2]) Désaguliers, *Cours de Physique*, vol. I., p. 300 1751.
([3]) Hunauld, Barthez, etc.

Désaguliers (*loc. cit.*); Schultze ([1]) and Gréhant ([2]) obtained an average of 45 kilogrammes as the force of traction with both hands.

The muscles of the neck can withstand up to 200 kilogrammes without bending, and on an average 150 kilogrammes. Quételet (*loc. cit.*) measured the "renal force" by means of "Regnier's" dynamometer (see § 206) the instrument is placed between the feet of the subject and fixed to the ground; he pulls the other extremity (fig. 128) first bending and then straightening himself. By experiments on thousands of people Quételet determined the renal force for various ages and sexes. The results between the ages of 6 and 60 are shewn in fig. 129. The average for an adult is 150 kilogrammes in man, and 78 kilogrammes in woman. Senile decay is observable from about 40 years.

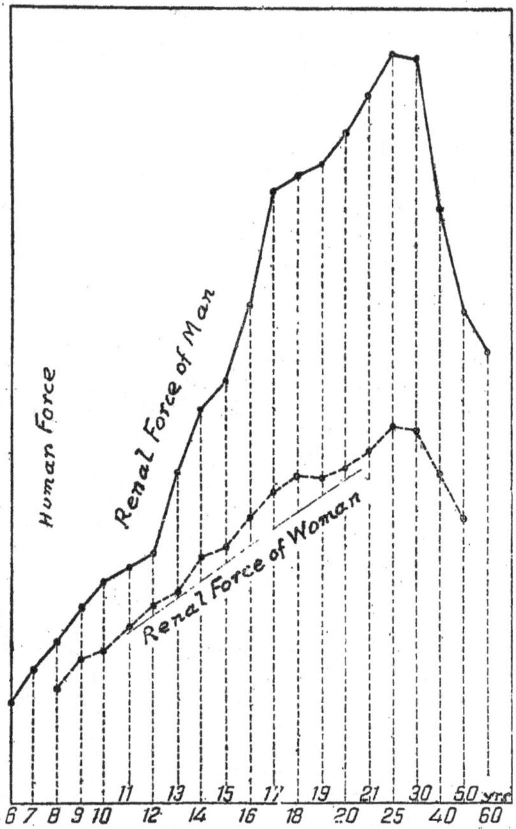

Fig. 129.
Variations of renal force with age.

The relative difference between the sexes is shown by the development of the muscles, which are larger in man than in woman, and also have a better functional adaptation. The same

([1]) Schultze (*Bibliotheque Britannique*, vol. lvi).
([2]) Gréhant (*Comptes Rendus Biologie*, 1897).

thing is noticed in the grip of the hand (pressure-dynamometer) ; it is a relation of the same kind, but $\frac{57}{100}$ according to Manouvriei. An equally important characteristic of force and of human effort is that man produces it quickly with its maximum value, and woman more slowly (according to Féré).

HUMAN STRENGTH.

AGE	MAN	WOMAN	AGE	MAN	WOMAN
Yrs.	kg.	kg.	Yrs.		
6	20	—	17	126	64
7	27	—	18	130	67
8	33	24	19	132	67
9	40	30	20	138	68
10	46	31	21	146	72
11	48	37	25	155	77
12	51	40	30	154	77
13	69	44	40	122	—
14	81	50	50	101	59
15	88	53	60	93	—
16	102	59			

Quételet's diagram shows a reduction of strength between 9 and 13 years of age. Grigorescu ([1]) analysing this period of childhood by measurements taken in schools, finds the development of strength is arrested between 11 and 13.

Whilst the preceding table shows a maximum renal force at the age of 30 in Europeans, Gould found it at about thirty-four in white Americans (soldiers) and 40 in Indians. He gives the following values :

WHITES	NEGROES	MULATTOES	INDIANS
144·400 kg.	146·700 kg.	158·300 kg.	159·200 kg.

Weisbach has given figures showing the " effort of pressure " of the hands in Asiatic and Negroid peoples ; these figures are inaccurate even as average values. It is interesting to notice, however, that these measurements, and those made by explorers, on various peoples, show that " the civilised nations are more robust than savage nations," and better developed, if not more resistant to physical pain. Environment has certain effects on human strength, being able to increase or decrease it. Therefore attention must be paid to it, as well as to the age of the subject.

90. The Periodicity of Voluntary Muscular Contraction —The muscle contracts voluntarily in a periodic manner ; and the contraction, real tetanus, is itself discontinuous, although the various

([1]) Grigorescu (*Comptes Rendus Biologie*, 1891, p. 547).

impulses of which it is the resultant, escape perception. The nervous flux acts in a periodic manner, and not continuously. The rapid succession of impulses in voluntary contraction can be observed, and can even produce a sound. If one finger is placed in the concha of the ear, and the biceps strongly contracted, a sound is heard; the impulses number about 50 per second.[1]   In the contraction of the masseter [2] (jaws) there are from 60 to 65 impulses; and in the flexor muscles of the fingers from 8 to 11 according to the finger.[3]

Voluntary contraction, whatever may be its rapidity, has therefore the character of a " physiological tetanus." Thus a series of excitations leave the nervous centres, which fuse the separate contractions of the muscular fibres into a single contraction, said to be voluntary. Treves has shown, in addition, that the rhythm of the impulses is not modified, whether the muscle sustains a small or a large load [4]. Fatigue alone can change it.

Hence static effort leads to a real vibratory movement, that is to say, to internal work. There must be an expenditure of work to produce an effort; for example :

1. The body of a pump in which slides a weighted piston, is connected to a water-pipe in which there is pressure; the piston will not descend because of the stationary flux or the force exerted by the water [5]. It is thus that the pressure of a jet of water can keep a door closed.

2. We have seen that the elastic work of traction is (§ 49) :

$$T = \tfrac{1}{2}\frac{ESl^2}{L} = \frac{Fl}{2},$$

the differential of the work in respect to the deformation will be :

$$\frac{dT}{dl} = \frac{ESl}{L} = F.[6]$$

91. The contraction of the muscle, and its tetanic character when voluntary, alternates, like the strokes of the piston of a steam engine. The number of alternations can vary within

---

[1] H. Piper (*Pflüg. Arch.*, 1909, vol. cxxiv., p. 591 ; *ibid.*, cxxvii., p. 474, and *Arch. f. Anat. u. Phys.*, 1910, p. 207).

[2] P. Hoffmann (*Pflüg. Arch.*, vol. cxxiv., p. 341). Helmholtz had found earlier, from 35 to 40 impulses instead of 60. But it must be admitted that the number varies according to the individual and the stature.

[3] Canney and Tunstall (*Journal of Physiol.*, vol. vi., p. xvii, 1885) ; S haefer (*ibid.*, vol. vii., p. 111, 1886).

[4] Z. Treves (*Arch. Ital. Biol.*, vol. xxxiii., p. 87, 1899) ; Simonelli and Coop (*Ann. di Neurol.*, vol. xviii., p. 310, Naples, 1900).

[5] Gariel, *Traité de Physique Biologique* d'Arsonval, Gariel, etc., vol. i., p. 994, 1901.

[6] Lebert (*Comptes Rendus Acad. Sciences*, 1904, p. 1481).

wide limits, and corresponds to different rhythms.   Thus, when the subject is in repose, the heart makes about 70 contractions a minute, which is its proper rhythm.

The "maximum rhythm" has been determined for several organs ; the fingers beat from 8 to 9 strokes a second, that is to say 480 to 540 per minute. This has been tested electrically, the fingers closing a circuit at each beat when tapping a metallic surface; [1] the jaw gives at most 360 contractions, the foot 210 flexions per minute [2] ; the great toe gives a little more than the foot, about 250 strokes [3] ; the fore-arm 230 to 240 flexions, the leg 120 (against the thigh).

Thus it is evident that the work of the fingers is the most rapid, which is confirmed by common experience. Also it can safely be said that there is a special rhythm for each muscle, or group of muscles. The speed of the movements of the joints is also of interest. The phalanges give at the very most 300 to 400 strokes to the minute, the wrist 690, the elbow 530, the shoulder 310. Thus the wrist and the elbow, in the act of writing, or in needle-work, are more rapid than the shoulder, or the fingers. [4]

These speed limits vary with age ; from 6 to 16 years they vary in the ratio of 2 to 3, with a retardation between 12 and 13 (as in the weight and strength of the body).

The example of the heart, which in health beats at the rate of 70 beats per minute, shows that there must be an indefatigable muscular rhythm, a " normal rhythm."

The following values relate to " unloaded " muscles :

Forearm	...	...	...	...	...	30 to 35.
Masticatory muscles		...	...	...	...	90 to 100.
Fingers	...	...	...	...	...	150
Heart	...	...	...	...	...	70

We shall see later (§ 120) that the " normal rhythm " is lowered when the muscles are loaded.

People of small stature are "relatively" stronger than tall ones, and quicker, because weight decreases as the cube of the size, whilst "force" only decreases as the square being proportional to the section of the muscle (see next para.). Borelli said : " Quo minora sunt animalia eo majores faciunt saltus." [5]   An interesting example [6] of the variation of the normal rhythm inversely to the stature is that of the muscles of mastication.

[1] Von Kries (Arch. f. Anat. u. Physiol., Suppl. B., 1886, p. 6)) ; Dresslar (Amer. Jl. of Physiol., vol. iv., p. 514, 1892) ; Bryan (ibid., v., p. 123).
[2] Von Kries (loc. cit.).
[3] Davis (Studies from the Yale Psychol. Lab., vol. vi., p. 11, 1898).
[4] Bryan (Amer. Journ. of Psych., iv., 514, 1892).
[5] Borelli, De Motu Animalium, 1710, Leyden, edn., p. 181.
[6] V. Ducceschi (Verworn's Zeitsch. f. Allg. Physiol., vol. ii., p. 482, 1903).

Ox	...	...	...	...	70 contractions per minute
Horse...	...	...	...	75	,, ,, ,,
Man ...	...	...	90 to 100		,, ,, ,,
Hunting dog...	...	...	102		,, ,, ,,
Cat ...	...	...	...	162	,, ,, ,,
Rabbit	...	...	...	240	,, ;, ,,
Guinea pig ...	...	...	300		,, ,, ,,
White mouse		...	...	350	;, ,, ,,

The same law is exemplified in the rate of the wing beats of various birds and insects which vary from the eagle—50 to 60 per minute—to the fly : nearly 20,000 (Marey). The speed is, as a rule, less in the female.

The causes which determine the rhythm are twofold : firstly, the nervous excitation accelerates or decelerates according to the resistance to be overcome ; secondly, the muscular fibre repairs itself in the intervals of repose. and the conditions of that reparation are not the same for all the muscles. According to M. Chauveau, the reparative work consists purely of re-establishing the elastic properties of the matter, of creating elastic force, or the force of contraction. The internal " physiological work," in the living cells, which never stops, achieves this definite result.

92. Similitude of Machines —One often uses, in the calculation of machines the idea of " similitude " (similis in Latin : similar) introduced into science by Newton [1], and of which Galileo had dreamed. It permits the study of a machine by a " reduced model." This is what is done, for instance, for the hulls of ships, for the planes of aeroplanes, etc. The reduced models of ships are generally to the scale of $\frac{1}{15}$. Suppose L to be the length of the arm of a statue, and l that of the same arm in the reduced model. The quotient $\frac{l}{L} = r$ is called the "relation of similitude."

Between the " surfaces " it is obvious the relation will be r^2, and between the volumes it will be r^3. Therefore :

$$\frac{s}{S} = r^2 ; \qquad \frac{v}{V} = r^3.$$

For example, the surface of the human body varies as the square of its height, but the volume varies as the " cube " ; so that the volume decreases less rapidly than the surface, when considering decreasing statures. (§ 91).

Considering two machines made of identical materials, there is the same relation for the " masses " or the " weights " as for

---

[1] Newton, *Philosophia Naturalis,* ii., Section 1, propos. 32.

the volumes. Therefore $\frac{m}{M} = r^3$. If the materials are not identical $\frac{m}{M} = \mu$.

The idea of similitude extends also to the movement of machines. Between the " durations " t and T necessary to describe two similar figures, there is the relation $\frac{t}{T} = \theta$. In the same way, the "speeds" u and U being, by definition, $u = \frac{l}{t}$, $U = \frac{L}{T}$,

$$\frac{u}{U} = \frac{l}{L} \times \frac{T}{t} \quad \text{or} \quad \frac{u}{U} = r \times \frac{1}{\theta} = \frac{r}{\theta}.$$

Finally, the " accelerations " γ and Ω, which express $\frac{u}{t}$ and $\frac{U}{T}$ will be to each other as :

$$\frac{U}{u} \times \frac{t}{T}, \quad \text{or} \quad \frac{\gamma}{\Omega} = \frac{r}{\theta} \times \frac{1}{\theta} = \frac{r}{\theta^2}.$$

Thus, if two similar parts of the machine, and its reduced model, take the accelerations, γ and Ω, by the action of the forces f and F, one would have $\frac{f}{F} = \frac{m\gamma}{M\Omega}$ by definition (§ 18) ; whence :

$$\frac{f}{F} = \mu \times \frac{r}{\theta^2} \quad \text{or} \quad \frac{f}{F} = \varphi = \mu \frac{r}{\theta^2}.$$

This last relation is called Newton's law of similitude. Its applications are very easy :

The speeds of the model, and of the machine are to each other as the durations $\frac{t}{T} = \theta$. θ is deduced from Newton's formula presuming identical materials. Then $\frac{f}{F} = r^3$ and $\mu = r^3$; whence

$$r^3 = \frac{r^4}{\theta^2}, \quad \text{or} \quad \theta = \sqrt{r,}$$

the ratio of the speeds is equal to the " square root of the ratio of the dimensions." Therefore :

$$\frac{u}{U} = \theta = \sqrt{r}.$$

For example, the speeds of the contraction of the muscles, or the "rhythm" (§ 91), of an adult of 1·69 metres high, and a child of 1·44 metres high will be in the relation :

$$\sqrt{\frac{144}{169}} = 0·923.$$

The speed therefore diminishes very little with the stature.

Now examine the " pressure " exerted by forces (such as the pressure of steam) : they are proportional to the surfaces which are subjected to them, that is to say, to r^2 ; therefore :

$$\frac{f}{s} = \frac{F}{S} = \frac{r^3}{r^2} = r.$$

Thus the pressures per unit of area are in the ratio of similitude r. Comparing the muscular forces, without regard to the sections of the muscles,

$$\frac{f}{F} = r^3 \quad \text{or} \quad \left(\frac{144}{169}\right)^3 = 0.618,$$

and as the weights of the subjects are such that $\frac{m}{M} = r^3$, it follows that

$$\frac{f}{F} = \frac{m}{M} = 0.618.$$

the muscular forces are therefore proportional to the weights of the individuals, or to the cube of the ratio of their heights.

As a matter of fact, the idea of similitude is here a little at fault. This is due very probably to the non-identity of organic materials from one age to another. Newton's law must therefore be applied with extreme caution, and, as the writer has always contended, experimental verification should invariably be applied. It was by experiment that Martine in 1720 found the relation $\frac{f}{F} = r^4$ between the muscular forces : the relation of forces being equal to the 4th power of the ratio of the heights [1] ; this is a relation which conforms better to the results of experiment than that which has been deduced from Newton's formula.

93. (*ii*) **Alimentation, the Combustible** —Any motor, to function and produce work, must be fed. It is fed by a stream of energy, and if it is to be always under pressure (as in the case of a steam engine) always ready for work, the stream of energy must be permanent.

In heat engines the energy expended is of a calorific nature ; it is developed by the combustion of a hydro-carbon (coal, oil, petrol, benzol, alcohol, etc). All combustion is necessarily a producer of exothermic heat ; on an average 1 gramme of oil burning in free air produces 7.50 great calories.

The combustible is only one of the factors of combustion ; the other factor is oxygen, a combustion supporting gas forming

---

[1] Martine *De Similibus Animalibus*, Propos, 24 and 25.

21% of the volume of the air. We must have, therefore, the simultaneous presence of the combustible and of the combustible supporting gas. The supply must be uninterrupted, and in sufficient quantity to maintain the motor in movement.

The action of oxygen, or oxidization is generally a rapid phenomenon, accompanied by flame, and producing a great quantity of heat in a short time, and causing an increase of temperature.

In the living motor, the combustible is the food, and the phenomenon of combustion is called nutrition. The name of *metabolisms* is reserved for the whole series of transformations which mark the evolution of food in the organism. There is no essential difference between the combustion of coal in a grate and that of food in the body. If oil could be burnt in our bodies, it would develop there just as much heat as under a boiler. If alcohol oxydised itself in our organs, it would liberate the same quantity of heat as in the cylinder of an internal combustion engine. This point, for a long time the subject of acute controversy, is now definitely proved.

Inter-organic combustion and all other combustions are of an identical nature; they are oxidizations.

At all times organic oxidization is slow; it is not accompanied by the emission of flame or an elevation of temperature. It takes place in all living beings—animal and vegetable—at almost any temperature, and in man at about 37° C. This extraordinary phenomenon of a slow reaction, taking place at a low temperature, is explained by the presence in the living tissues of oxydising agents. Their function is to serve as " primers," or perhaps to impart the small quantity of energy that a spark brings to an explosive powder. These oxidisers have been isolated, but their constitution remains obscure.

94. Although the exothermic character of the reactions of the whole of the organism may be indisputable, and the reality of the cellular combustion raise no more doubt, a fundamental characteristic distinguishes living beings from all mechanical heat engines. In the latter the nature of the fuel is indifferent, provided that it burns. In the former, on the contrary, the only acceptable food is that which the cells can assimilate and elaborate in a certain manner. The combustible is " reserved " by the organism, and thus it can undergo slow oxidization and become the source of all the energies of the being. If this reserve is not possible, the substance is rejected, and is useless as nourishment.

This important fact is demonstrated in the case of fasting, where the subject lives on his own substance, that is to say, develops heat and labour, without any help from outside aliments.

It is in this sense that the saying of Claude Bernard is true; " The muscle is a machine in perpetual renovation," ([1]) and the words of Chauveau : " It is not what one is actually eating that furnishes the energy employed in the physiological work of the organism, but the potential energy formed by what has been eaten previously."([2])   The fact that the bodily organism is, relatively, independent of the food which it is, at the moment, assimilating, has important results.   It ensures regularity of work, and makes possible an even tenor of existence, while irregularities in the supply of its fuel (food), which would cause irregular working or complete stoppage in the case of an inorganic heat engine, have no such effect on the human motor.

The previous elaboration of the aliment, without which there is no real nutrition or energy, and its utilisation afterwards, is what has been designated by the expression : "Labour or physiological energy" (Chauveau).   Physiological labour includes all the reactions of life, whatever may be the state of the muscles, in repose or in activity.   In man, this profound intimate labour, demands the conditions already defined for living matter in general (§ 65) : heat, oxygen, moisture, aliments.

The temperature of the body is assured by the exothermic phenomena of the organism, whose action it assists reciprocally.

The blood is the vehicle of the oxygen, with which it is charged at the lungs.

The body of man contains about 60% of water and loses 2 to 3 kilogrammes of water per day, in repose.   Lack of water may be a grave danger, and lead to respiratory, cardiac, and often nervous trouble.([3])

Besides the aliments the organism needs " mineral salts," especially Sodium Chloride.

The latter regulates the concentration of the organic liquids, provides the gastric juice, with its acid property, and aids the water to preserve the elastic state of the tissues.   The " alkaline salts " (phosphates, carbonates) consolidate the skeleton during its period of growth, and participate in the physico-chemical phenomena of life.   The insufficiency or absence of salts (mineral inanition) produces grave illnesses, which affect the nervous system.([4])   Finally, other mineral bodies such as iron manganese

---

([1]) Cl. Bernard, *Les Phénomènes de la Vie Communs aux Végétaux et aux Animaux*, vol. ii., pp. 506-509, 1879.

([2]) A. Chauveau, *La Vie et l'Energie chez l'Animal*, p. 50, 1894.

([3]) Pernice and Scagliosi (*Il Pisani*, part ii., 1895).

([4]) I. Forster (*Arch. f. Hygiene*, 1885, and *Zeitsch. f. Biol.*, vol. ix., pp. 297 and 381.)

and zinc (^{1}) seem to serve as cellular " excitants," and have a necessary part in the life of the micro-organisms.

Man requires from 25 to 30 grammes of sodium chloride per day, which he finds, as well as the other salts, in his food.

In noticing the essential functions of the different substances which have been mentioned (water, salts), it must be said that they are not true food combustibles.   However useful and indispensable they may be, their energetic value is nil. A real aliment or food is substance capable of constituting a cellular reserve, and which can eventually develop energy.

Amongst certain peoples there is found the peculiar custom of eating earthy materials of no alimentary value. This " geophagy " is found in Senegal, New Caledonia, Persia, Bolivia, South America and Java.   Even in Spain, (^{2}) eaters of alcaragas (baked earth) are to be found, and the women imagine that it gives them a perfectly white complexion!   It would seem probable that the origin of this peculiar habit is an attempt to provide a mechanical digestive stimulant, as in the case of birds.   Dr. Baudouin infers, from the condition of the teeth, that geophagy was a custom among the primitive races of man.(^{3})

95. Classification of Food Stuffs.—Our aliments are generally complex ; bread is made of " starch " and " gluten," perfectly definite substances to which are given the name of " immediate principles."   In the same way meat contains a principle analogous to gluten, derived from starch and fat.   Thus an aliment is formed of one or more immediate principles.

These are of " three kinds." Firstly, sugars and starches, which contain carbon associated with oxygen and hydrogen in the form of " water " ; and are called for that reason " carbohydrates."

Secondly, fats, which also contain carbon, hydrogen and oxygen.

Thirdly, all the quarternary principles which contain " azote " or nitrogen as well as the other elements named above.   They

---

(^{1}) In this way a mushroom, the *Aspergillus niger*, forms 1 gramme of vegetable in destroying 3 grammes of sugar, if it develops in a liquid containing a trace of zinc.   In the absence of this metal, it would take 28 grammes of sugar; the cell then growing less. G. Bertrand has shown in an analagous manner, the effect of manganese and iron, etc (*Comptes Rendus Acad. Sciences*, 5th Feb., 1912.)

(^{2}) Hellwald, *Ethnogr. Rosselsprünge*, Leipzig, 1891, p. 168.

(^{3}) *Comptes Rend. Acad. Sc.*, 29th Jan., 1912, p. 297.   The author admits that the men of the stone age (neolithic period) masticated food containing grains of sand.   The geophageous children of the Siamese Laos have to-day teeth worn like those of the children of the neolithic epoch. Geophagy was found by de Humboldt, Biot and Wallot respectively in Lapland, China and certain parts of Germany (*Comptes Rend. Acad. Sc.*, vol. iv., pp. 293, 301, 590, 1837).

are called proteids or azotes, and to indicate that they contain albumen, " albumenoids."

The combustion of an immediate principle developes heat, a definite number of calories per gramme of the substance. This number measures—as has already been said (§ 34)—" the heat of combustion." Its determination is made in practice by burning a certain weight of the substance with oxygen, in a special apparatus : " Berthelot's or Fery's calorimeter." The operation is violent and complete. But it is known that, in the human organism, reactions are gradual, and the aliment is not completely used up, for it leaves a residue capable of liberating more energy : the digestive transformations do not conduct the whole of the absorbed aliment to the cells. Also, each principle, each substance, or mixture of substances, possess " co-efficients of digestibility," or " co-efficients of proper nutritive utilisation " : by that, is meant the ratio of the quantity really utilised in cellular work, to the total quantity introduced through the mouth. Finally the "proteids" in their combustion furnish almost exclusively " urea," a substance not devoid of energy, that is to say, their combustion is incomplete.

Taking everything into account, it is found that the " calorific power " of food is inferior to the heat of combustion—the former being deduced from direct measurements on man and animals.

If we leave out of account the co-efficient of digestibility and consider only an organism burning its own reserves (the case of inanition), the calorific power would coincide with the heat of combustion of those same reserves, as there would be no waste.

96. Composition of Foods.—1. *Carbohydrates.*—These are : cellulose, starch, dextrine, sugars, glycocine, gums, and mucilages. They abound in the " feculents " and the " farinaceous foods " (potatoes, rice, etc.) They are eaten almost pure (honey, syrup) or absolutely pure (sugars). Their " co-efficients of digestibility " vary between ·9 and 1·. Experiment has given 4·1 calories per gramme of food ([1]) as their calorific power.

([1]) The determination of calorific power was initiated by Rubner in Germany (*Zeitsch. f. Biol.*, 1885, vol. xxi., pp. 250 and 377). Since 1896 the Department of Agriculture, Washington, has published, under the direction of Atwater and his collaboraters, a series of researches on the alimentation and labour of man. The title of these publications is *Proceedings of the American Agricultural Colleges and Experiment Stations.* They fill numerous numbered and dated bulletins. We shall often utilise them, quoting the number of the bulletin, the page, and the date. Since the death of Atwater (1908) Benedict directs this scientific enterprise. The institution also publishes numbered *Publications* distinct from the bulletins.

2. *Fats.*—These are oils, butter, and animal and vegetable fats. A fat is a composition representing the union of a fat acid with glycerine. Thus " stearin " is a combination of stearic acid and glycerine.

The co-efficient of digestibility of fats is from ·90 to ·97; the average calorific power being 9·1 calories. For equal weights, fats are the most exothermic substances.

3. *Proteids.*—These bodies, of the nature of albumen or white of egg, exist in milk (casein), cheese, also in meat, beans, peas, lentils, etc. These are quaternates, because of the inevitable presence of azote. The living matter—the protoplasma—is essentially nitrogenized.

Their co-efficient of digestibility varies from ·68 to ·98 according to the aliment considered its average value being ·91 : it is low in the vegetable aliments.

The average calorific power is practically the same as that of the carbo-hydrates 4·1 Calories.

Comparing the calorific powers, in inter-organic combustion, of 1 gramme of food, and the heats of combustion, according to Berthelot and André, the following average results are obtained.[1]

NATURE OF ALIMENT	CALORIFIC POWER	HEAT OF COMBUSTION
1 gramme carbo hydrates	4·10 calories	4·20 calories
1 — of fats	9·10 ,,	9·40 ,,
1 — of proteids	4·10 ,,	4·75 ,,

Rubner [2] obtained as calorific powers : 4·10 cal, 9·30 cal. and 4·10 cal. ; Atwater and Bryant, 4 cal. 8·90 cal, 4 cal.

Atwater and his collaboraters [3] determined the heat of inter-organic combustion of the habitual aliment as a mixture ; they estimated the heats of combustion per gramme at 4·10 cal. ; 9·40 cal., and 4·40 cal.; these values have been verified by Kintaro Oshima [4] who obtained identical results except for the carbo-hydrates, for which he gave a value of 4·20 cal. All these experiments show that, in the organism, the proteid matter, reduced by combustion to the state of urea, is not as exothermic as Berthelot assumed.

---

[1] A " bomb " calorimeter (see § 35) is used with oxygen under a pressure of 25 atmospheres (Berthelot and André, *Ann Chimie et Physique*, 1891, vol. xxii., p. 25).

[2] Rubner (*Zeitsch. f. Biol.*, vol. xxi., p. 377, 1885 ; xlii., p. 268, 1901).

[3] Atwater and Bryant (*Bull.*, No. 109, p. 86, 1899).

[4] Kintaro Oshima (*Bulletin*, No. 159, p. 223, 1905).

In spite of the diversity of the calorific co-efficients determined by numerous authors, the following values, in which special weight is given to Atwater's researches, are recognised :—

	CARBO HYDRATES	FATS	PROTEIDS
Heats of combustion	4·15′cal.	9·40 cal.	4·40 cal.
Calorific powers	4·10 cal.	9·10 cal.	4·10 cal.
Co-efficients of digestibility of the normal alimentation ([1])	0·98 cal.	0·95 cal.	0·91 cal.

97. The Origin of Vital Combustion.—Where is the combustion, the reaction of the combustible and the burning gas, produced? The food is absorbed by man, prepared and taken to the cells by the blood : this is " assimilation " and takes place chiefly in the motor organs : the muscles. Therefore it must be in the cells where the blood has deposited it, and where it constitutes a reserve, that the aliment undergoes combustion, because at the same time, the blood brings oxygen there. The vital combustion is therefore " inter-cellular," and although the motor muscles may be its active origin, it is general throughout the organism. Remembering that the expenditure of energy even takes place in a state of complete repose, as a consequence of life ; it is clear that alimentation is, in living beings, the source of their labour. The combustion and utilisation of the aliments, or the " disassimilation," takes place therefore in the cells. In what way does the oxygen carried by the " red corpuscles " of the blood, react on the alimentary molecules deposited in the cell ? This question has not received any answer, but one can imagine a "condensed " state of the combustible molecules which increases their " chemical force," or their " affinity " (§ 35). The matter in the red corpuscles, called " hæmoglobin," easily gives up its oxygen, and this "disassociation" results in the emission of "nascent " oxygen which is more active than the normal gas.

---

[1] Wait (*Bull.*, No. 89, p. 72, 1901 ; No. 117, p. 41, 1902 ; No. 136, p. 107, 1903).

CHAPTER III.

ALIMENTATION AND THE EXPENDITURE.

98. Alimentary Rations.—The name of alimentary ration is given to a determined weight of aliments. This ration can be pure or mixed according to whether it comprises one or several kinds of aliments. Its calorific power results from its immediate composition (§ 95) : thus a ration of a 100 grammes of bread and a 100 grammes of dried beans gives :

$$\begin{cases} \text{Carbo-hydrates} \dots107\!\cdot\!26 \text{ grms., or } 439\!\cdot\!77 \text{ Cal. } (= 107\!\cdot\!26 \times 4\!\cdot\!10) \\ \text{Fats} \dots\dots\dots\dots\dots 1\!\cdot\!60 \text{ grms. or } 14\!\cdot\!56 \text{ Cal. } (= 1\!\cdot\!60 \times 9\!\cdot\!10) \\ \text{Proteids} \dots\dots\dots 28\!\cdot\!23 \text{ grms. or } 115\!\cdot\!75 \text{ Cal. } (= 28\!\cdot\!23 \times 4\!\cdot\!10) \end{cases}$$

Calorific power of the ration   570·08 Calories

To facilitate the calculation of the energetic values of different rations, veritable encyclopedias have been published giving the immediate compositions of aliments. The following tables are drawn from the work of Balland [1] ; they especially concern French alimentation, as those of Kœnig [2] concern German products. It is superfluous to say that these tables are extremely practical.

TABLE OF COMMON ALIMENTS. [3]

In 100 grammes of:	Carbo-hydrates	Fats	Proteids	Calorific power
	grms.	grms.	grms.	calories
Fresh apricots	8·10	0·12	0·48	36·06
Dried almonds	18·00	54·20	18·10	641·23
Paris artichokes (bottoms).	13·07	0·21	3·68	70·00
Asparagus	4·72	0·41	3·38	36·94
Paris bananas	21·90	0·09	1·44	96·51
Isigny butter	—	83·58	2·52	770·91
Beef { Heart	2·20	4·84	15·25	115·59
Beef { Kidneys	2·54	1·82	16·30	93·81
Beef { Suet	—	90·94	·76	830·67
Cocoa from the Congo	30·25	42·40	11·35	556·40

[1] A. Balland, *Les Aliments*, 2 vols. Bailliére, Paris, 1907).

[2] J. Kœnig, *Chemie der Menschlichen Nahrungs und Genussmitteln*, Berlin, I., 1903 ; II., 1904 ; III., 1910–12 (2 Parts). Some tables by Kœnig are translated by Siedersky in the *Revue de la Soc. Scient. d'Hygiène Alimentaire*, vol. ii., p. 93–113, 1906.

[3] Except where specially noted, these are fresh foods bought in Paris.

Table of Common Aliments—*Continued*.

100 grammes of the Aliment	Carbo-hydrates	Fats	Proteids	Calorific power
Cocoa from New York (a)	37·70	28·90	21·60	506·12
Carrots	9·50	0·19	1·19	45·56
Carp	0·52	3·56	15·34	97·42
Cherries { sweet	14·12	0·09	1·02	62·89
Cherries { bitter	11·97	0·40	1·26	57·88
Mushrooms	3·68	0·32	4·50	36·45
Chestnuts (b)....................	33·16	0·89	2·47	154·18
Horseflesh......................	1·44	2·95	21·95	122·74
Chicory	4·02	0·10	1·04	21·65
Chocolate { ordinary	62·65	25·50	8·35	523·10
Chocolate { Meunier (c)	68·90	21·00	8·75	514·83
Cauliflower	4·89	0·38	3·51	37·90
Brussel sprouts	9·62	0·58	3·80	60·30
St. Julien Cream	1·60	26·52	2·58	258·47
Dates	67·10	0·06	1·96	283·69
Spinach	5·58	0·33	4·06	42·53
Dried beans	54·41	1·35	27·32	347·38
Dried figs	53·67	2·10	2·26	248·42
Calve's liver	1·83	7·13	19·12	150·78
Wild strawberries...........	8·85	0·99	1·36	50·87
Cheese { Brie	4·85	22·45	19·94	305·93
Cheese { Camenbert	5·95	21·65	18·72	298·16
Cheese { Gruyère	1·79	26·95	36·06	400·43
Cheese { Roquefort	3·00	38·30	25·16	464·00
Herrings { fresh	0·46	4·80	17·23	116·21
Herrings { smoked	0·71	14·97	51·62	350·74
Haricot beans { fresh ...	4·17	0·28	1·99	27·86
Haricot beans { dried	53·68	1·44	20·18	315·93
Oysters	7·33	1·43	8·70	78·74
Ham (Pâté of)	0·73	33·83	18·60	387·10
Cow's milk	4·83	4·12	3·23	70·54
Cos lettuce	1·74	0·15	0·92	12·27
Rabbit { leg	0·47	3·14	23·49	126·81
Rabbit { fillet	1·90	1·97	18·66	102·22

(a) According to Atwater and Woods (*Bulletin*, No. 28, p. 41, 1896).

(b) Limousin chestnuts, which are the most abundant; the chestnut is an important aliment in several departments (centre and midi); France produces about 4 million quintals.

(c) Chocolate contains cocoa, which gives it an alcaloid principle, a neuro-muscular excitant, cafein (see § 102); there is 0·16% of cafein in cocoa, and 1·40 gr. per 100 grammes of meunier chocolate, according to our personal investigation. American chocolate is very rich in fats; its composition is: carbon hydrates, 26·80; fats, 47·10; proteids, 12·50. It has a calorific power of 589·74 cal. (Atwater and Woods, *Bulletin*, No. 28, p. 41). But the calorific power does not show the quality of an aliment.

Table of Common Aliments - *Continued*.

100 grammes of the Aliment	Carbo-hydrates	Fats	Proteids	Calorific power
Dried lentils	56·07	1·45	23·04	337·55
Hare (leg)	2·55	3·35	29·88	163·36
Mackerel	0·28	15·04	15·67	202·26
Chestnuts	32·17	1·08	3·15	154·64
Melon	3·72	0·11	0·60	18·71
Whiting	1·25	0·46	16·15	75·53
Mutton (leg)	2·36	6·53	17·86	142·32
Turnip	5·57	0·06	0·47	25·31
Dried nuts	13·22	61·16	15·58	674·64
Walnuts	17·57	41·98	11·05	499·36
Macaroni	75·21	0·60	11·58	361·30
Hens' eggs	1·43	11·04	11·59	153·85
Goose (fat).....................	0·58	18·85	14·24	232·30
Sorrel	3·57	0·40	2·74	29·51
Bread { French roll	61·59	0·24	5·99	279·26
Household (*a*) ...	58·04	0·40	7·25	271·33
Army issue (*b*)	53·58	0·10	8·05	254·14
Vienna	57·29	0·11	7·03	264·71
Peaches	10·36	0·48	0·86	50·37
Pears	9·93	0·04	0·24	42·06
Peas { fresh	14·02	0·24	4·47	78·00
dried	57·76	1·40	20·56	335·85
Apples	14·41	0·06	1·44	65·53
Potatoes	17·58	0·04	1·71	79·45
Pork (leg)	1·58	3·10	20·30	117·92
Chicken (leg)	1·16	10·95	17·19	174·58
Prunes (pulped)	71·44	0·40	2·37	306·26
Ray or skate	0·17	0·45	22·08	95·32
Grapes { fresh..............	17·69	0·38	0·49	78·00
dried..............	76·70	0·56	0·45	313·41
White rice	75·22	0·30	8·89	347·58
Red mullet	2·29	0·98	22·85	112·00
Fresh sardines	0·57	2·33	22·12	114·23
Salmon	0·08	20·00	17·65	254·69
Sole	1·11	0·81	17·26	82·69
Red tomato	2·92	0·10	0·89	16·53
Caen tripe	4·73	16·79	19·06	250·33
Veal { breast	0·92	2·28	20·40	108·16
head	0·12	16·33	13·26	203·46
shoulder	1·22	4·08	22·27	133·43

(*a*) Five days old.
(*b*) A. Ballard (*Revue de l'Intendance*, 1907, p. 631).

99. Maintenance Rations.—By suitably increasing or decreasing the quantity of nourishment absorbed in twenty-four hours, the ration which assures " equilibrium of weight " (the body neither gaining nor losing in weight), can be found. " I hold," wrote Boussingault in 1844, " that an ' adult ' animal supplied with a ' maintenance ration ' yields, in the different products resulting from the vital action, a quantity of matter precisely equal and similar to that which he absorbs through the aliments." [1] Hence the weight is constant. The alimentation fills up the gaps made in the reserves by the inter-organic combustion.

If the alimentation is superabundant, there will be a formation of other and richer reserves and the person will gain in weight.

If, on the contrary, it is insufficient, the reserves will make up the deficit and the person will lose weight. The " expenditure " of the organism has a practically constant source ; its value not being modified by the alimentary flux, but, as we shall see, regulated by the energetic flux. In practice, the maintenance ration is easily determined. If the subject lives a regular life it does not take long to be able to decide it (see *Technics*, § 237).

Obviously the ration is not the same for everybody. It depends on the total bulk of the body (which varies according to age and sex), also on the external environment and the state of repose or of activity.

1. *The Mass of the Body.*—The necessary alimentary expenditure increases with the weight of the body.[2]   The wastage of the tissues, the inevitable consequence of life, has first to be made good. This is effected by the proteid elements. The emission of nitrogenous compounds takes place continuously through the urine (in the form of urea and uric acid), through the skin,[3] and by the processes of digestion. The minimum amount of proteids needed to repair this loss is 1 gramme per kilogramme of the weight of the body, *i.e.*, 65 or 70 grammes for an adult. Provided that the ration be sufficient,[4] this minimum need not be exceeded. It bears a constant relation to the weight of the body, independent of the activity of the subject [5] and of the external environment.

The question of the proteid minimum has formed the basis of a great deal of study for about thirty-five years. The re-

---

(1) Boussingault, *Economie Rurale*, vol. ii., p. 351, 1844.
(2) A child is in a state of growth ; its ration should therefore be superabundant (see § 81).
(3) Moleschott's *Untersuch*, vol. xii., p. 175, 1879).
(4) Atwater and Benedict (*Bulletin*, No. 136, pp. 121–6, 1903).
(5) Wait (*Bulletin*, No. 89, p. 70 ; No. 117, p. 40) ; Atwater and Benedict (*Bulletin*, No. 136, p. 175).

searches of Eijkmann ([1]) deserve attention, owing to the consistency of the results obtained. The average minimum, according to his experiments, is 1·20 grammes per kilogramme.

R. H. Chittenden,([2]) taking as his subjects students, gymnasts and soldiers, found that 0·75 grammes sufficed to maintain health, and vigour, and in addition caused an appreciable increase of muscular power. No loss could be found in the weight of his subjects after experiments lasting for several months.

When the alimentation is vegetable, ·7 grammes seems to be sufficient ([3]) ; it cannot be said, however, that animal alimentation necessitates a higher rate. In practice an unnecessary amount of proteids are consumed without any useful result. Taken as a whole, the quantity of food, per kilogramme of the weight of the body, needs to be more for tall than for short subjects,([4]) but each maintenance ration should contain about 1 gramme of proteids per kilogramme of the weight of the person.

2. *External Environment and Motor Activity.*—Man, as well as the homeothermic animals, must regulate his temperature at all times, so that it remains practically constant. The probable reason for this is that the speed of the interorganic reactions demands a constant temperature. This latter necessitates a diet of constant calorific value (§ 60).

If, however, the temperature of the "external environment" is reduced the flow of heat from the body will increase (§ 165). The supply of heat energy to the organism must therefore be correspondingly increased. Thus, as is well known, man needs a larger ration in winter than in summer.

Normally, and in repose, the organs of digestion, respiration, and circulation are in activity ; and perform internal work, a certain quantity of energy being dissipated into heat. The organism is, therefore, always working, and is maintained in thermal equilibrium by its total expenditure, relative to the external and internal environment, that is, by its "static expenditure." In order that the muscles may work and contract, there must be further expenditure to produce this external activity, namely, "dynamic expenditure." The alimentary ration is sufficient for both.

100. The Evaluation of the Ration.—This can be done in two ways for any given subject and conditions.

([1]) Eijkmann (*Virchow's Arch.*, vols. cxxxi. and cxxxiii., 1893).

([2]) R. Chittenden, *Physiol. Economy in Nutrition, with special reference to the minimum proteid requirement of man in health* : *an experimental study.* London, 1905.

([3]) L. Lapicque (*Arch. de Physiol.*, 1894, p. 596) ; H. Tissier (*Comptes Rendus Biologie*, 1910, p. 12).

([4]) Magnus Lévy (*Pflüger's Arch.*, vol. lv., 1893, p. 1).

(a) *The Method of Nutritive Equilibrium.*—Since, as stated in the preceding paragraph, the average composition of the ration is approximately constant, we have only to adjust the amount thereof until the weight of the body remains constant. The calorific power of such a ration expresses the energetic expenditure for twenty-four hours. But, as has been said, it is very important that the temperature of the external environment should be approximately constant. The subject must be in repose if it is desired to ascertain his " static expenditure "—or must always perform the same work, if it is desired to know his " dynamic expenditure."

Hence, with this method, exceptional care is required to obtain correct results. It is, however, useful if approximate results only are required.

(b) *The Oxygen Method.*—The preceding method determines the quantity and the quality of the combustible. By this method we measure the quantity of the combustion supporting gas, that is to say, the volume of oxygen used by the organism. This is very simple, for by passing the gases expired by the lungs through a " spirometer," the volume of air passing through the organism in a certain period of time can be obtained. The analysis of the gases expired gives their content of oxygen ; and as the outside air contains, normally, oxygen to the amount of 21% in volume, the difference shows the impoverishment of the air in its passage through the organism. The total volume of oxygen consumed is deduced from the reading of the spirometer.

An easy method [1] consists in breathing through the mouth

Fig. 130.
Chauveau's valve.

by means of Chauveau's valve (fig. 130) ; the air is inspired at I and expired at E, whence it goes into a little receptacle before making its exit through the meter. From this little receptacle one can take as small a sample as one likes, and analyse it after the experiment (see *Technics*, § 242, and fig. 131).

A male adult consumes, in repose, about 20 litres of oxygen measured at 0°C and at a normal pressure of 760 millimetres. The expenditure of oxygen is greatly increased by labour.

We have next to determine the ratio between the amount of energy actually expended and the corresponding volume of oxygen absorbed. The energy is, no doubt, proportional to the oxygen, and depends on the nature of the combustible : fats, carbo-hydrates, or proteids, and their proportions in the ration. Experiment has given for mixed alimentation a value of 4·90

[1] Jules Amar, *Journal de Physiologie*, March, 1911, p. 212).

Measurement of gaseous exchanges of a man carrying a load
(author's method).

Cal. for the energy developed by the consumption of a litre of
oxygen at 0° C. and 760 millimetres pressure.

101. The oxygen method needs very detailed examination.
Inter-organic combustion can be maintained, according to
circumstances, with one of the three kinds of aliments. Take a
molecule of "glucose"; its formula is $C_6H_{12}O_6$, and its molecular weight 180 grammes (§ 19). It burns, forming carbonic
acid gas and water and evolves heat. The equation of combustion is :

$$\underbrace{C_6H_{12}O_6}_{180\ gr.} + \underbrace{6O_2}_{192\ gr.} = 6CO_2 + 6H_2O + 677 \cdot 20\ Cal.$$

We deduce from this equation :

1. That 6 volumes of oxygen give 6 volumes of CO_2; as a
matter of fact, the carbon only has burned ; the ratio $\dfrac{CO_2}{O_2} = 1$
in volume. This ratio has been given the name of "respir-
atory quotient." If, therefore, the subject is fed on sugars,
his respiratory quotient would be equal to 1.

2. That a gramme of glucose evolves $\dfrac{677 \cdot 20}{180} = 3 \cdot 762$ Calories.

3. That a gramme of oxygen corresponding to 0·699 litres
(measured at 0°C and 760 mm) [1] evolves : $\dfrac{677 \cdot 20}{192}$ Cal. $= 3 \cdot 527$
Cal., i.e., 5·04 Cal. per litre of oxygen.

---

[1] A litre of oxygen at 0° and 760 millimetres, weighs about 1·42 gr.,
i.e., 0·699 litres per gramme.

4. Finally that, to burn, 1 gramme of glucose needs $\frac{192}{180}$ grammes of oxygen, which is :

$$\frac{192}{180 \times 1\cdot429} = 0\cdot746 \text{ litres of oxygen.}$$

Consider Glycogin, $C_6H_{10}O_5$, another carbo-hydrate, always present in the muscles, and of which the liver is a constant source (see § 107). Its equation of combustion is :

$$\underbrace{C_6H_{10}O_5}_{162\,gr.} + \underbrace{6\,O_2}_{192\,gr.} = 6\,CO_2 + 5\,H_2O + 684\cdot90 \text{ Cal.}$$

This gives 3·56 Cal. per gramme of oxygen or 5·08 Cal. per litre, and 4·22 Cal. per gramme of burnt glycogin. The respiratory quotient is again 1, as for all carbo-hydrates [1].

The equation of combustion for a fat, Oleïn, $C_{57}H_{104}O_6$. is :

$$\underbrace{C_{57}H_{104}O_6}_{884\,gr.} + \underbrace{80\,O_2}_{2,560\,gr.} = 57\,CO_2 + 52\,H_2O + 8,423 \text{ Cal.}$$

Hence the respiratory quotient is $\dfrac{57}{80} = 0\cdot712$, much less than unity; and the calorific energy is $\dfrac{8,423}{884} = 9\cdot52$ Cal. per gramme of material, or :

$$\frac{8,423}{2,560} \times 1\cdot429 = 4\cdot70 \text{ Calories}$$

per litre of oxygen, measured at 0°C and 760 millimetres.

The equation for the proteids, of which the chemical type is the albumin of Lieberkhün $C_{72}H_{112}N_{18}O_{22}S$ is

$$C_{72}H_{112}N_{18}O_{22}S + 77\,O_2 = 9\,CON_2H_4 + 63\,CO_2 + 37\,H_2O + SO_4H_2,$$

and 5·691 Cal. per gramme of albumin will be developed, from which must be deducted 0·845 Cal., dissipated in the urea formed, or an energetic production of 4·846 Cal. per gramme of the substance, and 4·53 Cal. per litre of oxygen consumed. The respiratory quotient will be :

$$\frac{CO_2}{O_2} = \frac{63}{77} = 0\cdot818.$$

All these theoretical values—the heat of combustion alone being experimental—give the following values :

---

[1] Glycogin is elaborated in the liver, which is traversed, before mingling with the circulation, by the liquid (chyle) extracted from the elements by the digestive process ; the chyliferic vessels go directly to the circulation, but the " portal vein " which has branches around the intestines, carries the salts, sugars, and soluble albumins to the storehouse of the liver, to await their final utilisation.)

	Carbo-hydrates	Fats	Proteids
Calorific power of a litre of oxygen at 0° and 760 milli-metres	5·05 Cal.	4·70 Cal.	4·53 Cal.
Respiratory quotient CO_2/O_2 ...	1·00	0·71	0·82

In reality, it is not known in which molecular state the albumen is oxydised or at what stage precisely the combustion stops. Numerous experiments show that hydro-carbonised alimentation raises the respiratory quotient almost to unity ; that fatty alimentation lowers it on an average to 0·73, and that the value is from 0·82 to 0·83 in a proteid alimentation.[1] This latter, for the same expenditure of energy, causes a higher consumption of oxygen,[2] because proteids are the least "thermogenetic."

Experiment has demonstrated the truth of this and has shown that the absorption of oxygen used in combustion is least in the carbo-hydrates, somewhat more in the fats, and most in the proteids. All this shows the value of the oxygen method.[3]

102. Limitations of the Energetic Value of Aliments : Nervine Aliments.—Whilst explaining that the alimentary substances turn into true combustibles, it has been stated that the organism is never indifferent to their character (§ 94) ; for it must be able to assimilate them, and draw reserves from them. Heat engines —whether they have an internal or external furnace—on the contrary, burn any combustible capable of developing heat. But there are substances whose action appears to act on living matter directly, that is, on the muscular or nervous fibre, and which are accompanied by effects depending very little on their calorific energy. They have been called "nervine aliments" ; and because certain of them reduce the energetic expenditure, they are also called "aliments of economy" or "dynamophores." They are notably the following : coffee, tea, maté, cocoa, kola, pimento, butyric acid, sodium chloride, ordinary alcohol, etc.

As a matter of fact, their action is singularly obscure : the majority of them, in strong doses, are toxic, as is shewn by the nervous troubles they cause.

Some of them play a part in the alimentary metabolism, perhaps as cellular excitants, analagous to the action of zinc salts on the "Aspergillus" (§ 94) ; and their toxic character is weakened in a number of people who absorb certain of these substances frequently.

---

[1] See particularly (§ 103) the experiments of Atwater on man (*Bulletin*, No. 136, p. 167, 1903).

[2] A. Chauveau (*Comptes Rendus Sciences*, 28th Jan., 1907, p. 173) ; Jules Amar (*Ibid.*, Feb. 19th, 1912, p. 528 ; *Journal de Physiol.*, 1912, p. 298).

[3] A. Chauveau (*Comptes Rendus Sciences*, vol. cxxxii., p. 194, 1901 ; Oct., 1904, p. 53).

The active principle of coffee, tea, kola or cocoa is " cafein," an alkaloid derived from an analagous body, " theobromin," both existing in the aliments above named. Other alkaloid products are also found in them such as: "kolatin," "kolanin," and " betain," closely related to cafein.

Tea in dried leaves represents about 3 Calories per gramme. Maté, the tea of Paraguay (also called the tea of the Jesuits or the missions) is the same ; and also the Catha Edulis of the Afghans.([1])

Coffee and cocoa give 4 Calories per gramme, and are as widely used as tea. Coffee has an almost universal character. Cocoa is very much in use in Paraguay and Bolivia ; tea in England, etc.([2])

The " kola nut " average weight 7 grammes, is widely spread in Africa, principally on the ivory coast ; its energetic value being 3·75 calories per gramme, in the dry state. It is taken infused, often mixed with cocoa, and the natives chew it, and draw from it a beneficial neuro-muscular excitation.([3])

Pimento (capsicum annuum) is a colonial product, biting to the taste, and containing an alkaloid, " capsicine " ; it develops about 2·75 Calories per gramme in the dry state. Great use is made of it in various countries of Africa and Asia.

" Butyric acid " is due to the slow oxydation of butter, to which it gives a rancid taste. Young, and later, Boussingault ([4]) noted the economic character which this substance possesses ; it tends to increase weight. Hence some peoples only eat butter in the rancid state.([5])

" Chloride of sodium " intervenes in the metabolism of the body to protect the proteids from waste,([6]) to stimulate the secretions, and to contribute to a better digestive utilisation.

Finally " common alcohol " or " ethyl alcohol " C_2H_6O, is found in all fermented liquors ; it develops 7·067 Calories per gramme ([7]) when burnt in a calorimeter.

A large dose is a dangerous poison. It is found in liquors which, by their sugary and proteid elements, are slightly nutritious.

([1]) J. Fr. Owen (*Journal of Soc. of Chem. Indust.*, vol. xxix., p. 1091, 30th Sept., 1910).

([2]) The consumption of tea in 1908, per head, was 2,850 grammes in England as against 32 grammes in France.

([3]) Auguste Chevalier and M. Perrot, *Les Kolatiers et les Noix de Kola*, Paris, 1911, see p. 253, *et sqq* ; *Bulletin, Soc. Géogr. Commerciale*, May, 1906, p. 304.

([4]) Boussingault, *Econ. Rurale*, ii., p. 473, 1844.

([5]) Jules Amar, *Le Rendement.*, *l. c.*, p. 76.

([6]) A. Pugliese (*Arch. d Farm. e Terap.*, vol. ii., 1895) ; *id.* and Coggi (*Riv. di Igiene e Sanita pubblica*, 1895, 6th year) ; Maurel (*Comptes Rendus Biol.*, 1897, p. 215) ; R. Tuteur (*Zeitschr. f. Biol.*, vol. liii., p. 361, 1909).

([7]) Atwater and Benedict (*Bulletin*, No. 63, p. 54, 1899).

TABLE OF NERVINE ALIMENTS.

PRODUCTS (100 gr.)	ACTIVE PRINCIPLE	PROTEIDS	FATS	CARBO-HYDRATES	CALORIFIC POWERS (¹)
					Cal.
Tea (dry)	Cafein ...... gr. 1·35	21·19	2·12	54·24	328·55
Coffee (roasted)	— 1·35	13·05	12·40	54·76	390·86
Maté (dry)	— 0·55	11·35	5·60	62·30	352·92
Cocoa (leaves)	Cocoaine 0·95				
Kola (dry)	Cafein ...... 3·11	11·64	1·41	73·16	375·86
Piments (dry)	Capsicine	12·77	8·45	35·58	275·13
					cal.
Strasbourg beer	Alcohol ...... gr. 4·80	0·409		5·487	24·174
Mans Cider	— 4·70	0·052	0·004	2·985	12·49
Normandy cider	— 4·40	0·046		3·582	14·87
Bordeaux wine {white	— 7·00				
Bordeaux wine {red	— 7·50				
Sauterne wine	— 15·00				
Champagne (sparkling)	— 11·60				
Madeira wine	— 20·40				
Chianti wine	— 8·35			0·180	
Old Pomard wine	— 11·90			0·400	

(¹) The calorific value of the active principle does not enter into the calculations.

In all the nervine aliments, two questions arise :

1. Are they consumed in the organism producing a measurable amount of heat ?

2. If not, what is their toxic dose, and what amount will perform the functions of·a digestive or neuro-muscular stimulant ? These questions will be answered later.

103. Alimentary Rations and Energetic Expenditure.—From analogy with other motors we deduce that the alimentation is the source of the energy of the living motor.   We are no longer at the stage when a German doctor, Reech, could venture to maintain the principle of " hereditary " animal heat.   This opinion elicited the following sally from Robert Mayer :   " I hope Reech will apply his principles and warm his room with a stove whose heat was gathered formerly in an ancestral blast furnace " (1843).

Moreover, experimental demonstrations have verified the principle of the conservation of energy in the animate matter.   These were begun by Hirn (1855) completed by Rubner (¹) and Chauveau (1899), and confirmed by Atwater's experiments.   The work of Atwater's school has been considerable ; its general results being contained in *Bulletins*, Nos. 136 (1903) ; 175 (1907), and 208 (1909).

The experimental method adopted by Atwater may briefly be described as follows (²) :—

The subject is placed in a calorimetric chamber of about 5 metres cube, this although a somewhat limited space causes no inconvenience for a single visit.(³)   The walls of the chamber are covered with a system of small tubes in which water at a known temperature of entry can be circulated.   The water tube system absorbs the heat radiated from the body of the subject.   The air in the chamber is renewed by a centrifugal fan, and arrangements are made so that periodical samples of the air can be taken both at its inlet and its outlet.   The heat evolved can be accurately evaluated by measuring the increase of temperature in the water, which can be read to an accuracy of one-hundredth of a degree.

Analysis of the gases and the volume of the circulating air gives the weight of oxygen consumed and of carbonic acid gas exhaled.   The proportion of water vapour in the air before and

---

(¹) Rubner (*Zeitsch. f. Biol.*, vol. xxx., 1894).
(²) Details of the apparatus are given in the 792 octavo pages of the above-mentioned *Bulletins*.   A clear and methodical summary has been given by Jules Lefeure in his remarkable *Traité de Bioénergétique* (p. 165, *sqq*), a work already quoted.
(³) A slight reservation must be made on this point, when the subject is doing any considerable work (see *Bulletin*, No. 136, pp. 81 and 109).

after its passage, and the quantity of water finally condensed in the room give the total weight of water evaporated by the lungs and exuded by the skin (perspiration). It is thus possible for the experimentalist to note and calculate the energetic expenditure of a subject in a determined time, either in repose (static value) or at work (supplementary or dynamic expenditure).

The accuracy of the apparatus, especially for static evaluations, is such that the combustion of alcohol therein gives the same heat of combustion as that found by the calorimeter.

In addition to the expenditure we have to determine the energetic value of the alimentary ration when properly metabolised. To effect this, the ration is analysed in samples, and its total heat of combustion determined ; that of the urine and rejected fæces is deducted. The equations of combustion are then utilised, the weight of the oxydised proteids being calculated according to the weight of " urea " contained in the urine, and the weight of the fats according to that of the carbon in the expired gases (CO_2), a deduction being made from the carbon of proteid origin. Atwater presumed that carbo-hydrates, in reserve in the cells, were not acted upon.[1] This postulate has been confirmed by experiment in the case of rations containing a sufficient quantity of carbo-hydrates.

Knowing the quantity and quality of all the substances utilised in the physiological labour of the subject, we can calculate the expenditure exactly. A comparison of the latter with the measured expenditure proves that the " principle of the conservation of energy " is fully applicable. The results of several hundreds of experiments, of a duration of 1 to 4 days each, on six to seven different subjects agreed very satisfactorily.

Thus the calorimetric chamber, being kept at 20°C, the results were :—

WEIGHT OF THE SUBJECT	STATIC EXPENDITURE		GROSS DYNAMIC EXPENDITURE	
	CALCULATED	MEASURED	CALCULATED	MEASURED
kilogrms.	Calories	Calories	Calories	Calories
65	2,119	2,133	3,559	3,544
70	2,279	2,283	3,892	3,861
70	2,305	2,337		
76	2,357	2,397	5,143	5,135
Error	+ 0·96%		− 0·43%	

(1) *Bulletin*, No. 136, p. 125.

The ration used was mixed, comprising bread, beef, milk, butter, and biscuits, and the drink consisted of weak coffee.

The static expenditure, that is to say, of the man in repose, only occupying himself, during 24 hours, by changing his clothes, making his bed, eating, reading and writing, represents on an average 32·56 Cal. per kilogramme of the weight of the body; so that, in an environment of 20°C, a male adult, weighing 65 kilogrammes, expends statically.

$$32·56 \times 65 = 2,120 \text{ Calories per day.}$$

But the gross expenditure of work (static + dynamic) varies with the weight of the subject and especially with the magnitude of his work. Muscular activity therefore, which will be considered later, is involved.

104. Analysis of Energetic Expenditure.—The following table gives an analysis of the results obtained by the American investigators with a subject of robust health, aged 22 years, and having a mean weight of ·76 kg. The temperature of the environment was 20° C. and a mixed diet was given.

HOURS	STATIC EXPENDITURE	WATER EXHALED AND PERSPIRED	CO_2 ELIMINATED	TOTAL OXYGEN CONSUMED = 689 gr.
	Cal.	gr.	gr.	Weight of urine : 1,421·80 gr.
DAY 7– 9	253·4	85·50	90·20	
9–11	232·9	74·50	73·60	
11–13	210·3	72·20	66·60	Volume of CO_2
13–15	231·3	75·80	85·90	$\dfrac{812·10}{1·9769}$ litres
15–17	224·8	74·70	70·90	
17–19	216·8	79·30	75·20	
NIGHT 19–21	219·8	71·50	67·60	Volume of O_2
21–23	213·0	74·20	69·50	$\dfrac{689}{1·429}$ litres
23– 1	145·2	70·80	59·50	
1– 3	154·9	69·10	50·20	Respiratory Quotient
3– 5	140·4	63·76	51·90	$\dfrac{CO_2}{O_2} = 0·853$
5– 7	154·2	69·70	51·00	
24 hours	2,397·0 Cal.	881·00 gr.	812·10 gr.	

It follows from this that the expenditure varies in the twenty-four hours, showing a minimum between 11 p.m. and 1 a.m., that being the time of deepest sleep. At that time, the expenditure is 145 Calories in two hours, which would make 1,740

Calories for a subject of 76 kilogrammes, and $\frac{1,740}{76} \times 65 = 1,488$ Calories for a normal adult of 65 kilogrammes in 24 hours. Thus, in complete repose, the muscles being in a state of relaxation, the expenditure per kilogramme of the weight of the body is $\frac{1,740}{76} = 22\cdot89$ Calories instead of $32\cdot56$ Calories, that is, about $\frac{7}{10}$.

The expenditure of the night (from 7 p.m. to 7 a.m.) is less than that of the day (from 7 a.m. to 7 p.m.), being 43 and 57 hundredths of the total expenditure respectively (fig. 132). In relation to the volume of oxygen the total energy corresponds to

$$\frac{2,397 \times 1\cdot429}{689} = 4\cdot97 \text{ Calories per litre } (0°C \text{ and } 760 \text{ millimetres}).$$

All the heat of interorganic combustion is dissipated externally and is found there as heat, since it has not been used in performing work. The expired air, entering the lungs at 20°C and leaving at 37°C contains this increased heat. As the " specific heat " of a substance is the quantity of heat that is required to raise one gramme of it 1°C, we can calculate that portion of the expenditure in calories; the specific heat of the air being $0\cdot2374$ calories. In the same way energy is dissipated through the urine and the fæces whose specific heats are taken as 1 calorie and $0\cdot9$ cal. The water vapor from the lungs and the skin dissipates a considerable fraction of the energy. This is calculated, by finding its heat of vaporisation, which is the quantity of heat needed for a gramme to pass into the state of vapour without changing temperature.

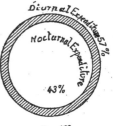

Fig. 132.

Regnault found for water the well-known relation $q = 606\cdot5 - 0\cdot695 \times t$, t being the temperature of vaporisation, and q the heat evolved expressed in small calories.

The expired gases carry away vapour which is formed at about 37°C, the temperature of the lungs; hence: $q = 606\cdot5 - 0\cdot695 \times 37 = 580\cdot8$ small calories.

This vaporised water enters the body at a temperature t' and rises to 37°C, hence the increase of temperature is $37° - t'$, $(37° - t')$ calories per gramme are absorbed (the specific heat of the water being unity). Hence:

$$\overline{q' = (606\cdot5 - 0\cdot695 \times 37)} + (37 - t') = 606\cdot5 - 37 (0\cdot695 - 1 + t').$$

or :

$$q' = 606\cdot5 + 37 \times 0\cdot305 - t'.$$

Thus, taking water at $t' = 20°$, $q' = 598$ small calories per gramme of water.

The total heat of vaporisation is thus measured.

Regnault gave a more complete formula, which would give, in this case, 595 calories, Atwater and Rosa adopted 592 small calories or 0·592 great calories[1], for the cooling of vapour from 37° to 20°.

The quantity of heat carried away in water vapour represents between 20 and 25% of the total expenditure. Thus in the above example :

$$881 \times 0·592 = 521·55 \text{ Cal.}$$

From the whole of their experiments, on men from 22 to 34 years old, the American professors concluded that the losses specified above amount to from 25% to 75% of the energy dissipated by radiation and convection from the surface of the body when the temperature of the surrounding atmosphere was 20°C.

An error is introduced if the temperature of the subject varies, if entering at 36·7°C, for instance, he came out of the calorimeter at 37·7° C. In this case rise of 1°C corresponds to an absorption by the body of 0·83 Cal. $\times$ 65 = 54 Calories, the specific heat of the human body [2] being 0·83 and the weight of the subject 65 kilogrammes. There will be a loss of 54 calories in the case of a similar fall of temperature. But, in repose, the temperature varies very little, and is usually the same at leaving as in entering the chamber. In any case, the temperature was noted every four minutes by means of an electrical thermometer placed in the "rectum." Temperatures could be read to $\frac{1}{100}$ of a degree [3] by the deflections of the galvanometer.

The daily variations of the rectal temperature of a man in repose and well fed, are shown on the chart (fig. 133).

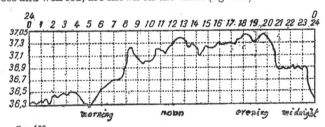

Fig. 133.
     Curve of the temperature of male subject during 24 hours.

[1] Atwater and Rosa (*Bulletin*, No. 63, p. 59, 1899).

[2] Pembrey : Schaefer's *Textbook of Physiol.*, i., p. 839, 1898. Rosenthal (*Archiv. f. Physiol.*, 1875).

[3] Benedict and Snell (*Pflüger's Archiv.*, vol. lxxxviii., p. 492 ; cx., 33, 1901-2).

The static expenditure is very much lower during the repose of the night, at the time when the temperature of the body is a minimum. It is only 1,488 Calories per twenty-four hours, and includes also the value of the radiation and convection from the body when the temperature of the surrounding atmosphere is 20° C. ; but this is very small for a man clothed in a fine cotton garment (Atwater) and covered by the sheets of the bed. It is not negligible, however. Let it be called x (see § 176). The expenditure $(1488 - x)$ is that of an adult absolutely at rest, the work performed by the body being strictly restricted to the internal operation of the organs of life (respiration, circulation, digestion). This is the minimum physiological expenditure. For example, an adult in repose, when the surrounding atmosphere is at 37° C. would expend $(1,488 - x)$ calories in 24 hours.

105. (ii).—The following table gives an analysis of the gross dynamic expenditure (static + dynamic) for the same subject as before. The work done in a period of eight hours being equivalent to 603·8 Cal. The work was done on the experimental bicycle. The principle of this instrument is that the back wheel drives a dynamo, the current generated being converted into heat in a suitable resistance (see also § 39). This amount of heat is added to the heat radiated by the human body in the calorimeter,[1] and the gross dynamic expenditure can be measured with the following results :—

	Hours	Gross dynamic expenditure	Water enhaled and perspired	CO₂ eliminated	Total oxygen consumed 1,558·80 grms.
		Cal.	grms.	grms.	Weight of urine
	7– 9	464·3	242·50	164·90	2,401·80 grms.
	9–11	785·1	529·90	276·50	
DAY	11–13	645·9	475·00	241·60	$\dfrac{CO_2}{O_2} = 0·815$
	13–15	536·0	288·80	154·90	
	15–17	813·1	579·40	283·00	
	17–19	645·4	488·60	215·10	Periods of work:
	19–21	292·6	125·00	98·70	8.15 to 10.15 a.m.
	21–23	282·0	138·40	91·10	= 145·50 Cal.
NIGHT	23– 1	193·9	113·30	63·30	10.30 to 12.30 a.m.
	1– 3	187·3	119·40	59·60	= 145·50 Cal
	3– 5	166·2	102·40	52·10	2 to 4 p.m.
	5– 7	164·4	94·90	58·90	= 154·90 Cal.
					4.15 to 6.15 p.m.
					= 157·90 Cal.
	24 hours	5,176·62 C	3,297·6 g.	1,759·7 g.	8 hours & 603·80 Cal.

[1] The wheel had a diameter of 0·405 m. (*Bulletin*, No. 208, p. 12, 1909), that is, a circumference of 1·27 m. ; at each stroke of the pedal the effort

This table shows clearly that the work has raised the expenditure, and that after its cessation the return to a state of repose is gradual (see § 126). The speed of the vital reactions does not resume its initial value immediately on the cessation of work.

Compared with a litre of oxygen, the total energy is—

$$\frac{5,176 \cdot 20 \times 1 \cdot 429}{1,558 \cdot 80} = 4 \cdot 75 \text{ Cal.}$$

This calorific power differs a little from that which was obtained in repose. The American professors obtained an average value of $4 \cdot 90$ cal. (§ 110).

The heat carried away by the vapourised water (from the lungs and skin) represents :

$3,297 \cdot 60 \times 0 \cdot 592$ Cal., $= 1,952 \cdot 18$ Cal. or $\dfrac{1,952 \cdot 18}{5,176 \cdot 20} = 37 \cdot 7\%$ of

the total expenditure. This proportion varies with the intensity of the labour, but not altogether regularly.

Deducting the static expenditure (2,397 Calories) from the 5,176·20 Cal. expended in performing work amounting to 603·80 Calories, the dynamic expenditure will be $5,176 \cdot 20 - 2,397 = 2,779 \cdot 20$ Cal.

The motive work is therefore only a small fraction :

$$\frac{603 \cdot 8}{2,779 \cdot 2} = 21 \cdot 7\%.$$

The temperature of the body during the work, varies sometimes 1°C ; but, whilst the stay in the calorimetric chamber raised the temperature of the man in repose by 0·03°C in twenty-four hours, it lowered it by 0·06°C during the working periods ; for the temperature tends to fall after work.[1]

Finally, it is seen that a ration producing 5,176·20 Calories is needed when the work is equal to 603·80 Calories or 260,000 kilogrammetres, the maximum which can be accomplished by workmen, with very rare exceptions.

106. Examples of Beneficial Combustibles used by Animated Motors.—The alimentary ration is generally mixed ; the reserves of the body, the source of its energy and its expenditure are, therefore, a mixture of fats, proteids and carbo-hydrates. None of these typical substances could serve alone as the exclusive source of energy. The living motor requires at least 65 grammes

reached 7·73 kg. A complete description of this bicycle has been given by Benedict and Cady in *Publication*, 167, of the Carnegie Institute, Washington, 1912 (not to be confused with the *Bulletin*).

[1] Atwater and Benedict (*Bulletin*, No. 136, p. 154, 1903).

of proteids. Even when fasting it obtains them from its own substance. Also the quantity of proteids utilised is never enough to cover the expenditure incurred when working. A demonstration of this was given by Fick and Vislicénus in their ascent of the Faulhorn ([1]) ; the urea of the urines collected, gave by calculation (§ 101) a value for the expenditure which was much lower than that of the work done. Therefore the organism does not accept a combustible exclusively proteid. Chauveau, and, later, Atwater (§ 99) confirmed this result; it is thus that in an expenditure of 9,314 calories, only 478 calories had a proteid origin ([2]) ; it rarely reaches 500 or 600 calories. Hence living motors consume ternary aliments abundantly—that is, fats and carbo-hydrates. Can we say that these behave in the same way as the proteids and are expended according to their calorific powers ? To take a numerical example, 1 gramme of reserve fat has a calorific equivalent of 9·4 Calories, while 1 gramme of carbo-hydrates is equivalent to 4·2 Calories. Can we, therefore, replace 1 gramme of the former by $\dfrac{9·4}{4·2} = 2·249$ grammes of the latter ?

To admit this is to accept the " isodynamic theory," by virtue of which the immediate principles can be substituted for each other, in proportion to their heats of combustion, 4·20, 9·40 and 4·75 respectively, according to Berthelot's determinations with a calorimeter. This would lead to the following proportions by weight: Carbo-hydrates 100, Fats 44·7, Proteids 88·4.

Experiment has not always confirmed this doctrine, for Atwater's method gave 4·40 cal. instead of 4·75 cal. for the heat of combustion of the proteids (§ 96). It also showed that, for the same amount of work done, under approximately identical conditions, the expenditure is less with carbo-hydrates than with fats ; or a sugar ration is more economical than a fat ration ; which presumes a lower value for fats than that assigned to them theoretically. In one case, it was even found that the calculation of the expenditure based on an isodynamic utilisation of 7,744 calories of fat, was 667 calories in excess of the measured expenditure.([3]) The isodynamic theory may be correct for a man in repose, nourished by a mixed ration abundant in carbo-hydrates, but is not justified if the man does a great amount of work or takes insufficient nourishment. In these conditions, Chauveau and Seegan considered that the reserves are transformed into glucose in the living cells, and are consumed in this state. Two quantities of aliments are thus energetically equivalent if

---

([1]) Fick and Vislicénus (*Arch. Sc. Nat.*, 1868, p. 273).
([2]) Atwater and Benedict (*Bulletin*, No. 136, **p.** 188, 1903).
([3]) Atwater and Benedict (*Bulletin*, No. 136, pp. 175 and 307, 1903).

they are transformed into equal weights of glucose, that is, if they are "isoglucosic." The doctrine of "isoglucosics" supplements that of "isodynamics."

The equations of transformation are not absolutely proved.

1. A fat, a Stearin, $C_{57}H_{110}O_6$, gives :

$$\underbrace{2\,C_{57}H_{110}O_6}_{\text{1,780 gr.}} + \underbrace{67\,O_2}_{} = \underbrace{16\,C_6H_{12}O_6}_{\text{2,880 gr.}} + 18\,CO_2 + 14\,H_2O,$$

or 1 gramme of glucose per 0·618 gr. of fat and the ratio

$$\frac{CO_2}{O_2} = \frac{18}{67} = 0\cdot27.$$

This shows that the fixation of oxygen in the course of this metamorphosis must lower the respiratory quotient. In fact, this lowering is observed both during violent exercise [1] and during sleep, an apparent period of glucose elaboration.

2. Take albumin.

$$\underbrace{2\,C_{72}H_{112}N_{18}SO_{22}}_{\text{3,224 gr.}} + \underbrace{54\,O_2}_{} + \underbrace{8\,H_2O}_{}.$$

$$= 18\,CON_2H_4 + \underbrace{14\,C_6H_{12}O_6}_{\text{2,520 gr.}} + 42\,CO_2 + 2\,S.$$
$$\quad\quad\underbrace{}_{\text{urea}}$$

That is, 1 gramme of glucose for 1·28 grms of proteids ; the ratio $\frac{CO_2}{O_2} = 0\cdot77$ shows a reduction of the respiratory quotient, which, normally, would be 0·82. This reduction takes place in the case of a ration rich in proteids, but insufficient for the work to be performed.

Finally, glycogen, starch, gives

$$\underbrace{C_6H_{10}O_5}_{\text{162 gr.}} + H_2O = \underbrace{C_6H_{12}O_6}_{\text{180 gr.}}$$

that is, 1 gramme of glucose is formed from 0·9 grms. of the glycogen, without variation of the respiratory quotient.

107. Isodynamics and Isoglucosics.—The equations of combustion and transformation permit the comparison of the energetic equivalents of aliments with regard to these two theories. By taking the gramme of glucose as unity, that is to say, 3·762 cal. (§ 101), we obtain the following results :—

---

[1] Atwater and Benedict (*l. c.*, p. 168 and 173). These authors appear to have adopted the theory of glucose transformations, (p. 173), but tentatively and with a much less clear idea of their reality than Chauveau (*Comptes Rendus Acad. Sciences*, 1897).

Substance	Isodynamic	Isoglucosic	Ratio
	gr.	gr.	gr
Glucose	1·00	1·00	1·00
Carbo hydrates (glycogen starch)	0·89	0·90	0·99
Proteids	0·792	1·28	0·62
Fats (average)	0·402	0·615	0·65

The proteids and the fats, therefore, are greater producers of energy according to the isodynamic than according to the isoglucosic theory, by ⅓ more on an average ; so that in substituting them for carbo-hydrates in a ration, they will be insufficient or sufficient according to the theory adopted. Chauveau found that, for a dog undergoing exercise, the isoglucosic estimation was the more correct, the other led to a diminution in weight of the animal. [1] On the other hand, numerous experiments of Atwater on man have shown, for instance, that there must be 2,874 Calories for the dynamic expenditure of work equivalent to 522 Calories, ff the ration is rich in carbo-hydrates; while 2,907 Calories are needed if the ration is fat, this estimation being isodynamic. This difference of 33 Calories signifies that, to cover its expenditure, the organism has transformed some fats into glucose with a waste of 33 Calories. The waste increases when the quantity of carbo-hydrates in the ration is reduced,[2] and especially as the body of the subject loses its glycogenic reserve. The intervention of this reserve can falsify the calculations in cases where the ration contains few carbo-hydrates.[3] Generally, the liver is a reservoir of glycogen which nourishes the muscles (Claude Bernard) and which feeds them at the moments when those muscles perform mechanical work. The proof is, that the respiratory quotient, about 0·85 in a mixed alimentation, is raised during work.

Carbo-hydrates appear, therefore, to have all the characteristics of a combustible beneficial to the muscular motor and to be the direct sources of its mechanical energy. It will be remembered (vide § 37) that the energy resulting from any chemical reaction consists of the " free " energy, which can be utilised to do work, and " bound " energy, which is dissipated in heat. Carbo-hydrates and glucose are examples of sources of free energy. The external work of the muscles, and the internal work of the organs (minimum expenditure of energy) utilise this form of combustible.

[1] A. Chauveau (Comptes Rendus Acad. Sciences, 1897).
[2] Atwater and Benedict (Bulletin, No. 136, pp. 184–5, 1903).
[3] Atwater and Benedict (Ibid., p. 189).

When the total mechanical work is moderate, that is, when the expenditure of free energy can be drawn solely from the carbo-hydrates of the ration and the reserve ; or when the external labour is zero, the subject only expending its minimum of energy (that needed for the internal organs) the isodynamic condition obtains ; the calculation of the rations being made exactly according to the co-efficients indicated above : 4·10 Cal., 4·10 Cal., and 9·10 Cal. But, in the case of excessive work, and of a ration and reserve poor in carbo-hydrates, isoglucosics intervenes to make up the deficit, by its glucose forming operations (glyco-genetics).

These two theories supplement and correct each other, and they show that, when studying a living motor, it is always necessary to give it food sufficient in carbo-hydrates. The " bound " energy taken indifferently from one of the three alimentary substances, maintains the body at a constant temperature. Thus it is clear that there is a carbo-hydrate minimum

Rubner [1] made some curious experiments on this point, by keeping an animal in a surrounding atmosphere of 37° C. after having freed it of its glycogenic reserves by a prolonged fast. He then observed that if the animal in repose expends 100 calories of carbo-hydrates for its maintenance (internal work) this physiological expenditure will be increased by 13 calories at the expense of the body with a diet of fats, and will be 131 calories if the ration is proteid.

Thus the minimum physiological expenditure is :—

For 100 calories of carbo-hydrates, 100 calories of " free " energy.

For 100 calories of fats, 13 calories of "bound" energy and 87 calories of "free" energy.

For 100 calories of proteids, 31 calories of "bound" energy and 69 calories of "free" energy.

The waste is therefore zero in the first case, or practically so (it would be absolutely zero in a glucose ration.) It follows that the expenditure of 100 calories of free energy, or carbo-hydrates corresponds to $\frac{100 \times 100}{87} = 115$ calories furnished in fats and $\frac{100 \times 100}{69} = 145$ calories in proteids. Rubner gave the name of "specific dynamic actions" to these wastes, equal respectively to 15% and 45%. Work uses the most economical form of energy.

---

[1] Max Rubner, *Die Gesetze des Energieverbrauchs bei der Ernährung,* p. 334 and Chaps. xvii. and xviii., Leipzig, 1902).

G. Weiss ([1]) came to the same conclusion : instead of man he took an animal which does not, normally, maintain its tempera-ture constant : namely, the frog. After feeding it with glucose, butter, or lean meat, he measured its consumption of oxygen. He obtained the following proportions :

100   107   153

which recall Rubner's specific dynamic actions

Atwater and Benedict ([2]) found that the consumption of oxygen by man when fasting (one lives, in this case, on one's reserves of fat) is 30·79 gr. to produce 100 Calories, and is 28·88 gr. with a ration containing 75% of carbo-hydrates. A ratio of 100 to 107. The experiment has not been attempted in the case of the pro-teids, because of the difficulties of ensuring the expenditure of pure proteids before the reserves of fat and carbo-hydrates are exhausted. *All* experimentalists have recognised that an excess of proteids causes an excessive absorption of oxygen, and Chau-veau summed up the facts when he said : " The digestion of food causes a superconsumption of oxygen, indicative of an increase of the energetic expenditure of the animal economy : an increase that is small with carbo-hydrates, larger with fats, but obviously the greatest in the case of albuminoids." ([3])

108. Variations in the Expenditure.—If the nature of the ali-mentation influences the magnitude of the expenditure, there are other causes of variation that are still more important :

1.—*The Amount of Mechanical Work.*—This is evident, and it will be analysed completely later.

2. *The Mass of the Body.*—This mass has as its dimension r^3, whilst the surface of the body has as dimension r^2 ; small statures have therefore relatively a greater surface ; and as the radiation increases with the surface, the heat will accordingly follow the same law. Hence, for small statures, it is necessary to regulate their temperature more actively and to have more intense com-bustion. This is called " The Law of Surfaces." It can be con-cluded that, per kilogramme of its weight, the child expends more than the adult. We give below a table giving the ex-penditure for various weights of the body. Some special subjects having an insufficient muscular bulk relatively to their surface (obesity), or an excess of that surface (very thin people), are in-cluded. They are all taken in a state of repose.

([1]) G. Weiss (*Journ. de Physiol.*, 1910, p. 408 ; *Rev. Gen. Sc.*, 1910, p. 19).
([2]) Atwater and Benedict (*Bulletin*, No. 136, p. 167, 1903).
([3]) A. Chauveau (*Compt. Rend. Acad. Sc.*, 28th Jan., 1907, p. 173).—*Cf.* Laulanié, *Eléments de Physiol.*, 1905, p. 561 ; J. Amar (*Journ. de Physiol.*, 1912, p. 307), Lafon (*C. R. Sc.*, March-April, 1913).

All the subjects are of the male sex and aged from 30 years to a few weeks. In old men between 69 and 84 years old the average expenditure is 28 Calories per kilogramme, or 910 Calories per square metre of body surface.[1] In the female sex the expenditure is generally 96% of that of man, for equal age and weight.[2]

WEIGHT OF BODY	EXPENDITURE		AUTHORITY	REMARKS
	Per Kilogram	Per sq. metre of surface		
kg.	C.	C.		
109·00	19·87	810·	MagnusLevy [3]	Subject fasting.
83·00	25·24	920·50	——	——
77·00	31·64	1,084·80		Subjects fed and in a
70·00	32·64	1,092·00	Atwater (4)	calorimetric chamber at 20°C.
65·00	32·88	1,072·80		
65·00	36·25	1,100·00	Rubner [5]	Subjects with free diet.
59·4	37·70	1,200	Amar	
52·8	39·80	1,220	Camerer	Der Stoffwechsel des Kindes, p. 108, 1894.
41·0	44·00	1,321	Rubner	(Beitrage z. Ern. im. Knabenalter, Berlin 1902.)
38·3	48·00	1,254	Sonden and Tiegerstedt	Skand. Arch. f. Physiol, p. 215, vol. 6; 1895).
34·0	47·40	1,250	Camerer	Loc. cit.
32·10	56·00	1,391	Sonden and Tiegerstedt	Loc. cit.
26·00	52·00	1,290	Rubner	Loc. cit.
23·20	63·00	1,499	Hellström	
18·00	76·70	1,680	Camerer	Loc. cit.
15·20	79·00	1,717	Uffelmann	Die Hygiene d. Kindes, p. 260.
12·20	81·00	1,568		
7·60	75·00	1,251	Heubner and Rubner	Average, (Zeitsch. f. Biol., vols. 36 and 38).
5·60	79·00	1,170	Camerer	Loc. cit.
4·40	100·00	1,370	——	——
3·20	81·00	1,000	——	——

[1] Sondèn (Skand. Archiv. f. Physiol., vol. xi. p. 60, 1910).
[2] Magnus-Levy and Falk (loc. cit.); Sondèn and Tiegerstedt (loc. cit.).
[3] Magnus Levy et Falk (Arch. f. Anat. un Phys., Suppl., p. 314, 1899).
[4] Bulletin, No. 136, p. 148, 1903.
[5] Rubner (Zeitsch. f. Biol., vol. xxi., p. 393, 1885); J. Amar, Le Rendement, etc.

3. *External· Environment.*—With equal surfaces, radiation increases with decrease in the temperature of the environment, and, consequently the expenditure is proportionately increased to compensate for this loss, this being a chemical law (Rubner). In an environment the surrounding temperature of which is higher than that of the body, bodies cannot reduce their expenditure, because they are, in this case, under the law of the *minimum physiological expenditure* ; they suffer, therefore, from the heat that they produce and defend themselves from it by active pulmonary and cutaneous vaporisation (see above, § 104). This is Rubner's [1] " physical law.'

There is a sensibility in every one that reveals the action of the " nervous centres."

EXPERIMENTS ON AN ADULT FOR 24 HOURS.

	Description of Experiment.	Energy (measured)	Oxygen consumed	Respiratory Quotient	Calories per litre of Oxygen
REPOSE	Fasting (reserves of fats)	Cal. 2,197	litres 473·60	0·727	Cal. [2] 4·638
	Ration with nearly 50% of carbo-hydrates ...	2,287	469·40	0·862	4·872
	Ration with 50% to 60% of carbo-hydrates ...	2,227	453·60	0·887	4·909 [3]
	Ration with 73% to 76% of carbo-hydrates ...	2,175	439·80	0·937	4·945
WORK	Ration rich in fats	3,570 5,128	737·50 1,058·90	0·833 0·809	4·840 4·842
	Ration rich in carbohydrates	3,699 5,142	757·10 1,025·90	0·865 0·906	4,885 5·012
	Insufficient ration (therefore fat reserves utilised)	9,134	2,032·40	0·770	4·582 [2]

109. Adaptation of the Respiratory Intensity to the Expenditure. The variations of the expenditure of the combustible cause equal variations of the gas, utilised in conbustion, namely, the oxygen : and the lungs are traversed by a current of air varying in rapidity the number of respirations being modified (see § 142). Coal placed in a grate needs a sufficient draught in the chimney ; but this draught, in industrial machines, cannot always be readily adapted for every kind of combustible. On the contrary, in man

[1] Rubner, *Die Gesetze.* (*loc. cit.*, Ch. viii.). *Kraft. und Stoff. im Haushalte der Natur*, p. 78. Leipzig, 1909 (very interesting little work).
[2] An average of 4·60 cal. is deduced from these figures.
[3] This is the value which corresponds to the normal ration in every day life (see § 105).

and animals, the admission of the gas utilised in combustion is perfectly regulatea and exactly adapted to the necessities of the expenditure, regardless of the quality of the food. The air circulates in a "respiratory chimney," whose shape provides numerous surfaces of contact between the oxygen and the blood. The work of the respiratory muscles increases with increased expenditure (dynamic state) and influences the value of that expenditure ; the regulation of the living machine is assured by the respiratory nervous centres ; without prejudice to the general control of the brain.

110. Recapitulation.—The combustible of the human motor must contain a proportion of 1 gramme of proteids per kilogramme of the weight of the body, and enough carbo-hydrates to suffice for the muscular work (external and internal) ; but, for the regulation of the temperature, the fight against cold, the nature of the combustible is indifferent. However, it will be noticed that fats, at equal weights, are the most exothermic, being 9·40 Cal. per gramme of reserve against 4·15 Cal. and 4·40 Cal. (§ 96). They are therefore economical, and experiment has, moreover, shown that the organism chooses them for its " thermogenesis " (§ 170). The above table shows the variations of the respiratory quotient, and the consumption of oxygen as functions of work and alimentation.[1] The expenditure is calculated from the volume of the gas consumed at 4·90 Cal. per litre measured at 0° C. and 760 millimetres barometric pressure, the alimentation being mixed. If the alimentation is pure the table in para. 101 can be used, and in the case of fasting an average value of 4·60 Cal. per litre of oxygen can be taken.

---

[1] Atwater and Benedict (*Bulletin*, No 136, p. 167, Table 97, 1903)

BOOK III.

HUMAN ENERGY.

CHAPTER I.

THE LAWS OF ENERGETIC EXPENDITURE.

111. Generalities.—From the point of view of utility, the energetic expenditure of man is that which corresponds to muscular activity only, but under certain circumstances, the muscles remain contracted without performing any work, in the mechanical sense of the word. The static effort thus expended causes a consumption of energy, and can be regarded as similiar to frictional work (§ 60) or vibratory work (§ 90). But the contraction develops some force ; dynamically it has variable degrees of speed and duration, its visible result being fatigue, which is itself susceptible to variation. If, however, only the kinds of activity which do not cause excessive fatigue are considered, then without forcing the muscles, it will be possible to estimate the amount of work according to the amount of energy expended. The one will increase with the other. In the variations of the expenditure will be seen the effect of the dynamic factors, force and speed, when the work done remains constant. It will also be seen how much the nature of the nutriment itself modifies the value of the expenditure.

On these lines the laws of the operation of the human machine were formulated by Chauveau, who devoted about 20 years to this study. His work is of great scientific value and practical importance. It is our starting point in the study of physical labour.

112. The Laws of the Muscular Function [1] : *Static Effort.*—Muscular contraction, whether periodical, as in work, or sustained and of a vibratory nature, as in a static effort, is prepared for by internal physiological work. Thus holding a dumbbell with the arm stretched and immobile, or lifting it and lowering it several times both necessitate an expenditure of energy.

As to static effort, Chauveau verified the expression given above (§ 84).

$$F = P \ (1 + r).$$

which shows that for the same effort F, and the same time the expenditure is :

---

[1] See G. Weiss, *Travail Musculaire et Chaleur Animale,* 1909, Paris, Masson.

1. Proportional to the weight lifted P ;
2.   ,,   to the degree of contraction r.

In the absence of mechanical work all the energy expended is dissipated into heat. Therefore, the only result of a static effort is the production of heat, which raises the temperature of the contracted muscles. Examples.[1] :

(a) A variable weight was lifted by contracting the biceps muscles uniformly. The temperature rise was as follows :—

Weight lifted	1 kg.	2 kg.	5 kg.
Temperature ⎰in 2′	0·17°C	0·32°C	0·98°C
rise ⎱in 4′	0·25°C	0·58°C	1·15°C

The relation of the temperature rise to weight and time is not doubtful, in spite of the difficulty of taking the measurements (a thermometer, capable of indicating to $\frac{1}{100}$ of a degree, was applied to the muscles).

(b) When a constant weight of 2 kilogrammes (P, fig. 134) was held with the forearm having angles of flexion varying from —40° to + 40°, for periods of two minutes. the following results were obtained :—

Angle	—40°	—20°	0°	+20°	+40°
	0·28°	0·50°	0·67°	0·78°	0·88°

We may also consider the effect of load and muscular contraction on the consumption of oxygen.[2]

(a) When sustaining a variable load by a constant muscular contraction the following results were obtained :—

Weight	1¾ kg.	3⅛ kg.	5kg.
Additional consumption of oxygen ...	119 cc.	204 cc.	319 cc.

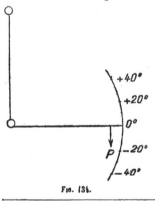

Fig. 134.

These are fairly exact proportions, the oxygen representing here the difference between the consumption during the static effort and the consumption before the experiment (in repose). The Calories may be estimated at 4·60 per litre, the subject having fasted. Then from the above table the expenditure may be calculated to be 0·547, 0·938 and 1·467 Calories respectively.

(b) For an effort of 5 kilogrammes and variable angles of flexion.

[1] A. Chauveau (*Journal de Physiol.*, 1899, p. 157 ; 1900, (313).
[2] A. Chauveau and Tissot (*Comptes Rendus Sciences*, vol. lxxiii., p. 1236 ; 1896, and *Arch. de Physiol.*, 1897, p. 78).

Angle (vide fig. 134) .... — 20°   0°   + 20°

Additional Oxygen   .... 212 cc.   344 cc.   360 cc.

The position of the muscles (the power) on the lever which receives the load and the number of muscles which take part in the same static effort, modify the expenditure, but, all things being equal, the latter is proportional to the static load and the duration of the action. This is generally written :

$$D_e = K \times P (1 + r),$$

D_e being the nett expenditure of the static effort (in excess of the expenditure in repose), and K, a co-efficient of proportion.[1]

113. Dynamic Contraction : Work. -If a load be displaced, the work of the muscles can either be motive or resistant. If D_d be the dynamic expenditure, it will be relative to the static effort D_e and to the work accomplished **T.** Chauveau gave the equation :—

$$D_d = D_e + \mathbf{T}.$$

the quantities being expressed in Calories, for instance.

He also found that the expenditure equivalent to **T** comprises the value (P × h), of the mechanical work (a weight lifted to a height or lowered from a height h) and the value of the friction R, which oppose the movement of the muscles. It also includes a fraction V, equivalent to the expenditure in starting the action. The equation will therefore be :

$$D_d = D_e + \mathbf{T} = D_e + Ph + R + V.$$

The term R, which is equal to the passive resistances, is assumed to be included both in the static contraction D_e and also in V. This term R therefore figures twice in the expenditure D_d, and remains to be known in D_e and in V. The exact values to be considered will be :

$$D_d = (D_e - R) + Ph + R + (V - R).$$

or :

$$D_d = D_e + Ph + V - R.$$

This is Chauveau's [2] formula, giving the analysis of expenditure for a work Ph.

All these values can be expressed in calories, or litres of oxygen, or in kilogrammetres.

114. A Proof of Chauveau's Formula.—Reduced thus to four terms, Chauveau's formula cannot be shown experimentally,

---

[1] The results of Bernstein and Poher, who obtained a more rapid increase of the expenditure in static effort (*Pflüger's Archiv.*, vol. xcv., p. 146, 1903) should be accepted with reserve.

[2] A. Chauveau (*Comptes Rendus Sciences*, 1902, vol. cxxxiv., p. 1266).

in the case of the muscles, because its terms cannot be separated, but for inanimate motors, Weiss and Chauveau have given the following example :

Take an electric motor. A weight of 10 kilogrammes was lifted in 1 second to a height of 2·50 centimetres. To effect this the expenditure, as shown by experiment, was 17·50 watts [1],

$$Ph = 10 \times 0·025 = 0·250 \text{ kgm.} = 2·45 \text{ watts.}$$

The expenditure needed to balance the weight was 8·50 watts, this being D_e.

At the speed of 2·50 cm., the motor running light consumed 11 watts $= V$, and $R = 4·50$ watts. Therefore :

$$D_d = 8·50 + 2·45 + 11 — 4·50 = 17·45 \text{ watts,}$$

which confirms the formula [2].

Consider, in the same way, a hydraulic motor. The starting up can be ignored.

To lift a weight of 10 kilogrammes 10 centimetres, at a speed of 0·001 m., the expenditure D_d was 63·01. By calculating the terms D_e, Ph and V separately, a total of 62·66 was found. This is a sufficient verification.[3]

This calculation, as well as the other, concerns the expenditure in positive or motor work only. Nothing accurate has been done on the subject of negative or resistant work. If we simply consider the work Ph as changing its sign we can write :

(2) $$D'_d = D_e — Ph + V — R.$$

That is to say, not only is there no expenditure on account of the work Ph, but there is even a regenerative effect.

It is said that resistant work returns energy. This restitution conforms to the law of equivalence (§ 34). The muscle, in resisting the production of work, destroys " *vis viva*," and dissipates it as heat, but that is not to say that, in resistant work one recuperates useful energy. The variation of energy or the muscular expenditure of muscle is expressed by :

$$U = Q — T, \quad \text{or} \quad D'_d = D_e — Ph + V — R.$$

Chauveau [4] and Hirn [5] were certain that calorific restitution took place. A man works a treadmill in a calorimeter. His expenditure, according to the oxygen consumed, reaches 257 Calories for a work of 68 Calories, and 193 Calories are registered on the calorimeter. Therefore, in this motor work,

---

[1] Remember that the watt (unit of power) equals about 0·102 kgm.
[2] A. Chauveau *Journal de Physiologie*, 1901.
[3] G. Weiss (*Comptes Rendus Biologie*, 1903, p. 426).
[4] A. Chauveau (*Comptes Rendus Sciences*, 1899, 2 sem., p. 249).
[5] A. Hirn *Recherches sur l'Equiv. M'éc. de la Chaleur.* Colmar, 1858.

$$D_d = 193 + 68 = 261 \text{ Calories,}$$

which agrees with the measured expenditure.

In descending the treadmill under the same conditions of speed, the man spends 125 Calories and the calorimeter registers 164 Calories. This is written

$$U = Q - T \quad \text{or} \quad 125 = 164 - 68 \ (= 96 \text{ Calories}).$$

It will be seen that some heat has certainly been restored, but in insufficient quantity. The experiment leaves something to be desired, although the principle of the conservation of energy is shown. Also the physiologist must admit some causes of of error in the experiment. The energetic expenditure is shown to be less in resistant work than in motor work, the muscles are less heated ([1]) and the respiration is less intense. Chronophotography shows a very slightly marked muscular relief (Richer).

The smaller expenditure in resistant work is explained by the fact that the muscles furnished an effort, which is less than the motor effort, and do so with a view to transforming the accelerated movement of the body due to gravity into a movement of uniform speed.

In a free fall, there would be no expenditure. The term V in Chauveau's formula decreases as the fall becomes more rapid.

115. Detailed Examination of Chauveau's Formula : Its Practical Results.—Chauveau studied the effects of speed and effort on energetic expenditure.([2]) A man weighing 50 kilogrammes worked a treadmill at a speed of 431 metres an hour. This constant speed was maintained, and the subject was progressively loaded by 10 kilogrammes at a time to modify the speed of ascension.

The following results per hour were obtained :—

WEIGHT OF SUBJECT.	EXPENDITURE OF OXYGEN.	EXPENDITURE PER KILOGRAMMETRE.	
kg.	cu. cm.	cu. cm.	Cal.
50	53,700	2·49 or	0·011454
60	63,550	2·45 ,,	0·011270
70	82,650	2·73 ,,	0·012558

The minimum expenditure here corresponds to a weight of 60 kilogrammes. When the load remained constant (50 kilogrammes) and only the speed varied:

([1]) A. Chauveau (*Comptes Rendus Sciences*, 1895, vol. cxxi., p. 26).
([2]) A. Chauveau (*Comptes Rendus Sciences*, 1901, 1st Sept., p. 194).

HOURLY SPEED.	EXPEND. OXÝGEN.	EXPENDITURE PER KILO-GRAMMETRE.	
metres	cu. cm.	cu. cm.	Cal.
302	44,900	2·97　or	0·013662
431	53,400	2·47　,,	0·011362
554	60,300	2·17　,,	0·009982

The economy, therefore, increases with the speed, and what takes place when the work is motive is also true in the case of exactly similiar resistant work. The expenditure of oxygen per kilogrammetre being :

	cu. cm.	cu. cm.	cu. cm.
With increasing weight	1·41	1·21	1·47
With increasing speed	1·68	1·32	1·12

By comparing motor and resistant work, it is found that the latter benefits more than the former, from the effects of the speed. Inversely if the movement is gradually reduced, a point can be found at which the expenditure is almost the same, whether ascending or descending a staircase, for example. Thus a man weighing 70 kilogrammes gave the following results ([1]) :—

HOURLY SPEED	EXPENDITURE PER KILOGRAMMETRE		RATIO
	MOTIVE WORK	RESISTANT WORK	
metres	cu. cm.	cu. cm.	
136·80	4·30	3·32	1·29
176·50	3·76	2·18	1·72
248·70	3·70	1·82	2·03

The expenditure for motor and resistant work respectively is about the same for a speed of about 100 metres an hour.

There is, therefore, no doubt that speed is an extremely important factor of economy. The labourer who works the fastest will expend the least. Increase of load has the opposite effect.

116. Analysis of Chauveau's Formula.—Reducing his formula to three terms :

$$D_d = D_c + Ph + V,$$

which is sufficient for a first approximation, Chauveau analysed it by experiment.([2]) By means of an ingenious contrivance, he

---

([1]) A. Chauveau (*Comptes Rendus Sciences*, vol. cxxii., 1896).
([2]) A. Chauveau (*Comptes Rendus Sciences*, 1904, vol. cxxxviii., June–July).

made the arm work so as to lift different weights, at variable heights and speeds, each lift being followed by a rest.

1. *Study of D_e.*—Increased weights can be sustained by contracting the flexor muscles 13 times a minute. No work is produced and it is found :—

	kg.	kg.	kg.	kg.
Weight sustained............	1·5	3	4·5	6
	cu. cm.	cu. cm.	cu. cm.	cu. cm.
Expenditure of oxygen	40	79	133	197

The effort of support is more onerous if the number of contractions or, what is identical, the number of excitations furnished by the nerves is increased. Thus :

Contractions	13	26	39	52
	cu. cm.	cu. cm.	cu. cm.	cu. cm.
Expend. of oxygen ⎱ 1·5	36	44	63	76
for ⎰ 4·5	98	125	163	187

This result is very interesting, as it shows that the frequent starts and stops increase the expenditure. One cannot, therefore, ignore the fact that the action of the nerve on the muscle necessitates a certain consumption of energy and the greater the effort to be produced, the greater will be that consumption. The expenditure of energy in setting in motion heavy weights is thus shown in another aspect.

2. *Study of Ph + V.*—This is the work itself, work estimated in quantity (Ph) and in quality (V). Chauveau varied Ph, leaving h constant, at 4·42 m. and also the speed, whilst P was varied from 1·5 to 6 kilogrammes.

By 13 contractions in 1 minute, the weight was lifted to 4·42 metres, *i.e.*, 0·34 metres per contraction of the flexor muscles. Under these conditions, the expenditure D_d was measured and knowing D_e, Ph + V can be found.

WEIGHT DISPLACED.	D_d	D_e [1]	Ph + V		
kg.	cu. cm.	cu. cm.	cu. cm.		
1·500	99	40	59	or	1·00
3·000	158	79	79	,,	1·34
4·500	241	133	108	,,	1·83
6·000	324	197	127	,,	2·15

The variations of Ph + V are less rapid than those of the weight lifted, while D_d varies more or less in proportion to the weight. Hence the static effort D_e is most felt in the expenditure.

Take next a constant weight, say 1·5, kg. and by increasing the number of contractions, carry it to 4·48 metres, 8·84 metres, 13·26 metres and 17·68 metres in the same time. The speed will therefore increase as 1, 2, 3, 4, also the work. The following results were obtained:

CONTRACTIONS	D_d	$D_e(^1)$	$Ph + V$.		
	cu. cm.	cu. cm.	cu. cm.		
13	91	36	55	or	1·00
26	151	44	107	,,	1·94
39	199	63	136	,,	2·47
52	243	76	167	,,	3·03

As might have been foreseen, there is increased expenditure, but there is an economy in the total expenditure, as the same amount of work is produced with a small load and a great speed, instead of as before when there was a heavy load and a small speed. This result is of geat practical utility, as it shows that a heavy load should be divided and this division compensated for by a suitable increase of speed.

Example.—A weight of 6 kilogrammes has to be transported to a sixth floor, situated at a height of 17·60 metres.

If carried up in a single journey the expenditure would be ... cu. cm. cu. cm. $324 \times 4 = 1,296$

If carried in fractions of 1·5 kg., the expenditure would be ... $243 \times 4 = 972$

In the second case there is an economy of ... ... —— 324 cu. cms. ——

representing $\dfrac{324}{1296} =$ about 25% of the total expenditure. At the same time the waste entailed by the return journeys empty handed must not be disregarded.

117. From the above tables, giving the value of D_d for increasing weights and speeds, the expenditure per kilogrammetre can be found :—

	cu. cm.	cu. cm.	cu. cm.	cu. cm.
For increasing weight ...	14·90	11·90	12·10	12·20
,, ,, speed ...	13·70	11·30	10·00	9·10

The economy increases with the speed and reaches a maximum value for a weight of 3 kilogrammes, which corresponds to an

---

(^{1}) D_e is taken from the preceding tables, p. 179).

expenditure of 11·90 cu. cms. With greater weights, carried to a height of 6 metres in 75 seconds, Laulanié, a pupil of Chauveau, obtained the following results[1] :—

Weight ... ...　20　40　60　80　100 kg̈s.

Expenditure per kilo-{ 3·32　2·38　2·29　2·08　2·13 cu. cms.
grammetre ... ...}

The minimum of expenditure is, in this kind of labour, with a load of 80 kilogrammes, at a speed of 0·08 metres. From all these experiments it is clear that there are certain weights and speeds which give maximum economy. It is most noticeable in the speed, not so much by the number of contractions and the rapid succession of movements, as by the extended displacements. In walking, for instance, small quick steps are less economical than big strides. As has been already pointed out, frequent starts and stops multiply the demand on the nervous system, and should be avoided where possible. Chauveau demonstrated this· experimentally. He caused the flexions of the arm to succeed each other in growing number, in the same proportion as the displacement of the weight decreased at each contraction, so that in the end the weight was carried at the same height all the time. The effect of the multiplicity of the contractions is shown in the expenditure : ([2])

Expenditure per kilogrammetre:

	cu. cms.	cu; cms.	cu. cms.	cu. cms.
Weight of 3 kilogrammes ...	8·10	8·80	10·10	10·70
,, 6 ,, ...	9·50	9·50	12·20	13·30

The expenditure, therefore, under these conditions, clearly increases. The combination of weight and speed which leads to the minimum expenditure is also found in the work of hydraulic motors, for instance.([3])

118. Resistant Work.—Chauveau undertook some experiments on resistant([4]) work corresponding to those on motive work. The weight, instead of being lifted, descends. The variations of D'_d and of $V - Ph$ were as follows:—

([1]) Laulanié, *Traité de Physiologie*, 1905, p. 792.
([2]) A. Chauveau (*Compt. Rend. Acad. Sc.*, 1904, vol. cxxxviii., p. 69 ; cxxxix., p. 13).
([3]) G. Weiss (*Comptes Rendus Biologie*, 1903, p. 426) ; A. Chauveau, *Rapport Scientifique. sur Trav. Entrepris en 1905 au moyen des subventions de la caisse des recherches scientifiques*, Melun, 1906.
([4]) A. Chauveau (*Compt. Rend. Acad. Sciences*, 1904, vol. cxxxviii., p. 108).

WEIGHTS DISPLACED	D'_d	D_e	$V - Ph$
kg.	cu. cms.	cu. cms.	cu. cms.
1·500	66	40	26 or 1
3·000	131	79	52 ,, 2
4·500	206	133	73 ,, 2·80
6·000	277	197	80 ,, 3·07

The increase of work with variation of speed was:

CONTRACTIONS	D'_d	D_e	$V - Ph$
	cu. cms.	cu. cms.	cu. cms.
13	68	36	32 or 1
26	114	44	70 ,, 2·18
39	161	62	98 ,, 3·09
52	201	70	125 ,, 3·90

These results confirm those obtained for motive work. Speed appears again as a dominating factor in the economy of energy.

From the above we can deduce the expenditure per kilogrammetre. This is :

	cu. cms.	cu. cms.	cu. cms.	cu. cms.
With increasing load ...	9·90	9·80	10·30	10·40
,, ,, speed ...	10·20	8·50	8·09	7·50

There is a minimum expenditure with a weight of 3 kilogrammes.

Calculating the economy in the transport of a load to a given depth, we find, for a load of 6 kilogrammes and a depth of 17·60 metres :—

	cu. cms.	cu. cms.
If the transport is effected in a single journey	$277 \times 4 =$	1,108
,, ,, ,, by fractions of 1·500 kg.		804
The difference		304

represents : $\dfrac{308}{1,108} = 27\%$ approximately of the total expenditure.

Comparing motor and resistant work it will be seen that the expenditure in the former case benefits less by the speed than in the latter. This has already been pointed out, but is here clearly exemplified.

119. Voluntary Work.—The accurate and ingenious experiments of Chauveau have shown the extreme importance of the speed at which work is done ; they have also shown that the expenditure, however great it may be, has a minimum value for certain conditions of load or effort. According to Trèves' experiments in Italy, on the flexors of the forearm, the determining cause of the effort, is found in the resistance to be overcome or the load to be displaced. It is the sense of resistance which regulates the functioning of the muscles,[1] that is to say, the motor nervous excitation. We have seen that the nervous excitation necessitates an expenditure of energy of not less than 2·5% of the expenditure of static effort (§ 116). Nervous excitation is costly, and must not be abused. Voluntary work, which reduces the effort to a minimum, regulates and conserves also the nervous intervention.

One characteristic of voluntary work is that it is always accomplished with minimum expenditure. The load to be displaced, or the corresponding effort, the speed, and the time must have certain very definite values to obtain an economical maximum. Muscular action is periodic (§ 90) on account of fatigue. Hence the absolute maximum can only relate to a definite period of time, or a succession of periods separated by intervals of repose.

These results, so valuable to industry, were obtained by means of the " ergograph " (from εργον, work), of which the first type was invented by Mosso (see *Technics*, § 222). The principle of the ergograph consists in opposing a resistance (a weight P) to the muscles, and recording the contractions graphically.

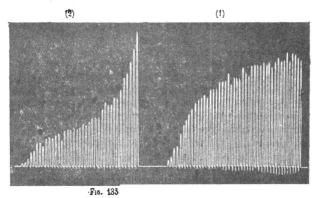

(2)   (1)

·Fig. 133

Types of Ergograms.

If h is the vertical height of the trace of a muscular contraction and P the weight, the work done in one contraction $= Ph$. If,

[1] Trèves (*Arch. ital. de Biologie*, vol. xxx., pp. 1 & 11 ; 1898).

before fatigue sets in, n contractions have taken place, the total work during that period is nPh. Fig. 135 shows two of these traces or *ergograms*. The traces of the contractions show a decreasing amplitude and varying rhythm. The voluntary muscular contraction lasts at least 6 to 7 hundredths of a second, *i.e.*, 1,000 contractions per minute approximately, but this rhythm is impossible in practice, as has already been shown (§ 91).

The rhythm of the contractions brings about an interval of repose necessary for the reparation of the muscles (see *Fatigue*, (§ 146). This is a fundamental fact, which explains why, in the living machine, the movements are reciprocating, although in the case of inanimate motion, rotary movements are the most economical and regular. In rotation, it is not possible to realise the indispensable organic reparation, nor to rid the cellular organs of their waste.

120. Ergograms have led to the following conclusions :—Each muscular group produces its maximum work for a definite value of the load. If the latter is modified, the rhythm of the contractions must likewise be modified. Thus the rhythm being 6 per minute, and the weight to be displaced being 3 kilogrammes, the flexor muscles of the middle finger could work almost indefinitely.

Double the weight and it will be necessary to double the interval of repose. If the rest periods are increased fourfold the preceding maximum of work done will be exceeded, but it must be remembered that the duration of the repose, necessary for the reparation of the muscle, increases more quickly than the weight lifted.

Instead of continuing the record until complete fatigue sets in (the amplitude being then almost zero) the work is often interrupted by a halt of a few minutes before fatigue sets in. For instance ([1]), under a weight of 3 kilogrammes and with a rhythm of 30 per minute, make 15 successive contractions and then rest for half an hour. Then a day's work will give :—28·164 kgm. (right middle finger) and 26·855 kgm. (left middle finger). But fatigue would have appeared sooner if, pushing the ergogram to its end, it had been followed by a rest even of two hours. The daily work would only have been :—

13·674 kgm (right middle finger) ; 14·742 kgm. (left middle finger).

From the above will be seen that frequent short intervals of repose are better than one long rest.

---

[1] A. Maggiora (*Arch. Ital. Biol.*, vol. xiii., p. 210 : 1890),

By modifying the weight, the complete ergogram, at a rhythm of 30, is:

Load	1	2	4	8 kg.
Work done	2·34	2·66	1·90	1·04 kgm.

A weight of 2 kilogrammes allows a maximum daily work at a rhythm of 30 and with a halt of one minute instead of half an hour. Finally the rhythm is of great importance as for the same load of 6 kilogrammes the daily work is 43 kilogrammetres or only 1 kilogrammetre according to whether the rhythm is 6 or 15. At the rate of 6, work can go on almost indefinitely if the load does not exceed 6 kilogrammes.

The maximum work is, therefore, the resultant of an effort and a rhythm suitable for practically continuous action. According to Trèves, this condition entails the minimum nervous expenditure, the latter being regulated by the effort of the muscles, but the resistance to be overcome must not necessitate too great an effort.[1] Also it is known that the resistance irritates the muscular fibres as they are seen to lengthen and shorten.[2] It is then that the nerves regulate the effort. The limit of load, compatible with maximum work, is smaller if the muscles have already been in action ; whence the tendency in work of any duration, to an effort of progressively decreasing value. Fick [3] recognised this, and Blix [4] showed later that a heavy load distends the muscular fibre and renders it unable to produce its utmost.

It is therefore of great practical importance always to work below the limit of the effort which would have produced the maximum amount of work.

This sub-maximum ensures a certain economy of force, and does not waste nervous energy by the too-frequently renewed intervention of neuro-muscular excitations (see also § 117 and 119). But if, instead of lightening the load, it is necessary to increase it after a short period of work, it is sufficient to reduce the rhythm of the contractions. The rôle of the will consists, precisely, in assuring the maximum work under the law of the least fatigue.

121. The Mechanical Maximum and the Economical Maximum. —It is natural to deduce from the preceding experiments that the

---

[1] Trèves (*Arch. Ital. de Biologie*, vol. xxxvi., 1901, p. 47 ; *Arch. di Fisiol.*, 1904).
[2] Von Anrep (*Pflüger's Arch.*, 1880, vol. xxi., p. 226) ; Blix, *Skand Arch.'f. Physiol.*, 1893, vol. iv., p. 399) ; Benedicenti (*Arch. Ital. de Biol.*, vol. xxv., p. 379 ; 1896).
[3] A. Fick (*Pflüger's Arch.*, 1891, vol. l., p. 189).
[4] Blix (*Skand. Arch. f. Physiol.*, 1895, vol. vi., p. 240).

maximum daily work is that which takes place in the most economical manner.

Laulanié, however, found that this was not the case.[1] Certain experiments with a man on the author's friction dynamometer (see *Technics*, § 221) gave the following consumptions of oxygen :—

WEIGHT	SPEED	WORK DONE IN 5 MINUTES	EXPENDITURE PER KILOGRAMMETRE.
1 kg.	1·49	448 kgm.	3·56 cu. cms.
2 ,,	1·07	642 ,,	2·44 ,,
3 ,,	0·80	726 ,,	2·18 ,,
4 ,,	0·61	778 ,,	2·16 ,,
5 ,,	0·54	812 ,,	2·21 ,,
6 ,,	0·44	853 ,,	2·26 ,,
8 ,,	0·37	896 ,,	2·44 ,,
10 ,,	0·29	905 ,,	2·86 ,,
12 ,,	0·24	906 ,,	3·12 ,,
15 ,,	0·13	570 ,,	5·31 ,,

The mechanical maximum of 905 kilogrammetres does not coincide with the economical maximum of 2·16 cu. cms. per kilogrammetre. It will be seen in the same way that the minimum expenditure in walking, without carrying a load, is at a speed of about 4·500 km. per hour.[2] Our muscles, as a result of long habit and acquired or hereditary experience, function so as to economise the store of energy, and adapt their effort and their speed with an inimitable precision and certainty to this end, by the regulating action of the nervous system.

122. The Maximum Work of Man. (1) *From the Mechanical Point of View.*—From the industrial point of view, the mechanical work estimated in kilogrammetres must be considered in most trades. As Montgolfier said, " It is live force that pays." This work is evaluated by determining the power of the subject, the product of his effort, and his speed in unit time, a second, and by multiplying this power (F × v) by the effective duration of the labour in seconds, whence :

$$T = F \times v \times t.$$

Particular values of these three factors can be found, so that the product F × v × t is a maximum. T will then represent man's greatest daily output.

[1] Laulanié (*Traité de Physiologie*, 2nd edn., Paris, 1905, p. 803).
[2] Jules Amar (*Journal de Physiologie*, 1911, p. 217). See A. Imbert, *Mode de Fonctionnement Economique de l'Organisme*, 1902 (*Coll. Scienta*).

Geometricians and natural philosophers (Daniel Bernoulli, Euler, Coulomb, etc.), found the maximum of $F \times v \times t$, theoretically.([1]) The greatest of all, Coulomb, knew how to ally theory to experiment. The principle of his method was as follows : a good labourer, without carrying a weight, could mount to a height H (on mountains) in a working day, the work done being PH. With a load, Q, he could only mount to H', or a work done of $(P + Q)$ H'. This is a diminution PH — $(P + Q)$ H', caused by the presence of the load Q. By means of the calculus, Coulomb found the value of the load Q, which gave the minimum diminution, that is to say, the maximum daily output.

The following is an example of this method, according to Coulomb : a man weighing 65 kilogrammes was able to ascend to the summit of the Peak of Teneriffe (2,923 metres) doing 189,915 kilogrammetres of work in the day. With a load of 68 kilogrammes he was only able to do 105,336 kilogrammetres of work, a decrease of 84,579 kilogrammetres, or $\dfrac{84,579}{68}$ per kilogramme, or, $\dfrac{84,579}{68} \times Q'$ for a load Q'. Let $\dfrac{84579}{68} = b$, and the work done without a load a. Then $a — bQ'$ is the expression of the possible work which can be done. If the height, in these conditions, is reduced to h there will be a new expression $(65 + Q')$ h for the same amount of work : whence the equation :

$$a - bQ' = (65 + Q') h, \text{ and } h = \frac{a - bQ'}{65 + Q'}.$$

The useful work being that of the load $Q'h$,

$$Q'h = Q' \frac{a - bQ'}{65 + Q'} \text{ or } \mathbf{T} = Q' \frac{a - bQ'}{P + Q'}.$$

For $\mathbf{T}$ to be maximum the value of Q' will be :

$$Q' = P \left[\left(1 + \frac{a}{bP} \right)^{\frac{1}{2}} - 1, \right]$$

Taking numerical values, $Q' = 53$ kilogrammes and $Q'h = 55,350$ kilogrammetres ; which gives $h = \dfrac{55,350}{53}$ and a total

---

([1]) Following Coulomb, various authors have accused Daniel Bernoulli of ignoring this physiological law, that it is not immaterial to compensate the speed by the effort, in such a way that the power remains constant. The writings of Bernoulli bear witness that this was never his error (*Hydrodynamica*, 1738, § 13, § 21. *Prix. Acad. Sciences*, 1768, vol. viii., p. 7). He obtained $F = 15 K$ and $v = 0·66$ m. as the maximum daily work of the arm.

amount of work done :

$$(65 + 53) \; h = \frac{(65 + 53) \; 55{,}350}{53} = 123{,}232 \; \text{kilogrammetres.}$$

This maximum work done with a load is about $\frac{123{,}232}{189{,}915}$ or 65%, practically two-thirds, of the work done without a load.

Coulomb determined the maximum amount of work in a great number of trades, by experiment and calculation,[1] as will be detailed later.

To obtain useful results by the above method it is necessary —Coulomb said so clearly—to take a strong workman working on piecework. It may be added that it is advisable to multiply the experiments and only to submit incontestable average values to calculation. Those of Coulomb, always taken from single observations, and sometimes borrowed from none too reliable observers, are not sufficiently reliable, in spite of the indisputable authority of that celebrated natural philosopher.

At the same time, his is the honour of having introduced into science this kind of research, which others, at a later date, such as Frederick Taylor, Gilbreth, etc., applied to industrial problems. (See § 303).

123. Another method, first employed by De la Hire [2] in 1702, and developed by Coriolis [3] in 1829, is similar to that which hydraulic engineers use to calculate the work of a current of water acting on the paddles of a water wheel. These scientists assumed that a fluid circulated in the muscles with a speed u. A man of a weight Q does a maximum amount of work unloaded at a speed V. If he is loaded with a weight P he will work at a speed v. Assuming that the efforts are proportional to the squares of the speeds, calculation will lead to the following results :

1. The man produces a maximum amount of work in lifting a load scarcely equal to ⅔ of the weight of his body.[4]

2. The speed is, in these conditions 48% of his speed without a load.

The calculation is very simple, the proportion of the efforts to the squares of the speeds giving :—

$$Q = K \; (u - V)^2,$$

---

[1] C. A. Coulomb (1736–1806), *Mémoire sur la Force des Hommes*, written in 1786, on his return from a voyage to Martinique, but published in 1799 in the *Mémoires de l'Institut.*, vol. ii., and in *Theorie des Machines* (Bachelier, 1821).

[2] De la Hire (*Mém. Acad. Roy. Sciences*, 1702).

[3] Coriolis : *Du Calcul de l'Effet des Machines*, pp. 278–9, 1844 (2nd edn.).

[4] Coulomb's method gave ⅔, or a little more than ⅘ for ascending with loads.

and the maximum work done per second will be :

$$QV = K(u - V)^2 \, V,$$

K being a constant.

In the same way $(Q + P) = K(u - v)^2$ and $(Q + P) \, v = K (u - v)^2 \, v$.

For QV to be a maximum V must equal $\dfrac{u}{3}$, hence $Q = \dfrac{4}{9} \, Ku^2$.

To have $(Q + P) \, v$ maximum it is necessary that

$$v = \frac{2}{3} \, u - \sqrt{\frac{u^2}{9} + \frac{P}{3K}}.$$

Replace Q by its value $\dfrac{4}{9} \, Ku^2$, then

$$v = 0 \cdot 474V, \quad \text{about} \quad \frac{48}{100} \, V,$$

and from $(Q + P) = K \, (u - v)^2$.

$$P = 0 \cdot 597Q \quad \text{or practically} \quad P = \frac{3}{5} \, Q.$$

124. The work done per second, that is, the product $F \times v$, has a maximum value which various authors have attempted to determine *a priori*. According to Euler, it can be represented by one of the following formulæ :—

$$F = F' \left(1 - \frac{v}{v} \right)^2 \quad \text{or} \quad F = F' \left(1 - \frac{v^2}{v'^2} \right).$$

F' and v' being respectively the greatest (absolute) effort and speed, which will render all work impossible.

From the first formula :

$$v = \frac{v'}{3} \, ; \quad \text{hence} \quad F = \frac{4}{9} \, F' \quad \text{and} \quad Fv = \frac{4}{27} \, F'v' \, ; \quad \text{this being}$$

the maximum power.

From the second formula :

$$v = \frac{v'}{2} \quad \text{and} \quad Fv = \frac{3}{8} \, F'v'.$$

Schultz ([1]) obtained by experiments on the haulage of loads :

$$F' = 48 \text{ to } 49 \text{ kilogrammes} \, ; \quad v' = 1 \cdot 60 \text{ metres.}$$

Hence the first formula gives $v = 0 \cdot 53$ metres, and $Fv = 11 \cdot 5$ kilogrammetres approximately.

He found by experiment that man develops in continuous work an effort of 13·7 kg. at a speed of 0·76 m., that is a power of 10·4 kgm. in accordance with Euler's theory.

([1]) Schultz (*Bibliothèque Brittannique*, 1783, vol. lvi.).

Langsdorf ([1]) obtained :—

$v = 0·757$ m. ; $F = 13·30$; hence $Fv = 10$ kilogrammetres.

Euler's first formula, which is represented graphically by a parabola (fig. 136) is therefore sufficiently correct, but the time should be introduced into these relations if they are to have a practical significiation. Calling the factors of the daily maximum work F_1, v_1, t_1 similar formulæ are obtained to that of Mascheck ([2]) :

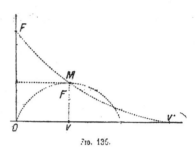

Fig. 136.

$$F = \left(3 - \frac{v}{v_1} - \frac{t}{t_1}\right) F_1,$$

and that of Gerstner ([3]) :

$$F = \left(2 - \frac{v}{v_1}\right) \left(2 - \frac{t}{l_1}\right) F_1.$$

These formulæ are unsatisfactory. The German engineers ([4]) stated that, for 8 hours of work per day, the normal effort of a man represents a third of his weight, 20 to 25 kilogrammes. It will be seen that this is not often the case, and that calculation cannot replace experiment.

125. (ii) *The Energetic Point of View.*—The idea of fatigue had, in Coulomb's mind, the value that we attribute to the idea of energy. " The whole question," he wrote, " resolves itself into how to find the combination with each other of the different degrees of pressure, speed and time, so that a man, with equal fatigue, can produce the greatest amount of work." But fatigue is not a precise thing, and is difficult to define. Fatigue occurs in walking, for example, from the first kilogrammetre accomplished, because each unit of work has an effect, often negligible, but still real, on the organism. At the limit at which the human forces are incapable of further exertion, fatigue is more a pathological than a physiological state, and the degrees of fatigue, prior to that state, are not susceptible of precise measurement (§ 146), sensation not having physical dimensions.

It is therefore desirable to substitute for a sensation, fatigue, the direct estimation of possible work. This is often difficult, all the more so as the work of the muscles is greater than that of

([1]) Quoted by Rhülmann (*Allg. Maschienenlehre* vol. i., p. 268, note).
([2]) Quoted by Simms (*Proc. Instit. of Civil Eng.*, vol. ii., p. 112.
([3]) Quoted by Simms (*loc. cit.*) and Gerstner's *Mécanique*.
([4]) Weisbach, *Lehrbuch d. Ingen. und Maschienen-Mechanik.*

the tools on which they act, and because, it is compounded of uncertain elements, such as the skill of the workman and the perfection of the tools. It follows that the estimation of the energetic expenditure, either according to the consumption of oxygen, or according to the living ration, is the most reliable guide to the magnitude of the muscular work and the degree of fatigue at any moment, and for the relative comparison of operations that are not directly comparable. The appearance of physiological troubles will mark the limits of fatigue. This indication will be developed further in regard to the subject of industrial work.

126. The Running of the Human Machine.—The Law of Repose. —The evaluation of the expenditure of energy—the accurate criterion of the amount of work performed by the muscles—must be made when the subject is in a normal state, as to his mechanical action, his respiration, and his gaseous exchanges. It is difficult to obtain a perfectly constant speed in ordinary machines. Man readily attains it, owing to the co-ordination of sensations and movements, and to what is also called the muscular sense or the sense of resistance, in short, to the nervous centres.[1] The initial period of getting into action is all the quicker, the longer experience the subject has had of the work and the smaller his personal equation (§ 83). Normal working continues as long as fatigue has not decreased the nervous excitability. In extreme cases this fatigue is felt in the nervous centres themselves and disturbs the co-ordination.

Certain features in the operation of the human machine must be pointed out ; they reveal themselves in the energetic expenditure. This expenditure, after the commencement of an action, accelerates rapidly and the oxygen consumed in the first two minutes so far exceeds the quantity of carbonic acid gas eliminated that the respiratory quotient $\dfrac{CO^2}{O^2}$ undergoes a fall of about 15%.

Then the respiration rapidly becomes regular.

In recommencing an action several times, after intervals of repose of a few minutes, a less noticeable lowering of the respiratory quotient is found, which would seem to indicate an adaptation of the subject which lessens the expenditure.[2]

The normal state being once attained, the expenditure increases little by little ; muscular groups, up till then inactive, intervene in the work ; the chemical reactions which furnish the energy are wider and more rapid. At the end of half an hour,

[1] S. A. Pari and Farini (*Atti del Real Istitute Veneto*, vol. xiv., p. 929, 1904–5).

[2] Jules Amar (*Comptes Rendus Sciences*, 1910, vol. cli., p. 680).

however, the expenditure is almost uniform [1] and can be measured. Finally, if a stoppage of work takes place, the expenditure does not fall back to its static value, but is maintained longer the higher it has been raised, that is to say, the more intense has been the work. The law of repose takes the same course as Newton's law for the cooling of hot bodies.[2] This is very important, because rapid work, besides being economical, will also be the least persistent in its after effects.[3] The proportion of CO_2 to O_2 becomes higher and the respiratory quotient therefore increases.[4]

All these disturbances which affect the exchanges of gas seem to affect the elimination of carbonic gas much more than the consumption of oxygen, and under normal conditions it can always be assumed that the oxygen gives the most correct measurement of the energetic expenditure.

127. The rate of the expenditure varies at different hours of the day, the minimum taking place from 3 to 7 o'clock in the morning for a man in repose or a man at work (§ 105 and 106). On the other hand, partaking of meals raises the expenditure in a proportion which is modified by the nature of the nutriment.

By beginning from the time of the meal it is possible to find the moment at which it no longer has any appreciable influence on the rise of the expenditure and to see whether the time elapsed is independent of the nature of the nutriment. The procedure is as follows :—The subject fasts from 8 o'clock in the evening, to 8 o'clock in the morning and then takes a carbohydrate meal, his exchanges of gas, whilst fasting, being previously measured for five minutes. From the moment of the meal, similar measurements of the consumption of oxygen are made from hour to hour.

Similar determinations can be made after a nitrogenous meal.

A series of similar experiments were carried out with the experimental bicycle, work equivalent to 2·72 Calories being performed in 10 minutes. The subject was fed both with carbo-hydrate and nitrogenous diets, and tests were made for various intervals of time between the meal and the work.

These results may be summarised as follows :—

1. The rise of the expenditure following a meal ceases at once if the latter is of carbo-hydrates ; the expenditure, in other cir-

---

[1] Jules Amar (*Ibid.*, p. 892 ; *Le Rendement de la Machine Humaine*, pp. 64–5, Paris, 1910).
[2] *Ibid.* (*Comptes Rendus Sciences*, vol. cliii., p. 79).
[3] The measurements of Atwater on the energetic expenditure at intervals of two hours (§ 105) confirm the law of repose.
[4] Katzenstein (*Pflüger's Archiv.*, 1891, vol. xlix., p. 330).

cumstances progressively decreases until the third and fourth hour.

2. The initial rise increases until the third hour if the diet is nitrogenous.

3. In consequence of 1 and 2 a carbo-hydrate diet is more economical than an nitrogenous diet, the materials of the first being more quickly utilised than those of the second ;

4. All things being equal, the expenditure, in nitrogenous foods, is greater than the expenditure in carbo-hydrates. Briefly stated, a day's work with a carbo-hydrate diet is 4·5% more economical than with nitrogenous diet.[1] The difficulty of feeding for several days on fats makes any experiments with these impossible.

128. Conclusions and General Laws.—

1. Work compared to the simple support of a load necessitates a higher energetic expenditure in the same time, and motive work, other factors, being constant, is more expensive than resistant work.

2. An economy of expenditure is attained by working quickly that is, by dividing the loads into fractions and taking short and frequent rests.

3. Movements of great amplitude are more economical than those of small amplitude, more often repeated. There is a rhythm which gives best results for a day's work.

4. In a given time, a maximum amount of work will be produced if the resistance to be overcome decreases progressively, that is, if the sensation of fatigue itself regulates the effort of the muscles.

5. Carbo-hydrate alimentation leads to an economy of 4·5% per day in the expenditure of energy, as compared with a nitrogenous diet.

6. The law of repose must regulate the duration of the intervals of repose in the course of the working day in accordance with the demands of various trades. This is a fundamental principle, but it has not yet been much studied.

The application of the six preceding laws to the scientific organisation of industrial work allows a man to utilise his muscular force to the best advantage without prejudice to his intellectual capacity, always a great asset. It prevents him from overstepping the physiological limits of normal activity.

---

[1] Jules Amar (*Comptes Rendus Acad. Sc.*, 1912, 19th Feb., p. 528; *Journal de Physiol.*, 1912, p. 298).

CHAPTER II.

YIELD OF THE HUMAN MACHINE.

129. Definition.—The yield is the relation of the mechanical energy produced, to the energy expended. It has been explained that the industrial yield, r, is a gross value deducted from the relation of useful energy to the total energy (static and dynamic) ; whilst the net yield R only includes the dynamic expenditure. Then (see § 61) :

$$r = \frac{T}{D_s + D_d} \qquad R = \frac{T}{D_d}.$$

Example : An adult expends 100 calories per hour in repose, performing work to the amount of 25,500 kgm (*i.e.* 60 calories per hour), he expends altogether 340 calories. Therefore :

$$D_s = 100, \quad T = 60, \quad D_d = 240, \text{ and }$$

$$r = \frac{60}{340} = 17 \cdot 6\%, \quad R = \frac{60}{240} = 25\%.$$

If the value of the net yield of the subject is once definitely determined the amount of his expenditure will give the value of the work performed :—

$$T = R \times D_d$$

To obtain D_d the consumption of oxygen before the trial, and afterwards, when normally working is measured. From the ratio of 4·90 Calories per litre (at 0°C and 760 millimetres of mercury barometric pressure) can be calculated the energy expended D_s and D_d in a period of time or a few minutes (thirty minutes in the course of work).

This method of operation is the only correct one, seeing that the initial state of the subject is always difficult to define. By coming to the workshop in a certain state of fatigue, the workman has already a high static expenditure. It is therefore impossible to take his gross expenditure $D_s + D_d$ as a basis from which to calculate the amount of work he performs, in other words, r is very variable, much more so, as will be shown later, than the net yield R.

Before proceeding further, the terms whose quotients give the net and gross yields must be accurately defined. First of all there is the useful mechanical work, the industrial effect, a quantity which can generally be calculated without difficulty. The work done in ascending a mountain, a staircase, or a ladder is the product of the weight of the body (with or without a load) and the vertical height ascended.   The work done by a cyclist is the product of the distance covered, and the passive resistances of rolling, friction, etc.   The work done by the arms or legs in operating tools, or the work done in producing locomotion are also measurable more or less exactly.   It is found, nevertheless, that this mechanical quantity is more difficult to measure in some cases than in others, and when the movements are diverse or complicated, the problem becomes acute, all the more so because any static effort of the workman escapes the measurements, although the whole muscular activity consists of static efforts.

Hence, in a given occupation or trade, it is only possible to compare the quantities of useful work done by several workmen if the conditions are approximately identical.   It is impossible to make comparison between different occupations or trades.

130.   It must be stated, in fact, that the sum of human activity bears more relation to the muscular work done than to the mechanical work performed by the tool.   The manufacturer may estimate the latter quantity, but that will not prevent the workman from estimating the former on the purely subjective but pertinent indications of fatigue.   Take, for example, a man occupied in filing ; the useful work that he performs is the result of his effort to overcome the resistance of the metal in displacing the file.   But this result is only obtained by an effort which presses the file on the metal and obliges it to bite, by the return stroke of the tool, by the speed, by an appropriate attitude at the bench, by the swaying of the body, by a certain inclination of the vertebral column and a tension of the muscles of the upper limbs.   These multiple muscular efforts vary in direction and extent in different trades.   All, from the greatest to the smallest, necessitate an expenditure of energy, a consumption of oxygen ; and their effects must be added in determining the fatigue.   Thus, in any given occupation man's maximum output is conditioned by his maximum expenditure of energy, an expenditure whose value will be given later (§ 342) and the quantities of work performed by two different workmen are proportional to their respective expenditures.[1]

131.   We will now consider further the net yield of the muscles.

In the equation: $R = \dfrac{T}{D_d}$,

T stands for the product Ph of the weight of the subject and of the height h of a staircase mounted by him.   Now D_d does not correspond solely to this amount of work, because the ascension

---

[1] If it is a case of the same occupation and conditions of work as similar as possible.

involves an increased performance of work by the heart and the respiratory muscles. In round figures the beats of the heart increase from 72 to 110 per minute in the performance of a large amount of work (250,000 kilogrammetres in eight hours), and the volume of air breathed from 500 to 2,000 litres per hour. According to the average of experiments by various authorities, the heart pumps 150 grammes of blood per cycle at a pressure of about $\frac{1}{10}$ of that of the surrounding atmosphere equivalent to height of 1·25 metres. This is $0·150 \times 1·25 = 0·1875$ kgm. of work done. In repose it will be :

$$0·1875 \times 72 = 13·75 \text{ kgm. per minute.}$$

and at work (value above),

$$0·1875 \times 110 = 20·625 \text{ kgm. per minute.}$$

an increase of 6·875 kgm. per minute, or

$$6·875 \times 60 = 412·50 \text{ kgm per hour.}$$

As to the respiration, the pressure of the air expired varies from 0·06 m. to 0·30 m. of water (see § 337) in repose and work respectively, which gives :—

$$500 \times 0·06 = 30 \text{ kilogrammetres, in one case, and}$$

$$2,000 \times 0·30 = 600 \text{ kilogrammetres}$$

in the other, per hour. The increase of work done is therefore 570 kilogrammetres per hour on the average. As the volume of air, both inspired and expired, there is a double amount of muscular work done.

$$570 \times 2 = 1,140 \text{ kilogrammetres.}$$

Hence the expenditure D_d covers an increase of work done by the organs equal to :—

$$412 + 1,140 = 1,552 \text{ kilogrammetres per hour.}$$

As regards the circulation of the blood this work is dissipated into heat by friction (see § 60). In accurate calculations of the work done and the muscular yield, these 1,552 kilogrammetres must be added to the work done by the muscles per hour ; the yield, in consequence, will be higher than the quotient $\frac{T}{D_d}$

The circulatory and respiratory activity determined by the working of the muscles is due to a secretion of the latter, which is carried to the nervous centres controlling the heart and the lungs. This causes a greater quantity of oxygen to be placed at the service of the muscles because, in passing more frequently through the lungs, the blood absorbs more oxygen there, which latter is also renewed frequently on the surface of the lungs.

132. An Important Observation. —In stating that the yield is the quotient of the useful work by the expenditure, it has not been specified whether the question involved was of motor or resistant work. As a rule, only the former is considered, but it is known that the latter produces a smaller expenditure. A man mounting a staircase makes a larger expenditure of energy than that necessary for descending the stairs, but the descent is more or less restrained by the muscles, which fact modifies, within wide limits, the corresponding value of the expenditure. Therefore, the yield of a resistant work is not a correct statement, since the motor does not perform the work ; it acts against the acceleration of Gravity in the manner of a brake. As for the muscular work, it is obvious that its value is less in this case than in the other where Gravity has to be overcome and the expenditure is less in about the same proportion. Therefore R is taken as the yield, both of motor and resistance work.[1]

133. Examples of Yield.—(a) **The Use of an Experimental Bicycle Dynamometer.**—The following results were obtained by some American observers with a robust student, weighing 76 kilogrammes and from 20 to 23 years old. His static expenditure D_s was 2,397 Calories in the calorimetic chamber at 20° (see § 104). By causing him to perform work to the amount of 200,000 to 250,000 kilogrammetres the following results were obtained, the average being given at the foot of each column :—

EQUIVALENT OF WORK DONE	$D_s + D_d$ OR $2,397 + D_d$	$r = \dfrac{T}{D_s + D_d}$	$R = \dfrac{T}{D_d}$
Cal.	Cal.	%	%
505·75	4,764	10·61	21·36
517·82	5,223	9·09	18·32
547·52	5,205	10·51	19·49
562·07	5,248	10·70	19·71
587·33	5,178	11·34	21·12
594·76	5,215	11·40	21·10
607·00	5,309	11·43	20·84
1,481·70	9,314	15·90	21·42
675·50 [2]	5,682	11·82%	20·50%

The average value of R is 20·5% ; that of r is 11·82%.

The duration of the experiment was eight hours, except in the last trial, which lasted sixteen hours. The net yield appears to be practically constant, but it rose in certain cases,[3]

---

[1] Jules Amar (*Comptes Rendus Sciences*, June, 1911, p. 1618).
[2] Atwater and Benedict (*Bulletin*, No. 136, p. 51, 66, 97, 184, 307, 1903).
[3] Atwater and Benedict (*Ibid.*, p. 59).

to 23·8%. However, the average value of 20·5% is small. According to Frey, the muscles of the body would have to be kept in a state of tension (static expenditure) to maintain equilibrium on the apparatus for eight hours. Also it must be added that the friction of the feet on the pedals developed a quantity of heat which the calorimeter registered as dynamic expenditure ; that the exactitude of the ergometer is not always

Fig. 137.   Bicycle Dynamometer (J. Amar).

what one could desire,[1] and finally that a prolonged stay in the calorimeter is unfavourable to the performance of a large amount of work (§ 105). Also the average effort 7·73 kg., was a high value.

At least a hundred agricultural labourers, men used to an active life, have ridden on the bicycle dynamometer, which will be described in *Technics* (§ 221). The arrangement of the apparatus is shown in fig. 137. The experiments took place in the open air, the average effort rarely attaining 400 grammes, and the duration of the experiments not exceeding four hours for a daily amount of work of about 55,600 kilogrammetres, made at a normal rhythm of 90 to 92 strokes of the pedal per minute. As a rule, the subjects worked two hours in the morning and two in the afternoon. Under these favourable conditions

$$R = 32·5\%.$$

(see also § 290). The expenditure was estimated according to the maintainence rations in repose and at work.[2]

---

[1] Atwater and Benedict (*loc. cit.*, p. 34–35)
[2] Jules Amar (*Le Rendement de la Machine Humaine*, p. 60. Jules Lefèvre, in his *Traité de Bioénergétique*, gave an erroneous interpretation of our calculation of the yield ; this was pointed out in *C. R. Sciences* of June, 1911.

134. (*b*) **Use of a Lifting Gear.**—The subject worked a kind of quarrier's winch, *vide* fig. 216, when enclosed in a calorimetric chamber, his expenditure being calculated by the oxygen consumed. At the commencement of study of human thermo dynamics, Hirn [1] made some experiments in which the calorimetric measurements are probably wrong, but there remain those relative to the oxygen, the respiratory quotient being 0·99 since the subjects were fed on feculents. Taking 5·05 Calories per litre of oxygen, the expenditure can be calculated fairly exactly. Chauveau [2] corrected Hirn's method later. Here, first of all, are the latter's figures :—

WEIGHT OF THE SUBJECT	STATIC EXPENDITURE D_s	$D_s + D_d$	EQUIVALENT OF WORK	R %
kg.	Cal.	Cal.	Cal.	
⎡52............	115·25	348·90	60·97	26·09
I ⎨ —	115·25	311·98	54·09	27·49
⎣ —	115·25	301·14	46·09	24·79
⎡61	84·02	446·34	64·90	17·91
II ⎨ —	89·55	460·95	64·58	17·38
⎣ —	107·00	407·34	54·96	18·29
III 62	108·95	381·11	69·96	25·70
IV 73	95·22	435·35	76·59	22·51
V 85	115·28	410·12	78·42	26·59
				25·53

The two last subjects were well developed and robust ; the first and third (women) were young people of 18 years old ; Number II. was Hirn himself. It will be seen that, in this case, the yield has dropped to about 17·50%. Atwater and Benedict obtained equally low results in experimenting on chemists and other men belonging to the laboratory.

Hirn made his experiments last from 41 to 90 minutes, in a calorimeter maintained at temperatures ranging from 17° to 23°C.

Chauveau, in his trials of one hour, found that the net yield rose to 26·4% (§ 114) ; but for durations of eight to ten minutes he found an average of 20·2% only.

Thus :

Work (Calories) ...	35·52	50·47	65·09	60·74	71·06
D_d (Calories)	206·50	245	277	292	380
R	17·50%	20·60%	23·50%	20·80%	18·70%

---

[1] Ad. Hirn, *Recherches sur l'Equiv.* (*loc. cit.*) ; *Revue Scientifique*, 1887.
[2] A. Chauveau (*Comptes Rendus Sciences*, 1901, first half year, p. 194).

The whole of the preceding researches, especially in view of the yields of 24 and 24·6% obtained, by Atwater and his collaborators, Benedict and Carpenter,[1] lead to a value of at least 25% for the useful effect of the muscular energy of the legs.

135. (c) *Ascents of Mountains* : *Walking.*—Dumas and Boussingault [2] quote an ascent of Mont Blanc, made in twelve hours, which necessitated a dynamic expenditure of 2,425 Calories, that is a net yield.

$$R = \frac{4,810 \times 65}{2,425 \times 425} = 30\% \text{ approximately.}$$

The height of Mont Blanc is 4,810 metres, and the weight of the subject was 65 kilogrammes. Fick and Vislicénus, in their ascent of the Faulhorn (1,956 metres) calculated a yield of 50%, but on very doubtful data (§ 106).

In walking, Katzenstein [3] obtained a dynamic expenditure of 1·957 c.c. of oxygen per kilogrammetre, that is,

$$0·001957 \times 4·90 \times 425 = 4·075 \text{ kgm.}$$

From this :—

$$R = \frac{1}{4·075} = 25\% \text{ approximately,}$$

a result which agrees with the preceding ones. However, Frentzel and Reach,[4] studying six different subjects on climbing expeditions, obtained an average of 32% with a minimum of 28% and a maximum of 36%.

Undoubtedly, the lower limbs have a peculiar impulse which reduces their expenditure of energy if they are not caused to exceed their natural effort and their normal speed. In ascending an inclined plane (see § 298) R has been found to be 29·40% approximately.[5]

136. (d) *Use of the Muscles of the Arm.* —There are very few good experiments on the useful work produced by the muscles of the arm. The use of the ergograph (§ 119) does not allow the separation of motor from resistant work, and the expenditure therefore, refers to a heterogeneous, mechanical whole. An exception must be made in favour of Hall's [6] ergograph, which makes this distinction, although the use of this ergograph is restricted.

[1] Benedict and Carpenter (*Bulletin*, No. 208, p. 39 ; 1909).
[2] Dumas and Boussingault, *Essai de Statique des êtres Organisés*, 1344.
[3] Katzenstein (*Pflüger's Archiv.*, vol. xlix., p. 330, 1391).
[4] Frentzel and Reach (*Ibid.*, vol. lxxxiii., p. 477, 1901).
[5] J. Amar (*Comptes Rendus Sciences*, May, 1911, p.p. 13-27).
[6] W. S. Hall, *Experimental Physiology*, 1904, p. 227.

Atwater and Benedict ([1]) first thought of having a weight (a block of iron of 5·7 kg.) lifted by means of a cord passing over a pulley, and pulled by the arms. They had to abandon this idea, because the work of the arms would have been unequal, and also because of the negative work in the restrained descent which cannot be accurately measured.

By lifting weights to a certain height and letting them fall again Hanriot and Richet ([2]) calculated $R = 16\%$ approximately, from the measurements of the exchanges of gas, but without great experimental accuracy.

Laulanié ([3]) made some experiments, unfortunately of too short duration, on the working by the arms of a special brake. In trials lasting from two to five minutes, and for work done amounting to 560 to 1660 kilogrammetres, he found the net yield R to be 21 to 23% (see § 121).

Armand Gautier ([4]) estimated the dynamic expenditure from the maintenance ration, on workmen employed in wine warehouses in the south of France, working ten hours a day at pumping water. A vat (holding 15,000 litres) had to be filled, the water being raised to a height of 10 metres, i.e. :

$$T = 15,000 \times 10 = 150,000 \text{ kilogrammetres.}$$

The minor supplementary work was estimated at 10,000 kilogrammetres. Hence :

$$D_s = 2,643 \text{ Cal.,} \qquad D_s + D_d = 4,218 \text{ Cal. in 24 hours.}$$

Consequently :

$$R = \frac{160,000}{425\,(4,218 - 2,643)} = 24\%, \qquad r = \frac{160,000}{425 \times 4,218} = 9\%.$$

This hard and continuous work causes many losses (such as the friction on the handle, losses in the pump, and the raising of the upper half of the body about 1,200 times) which Gautier estimated at 100,000 kilogrammetres.

Finally, Heinemann ([5]) gives

$$R = 22 \cdot 6\%$$

for the muscles of the arms.

137. Variations of the Yield.—Chauveau's experiments have shown the influence of speed and load on the amount of expendi-

---

([1]) Atwater, Benedict and Woods (*Bulletin*, No. 44, p. 51, 1897).
([2]) Hanriot and Richet (*Comptes Rendus Sciences*, vol. cv., p. 78).
([3]) Laulanié, *Traité de Physiologie*, pp. 792, 801, 803, Paris, 1905.
([4]) A. Gautier, *L'Alimentation et les Régimes*, Paris, 1908.
([5]) Heineman (*Pflüger's Archiv.*, vol. lxxxiii., p. 441, 1901).

ture. By reducing the latter, the yield is improved (§ 115 and following), and what is even more important, the yield improves in proportion to the work done.

Example : 54,993 kilogrammetres of work done on the bicycle dynamometer.[1]

TIME	WORK DONE	NET YIELD %
1st hour	13,748·25 kgm.	29·33
2nd —	,, ,,	31·23
3rd —	,, ,,	33·81
4th —	,, ,,	35·03
4 hours	54,993·00 kgm.	32·20

And, with varying speed (fig. 138) :

SPEED PER MINUTE		WORK DONE	NET YIELD %
1 {	70 strokes of the pedal	32,079 kgm.	25·10
	80 ,, ,, ,,	38,592 ,,	26·70
	90 ,, ,, ,,	48,481 ,,	28·40
2 {	90 ,, ,, ,,	66,661 ,,	30·60
	100 ,, ,, ,,	71,636 ,,	25·80

so that increase of speed increases the yield up to a certain limit and thereafter decreases it.

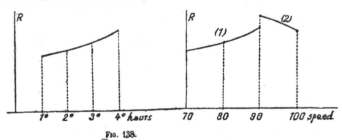

Fɪɢ. 138.

Variations of the Yield.

Speed can exercise the same influence on the yield of inanimate motors. The following results were obtained with an internal combustion engine [2] :

---

[1] Jules Amar, *Le Rendement*, pp. 61–3.
[2] Hopkinson and Ricardo (*Génie Civil*, 4th May, 1907).

SPEED PER MINUTE	EFFECTIVE YIELD %
400 revolutions	16·10
600 ,,	18·80
1,000 ,,	19·30
1,100 ,,	18·40
1,225 ,,	15·40

No doubt the increase in efficiency is due to the reduction of the calorific losses and the better utilisation of the combustible.

G. Weiss and Chauveau found a similar result in hydraulic motors (§ 114). The analogy between the muscles and heat engines, however tempting it may be, cannot be pressed, since the cause which limits the effects of speed cannot be the same. An extreme value of the speed prevents the reparation of the tissue and arrests the muscular contraction by fatigue.

In a cannon a yield of 44% is obtained, far above that of other heat engines, the reason being that the combustion is so complete, in spite of the rapidity of the explosion, whilst only a slight thermic loss takes place through the barrel owing to the speed of discharge. Perhaps this is somewhat analogous to the contraction of the muscles.

138. The variations of the yield are also due to other causes. In normal continuous work, without excessive fatigue, the muscular fibre becomes more irritable and the fibres and nervous cells more excitable. This is shown by an increase of force [2] and by a smaller consumption of oxygen.[3]

Voluntary work, with a suitable load and at a suitable speed—they vary according to the active organs—leads to a better energetic yield.

139. Finally the loss of work due to the passive resistances of the tools or apparatus must be considered. To run the bicycle dynamometer unloaded necessitates an expenditure of energy which is dissipated as heat in Atwater's experiments. Benedict and Carpenter [4] found this to be 6·50% of the measured mechanical work. It is a fraction of the work done for which the muscles have made a very appreciable expenditure of energy. It is obvious that, when using the bicycle dynamometer, or, indeed, any other ergometric instrument, we must know accurately the frictional losses in the apparatus so that we can add them to the

[1] Aimé Witz (Dernière Evolution du Moteur à Gaz, p. 144, 1910. Paris.
[2] Manca (Arch. Ital. Biol., vol. xvii., p. 390) ; Kronecker and Cutter (Comptes Rendus Sciences, vol. cxxix., p. 492, 1900).
[3] Grüber (Zeitsch. f. Biol., vol. xxviii., p. 466, 1891).
[4] Benedict and Carpenter (Bulletin, No. 208, p. 27, 1909) ; (Benedict and Cady (Publication, No. 167, 1912).

readings of the instrument to obtain the total output of muscular energy, and the real yield (§ 61). Thus Benedict and Carpenter [1] corrected their nett results for R by the amount of 6·50% above mentioned.

Witz [2] gave a simple method for evaluating the frictional losses in the apparatus.

In the case of the bicycle dynamometer the machine is run up, unloaded, to the required speed and the motive force, in this case the pressure of the feet on the pedals is then suddenly withdrawn. The machine continues to revolve until it has exhausted the energy imparted to it. Let it make N revolutions in time t before it stops, the initial speed being n_0 revolutions per second. Let K be the moment of inertia of the rotating system. Then the work done in overcoming the internal friction W, is represented by the equation :

$$W = \cdot 0055K \, \frac{n_0{}^2}{n} \text{ kilogrammetres.}$$

Where $n = \dfrac{N}{t}$.

If the normal speed is n' revolutions per second, the power absorbed by friction is $W \times n'$. The measured power being W', the organic yield, $\rho = \dfrac{W'}{n'W + W'}$ can be deduced for the whole system in movement.

Example: Let $K = 0·28$, $n_0 = 2$, $n = 0·40$, $n' = 2·05$. Then:
$$Wn' = 0·032 \text{ kgm.}$$

W' has been measured as 1·93, therefore :

$$\rho = \frac{1·93}{1·93 + 0·032} = \frac{1·93}{1·963} = 0·98.$$

The above test was made on the before-mentioned bicycle dynamometer, the speeds being registered electrically (§ 321). As a general rule, " coasting " with French bicycles absorbs nearly 5% of the total work.

140. Summary : Chauveau's Ratio.—The most complete experiments on the work done by man under conditions as to load, duration and alimentation give an average net yield of 25%, *i.e.*

$$R = \frac{T : 425}{D_d} = 0·25.$$

This is the maximum in the case of the arms.

---

[1] Benedict and Carpenter (*Bulletin*, No. 208, p. 39, 1909).
[2] Aimé Witz (*Comptes Rendus Sciences*, 3rd Aug., 1908) ; *Dernière Evolution du Moteur à Gaz*, p. 225.

On the other hand any method of activity (walking, ascending, bicycling, moving the pedals of machines with the feet) which utilises exclusively the muscles of the legs, gives an average net yield of 30%.

In order to include both resistant and motive work, whose expenditures are so different, it is assumed that the former equals $\frac{52}{100}$ of the latter.

In fact, in his experiments on the quarrier's winch (§ 134) Chauveau found the following relation between the expenditures :

$$\text{Cal,}$$

$$D_d \begin{cases} \text{Ascent} \dots \dots & 206 \cdot 50 \quad 245 \quad 277 \quad 292 \quad 380 = 1{,}400 \cdot 50 \\ \left.\begin{array}{l} \text{Restrained} \\ \text{Descent} \end{array}\right\} \dots & 117 \quad 131 \cdot 50 \ 143 \cdot 50 \ 144 \quad 203 = \quad 738 \end{cases}$$

hence :

$$\frac{738}{1{,}400 \cdot 5} = \frac{52}{100};$$

but this ratio only holds good if the speed is the same in the two directions of movement and does not exceed 0·12 metres per second (§ 116). Thus, if 152 calories is expended in the work of lifting, followed by a descent, 100 calories would be attributed to the motor expenditure and 52 calories to the expenditure during the descent. Finally, in the case of the arms, we have :—

$$\frac{T}{100} = 0 \cdot 25; \quad \text{whence} \quad T = 25 \text{ Calories.}$$

The useful effect is often in these 25 calories alone. In any case the muscular work is :

$$25 \text{ Cal} + (52 \times 0 \cdot 25) = 38 \text{ Calories.}$$

and the total mechanical work :

$$25 \times 2 = 50 \text{ Calories.}$$

It goes without saying that the muscles should always be worked under the least onerous conditions, and that the estimate of the work done should be made according to the expenditure of energy, as has been shown since 1909 ; which has an eminently practical value ([1]). The idea has been revived by Jules Lefèure, under the title of *The Motor Equivalent* (?) of the resistant work (see also § 300).

There is nothing definite to note on the subject of the industrial yield ; it varies from 4 to 10% in proportion as the quantity of daily work increases, and reaches 16% with difficulty. In a working day of 8 hours, unless there is inefficient use of the muscular forces, a waste of energy, or insufficient work, it should not be less than 10%. Its consideration has no scientific interest, whilst under definite conditions of work, a knowledge of the

---

([1]) Jules Amar, *Le Rendement*, p. 73–74.

net yield R is extremely useful. A distinction can then be made between various subjects according to their degree of ability, that is, their social utility.[1]

The idea of yield ceases to be applicable if the forms of muscular activity are of the static order, and if the subject fatigues himself without producing any mechanical work in the strict sense of the word. In true muscular work great resistances have to be displaced, and the work is evaluated in kilogrammetres according to the yield.

[1] Ernest Solvay : *Formules d'Energétique*, p. 9 ; Bruxelles, 1906.

CHAPTER III.

PHYSIOLOGICAL EFFECTS OF LABOUR : FATIGUE.

141. Conditions of Normal Activity.—Any muscular action is accompanied by various physiological effects, which modify the intensity of the respiratory, circulatory and nervous phenomena.

These modifications often attain a degree which is shown by fatigue, this being the normal case. The extreme degree is exhaustion, a pathological state.

With lesser degrees of fatigue the organism recovers its equilibrium and is completely repaired by rest, notably by the calm and sleep of the night.

It is therefore important to indicate the physiological effects which are exhibited in a state of activity which is normal, and such that the vital energy is not permanently diminished.

142. Effects of Work on the Respiration.—To study the rhythm and amplitude of the respirations a graphical method is employed. A single or double tympan is secured to the chest by means of a strap. It communicates with another tympan provided with a style, the whole apparatus being called the pneumograph (see *Technics*, § 195). A pneumographic trace indicates the following :—

15 to 18 respirations take place per minute when a man breathes in a state of repose. This rhythm varies with age.

On an average the following results are obtained :—

AGE	RHYTHM	AGE	RHYTHM
1 to 5 years ...	40 to 25	15 to 25 years ...	20 to 18
5 to 15 years ...	25 to 21	25 to 50 years ...	18 to 17

It will be seen from the pneumographic curve (fig. 139) that the expiration lasts a little longer than the inspiration, and that the two phases succeed each other fairly regularly.

When working, the rhythm increases and can attain twice its value in repose, *i.e.*, 25 to 35 respirations instead of 18 in an adult, at an external temperature of 12° to 15° C. Also the exercise of effort is marked by prolonged inspirations and short expirations, which is the reverse of the state of affairs in repose.

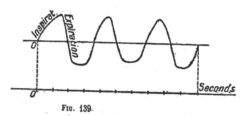

Respiratory Curves.

With this increase of rhythm there is a corresponding increase of the pulmonary ventilation, which tends to eliminate rapidly, the carbonic gas, which is a poison to the neuro-muscular organs.

If the work is very heavy, or takes place under bad conditions, CO_2 accumulates in the tissues ; hence the ratio $\dfrac{CO_2}{O_2}$ diminishes and, the subject becomes breathless.[1]   Therefore anything that impedes the respiration should be avoided in order that breathlessness shall not interfere with the work.

The following table gives the respiration per hour during a total of 45,000 kgm. of work done in five consecutive hours on the bicycle dynamometer : [2]

HOURLY FLOW OF THE RESPIRATION.

DAYS	1ST HOUR	2ND HOUR	3RD HOUR	4TH HOUR	5TH HOUR
1st	842 l.	1,051 l.	1,074 l.	1,079 l.	1,080 l.
2nd	878	1,139	1,167	1,187	1,188
3rd	896	1,063	1,122	1,128	1,133
Average	872 l.	1,084 l.	1,121 l.	1,131 l.	1,133 l.

It will be seen that the flow finds its level in the second hour of working.   Whilst in repose it is 500 litres on the average.   The production of 9,000 kilogrammetres of work per hour brings it to 1,100 litres.   A large amount of work causes 1,500 to 2,000 litres to pass through the lungs per hour.   In order that such volumes of air may be constantly pure, the workshops must be large and thoroughly ventilated.

From a practical point of view, the rhythm of the movements must not be such as to produce breathlessness, a cause of prompt

[1] F. Lagrange (*Revue Scientifique*, 1887, p. 718).
[2] Jules Amar, *Le Rendement*, p. 64.

fatigue, the force exerted must not impede the expiration (dyspnœa) and the clothing must allow free play to the thoracic walls. This problem of respiration is of prime importance. Its irregularity gives the first indication of fatigue.

143. Effects of Work on the Circulation.—The graphic method is also used to register the movements of the heart. The tracing obtained by the *cardiograph* (*Technics*, § 195) gives the phases of the complete cycle of movement of the heart : the systole, which is the contraction necessary to pump the blood into the arteries, and the diastole, which is the phase of repose.

The cardiac pulsation corresponds to the systole of the ventricles (the lower extremity of the heart).

This systole is shown by an elevation in the trace and some undulations, generally three in number which indicate a sustained contraction, of tetanic form. Its duration represents the quarter of the total period, the diastole covering the other three quarters (fig. 140).

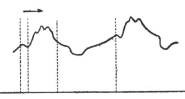

Fig. 140.
Cardiographic Record.

about the level of the left nipple.

The cardiac pulsation can be felt, and even seen, at It is occurs 72 to 75 times per minute in an adult in repose.

The beats of the heart cause the beats of the arteries to take place at the same rhythm. On the radial the pulsation is found to be ⅓ second later than the movement of the heart. The record of the pulse is taken by means of the *sphygmograph* (*Technics*, § 195). After the systolic phase there is a little jump due to the arterial elasticity, this being called the dicrotism (fig. 141). The ascending

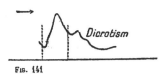

Fig. 141
Sphygmographic Record.

portion of the curve corresponds to the cardiac impulse and the descending portion marks the passage of the blood into the capillary vessels. As to the dicrotism, it is sometimes duplicated or triplicated, and is then called the polycrotism. It is more noticeable under the effect of a high temperature, or when wearing very thick clothes, as also after taking alcoholic drinks.

Another very important element in the pulse is the arterial pressure. If an artery (the brachial artery, for instance) be attached to a manometer a pressure of 120 millimetres of mercury would be measured. If a little rubber bulb is attached to the pulse and compressed until the pressure of the pulse is balanced, a manometer attached to the bulb will indicate the amount of the arterial pressure. This arrangement constitutes Potain's sphygmomanometer.

Pachon's oscillometer achieves the same result with more precision (see *Technics*, § 248).

For man in repose the following results have been found:

AGE	PULSATIONS PER MINUTE	AGE	PULSATIONS PER MINUTE
5 to 6 years	98	14 to 19 years	82 to 77
6 to 8 ...	93	19 to 80	75 to 70
8 to 14	89 to 87	80 years and over	79

The relation between the durations of the diastole and the systole is:

$$\tfrac{3}{4} : \tfrac{1}{4} = 3 \text{ approximately.}$$

The arterial pressure increases with age. It is 13 to 14 centimetres of mercury between 10 and 20 years, 17 to 19 centimetres between 20 and 40 years, and it exceeds 20 centimetres after 50 (Potain); the systolic pressure is taken in these measurements, the diastolic pressure being smaller.

When a man performs work, the rhythm of the pulsations increases to 100 and 120 per minute, and attains a steady value if the work is normal and regular. This is 112 to 114 for work amounting to 200,000 to 250,000 kilogrammetres in eight hours.[1] According to Otto Weiss[2] the extreme limit is 167. In this activity the organism finds the condition of its resistance to fatigue and the blood circulates oftener, so that, in unit time, 5 or 6 times more blood passes through the same organ.[3] The following observations on the rhythm of the pulse are of interest.[4] A subject covered 38 metres on the level at increasing speeds; his pulse, which was 75, becomes successively:

84 85 88 90 90

increasing by

9 10 13 15 and 15

The duration of the walk was:

30 27 26 19 18 seconds.

i.e. inversely proportional to the increases of the rhythm.

[1] Atwater and Benedict (*Bulletin*, No. 136, p. 357, table 127).
[2] Otto Weiss (*Pflüger's Archiv.*, vol. cxxiii., p. 341, 1908.)
[3] Chauveau and Kaufmann (*Comptes Rendus Sc.*, 1886 and 1887).
[4] J. Amar, (unpublished observations).

In climbing a slope of 11·50 cm., rise in 80 metres, the pulse, originally beating at 70, the successive results were :

an increase of	96	106	112
	26	36	42
The duration of the walk was	40	33	30 seconds.

which verifies the preceding relation between these quantities, and also shows the effect of the slope of the ground and the speed. The increase in the pulse for the same duration of 30 seconds was 42 instead of 9.

Finally, the systolic phase is prolonged during heavy work, and the relation $\dfrac{\text{diastole}}{\text{systole}}$ diminishes gradually, the dicrotism becomes less, but the arterial pressure, on the contrary, increases. If, however, the exercise is violent, the pressure becomes considerably less. During the performance of work on a bicycle, amounting to 10,000 kilogrammetres in 10 minutes the arterial pressure increased by 30% measured by the Pachon method.

All these elements taken together indicate the degree of fatigue. Lavoisier was the first to draw attention to a remarkable relation between the quantity of work done and the number of respirations and of pulsations. According to this illustrious scientist " the first quantity is proportional to the product of the other two."[1] Nevertheless this observation cannot be strictly applied. It is only true when the work progresses quietly and produces no fatigue. It is fairly correct for moderate degrees of activity.

144. Effects of Work on the Muscular Power.—It is a fact of common observation that normal work " trains " (*entraine*) the muscles, provoking a greater irritability of their fibres (§ 138) and reducing, perhaps, the period of getting into action which shows itself in beginners by the stiffness of their movements.

Before a detailed examination of the nature of muscular " training " (*entrainement*) it must be pointed out that, according to various authorities, it is accompanied by a gain of force. Thus, if the arms are worked until fatigue ensues, lifting dumb bells of 5 kilogrammes each above the head, at the beginning five movements can be made in four seconds, but gradually this number can be increased up to 120 movements.[2]

---

[1] Lavoisier, *Œuvres Complètes*, vol. ii., p. 696 (édition officielle).
[2] G. Manca (*Arch. Ital. Biol.*, vol. xvii., p. 390) ; Henry (*Comptes Rendus Sciences*, vol. cxii., p. 1473) ; W.–C Lombard (*Journal of Physiol.*, vol. xiii., p. 1, 1892).

According to Kronecker and Cutter [1] the work of the legs in walking increases the strength of the arms. The merit of all these observations is that they are founded on figures. But the general doctrine of the gain of strength in the organs in the course of, or as the result of, normal activity, was formulated in the xviiith centuiy by Cheyne and Ramazzini as the result of their observations on artisans.[2] They stated that the artisans must be suitably nourished.

The internal massage which the muscles undergo in consequence of their repeated movements during exercise has also, doubtless, a beneficial effect. External massage produces a still more appreciable effect which will be examined later (§ 159).

The nature of the training itself,[3] is both mechanical and physiological, mechanical because the work diminishes the natural inertia of the muscular fibre, and physiological because the work increases the irritability of the muscles and of the nerves just as inactivity blunts them and leads to atrophy and degeneration. Also it stimulates the circulatory phenomena, the action of the blood and of the lymph, to the point of giving rise to what has been called functional hypertrophy. The mass of the muscles increases, not by the addition of new fibres, but by the thickening of the old ones, which increase in size and form, a larger reserve of nitrogenous *substances.[4] The albumin thus becomes really an energy-supplying food.[5] The economy of expenditure which results from this increase of muscular power has been discussed in connection with the yield (§ 137).

145. The Effects of Work on the General Metabolism.—The real repercussion caused by the exertion of the muscles in the organism has an entirely general character. This is metabolism, and is what has been called physiological work (§ 60). It includes all the intimate reactions of the cells, which increase in intensity, like a chemical reaction which gains speed in proportion as the temperature rises.

Work increases the intensity of the cellular reactions, as heat increases the temperature of a body, and it has been seen (§ 126) that when the organism returns to a state of repose, its internal reactions and its expenditure decrease according to Newton's law for the cooling of bodies (the law of repose).

[1] Kronecker and Cutter (*Comptes Rendus Sciences*, vol. cxxix., p. 492 ; 1900).

[2] G. Cheyne, *Rules for Health and The Method of Prolonging Life* ; B. Ramazzini, *De Morbis Artificum Diatriba*, Modena, 1701 (translated into various languages).

[3] Boyet-Collard defined "*entrainement*" as "a disposition to perform certain work" (*Bulletin, Acad. Med.*, 1842).

[4] Morpurgo (*Arch. Ital. Biol.*, vol. xxix., p. 65, 1898).

[5] Zuntz and Schumburg (*Pflüeger's Archiv.*, vol. lxxxviii., p. 557, 1901).

The increase of energy expended is the corollary of the increase in the material operations of the organs. A greater acidity of the muscles is found after work, and this is attributed ([1]) to the formation of lactic acid (?), but this acidity is slight in moderate exercise with suitable intervals of repose. In the urine an increasing elimination of phosphorus is observed. This is very interesting, because some phosphoretted albumins exist in our cells, and Siegfried attributes to one of them, which is a part of the cellular nucleus, the power to decompose, giving out phosphorus, carbonic gas and lactic acid ; the centre of those oxydations, he says, is this nucleo-proteid,([2]) because it decreases in the muscles during work of any duration, whilst their acidity increases. Also the oxydation in organs, rich in nucleo, is extremely intense.([3]) There are, therefore, in the cells certain proteid reactions which are only manifested by an excretion of urates, as many experiments have proved. To these same reactions must, no doubt, be attributed the presence in the urine of a proteid derivative, creatinine, a derivative which is eliminated when the muscles are contracted statically, and not when they are working. This is an example of the variety of phenomena which take place in living substance,([4]) and of the part played by the proteids in the production of muscular force.

Work increases the elimination of water by the skin and the lungs, chiefly by perspiration. A subject who, in repose, lost 881 grammes of water in this way lost 2,475, 3,230 and even 7,381 grammes, after having performed increasingly hard work.([5]) A decrease of water in the blood is the result,([6]) accompanied by an irresistible need to restore the loss which gives rise to thirst. The density of the blood is slightly raised.([7])

In any study of the phenomena which occur during work we need to give particular attention to the nature of the food so that the proper proportions thereof in fats, proteids, and hydro-carbons may be discovered.

Metabolism both in repose and during work draws on the proteids in a fairly constant proportion of 60 to 65 grammes a day. It affects the carbo-hydrates, since they are the source of

([1]) Dreser (Centralblatt f. Physiol., vol. i., p. 195, 1887).
([2]) Siegfried (Hoppe-Seyler's Zeitsch., vol. xxi., p. 360, 1895–6).
([3]) Ralph Lillie (Amer. Journ. of Physiol., vol. vii., p. 412, 1902) ; Bonanni (Arch. di Farm Sper. e Sc. Affini, vol. ii., p. 8, 1902).
([4]) Harkink (C. R. Acad. Sciences d'Amsterdam, 30th Sept., 1911).
([5]) Atwater and Benedict (Bulletin, No. 136, p. 307 sqq.).
([6]) Kuthy, Zuntz and Schumburg, Lloyd Jones (Journ. of Physiol., vol. viii., 12).
([7]) Perspiration eliminates a few urates. The material expenditure is 0·80 grammes to 1·40 grammes of proteids per day, which can rise to 4 grammes (Atwater).

free energy transformable into mechanical work. At the same time it maintains the temperature of the body at about 37° C because this is a necessity. This expenditure in regulation appears to be at the expense of the fats in preference to all other alimentary substances (§ 110).

The activity of the muscles increases the activity of the humoral circulation,[1] (blood and lymph) provokes a speed of bodily combustion which can raise the general temperature by about 1°C [2] (§ 105), and assists the digestive functions to an appreciable extent.

Even the nervous centres profit by this general movement of the internal life as is shewn by their accentuated responsiveness to the rapidity of sensations or actions. It has been recognised, for instance, that the tactile sensibility is increased and rendered more delicate, notably in the case of typographers.

Men who devote much time exclusively to brain work feel the need of stimulating, by means of physical work, the nervous system, the respiratory organs, and the muscular power, which is almost suspended during the period of concentrated thought.

Any person who has the aptitude for work is fit to succeed in all professions or occupations because his muscles and his nerves are disciplined for this manifold end. Physiologcially, work breeds the aptitude for work.

146. The Limits of Work : Fatigue.—Fatigue can be defined as the effect which limits the duration of work. In the case of inanimate motors, owing to molecular alterations of a physical order, fatigue attacks all parts subjected to stresses, though very slowly. In the case of living motors, man and animals, the fatigue either decreases the intensity of the muscular effort, or reduces the contraction of the muscle. This will be further explained later. The result of fatigue is a lessened aptitude for work. The ergographic tracing (§ 119) shows this decrease in the quantity of work done by contraction. As already shown, the curve will descend quicker or slower according to the rhythm of the contractions and the intensity of the effort. It must be noted, as Imbert showed, that the real muscular fatigue is slow, although it is shown very quickly on the ergograph in consequence of the sensation of pain.[3] The conditions of the ergographic work of the finger generally cause discomfort and the traces in fig. 142 show this discomfort rather than the real fatigue of the flexor muscles.

---

[1] Mossu (*Comptes Rendus Biologia,* 1900).
[2] Forel (*Revue Scient.,* 1885) ; Marcet (*Archives Sc. Nat. de Geneva,* 1885) ; Woodhead (*Journal of Physiol.,* vol. xxiii., 1898–99) ; Atwater and Snell (*loc. cit.*).
[3] A. Imbert (*Comptes Rendus Acad. Sciences,* 31st October, 1910.)

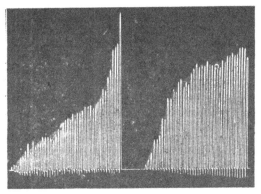

FIG. 142.

The curve of the fatigue varies very little, as a rule, in the same individual. The shape has been found to be the same for several years,[1] although sometimes it has undergone variations which

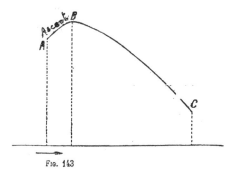

FIG. 143

rendered it unrecognisable. If a close examination is made of an ergogram, it will be found that its initial portion rises (fig. 143). This ascent is due to the fact that the nervous excitation produces, by its frequency, an internal massage of the muscles, and soon induces more regular functioning (Mosso, Richet), or, in other words, causes a latent addition to the excitations (Richet). It is known that, by strong electric excitations on the nerve the muscle can be caused to contract without any ascent.

As to the descending portion of the curve (BC), its decrease is all the more rapid the more defective the mechanical conditions under which the work is done or the physiological state of the

[1] A. Mosso (*Arch. Ital. Biol.*, vol. xiii., p. 123, 1890) ; A. Maggiora (*ibid.*, p. 187).

subject.[1] Hence after a prolonged period of work the ergographic curve falls rapidly. If we make use of the curve to estimate the degree of fatigue, it is important to remember that due allowance must be made for the effect of pain or discomfort.[2] Thus a very intense effort can provoke muscular or nervous pain, so that the curve may show pronounced fatigue before any considerable amount of work has been done.

Furthermore, in some occupations the fatigue is localised in a single limb, the arm, leg, or fingers. If so, the curve can only show a simple local fatigue. However, the ultimate effect is general, and the fatigue spreads to several muscular groups slowly and progressively.

" The muscles of the forearm tire the most rapidly, and give a lesser quantity of mechanical work as the result of the general fatigue produced by a walk of 10 kilometres." [3]

The secret of attaining the maximum yield from a workman is to proportion the elements of the work so that the muscles contract without pain or excess of local fatigue.

Ergograms reveal also, by their shapes and the quantities of work they represent, the influence of the numerous factors of human activity: the nature of this or that food, external temperature, position of the body, the magnitude of the effort to be produced, speed of walking, and the rhythm of the movements. By their means (§ 120) the speed of economical work and, to some extent, of muscular indefatigability, can be determined, of which the heart offers a curious example.

An ingenious observation of Galileo [4] may be quoted (1564-1642) : " The fatigue of the body of an animal depends, according to my idea, on the fact that he uses one of his parts to move the whole ; you will find, on the other hand, that the heart is indefatigable, because it only moves itself."

In feats of strength, such as wrestling, accidents are frequent : fractures, dislocations and abrasions ; hence the need for great resistance, so that the man only yields to fatigue. If, on the contrary, the man has organic defects, an accident will soon limit his activity, and he stops working without being as yet fatigued. The state of the heart and the lungs also contributes to the exertion of force, and the flow of blood and the respiratory flow are in proportion to the effort. The man capable of a great display of muscular force is characterised by the following features :—

[1] Grandis (*Arch. per le Science Medicihe*, vol. xxvi., p. 269, 1902).
[2] Pain is often the result of bad tools and a lack of workmanlike ability.
[3] A. Maggiora (*loc. cit.*, p. 217).
[4] Galileo *Opere*, Milan Edn., 1811, vol. xi., p. 558.

arched chest, upright stature, larger chest expansion than the average, and prominent muscles.

In exercise or work involving great speed, fatigue is due to the frequency of the nervous excitation, to the effort needed to attain the necessary speed. The exact nature of this fatigue is not known, but it is suspected that it takes its rise in the termination of the motor nerves. This kind of work draws on the nervous energy ; for example, stenographers and typists, etc., when working at great pressure, may make mistakes and miss out words. Men addicted to working at high speed do not develop muscularly, but have slim, rather thin, bodies, such as runners, dancers and fencers. They have generally less appetite than other men. Unfortunately, no precise rule can be formulated to estimate the degree of nervous fatigue.

147. Causes of Fatigue.—[1] Two phenomena, the one physical and the other chemical, appear to be the determining causes of fatigue. There is, on the one hand, an alteration of the elastic properties and of the cohesion of the muscular fibres. Their elastic force is greatly decreased, and they become pliable.[2] On the other hand, the matter of the muscles changes its chemical properties. It is clearly acid, and in its alcoholic extraction are found several toxic bodies capable of giving fatigue, if injected, into the bodies of animals.[3] The ponogeneous, toxic products (from πονεω I force myself) diminish the irritability so that the muscles no longer react except to stronger nervous excitations, and there follows, therefore, an excessive expenditure in getting into action, the origin of a new fatigue.[4] It has nearly always been stated that nerves, in contrast to the muscles, are indefatigable, even such important nervous centres as the brain. It would seem that this is not absolutely true, although [5] the nervous fibres are much less easily tired than the cells, and, as has been shown, all fatigue, in whichever organ it is localised, corresponds to the formation of toxic substances in the organism. Further, these latter increase, owing to the fact that the albuminoid reserves are drawn upon when the respiration is impeded (dypsnœa), as in the case of a tired man. And it has been found

---

[1] See an interesting article by Lee, " The Nature of Muscle Fatigue " (*Amer. Journ. of Physiol.*, vol. ii., p. 11, 1905).

[2] Boudet *De l'Elasticité Musculaire,* Thèse, Paris, 1880 ; A. Mosso (*Arch. Ital. Biol.*, vol. xxv., p. 371, 1896) ; Ioteyko (article, "Fatigue," in *Dictionnaire de Physiol.*, of Ch. Richet, 1904).

[3] A. Mosso, " La Fatigue," translated by Langlois, Paris, 1894.

[4] Trèves *Arch. Ital. Biol.*, vol. xxx., p. 1; 1898.

[5] J. Carvallo (*C. R. Sc.*, vol. cxxvii., p. 774, 1900) ; Frœhlich (*Zeit. Allg. Phys.*, vol. iii., p. 468, 1904).

that, under these conditions, the quantity of poisons in the muscles, the blood, and the urine increases considerably.[1]

The blood, by circulating more quickly during work, washes the poisons out of the tissues, and carries them to the suprarenal glands which secrete adrenalin by which they are neutralised [2] ; it oxydises them itself by the oxygen which it contains.

A state of repose is therefore necessary for this purification to take place. It allows, in addition, the elimination of the carbonic gas accumulated in the blood in consequence of the inter-organic combusions, which gas also acts as a muscular poison and lowers the power of the subject.[3] Finally, it allows the irritability to re-establish itself under the action of the oxygen gas.[4]

Fatigue necessitates rest, and is its determining circumstance ; it progresses with the work, and becomes eventually the cause of stoppage or of inhibition. From this point of view it safeguards the health of the subject.

148. Resistance to Fatigue : Endurance.—The resistance to fatigue is generally defined, as the product $F \times t$, in which F is the effort expended, the weight lifted, and t, the time, occupied by the effort. Thus, according to Gaillard, one cannot hold the arms stretched out for longer than 19 minutes. Haughton and Nipher [5] obtained the relation :

$$F^2 \times t = C^{te}.$$

From experiments on nearly 80 subjects, we have found that t varies from 20 to 78 seconds when a weight of 5 kilograms is held in each hand with extended arms until fatigue compels the subject to lower them ; t decreases all the quicker, the shorter the intervals of repose. Thus the product, $F^2 \times t$, varies very much from one subject to another, its highest value being found in sailors and dock labourers. Subjects having a strong will have more endurance than others. According to Chauveau, the resistance to fatigue is a function of the muscular elasticity, and according to Trèves, it is a functional tonus of the spinal cord, a reserve of nervous energy.[6] Waller claims that the centres of the spinal cord are the first to feel fatigue,[7] whilst Ioteyko holds that it is the motor terminations of the nerves.[8]

---

[1] Oddi and Carulli (*Arch. Ital. Biol.*, vol. xix., p. 384, 1893) ; Aducco (*Ibid.*, vol. viii., p. 238, 1887) ; Moitessier (*C. R. Biol.*, 1891, p. 573) ; Casciani (*La Riforma Medica*, 1896).

[2] Abelous (*Internat. Med. Congress at Rome*, 1894, vol. ii.) ; Langlois ; *Thesis*, Paris, 1897).

[3] Lothak de Lotha (*Comptes Rendus Sciences*, Aug., 1902).

[4] Spallanzani, *Mémoires sur la Respiration*, p. 352, Edition 1803.

[5] Haughton and Nipher (*Proceed. Roy. Soc.*, vol. xxiv.)

[6] Trèves (*Arch. Ital. Biol.*, vol. xxx., pp. 1–34, 1898).

[7] A. D. Waller, " The Sense of Effort " (*Brain*, vol. xiv., p. 179, 1892),

[8] J. Ioteyko (*Travaux Instit. Solvay*, iii., book 2, 1900).

There is, as already stated, a tendency, with most physiologists, to carry the seat of fatigue into the extreme points of the nervo-motor filaments, but the medullary centres seem more likely than the preceding, as, after a tiring period of work, a sensation of resistance which lasts for several hours is experienced.

During work lasting several days, the daily maximum is reached by the workmen who can the best resist discomfort, because the sensation of pain is often mingled with the sensation of fatigue. A sort of blunted sensibility protects men in certain occupations from the more or less painful efforts that they exert. To get an idea of a subject's resistance to fatigue, we should consider the sum of the work done or the expenditure of energy each day, rather than the static effort Ft. Neither the static nor the dynamic idea of endurance apply in a state of extreme fatigue or overwork, which springs from physiological causes and denotes bad organisation.

149. Nervous Fatigue : Intellectual Activity.—The activity of the muscles give rise to an expenditure of energy which is measurable in calories and an equivalent consumption of oxygen. The activity of the nerves is more obscure.

However, since there is a respiratory action in nervous matter, as in all tissues, Thunburg, of Lind, invented a little instrument, the *microrespirometer*, by means of which he found that the filaments of the nerves consume in pure air, at a temperature of 20° C., 22·20 cubic millimetres of oxygen per gramme per hour, and exhale 22 cubic millimetres of carbonic gas.[1] These exchanges of gas are a little more active when the tissue is in its place in the living animal.[2] surrounded by nourishing liquids. Even allowing a double expenditure of oxygen, 45 cubic millimetres per gramme-hour, it would be found that for the 1,700 grammes that the nervous mass of an adult represents, and in 24 hours :

0·045 c.c. × 1,700 × 24 = 1,836 cubic centimetres.

equals : 1,838 × 5·05 Cal. = 9·27 Cal.

This calorific production is about $\frac{4}{1000}$ of that of the entire organism taken in repose. It will be understood that no appreciable rise of temperature of the brain or of the nerves can be detected when they are excited electrically.[3]

[1] Thunberg (*Centralblatt f. Physiol.*, vol. xviii., p. 553, 1905), experiment on the brain of a dog ; Batelli and Stern obtained higher values (*Journ. de Physiol.*, 1907).

[2] A. Waller, *Lecons sur l'Electricité Animale*).

[3] De Boeck, *Thèse de Bruxelles*, 1893 ; Cremer (*Sitzungsb. d. Gesellsch. f. Morph. u. Physiol. zu. München,* 1896) ; A, Mosso (*Arch. Ital. Biol.*, vols. xviii. and xxii).

Benedict and Carpenter, [1] and Atwater [2] used the calorimetric chamber to measure the increase of calorific production of a man performing difficult intellectual operations. They obtained an excess of 1·32 cal. in three hours, about 4 per 1,000 exactly. The details of the observations are as follows :—

AVERAGE OF 22 EXPERIMENTS	REPOSE	INTELLECTUAL ACTIVITY.
Heat expended per hour	98·43 Cal.	98·80 Cal.
Vaporised water	37·80 gr.	39·23 gr.
Oxygen consumed	25·86 ,,	27·30 ,,
Carbonic gas exhaled	32·76 ,,	33·42 ,,
Temperature of the body (variation)	0·980°C	0·989°C
Pulsations per minute	74	79

" From the accumulated data of this series of experiments on the effects of intellectual work and its metabolism, it was found that the number of pulsations, as well as the temperature of the body, was slightly increased, and that the increase of the quantity of vaporised water was about 5%, that of the exhaled carbonic gas 2%, that of the oxygen about 6%, and that of the heat produced 0·50%, all under conditions of sustained cerebral effort, such as those of students during examinations.

" We are very strongly of the opinion that the results obtained in the course of these experiments do not indicate that the cerebral effort exerts any positive influence on the metabolic activity." [3]

Some unpublished experiments on the expenditure of oxygen of students doing mental work have led to the same conclusion. It can be stated that intellectual activity involves no corresponding measurable energetic expenditure.

In view of this small calorific expenditure, it is remarkable that intellectual activity produces fatigue, an undeniable fatigue, often more maiked than that of the muscles. We cannot indeed numerically compute that activity, but it does not follow that it cannot give rise to toxic wastes as in the working of muscles (Mosso). Mental activity must entail a material exchange and disassociation of various substances, generally phosphates, and it would seem to have an influence on the fatigue of the nervous terminations which make contact with the muscles, that is to say, it makes work more troublesome and sometimes even painful.

[1] Benedict and Carpenter (*Bulletin*, No. 208, p. 45–100, 1909).
[2] Atwater and Benedict (*Bulletin*, No. 136, p. 101 and 121).
[3] Benedict and Carpenter (*Bulletin*, No. 208, p. 100, 1909).

The excitability of the nervous centres is then lessened, and they show increasing inertia. It is thus that thought has more force in the morning than in the evening.[1] The sensitiveness of the skin has been measured by means of the *esthesiometer*, and it was found, with school children, that it diminished progressively in the course of the day's studies[2] or after prolonged mediation (§ 249). Whilst the liminal distance is 3·5 millimetres on the lower lip on the days of study, it is only 1 on Sunday, the day of repose. In young workmen (apprentices) the difference, on the contrary, is hardly appreciable. Finally, account must be taken of attention and reflexion which bring into play various muscles of the face, and the sustained contraction of which is a cause of fatigue. It can be stated, without presumption, that these muscular contractions have led several experimentalists astray who observed a rise of cerebral temperature (Mosso, Gley) or more active exchanges of gas when the nervous centres were either excited normally[3] or by an absorption of liquids, such as absinthe, which provoke epileptic fits.[4] Whatever may be its nature nervous fatigue is real and shows itself in proportion to the degree of attention demanded. Thus work which makes demands on the intelligence is certainly more onerous than operations which can be effected automatically. The intervention of thought is not a factor of economy in the human organism.

Cerebral fatigue diminishes not only the tactile sensibility, but also the general sensibility ; the personal equation increases and the aptitude for work weakens. It is good to vary occupations, so that the same nervous centres are not constantly called upon. The endeavour should be made to vary the occupations of the workman, and his leisure should be spent in pursuits which call forth different thoughts and feelings from those which his daily work brings to him. The weekly day of rest, which, through the ages, the Divine will has laid down as a sovereign physiological law, gives the needed opportunity for rest and recuperation, and is a check to the avarice of the employer. Thus the re-establishment of nervous and muscular energy results from repose. Too long an interruption produces a real need for activity, to which the return should be progressive. But, after a rest of 24 hours, a man can rapidly get into action again, unless bad use has been made of the holiday.

To sum up, fatigue is of a unique nature, being principally an intoxication : " The greatest pleasure that I have experienced

[1] A. Mosso, *Les Exercises Physiques et le Développement Intellectuel,* trans. Jaquet, 1904 ; Binet et Henri, *La Fatigue Intellectuelle.*

[2] Griessbach, *Energetik und Hyg. d. Nerven-Systems in die Schule,* Leipzig, 1895 ; R. Abelson, " Mental Fatigue " (Thèse de l'Univ. de Rennes, 1909).

[3] Becker and Olsen (*Die Umschau,* No. 19, 1912).

[4] Hill and Nabarro (*Journal of Physiology,* vol. xviii., p. 218. 1895).

in the course of my studies on fatigue," wrote Mosso, " is to have discovered that the lowering of force, due to the action of thought or of movement, produces identical effects. Whether man works muscles or brain, the nature of the fatigue is always the same, because there is only one actuating force in existence—nervous force." (1)

(1) A. Mosso (*loc. cit.*, p. 216) ; W. Weichardt, *Ueber Erdmüdungs-stoffe*, Stuttgart, 1910.

BOOK IV.

MAN AND HIS ENVIRONMENT

CHAPTER I.

The Internal Environment.

150. The Internal Environment.—Claud Bernard defined the blood as " the internal environment." Indeed, the blood distributes food and oxygen to the issues, and carries away the waste products of the interorganic combustion, the cells of the body living in it as in an atmosphere. But also everything which decreases the useful elements of this internal environment, and even more so, all substances capable of vitiating it, have a serious effect on the organism. From this point of view we must consider the quantity and the quality of the aliment, as well as the rôle of the nervines and the toxic products. Life itself is an incessant evolution, whose rapidity depends on various factors : the variable activity of the subjects, their age and their sex. There are many distinct problems which merit a detailed study, but which cannot be dealt with in this book. For these the reader should consult treatises on Hygiene. This book will only sum up the ideas concerning the relations of the internal environment of man to his work.

151. Influence of the Aliment.—It has already been shown that, unlike inanimate motors, the human machine does not feed entirely on a single combustible, whatever it may be. Its fuel must realise the fundamental condition of being capable of maintaining a reserve. Thus the " calorific power " does not alone define the aliment (see § 94).

From this point of view we will consider alcoholic drinks and the use of alcohol in general. The element in fermented liquids is ethyl alcohol, its formula being $C_2H_6O = 46$ grammes, and its heat of combustion reaching 7·069 Cal. per gramme.([1]) A dose of 1 gramme per kilogramme of a man's weight is not toxic. Therefore we desire to know the effects of a dose of 65 to 70 grammes a day. Theoretically, there are no chemical transformations by which sugar or any other really alimentary kind of substance can be derived from alcohol. Its part in the mechanical energy of the muscles is therefore doubtful. But it can burn directly and provide calorific energy.

([1]) Atwater and Benedict (*Bulletin*, No. 63, p. 54, 1899).

Is alcohol, therefore, a useful aliment ? Can it take the place of carbo-hydrates, fats or proteids in the ration ? This is how Atwater and Benedict [1] replied to the question : The subject, thirty-one years old, and weighing 68 kilogrammes, received 72 grammes of alcohol (equivalent to a bottle of Rhine wine) in an infusion of coffee (650 grammes) in the following manner: 11·50 grms. for breakfast, 7·60 grms. at 10.30 a.m., 19·10 grms. for lunch, 7·60 grms. at 3.30 p.m., 19·10 grms. for dinner, and 7·60 grms. in the evening. Making a deduction of about 3 grammes, which were eliminated naturally, by the lungs, the kidneys, and the skin, the dose was equal to 491 Calories, and it was substituted for a part of the ration. The American investigators observed that 2,283 Calories was registered in the calorimeter. The calculation relative to the metabolism of the ration containing alcohol led to 2,268 Calories. These results are fairly consistent, for in another experiment 2,394 Calories and 2,434 Calories were obtained.

In consequence, all, or nearly all, the alcohol was consumed in the organism and it was noticed that the subject got slightly fatter. Therefore Atwater and Benedict concluded that the kinetic energy resulting from the oxydization was absolutely equal to that of the combustion of the alcohol and that the latter served to protect the proteids and the fats against oxydization.[2] No reasoning prevails against the fact that " bound " energy, calorific, can have alcohol as its origin in the living cells.

Some experiments undertaken by Chauveau [3] also show that alcohol can be substituted for the aliments composing a ration, to a certain degree, but that this substitution is disadvantageous to the production of mechanical labour. Therefore, in a ration properly adapted for the performance of work by the subject, alcohol cannot replace carbo-hydrates and in this respect the conclusions of Atwater and others need emendation.[4]

Glycerine (triatomic alcohol) in small doses causes an economy in fats and carbo-hydrates, if sugar could be derived from it, it might even be a source of mechanical energy.[5]

The use of alcohol as a drink, in moderation, is not therefore to be condemned in principle. It stimulates the digestive

---

[1] Atwater and Benedict (*Bulletin*, No. 69, p. 23, *sqq.* ; *The Physiological Aspects of the Liquor Problem*, Part II., p. 149, *sqq.*).
[2] *Loc. cit.*, p. 112.
[3] A. Chauveau (*Comptes Rendus Acad. Sciences*, vol. cxxxii., p. 65, 110, 1901).
[4] Rosemann (*Pflüeger's Archiv.*, vol. lxxxvi., p. 327, 1901 ; xciv., p. 557, 1903). etc.
[5] Munk (*Pflüeger's Archiv.*, vol. xlvi., p. 303, 1890) ; Leo (*ibid.*, vol. xciii., p. 269, 1903).

mucus, provokes the flow of the (¹) gastric and pancreatic (²) juices, and is also a general stimulant to the nutritive operations, promoting the growth of the organism.(³)

Finally, it is an excitant of the muscular fibre, probably by a nervous route, increasing its power and retarding its fatigue,(⁴) at least for some time.(⁵)

152. Unfortunately alcohol is abused ; a physiological dose is soon exceeded and becomes a poisonous dose. All the effects a.e then disastrous. The organism cannot defend itself, because it only eliminates, very slowly, small quantities of alcohol by the urine, the perspiration and the respirations.(⁶) The mechanical activity of the muscles increases the elimination (⁷) a little, but never sufficiently to neutralise the dangerous action of this poison on the nervous centres. In strong enough doses, more than 100 grammes a day, alcohol is a na_cotic, and a very penetrating, posionous substance. It is often as poisonous in itself as in the essences known as "spirits." Some of these essences are *convulsive*, others *narcotic*. In the former category are, in decreasing order of their power, the essences of sage, absinthe, hyssop, rosemary, savory, fennel, sweet marjoram, calamint, and barilica. In the latter are thyme, wild thyme, lavender, rue and balm-mint.

Thus 5 centigrammes of essence of sage, introduced into the blood of a dog weighing 7 kilogrammes would give him three epileptic fits, and 25 centigrammes would kill him quickly. Man is more sensitive to these effects, for whilst it requires 3 grammes of essence of hyssop to cause convulsions in a dog weighing 7 kilogrammes, 2 grammes would be sufficient for a vigorous man if he were fasting.(⁸)

According to Triboulet and Mathieu,(⁹) it would need to kill a dog weighing 7 kilogrammes.

Real cognac	108 cc.
Kirsch	109
— Cider	108
— Wine lees	103
— Plum brandy	103
Heady alcohol (bad taste)	106

(¹) Radzikowski (*Ibid.*, vol. lxxxiv., p. 513, 1901).
(²) Gizelt (*Centralb. f. Physiol.*, vol. xix., p. 851, 1906).
(³) G. Pierrotti (*Giornale della Reale Soc. Ital. d'Igiene di Milano*, 1906).
(⁴) Lee and Salant (*Amer. Journ. of Physiol.*, vol. viii., pp. 61–74, 1903).
(⁵) E. Destrée (*Journ. Méd. de Brux.*, 1897, p. 537), L. Schnyder (*Pflüger's Arch.*, vol. xciii, p. 451, 1903).
(⁶) Gréhant and Nicloux (*Comptes Rendus Biologie*, 1899, 1900, 1903).
(⁷) W. Woelz and A. Baudrexel (*Pflüger's Arch.*, vol. clxii., parts 1 and 2, 1911).
(⁸) Cadéac and Meunier (*Comptes Rendus Biologie*, 1891, p. 213.
(⁹) Triboulet and Mathieu (*Ibid*, 1901).

Besides being nervous poisons, alcoholic drinks decrease the muscular power very materially,[1] by simple ingestion in the stomach. In view of their injurious effects on the organs and the general depression of strength which they cause [2] their use ought to be strictly forbidden.

Intoxicating drinks constitute a source of distraction, in the strict sense of the word ; they drive away the cares that assail the spirit of man ; they stupify him momentarily, and are the refuge of the weak minded.

Every people has its favourite drink. For example, there is the "koumiss" (fermented mare's milk) of the Turks and Mongolians ; the millet beer of the Negroes ; the sago wine of the Malays ; the aloe wine of the Mexicans ; the spice wine of the Polynesians ; the palm wine of the Arabs ; the "betsabetsa" (the juice of the sugar cane fermented) of the Malgaches.

The conclusion drawn from the preceding facts is that alcohol is a thermogeneous aliment, and not a dynamogeneous aliment. In addition, even in comparatively small doses, it constitutes a danger to the human economy. The workman would therefore do well to abstain from it completely, because it is he, as statistics show (§ 343) who has a tendancy to abuse it.[3]

153. Aliments of Economy.—Alcohol in small doses is therefore an aliment of economy relatively to any one of the three kinds of aliments.

Is this same character found in coffee, tea, kola nuts, etc ?

Here are the facts on the subject.[4]

Three persons, adults, accomplished work of 50,000 kilogrammetres each on the bicycle dynamometer ; they consumed a maintenance ration. Then 5 grammes of "dried" tea (taken infused) was substituted isodynamically for the bread in that ration. Equilibrium was realised with an economy of 125·50 Cal., 157·56 Cal., and 161·59 Cal. respectively on the daily expenditure.

This economy was constant during several days.

Numerous populations (Russians, Moroccans) make a continual use of strongly sugared tea. According to our own observations, the Moroccan of average condition absorbs, per day, 15 to 20 cups of tea, representing nearly 12 grammes of dried tea and 400

---

[1] Gréhant and Quinquaud (*Comptes Rendus Sciences*, 1891, p. 416).
[2] De Boeck and Günzburg (*Bull. Soc. Med. Mentale Belg.*, 1899, p. 307) ; Kurg, Büdin, Mayer, etc. (*Psych. Arbeiten*, vols. iii. and iv., 1900-1).
[3] See Louis Jacquet, *L'Alcool* ; Preface by G. Clemenceau, Paris, 1913 (Masson).
[4] Jules Amar, *Le Rendement de la Machine Humaine*, p. 76.

grammes of sugar. His strength and resistance to fatigue are remarkable. Afghans use a substitute for tea called "catha edulis," which enables them to make long night marches and increases their muscular strength.[1]

154. Coffee taken as an infusion and isyodynamically to bread, into the ration of two persons who produce 52,147 kilogrammetres of work each, gave an economy of 139. Calories and 246 Calories. Thirty grammes of roasted coffee being taken.[2] In this rôle of economy it seems certain that coffee, taken in small quantity, stimulates the muscular and nervous functions,[3] provokes the digestive secretions, and aids the general metabolism.

155. Cocoa, which contains 16% of theine, as used to make chocolate, acts less energetically than coffee ; but it is more nutritive.

Kola nuts are richer in cafein by 2 to 3%, and their favourable action on muscular work and intellectual activity is most marked.

"In the evening," writes Chevalier, the explorer of the Congo and the Ivory Coast, "when we had to keep awake, not only did we do so easily by chewing a kola nut, but the mental activity was stimulated, and the thoughts flowed from our pens. Our work finished we went to sleep as easily as usual, and we felt no depression the next day." [4] Fatigue is retarded, and endurance is considerably increased.[5]

156. Pimento (*capsicum annuum*) and butyric acid have also proved to be aliments of economy. Four capsicums introduced into a living ration produced an economy of 298 calories. If the ration is not diminished the weight increases 400 grammes a day on an average, and yet the energetic contribution of these four capsicums only equals 21 Calories.

Finally, rancid butter, representing 4·21 grms of butyric acid enabled a subject, who produced 48,290 kilogrammetres and expended 3,576·64 Cal. to realise an economy of 485 Calories.

These few experiments demonstrate the general effect of the nervine aliments on the expenditure. They afford protection to the organic reserves, whose co-efficient of energetic transformation they appear to modify. If condiments—salt, vinegar, pepper, etc.—are examined in the same way, it is found that they lower the muscular power a little.[6]

---

[1] J. F. Oven (*Journ. of Soc. of Chem. Ind.*, vol. xxix., p. 1091., 30th Sept., 1910).
[2] Jules Amar, *loc. cit.*
[3] F. Ranson (*Journal of Physiol.*, vol. xlii., p. 144, 1911).
[4] A. Chevalier and Perrot, *Les Kolatiers*, p. 471, Paris, 1911.
[5] W. Barr (*Ther. Gazette*, vol. xx., p. 221, 1896).
[6] Féré ,*Travail et Plaisir*, 1904, Paris (Alcan).

157. Fasting and Inanition.—The insufficiency of the quantity of food, the state of fasting itself, does not reduce the expenditure in 24 hours appreciably, the reduction being 5% to 6% the first day, according to Atwater's measurements, after which the value tends to become constant. Thus the organism shows a certain independence in regard to the amount of food taken. But the general forces diminish progressively. The contraction of the muscles is retarded, and they become tired without having done any work.[1]

In a state of inanition, it is especially the muscles which suffer, and lose their power. The intellectual faculties resist, because the nervous substance is the least tried. Thus determinations made on a pigeon, a cat, and a dog gave a very significant percentage of utilisation, at the end of a long fasts:

Skeleton	21%	to	19%
Muscles	42%		70%
Heart,	45%		55%
Spleen	71%		75%
Pancreas	64%		39%
Lungs	22%		30%
Brain and spinal column	2 (Chossat) [2]		1·1 (Seldmair) [3]

Clearly this shows that the organs which sustain physical life are more affected than those which support intellectual life.

An inanitiated subject regains his weight more quickly by absorbing ternary substances rather than proteids, provided that the latter are in the proportion of 2 grammes per kilogramme of weight. For example, after fasts of forty hours at a time, a man weighing 54 kilogrammes who produced 36,089 kgm. = 85 Calories of work on the bicycle dynamometer in four hours, was given regularly a ration of 2,600 Calories comprising 1,750 Calories of carbo-hydrates. The results were as follows :—

	Cal.	Cal.	Cal.	
Proteids	93	652	330	Averages
Fats	750	191	513	of several days.
Gain of weight	433 gr.	707 gr.	1,218 gr	

The fats assure the conservation of the weight of the body better than the proteids, but carbo-hydrates are even better.[4]

The effect of an insufficiency of aliments is more apparent in children than in adults, because of the greater speed of growth in the former (§ 99).

---

[1] Gaglio (*Arch. p. Les Sc. Méd.*, vol. xvii., p. 301, 1884).
[2] Chossat (*Mém. Acad. Sc.* vol. viii., p. 438, 1843).
[3] Seldmair (*Zeitsch. f. Biol.* vol. xxxvii., p. 41, 1899).
[4] Jules Amar, *Le Rendement*, pp. 79-82.

158. Influence of Physiological Troubles.—In all the preceding circumstances, the physiological functions (circulation, respiration, etc.); were presumed to be normal. The blood fulfils its function as the vehicle of the oxygen and is the purifying stream of the tissues. Therefore a compression which impedes the circulation (tight clothes or defective attitudes when working ([1]) decreases the muscular activity. Anæmia aggravates this symptom and produces fatigue ([2]) ; the fibres and nervous cells becoming less excitable,([3]) without doubt through insufficiency of oxygen.

Nothing must interfere with the respiration which assures the constant supply of oxygen. The accumulation of carbonic gas in the blood as a consequence of incomplete expiration, as sometimes happens in the course of work, causes muscular weakening of toxic origin,([4]) and lowers the nervous excitability.([5]) An intoxication, from the same cause, produces breathlessness ; this happens in work which is so rapid that insufficient time is given for the elimination of all the carbon dioxide (§ 112).

It is an accepted fact that fatigue accompanies this toxic phenomenon that has its source in the blood. For instance, the poisons in the urine and sweat will injure the organism specially the muscular activity unless they are eliminated.([6]) The cleanliness of the skin and a suitable quantity of drink assist that elimination.

Returning to one of the causes of fatigue, auto-intoxication (§ 147), it will be noted that the muscular power of a subject lessens with fatigue.([7]) Extreme fatigue leads to exhaustion and then grave troubles, with symptoms of momentary paralysis show themselves ([8]) ; some of the muscular and nervous fibres being lacerated internally.([9]) Often contraction appears, giving pain for some time. Over-exertion can be fatal. The example of the soldier of Marathon—see the admirable statue in the gardens of the Tuileries by the sculptor Cortot—who, after running an almost superhuman race to bring the tidings of victory, fell

---

([1]) Atwater and Benedict (*Bulletin*, No. 136, p. 180, 1903), etc.
([2]) A. Maggiora (*Arch. Ital. Biologie*, vol. xiii., p. 217) ; Jensen (*Pflüger's Arch.*, vol. lxxxvi., p. 47, 1901).
([3]) Aducco (*Arch. Ital. Biol.*, vol. xiv., p. 136, 1890 ; Baglioni (*ibid.*, vol. xlii., p. 83, 1904).
([4]) Lothak de Lotha (*Comptes Rendus Acad. Sc.*, Aug., 1902).
([5]) G. Weiss (*Comptes Rendus Biol.*, 1900, p. 444 ; *Journal de Physiol.*, 1903, p. 239).
([6]) Aducco (*Arch. Ital. Biol.*, vol. x., p. 1, 1888) ; Casciani (*La Riforma Medica*, 1896, June).
([7]) Benedicenti, *loc. cit.*
([8]) Tréves (*Arch. Ital. Biol.*, vol. xxx., p. 1, 1898).
([9]) Th. Hough (*Amer. Journ. of Physiol.*, vol. vii., p. 76, 1902).

down dead as soon as he had accomplished his mission, is often quoted, and not without reason.

Before the extreme limit of exhaustion is reached, tiring work gives rise to feverishness accompanied by pains in the joints, which are also of toxic origin.[1] Moreover, intense labour raises the temperature of the body a little, from 1° to 1·5° C., and that without any inconvenience.

Age only causes insignificant modifications to the organism between 20 and 50 years of age ; human strength progresses up to 40, but is not marked by any physiological troubles. As has been seen already (§ 142) the rhythms of the respirations and the pulse alone are modified. There are also differences in the two sexes ; in particular, the rhythms are slightly quicker in woman and the blood not quite so rich in red corpuscles. The physiological state presents greater differences in the period of pregnancy, the muscular power of the woman then decreasing. All fatigue should then be spared her, otherwise both mother and offspring will suffer.[2]

There are also individual characteristics ; thus obese subjects have blood that is less rich in red corpuscles ; the blood of muscular subjects on the contrary is very rich in red corpuscles (Malassez), and they tire less quickly. Of course normal internal conditions are not found in all workmen, for intemperance brings troubles which predisposes them to work but feebly. It is profitable to watch over their health, and to do what is necessary to protect it, in spite of themselves.

158. Influence of the Senses.—The rôle of the senses is obvious, notably that of sight, of hearing, and of touch. They can be developed and rendered more useful.

Good sight contributes to the perfection of work. Workmen have not all got the same eyesight ; therefore the short-sighted should not work without glasses, because they stoop to see better. what they are doing, and are fatigued by that defective attitude. Sight permits a better equilibrium of the body.

In certain trades—painters, dyers, decorators, etc.—the workman must be able to distinguish colours, and this often needs education. " *Daltonism* " (colour blindness) is the inability to distinguish between red, yellow and green. About 4% of men are Daltonists, but women very seldom.

Hearing assists the workman in his normal conduct in the same way that it gives the note to the singer ; thus it assists the periodic action of the tools, as smiths swing their hammers to a

<hr>

[1] A. Mosso (*Arch. Ital. Biol.*, 1890, vol. xiii., p. 165),
[2] René Laufer (*Nouvelle Revue*, 1907, p. 11).

rhythm which increases their work and prevents their hammers interfering with each other.

Finally touch helps the execution of the task by developing agility, ability and precision ; it is the eyesight of the blind man.

159. Favourable Influences : Massage, Sleep, Rest.—Amongst the influences which are favourable to muscular power are massage and sleep.

Massage, or kneading of the muscles, repairs them. This fact, ascertained by ancient scholars and utilised by the athletes of all times, is absolutely true. The following facts are the result of the ergographic researches of Maggiora :

Massage relaxes the muscles, made stiff by work, increases their resistance, and retards their fatigue.

Its effect is proportional to its duration, within certain limits.

Kneading is better than percussion and friction.

Muscle, weakened by fasting, is made resistant by massage.

Muscle, weakened by walking, want of sleep, or excessive intellectual work, is restored by massage.

Finally, massage, without circulation of the blood is useless. [1] Combined with the action of a hot bath, it re-establishes the muscular power in its integrity.[2]

The Chinese have the reputation of being very able masseurs.

The influence of sleep is restorative no less than that of massage. Sleep is complete repose, reducing the energetic expenditure by $\frac{14}{100}$ of its static value (§ 103) reducing also the sum of nervous excitations which reach us when awake, and suppressing all communications of external stimuli. An excess of aliment can not replace sleep,[3] seeing that the repose of the nerves and the muscles is necessary for their restoration. Benedicenti found out by means of the " myotonometer " (§ 70) that the muscles are more retractile and resist distension better after a deep sleep.[4]

The duration of sleep is an important factor in the re-establishment of the equilibrium of the forces which have been upset by work. At least seven hours is necessary. It should be at night and free from disturbances. In that period the energetic expenditure is lowered, as we have already said, and the temperature of the body decreases by 0·8°C. between 8 and 12 o'clock (§ 103).

[1] A. Maggiora (*Arch. Ital. Biol.*, vol. xvi., p. 245, 1891) ; Ruge (*Englemann's Archiv. f. Phys.*, 1901, p. 466).
[2] Trèves (*Arch. Ital. Biol.*, vol. xxx., p. 14, 1898).
[3] A. Maggiora (*Arch. Ital. Biol.*, vol. xiii., p. 187).
[4] Benedicenti (*Arch. Ital. Biol.*, vol. xxv., 1896).

Repóse and sleep are inevitable consequences of the law of rhythm which appears to govern life and constitute its means of defence (see § 149 as to the weekly rest).

160. Moral Influences.—The effect of the moral and mental condition of the workman on his physical strength and output must not be overlooked. If he is in a contented frame of mind, the effects of fatigue are less felt and the reparation of his tissues is more rapid. " The happy always recover," said Ambrose Pare! If, in his leisure hours, he can be interested and amused, he is likely to show more energy in his daily work. Both the financial incentive of higher wages and the innate pride in good work lend to improve his output.

On the other hand, there are many moral factors which tend to decrease his output, such as anxiety and sickness in his family. Among some peoples even religious prejudices, which forbid work on certain days and prohibit certain forms of food, unfavourably affect output.

In a person suffering from mental trouble the contractability of the muscle decreases. Lombard showed this in the following manner : one knee being placed on the other, whilst one foot touches the ground, the extensor muscle of the upper leg is tapped with a hammer. At each stroke the foot lifts and an apparatus attached to the toes registers the force of the contraction. When the subject is suffering from mental trouble the movement decreases perceptibly.[1]

Interest in his trade has also a powerful moral influence ; therefore a master should see that a workman is not removed from a task that he likes and to which he is accustomed, and given one to which he is not suited by temperament. A man's natural bent should not be thwarted, and since the love of money has replaced the love of occupation or trade, it is necessary to ascertain his vocation and to make it permanent by enlisting his self-interest.

161. Professional Influences.—Amongst the internal factors in work must be mentioned ability and skill. These are qualities which will increase output, and are only acquired by habit and thought. The workman who pays no attention to his work accomplishes it without benefiting his education and will not make progress. He will become a mere machine, and he will not notice the defective attitudes which tire him, or eliminate unnecessary action of muscles ; he will not follow the example of the good, skilful workman who, next to him, performs his task by economising his strength, thereby producing more work.

---

[1] W. C. Lombard (*Journ. of Physiol.*, vol. xiii., p. 1, 1892),

Therefore employers, notably American engineers, distinguish very clearly between the first-class workman, who studies and rectifies faults in his movements and the second-rate workman who entirely lacks this perspicacity.[1]

This distinction is necessary, because only the men of the first category are capable of considerably increasing their work and hence deserve to be well paid.

162. Morphological and Dynamic Influences.—A classification of human types can be made on the basis of the development and the structure of the body, with regard to aptitude for activity, requiring either strength or speed. On this basis rests the new science of dynamic morphology, which treats of the possible relations between the plastic and functional aspects of the human body. It does not deal with differences of temperaments, a very vague subject, but with the predominance of this or that physiological function. One man may be of the digestive type, eating much and working slowly but for a long time ; another of the muscular type, that is to say, able to bring into a play a considerable force, never of very long duration ; a third belongs to the respiratory type, which offers the advantage of being able to keep up a relatively large effort for a long time ; finally there exists a nervous type, which, by his power of rapidly initiating movements, works with economy.

There is no doubt that each of the above four types of men is suited to a certain form of activity more than to any other. Everyone has noticed that dockers, navvies, and others who do laborious work, do it without haste, as a rule, but also almost without respite ; this class of men must be abundantly fed. The Americans (Taylor), to distinguish them, called them the " bovine " type. Their appearance is robust, the limbs of average length, or short, but thick and strong, with solid and massive joints ; the chest is wide, the legs well apart, forming a good basis of support. Nevertheless, this digestive type is not very muscular. If his muscles develop, he passes into the muscular type, but the gain in " power " is less than the loss in continuity of action. This is why wrestlers with highly-developed muscles are bad workers.

The digestive type can also have long limbs which allow him to perform movements of great amplitude. The runners of the East cover very long distances with a long and rapid stride, without resting. For carrying small weights constantly, such men have a big yield.

The man of respiratory type is more like the nervous type than the preceding ; he can undertake work of a certain duration, and

---

[1] Gilbreth, *Motion Study*.

display great staying power, but he is not fit for exertions of strength. The nervous type can sustain, however, a considerable effort, provided that it does not last long ; this rapid exhaustion is due to the double expenditure, muscular and nervous, especially to the latter. The resistance of his organs of movement is not very great.

In considering the physical qualities of individuals we must classify them according to their degree of intelligence and their personal equation, and distinguish between naturally quick and naturally slow workers. Satisfactory selection in industry means that each individual shall be given that work which shall make the best use of all his qualities, with a consequent increase in his productive power. Increased output, however, should logically bring a higher wage.

163. Social Influences.—Amongst the internal factors of human activity can be included those which are derived from social hygiene, namely: 1. The hygiene of the body, rational feeding, prophylaxis, the well-being of the man from the physiological point of view: 2. The hygiene and the development of the mind, or, rather, the moral qualities of the worker, which are a result of his well-being and his environment. The action of the social environment is obvious; man is influenced by it, and he acquires a tendency to do that which he sees others do, be it good or bad. (¹)

As solidarity becomes more and more the law of workmen's organizations, the syndicates impose on all their adherents the acceptance of long-studied tactics, in which the master insists in seeing a real danger to his own interests. We are convinced, on the contrary, that these interests agree with those of the employers. The science of energy estimates exactly the daily sacrifices of the workers and professional technics teach the methods of increasing the human yield. Both demonstrate the possibility of lowering the cost price of the unit of work, and consequently of raising wages in a certain measure, or, of reducing the day's work judiciously. Such is the result of the scientific progress of the last few years (see Book VI., Chap. iv.). It would be in vain to deny it and not to wish, by better conditions, for the workmen to contribute to the necessary work of social hygiene, which must result in justice, concord, and common prosperity.

(¹) Pilker, *Die Grundgesetze des Neuro-Psych.*, Berlin, 1900.

CHAPTER II.

THE EXTERNAL ENVIRONMENT.

164. The Atmosphere.—Human life develops in an atmospheric environment which extends to a distance of 150 to 160 kilometres from the earth's surface. At the inhabited levels of the earth, the composition of the air, not counting rare gases and impurities, is :—

Nitrogen ([1]) : 79%   Oxygen : 21% (in volumes).

There is a trace of carbon-dioxide about 0·3%. The amount of water vapour in the atmosphere varies and gives the hygrometric state of the environment (see § 173). Finally, microbes, solid and invisible particles, "*electric grains*" ([2]) are disseminated in the normal atmosphere. Accidentally the air may contain more or less toxic or deleterious gases (sulphurous acid gas, chlorine, carbon-monoxide, etc.).

The purity of the air increases with altitude ; the disturbing effect of the nearness of the earth from this point of view, can still be felt at a height of 3 kilometres. Clouds are found below this level and up to 10 kilometres.([3])

The temperature of the air varies in the twenty-four hours : the maximum occurring towards 2 o'clock in the afternoon, and the minimum about sunrise, at 8 o'clock in the morning in January, and at 4 o'clock in the morning in July :

There is, in consequence, a variation of temperature equal to 3·6° C. in January and 9·3° C. in July.

The temperature of the air varies with altitude and latitude.

The weight of air pressing on the surface of a body (that of a man, for instance) at a given altitude, is called the atmospheric or barometric pressure. The normal pressure at sea level is capable of sustaining a column of mercury 760 millimetres in height. The weight of a cubic centimetre of mercury being 13·6 grammes, the corresponding weight of the barometric column is 1033 grammes. The average surface of an adult's body being about 2 square metres, the total atmospheric pressure on the body is approximately :

$$20,000 \times 1,033 = 20,660 \text{ kilogrammes.}$$

([1]) This includes 0·94% of argon, according to Leduc.
([2]) A term due to M. Langevin. They are usually called ions.
([3]) See Wegener's interesting monograph, *Fortschritte der Naturvissenschaft-forschung der Abderhalden*, vol. iii., 1911).

The effect of this great pressure is nil because it acts equally both inside and outside the body.

The influence of the various factors in the external environment will now be considered in detail, so far as they affect the conditions of industrial labour.

165. Influence of Temperature.—The influence of the temperature of the environment on the vital organism is of first importance. Numerous observations have demonstrated that decrease in the temperature of the environment causes a proportionate increase in the expenditure of the organism. Cold stimulates vital combustions; heat relaxes them.

Bodies cool by radiation. The lower the external temperature, the more the cutaneous surface of the animal radiates and tends to lose heat. The speed of cooling of hot bodies increases proportionally to the excess of their own temperature over that of the external environment. This is Newton's law. If the human body is represented by a circle of hot water (fig. 144), the radiation is measured by the number of small calories emitted by a surface of 1 square centimetre. As the emission, according to Newton's law, is proportional to the difference of temperature between the surface, and the external environment, the emissive power, K, is the number of calories per second per degree difference.

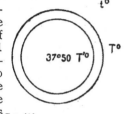

Fig. 144.

T′ and T are the internal and external temperature of the skin : t is that of the surrounding air.

Thus for a difference of temperature $(T - t)$, the loss per second per square centimetre of the radiating surface will be:

$$q_1 = K_1 (T - t) \text{ small calories.}$$

Radiation tends to diminish the temperature of the body, and therefore more heat has to be produced by the body in order to maintain its temperature constant (about 37·50° C.) by producing more heat (chemical regulation). The value of the emissive power K varies according to the nature and the colour of the radiating surface.

In addition to the radiation, the air, in contact with the skin and constantly changing, carries away a quantity of heat by convection. The loss due to convection depends not only on the difference of temperature $(T - t)$ and on the area of the surface, but also on the shape of the latter. According to Péclet's classic researches, this factor can be represented by a co-efficient, $K_2 = $ ·000066 $c.$ per square centimetre per second; whence :

$$q_2 = K_2 (T - t)$$

in small calories.

The calorific loss per square centimetre per second is, therefore, in all :

$$q_1 + q_2 = (K_1 + K_2)\ (T - t).$$

Let it be noted that the temperature, T, of the external surface of the skin is neither easy to measure nor constant. The temperature of the organism, about 37·50°C, is maintained by a calorific regimen, a permanent flow of heat. The characteristic of the regimen is that the skin receives on its internal surface as much heat as it loses on its external surface. It is easily proved that it receives :

$$q_3 = (K_1 + K_2)\ (37·50°C - T'),$$

T' being the internal cutaneous temperature (see fig. 144). Hence :

$$q_3 = q_1 + q_2.$$

But the transmission of the heat takes place through a thickness e, of the skin, whose conductivity has to be ascertained. The number of small calories able to traverse a surface of 1 square centimetre with a thickness of 1 centimetre in one second, and for a difference of temperature equal to 1°C between the internal and external walls, is called the co-efficient of conductivity c. In these conditions the heat transmitted is :

$$q_4 = c\ \frac{(T' - T)}{e}$$

in small calories, and

$$q_4 = q_3 = q_1 + q_2 = q \text{ (generally).}$$

The advantage of thus having three expressions for the same calorific loss is that we can eliminate T and T', which are not known, and solve the problem with known temperatures only ; 37·50° C. for the internal, and $t°$ for the external (the air temperature). A very simple operation will give :

$$q = \frac{cK_2\ (K_1 + K_2)\ (37·50°C - t)}{c\ (K_1 + 2K_2) + eK_2\ (K_1 + K_2)}.$$

The average thickness of the human skin $e = 0·2$ cms. The co-efficients are :

$c\ (^1) = 0·00060\ c$; $K_1 = 0·00015\ c$; $K_2 = 0·000066\ c$. This gives :

$$q = 497 \times 10^{-7} \times (37·50°C - t°).$$

Per twenty-four hours, or in (3,600 × 24) seconds, a square centimetre of skin will lose a quantity of heat :

$$Q_1 = 0·004294\ (37·50°C - t°) \text{ in great calories.}$$

(¹) Jules Lefèvre estimates c at 0·00060 c ; Adamkiewiez found for the muscles 0·00012 c., certainly too small a value, and Bordier's experiments also resulted in 0·00014 c.

As the surface of an adult is 19,900 square centimetres approximately, the loss will be :

$$Q = 85 \cdot 450 \text{ Cal. } (37 \cdot 50°C — t°)$$

in an external environment of $t°$. This formula should be remembered.

166. Examples.—Let there be an environment at 9°C. Replacing $t°$ by 9°C in the expression for q we have :

$$Q = 2435 \text{ Calories.}$$

At this same temperature, Jules Lefèvre [1] measured a total of 3,216 calories. From which we can infer a physiological expenditure of 781 Calories, independent of the thermic influences of the exterior.

Let $t = 20°C$ (as in the American experiments). Then: $Q = 1,496$ Calories, which gives :

$$1,496 + 781 = 2,277 \text{ Calories.}$$

as the total static expenditure, of which about ⅔ are expended in the regulation of the temperature.

In a hot environment (in the tropics) at 37·50° C. we have $37 \cdot 5° — t° = O$; the loss being zero and the organism reduced to its minimum expenditure of energy. Further, suppose a temperature, t, higher than 37·50° C. The organism would not gain by it, because outside its thermic regulation, it could not employ the heat for any physiological service. On the contrary, it is a source of embarrassment, owing to the excessive perspiration which results (Rubner's Physical Regulation, § 108).

Some special examples are interesting. In the case of children as their surface is relatively large, the calorific loss is relatively higher than in the adult. Very thin people experience, for the same reason, an excessive loss, to which they respond by more calorific production. Fat men, on the contrary, have a relatively small surface.· Nevertheless, the intensity of their combustions does not suffice to cover the necessary expenditure, and it is the same with emaciated subjects with very little muscle.

167. Other Effects of Temperature.—It has been recognised that the contractions of the muscles become rapid and energetic in an environment of + 20° C., and that at this same temperature the resistance to fagitue is a maximum.[2] In addition, cellular renovation is accelerated between + 37° C. and + 40° C. Directly opposite effects are observed at low temperatures.[3]

---

[1] *Bioénergétique*, p. 405.
[2] J. Carvallo (*Comptes Rendus Acad. Sciences*, vol. cxxx, 1900).
[3] R. Penzo (*Arch. p. le Sc. Med.*, vol. xvi., p. 129, 1892) ; Bizzozero and Sacerdotti (*Giornale della R. Acad. d. Med. di Torino*, vol. lix., No. 5, 1896.).

The excitability of the nerves increase at temperatures from 0° up to 40° C., so that a rise of temperature is felt more particularly in the nervous properties,[1] the movements of man.

A very hot day in Paris, for example, is distinguished by the same effects on the people as in a tropical town. This was the case in July and August, 1911.

168. Temperature retards or accelerates the respiration according to whether it is high or low. The gaseous exchanges which increase with the lowering of the temperature,[2] are due to the increasing intensity of the combustions.

Intense heat increases the rhythm of the respirations, and gives rise to a veritable palpitation (Richet). It is seen in dogs when they pant in the sun. It causes profuse perspiration,[3]

The gaseous exchanges, within certain limits of temperature, are easier when the external environment is cold ; the cold air penetrates the pulmonary membrane by a sort of *thermo-endosmosis*, towards the warmer surrounding matter.[4] In addition, it contains more oxygen than the same volume of hot air, which is a favourable condition for the economical expenditure of the organism.

Respiration in an overheated atmosphere is therefore unfavourable to physiological labour. In regard to the discomfort due to high temperatures Coulomb made some observations on the work carried out by French soldiers in Martinique.[5] He concluded that in such a tropical climate, where exertion caused profuse perspiration, the daily output of work was less than half that which could be effected in a temperate climate.[6]

169. When the temperature exceeds certain limits, the organism suffers. Extreme cold demands intense calorific production to maintain the internal temperature constant, while excessive heat induces profuse perspiration.

In inhabited countries the extremes of the average monthly temperature rarely exceed + 36° C. and — 22° C. The variation is at the outside 60° C. In Europe and Northern Africa the greatest cold only reaches — 14° C., and the most intense heat + 36° C. Such temperatures do not trouble the physiological

[1] G. Weiss (*Journal de Physiol.*, 1903, p. 31).
[2] Vernon (*Journal of Physiol.*, 1897, p. 443).
[3] Ch. Richet (*Dictionnaire* of Richet, article *Chaleur*, vol., iii., p. 175) ; Langlois and Garrelon (*Journ. de Physiol.*, 1906, p. 236, 1907, p. 640).
[4] G. Lippmann (*Comptes Rendus Acad. Sciences*, vol. cxlv., p. 104, 1907) ; Aubert, Thesis for Doctorate, Paris, 1912).
[5] Coulomb (memoire quoted, end) 1785 (date of publication).
[6] The real average temperature of Martinique is 25·60°, a maximum of 27° and a minimum of 24°. It must be added that the natives of hot countries suffer less from the high temperature than strangers ; (see § 171).

functions, but they modify appreciably the expenditure of energy, and reduce the amount of work. A low temperature raises the expenditure of energy, or the living ration, to a very high value ; a high temperature limits the production of work.

The rôle of climate is defined by what has been said above, apart from other characteristics—the hygrometric state, the altitude, and the latitude. Arctic climates, where the cold reaches — 50°, and sometimes even — 80° C., have a curious effect on the nutritive exchanges. Then, when the organism has to feed well and breathe deeply, the action of the polar temperature retards the rhythm of the respiration and disturbs slightly the expiration of the gases (Nansen, Amundsen, etc.). In spite of this, by the protection of furs, man contrives to keep a constant central temperature.

When, owing to insufficient protection, or defective organic resistance (alcoholism) the organism cools internally, life is in danger. If the internal temperature reaches 32° C. a fall of 5·5° C., death is practically certain. In the same way, if the central temperature rises from 37·50 to 43° or 44° C., there is also danger of death. Poisoning often leads to hypothermia.

Under strictly physiological conditions, with a normal subject, and for the usual ranges of temperature, the action of the latter is balanced by the nutritive exchanges, and is complicated or corrected by clothes, the humidity of the air, and the speed or the atmospheric currents ; this last factor affecting the convection and pressure exerted on the muscles.

170. Influence of Clothes.—The human skin and hair protect the central temperature inefficiently. Therefore man protects himself artificially by means of clothes. It is obvious that the protective power of the latter depends on the nature and the thickness of the material, that is to say, on its conductivity. We know that the conductivity of the human skin is 0·0006, $i.e.$, this is the quantity of heat in small calories that will pass per square centimetre through a thickness of 1 cm. with a temperature difference between the two surfaces of 1° C. It is recognised that the conductivity of the skin decreases in glacial regions, because of the fatty tissue which lines it.

Various measurements have been made of the co-efficient of conductivity of various materials. The most complete and correct are those of Rubner,[1] who used several calorimeters of different sizes. Rubner showed, first of all, that the best heat insulator is the air ; its co-efficient of conductivity being ·0000532. If it were possible to surround the body with a layer of air of a suitable thickness it would be better protected than by any garment of equal thickness.

[1] Max Rubner (*Arch. f. Hygiene*, vol. xxiv., p. 265 *sqq.*, 1895).

The co-efficient, c., for various materials depends, therefore, much less on their nature than on the air, which they can imprison. Skins, furs and various porous tissues are bad conductors of heat, because of the air in their interstices. The less dense the tissue the better the material as a heat insulator. See the tables (§ 251) in *Technics*.

Here are a few average co-efficients of conductivity obtained by Rubner [1],

SUBSTANCES.	CO-EFFICIENT OF CONDUCTIVITY
Air	0·0000532 c.
Hair { brown } (of peasants) .... {	0·0000763
Hair { grey }	0·0000745
Feathers (eider down)	0·0000574
Skins and horse hair	0·0000570
Smooth cotton fabric	0·0000810
„ wool „	0·0000686
„ silk „	0·0000684
Cashmere	0·0000686
Linen cambric (Batiste)	0·0000810
Flannel	0·0000723
Knitted wool	0·0000650
Flannelette	0·0000757
Knitted cotton	0·0001002
Tricot linen	0·0001158
„ silk	0·0000916
Blue winter stuffs	0·0000756
Winter cloth	0·0000733
Summer cloth	0·0000714
Winter overcoat	0·0000676
Rabbit skin { fur outside.....................	0·0000689
Rabbit skin { fur inside	0·0000682
Water [2] (at about 37°C).....................	0·001350
10% Solution of sea salt [3]...................	0·001080
Human skin [4]	0·000600
Lard (solid fat) [5].............................	0·000480
Ox hide [6]	0·000420

(See a supplementary table in *Technique*).

---

[1] Rubner (*loc. cit.*, p. 350 to 380.
[2] Lees (*Proceed. Roy. Soc.*, vol. lxii., p. 286, 1898 ; *Phil. Trans.*, vol. cxci, p. 399, 1898).
[3] Winckelmann (*Wied. Ann.*, vol. x., p. 668, 1880).
[4] Jules Lefèvre, *Bioénergétique*, p. 398.
[5] Lees (*loc. cit.*):
[6] Lees and Chorlton (*Phil. Mag.*, vol. xli., p. 495, 1896).

Take, as an example, a man wearing a woollen garment (c = 0·0000686) with a total surface of 19,000 square centimetres, a thickness of 0·75 cms., and let the difference of temperature between inside and outside be 10°, what will be the amount of heat lost by conduction in 24 hours ?

We have

$$Q = \frac{0·0000686 \times 19,000 \times 3,600 \times 24 \times 10}{0·75 \times 1,000} = 1,528 \text{ Calories.}$$

It has been divided by 1,000 so as to express Q in large calories.

171. In regard to the emissive powers of various materials we have only some results obtained by Peclet.[1] He agreed with Melloni that the colour of the tissues is immaterial, except for the fact, demonstrated by all authorities, that black is the most radiant.

A table of known emissive powers is given later (§ 250 of *Technics*). But Péclet's measurements are not beyond criticism ; they are also rather old (1841). Thus Péclet finds, in opposition to more modern experimenters :

Smoke black $K_1 = 0·00011$ c., instead of 0·00016 c. found by Stefan and Christiansen. For the skin, we will take $K_1 = 0·00015$ c. For the air, recent determinations[2] have given $K_1 = 0·000040$c, Glogner,[3] using a water calorimeter, studied the radiation of the skin of Europeans and of negroes (Malays). Black skin was found to be more radiant. Thus per hour and per square metre the former gave 17·40 Cal. and the latter 21 Calories for the fore-arm, a ratio :

$$\frac{21}{17·4} = 1·20.$$

In the same way in an air calorimeter, the rise of temperature of a given volume of air in a given time was 1·21, more for black than white skin (the thigh).

This very distinct difference explains also the resistance of the black races to the effects of the tropical climates which they inhabit.

An estimate of the radiated heat is easily made by Stefan's law, so often verified,[4] which is this :

The radiation from a surface is proportional to the 4th power of its absolute temperature.

[1] Péclet, *Traité de la Chaleur*, 3rd Edn.. 1860, vol. i., p. 373 (reviewed by L. Ser).
[2] Average, according to Wellanmann and Exner (*Acad. Sciences de Vienne*, 19th Jan., 1911).
[3] Glogner (*Virchow's Arch.*, vol. cxvi., p. 540, 1889).
[4] For instance, recently Wamsler (*Zeitzch. d. Ver. Deutsch. Ing.*, No. 15 and 22, 1911).

Let T be the ordinary temperature of the surface, t that of the external environment. Then :

$$q_1 = K'_t \ [(T + 273)^4 - (t + 273)^4].$$

The factor of proportionality $K'_t = 1\cdot355 \times 10^{-12}$, according to A. Shakespeare, $1\cdot27 \times 10^{-12}$, according to Bauer, for perfectly black surfaces. In the case of the human skin, the co-efficient $K'_t = 1\cdot02 \times 10^{-12}$ approximately.[1]

172. Co-efficient of Utility of Clothing.—To estimate the protective effect of a garment, without taking into account its matter or its thickness, Coulier [2] covered a cylindrical brass vessel, filled with hot water, with the material to be studied. Bergonié [3] used a copper bust in which the water was at a temperature of 37° C. He noted the time t in which the temperature of the bust, when covered with a given garment, fell 1°C.

The external temperature was 12°C.

The time taken in a fall of temperature of 1°C, when the bust was bare was θ. The ratio $\frac{t}{\theta} = c'$ gave the co-efficiency of utility or the protection afforded by the garment.

Bergonié obtained the following practical co-efficients :—

GARMENTS.	c'
Cyclists' costume, (close fitting)	1·10
Woollen shirt	1·50
Swanskin waistcoat	1·55
Hunting waistcoat	1·60
Leather jacket, black, lined	1·60
Flannel shirt	1·75
Coarse cloth jacket	1·90
Rainproof cloak (Inverness)	2·10
Pyrenese wool waistcoat	2·50
Winter overcoat silk lined	2·50
,, ,, fur lined	4·50

Rubner's tables can be used to calculate the protective power of a garment according to the nature of its tissue and its thickness.

At the same time the practical, hygienic value of a material also depends on the way it behaves as regards perspiration. This is an important though not absolutely essential factor in the utility of the garment. One must not neglect to be well covered, though the workman and the peasant, although badly clothed

[1] G. A. Shakespeare (*Proced. Roy. Soc.*, 11th Jan., 1912. Bauer and Moulin (*Journ. de Physique*, 1910, p. 468). Rubner (*Arch. f. Hygiene*, vol. xvi., p. 357, 1893).
[2] Coulier (*Journ. de Physiol.*, 1858, vol. i.).
[3] Bergonié (*Comptes Rendus Biologie*, 1904, pp. 265, 314).

and insufficiently wrapped up, do not suffer thereby. Montaigne tells of a man, sensitive to cold, warmly clad, who saw a beggar gaily walking in nothing but his shirt in winter weather. He was astonished. " But you, sir," replied the other, " have your face uncovered : as for me, I am all face." The adaptability of the body to external conditions is marvellous. Resistance to inclement weather is a characterisitc feature in men accustomed to laborious work.

CHAPTER III.

THE EXTERNAL ENVIRONMENT (*continued*).

173. The Influence of the Hygrometric State.—The hygrometric state or humidity of the air at a given temperature is the ratio of the weight of water vapour which it contains to the maximum weight which it could contain in the same volume.

Let p and P be those two weights, the hygrometric state will be :

$$e = \frac{p}{P}.$$

It is, in fact, the relative humidity. In different publications the state of relative dryness or the relation $\frac{P - p}{P}$ is given.

It is obvious that the state of dryness increases as that of p is reduced.

In practice the weights p and P of vapour are not considered, but its tensions f and F, that is to say, its "elastic force," as it is observed, and as it would be if it were the maximum, for a given temperature $t°$. The hygrometric state will be :

$$e = \frac{f}{F}$$

the value of F can be found for all temperatures in Regnault's tables (see *Technique*, § 253) ; f is measured by means of a hygrometer, of which that of Crova is the simplest and best ; its principle being the following:—In cooling the vapour of the air, there will be a temperature t', at which the elastic force is a maximum ; t' therefore will be found at the " dew-point," when the vapour starts to condense. The tables give the force corresponding to t' as f.

Example : In a locality at 15° C. the dew point or the hygrometer is found when $t' = 5°$ C. The tables give, for this temperature: $f = 6.55$ mm. ; for $t = 15°$, F = 12.70 mm. Hence :

$$e = \frac{f}{F} = \frac{6.55}{12.7} = 0.514, \text{ or } 51.4\%.$$

Knowing f or e we can calculate the weight of water vapour per cubic metre at $t°$C.

$$p = \frac{290.2 \times f}{273 + t} \text{ grammes, } \quad \text{or} \quad p = \frac{290.2 \times F \times e}{273 + t} \text{ grammes.}$$

The mode of operation will be seen later. In spinning mills, where there is always great moisture, a skein of wool is placed in the scales ; the heavier it is the greater the humidity. The working of textiles requires a humid atmosphere which is artificially maintained. Here are some examples or the humidity maintained in cotton mills :

		%
Preparing room..$e =$		60
Combing ,, ...		80
Carding ,, ...	55 to	60
Finishing ,, ...	65 to	70
Cotton weaving	75 to	80
Spinning and weaving of linen, jute, hemp	80 to	85
Spinning of silk	70 to	75
Spinning and weaving of wool	80 to	90

It will be seen that very often the air of these mills is almost saturated.

174. Perspiration.—Rubner [1] made the best researches on this question. Conformably to the idea of physical equilibrium, he recognised that the pulmonary and cutaneous evaporation increases with the state of dryness of the atmosphere. It becomes almost double when there are 5 grammes of water vapour instead of 9 in one cubic metre of air. In short, the value of the elimination of water vapour by the organism varies inversely with the hygrometric state. It is the same with fasting or fed subjects, but the elimination is more rapid in the case of overfeeding.

Comparing the influence of the hygrometric state with that of the temperature, Rubner shows that—all things being equal—the temperature increases the emission of water ; the minimum takes place between 10° and 15° C., while from 25° C. onwards the emission is rapid. Wolpert finds a minimum at about 18° and a maximum at 37° C.

An analogous phenomenon has been found amongst vegetables, especially in those which grow in the desert and are called xerophytes (from χερος dry). The perspiration of plants is more intense in the sun than in the shade, because of the absorption of red rays, which are calorific, while it can be stopped by a saturated environment.

In man and animals, the emission of water vapour appears to be a complex physical and physiological phenomenon, subject, undoubtedly to the action of the nervous centres. The rôle of these centres is to regulate the perspiration so as to adapt it to

[1] Max Rubner (*Arch. f Hygiene*, vol xvi., p. 101, 1892). H. Wolpert (*Ibid.*, vol. xxvi., p. 32, 1896 ; vol. xxxiii., p. 206, 1898) ; Wolpert and Broden (*Ibid.*, vol. xxxix., p. 208, 1901) may also be consulted.

the defence of the organism against heat. The rejected water evaporates on the surface of the skin at the same time absorbing a quantity of heat.

Sudation is therefore a factor in the equilibrium of the organism which obeys, like all the others, the nervous co-ordination. It would be very serious if it were not so, for sweat is a toxic waste, and is produced during fatigue (§ 158). The poisons which it eliminates in twenty-four hours would be sufficient to endanger an adult subject.[1] Poisoning sometimes takes place in a hot, humid atmosphere if the sweat has not been able to leave the body.[2] Therefore the necessity for the regulation or of the emission of water vapour in a manner adapted to biological ends will be understood.

In an environment at a temperature of 20° C. a male adult eliminates about 900 grammes of water in the state of repose ; 3,000 grammes in an average amount of work of 200,000 kilogrammes ; in the case of exceptionally hard work 7 to 8 kilogrammes of water. Walking in the desert causes an enormous sudation, often disastrous to the health. The evaporation of these considerable quantities of water corresponds to a great expenditure of heat.

Any circumstances which impede perspiration are dangerous ; such as the humidity of the rooms of cotton mills (on an average 85% at a temperature of 23° C.) [3] or dust which obstructs the pores of the skin. One suffers from damp heat,[4] says Rubner, because of the inability to evaporate sufficiently. One suffers from damp cold, because it causes too much loss of heat.[5]

It is desirable to reduce humidity by adequate ventilation ; because, on the one hand, sudation will then take place normally, and on the other, the heat will be more bearable in a relatively dry environment, as damp air retains the heat longer.[6]

A dry state of the atmosphere is favourable to work, especially at an average temperature of 15–16°C ; it is only in very particular cases that extreme dryness is accompanied by trouble

---

[1] Arloing (*Journ. de Physiol.*, 1899, pp. 249, 268).
[2] Haldane (*Revue Scientifique*, 8th Oct., 1910).
[3] P. Boulin (*Ibid.*, 8th April, 1911, p. 430).
[4] In various countries, as at Buenos-Ayres, the moisture combined with a temperature of 39° and 40°, caused numerous deaths in 1900. (Grandis and Mainini, *Arch. Ital. Biol.*, vol. xxxvii., No. 281, 1901).
[5] Rubner (*Arch. f. Hygiene*, vol. xxxviii., p. 120, 1900).
[6] Hoorweg, Haga (*Journal de Physique*, 1877).

some characteristics. It may then cause wood to split, bodies to become electrified,[1] and the skin of the hands to peel in places.[2]

Finally, garments absorb water [3] in varying quantities, according to the nature of the material, thereby moderating the evaporation and preventing too rapid cooling.

Rubner found that the maximum quantity of water retained, per gramme of material was :

Flannel	.... 10·30 gr.	Silk tricot	...... 3·80 gr.
Flannelette	.... 6·00	Linen ,,	...... 2·10
Wool tricot	.... 4·80	Cotton	.........0·80
Cotton ,,	.... 4·20		

Wool, from this point of view, is equally as valuable in summer as in winter ; the Arabs, for instance, always wear it.

175. The Influence of Air Currents.—The air acts on man and animals by its temperature ; but it also affects them by its speed and its bulk. In a still atmosphere the resistance of the air is due to the speed of movement. The speed of a pedestrian, walking at a good pace, is 1·50 metres per second. The resistance offered by the air, that is to say, the pressure that it brings to bear on the body in movement, is :

$$R = K \times S \times V^2,$$

R being in kilogrammes, V in metres, and the surface S in square metres. The co-efficient of resistance, K [4], is 0·079 up to a speed of 42 metres. A man's effective surface, S, when walking, is about 0·75 m². Hence :

$$R = 0·079 \times \overline{1·50}^2 \times 0·75 = 0·133 \text{ kg.}$$

This represents, per second, a useless labour of :

$$0·133 \times 1·5 = 0·20 \text{ kgm.}$$

In reality, the speed to be considered is that of the wind, which can vary between 2 and 40 metres, according to the momentum and also according to the altitude, increasing with the latter. Of course the speed of the pedestrian is, in these cases, negligible. Exceptions must be made for races, on bicycles, in motors, etc., or even on foot.

We can take 6 metres as the normal speed on the level. There is, therefore, a pressure, R = 2·133 kg. and the work done is 12·80 kgm. per second.

---

[1] Mlle. de Harven (*Bull. Soc. Astron. de France*, 1904, p. 173).
[2] Jean Mascart (*Revue Générale des Sciences*, 1910, p. 906).
[3] Rubner (*Arch. für Hygiene*, vol. xv., p. 54, 1892).
[4] G. Eiffel, *La Résistance de l'Air*, 2nd Edn., 1911.

In a storm the pressure of air reaches 95 kilogrammes, sufficient to overturn an adult man, if he did not bend, so as to reduce his surface and thus offer a smaller resistance.[1]

The speed of the wind [2] is measured by means of the anemometer, which will be described later (*Technique*, § 200).

176. The influence of the speed of air currents, at a given temperature, has been studied by Jules Lefèvre [3] after d'Arsonval's methods. He placed his subject in his physiological calorimeter (see *Technics*, § 250) in a draught of air of known mass and speed ; he noted the temperatures of the air at entry and exit. Let M be the total mass of the air which has circulated in t minutes and been raised to a temperature of $\theta°$. By multiplying this excess of temperature θ by the specific heat of air, 0·237 (§ 104) the number of calories absorbed by the air, that is to say, eliminated by the subject are obtained. This is, per hour :

$$Q = \frac{0·237 \times \theta \times M}{t} \times 60 \text{ calories.}$$

Here is a table of some results obtained with an adult :

Velocity of the Air	Temperature of the Air	Per hour in Great Calories		Ratios	
		Naked Body	Clothed Body	A	B
metres 1·20	9°C	134	98		
3·80	,,	201	130	$\frac{201}{134} = 1·50$ $\frac{130}{98} = 1·32$	$\frac{134}{98} = 1·36$ $\frac{201}{130} = 1·54$
1·50	5°C	185	143		
3·80	,,	277·50	172	$\frac{277·5}{185} = 1·50$ $\frac{172}{143} = 1·20$	$\frac{185}{148} = 1·30$ $\frac{277·5}{172} = 1·61$
4·00	4°C	313	170		$\frac{313}{170} = 1·84$

[1] This inclination to the horizontal constitutes «the angle of attack *a*». The resistance R will therefore be expressed as :
$$R = K \times S \times V^2 \times \sin a.$$
it diminishes in consequence with the value of the angle *a*. but only up to $a = 30$ (G. Eiffel).

[2] One can equally well say : "force" of the winds, substituting pressure for speed.

[3] Jules Lefèvre, *Bioénergétique* (*loc. cit.*, pp. 103, 405, 426). Consult also d'Arsonval (*Arch. de Physiol.*, 1894, p. 360).

It is easily seen that the thermogenesis has increased with the fall of the temperature and also with the increase of wind velocity. The increase in question is, all things being equal, less for a man clothed (rather lightly) than naked (ratio A).   This demonstrates the protective rôle of clothing.   The protection is all the greater the colder the current (ratio B).   The co-efficient of utility is 1·54 at 9°, 1·61 at 5°, and 1·84 at 4°, the speed being practically constant (3·8 to 4 metres).

The first of these results—protection against the effects of wind velocity—is explained by the fact that the air buries itself better in the garments and forms there a non-conducting mattress. The second—the increasing protection with cold—is because cold air is a worse conductor than hot air.

The increase of the calorific expenditure, with the increase of the speed of the current of air, corresponds to the work of the latter on the body of the subject, a work which rises to 10,000 or 12,000 kilogrammetres per hour, about 30 Calories (for V = 3 to 4 metres per second), and also to the convection.

At great altitudes and in the open air, the calorific expenditure is therefore clearly higher than in the case of indoor town life, in office or workshop.

177. For a constant speed of 3·50 to 4 metres, the increase of the expenditure with temperature is shown in fig. 145.   The curves are for a male adult subject.

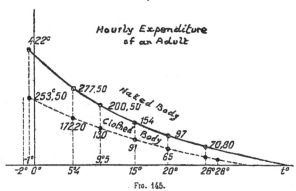

FIG. 145.

These quantities represent the loss by transmission or the total calorific expenditure.   In an environment of 20° C. the loss per diem is 97 × 24 = 2,328 Calories.   The average loss in the radiation and convection being 1,500 Calories, there remains 828 Calories for the minimum physiological expenditure (§ 166) ; this expenditure is therefore nearly 900 Cal. in an adult, but not more.

178. Influence of Water and of Baths.—The circumstances in which a man works immersed in water are rare. In swimmers the calorific expenditure is modified by the force of the current and the température of the water ; the resistance to be overcome is :

$$R = K \times S \times V^2.$$

K may be taken as 73 and S as ·034 square metres.[1] Hence if the velocity of the current is 4 metres we have :

$$R = 73 \times 0·035 \times 16 = 41 \text{ kilogrammes.}$$

If the water is calm, only the chemical and thermic actions need be considered ; the former intervene by phenomena known of osmotic exchanges between the salts of the organism and the water especially when the latter itself is salt. The thermic actions are more appreciable. Jules Lefèvre made a thorough study of them : a subject was immersed in a mass of water, M, contained in a bath ; and the temperature was raised by $\theta°$ in t minutes. The specific heat of water being unity, the hourly expenditure :—

$$Q = \frac{M \times \theta}{t} \times 60.$$

Lefèvre established that the calorific production varies inversely with that of the temperature of the bath. The thermic expenditure per minute would be given approximately by the following formula :—$q = 22·556$ Cal. $- 0·843\,t - 0·0178\,t^2 + 0·00124\,t^3 - 0·000016t^4.$

This is true between $+ 5°$ and $+34°$ C. ;

The expenditure per minute was :

Temperature	$+5°$	12°	18°	24°	30°C
q per minute	18·05	11·7	7·2	4	2 Calories.

Lefèvre's law, as fig. 145 shows, would lead to a calorific production of 1,200 calories in 24 hours for a temperature of 35°. By experiment he obtained a value of 1,500 Calories, on the average, both by the preceding method and by the expenditure of oxygen.[2] The physiological energy was therefore estimated, by him, to be 1,500 calories, instead of 900 calories, which is the largest value which the writer can accept.[3]

The influence of water, like that of the air, is relatively greater on short subjects than on tall, because it is a surface action.

---

[1] Other authorities take K = 55, which lowers the value of the resistance R. Also note that S is the surface of the biggest section of the immersed body, and that R is expressed in kilogrammes).

[2] Jules Lefèvre (*loc. cit.*, pp. 907, 908) and for the action of baths (pp. 417-422). See also § 252.

[3] The value, 1·500 Cal. is even greater than the *total* calorific expenditure during sleep (§ 104).

179. The Influence of Altitude—Atmospheric pressure is measured by the barometer (*Technics*, § 245). This pressure is a function of the altitude decreasing as the altitude increases, and increasing consequently in proportion as one descends below the surface of the earth.

The temperature of the air does the same. It becomes colder as we ascend, and inversely it gets hotter as we descend. The temperature is 1° C. lower at 180 metres above sea level, and it increases by 1° when 33 metres below the ground.

More exactly, the barometric pressure and the temperature of a place are functions of its altitude and latitude. Knowing the pressures of the barometer at the foot and at the summit of a mountain, as well as the temperatures, H, H' and t, t', respectively, and knowing the latitude λ, Laplace's formula allows the altitude A to be deduced :

$$A = 18,405^{\,m} \left(1 + 0 \cdot 002552 \cos 2\lambda \left(1 + \frac{t + t'}{500}\right) \log \frac{H.}{H'}\right.$$

Conversely, the value of H' can be deduced from A and the other factors. The height A thus calculated must have added to it the height of the foot of the mountain above sea-level ; if this is B metres, the true height will be : A + B. This is called the reduced altitude (reduced to sea-level).

The variation of temperature with altitude is affected by numerous factors, which it is difficult to determine exactly. The winds and the position of the place itself in regard to its surroundings are variables not easily determined.

The variation of temperature with depth is quite as irregular. Experience has shown that at about 30 metres below the surface in our climates, there is an " invariable stratum " ; for example, a cave at that depth would have a fairly constant temperature both summer and winter.

Below this invariable stratum, the temperature of the earth increases with the depth about 1° C. per 33 metres. The differences are remarkable. Thus we find 1° per 25 metres in the Sperenberg mines, near Potsdam, up to a depth of 628 metres ; below that the rise is 1° per 31 metres and 1° per 64 metres. In the Anzin pits it is 1° per 15 to 26 metres ; in the Neuffen mines, in Wurtemburg, 1° per 11 metres. More exact results can be obtained by measuring the temperature in Artesian wells, that of Grenelle, 548 metres deep, shows an increase of 1° C. per 30 metres. A man who climbs a mountain, goes up in a balloon, or descends the shaft of a mine, experiences a change of atmospheric pressure and of temperature. This change will be slow or rapid, according to the speed with which he moves. It is useful to remember this factor of speed, to which one attributes, not without reason, certain consequences of high altitudes.

The variations of pressure modify the amount of oxygen in the air. Normally there are 300 grammes of oxygen per cubic metre of air at a pressure of 760 millimetres and at 0°C. If the pressure falls by half to 380 millimetres there will only be about 150 grammes of oxygen. Has this any physiological effect on man ? Compressed air, on the contrary, is richer in oxygen than free air. What is its effect on the organism ? These questions will be answered briefly.

180. Effects of Atmospheric Pressure.—Take first of all the case of barometric depression. It causes a decrease in the normal proportion of oxygen. Up to 115 grammes per cubic metre the respiration is in no way troubled. This is true whether the pressure is maintained constant at 760 and the proportion of oxygen reduced,[1] or if both the pressure and the proportion of this gas fall at the same time.[2]

The limit of 115 grammes corresponds to a pressure of about 290 millimetres, or an average altitude of 7,680 metres. Up to this point the red corpuscles of the blood fulfil their normal function as vehicles of oxygen, and the inter-organic combustions preserve their character of regularity.

At altitudes of 1,500 metres and upwards the number of red corpuscles increases,[3] and by this increase of their total surface, they make up the deficit created by the fall in the proportion of oxygen. For instance, Mercier[4] noticed at Zurich (Z) at an altitude of 412 metres, that a cubic millimetre of his blood contained 5·4 millions of red corpuscles approximately ; on Mount Arosa (A), at an elevation of 1,800 metres, the number rose to 7 millions and more ; at Bâle (B), where the altitude is 266 metres, it fell to 6 millions, still feeling the effects of the stay on Mount Arosa, which had lasted ten months (see diagram, fig. 146). The stay must needs have a certain duration,[5] at least if the altitude is not more than 2,800 metres.[6]

By making good the deficit in oxygen consequent on the rarefication of the atmosphere, life can be sustained at a height of 11,650 metres without difficulty. The experiment consists [7] in breathing from a pneumatic receiver air rich in oxygen, while the barometric pressure is reduced to 192 millimetres, which corresponds to an altitude of 11,690 metres.

(1) Paul Bert, *La Pression Atmosphérique*, 1878, p. 654; Speck, *Physiol. d. Menschl. Athmens*, Leipzig, 1892, p. 123 ; J. Tissot (*Comptes Rendus Biologie*, 1901, pp. 876, 941).

(2) J. Tissot (*Ibid.*, 1902, pp. 682, 688).

(3) Viault (*Comptes Rendus Acad. Sciences*, 1890, vol. cxi., p. 917).

(4) A. Mercier (*Arch. de Physiol.*, 1880, p. 769).

(5) Giacosa (*Rend. R. Instit. Lomb. d. Sc. and Lett.*, 1897, p. 410).

(6) Kronecker and Marti (*Arch. Ital. Biol.*, vol. xxvii., p. 333, 1897).

(7) A. Mosso, *Fisiologia del Homo sulle Alpi*, Milan, 1897.

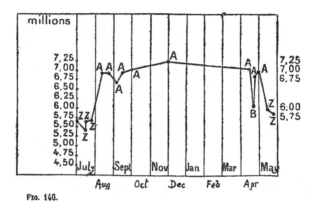

FIG. 146.

Effect of altitude on the richness of the blood in red corpuscles.

The relative independence of the inter-organic oxydizations of the atmospheric pressure is an experimental fact of great importance ; life, which is combustion, is not therefore seriously affected by the oscillations of the barometer. But it goes without saying that to consume the same amount of oxygen, the ventilation must needs, be greater and the respiratory labour more intense. This is probably why Zuntz and Durig, in their ascent of the Tylde Peak (3,700 metres) at Teneriffe, found that, whether resting or working, the expenditure of oxygen was greater at the summit than at the foot of the mountain.[1] Mosso [2] found on Mount Rose, at a height of 4,500 metres, equivalent to a pressure of 428 millimetres, that the pulsations and the respirations were modified, and that the vital capacity was subject to slight decrease. By taking an ergographic tracing of the fatigue, irregularities were revealed which seem to show that at a height the nervous system does not function so well as regards its motor centres. In the case of a man having to produce a moderately large amount of mechanical work at any considerable altitude, it is obvious that the respiratory activity will be troublesome.[3] The expired gases are seen to be relatively rich in carbonic gas and poor in oxygen ; in contrast, the blood is poorer in carbonic gas the higher one climbs ; there is, to use Mosso's word, a tendency to *acapnie* [4] χαπος, smoke). The nervous centres, irrigated by acapnic blood, exhibit the irregularities of action, which we have pointed out.

[1] Jean Mascart (*Rev. Gén. Sciences*, 1910, p. 633).
[2] A. Mosso, (*Fisiologia del Uomo sulle Alpi*, 1897, Milano, pp. 7, 11, 37-46).
[3] L. Hill (*Nature*, vol. lxxxiv., 1910).
[4] A. Mosso (*Arch. Ital. Biol.*, 1901) ; Haldane (*Proceed. Roy. Soc.*, 18th Jan., 1912).

181. Mountain Sickness.—The troubles due to altitude are called mountain sickness, or altitude sickness (the " puna " of South Americans ([1]), or, again, aviators' sickness. At a pressure of about 400 millimetres, nausea, acceleration of the heart, and the respiration, and difficulties of movement are apparent ; the sensibility and the intelligence are slightly blunted ; and there is a danger of asphyxia causing death at a height of 8,500 metres.

Raoul Bayeaux ([2]) shewed that the fall of pressure reduces the oxy-hœmoglobin of the blood, as is seen by autochrome photographs of this blood, and that the altitude sickness is cured by hypodermic injection of superoxygenated liquids in small quantities.

A unreliable experiment by the Weber brothers led De Humbold to state ([3]) that atmospheric pressure maintained the contact of articular surfaces,([4]) and that this was the reason for movements being difficult when the pressure was low, as on the top of mountains.

In reality, the fatigue is here of respiratory origin, and the greater the effort of climbing the more acute will be the altitude sickness. When carried to the top of Mont Blanc, Janssen experienced no discomfort ; Alpinists experience sickness at 2,000 metres, and sometimes at 1,500 metres. Balloonists, whose expenditure of energy is very small, do not feel it until much higher. Aviators, whose nerves and muscles are subjected to a permanent tension, are the most exposed to altitude sickness.

At greater heights than 1,200 metres travellers suffer from buzzing in the ears, from headaches, and from a keen smarting of the face ; they are fatigued, and their eyes close with sleep as soon as they reach lower altitudes.([5]) In the case of aviators the effect of the change of pressure is sudden, especially in the descent. For example, the aviator Chavez took 19 minutes to rise from 880 metres to 2,010 metres ; Morane reached 2,600 metres in 24 minutes, from which distance he descended in only 2 minutes (!) etc. These sudden variations of pressure are one of the causes of the troubles observed. To finish the explanation of this subject one must note the cold and the wind, which increase with the height of the ascension, the dryness, and, if one believes Knocke, the ionisation of the air. Nevertheless, no one fact will account for altitude sickness.

([1]) V. Ducceschi (*Arch. di Fisio* 1st Jan., 1912).
([2]) R. Bayeux (*Comptes Rendus Sciences*, 3rd June, 1912).
([3]) *Comptes Rendus Sciences*, vol. iv., p. 181 ; 1837.
([4]) It was a question of the coxo-femoral joints (hips).
([5]) René Cruchet and H. Moulinier (*Revue Scientifique*, 1911, p. 740).

182. Fatigue is the true source of the physiological troubles which characterise this sickness.[1] It is produced quickly, in consequence, perhaps, of the lowering of the tension of oxygen and the rarefication of the atmosphere. It follows that man is not capable of performing the same amount of mechanical work at great heights as at normal elevations. In the Burlard mines, at Sentein, at 2,600 metres, a walk of only 600 metres to reach the galleries, produces breathlessness.[2]

Bayeux's experiment explains this fatigue. Bancroft [3] also showed that the affinity of the hœmoglobin of the blood for oxygen diminishes with altitude at the same rate as the alkalinity of the liquid, which latter is conducive to the fixation of the oxygen.

We may estimate that the diminution of power of workmen living at a height of 2,500 metres is 15%, even when they come from heights of 700 to 800 metres. The Caylloma mines, South Peru, are at 4,500 to 4,900 metres above sea level, and the work of smiths, carpenters, wood workers and mechanics is there lowered by half. In practice, say Tréfois and Fox, one must admit that at great altitudes the dynamic equivalent of a workman is considerably lowered by the rarification of the air alone.

Cold has also a share in this reduction of output. Leaving out of account the exceptional cold ($-40°$) of the mines in Lapland, Siberia, Alaska and Greenland, one must reckon with the abundant snow, which is found between 2,000 and 3,000 metres altitude, and which attains a thickness of 8 to 10 metres in winter (the mines of Pieos, in Spain ; of the Pyrenees in France ; of Vallauria, in Italy, etc.). The best paid workmen refuse to work in such regions ; the soldiers on the Alpine posts resist the climate but feebly, and, in consequence, fill the hospitals. In fact, in the temperate zone, a mine at an altitude of 5,000 metres would be absolutely unworkable, even if it contained golden sovereigns ready minted.

Therefore cold, fatigue, lack of oxygenation of the blood, and, perhaps, the fear of danger [4], produce altitude sickness.

It is interesting to note that the power of internal combustion engines decreases from 11% to 25% at altitudes of 1,000 to 5,000 metres (§ 168).

---

[1] See an interesting article by Kronecker *Nature du Mal des Montagnes et un Cas rare de ce Mal*, in *Biologische Centralblatt* (vol. xxxi., 1911).

[2] G. Tréfois (*Revue Univ. des Mines*, July, 1910, p. 38, Liége).

[3] Bancroft (*Journal de Physiol.*, vol. xlii., p. 44, 1911. *Proceedgs. Roy. Soc. Lond.*, 18th Jan., 1912).

[4] D'Hombres Firmas (*Comptes Rendus Sciences*, vol. iii., p. 382, 1836).

The problem of altitude sickness would not be amongst the preoccupations of science if aviation had not become an arm for national defence and an industry of importance.[1]

The phenomena which accompany the rapid descent of the aviator are most curious ; and they merit a more careful study now that an aeroplane can rise sometimes to more than 5,000 metres. Descending rapidly gives rise to troubles which are expressed by the smarting of the face, etc. (see above). There is a mechanical explanation of this. First of all, consider the fall of a body animated by an acceleration γ ; if this body supported a weight, the pressure of that weight would be reduced to m $(g - \gamma)$ instead of being mg. Compare this to what takes place in the human body ; the blood is a liquid of which every particle pushes internally with a force mg ; in the accelerated descent of the aviator, this force is reduced to m $(g - \gamma)$, and in a great acceleration everything would take place as if our blood had no longer any weight ; there must result from it a peculiar sensation of smarting in the face where the blood arrives with an apparently stronger cardiac impulsion, and very probably a sensation of cold in the legs. Of course, if this explanation is correct, it follows that a descent at a constant speed, without acceleration, would do away with the aviator's troubles.

---

[1] H. de Graffigny, *Hygiène Pratique et Physiologie de l'Aviateur et de l'Aéronaute*, Preface by Ch. Richet, Paris (*Maloine*), 1912.

CHAPTER IV.

THE EXTERNAL ENVIRONMENT (continued).

183. Atmospheric Pressure below Ground Level.—Below the ground, in a mine, the atmospheric pressure is greater than on the surface. The increase of the proportion of oxygen in the air, which follows, does not modify in the least the value of the respiratory exchanges. At the ordinary depths of a mine it cannot be the pressure which causes physiological troubles. All the more so that the increase is very small ; the rate of the oxygen varies, therefore, very little, and experiment has shown clearly that the respiration remains normal.[1] It was found, in this latter case, that the blood was merely momentarily over-saturated ; [2] but this phenomenon must be absolutely uncertain, having escaped a number of observers.[3]

Far from being in contact with a super-oxygenated atmosphere miners are exposed to breathing deleterious gases. Notably carbon-dioxide and carburetted hydrogen (fire damp). The heat the humidity and the darkness of underground workings exert a certain influence on the workers.

The heat is due to the depth. If the outside temperature at the surface is 10° C., that at 1,500 metres is 50°–55°. There is also a higher degree of humidity. Labour in a hot and humid atmosphere is, from what has already been explained, very troublesome (§ 174). In such conditions 25° is a hardly bearable limit ; so that after a depth of 700 to 800 metres the hottest parts of the mine have to be cooled by sending down cold air to mix with the hot.[4]

The effect of darkness will be examined later (§ 187).

Highly compressed air presents more dangers than the slightly overcharged air of the mine. The proportion of oxygen, which is notably increased, is not the cause, and entails no evil consequences. But it is in no wise immaterial that the organism should suffer successive compressions and relaxations, especially if these are produced suddenly and without very great precautions. The troubles which follow from a stay in compressed air can be extremely serious. They are shown in workmen employed in caissons and in divers. They suffer from caisson sick-

[1] Regnault (*Ann. Ch. Phys.*, 1849, vol. xxvi., p. 299) ; de Saint-Martin (*Rech. Expér. sur la Respiration*, Paris, 1893, p. 96),
[2] Falloise (Trav. Lab. Frédéricq, 1896-1901) ; A Durig (*Arch. f. Physiol.*, 1903, suppl. p. 209).
[3] Schaternikoff (*Arch. f. Physiol.*, 1904, suppl. p. 135).
[4] Dietz (*Zeitsch. f. Die Gesamte Kaelte-Industrie*, Dec., 1911).

ness. The workmen enter the diving bell after the compressed air has gradually driven out the water. The pressure depends on the depth at which they have to work. It is 1 atmosphere per 10·33 m. But work is rarely carried out under a pressure of more than 5 atmospheres.

In these circumstances, the breathing becomes slower, and, consequently there is less intensity of interorganic combustion. The blood dissolves a greater quantity of gas, that is to say, of nitrogen and oxygen. Thus we find, in the blood :

	OXYGEN	NITROGEN
At normal pressure	20%	2·2%
At 6 atmospheres	23%	6·5%

In other words, there is an excess of 30 cubic centimetres of oxygen and of 43 cubic centimetres of nitrogen per litre of circulating blood. For an adult, the blood represents a total volume of about 4,500 cubic centimetres, of which 135 and 194 cubic centimetres of gas tend, at the moment of decompression, to leave the blood and to be evolved in the cellular tissue. This causes pricks, itching and sometimes tumefaction in the workmen. The moment of decompression is certainly the most to be feared.

These gaseous embolisms can be fatal ; they are more serious and more frequent in fat persons. The constituent element is nitrogen, because the oxygen remains fixed in the tissues. Hill even recommended inhalations of oxygen to facilitate the departure of the nitrogen without serious danger.[1] Other accidents, not really very serious, also occur in diving ; there is a singing in the ears, sometimes painful, but which the workmen get rid of by a swallowing movement. Other facts which belong to industrial hygiene cannot be mentioned ; it is enough to point out the diminution of the phenomenon of oxydation (the sole source of energy) which must result in a decrease of dynamic capacity. This decrease has not been exactly estimated. Men who work in compressed air complain also of a certain rigidity in the joints which impedes their movements.

184. Influence of Deleterious Gases and Vapours.—The atmosphere, whose theoretical composition has been previously given (§ 164), and which was then considered to be in a state of purity, is, as a matter of fact, never pure in a place where men are gathered working. Carbonic acid gas and carbon-monoxide are the most frequent causes of vitiation ; the former is only dangerous in large quantities ; but the latter, which has the property of fixing itself energetically on the hœmoglobin of the blood, is a formidable poison, even in the proportion of 0·2 to 0·3% of the atmos-

---

[1] *Revue Gén des Sciences*, 1910, p. 954. See an article by Hill in the *British Medical Journal* of 17th Feb., 1912.

pheric mixture ; it is all the more so when a man is tired.([1])
Unfortunately there is carbon-monoxide about nearly everywhere, for there is 5% to 9% in the gas used for lighting purposes,
and it forms in ore mines, limekilns, blast furnaces, badly ventilated tunnels, in the combustion of braziers and stoves without
a flue, in fireplaces with a bad draught or with incomplete combustion. Illnesses naturally occur to gas workers, miners, bakers,
etc., from the presence of this gas. The symptoms are : blue-
ness of the face (cyanosis), giddiness and hallucinations, and a
considerable decrease of strength.

Dangerous vapours also arise in the working of metals : those
from lead and mercury being the worst. Dr. Holland, of Cham-
béry, has also pointed out that the vapours, which arise in the
treatment of aluminium, cause a kind of diabetes in the workman.([2])

The sulphuric vapour given off by electric accumulators is
very strong and corrosive. Variations of atmospheric pressure
and temperature increase the effect.([3])

Drains and sewers are a cause of asphyxiation ; but it appears
in this case that it is the lack of oxygen which causes the trouble,
and not the presence of insignificant traces of sulphuretted
hydrogen.([4])

The gasses and the vapours above mentioned impede the
respiratory exchanges and cause incipient anesthesia ([5]) (carbonic
acid gas), or asphyxiation, an enervation which depresses the
muscular force.

185. Workmen (engravers, turners, etc.) who make articles
of boxwood (Gonioma Kamassi) are exposed to a poisoning
of the nerves, for boxwood contains a paralysing alkaloid,
analogous to curare, which attacks the centres of the brain and
of the spinal cord. There is a proportion of 0·07% of this alkaloid
and exotic boxwoods, those of the Cape, for instance, are the most
harmful.([6]) But its action on the muscles is very small.

There are numerous toxic woods, such as yew, ebony, the
various rose woods, acacia wood, etc. The working of all these
woods causes a certain lassitude,([7]) headache and torpor, which
reduces the work done by the workmen.

([1]) Haldane (*Journal of Physiology*, vol. xviii., p. 463, 1895) ; A. Mosso
(*Comptes Rendus Acad. Sc.*, 1900 ; *Arch. Ital. Biol.*, vol. xxxv., p. 1, 1901).
([2]) *La Nature*, 16th Sept., 1911.
([3]) Boudouard (*Comptes Rendus Acad. Sc.*, 22nd Jan., 1912, p. 238).
([4]) Hanriot (*Comptes Rendus Biologie*, 1902, pp. 208-10).
([5]) Paul Bert (*Comptes Rendus Biologie*, 1884, p. 565).
([6]) E. Dixon (*Proceedgs. Roy. Soc. Lond.*, 19th Jan., 1911).
([7]) Grossman (*Journal de Pharmacie et de Chimie*, 1911).

Opium and tobacco also affect the body. The principle of opium is morphia, which acts as a narcotic.

The active principle of tobacco is nicotine, of which there is 2% in Havana tobacco, 2·3% in Virginia, and in French tobacco an average of 5%. The Frenchman consumes per year about 1 kilogramme of tobacco, that is to say, he absorbs in that time 50 grammes of nicotine. Féré [1] found that, in very small doses, tobacco stimulates the muscular power ; it helps the association of the ideas according to Claparède.[2] But some careful observations made by Weley [3] have established that nicotine, in a solution of its tartaric salt, produces a typical effect on the muscles, which consists of an initial diminution of their power, and then an increase followed by a gradual fall. Altogether, there is a reduction in the contractability of the muscles, the increase of power being quite temporary.

The smoke of tobacco, writing paper, straw, and wood all contain carbon dioxide [4] and "furfurol."[5]

186. The Influence of Dust.—The atmosphere, especially in industrial towns, is always vitiated by dust and smoke, which remain in suspension owing to the moisture in the air and form a veritable fog. In gas works and foundries the air may contain grains of coal, iron, oxide of lime, silica, etc.

Some smoke is corrosive, because it contains hydrochloric, hydrofluoric, or sulphuric gases ; in other cases it is sharp and penetrating, thus facilitating the ingress of microbes into the organism ; and some are pathogeonus, causing, for instance, anthracosis, the pneumoconiosis of miners, silicosis of the lungs, the illness of mill stone cutters, etc.

In Paris, these industrial fogs are sometimes 400 to 600 metres thick. They come from the north-east district, where the factories are, blown by a gentle wind (velocity 2 to 3 metres), over Paris. They disperse with a stronger wind (4 to 5 metres), which blows from west south-west. The lowering of the barometric pressure, the humidity and the temperature increases these fogs.[6]

Dry dust is easily combustible when held in suspension in the air. One must distinguish [7] between oil dusts, containing less

[1] Féré (*Arch. de Neurologie*, 1901, p. 463).

[2] Claparède et Isaïlowitch (*Comptes Rendus Biologie*, 1902, pp. 758-60).

[3] Weley *Proceedgs. Roy. Soc.*, vol. lxxxii., p. 333, 1910 ; series B).

[4] H. Molisch (*Anzieger d. K. Akad. d. Wiss in Wien*, vol. xlviii, p. 20, 1911).

[5] Furfurol is a toxic aldehyde $C_5H_4O_2$; methyl alcohol and wood vinegar contain some of it.

[6] Jaubert (*Revue Gén. Sc.*, 1910, p. 842).

[7] Experiments made at Frameries, Liévin, Altofts (Yorkshire), Glesenkircken (Germany), Rossitz (Austria), and at Berlin sugar works and distilleries. (*Rev. Gén. Sciences*, 1911, p. 477).

than 18% of volatile matters and those which contain 19% to 30% ; the latter explode violently, the more so if the grains are small.

The combustibility of dust is due to the fact that the individual grains have a big surface in proportion to their mass. Chauffeurs have been known to have eye troubles, due to the fact that the dust of the roads contains particles of tar. In fact, whilst ordinary dust (silica or calcium) only cause a slight inflammation of the eyelids, tar dust cause a more serious conjunctivitis of a purulent character.[1] The same occurs with workmen who work certain coals, because of the bituminous dust.[2] Apparatus for sucking up the dust by means of compressed air has already been installed in coal mines. One such apparatus working 20 days a month is sufficient for the clearing of galleries of a total length of 1,600 metres.[3]

Exhaust fans are used to get rid of the dust in cotton mills, which would injuriously affect the workpeople. In this way the frames of the machinery can be properly cleaned without interrupting work.[4]

187. The Influence of Radiation. Solar Action.—Radiation is of many kinds. Calorific radiation has been studied in connection with temperature (§ 165). It is most intense at the red end of the spectrum. Radiant heat is almost entirely arrested by glass. The heat which is experienced in a green house, or in any environment bounded by panes of glass is not caused by the opacity of the latter; in fact, there is the same elevation of temperature behind slabs of rock salt, which is most transparent to heat (diathermic). Wood has shown that the enclosed air is heated because it does not circulate.[5]

Calorific radiation is present in all sources of light, beginning with the sun. A calorific radiation of 0·0036 c. per square centimetre per hour produces a sensation of heat whilst, if it were 6·5 times more intense, say ·024 c., it would be intolerable. An ideal source of light should not radiate more than 0·0021 c., according to Rubner.[6] In comparing the various methods of lighting, one finds that all, except lighting with kerosine oil, satisfy this condition.[7]

The luminous part of the spectrum, or, more exactly, the whole light produces various effects on the organism, some of which

[1] Truc et Fleig (*Comptes Rendus Acad. Sc.*, Sept., 1910).
[2] *Congrés des Maladies Professionnelles de Bruxelles*, Sept., 1910
[3] *Génie civil*, 19th Aug., 1911, p. 337.
[4] *Génie civil*, 12th April, 1911, p. 319.
[5] Wood (*Phil. Magazine*, 1st Sept., 1909, p. 319).
[6] Rubner (*Arch. f. Hygiene*, 1895, vol. xxiv., p. 193).
[7] V. Woege (*Journal für Gasbeulechtung*, 1911, No. 13).

are still disputed. In particular, it is not absolutely proved that luminous radiation raises the rate of the respiratory exchanges, increasing the consumption of oxygen.[1]

However, light is a muscular excitant,[2] and it is incontestible that it is a cell-stimulant. In fact, it assists the development of the body and in particular the organ of sight.[3] It determines the pigmentation of the skin, and it appears to assist the multiplication of red corpuscles.

On the contrary, darkness impedes the development of the organs, atrophies that of the sight, depigments the skin [4], and lowers the number of red corpuscles.[5] The general sensibility of people who live in the dark is blunted, so much so that the return to light causes shock, [6] and the muscular power diminishes as in the case of the blind.[7] Colours seem to have various effects on the subject, although it is not proved that they modify the respiratory exchanges [8] or the rate of development of the organisms.[9] It is not, either, quite certain that their influence on the psychic state of man, is constant. It is said to have been found that in photographic developing rooms men working in a red light were gay and talkative, whilst in a violet light they became melancholy and apathetic and less disposed to work.

The violet and ultra-violet rays of the spectrum exercise a chemical action, which is probably the important factor in the phenomena of pigmentation. These rays abound in electric light and cause various diseases such as electric opthalmia [10] and facial erythemia, aggravated sometimes by cerebral congestion. Sources of light that are very rich in ultra-violet rays can cause veritable sunstrokes.

188. The above remarks apply to solar radiation. The sun gives out a flood of radiations. It has a beneficial (microbicide) effect, but its chemical rays can cause sunstrokes.[11] By using

---

[1] Moleschott admitted it and also Fubini (*Arch. Ital. Biol.*, 1891, vol. xvi., p. 80). Against it are the works of Speck (*Arch. f. Exper. Path. Und Pharmak*, 1880, vol. xii., p. 1) Adducco, Loeb, etc.

[2] D'Arsonval (*Comptes Rendus Biologie*, 1891, p. 318).

[3] W. Edwards, *Influence des Agents Physiques sur la Vie*, 1824 ; Humboldt ; Vicarelli ; (*Ann. d. Ostetr. e. Ginecol.*, 1890).

[4] Armand Viré (*Comptes Rendus Acad. Sc.*, 14th March, 1904).

[5] Kronecker Marti (*loc. cit.*).

[6] See an article, *Nature*, 11th May, vol. lxxxv i., p.349, 1911.

[7] Griesbach (*Pfl. Arch.*, 1899, vols. lxxiv.-v.) ; Féré *Travail et Plaisir*, p. 100 (*loc. cit.*).

[8] Selmi et Piacentini (*R, Ist lomb. d. Sc. e Lett.*, *Rendic.*, 1870, pp. 57-63).

[9] E. Yung (*Comptes Rendus Acad. Sc.*, 1880, vol. xci., p. 440).

[10] Terrien (*Arch. d'Ophtalm.*, 1902, p. 692, 1908, p. 679).

[11] Widmark (*Skand. f. Physiol.*, i., p. 264 ; iv., p. 281) ; Ch. Bouchard (*Comptes Rendus Biologie*, 1877).

coloured screens, von Schrotter ([1]) proved that it is the portion of the spectrum from blue to ultra-violet, which produces cutaneous erythemia, and this action is very marked at great altitudes.

Negroes are less exposed to this disease than white races, because their pigment changes the chemical rays into calorific rays; "the negro lives in the shelter of his skin" (Ch. Ed. Guillaume).

Solar light, when it is mild, favours visual acuteness, the perception of colours, and a clear view of details. When it is intense, which is the case, for instance, in the Mediterranean countries, it provokes ocular diseases, and a slight deformation of the ball of the eye (inverse astigmatism), which is rare in Northern countries.([2])

The solar heat,([3]) in the tropics can raise the temperature of the human skin from 3° to 4°. It has been observed that, in these circumstances, negroes perspire enormously to counteract hyperthermia.

In short, owing to its heat and its chemical radiations intense sunlight is a danger to man and animals.

The units of light, photometry and the lighting of workshops will not be discussed here. They are essentially matters of industrial hygiene.

189. Influence of Electric and Magnetic Fields.—The sun, thunderstorms, and industrial electric machinery pour into the atmosphere a prodigious quantity of electrified particles called ions. The ionisation of the air is a permanent phenomenon, which has no effect on man. It is not known whether or not it increases his muscular force and his expenditure of energy.

The electric current excites the muscles and the nerves by acting locally as a shock; the application of a moderate current appears to increase the power of the muscles, an effect which lasts for several days.([4]) The action of an electrified environment as after a violent thunderstorm, or in a radiotelegraphic station, produces a reverse effect, a slight depression of the nervous system, anæmia and a sort of apathy. Is this due to the electrification of the air or to the presence of ozone? It has been found that ozone has microbicide, cellulocide,([5]) and probably nervous ([6]) effects. One might therefore say that the effect of

---

([1]) Mission to Teneriffe, Jean Mascart (*loc. cit.*).
([2]) Jules Amar (*Journal de Physiologie*, 1908, pp. 231-7).
([3]) Hans Aron *Philippine Journal of Science*, vol. vi., April 1911).
([4]) Capriati (*Riv. Sper. di Frenol. e Med. Leg.*, vol. xxvii., p. 285, 1901).
([5]) Candiotti (*Revue Gén des Sciences*, 1911, p. 224).
([6]) *Elektrotech. Zeitsch.* of 17th April, 1913.

an electric field is not favourable to the organism, and can at length compromise the health. The effects of lightning are familiar, but it is interesting to note that the liability to be struck by lightning seems to vary with different trees. The effects on human beings are terrible. For instance, two labourers were hit in a field ; one died on the spot, the other survived but a few hours ; their clothes were burnt ; the skull was broken as by a stroke of a club ; often the man who is hit is thrown some distance.

Prévost and Batelli ([1]) have shown that an alternating current of low tension stops the heart, but the respiration continues for a few minutes ; at average tensions both stop ; at high tension the current stops the respiration but the heart continues to beat. In these conditions artificial respiration is indicated. An alternating current is much more dangerous for equal voltages than a continuous current.

Severe shocks ([2]) can cause stoppage of the heart and anæmia of the nervous centres ; or, by paralysing the respiratory organs produce asphyxiation ; in this case especially artificial respiration is of use.

A statistic of 55 fatal accidents caused by electricity in mines has shown that 53 of them, that is, 96%, are due to defective insulation of cables and bad earth connexions.

The effects of a magnetic field are obscure and doubtful. Schiff could observe no effect on the muscles and the nerves when exposed to a magnetic field in any direction.([3]) Peterson and Kennely ([4]) operating in Edison's laboratory with very powerful electro magnets, could perceive no action on a normal man. Lord Lindsay and Cromwell Varley found that there was no effect whatever when the head of a man was placed between two magnetic poles.

At the same time Féré ([5]), by means of an ergograph, found an increase of muscular force in an arm when brought within a distance of 1 metre from a magnet ; while in the other arm the force diminished. Finally, Danilewski and Grandis ([6]) claim that magnetic field can excite the muscles if its lines of force act per-pendicularly to the fibres. This phenomenon is contested, and in any case diversely interpreted.

([1]) Prévost and Battelli (*Journ. de Physiol.*, 1899, 1900). G. Weiss *Bull. Soc. Intern. des Elect.*. 3rd Series, vol. i., No. 8, 1912. Gerbis (*Elektr. Zeitsch.*, July, 1913).

([2]) *Electrician*, 7th April, 1911. For accidents due to electric shock see Langlois (*Rev. Gén. Sc., April*, 1913).

([3]) Schiff (*Arch. Sc. Phys. et Nat.*, 1888, 3rd Series, i.).

([4]) Peterson and Kennely (*New. York Med. Journ*, 31st Dec., 1892).

([5]) Féré (*Comptes Rendus Biologie*, 1902, pp: 388, 509).

([6]) Grandis (*Arch. Ital. Biol.*, 1902, vol. xxxvii., p. 313).

190. The Influence of an Acoustic Field : Sounds, Noises.—The influence of sounds on man's labour is allied to that of rhythm and cadence. There is no doubt that our muscles exert their activity in a rhythmical fashion, and that such is essentially the method of nervous action.

The cadence of sounds, harmony and music, have rules analogous to those of poetry, and their influence is of the same nature. There is nothing more interesting than to follow the rôle of the melody of rhyme in the numerous forms of human labour, at all epochs, in all civilisations and at every age ([1]). According to whether the cadence is slow or rapid, it accelerates or retards the pace of the soldier or the movements of the workman. A gay, quick tune enlivens a column of soldiers ; a slow, heavy sound leads to sadness and drowsiness. A whole workshop stops working at the rolling of the drums of a funeral. Every kind of activity has its own cadence. There is that of sawyers, who work a double-handed saw, in a certain rhythm ; there is the cadence of the blacksmith's hammer, which allows two men to strike alternately on the anvil without hitting each other or getting in each other's way ; whereby the speed and the quantity of labour is increased. Further, there is the rhythm of the carpenter using a plane, of even the writer, in the manual sense of the word, of the orator, etc. Song, melody, or a refrain add very often to the rhythm of the tool ; the words are unimportant ; the rhythm to which the worker attaches in a way the thread of his activity is the only thing that counts. Foremen can judge of the intensity of their workmen's labour by the sounds of the tools. What more pleasing allegory than that of the walls of Jericho falling at the sound of the trumpet or that of the walls of Thebes rising at the accents of the musician-poet, Amphion !

The musical intervals, according to whether they are consonant or dissonant, stimulate or retard the labour measured by the ergograph. Major keys are better than minor keys ; the major sixth giving the greatest stimulus.([2]) Rhythm leads to a greater accuracy of movement, to an increased output of work, and to a better utilisation of force. Is it necessary to say that the silence of the workmen, which characterises English workshops, is more advantageous in this respect than any songs

([1]) See a curious book by Karl Bücher, *Arbeit und Rythmus*, Leipzig, 1909. The author discusses the rôle of rhythm in human activity through the ages and in different countries ; it is a compilation of all the melodies, poetry and pieces of music which have been used or are still used in the muscular and intellectual labour of man.

([2]) Féré et Mme. Jaëll (*Comptes Rendus Biologie*, 1902, *passim* ; Féré *Travail et Plaisir* (*loc. cit.*). A nervous excitation acting on a muscle can, in certain cases, be reinforced by a sound. This reinforcement is the *Bahnung* of the Germans. (See *Yerkes, Pflüger's Archiv.*, vol. cxvii., p. 207, 1905).

and that the influence of rhythm is the best of all when it comes from the movements of the tools alone ?

191. The influence of noise, shocks, and vibrations is entirely different. No kind of human activity can be regulated by them because of their lack of periodicity. The effects of vibration and shock are inconvenient and even harmful. Thus the vibration and jolting of motor omnibuses is trying to the drivers, and especially to the conductors, since they are standing for considerable periods. The result is muscular fatigue and nervous exhaustion, to which latter the incessant noise no doubt contributes. In workshops, badly balanced machinery, running at high speeds, is a fruitful source of vibration, affecting both persons and buildings in the vicinity. The natural elasticity of the human frame cannot completely deaden vibration.

Although familiarity greatly diminishes the sensitiveness to vibration and noise, yet both are unfavourable influences in the workshop, and it is very desirable to avoid them as far as possible.

192. The Influence of Tools.—The output of a workman is obviously affected by the quality of the tools with which he works. Dupin remarked, in 1825, that the superiority of the British workman was due to the high quality of his tool equipment.

The weight of hand tools is also a matter of importance. To permit of rapidity of movement and maximum output, the tool must not exceed a certain weight. The proper weight for each trade or occupation is a matter to be decided by experiment, in which the age and physique of the worker must have due consideration.

In fact, the whole outfit of the workshop, both machine and hand tools, should be designed on natural lines so as not to interfere with the speed of the movements nor cause anything which is not strictly profitable to the work, nor entail interruptions other than those of the rest intervals ; The useful efforts must be reduced to a minimum, and useless contractions of the muscles must be suppressed. Thus the transport of earth in a wheelbarrow with only one wheel causes oscillations which bring about rapid fatigue ; therefore a wheelbarrow with two wheels should be employed.

Study and knowledge must assert themselves in proportion to the needs of the scientific organisation of industrial labour, in order to substitute rigorous methods for the guesses of empiricism. An eminent American engineer, Frederick Taylor, [1] applied the above principles in engineering workshops, where, thanks to the

---

[1] Frederick Winslow Taylor, *Principles of Scientific Organisation of the Workshops* ; *and Publication of the Review of Metalurgy,* 1907.

patient efforts of a quarter of a century, he made a veritable revolution. Frank Gilbreth (1) applied these same principles to bricklayers' work with great success. Human labour is a very complex thing, in which numerous factors, internal and external, to the workman, have influence. Their study must not be merely left to chance observation. It demands the methodical co-operation of the laboratory and the workshop.

---

(1) Frank B. Gilbreth, *Motion Study*, London, 1911.

BOOK V.

EXPERIMENTAL METHODS.

CHAPTER I.

MEASUREMENTS : INSTRUMENTS.

193. Measurements and Errors.—Under the heading of *Experimental Methods* will be set forth the elements of experimental measurements and the instruments already mentioned will be described. A measurement is never absolutely correct; an error, no matter how small, always exists, no matter with what care the measurement is carried out, or however perfect the instruments. The art of measurement consists in knowing how to reach the extreme limit of experimental exactitude, or the smallest error. The difference between the value found and the real value is called the *absolute error*. Suppose, for example, it is desired to determine the exact weight of a man of 65 kilogrammes. If the scales indicate 64·900 kg., there is an absolute negative error of 0·100 kg. If they indicate 65·100 kg. there is again an absolute positive error of 0·100 kg. The reduction of absolute errors depends on the degree of perfection of the instruments.

The relation of the absolute error to the total dimensions to be measured is called the relative error. In the preceding example it is $\dfrac{0·100}{65} = \dfrac{1}{650}$. It will be seen that the relative error decreases in proportion as the total quantity increases. For a weight of 130 kilogrammes, it would be :

$$\frac{0·100}{130} = \frac{1}{1,300}$$

In experiments the permissible relative error depends on the end in view. Thus, if a gas meter had a constant error of half a litre (minus), 100 litres of gas would be read as 99·5 litres. The error being ·5% (half of 1%), which would be permissible. The same error in a measurement of 10 litres would amount to 5%, which would not be permissible.

A variable and increasing error can also be introduced by wear in the moving parts of the instrument. Also, in the course of any experiment, errors may occur owing to external interference. Thus, in delicate measurements of temperature, the heat of the experimenter's body may affect results. It is often difficult, if not impossible, accurately to evaluate the amount of such errors.

Whatever precautions may be taken, a single measurement is insufficient ; there must be at least two, from which the average may be taken.

194. In practice the concordance of several observations is not absolute ; there will always be differences between them. We can take the arithmetical mean of n readings, a_1, a_2, a_3..., a_n ;

$$a_m = \frac{a_1 + a_2 + a^3 + \ldots + a_n}{n},$$

Each of these observed values will differ, more or less, from the average a_m. We shall have n differences, represented by δ. If the differences are small, and the number n of the observations comparatively large, the average a_m will give approximately the desired quantity. But for greater precision we apply the calculus of probabilities.[1] Let S be the sum of the squares of all the differences, a sum obviously positive, and e be the average error, then

$$e = \pm \sqrt{\frac{S}{n\,(n-1)}}.$$

It can be shown that the probable error is about $\frac{2}{3}$ of e. Consequently, the desired value will be :

$$a = a_m \pm \frac{2}{3}\,e,$$

a_m being the arithmetical mean. We endeavour to make the sum of the squares of the differences, S, as small as possible. Hence the name, *the law of least squares*, given to the method.

It is a good plan to make calculations without waiting till the end of a series of experiments, so as to make sure, before going further, that there has been no error. Note should always be made of the temperature, the atmospheric pressure at the time, the date and the place. If the experiment is on man, the sex, name, occupation, age, stature, etc., should be noted.

195. Methods of Graphical Registration.—Errors are reduced both by the accuracy of the instruments employed, and their frequent calibration, and also by arranging that, where possible, they shall be self-recording. The demands on the attention of the observer are thereby greatly reduced and the possibility of visual errors in observation eliminated. The apparatus employed in producing the various graphical records described in

---

[1] E. Carvallo, *Le Calcul des Probabilités et ses Applications*, 1912, p. 118 (*Gauthier-Villars*, Paris). This work is distinguished by its clearness and simplicity.

this book is always, in principle, similar to Marey's tanbour or tympan (*vide* § 5). The movement caused by the heart, the pulse, or the respirations, etc., induces corresponding movements in an elastic membrane. The motion of the latter is transmitted pneumatically to a similar tambour, which acts upon a stylus, by means of which the movement can be recorded, and also, if desired, magnified. Examples of such instruments are the *sphygmograph*, the *cardiograph*, the *pneumograph*, etc.

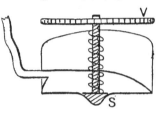

Fig. 147 shows Marey's cardiograph which is used to record the pulsations of the heart. An ivory button S is fitted in contact with the membrane, as

Fₗₒ. 147
Marey's Cardiograph.

shown, against which it is pressed by means of a spiral spring, the tension of which can be regulated by the screw V. The apparatus is applied to the chest, so that the button, S, is against the heart, at about the fifth intercostal space, and the pressure of the air is transmitted to a recording tambour.

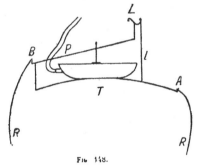

Fₗₒ 148.
Pneumograph.

The *pneumograph* shows the rise and fall of the chest. Laulanie's model has a tympan, T, soldered to a piece of metal which is applied to the chest. An inextensible ribbon, R, passes round the chest and is fixed to the metal at A, and to the teeth, B, of a jointed plate P. This plate receives the button of the membrane and stretches it by means of the lever L. and the elastic strap l. It is easy to understand that in inspiration the plate is pushed at B and tends to rock, pulling on the membrane, from which an aspiration of air is transmitted to the receiving typman. The contrary takes place in expiration (fig. 148). *Double pneumographs* are also used. Fig. 137 shows a pneumographic record being made during work.

Marey's *sphygmograph* shows the pulsation or the pulse, that is to say, the pressure of the flow of blood in the radial artery.

In fig. 149 a spring holds a little ivory disc against the artery and slightly compresses it, and the oscillations of the disc are transmitted to a rocking member B, which acts on the membrane

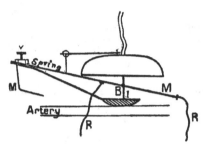

Fig. 149.
Marey's Transmitting Sphygmograph.

of the tympan. The sphygmograph of the transmission type is fixed to the arm by means of bands R, attached to the mounting M.

The pressure of the spring regulated by the screw V.

Marey's tambour can be used for the registration of any motions. Thus it can be used to record the swelling or shortening of a muscle and for the general study of *myography*. There is no need, therefore, to describe further applications, as they depend on the ingenuity of the user and on various circumstances.

196. The record is obtained by bringing the style of the receiving tympan in contact with smoked paper, covering a cylinder which turns at the desired speed.

The friction of the style on the paper must be negligible, styles made of bamboo or straw being very suitable. Glazed commercial paper is used covered with a relatively thin coating of lamp black,

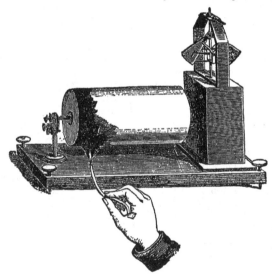

Fig. 150.

How to blacken a registering cylinder.

preferably of petrol black, although one can use essence of turpentine, or it can be smoked with a piece of small wax taper, as shown in the illustration ([1]) (fig. 150).

The deposit should be brown or chestnut-coloured, if possible, In most of the lever tympans, a screw adjustment allows the style to be gradually and delicately brought into contact with the paper. The receiving elements are mounted in front of the cylinder and fixed to supports of which it is best to have several mounted on an automatic slide capable of being moved from one end of the cylinder to the other (fig. 151). The tracings can then follow each other in a helicoidal manner and cover all the paper. There are generally three changes of speed; but in the latest models a wider range of speed is possible. The regularity of the rotation is assured by a Foucault governor with small vanes (see preceding figures).

The graphs, when obtained, are fixed by soaking the sheet in a fixing bath. The bath is composed of a filtered solution of gum-lac in alcohol, with a little Venetian turpentine, at 36°C. Before fixing, all notes (date, temperature, etc.), should be written on the sheet. When fixed and dried, the records are almost indelible.

The graphic method reveals, by its sensibility, details which escape our senses; in fact, the movements can be amplified by longer levers receiving the oscillation of the membrane nearer to their joints (§ 5).

Fig. 151.

Automatic slide on which the support is moved parallel to the cylinder.

([1]) Ch. Fleis (*Phys, Zeitsch.*, vol. xii., p. 391, 1911).

197. Measurement of Time.—The unit of time is the second. It is rarely necessary, in the phenomena under consideration, to measure small fractions of a second. However, in walking at 100 or 150 steps a minute, or in operating the keys of a piano, or a typewriter, etc., the duration of each movement may be from, say, $\frac{1}{4}$ to $\frac{1}{6}$ of a second. It suffices in most cases to use a metronome, which will give the cadence of the work, will regulate it invariably, and will indicate the duration of any isolated, mechanical act. Generally a metronome can hardly measure a quarter of second, as it makes 40 to 208 beats a minute (fig. 152.) The various cadences are obtained by moving the weight B on the pendulum and fixing it at the desired position (see § 26).

The metronome is wound up, and goes for about three-quarters of an hour, but it can also be actuated by electricity.

To record the time, on a registering cylinder, at the same time as the graphs of the movement, the *chrono-graph* is used. In Jacquet's chronograph a beat takes place every second or fifth of a second, and displaces the style, which is usually made of aluminium (fig. 153). It has two dials, of which one marks the seconds and the

Fig. 152.

Metronome.

other the minutes, and is mounted on a support like the tambours. The style makes a horizontal mark at each fifth of a second. To measure time, without registering it, the stop watch is used. It is started or stopped by pressing a button in one direction,

Fig. 153.

Jacquet's Chronograph.

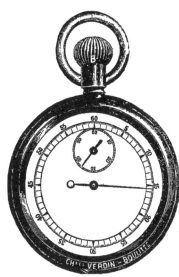

FIG. 154.
Stop Watch.

or by pressing once or twice on the button (fig. 154).

When the experiment lasts more than ten minutes, clocks are used with a loud tick, which produce a definite sound at the end of each minute. With care an ordinary watch can be used. The error here, is at the most two or three seconds per hour, or a relative average of $\frac{1}{1800}$. For instance, a man working hard would eliminate 1,500 litres of gas, and the relative error would be 1 litre per hour.

198. Experiments concerning the measurement of very rapid occurences, especially nervous phenomena, and the phenomena of shock, necessitate the use of chronographs reading to the $\frac{1}{100}$, and even the $\frac{1}{1000}$ of a second. Electrically driven tuning forks can be used. The vibrations of the tuning-fork can be registered directly, by the intermediary of an electric indicator, of which the best known is that of Marcel Deprez.

In the former case, the two prongs of the fork have between them an electro-magnet, connected to a battery, P, as shown (fig. 155). The circuit

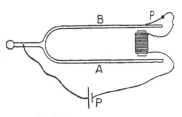

FIG. 155.
Electro-tuning Fork.

being closed the prong B is attracted by the magnet and breaks contact with a platinum point p. The circuit is then opened and the fork returns to make contact again with the point p.

A tuning fork can thus be made to vibrate continuously at the rate corresponding to its pitch. By attaching a very light style to one of the prongs, intervals of time corresponding to the period of the fork can be registered.

In the latter case, Deprez's indicator is introduced in the circuit of the battery. The indicator comprises a very small electro-magnet, E (fig. 156), which receives current from the same battery as the tuning fork, and attracts an armature, D, of soft iron, carrying a style S. This armature oscillates, therefore, at each vibration of the tuning-fork, being brought back to its initial positions by a small spiral spring R. The indicator, mounted on a supporting pedestal, is placed against the registering cylinder,

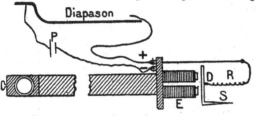

which allows the transmission of a time record from a long distance (see fig. 137). As has been said, Ja-quet's chrono-graph, reading to $\frac{1}{8}$ of a second, is quite sufficient

Fig. 136.

Registration of time by an electro-tuning fork.

in practice, the probable error being rarely $\frac{1}{2000}$.

When the time has to be read by a watch, the error must be reduced by increasing the duration of the phenomenon. Thus we observe n, similar movements in a time t; the duration of one movement is $\frac{t}{n}$, with a probable error of $\pm \frac{1}{t}$.

199. Measurement of Speed.—In uniform movement, speed is the relation of the distance to the time, the distance covered in a second.

When a movement is periodic, such that in each period it is uniform, the distance divided by the duration of the period gives the average speed. The walk of a man obeying a determined cadence is an example. The average speed of walking is there-fore easy to find. More often it is expressed in steps, the size of the step being estimated in centimetres.

In the case of a bicycle it suffices to count the numbers of strokes of the pedal. A tachometer or speedometer can also be used.

There are also acoustic timekeepers analogous to the metro-nome, which can be placed on the handle-bars, to beat the measure of the stroke of the pedal, thus regulating the speed. Also we can register electrically the revolutions of the wheel, especially if the bicycle is mounted on a fixed framework, as in certain experiments (§ 221).

Marey ([1]) evolved various arrangements for counting the number of steps and measuring their length in human locomotion. He utilised the old pedometer in conjunction with air transmission. A full description of this odograph (from the Greek οδος, distance) is not necessary.

([1]) Marey, *La Méthode Graphique*, p. 183, 1878.)

Marey also used a track, with electric contacts, to obtain a trace of walking, from which he was able to deduce the speed in terms of the cadence.[1]

Industry makes great use of revolution counters for machines, and of tachometers for bicycles and motor vehicles. As an example may be mentioned the meters which are used in weaving mills to indicate the quantity of thread unrolled and inserted by the shuttle of the weaver, from one selvage to the other, or the length of weft.

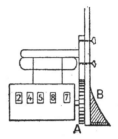

Fig. 157.
Plank Counter.

The weft meter is fixed by means of a bracket to the frame at a height at which it is easy for the workman to read the figures. He then knows the amount of work produced.

In the mechanical working of wood, a meter capable of counting the lengths of the planks planed or sawn is used (fig. 157).

This counter comprises a toothed wheel, A, which is set in motion by the planks. A support, B, fixes the meter to the frame of the machine. The readings are in metres.

200. The Anemometer.—The linear speed of gases is measured by the anemometer, especially when an estimation of the force of an air current is required. In this way, in the mining industry the quantity of air driven into a mine can be ascertained at any given moment. If it is desired to find the speed in a mine gallery, the average value is taken, because this speed varies at different points of the section, being generally greater in the centre than at the wall.

For speeds of $\frac{1}{2}$ to 10 metres per second, Combes' classic anemometer is sufficient (fig. 158). This instrument consists of a number of flat vanes, mounted at an inclination of 30° on a very thin spindle turning in agate bearings. The vane wheel is exposed to the wind so that the direction of the speed of the latter is parallel to the axis oo'. Its motion is communicated to a dial, C, graduated in revolutions. If N revolutions are recorded in time t, the speed is:

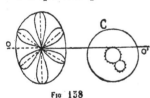

Fig 158
Combes' Anemometer.

$$V = a + bN ;$$

[1] Marey, in *Traité de Physique Biologique* (Marey, D'Arsonval, and Garcel vol. i., p. 187, 1901 Masson. Paris).

Where a is an instrumental co-efficient and b depends on the density of the air. The apparatus must therefore be tried at known speeds, in still air. Given the speeds V_1 and V_2, for which the corresponding number of revolutions are N_1 and N_2 in the same time, it will follow that:—$V_1 = a + bN_1$ and $V_2 = a + bN_2$, from which the values of a and b can be deduced.

There are numbers of types of anemo-meters : those of Casartelli, Biram, Robinson, Rosenmüller, Richard, etc. The latest anemometer of Lea-Biran's [1] has a vane wheel, p, operating a pointer which moves over a dial, c, a system of gears reducing the speed of rotation of the pointer, so that it does not make more than 20 revolutions per minute, when the speed of the wind is 10 metres (fig. 159).

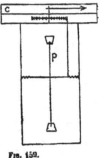

Fig. 159.

If there are N revolutions in t seconds, the speed in metres is given by the equation :

$$V = \frac{30N}{t}.$$

In Robinson's model the vane wheel is formed of hemispherical cups instead of flat vanes ; but the apparatus is too heavy and has too much friction whilst the indications are not accurate.

Richard's anemometer, like the Biram type, has a very light vane wheel, with aluminium wings ; it indicates the speed of the wind in metres.

201. Static Elements of the Human Machine : Stature.—The stature (§ 77) is determined by the use of Alphonse Bertillon's methods.[2] For the total stature the subject, with naked feet, is placed against a vertical wall with the heels together, the head held straight, and looking straight in front of him. A 2-metre scale is applied vertically on the wall, from the ground ; a set square is held against it and caused to slide down into contact with the top of the head, when the measurement is shown on the scale. It is better to take it twice, and it is especially essential to watch that the subject does not assume bent attitudes, hollowing his back, pushing out his stomach or shortening his neck. The feet being flat on the ground, this method gives the *whole* vertical development (fig. 160). The anthropmetric measurer is easily handled.

---

[1] *Engineering* of 20th Oct. 1911.
[2] Consult *Anthropologie Metrique* by Bertillon et Chervin Paris, 1909. We owe the three following illustrations to M. Bertillon

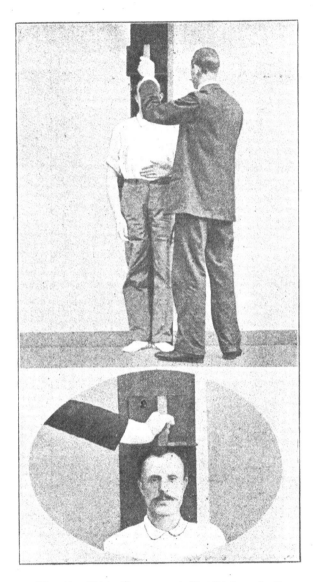

Fig. 160.—Height Measurement (Bertillon's method).

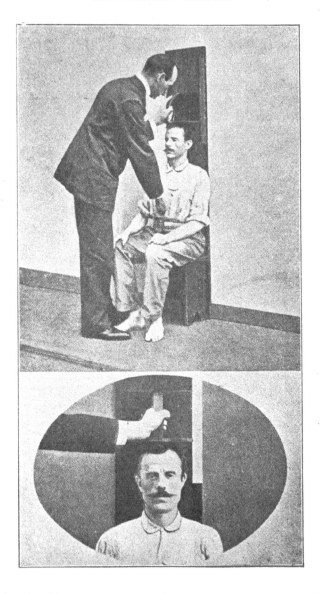

Fig. 161.—Measurement of sitting figure or bust (Bertillon method).

Fig. 162.—Measurement of the spread of the arms (Bertillon method).

In France the average stature varies between 167·20 cm. and 162·60 cm. For instance :

DEPARTMENTS	STATURE	DEPARTMENTS	STATURE
Ain	166·50 cm.	Lot-et-Garonne	166·10 cm.
Alpes-Maritimes	166·50 ,,	Meurthe	166·40 ,,
Côte-d'Or	167·20 ,,	Seine	165·80 ,,
Eure	166·30 ,,	Tarn	162·60
Haute-Savoie	166·20 ,,	Vosges	165·70 ,,
Jura	165·00 ,,		

In different countries, the following heights have been found:

Americans ([1]) {	Whites............................	171	cm.
	Indians	172	,,
	Negroes	168	,,
Annamites		158·50	,,
Arabs { Algeria ([2])		165·60	,,
{ Tunis ([3])		166·20	,,
Basques { French		165·80	,,
{ Spanish		163·8u	,,
Cochin Chinese		157·10	,,
Corsicans		163·30	,,
Scotch { towndwellers		174·60	,,
{ peasants		179·20	,,
Spaniards		164·50	,,
French		165·00	,,
Italians		164·50	,,
Japanese		157·00	,,
Akka Negroes		137·80	,,
Portuguese		163·70	,,
European Russians		164·20	,,

202. Measurement of the Bust and the Sitting Figure.—This measurement is taken with the subject sitting on a stool 0·40 m. high, so as to have the buttocks against the wall, the legs set square, and the shoulders falling. A scale and set square are used as for the height, and a deduction of 0·40 m. is made (Fig. 161).

The span is taken with the arms fully stretched horizontally against the wall (fig. 162). Finally the thoracic perimeter is

([1]) According to Gould (1869) and Baxter (1875).
([2]) The Berber average is higher—168 centimetres.
([3]) From statistics of 800 cases compiled by the author by the assistance of M. Louis Chenay, Director of the *Anthropmetric* Service ; the subjects were from 20 to 45 years old.

obtained with a tape measure passed round the lower part of the shoulder blades at the level of the nipples. When reading this measurement the respiration of the subject should be stopped.

The thoracic perimeter and the vital capacity vary according to the race. The following results have been found, for example, on adults :—

		THORACIC PERIMETER	VITAL CAPACITY
French	....	0·86 m.	3·750 litres
Americans {	Whites	0·84 ,,	2·709 ,,
	Indians	0·86 ,,	3·009 ,,
	Negroes	0·85 ,,	2·649 ,,
Germans	....	0·86 ,,	3·222 ,,
English	....	0·88 ,,	3·772 ,,

Generally the perimeter varies between 0·80 m. and 0·90m. in Europeans and the vital capacity between 3 and 4 litres.

203. Measurement of the Surface and Volume of the Human Body.—The area of the surface is usually obtained by Meeh's formula (§ 80).

The volume is given by the volume of water displaced when the subject plunges up to the ears in a bath fitted with an overflow, the initial level of the water being flush with the overflow (fig. 163). The plunge should be made gently after having turned off the tap, and the temperature of the bath,

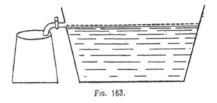

FIG. 163.

which should be between 20° and 25°C, should be noted. The water displaced and weighed will give the volume of the immersed body at the rate of (1 cm.³ + α) per gramme. The following table gives the values of 1 + α for various temperatures :

T	1 + α	T	1 + α
+ 10°	1·000273 cm³	+ 19°	1·001571 cm.³
11	1·000368 ,,	20	1·001773 ,,
12	1·000476 ,,	21	1·001985 ,,
13	1·000596 ,,	22	1·002208 ,,
14	1·000729 ,,	23	1·002441 ,,
15	1·000874 ,,	24	1·002685 ,,
16	1·001031 ,,	25	1·002938 ,,
17	1·001200 ,,	26	1·003201 ,,
18	1·001380 ,,	27	1·003473 ,,

As the subject's head remains out of the water, it must be taken into account, which is a rather difficult matter, the simplest way being to stop the ears with cotton wool, and only leave the nose above water. The correction is then insignificant.

204. Measurement of Weight.—It is a difficult operation to weigh the human body exactly. The subject must be weighed nude instead of deducting from his weight with clothes, the weight of the latter. He should be fasting, otherwise the weight of the food and the drink will make the result incorrect. For every reason it is better to take the weight on awaking in the morning before any food. To compare different weights from day to day they should always be taken at the same time, seven o'clock in the morning, for instance.

The balances used are sensitive to 5 grammes per 100 kilogrammes, but even this is insufficient in some cases. The total error being 10 grammes, if from one weighing to the next a subject gains 100 grammes, the maximum relative error would be 10%.

Care should be taken that the subject stands centrally on the platform of the scales, with his back to the graduation and that he keeps quite still.

The scales for weighing young children and babies must be very sensitive, and this is easily done. Many good models are on the market ; they are of the Roberval type, and sensitive to one gramme per 10 to 15 kilogrammes.

205. Dynamometric Measurements.—Dynamometers are springs whose deformations are proportional to the forces which

Fɪɢ., 164

Ordinary balance.

produce them (see § 11). The general type is the ordinary spring balance. It comprises a blade, AB, of tempered steel, of V-shape. At the extremity of the arm B is fixed an iron arc, *n*, which is prolonged and passes freely through an eye formed in the extremity of the other arm, A. From the latter a similar arc, *m*, passes in the same way through B, and is terminated by a hook, *c*. The arc, *n* carries a ring, *o* (fig. 164).

The balance is graduated by hanging it up by the ring *o* to a fixed point, and by suspending on the hook *c* increasing known weights. On the sector *n* notches are cut corresponding to the flexions of the arm A for the given weights.

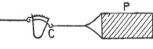

Fig. 165.

In order that the weight shall not exceed the limit of elasticity of the spring, the arc *n* has a stop *t*, against which the arm A will abut if the force is too great.

Suppose, for example, it is desired to measure the tractive effort in the transport of a load P. The hook C would be attached to the load, and a pull exerted on the ring until movement begins. The value marked would be that of the tractive effort (fig. 165).

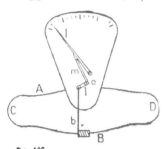

206. Regnier's Dynamometer.— This was constructed to Buffoon's requirements. It consists of two steel springs, A and B, united at their extremities by iron stirrups,

Fɪɢ. 166

Regnier's dynamometer.

C and D. In the middle of B is a small piece of metal which can move the jointed lever *lom*, by means of the crank *b*. The arm *m* of the lever guides the pointer I over a graduated scale supported by the spring A. The graduations serve a double purpose, one corresponding to the efforts of traction as when C is fixed and a pull exerted on D (renal force) and the the other to efforts of pressure as when pressure is exerted on B (see § 89 and fig. 166).

207. There are a considerable number of dynamometers, but it is impossible and unnecessary to describe them all. Various models are used in clinics, such as that of Bloch, the *sthenometer*.[1] In this case the deformations of an elliptical spring are transmitted by a pinion carrying pointers. The graduation is double for traction and pressure (fig. 167).

208. Dynamometric Registers or Dynamographs.— To observe the variations of force, Morin constructed to Poncelet's instructions,

Fig. 167. Bloch's Sthenometer.

a dynamometric register, the moveable end of the spring carrying a tracing point, which moves over the paper in pro-

---

[1] Bloch (*Comptes Rendus Biol.* 1895).

portion to the deformations. Thus ordinates are found proportional to the efforts, provided that the paper unrolls in front of the point parallel to the line of the abscissa xx'. The average value of the effort is the arithmetical mean of the ordinates :

$$y = \frac{y_1 + y_2 + \ldots + y_n}{n}.$$

And its intensity, at any moment, is given by the corresponding ordinate (fig. 168). On this principle the dynamographs of Marey [1] (fig. 202), Héséhous [2], Gréhant,[3] Charles Henry,[4] Hulss,[5] Verdin,[6] and Waller [7] have been constructed. The latter is in use in clinics in England, and gives the effort of the pressure of the hand (fig. 169).

In spite of their number and variety, the existing types of dynamometers in no way suffice to register all the forces and components of forces, found in the exercise of trades. Special devices have had to be got out to obtain records of efforts in all the possible circumstances, the nature of which is described later.

Fig. 168.

209. Registration of Muscular Efforts in different Occupations.—Marey's method is the foundation of all apparatus for these measurements. A spring suitably disposed and of appropriate strength, acts directly on an indiarubber bulb or on a Marey's tympan, the deformations being transmitted by the movement of the air and the elastic membrane, to a receiving tympan with a style acting on a registering cylinder. The record can thus be amplified and the ordinates will be proportional to the efforts (see § 215). Professor A. Imbert was the

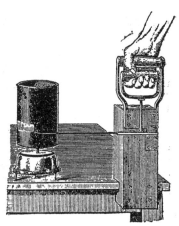

Fig. 169. — Waller's dynamograph.

[1] Marey (*Trav. de Laboratoire* i., 11, 1875).
[2] Héséhous (*Journ. de Physique* 1889).
[3] Gréhant (*Comptes Rendus Biologie*, 1891, 1892, 1897).
[4] Ch. Henry (*ibid.* 1895).
[5] Quoted and described by Krummacher (*Zeitsch. f. Biol.* vol. xxxiii. p. 135, 1896).
[6] Ch. Verdin (*Comptes Rendus Biologie*, 1896).
[7] A. Waller, *Physiol. Humaine.*

first to show the use that could be made of the graphic method to register the efforts of the workman's muscles on his tools.

210. Use of the "Cabrouet" and the Wheelbarrow.[1]—The *cabrouet* possesses two wheels, which maintain its lateral equilibrium (fig. 170), and these wheels have a small diameter, which requires the man holding the handles to bend his arms very little, the horizontal component of his effort being thus reduced (§ 12), although the equilibrium is stable.

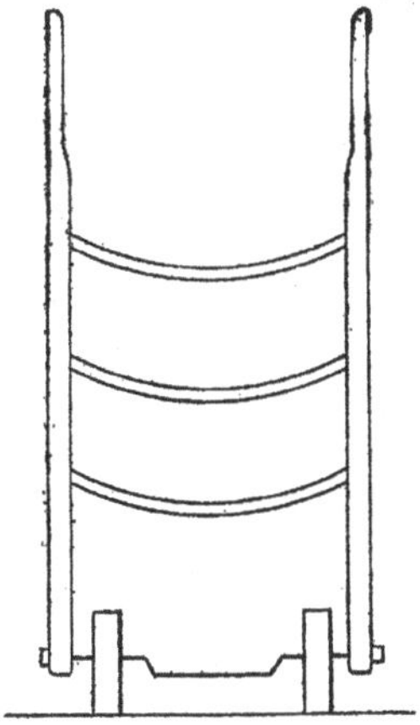

In the wheelbarrow, on the contrary, there is one wheel of larger diameter (fig. 171). The lateral equilibrium is therefore unstable, and the effort of support is greater, but the effort in the direction of the movement has a greater horizontal component. The *cabrouet* is designed to transport heavy weights, generally in single pieces, whilst the wheelbarrow is used to transport divided objects, such as stones, sand, gravel, earth, mortar and other materials of construction. The former of these objects is heavy, and its handling often requires two or three men. The latter is of an average weight of 30 kilogrammes, a capacity of $\frac{1}{20}$ to $\frac{1}{30}$ of a cubic metre, and one man handles it.

Fig. 170.

Cabrouet.

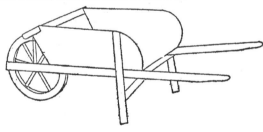

Fig. 171.

Wheelbarrow.

The muscular efforts to be registered are exerted perpendicularly to the handles, to support the load, and parallel to the handles to give the tractive force or the pressure necessary to move the vehicle.

[1] A. Imbert (*Bulletin de l'Inspection du Travail*, No. 5, 1905; Nos. 1 and 2, 1909; *Revue d'Hygiène et de Police Sanitaire*, vol. xxxi., 1909, No. 8).

1. Efforts Exerted Perpendicularly to the Handles.—One of the handles of the truck is sawn on the line S-S' at 0·30 m. from the free extremity. The fixed part, I, then has attached to its lateral sides two metal plates,

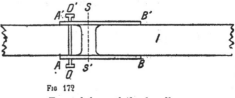

Fɪɢ 172

Frontal face of the handle.

AB and A′B′, which hold the detached part and are jointed by a pin, OO′, which works without friction (fig. 172). Further, on the front face of the handle, an oval spring, R, is fixed, and is screwed to the vertical ends of two metal angle plates, Q and Q′, fixed on the same face (fig. 173), whilst on the opposite side two similar metal angle plates are fixed, whose vertical edges support, the one a Marey's tympan and the other a rod *m*, which works the membrane (fig. 174). In reality the connexion of the rod *m* with the membrane of the tympan is more complicated and indirect, and includes a lever which allows modifications of the oscillations of the membrane of the tympan. For a similar rotation of the handle round the axis OO′, the membrane could receive an easily-regulated displacement and the tympan transmit movements of greater or less amplitude. It is sufficient to fit one only of the handles, with these attachments the effort of the man being practically symmetrical.

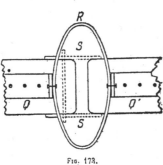

Fɪɢ. 173.

Front face with the oval spring R.

2. Efforts Exerted in the Direction of the Handles.—For this second measurement, one handle is made cylindrical and enveloped in a metal sleeve, M, carrying an angle bracket, H opposite a second angle bracket, H′ the brackets being connected by an oval spring, R. On the opposite side a tympan and rod system, as described in the preceding paragraph, is fixed.

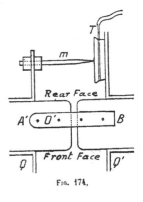

Fɪɢ. 174.

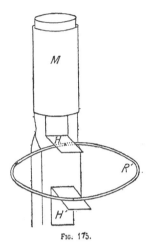

FIG. 175.

In these conditions, "when the workmen, holding the handle of the truck by the sleeve, M, exerts a pushing or pulling effort, this effort causes the sleeve M to slide to a degree limited by the spring R, the movement being transmitted to the membrane of the tympan [1] (fig. 175). Thus the efforts that are perpendicular and parallel to the handles will be inscribed on a cylinder by receiving tympans connected to the transmitting tympans.

211. In the handling of the *cabrouet* as in the displacements of loads in general, the load should be carried on a vehicle by pulling it. Imbert uses for this purpose an oval spring with a handle, P, and a Marey's tympan on one of its branches, joined to the other branch by a rigid rod, *t*. The man grasps the handle P (fig. 176).

The effort is registered by a receiving tambour connected with T.

A handle of the same kind can be used to measure the effort in supporting the handles of a wheelbarrow. Prof. Imbert fixes the spring to two metal pieces, M and M', the one soldered to the handle P (fig. 177)

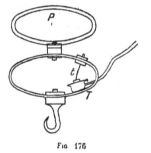

FIG 176

and the other to a ring, A, fixed to the handle of the wheelbarrow.

Thus the effort of support will deform the spring, and the deformations will be transmitted to an indiarubber bulb, C, placed in a metal cup, through the medium of a small disc, the bulb being connected to a receiving tambour.

The learned professor, of Montpellier, improved the method of measuring the effort parallel to the

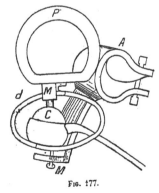

FIG. 177.

[1] A. Imbert (*loc. cit.*, p.p. 3-5 ; separate reprint, 1906).

handles. Two metal laths, PQ and P'Q'. are fixed across the latter, and have two rings underneath, in which slide two strong iron rods terminated by the handles I and I' (fig. 178).

These two rods are riveted to a transverse metal rod, HL, absolutely detached from the wooden handles, but to which is attached one end of a strong spiral spring, R, the other end

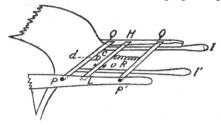

being fixed on the rod P'Q'. Hence, when holding the handles I and I', the workman will exert an effort on the transverse rod HL, whose displacements will be limited by the spring R. These displacements are translated by the deformations of a small indiarubber bulb, c, placed in a cup and in contact with a small disc, d, contact being made by the screw v. This arrangement is both sensitive and accurate.[1]

Fig. 178.

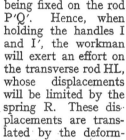

Fig. 179.
Shoe for measuring the pressure of the foot on the ground (Marey).

212. Marey's Experimental Shoes.—

The effort exerted by the foot on the ground, on a pedal, and so forth, can be registered by fitting the shoes with appropriate tambours. Marey's [2] model comprises a thick indiarubber sole, inside which is a small, hollow chamber. The fall and rise of the foot give rise to an expansion or compression of air which is communicated to a receiving tympan.

When walking, the subject carries a small registering cylinder in his hands (figs. 179 and 180). It should be recognised that the air chamber is not in contact with the entire surface of the foot, and therefore on this account the readings of the effort produced are rather uncertain. Besides

Fig. 180.

which, this kind of footwear will not allow long walks.

[1] A. Imbert (*Bull. Insp. Travail* Nos. 1 and 2, 1909 ; separate reprint pp. 8-9).

[2] Marey *La Méthode Graphique* pp. 155 and 497, 1878.

Marey also used another contrivance. The air vessel, containing a brass spring, is placed inside the heel of an ordinary shoe. A tongue of steel forming the sole is introduced under the foot of the subject and rests on projecting button which works the membrane of the apparatus. The pressure of the foot sends a certain amount of air through an indiarubber tube, which goes up behind the heel (fig. 181). This arrangement is especially adapted to the study of walking. Tatin (1843–1913) devised a " bellows " sole, which can be adapted to the footwear, and is of an extremely simple construction.

Marey used a dynamographic stage, or gangway, to study locomotion (§ 269).

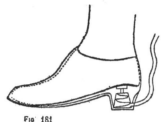

Fig. 181
Recording sole.

213. Tools provided with Recording Devices. — Professor

Imbert[1] applied Marey's system of registration to a tool much in use in the Midi, namely, the pruning shears, which are used to cut the long vine shoots into slips of a variable thickness. They are in the form of scissors, that is to say, a lever of the first order (fig. 182 and see § 51), the fulcrum being at the joint ; consequently, the effort will be all the greater the further away from the joint the vine-shoot is cut.

The measurement of this effort, therefore necessitates the choice of a constant position for the vine-shoot relatively to the tool. This is how Prof. Imbert proceeded. The handle, MN, of the pruning shears is cut at S, and the two parts are joined by means of a hinge which allows the portion SN to turn round the axis O, thereby drawing

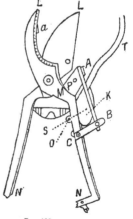

Fig. 182.
Pruning Shears.

[1] A. Imbert (*Revue d'Hygiène et de Police Sanitaire* vol. xxxi. No. 8, 1909 ; separate reprint p. 18 ; *Revue d'Economie Politique* 1909 ; *Revue Générale des Sciences* 1911, p. 481).

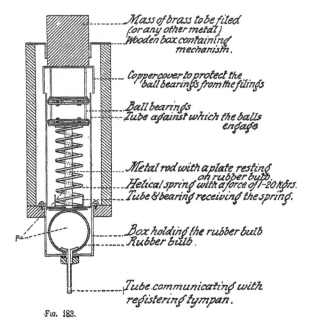

Mass of brass to be filed (or any other metal)
Wooden box containing mechanism.

Copper cover to protect the ball bearings from the filings

Ball bearings
Tube against which the balls engage

Metal rod with a plate resting on rubber bulb.
Helical spring with a force of 1-20 kgrs.
Tube & bearing receiving the spring.

Box holding the rubber bulb
Rubber bulb.

Tube communicating with registering tympan.

Fig. 183.

The Author's dynamometric support.

a steel blade, AB, which is riveted to the part P at one end, and at the other joins a bar, BC. The movement of the steel blade AB, in the effort of cutting, is transmitted to an indiarubber bulb, K, placed between it and the handle MN of the pruning shears. The bulb is connected by an elastic tube to a receiving tambour.

A stop, *a*, soldered to the blade L, assures that the vine-shoots are always placed at the same point.

214. Imbert was equally successful in registering the efforts made in filing, that is to say, the pressure exerted on the vice, the efforts of the left-hand which guides the tool and the effort of the right hand on the handle, but he did not publish his methods.[1] The author's arrangements for the same investigation were as follows [2] :—The part to be filed, a brass rod, for

[1] A. Imbert (*Revue Générale des Sciences*, 1911, p. 485).
[2] Jules Amar (*Journ. de Physiol.*, Jan., 1913, p. 62).

instance, is arranged in a dynamometric support such as that
shown on fig. 183, which is self-explanatory. The vertical pressure on the vice is thus registered. The special attachments for
the file (fig. 184) allow the registration of the effort of the right

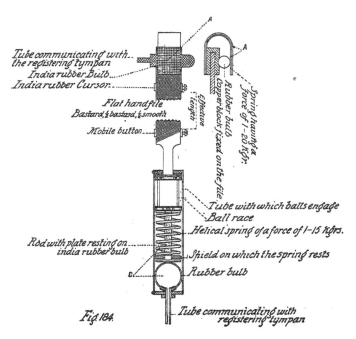

Dynamometric attachments for file.

hand on the handle (the horizontal component) and that of the
left hand (see § 311).

The dynamometric support, placed in the vice, gives the
vertical pressure of the two hands necessary to cause the file to
bite.

The spring attachments give the pressure of the left hand at
A and the horizontal component at B (fig. 185) ; also the horizontal component of the right hand at C. (fig. 184). Ball bearings
reduce the friction, and the strength of the springs is adjusted to
suit the nature of the work.

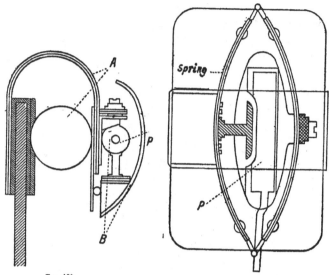

Fig 185

FIG. 185.—Elliptical spring for receiving the pressure of the left hand
[(B is seen in elevation and plan).   The rubber bulbs, which are connected
to receiving tympans of the Marey type, are placed at the points of application of the efforts, which deform them through the medium of small
tangential metal discs.

215. Evaluation of Efforts in Kilogrammes.

—To make use of any graph, such as Fig. 186, for quantitive purposes, we must know its scale, *i.e.*, to what weight a vertical distance of, say, 1 millimetre, corresponds.

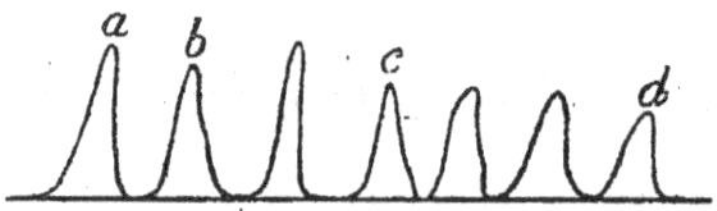

FIG. 186.
Graph of efforts.

In the case of the spring hook, this calibration can be very easily effected by rigidly fixing the handle, hanging various . standard weights thereto, and finding the corresponding heights of the ordinates from a graph such as fig. 187.

This calibration should always be carried out before each series of experiments.

Consider, first of all, the *cabrouet* the wheelbarrow, and

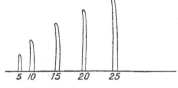

Fig 187.
Gauging of efforts.

similar vehicles. It is necessary to determine the effort of the support and that from which the progression results. For the former it will be sufficient to replace the muscles of the arm by a rope tied to the handles at its two extremities and hooked in the middle on to an ordinary balance (§ 205). For the effort of progression the inclination of the handles during transport must be taken into account. In fact, the effort exerted on a handle, in progression, acts by virtue of its horizontal component, OF',

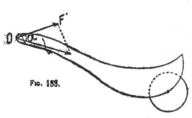

Fig. 188.

Effort of progression of a cabrouet.

and it is known (§ 3) that OF' varies as the cosine of the angle α, But the cosine varies inversely with the angle α, that is to say, the inclination. The necessary value OF' to overcome the friction of the wheel on its axis and on the ground will therefore depend, to a large extent, on the inclination (fig. 188).

Again, the friction varies according to whether the centre of gravity is nearer to or further from the axis of the wheel, and whether part of the weight has a greater or lesser effect on the workman's arms.

Thus the measurement of the effort must be made under perfectly definite conditions. Prof. Imbert was content to measure the effort of progression when the centre of gravity of the load was vertically over the axis of the wheels : he joined the handles by a rope whose centre was attached by another rope to a scale pan after having passed over a pulley. Weights were put into the scale until the progression of the truck started (no notice was taken of the effort of the start, which is always a little more).

The real measurement of the muscular effort should be obtained by introducing a graduated dynamometer between the handle and the hand and pushing until the inscribing style traces ordinates equal to the ordinates resulting from the progression.

216. The calibration is very simple in the case of the pruning shears (fig. 189). The handle N'L' is fixed into the jaws of a vice, so that the part SN is horizontal, and the spring of the pruning shears (shewn dotted) is replaced by a rigid piece. The calibration can then be effected by hanging weights from the middle of SN. If the weights are plotted, as abscissæ, a curve like that of fig. 190 would be obtained. The other tools are calibrated on the same principle.

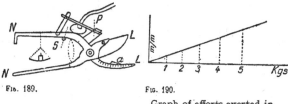

Fig. 189.

Fig. 190.

Graph of efforts exerted in
operating pruning shears.

The minimum effort needed for the manipulation of a tool is
a value that must be known, in order not to expose subjects who
have not the necessary muscular strength (women and children)
to too tiring a task, nor to cause them excessive fatigue.

CHAPTER II.

MEASUREMENTS : THE DYNAMIC ELEMENTS OF THE HUMAN MACHINE.

217. The Evaluation of Work.—The dynamograph, if it is arranged so as to indicate the effort, and the displacement at the point of application of that effort, is the proper instrument to measure the work done. Its graph shows the value of the effort and the amount of the displacement at any moment. Suppose the muscles pro-

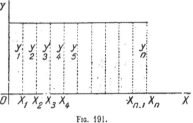

Fig. 191.

duce a constant effort, represented by the ordinates $y_1 \ldots, y_n$, in n seconds, and displace the resistance opposing them by distances $ox_1,\ x_1x_2 \ldots,\ x_{n-1}x_n$. The total work done by the muscles will be the sum of the products $ox_1 \times y_1 + x_1x_2 \times y_2 + \ldots$, say $ox \times y$ (fig. 191). If the effort were variable, the total area would be that of fig. 192.

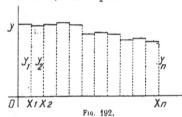

Fig. 192.

If the variation of the effort is continuous, the graph would take the form of a curve C (fig. 193) and the area to be found would be that of OABx.

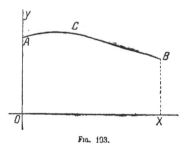

Fig. 193.

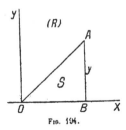

Fig. 194.

Area of right-angled triangle.

When the displacements are very great they can be reduced in any desired proportion *i.e.*, 1 millimetre can represent 10 centimetres, or 1 metre, or even 1 kilometre. This is the principle employed in a steam engine indicator : a curve is obtained of which any one point represents both the position of the piston (distance covered) and the pressure of the steam. The area of the curve is the measure of the work done during the stroke (§ 61) of the engine. The shape of the curves obtained varies. Sometimes it is that of regular figures, such as a right-angled triangle (fig. 194) (R), a trapezium (T), an ellipse or circle (E,c), a segment of a parabola (P), a sinusoidal curve (S), etc. The areas are respectively as follows :—right-angled triangle

$$S = \frac{OB \times AB}{2} \; ;$$

Trapezium (fig. 195) :

$$S = \frac{AB + OC}{2} \times AD \; ;$$

Semi-ellipse :

$$S = \frac{\pi \times OA}{2} \times AB \text{ (or AB}') $$

(fig. 196) ;

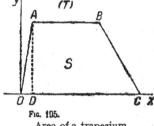

Fig. 195.
Area of a trapezium.

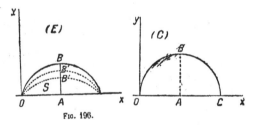

Fig. 196.

Area of ellipse and circle.

Semi-circle (fig. 196) :

$$S = \frac{\pi \times \overline{AB^2}}{2}$$

Segment of parabola (fig. 197) :

$$S = \frac{2}{3} OA \times AB$$

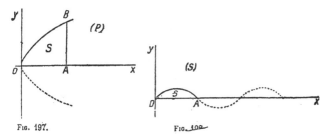

Fig. 197.   Fig. 198.

Area of a parabola.   Area of a sinusoidal curve.

Area of the sinusoidal curve (fig. 198) :

$$S = 2.$$

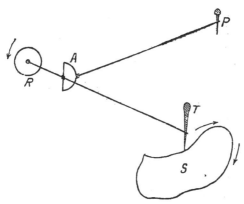

Fig. 199.

218. The problem of the determination of the areas or plane surfaces, that is to say, of the curves traced in a plane and whose equation usually is :

$$y = f (x),$$

is called the problem of the *quadratures*. It resolves itself always into the integration of the equation $y = f (x)$. Mechanical integrators or planimeters have been constructed, by which areas, or, in other words, work done can be measured. They comprise systems of jointed levers, turning round a fixed axis, and carrying a graduated cylinder and a tracing point. Whilst the tracer passes over the boundary of the area to be measured, the cylinder turns through an angle proportional to the area and gives its value. Amsler's planimeter is one of the best known. The present model consists of two rods AP and AT (fig. 199), jointed at

A by a universal joint. The point P is fixed at a point in the plane of the curved figure S, whose area it is desired to ascertain, and the point T is moved over the boundary of the figure.

During this movement a roller R, fixed to the rod, turns through an arc proportional to the area to be measured. Then S = K × n, K, being an instrumental constant, n the number of revolutions and fractions of revolutions of the roller. A counter on the rod AP gives the number of complete revolutions and a vernier, fixed to the roller, the fractions of a revolution.

Suppose 2,500 units to be indicated before, and 2,560 after the measurement. Then n = 2,560 — 2,500 = 60. Again the joint A, being placed at a point of the rod AT, the value of K is found at this point ; it is marked thereon in square millimetres.

Let K = 9 square millimetres. Then :

$$S = K \times n = 9 \times 60 = 540 \text{ square millimetres.}$$

The correction of the errors, or the compensation, is made by leaving the point P where it was, and bringing the roller to a position symmetrically opposite to the first position (fig. 200). In reality, therefore, two measurements, S_1 and S_2, are made ; the exact value will be :

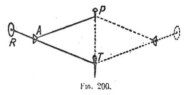

Fig. 200.

$$S = \frac{S_1 + S_2}{2}.$$

A simple way of finding areas is that of weighing the graphs (§ 80) and comparing them with the weight of a square centimetre of the same paper. Homogeneous paper must be used. The error is about 5%.

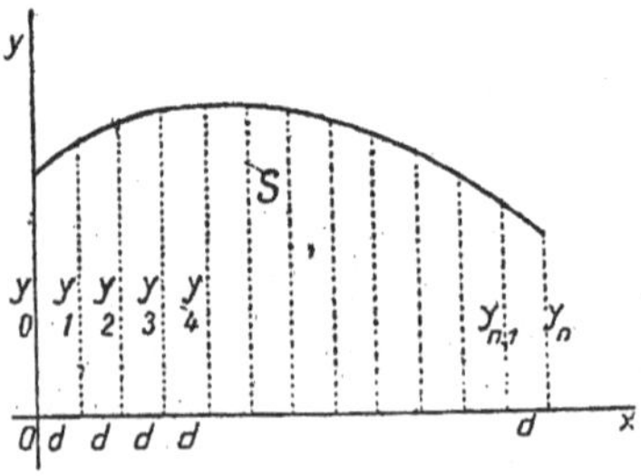

Finally, it can be seen that the area of a graph is equal to the sum, either of a series of small equal rectangles, as already seen, or more exactly of a series of small trapeziums. In this case, divide the base or the line of the abscissæ Ox into a sufficiently large number

Fig 201

Area of a graph (quadrature)

of equal parts, d (fig. 201). The value of S is furnished by Poncelet's formula :

$$S = d \left[2 \ (y_1 + y_3 + \ldots y_n\text{-}1) + \frac{y_o + y_n}{4} - \frac{y_1 + y_{n-1}}{4} \right].$$

This is the product of the distance d between any two consecutive ordinates by double the sum of the odd ordinates, plus a quarter of the extreme ordinates, and minus a quarter of the ordinates immediately adjacent to the extremes.

The even ordinates need not, therefore, be considered. The highest limit of error is :

$$\frac{d}{4} \ (y_1 + y_n\text{-}1 - y_o - y_n).$$

The application of Poncelet's method is easy and gives good results.

219. Ergometry and Ergography.—Ergometry is the name given to the procedure for the measurement of work done, and ergography is that given to the graphical registration of work done. In testing the output of ordinary machines Prony's brake or some modification thereof, is generally employed (§ 39). In the case of a man using a crank handle, a pulley could be fixed on the axis of the crank handle to transmit the work to a Prony brake, and the same could be done with a bicycle. But the results would be inexact. In fact, in an inanimate machine, we can balance the motor momentum gradually, by tightening the brake, and that momentum has a constant value. The muscles modify their power according to the resistance to be overcome, so that this power varies gradually in proportion to the tightening of the brake, and takes the value which corresponds to the friction at a given moment. An exact estimation of human work, by a Prony brake, is therefore necessarily difficult. The brake is also not very sensitive, and has been of little use in the study of muscular dynamics.

220. Ergographic apparatus is more numerous and more satisfactory than ergometric apparatus.[1] General Morin was the first to take up the subject, and on Poncelet's advice (about 1839 or 1940) he had a dynamographic machine constructed to measure the work done during the traction of carriages.

Marey applied his system of transmission by air as follows :— Suppose it is required to lift a load by means of a rope passing over a pulley. In the portion of rope which is moved by the muscles is interposed a dynamograph consisting of a piston P, held in equilibrium between two coiled springs, of which one, which is stiffer than the other, sustains the effort exerted at A. The rod of the piston is attached to a membrane of indiarubber,

---

[1] See below and also Zuntz (*Arch. f. Physiol.* 1899 p. 375) ; Johanssohn (*Skand. Arch. f. Physiol.* vol. xi. p. 273, 1901) ; Blix (*ibid.* vol. xv. p. 122, 1904).

which closes a metal case C. A strong iron casing carries the rings A and B. The resistance to be displaced acts at B and the effort is exerted at A raising the membrane slightly and producing a rush of air which acts on a receiving tambour (fig. 202). The graph will give the value in kilogrammes of the efforts of traction. The rotation of the pulley is transmitted by a system of reduction to the registering cylinder and, as a result, the area of the curve described gives the amount of work done. The distances covered can be reduced by combinations of gears or by pulleys of different diameters as required. Marey verified that the amount of work required to lift a load is greater than that for lowering it.

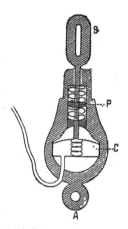

Fig. 202.
Marey's dynamograph.

221. Ergometric Apparatus.—Laulanié's dynamometer is as follows [1] ; Around the groove of a large pulley a metal strap passes, with equal weights, P and P′ at either extremity. The weight P is attached to a special weighing machine p (fig. 203). The subject turns the pulley at a constant speed. The work done is equal to the product of $2\pi r n$ (n = number of revolutions) by the friction indicated on the dial of the weighing machine. This apparatus was used for measuring work done by the arms. Atwater and Benedict [2] used an ergometric bicycle whose arrangement was such that the whole of the friction was converted into heat in a calorimetric chamber and was thus measured. This apparatus cannot therefore be used independently of a calorimetric installation. The reader interested in this technique can refer to the original memoir (see § 103).

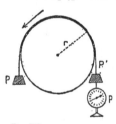

Fig. 203.
Laulanié's weight brake.

The ergometric bicycle [3] can be more simply and correctly employed as follows :—A bicycle is mounted on a rigid frame (fig. 204), the back wheel being weighted and well balanced so as

---

[1] Laulanié (*Comptes Rendus Biologie*, 1903, p. 880).
[2] Atwater and Benedict (*Bulletin*, No. 136, p. 30, 1903 ; No. 208, p. 11, 1909) and *Publication* No. 167, 1912).
[3] Jules Amar (*Journ. de Physiol.*, 1912, p. 303). *Cf. Le Rendement de la Machine Humaine* p. 30, Paris, 1910.

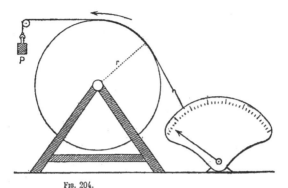

Fig. 204.

Diagram of Amar's braked bicycle.

to act as a fly-wheel. A steel band which carries weights at one of its extremities, and is attached at the other to a dynamometer with a dial, passes around a groove in this wheel. For a given weight P, P will be indicated on the dynamometer when stationary, but at a normal-pace, at a known speed $(P + p)$ grammes is indicated. The value p depends on the friction. The work done is:

$$T = 2\pi rn \times p \text{ (see also fig. 137).}$$

The work done by the muscles of the legs is thus measured, but the pedal could be replaced by a crank handle and the arms made to work by placing the whole frame at a convenient height. The number of revolutions is taken per minute. For greater exactitude an electric device can be fitted to the fork and the wheel at the point c, which will indicate by notches on smoked paper the revolutions of the wheel. A Deprez indicator may be introduced in the circuit (fig. 205). Other types of brakes are explained by figures 206 and 207. Finally, it may be mentioned that Langlois used a bicycle as a Prony brake which absorbs all the work transmitted to an auxiliary pulley.[1] It has already been shown why this arrangement is unsatisfactory ; it is particularly so at speeds of 90 to 120 strokes of the pedal per minute (§ 219).

Fig. 205.

Electrical registration of the speed of rotation of a bicycle wheel.

[1] Langlois (*Comptes Rendus Soc. Biol.* 1910-1).

222. Ergographic Apparatus.—These are undoubtedly the most useful, because they are the most practical and correct. The classic ergograph is that of Mosso,([1]) an Italian physiologist, who gave it his name. It comprises two parts :

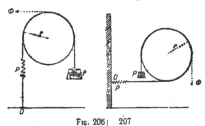

Fig. 206 | 207

The point O is fixed ; when stationary the spring balance shows the value of P which will overcome the effort of friction ϕ; in action it will indicate P — ϕ, from which ϕ can be deduced. The work done per revolution will be : $2\pi r\phi$.

1. *Fixed Portion.*—In Mosso's model assume that the registration of the flexor muscles of a finger is to be taken; the hand is laid, palm upwards, on a cushion, A (fig. 208), whilst the index and ring fingers are introduced into the rigid tubes G and N; the back of the forearm resting on B. Next a bracelet, CD, is tightened round the wrist, and sometimes a second in the middle of the forearm. The whole hand and forearm are therefore sufficiently fixed, while the middle finger remains free.

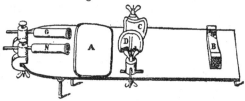

Fig 208
Fixed portion of Mosso's ergograph.

2. *The Inscribing Slide.*—The moving portion is a slide travelling on two bars, N, N', and carrying a pen, PQ. To the base of the slide is attached, on one side, the cord S, which is connected to the middle finger, and on the other side a cord T, passing through the axis of a screw C and over a pulley V, to sustain a weight P. The screw C regulates the initial position of the slide so that, when stationary, the finger does not undergo traction (fig. 209).

([1]) Angelo Mosso (*Arch. Ital. Biol.* vol. xiii. p. 123, 1890. *La Fatigue,* French translation, 1894).

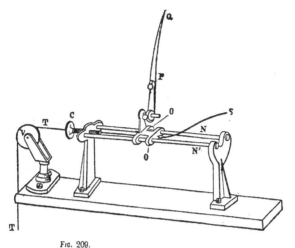

Fɪɢ. 209.

Inscribing slide of the ergograph.

The two parts of Mosso's ergograph are mounted securely on a table, and the pulley projects over the end of the table ; the fixed portion, parallel to the side edge of the table, is inclined to the right for the right hand. The finger is attached to the cord S by means of a leather ring round the second phalange. The position of the screw C is adjusted and a weight, P, say 3 kilo-grammes, is suspended at the end of the cord T. The pen is put in contact with a registering cylinder rotating slowly (fig. 210).

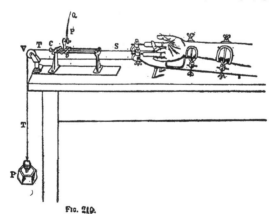

Fɪɢ. 210.

Complete Mosso ergograph.

At each flexion of the finger, a curve is registered whose ordinate expresses the displacement l of the weight P ; the motor work done by contraction is therefore P $\times$ l. The intensity of the contractions becomes progressively less because of the fatigue, and the general trend of the curves is descendant, especially when the rhythm of the movements is accelerated. The whole of the contractions registered up to the point of fatigue is called an ergogram. Fig. 142 shows a few ergograms.

223. Various Ergographs (on Mosso's Principle).—There are a considerable number of ergographs having the same principle as that of Mosso. Most experimentalists have used the mesial finger for their experiments,([1]) except Storey,([2]) who, noticing the constraint of this finger when the others were immobilised by the apparatus, used the index finger ; this is certainly more normal.

Trèves designed a brachial ergograph,([3]) shown in fig. 211. The subject leans against a vertical wall A, whilst his right arm is fixed in a saddle, B, by means of a strap. A bracelet, G, attaches the forearm to the crank-handle E, of a wheel C, whose axis lies in the prolongation of the transverse axis of the elbow joint. The weight P to be lifted is suspended from a cord which runs in the groove of the wheel C. Finally from the axle H of the latter, a cord runs to the inscribing slide.

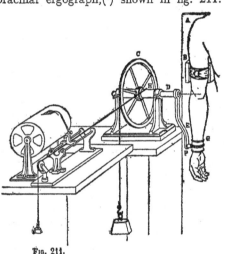

Fig. 211.
Trèves brachial ergograph.

To obtain the value of the work done, the radii R of the crank handle, r of the wheel, and r' of the axle, must be taken into

([1]) Lombard (*Journ. of Physiol.* vol. xiii. pp. 1-58 1892) ; Pantanetti, (*Arch. Ital. Biol.*, vol. xxii., p. 17, 1898) ; Trèves, (*Ibid.*, vol. xxxvi., p. 44, 1901) ; Binet and Vaschide (*Année Psychol.*, 1898, p. 303) ; Grandis (*Arch. Sc. Med.* vol. xxvi. p. 269, 1902).

([2]) Storey (*Amer. Journ. of Physiol.* vol. viii., p. 355, 1903.

([3]) Trèves (*Arch. Sc. Med.*, vol. xxii., p. 373, 1898).

account. If h is the ordinate of a curve due to the flexion of the forearm relatively to the arm, the corresponding work done will be :

$$\mathbf{T} = \mathrm{P} \times h \times \frac{r}{\mathrm{R}} \times \frac{r}{r'} = \frac{\mathrm{P}hr^2}{\mathrm{R}r'}.$$

224. The modifications of Mosso's apparatus necessary to make an ergograph of the legs will now be considered. These were due to Capobianco ([1]) (fig. 212): The fixed portion is a boot made of fine and strong cloth with a rigid sole of wood or iron. This is fixed on a support of convenient size, having a spur to which is attached catgut passing over a pulley r on a level with the support.

The cord is attached to the usual Mosso slide, with its style S and weight P. The subject sits on a chair, the thigh being held by a strap, and the leg being a little bent. He raises the heel whilst the point of the foot remains fixed to a hinge. Under a weight of 20 kilogrammes, the contraction of the crural triceps causes rapid fatigue, and the ergograms obtained are very similar to those for the middle finger.

The technique of ergography need great attention to avoid muscular associations and pain.([2])

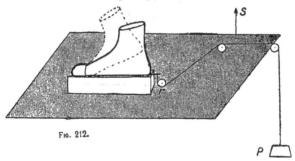

Fig. 212.

Capobianco's ergograph for the leg.

225. The Measurement of Industrial Work.—The principal object of ergographs is to investigate the decrease of work under the influence of fatigue.

Marey's graphic method only allows the measurement of the muscles applied in the handling of a given tool. The arrangements described herein for the measurement of muscular effort are also applicable for the measurement of work.

([1]) F. Capobianco (*Arch. Ital. Biol.*, vol. xxxvii., p. 123, and especially *Monitore Zoologico Ital.* No. 7, 1901).

([2]) Consult Holmes (*Journ. of Amer. Med. Assoc.*, Dec. 1903), and Hellsten (*Skand. Arch. f. Physiol.*, vol. xvi., 139, 1904); A. Imbert (*Comptes Rend. Ac. Sc.*, 31st, Oct. 1910).

Consider the different cases already mentioned (§ 209 *et seq.*) and distinguish carefully the useful work of the instrument on the one hand, and the muscular work on the other. For example, the useful work of a truck, a wheelbarrow, or any vehicle, is the product of the friction by the distance covered. The manner of measuring the effort due to the friction F is known. Measure the distance covered L, then

$$\mathbf{T} = F \times L.$$

But it is the horizontal component of the muscular effort which gives the value F ; if it is a fraction $\frac{1}{m}$ of that total effort, it can be said that the muscles make an expenditure of force, $m \times F \times t$ in the time t, during which the work is performed.

The diagram, fig. 213, gives an example of the method of analysing the effort exerted on the tool.

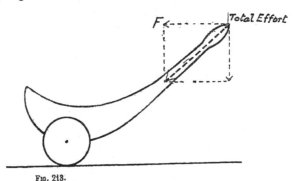

FIG. 213.

Analysis of the effort in pushing a truck.

The maintenance of the handles at a certain height constitutes a static effort, $F' \times t$, so that for work done, $\mathbf{T} = F \times l$, in the time t, the expenditure of muscular force is :

$$\sqrt{F^2 + F'^2} \times t.$$

226. The measurement of the work done in using pruning shears was made by Prof. Imbert by finding the distance fallen by a weight capable of cutting a given vine-shoot. For this purpose the pruning shears were arranged as if for the measurement of the effort of cutting (fig. 189). In the centre of SN was suspended a flexible cord, terminated by a hook to receive the weight, the latter being caused to fall along a vertical scale, giving the height of the fall.

Let P be the weight and h the height ; the work done in cutting will be :

$$\mathbf{T} = Ph.$$

It is important 'to remember that this work varies according to the position of the vine-shoot in relation to the pivot of the pruning shears and according to the thickness to be severed.

227. Consider again the case of the work done in filing. The workman leans on the file to make it bite, but the work done is the product of the distance travelled by the file and the sum of the horizontal efforts of the right and left hand, which overcome the resistance of the metal. If the value of these efforts is F, and if the distance traversed by the file is l, the work done per stroke of the file will be

$$T = Fl.$$

It is not necessary to add that the same principle can be applied to the measurement of the work done by the plane, saw, etc. However great the static efforts of the muscles, they cannot, properly speaking, figure in the useful work.

228. Classification of the Work done by Man.—Considering mechanical work only, a classification could be based on the group of active muscles employed according to whether they are the muscles of the arms, of the legs, of the fingers, or several groups at once, or, finally, whether the whole weight of the body is utilised.

The work of the arms is the most varied, being used to push or pull, either directly or through the medium of levers, crank handles, ropes, and pulleys, and to actuate numerous tools and apparatus.

The file, saw, plane, pruning shears, clippers and scissors are levers of the first order, having consequently the fulcrum at the pivot. The example of the pruning shears gives the procedure for measuring the effort of the hand and its work.

Pump handles, sculls of boats, large vegetable or bread cutters and nut crackers are levers of the second order. The effort can be measured by applying to the arm of the lever, at the point where the power will act, a steel blade covering a small rubber bulb, the variations of pressure of the air being transmitted to a receiving tambour, this being the system adopted to measure the vertical effort of the left hand acting on a file (fig. 185). In the case of an oar the fulcrum is the water, the effort of the rower is the power, and the boat that he propels constitutes the resistance. In this case the effort could also be easily measured if the relative positions of the surface of the water, the oar, the boat, and the rower remained constant throughout the experiment. The registering cylinder could be placed in the boat by holding it suitably, as Marey's register is held in walking (fig. 180).

The pile-driver consists of a very heavy mass called the "monkey," which is first raised to a certain height and then let fall on to the pile to be driven into the ground. In the hand pile driver each labourer pulls on a rope, and if there are n workmen and the weight of the monkey is P, each of them will sustain on an average a weight, $\dfrac{P}{n}$.

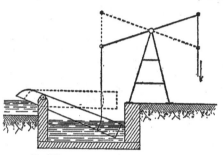

Fig. 214.

Dutch scoop.

By inserting a strong spring balance, or, better still, a Marey's dynamograph, in the rope, suitably cut, we can measure at any moment the effort exerted by the labourer. The inclination of the rope to the vertical modifies the value of that effort.

Knowing the height to which the monkey is lifted, we can find the work done per blow of the pile driver. It is easy to find out how many blows of the pile driver a man makes in the course of a day's work.

In the Dutch scoop, by which water is raised by hand, the height to which the water is lifted and the depth of the sumph are known. A dynamograph could be inserted in the rope, which is attached to the bucket to measure the effort. If the effort is applied through the medium of a lever, as in certain methods of drawing water, the work done can be calculated from the displacement of the power arm, which is known (fig. 214).

229. The action of the muscles of the arms can be exerted on windlasses either through the medium of a rope wound round a drum, or by means of a crank handle, BA, mounted at the extremity of the shaft BC of a winch (fig. 91. The effort can be measured by interposing a spring balance or a dynamograph in the rope and by applying a spring with an indiarubber bulb to the crank handle.

Let F be the power exerted by the workman ; the arm of the lever in relation to the axis of the windlass is BB′ ; call it r. It is obvious that the work done per revolution is :

$$T = 2\pi r \times F.$$

The effort F acts tangentially to the barrel, in the first case, and to the circumference described by the crank handle in the second case.

The work thus estimated includes that of the friction of the axle of the windlass, and of the stiffness of the rope which is wound round the barrel. In the same way we can calculate the work done, and measure the power, in the case of a capstan, which is, in fact, a windlass with a vertical axis. A man turning a capstan would exert on one of the bars an effort F ; let l be the length of the bar ; then the work done is $2\pi l \times F$ per revolution. Several bars are thus fitted to the head of the apparatus, and by the efforts of several men the cable that carries a ship's anchor is wound up.

A winch is often used to raise the monkey of a pile-driver. The rope is coiled round the barrel of the winch, and when the monkey has attained the desired height it is released automatically and falls on to the pile.

In the lifting jack, by which heavy loads are lifted to a small height, the power is exerted on a crank handle.

Finally, in the coining press, the power is exerted on a horizontal lever actuating a screw. None of these operations presents any complications as regards the measurement of the effort and the muscular work (see Book VI.).

230. Smith's bellows are even simpler in that respect, owing to the method by which they are worked. A dynamograph will give the effort exerted on the operating cord, and a stop can be provided to limit the travel of that cord so that the work done can be measured.

Various tools, worked by hand, such as pincers, screw-drivers, augers, graving tools, centre bits, turning chisels, planes, nippers, bow drills, violin bows, etc., either do not require much effort, or are rarely used continuously. It would be interesting, however, to fit them with dynamographic apparatus to obtain an idea of the effort which each of them requires. For the violinist's bow, in particular, the effort is small, but it is continuous and rapid, and the registration by means of a dynamograph placed in the closed hand, should therefore indicate also the speed of the movement of the bow.

The handling of the hammer and the mallet is sometimes fatiguing. They are, in the majority of cases, made so that at the moment of the percussion there is no appreciable reaction on the hand (§ 41). The useful work of the hammer is easily calculated from the speed

$$T = \tfrac{1}{2}Mv^2$$

at each blow. The force of the blow is : $Mv = Ft$. If t is registered electrically F can be estimated.

In the construction of earth-works, in agriculture, etc., the tools used comprise picks, spades, and shovels. The measurement of the work done requires the knowledge of the weight displaced (the tool and its load), as well as the height to which it is lifted. The strictly useful effect is the work done and the weight of earth displaced, etc. To drive a pickaxe or spade into the earth a certain resistance has to be overcome. It is therefore necessary to divide the handle into sections and adapt an appropriate dynamograph to it in order to find the expenditure of energy.

231. Exercise of the Fingers.—Here speed is an important factor, as in the work of instrumental musicians, writers (in the manual sense of the word), engravers, sempstresses, embroiderers, etc. When the fingers have to operate keys (fig. 215) the latter can be fitted with small tambours, which will indicate the pressure applied. In addition, by means of a wire and a light counter weight, the displacement can be registered and the amount of work done calculated. Marey himself proceeded as follows : — Above each key of the keyboard of a harmonium, small bellows were arranged, each connected by a special tube to a similar bellows, operating an inscribing style.([1]) Thus a record of the notes played was obtained, with their durations represented by longer or shorter marks. In reality, these measurements are not very useful, the real factor to be considered in this kind of fatigue being the speed of the movements.

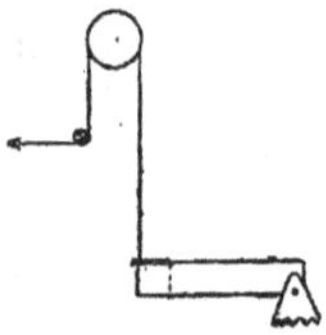

Fig. 215
Piano action

232. Work of the Muscles of the Leg.—These are certainly the strongest of the human muscles. Their normal rhythm and fatigue can be studied by means of Capobianco's ergograph. The work done on a bicycle or on a treadle of a grindstone, for example, is easily estimated (§ 221), especially if the foot is fitted with an experimental shoe and the pedal with a Marey tambour with an internal spring (§ 212).

In the case of bicycles, special dynamographs are used, such as Scott's *cyclograph* or Marey's *dynamometrical pedal*.([2])

If F is the uniform pressure on each pedal and d is the diameter of the circle of the pedal, the work done will be F $\times$ d. Per stroke of the pedal (both legs working) it is approximately :

$$T = 2Fd.$$

This is the work performed by the legs, and it is also the work done in advancing the loaded bicycle. It is clear that, by each stroke of the pedal the bicycle advances a distance D, depending on the gear. If R is the sum of the resistances overcome (resistance to rolling, passive resistances of the bearings and of the transmission, and resistance of the air) then

---

([1]) Marey : *Le Mouvement*, p. 12, 1894.
([2]) Bowny (*Comptes Rendus Sciences*, 15 June, 1896).

$$R \times D = \mathbf{T} = 2Fd..$$

So that, knowing $\mathbf{T}$ or R, we can deduce the value of the average pressure F on the pedals. A value of R, sufficiently accurate for practical purposes, is given by the equation :

$$R = 0{\cdot}012P + 0{\cdot}0738SV^2,$$

P being the total weight of the bicycle and the rider, S the surface area of the latter, about $0{\cdot}60$ sq. metres and V the speed in metres per second.

If the slope is inclined by i per metre :

$$R = P\ (0{\cdot}012 \pm i) + 0{\cdot}073SV^2.$$

Example : A speed of 18 kilometres an hour is maintained on a slope where $i = 0{\cdot}02$ metre; the bicycle weighs 15 kilogrammes and the rider 65 kilogrammes.

Then $\qquad P = 65 + 15 = 80$ kilogrammes.

$$V = \frac{18,000}{3,600} = 5 \text{ metres per second.}$$

Therefore :

$$R = 80 \times 0{\cdot}032 + 0{\cdot}073 \times 0{\cdot}6 \times 5 \times 5 = 3{\cdot}655 \text{ kilogrammes.}$$

The work done will be

Per hour :

$$3{\cdot}655 \times 18,000 = 65,790 \text{ kilogrammetres.}$$

Per metre :

$$\frac{65,790}{18\ 000} = 3{\cdot}655 \text{ kilogrammetres.}$$

In the descent the value of R will be :

$$R = 80 \times (-0{\cdot}008) + 0{\cdot}073 \times 0{\cdot}6 \times 5 \times 5 = 0{\cdot}455 \text{ kilo-}$$
grammes.

Of course the nature of the ground, and the state of the tyres will modify the preceding values.

The ordinary work of the legs is that of locomotion (see below, § 263) ; they then support the weight of the human body with variations depending on the nature of the movement. They often have to resist, in addition, the weight of loads carried, whilst displacing this total weight on the horizontal or on a slope. The useful work is obviously the product of the weight displaced by the sum of the amplitudes of the vertical oscillation of the body walking on level ground, or by that sum increased by the total slope that has been climbed. But the horizontal journey modifies the expenditure of energy to such an extent for a similar amount of mechanical work that it is advantageous to use as Coulomb did, a unit other than the kilogrammetre, one which is the product of 1 kilogramme of weight displaced per metre covered, horizontally or on a slope. This unit will be known as the metre-kilogramme (symbol : Mkg.).

When it is only a question of lifting a weight to the top of a staircase of height H, the work done will be P × H, because the subject really lifts his weight, exerting an effort P in the direction of the displacement H.

If he mounts a ladder, H will be the vertical distance in relation to the ground, and not the length of the ladder.

But according to the speed of the ascent, the subject will expend an effort greater than P, so that the muscular work is greater than the mechanical work.

When the subject descends from a height, H, the mechanical work due to the action of gravity on his total weight, P, is obviously P × H. The muscular work done depends on the effort exerted in resisting the force of gravity. (See the following chapter).

233. Various Work due to the Muscles of the Legs.—The treadmill or quarrier's windlass (fig. 216) is used to lift stones. It comprises a wheel having steps projecting laterally around its circumference. The labourer climbs these steps, and thus works it by his weight acting at the extremity of a very long radius R. The work done per revolution is :

$$T = 2\pi R \times P.$$

The ascension is in this case virtual, the subject not really mounting at all.

In working the treadle of a sewing machine or a grindstone, (which are levers of the third order) the experimental shoe will give the value of the effort. The effort varies according to the hardness of the material to be worked, the pressure of the tool on the stone, etc.

Fig. 216.
Treadmill or quarrier's windlass.

234. The Complexity of Industrial Labour.—The analysis of the methods of measurement has necessitated a classification by active muscular groups. In reality the workman moves his arms at the same time as his legs in many occupations.

This is always the case in sports such as gymnastics, fencing and boxing. In these the speed of the movements is, as a rule far more important than the magnitude of the effort.

Public speaking entails a certain amount of work, which reaches high values in the orator, the actor and the singer.

The work of speech has been measured by Marage [1] from the volume of air V expelled by the lungs and its pressure H in the trachea. It is expressed by the product VH. But this estimation gives only a fraction of the work performed by the orator, all the muscular energy being excluded from it. The total work done must apparently elude any experimental determination.

235. Power of Man.—This is estimated, in the case of continuous labour, or for a period of time t, by dividing the work done by its duration expressed in seconds. This is the speed of work. A scientific organisation of labour must assure that the power of the workman is practically constant at each period, and that it is not reduced by too rapid fatigue, due to bad mechanical or physiological conditions.

---

[1] Marage (*Journal de Physique,* 1908, p. 298).

CHAPTER III.

The Measurement of Energy.

236. General Remarks.—The two forms of energy with which we are concerned in our study of the human machine are, firstly, that which is manifested externally in work or heat, and, secondly, that energy which acts from outside on the organism.

The first is the expression of physiological work or physiological energy. The second is due to natural and meteorological actions. The latter react on the former so that the measurement of physiological energy, that is to say, of the expenditure of the human motor gives exactly the resultant of its functions at a definite moment. In addition, it indicates the quantity of energy that a certain amount of work entails, a certain form of activity whose mechanical estimation would not be possible.

This kind of measurement will first be considered.

237. Measurement of Physiological Energy.—There are two methods, that of the maintenance ration and that of the consumption of oxygen (§ 100).

(A) *Method of Maintenance Rations.*—The subject of the experiment follows his usual alimentary diet. The approximate quantity and quality of the rations consumed is noted. Then, by trial, he is given a ration such that every day, at the same hour, his weight is appreciably the same. That hour will be preferably on rising in the morning.

In addition, if it is desired to find the ration corresponding to a definite dynamic expenditure, the daily work should be as constant as possible, and performed at the same period of each day.

As soon as the subject has began to work, it may be found that the trial ration may allow him to maintain his weight even on the following day. It would be a mistake to stop there. We have always found that the ration would not maintain the weight on next day but one. It must then be slightly increased. On the other hand, seven to eight days of the same work diminish the living ration. These variations are small, as the following figures show :

Weight of subject in repose...........................	80·200	kg
1st day of work	80·200	,,
2nd ,, ,, ...	79·980	,,
3rd ,, ,, ...	80·100	,,
4th ,, ,, ...	80·180	,,

5th day of work	.... 80·200	kg.
6th ,, ,,	.... 80·200	,,
7th ,, ,,	.... 80·200	,,
8th ,, ,,	.... 80·280	,,
9th ,, ,,	.... 80·300	,,

The reading for the seventh day is used, but frequently constancy of weight is attained on the third day.[1]

The living rations are estimated in great calories.

The preceding conditions are applicable to laboratory researches. Ordinarily a man's labour is not constant and the energetic estimations are no longer correct.

As a rule, therefore, inquiries are made as to the average rations of workpeople of different ages, occupations, and sexes. The Solway Institute [2] organised its inquiries as follows : Through the medium of trustworthy people, inquiries were made in the homes of workpeople who were neither very poor or in easy circumstances. The household was considered to be all those who normally had their meals together. The information usually related to a period of fifteen days, some being furnished by the note book of the observer, and others by the household consumption book kept regularly by the house-wife. When the inquiry was finished, the quantities of proteids, fats, and carbo-hydrates and the corresponding energetic values were determined from tables (§ 98). Finally, to take into account the age and the sex, Atwater's co-efficients were employed [3] :

The consumption of an adult man being   1·00
That of a woman will be.....................   0·80
Boy of 14–16 years   ....   0·80
Girl of 14–16 years   ....   0·70
Child of 10 to 13   ....   0·60
    —   6 to 9   ....   0·50
    —   2 to 5   ,, ...   0·40
    —   below 2 years   ....   0·30

We can thus estimate the average energetic expenditure of a man in a known occupation. This method obviously lacks exactitude.

238. (B) *Oxygen Method.*—This method is both more convenient and more accurate than the other. In fact, it allows the measurement of the energetic expenditure of subjects with a free diet, and, if required for short periods of a few minutes only.

---

[1] Jules Amar., *Le Rendement* (*loc. cit.*, pp. 45-6).

[2] Slosse and Waxweiler : *Enquête sur le Régime Alimentaire*, part 9 ; Bruxelles, 1910, p. 14).

[3] Atwater (*Bulletin*, No. 142, p. 33, 1903). Engel gave the same coefficients (*Bulletin, Soc. Internat. Statist.*, vol. ix., p. 5, 1895).

The principle has already been stated. We have to determine the consumption of oxygen, in repose and at work, of a subject placed in an environment of known temperature.

To avoid uncertainty, it is better to operate in the morning, after the fast of the night (about 10 hours). The calorific power of a litre of oxygen, at $0°$ and 760 mm., will then be 4·6 cal. (§ 110).

We can also give a certain quantity of carbo-hydrates to the subject and not begin the determination until 2 hours afterwards. In that case the calorific power will be nearly 5 calories (§ 101).

If, finally, the subject feeds as he likes, and it is not possible to submit him to a known diet, we are guided by the respiratory quotient (§ 101). The calorific power power is then 4·90 cal. on the average. The experiment should last at least 10 minutes so that the respiratory regimen may become normal.

239. Measurement of Respiratory Exchanges.—In the mouth

Fig. 217

Chauveau's respiratory valve.

of the subject Chauveau's inhaler is placed, the valves of which combine tightness with great mobility. At inspiration the external air opens the valve I and passes to the lungs ; at expiration, I closes and the gasses pass through the valve E, an indiarubber tube leading them to the meter (figs. 217 and 218).

Fig. 218.—Chauveau's respiratory valve.

The part of the valve B, which enters the mouth, has a ring of indiarubber which fits against the teeth, under the lips, and prevents any leakage. The nose is pinched by a clip in the form of a small wooden clothes peg covered with felt. Before the experiment, the parts of the valve are carefully cleaned to prevent the adherence of the valves to the seatings ; these seatings are made narrow to diminish their adherence to the valves.

The external air which the subject is to breathe must be pure, composed of 21% of oxygen and 79% of nitrogen by volume. He should therefore be placed in the middle of a large room, well ventilated, or, better still, fresh air from outside, taken at a certain height from the ground, is brought in by a glass or rubber tube (see fig. 137).

In experiments on locomotion the preceding installation is not suitable if the subject covers any great distance. Therefore the study of walking requires special arrangements, to which further reference will be made.

240. When the valve is in place, the expired gases are conducted by a rubber tube to a meter called a spirometer. The ordinary spirometer indicates, in decalitres, litres and centilitres, the air expired in a given time. Two readings, taken before and after the experiment, give the volume of the air that has circulated in the lungs. A deep expiration through the spirometer gives what has been called the vital capacity (§ 79). The rhythm of

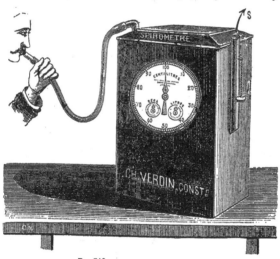

Fig. 240.

Ordinary spirometer.

the respiration can be ascertained by counting the number of movements of the large pointer in a minute.

The ordinary spirometer is not generally accurate, nor is its error constant. If a known volume of air, V, is passed through it and the dial indicates $V + a$, the quantity a will equal the

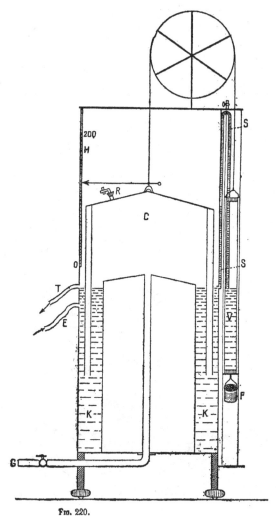

Fig. 220.

Tissot's automatic spirometer.

amount by which the indication is defective. According to whether a is positive or negative, it is added or subtracted from the volume indicated (fig. 219).

Tissot's automatic spirometer (fig. 220) can be relied upon for correct measurements. It consists of a very thin ($\frac{2}{10}$ of a millimetre) copper bell C. fitted on its internal wall with two very light

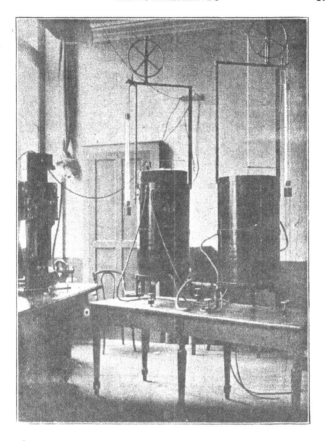

Fig. 221.—Two automatic spirometers coupled together (on the left is a eudiometer for analysis.)

hollow metal tubes to increase the displacement of the water. It is suspended within a receptacle K, of which the annular part is filled with water. A tube, G, leads in the expired gases. The bell rises, and is exactly balanced in every position by an automatic counterweight. The bell is suspended by a thin steel wire, which passes over an aluminium pulley, with practically no friction, and carries a counterweight, consisting of a cylindrical glass tube, V, closed at the bottom and having a section exactly equal to that of the hollow tubes of the bell, to which is suspended a receptacle P, full of lead shot. A syphon tube, S, connects K with the tube V. As soon as the syphon is started, a rise of the bell will produce an equal lowering in the tube V, and the water

will run into the latter through the syphon balancing the apparent
increase in weight of the bell. Also the vessel K receives a flow
of water through E, which assures a constant level, the excess
passing off by the overflow T.

The capacity of the bell is, as a rule, from 50 to 250 litres. The
volumes of gas expired are read on a graduated scale, H, over
which moves an aluminium pointer. An apparatus of 200 litres
capacity is sufficient, but if necessary two may be coupled
together (fig. 221). Another advantage of the counterweight
spirometer is that the gases are preserved in it and samples for
analysis can be taken from the top of the bell by unscrewing the
cap R. Fig 221 indicates the manner in which this can be done..

242. With the ordinary meter samples of the gas are taken
during the experiment in the following manner :—Before entering
the spirometer, the gases pass through a small vessel, F, which
holds about 1 litre (fig. 222). Into this vessel penetrates a
capillary tube, AA′, which is prolonged externally to form a bend
terminated by an elbow immersed in mercury. A three-way

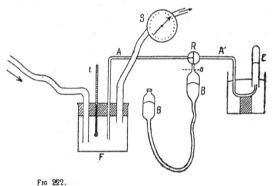

Fɪɢ 222.

Apparatus for sampling expired gases.

cock, R, is fitted, as shown, which can connect A and B, A and A′
or B and A′ (fig. 223). With the cock in the first position, the
mercury reservoir, B′, is raised to fill B up to the line a and the
opening is regulated so that by hooking the reservoir B′ to a low
support, the mercury runs slowly from B to B′. When the experiment is terminated, the cock is turned to position No. 2,
which isolates the gas.

Fɪɢ. 223.

By placing the cock in the third position and lifting B′, the air in B is driven into the test tube E. The first bubbles of gas should be allowed to escape outside the test tube so as to insure that RA is filled with expired gas only.

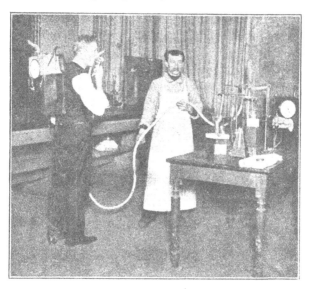

FIG. 224.—Apparatus for sampling and measuring respiratory gases
(J. Amar).

Whilst these operations are proceeding all the rest of the expired gases pass to the spiromerer S, which indicates the quantity. The average temperature of these gases is given by the thermometer t.

A very practical arrangement, for certain experiments, is to take two connections from the vessel F. This is shown in figure 224.

243. Analysis of the Gas.—Suppose, for example, 150 cubic centimetres of gas to have been retained in the test tube E, or a sample to have been taken in Tissot's automatic spirometer, and that it is desired to analyse this sample. The two following eudimeters, can be employed for the purpose, both being charged with reagents to absorb the carbonic gas and oxygen.

1. *Laulanié's Eudiometer*.[1]—The usual and most practical model consists of two glass vessels, K and P, the one containing potash solution to absorb the carbonic gas ; the other phosphorus, immersed in water, which has the property of rapidly fixing the oxygen of the air. The two graduated tubes, m and g, serve,

[1] Laulanié (*Arch. de Physiol.*, 1894, p. 740).

the one as a manometer and the other for measuring the gas, and communicate below by a curved portion, receiving water from the vessel R. When R is raised, a three-way cock, r, allows the gas contained in the glass bulb a to pass either into K or into P (fig. 225).

All the cocks being open, the reservoir R is raised by means of the hand-wheel, MI, and air is driven through the tube $r'i$. The cock, r', is then turned to open to s, the reservoir is lowered, and the gases are drawn in through s, which is connected with the spirometer or the test tube containing the gas (see fig. 221). The water level is brought to zero on the graduation, on the lower part of the apparatus, the whole capacity available for the gas being then 100 cubic centimetres, of which 25 are represented by the graduated tube g. By closing r' and opening r to the glass vessel containing potash, the gas is driven into it and the solution is driven out into B. The vessel R is lowered and raised to renew the contact with the solution. Meanwhile r'' has been closed. It is opened at the moment when, bringing the gas to g, its volume is read by the atmospheric pressure, the level of the water then being the same in m and in g. Let the reading be 3 cubic centimetres. That means that 3% in volume has been absorbed by the potash and represents the proportion of carbonic gas.

The same operation is carried out with the phosphorus, but the gases are left there a little longer. Let the new reading be 20, then the difference 20 — 3 = 17 represents the volume absorbed by the phosphorus; 17% is therefore the proportion of oxygen. Let it be noted that the graduated tubes are immersed in a vessel full of water, which re-

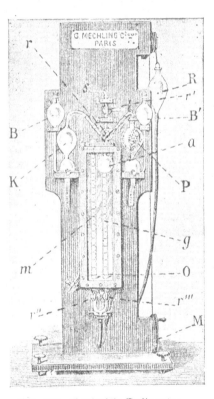

FIG. 225.—Laulanié's Eudiometer.

duces the variations of temperature during the experiment. The atmospheric pressure at the moment is also ascertained.

As a precaution, two readings should be made to ensure that each absorption has been complete, whilst beforehand the free air should be analysed, and should give 21% of oxygen and practically no carbonic gas (0·03%). The slightest trace of turpentine should be avoided, because it destroys the absorbent power of the phosphorus. The cocks should be greased.

244. 2. *Bonnier and Mangin's Eudiometer*—The principle of this apparatus is the same as that of the preceding, except that the absorption of oxygen is effected by a concentrated solution of potassium pyrogallate instead of phosphorus. It comprises a capillary tube *dfg* bent into U-shape at its free extremity, which enters a vessel of mercury (fig. 226), the other extremity being soldered to a metal cylinder also filled with mercury and closed by an air-tight piston actuated by a hand wheel *a*. The capillary tube is accurately graduated from 0 to 600. By pushing in the piston the tube of mercury is filled to its orifice *i*, which should be a few millimetres below the mercury level.

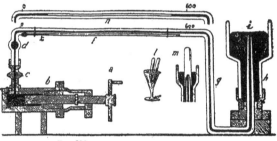

Fig. 226.

Bonnier and Mangin's Eudiometer.

The solutions of the reagents are prepared in small test tubes inverted in mercury (*l*). The solution of potash is made by melting tablets of potash in a test tube containing water. The solution of pyrogallate is made by dissolving pyrogallic acid and adding a few tablets of potassium to the test tube containing the liquid, the solution has a clear brown colour. It is essential that the two solutions be saturated.

Operation.—To make an analysis, the test tube (*m*) is sunk over the tube *i* until the point of the latter appears within it. If the piston be slightly pressed in, a sample of gas can be taken. The test tube is withdrawn, and by the movement of the piston, the air to be analysed is brought into the graduated tube and enclosed between the final division marked 600 and a division which will be read to the left, say 150. Therefore there are 600—150= 450 divisions or volumes of air to analyse. This is represented by N. A reading thus made backwards will prevent the gas stopping in the tube d, which would give rise to small errors.

By a similar operation, a sample of the solution of potassium can be taken, bringing it to the middle of the tube g and then expelling it immediately. If, afterwards, various samples of air are passed through it, all the carbonic gas will be absorbed. Bring it to 600, the division on the left being, for instance, 165 ; therefore $N' = 600 - 165 = 435$ volumes. It will be seen that $450 - 435 = 15$ volumes in 450 represents the carbonic acid gas content.

Next take a sample of pyrogallate and absorb the oxygen :— Let $N'' = 600 - 240 = 360$ volumes.

The oxygen content is, therefore : $435 - 360 = 75$ volumes in 450.

The proportions will be :

$$CO_2 = \frac{15}{450} \times 100 \text{ or } 3 \cdot 33\% \; ;$$

$$O_2 = \frac{75}{450} \times 100 \text{ or } 16 \cdot 66\%.$$

The calculation is therefore very easy. N, N' and N'' being obtained ; then :

$$CO_2\% = \frac{N - N'}{N} \times 100 \; ;$$

$$O_2\% = \frac{N' - N''}{N} \times 100.$$

The rapidity of the operations (about 15 minutes) render it possible to dispense with any correction for temperature variations. It should be noted, however, on the thermometer t. The absorption of oxygen will be accelerated by shaking the column of gas, which will reduce the total duration to 10 minutes. The sensibility of the measurements can be increased by reading to half divisions.

Precautions.—Make two or three readings before passing from one reagent to the next. After having shaken the gas, bring it quickly to the graduated part, and take at least 400 volumes for each analysis.

The movement of the reagents should be very slow. At the end of the experiment, draw in a drop of hydrochloric acid, clean the tube, and finish the cleaning with distilled water and dry air.

In view of the small capacity of the tube, one cubic centimetre of air will be sufficient for several analyses, and in addition the whole apparatus is quite portable.

245. Calculations and Corrections.—The experiments are made at a temperature t and at an atmospheric pressure H. To compare the quantities with each other, and to calculate the energetic expenditure by the oxygen consumed (§ 101) the volume V_t thus measured must be reduced to a temperature of 0° C. and a barometric pressure of 760 millimetres of mercury. The volume of a gas increases with the temperature by $\alpha = \frac{1}{273}$ per degree C., and diminishes as the pressure rises. The volume at 0° C. and 760 mm. is :

$$V_o = \frac{V_t}{1 + \alpha t} \times \frac{H}{760}$$

or, approximately,

$$V_o = \frac{0.36 \times V_t \times H}{273 + t}.$$

In the case of Laulanie's eudiometer, H is a measure of the pressure of the air, presumed to be dry, and the tension F of the water vapour at the temperature t, since water is used The tension F can be found from Regnault's tables (§ 253). There fore :

$$V_o = \frac{0.36 \times V_t (H - F)}{273 + t}$$

H being the atmospheric pressure at the moment, F the tension of the water vapour at the temperature t^0. The volume of the dry gases is therefore obtained at 0^0 and 760 millimetres. H is

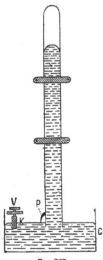

FIG. 227.
Perpendicular barometer.

read on the mercury barometer, the only really correct one (fig. 227). It comprises a tube of 2 to 2·5 centimetres diameter, closed at the top and open at the other end and inverted, full of mercury, in a cup of mercury, C. The tube is fixed by strong bars on to an oak case, and is graduated from 0 to 800 millimetres, its total length being about 90 centimetres. The level of the mercury is adjusted to the point p, corresponding to the zero of the scale by means of a plunger K operated by a micrometer screw, V. If the height of mercury is H_t at the temperature of t^0, it can be reduced to 0°, by taking into account the co-efficients of expansion of mercury and glass. Then :

$$H_0 = H_t \pm \alpha,$$

according to whether t is lower or higher than 0°. α can be found from tables. Approximately

$$\alpha = 0.000168 t H_t.$$

Finally, as a precaution, always verify that the zero of the barometer corresponds to the level of the point p, and bring the mercury flush therewith by turning the screw.

If Tissot's spirometer is used, a thermometer immersed in the water will give the temperature, and the barometer will show the pressure at which the gases are measured.

If the derivation apparatus is used, the temperature of the gases will be, on an average, that of the receptacle in front of the meter, but a certain error in regard to both temperature and pressure is unavoidable.

246. Knowing the volume of the gases V_0 for the duration of the experiment, and the analysis having given the values of CO_2 and of O_2, it will be easy to deduce :

1. The respiratory quotient $\dfrac{CO_2}{O_2}$;

2. The total oxygen consumed. In the pure inspired air, there is 21% oxygen, and if the analysis gives 17% then 4% has been consumed by the organism. Therefore, the proportion r in the expired gases being determined, the quantity remaining in the body will be :

$$\frac{(21 - r) \times V_0}{100} ;$$

3. The total carbonic acid gas eliminated. Here all the CO_2 in the expired gases is taken, since there was practically none in the inspired air (0·03%).

For example, let v_0 be the consumption of oxygen in 10 minutes, of a man in repose, and let $\dfrac{CO_2}{O_2} = 0\cdot98$. This respiratory quotient indicates a utilisation of carbo-hydrate reserves. A litre of oxygen equals, therefore, 5·05 Cal., and v_0 litres represents the static expenditure of the subject. Then :

$$q_s = v_0 \times 5\cdot05 \text{ Cal.}$$

Let v'_0 be the quantity of oxygen absorbed during work equal to T for 10 minutes, and let $\dfrac{CO_2}{O_2} = 0\cdot97$. The co-efficient 5·05 Cal. will also be applicable to this gross expenditure :

$$q = v'_0 \times 5\cdot05 \text{ Cal.}$$

It follows that the dynamic expenditure will be :

$$q_d = (v'_0 - v_0)\ 5\cdot05 \text{ Cal. or } q - q_s.$$

247. Vital Capacity and Respiratory Rhythm.—The vital capacity (§ 79) is measured by the spirometer and the volume reduced to 0° and 760 millimetres.

The rhythm of the respirations may be traced by Tissot's spirometer, for instance, by fitting the glass tube with a style rubbing lightly on a level surface of smoked paper moving horizontally. At the same time, the volume of each respiration can be found.

The respiratory curves can also be registered by the pneumograph. This apparatus must be fixed to the subject so that it is not shaken by his work and exploratory tambours can be placed on the workman's back instead of on his chest. After having obtained the registration when in repose, leave the pneumograph in place for a registration when working, and the traces may then be strictly comparable.

248. Circulatory Activity.—The rhythm of the beat of the heart and the pulse can be registered by the cardiograph and the transmitting sphygmograph (§ 195). It is difficult to place the various apparatus in precisely the same position for each experiment so that the curves obtained may be strictly comparable.

It is best to determine the arterial pressure before and after work, using, for instance, Pachon's oscillometer (fig. 228). This consists of a rubber tube B covered with fabric placed round the wrist and connected by a rubber tube a to the oscillometer. The latter consists of a vessel E, in which air is compressed by means of a pump, P, to a pressure always higher than that which is to be measured, 20 centimetres, for instance, which is read on the gauge M. The passage fba being open, there will be the same pressure in the wrist tube B as in the aneroid box c, and the needle, l, attached to the metal diaphragm, will be stationary. Lower the pressure of the air a little by unscrewing the valve V, and at intervals tighten the contact S to close the passage. As soon as the pressure of air has attained that of the blood, the needle will be ready to oscillate. The beginning of that oscillation marks the systolic pressure, the strongest pressure of the artery.

Again decrease the pressure of the air and the oscillations will indicate the diastolic pressure. These pressures are read on the gauge M.

249. Measurement of Tactile Sensibility : The Esthesiometer.—If the skin is touched with a metal point, it is possible, with closed eyes, to indicate with greater or less accuracy the spot touched. This is what Weber called the sense of place or capacity of localisation.[1] This capacity can be measured by two methods :

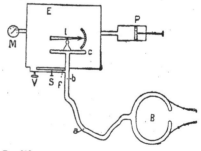

Fig. 228.

Pachon's sphygmometric oscillometer.

---

[1] Weber *Wagner's Handbuch d. Physiol.*, iii., 2 Abt., p. 524.

1. The skin, being well stretched, is touched with a metal point. The subject then indicates the point touched. The capacity of localisation is then inversely proportional to the distance in millimetres between the actual point of contact and that indicated by the subject.

2. By Weber's esthesiometer.—This consists of a caliper gauge with pointed arms, which are applied slightly and simultaneously to the skin.

FIG. 229.

The degree of sensibility is given by the smallest distance between the points at which they are both distinctly felt (fig. 229).

Various types of esthesiometers are used at the present time. The localising capacity is highly developed in the blind, and is greater in children than in adults, vide the following table, due in part to Weber ([1]).

	ADULTS	CHILDREN
Tip of the tongue	1·10 mm.	1·10 mm.
„ „ nose	6·80 „	4·50 „
Palm of the hand	8·90 „	„ „
Eyelids	11·30 „	9·00 „
Back of the hand	31·60 „	22·60 „
Sternum	45·10 „	33·80 „
Middle of the back, arms, and thighs	67·70 „	40·60 „

250. Measurement of the Thermal Energy of the Body.—The exact measurement of the thermal expenditure would necessitate an expensive installation, such as Atwater and Benedict's calorimetric chamber, d'Arsonval's calorimeters, etc., for which the reader must be referred to the original memoirs.([2])

Thermal energy comprises the energy of physical waste and that of the physiological minimum. The waste is calculated from the theoretical relations of the radiation and of the convection in the air at an external temperature of $t°$ (§ 165). If Newton's law is applied K_1 will be taken as equal to 0.00015c for the emissive power. If Stefan's law is used (§ 171) K'_1 will be taken as $1·02 \times 10^{-12}$ in the formula :

$$q_1 = K'_1 \left[(T + 273)^4 - (t + 273)^4 \right].$$

([1]) Consult Victor Henri (*Arch. de Physiol.*, 1893, pp. 619-27) ; Marillier et Philippe (*Journal de Physiol.*, 1903, p. 65).
([2]) Jules Lefèvre, in his *Bioénergétique* (*loc. cit.*, pp. 77 *sqg.*) gives a complete and methodical study of the subject.

The following table gives the emissive powers of various substances as obtained by Péclet. The accuracy of the values has, however, been disputed (Wiedelburg, 1898) ;

Polished silver	$K_1 =$	0·0000036 c.
Copper		0·0000044
Glass		·0000808
Fine sand		·0001000
Oil paints		·0001030
Paper		·0001040
Wood		·0001000
Woollen fabrics ([1])		·0001020
Calico		·0001010
Silk fabrics		·0001020
Water		·0001470
Oil		·0002010

The above figures give the radiation in still air. In moving air, the calorific loss is greater, being proportional to the speed of the horizontal air current, as Oberbeck ([2]) found with inanimate bodies and Jules Lèfevre ([3]) with man (§ 175).

Lèfevre's physiological calorimeter comprises a large zinc casing 3 metres long (fig. 230) supported internally by a wooden framework and composed of three parts, namely : a cylindrical central chamber for the subject and inlet and outlet compartments for the air.

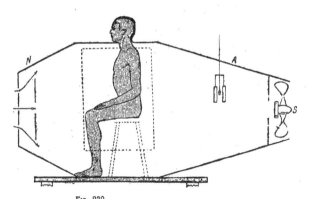

Fɪɢ. 230.

Lefèvre's Physiological calorimeter.

([1]) As the radiation of clothing, Rubner takes $K_1 = 0·000113$ c. (*Die Gesetze*. Ch. xiii).
([2]) Oberbeck (*Wied. Ann.*, vol. lvi., p. 397, 1895).
([3]) Jules Lefèvre (*loc. cit.*, p. 103).

The air has free access to the central chamber, the latter has a large side door, shown in dotted lines, to allow the subject to enter the apparatus, which is afterwards hermetically sealed during the experiment.

The subject is seated in the interior on a stool. His head projects through a circular hole, round the edges of which is fixed a rubber cap which goes over the head. Respiration, therefore, takes place in the open air, although the atmosphere inside the calorimeter is separated from the external atmosphere.

The outlet chamber contains a fan S, capable of exhausting 600 cubic metres of air per hour.

The inlet chamber N has three air intakes open to the external atmosphere, and an anomometer can be fixed to each of these openings (§ 200).

Knowing the sections, s_1, s_2, s_3, of the air intakes and the average speeds, v_1, v_2, v_3, of the air current, the volume of air can be calculated by the sum of the products :

$$s_1 v_1 + s_2 v_2 + s_3 v_3 \ldots = SV.$$

Accurate thermometers reading to $\frac{1}{10}$ of a degree are placed in front of and behind the subject to give the amount θ by which the air is heated. Let V be the average speed of the air during the experiment and SV is the volume in litres. The weight of a litre of air being 1·293 gr., the total mass M will be :

$$M = S \times V \times 1\cdot293 \text{ grammes.}$$

Correcting for the atmospheric pressure H and the temperature t of the air, the expression becomes :

$$M = S \times V \times 1\cdot293 \times \frac{0\cdot36 \times H}{273 + t}.$$

The increase in temperature θ will therefore correspond to :

$$Q = M \times \theta \times 0\cdot237 \text{ cal.}$$

0·237 cal. being the specific heat of air.

It is possible, with this simple and accurate apparatus, to measure the thermal waste at different speeds and temperatures of the air current (§ 175).

251. Thermal Conductivity.—We can estimate this waste with various garments by taking into account their co-efficient of conductivity or of transmission c (§ 170). The following are some values of that co-efficient, in addition to those already given :

SUBSTANCES	C.	AUTHORITY
Air	⎧ 0·0000500	Winkelmann (*Wied. Ann*, 1880 vol. x., p. 668).
	⎩ 0·0000532	Rubner (see § 170).
Copper	1·0400000	H. F. Weber
Iron	0·1587000	Berget (*Comptes Rend. Sc.* tr., cvii., p. 227, 1888)
Marble	0·0018000	Forbes *Prco. Ed. Soc.*, 1872-75).
	0·0022000	Herschell
Chalk	⎧ 0·0002900 (1)	Lees (*Proceed. Bay, Soc.*, 1901, tr lxxiv.)
Oak	⎰ 0·0001300 (2)	,, ,, ,,
	⎱ 0·0001500 (3)	,, ,, ,,
Maple	⎰ 0·0003500	,, ,, ,,
	⎱ 0·0001500	,, ,, ,,
Pine, fir tree	0·0000900	Forbes (*loc. cit.*)
Cork	0·0001300	Forbes, Mauro (*Il Polidermes*, Dec., 1910)
Hard gum	0·0000890	Stefan (*Wien Ber*, vol. lxxiv., p. 438, 1879.
Beeswax	0·0000870	Frobes (*loc. cit.*)
Horn	0·0000870	,,
Pasteboard	0·0004530	,,
Paper	0·0003100	Lees (*loc. cit.*)
Vulcanised Rubber	0·0000890	Forbes (*loc. cit.*)
Wood sawdust(4)	0·0001230	,,
Felt	0·0000900	,,
Wool	0·0000550	Lees (*loc. cit.*)
	0·0000400	Forbes (*loc. cit.*)
Compressed cotton	0·0000330	,,
Cotton (loose)	0·0000433	,,
Cotton wool	0·0001250	Mauro (*loc. cit.*)
Olive oil	0·0003900	Waschmull (*Phys. Zelt.*, 1901, vol. 111, p. 79)
Snow	0·0003600	Okada (*Meteor Zeit.*, 1905, vol. xxii., p. 336

For ordinary clothing, Rubner's table (§ 170) is the most trust-worthy. The co-efficient of protection (§ 172) or the heat transmitted by a tissue, must depend on the thickness of that tissue. But it must be pointed out that the volume of air imprisoned in fur is very important as a heat insulator even though the

(1) Parallel to the fibres.
(2) Perpendicular to the fibres and following a medullary ray.
(3) Perpendicular to the fibres and to a medullary ray.
(4) For fir tree sawdust Mauro (*loc. cit.*) found a higher value 0·000, 1830.

skin itself may not be very thick. Hence the conducting power diminishes with the lowering of the density of the tissue, *e.g.* :

	DENSITY	C.
Linen Tricot	0·302	0·0001181
—	0·420	0·0001523

The following table compiled by Rubner, is very instructive :

Designation	Thickness		Average Density:	Volume of air imprisoned
	total	of the skin		
	mm	mm		%
Black cat's skin	12·60	0·60	0·0429	96·7
Black lamb's skin	13·00	0·30	0·0484	96·4
Rabbit skin	13·00	0·50	0·0304	97·7
Musquash rat skin.................	14·00	0·60	0·0576	95·6
Otter skin	17·00	0·90	0·0638	95·1
White bear skin	21·00	0·90	0·0582	95·5
Beaver...............................	22·00	0·80	0·0514	96·1
Skunk	26·00	0·50	0·0410	96·8
Sheepskin	40·00	0·70	0·0461	96·4
Cashmere	0·37		0·364	72·0
Muslin	0·29		0·179	86·7
Silk	0·25		0·329	74·7

252. Calorific Loss of Water.—To estimate this loss in the case of a bath of water at a temperature t, the procedure is simple and has already been indicated (§ 178). According to Boussinesq's [1] theory, verified by various authorities [2] the loss of heat in a liquid at rest has as its expression :

$$Q = A \times \Delta^{0.233} \times K^{0.533} \times C^{0.467} \times (T - t)^{1.233},$$

in which A is a constant, Δ the co-efficient of expansion of the liquid, a co-efficient that varies with temperature, K the heat conductivity, and C the specific heat. It is not proposed to apply to man, a formula which especially requires the discussion of each of its terms.

Aimé Witz [3] found that the rate of cooling of a surface in contact with water was :

$$v = K' \frac{S}{V} \times \alpha^{1.203} + 0.00048\alpha,$$

α being the difference of temperature, S the surface, V the volume of the body and K' a constant.

---

[1] Boussinesq (*Comptes Rendus Sc.*, vols. cxxxii., cxxxviii., cxl.).
[2] L. Ser. *Physique Industrielle*, vol. i., p. 160, 1888.
[3] Aimé Witz, *Thèse de Doctorat*, Paris, 1878.

Assume $\frac{S}{V} = 32$ and $v = 18 \cdot 05$ Cal. for an adult.   Then

$\alpha = 35 - 5 = 30°$ (according to Lefèvre) and $K' = 0 \cdot 009$.

Taking $\alpha = 35 - 12 = 23°C$, $v = 12.8$ Cal.   Lefèvre obtained 11·70 Cal.

253. Measurement of the Hygrometric State—The use of Crova's hygrometer (fig. 231) has already been recommended (§ 173).

This instrument consists of a brass tube, polished internally, closed in front by a sheet of ground glass V and at the back by a lens L, which allows a view of the interior.   The tube is immersed in a brass vessel containing carbon bi-sulphide, and crossed from A to C by a current of air, which causes a fall of temperature indicated by the thermometer T.

By means of the bulb P, air is drawn through the tube B, and the formation of dew can be observed through D.   As soon as dark patches appear, the temperature t' is read by the thermometer T, the external temperature t being known.   Regnault's tables give the values f and F, the following being a portion of these tables for temperatures between $- 10°$ and $+ 50°$ C.

TABLE OF THE TENSIONS OF VAPOUR IN MILLIMETRES OF
MERCURY (REGNAULT, THIESEN and SCHEEL.)

Temperature Centigrade	Tension	Temperature	Tension	Temperature	Tension
	mm.		mm.		mm.
— 10°	2·13	+ 11°	9·86	+ 31°	33·59
— 9	2·30	12	10·53	32	35·55
8	2·49	13	11·24	33	37·61
7	2·69	14	11·99	34	39·77
6	2·90	15	12·79	35	42·04
5	3·13	16	13·63	36	44·42
4	3·38	17	14·52	37	46·92
3	3·65	18	15·47	38	49·54
2	3·94	19	16·47	39	52·29
1	4·25	20	17·52	40	55·16
0	4·58	21	18·63	41	58·17
+ 1	4·93	22	19·80	42	61·32
2	5·30	23	21·03	43	64·62
3	5·69	24	22·33	44	68·07
4	6·11	25	23·71	45	71·68
5	6·56	26	25·16	46	75·46
6	7·03	27	26·68	47	79·41
7	7·53	28	27·28	48	83·54
8	8·06	29	29·96	49	87·85
9	8·62	30	31·73	50	92·35
10	9·22				

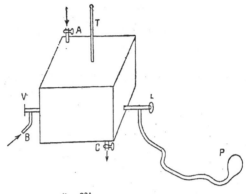

Fig. 231.
Crova's Hygrometer.

In using Crova's hygrometer, it is as well to wait for the disappearance of the drop of dew, which takes place at a temperature t'_2, slightly different from t'_1, and to take the average $\dfrac{t'_1 + t'_2}{2}$ as t'. The brass tube should be very clean.[1]

Knowing the tension f the weight in grammes of the water vapour in a cubic metre of the air can be calculated. This is the absolute humidity, whilst $\dfrac{f}{F} = e$ is the relative humidity.

Now the weight of a litre of gas or vapour is equal to 1·293 gramme (the weight of a litre of air), multiplied by the density of the fluid in question. The pressure and the temperature are also taken into account by writing :

$$p = 1·293 \times d \times \frac{H}{(1 + \alpha t) \times 760}.$$

For water vapour $d = 0·622$, about $\frac{5}{8}$; $H = f$. Therefore :

$$p = 1·293 \times \frac{5}{8} \times \frac{f \times 273}{(273 + t)\,760},$$

or :

$$p = \frac{0·2902 \times f}{273 + t},$$

or, per cubic metre :

(1)
$$p = \frac{290·2 \times f}{273 + t}.$$

Knowing that $e = \dfrac{f}{F}$ or $f = Fe$, the expression could be written :

[1] Cantor (*Wied, Ann.*, vol. lvi., p. 492, 1895).

(2) $$p = \frac{290\cdot2 \times F \times e}{273 + t}.$$

254. The pyschrometer is in common use, but it is a troublesome and incorrect instrument. Its use will be explained in order that its only useful aspect may be seen.

It consists of two thermometers, the one dry, the other moistened by a piece of rag, which covers its bulb and receives water from a cotton wick immersed in a tube. The evaporation of this water cools the reservoir and brings it to a temperate θ lower than that of the atmosphere t (fig. 232).

To find the tension F′ corresponding to a temperature θ, the atmospheric pressure H is noted. The tension f will be :

$$f = F' - AH\ (t - θ).$$

A being the constant of the psychrometer, which is determined by a hygrometer; the latter giving f the equation will be written :

$$A = \frac{F' - f}{H\ (t - θ)}$$

It is unnecessary to give the principle of this instrument, a principle which is marred by a great lack of precision. But let it be said that the value of A is far from being constant as it varies with the velocity of the wind, the radiation from the walls of the tubes etc., and the place of the observation itself. The psychometer cannot be used below O°C.

If the instrument is rapidly moved resulting in a high air velocity, we can write in general terms :

A = 0·00082 for θ above 0°C.
A = 0·00069 for θ lower than 0°C.

Example : The dry bulb thermometer shows 20° or t = 20°C. The wet bulb thermometer shows 16°, and H = 758 millimetres. Assume that A = 0·00082. Since at 16°C, θ = 16° and F, = 13·63, we have :

$$f = 13\cdot63 - 0\cdot00082 \times 758 \times 4 = 11\cdot16\,\text{mm}.$$

The maximum tension corresponding to 20°C is 17·52 mm. Therefore the hygrometric state is :

$$\frac{11\cdot16}{17\cdot52} = 0\cdot637.$$

Fɪɢ. 232.
Psychrometer

255. Friction.—A few indications concerning the co-efficients of friction appear to be necessary (§ 39). Only a few rather old values are available.

Co-efficients f of Sliding.

NATURE OF BODIES IN SLIDING CONTACT.	VALUE OF f DURING THE MOVEMENT.
Sandstone on sandstone (smooth and dry)	0·71 (Rennie)
Limestone on limestone (hard and polished) ...	0·58 (Roadelet)
Granite (smooth) on granite (rough dressed)...	0·66 (Rennie)
Wooden chest on pavement	0·58 (Regnier)
,, ,, beaten earth	0·33 (Hubert)
Iron on iron or brass, dry	0·18 (Various)
Brass on brass, dry	0·15 —
Iron on ice (skates)	0·02 (Cheuller)
Metal on metal (with lubrication)	0·10 (Various)
Leather straps on metals (dry)	0·56
,, ,, ,, (greased)	0·23

The values of these co-efficients are modified by the use of lubricants, notably oils and tallow. They increase with the speed.[1] It is so difficult to assure constancy in the state of rubbing surfaces that the concordance of the measurements cannot be satisfactory. Friction is greater at the start than in the course of motion.

256. In the rolling of cylindrical bodies (wheels, rollers, castors) the value of the friction is much less than in sliding. To overcome it, there must be an effort proportional to the pressure between the bodies and inversely proportional to the radius. It is presumed that this effort acts at the centre (in the case of wheels) *i.e.*, tangentially to the surface. A few values of the co-efficient φ, for ordinary wheels have been given (§ 39). For brass rollers on brass or wrought iron, it has been found that [2] :

$$\varphi = \frac{0\cdot0039}{\sqrt{r}} \quad \text{and} \quad \frac{0\cdot0044}{\sqrt{r}}, \text{ respectively,}$$

r being the radius in centimetres.

With steel rollers on brass or on steel :

$$\varphi = \frac{0\cdot0045}{\sqrt{r}} \quad \text{and} \quad \frac{0\cdot0039}{\sqrt{r}}, \text{ respectively.}$$

For wrought iron rollers on brass :

$$\varphi = \frac{0\cdot0075}{\sqrt{r}}$$

---

[1] Rennie (*Phil. Trans.*, 1829) ; Morin (*Mém. Sav. Etr.*, vols. v., vi) ; Jenkin (*Journ. de Physique* 1st Sept. vol. vi.) ; Müller (*Pogg. Ann.* vol. cxxxix, 1870) ; Kimball (*Amer. Journ.*,1877); *Bulletin, Technol. des Anc. él. Arts et Métiers*, 1895, p. 657 ; 1897, p. 1228.

[2] John Perry: *Applied Mechanics*.

Doubtless the idea of the co-efficient of traction, already defined (§ 39) is more useful. It has been found in normal conditions :

NATURE OF BODY IN SLIDING CONTACT	CO-EFFICIENT OF TRACTION
Iron wheels on iron rails	0·005
— or tyres on main roads	0·030
The same on paving stone	0·015
The same on a stony road	0·040
—— — non-stony road	0·068

257. Table of Sines and Tangents.—It will be recalled that the cosine of an angle is equal to the sine of the complemental angle (two angles whose sum equals 90° are said to be complementary) and that

$$\tan \alpha = \frac{\sin \alpha}{\cos \alpha}$$

DEGREES	SINES	TANGENTS	DEGREES	SINES	TANGENTS
1	0·017	0·017	46	0·719	1·036
2	0·035	0·035	47	0·731	1·073
3	0·052	0·052	48	0·743	1·111
4	0·070	0·070	49	0·755	1·151
5	0·087	0·088	50	0·766	1·192
6	0·105	0·105	51	0·777	1·236
7	0·122	0·123	52	0·788	1·281
8	0·139	0·141	53	0·799	1·328
9	0·157	0·159	54	0·809	1·377
10	0·174	0·177	55	0·819	1·429
11	0·191	0·195	56	0·829	1·483
12	0·208	0·213	57	0·839	1·541
13	0·225	0·231	58	0·848	1·601
14	0·242	0·250	59	0·857	1·665
15	0·259	0·268	60	0·866	1·733
16	0·276	0·287	61	0·875	1·805
17	0·293	0·306	62	0·883	1·882
18	0·309	0·325	63	0·891	1·964
19	0·326	0·345	64	0·899	2·052
20	0·342	0·364	65	0·906	2·146
21	0·359	0·384	66	0·914	2·248
22	0·375	0·404	67	0·921	2·358
23	0·391	0·425	68	0·927	2·477
24	0·407	0·455	69	0·934	2·607
25	0·423	0·467	70	0·946	2·750
26	0·439	0·488	71	0·946	2·907
27	0·454	0·510	72	0·951	3·081
28	0·470	0·532	73	0·956	3·274

DEGREES	SINES	TANGENTS	DEGREES	SINES	TANGENTS
29	0·485	0·555	74	0·961	3·481
30	0·500	0·578	75	0·966	3·736
31	0·515	0·601	76	0·970	4·016
32	0·530	0·625	77	0·974	4·337
33	0·545	0·650	78	0·978	4·711
34	5·559	0·675	79	0·982	5·152
35	0·574	0·701	80	0·985	5·681
36	0·588	0·727	81	0·988	6·326
37	0·602	0·754	82	0·990	7·130
38	0·616	0·782	83	0.992	8·164
39	0·629	0·810	84	0·994	9·541
40	0·643	0·839	85	0·996	11·468
41	0·656	0·870	86	0·997	14·361
42	0·669	0·901	87	0·998	19·188
43	0·682	0·933	88	0·999	28·640
44	0·695	0·966	89	0·999	57·290
45	0·707	1·000	90	1·000	∞

BOOK VI.

INDUSTRIAL LABOUR.

CHAPTER I.

THE HUMAN BODY IN EQUILIBRIUM AND MOVEMENT.
LOCOMOTION.

258. General Remarks.—The study of Industrial Labour has two main divisions. In the one we consider the human body in equilibrium and in motion. In the other we investigate the influence which is due to the nature and quality of the tools and appliances employed. Herein we shall confine our attention almost exclusively to the former division.

The human body is an articulated, or jointed, system. But its various members are not interconnected so as to form a rigid whole like a marble statue. It is, indeed, never truly at rest. When nominally in repose, the body is yet in continual movement owing to the functions of respiration and circulation.[1] The muscles, also, being always more or less contracted, are in a continued state of vibration. The oscillatory movement due to these vibrations can even be recorded if a style is fixed to the top of the head [2], or, if a person is placed in a very sensitive weighing machine, a periodical disturbance of equilibrium can be detected.

The human body is a material system subject both to exterior forces (of which the most important is Gravitation) and also to the interior forces of the muscles. Further, it is a heterogeneous body, whose density varies in different parts. Its shape is irregular. Finally, it is not isolated in space, but is posed on the earth's surface supported by a base formed by the feet.

In short, the human body is a system to which the ordinary laws of mechanics can be applied, and which can be studied both in its static and dynamic states.

---

[1] A. Mosso, *Arch. Ital. Biol.*, vol. v., 1884.
[2] Vierordt *Grundriss d. Physiol. d. Menschen*, p. 364, 1862, 2nd edition.

259. (A) Statics of the Human Body.[1]—The human body is obviously at all times under the influence of Gravitation. Its centre of gravity cannot, however, be deduced from its shape, but can only be found experimentally.

If a plank, on which a man is lying is arranged to project over the edge of a table ; by gradually advancing the plank, a position of equilibrium can be found and the centre of gravity will be in a vertical plane cutting the above edge. If we determine the position of equilibrium for two further positions, the required centre of gravity will be at the point of intersection of the three planes. (*Borelli*, 1679).

It will be obvious that the position of the centre of gravity of the body must depend on the relative disposition of its constituent masses, *i.e.*, on the attitude of the body. Thus *Otto Fischer* found the centres of gravity of the various members of the body in known relative positions and reduced these to a single centre. He used for his experiments corpses in a state of rigidity.

When a man stands in an upright position the segments of his body, the double curvature of the vertebral column, and his pyramidical shape result in a state of instability, so that the muscles have to be continuously (though unconsciously) exercised to maintain equilibrium.. The instability is due both to the small area of the base of support (§ 21) and to the fact that the centre of gravity is comparatively high.

According to Braune and Fischer, when the body is at rest in the upright position the centre of gravity will be found to lie at the level of the top of the third sacral vertebrae, or of the umbilicus. From an anatomical point of view the upright position is either *symmetrical* or *asymmetrical*. . In the first of the symmetrical poses (fig. 233) the body is straight, the heels are in contact, and the line of gravity passes through their centre (this is the " erect attitude " which Braune and Fischer call *Normal-Stellung*).

In the second symmetrical pose (fig. 234) the line of gravity falls in front of the heel (this is the " easy attitude " or the *Bequeme-Haltung*). Fig. 235 shows the asymmetrical pose, other-

---

[1] Numerous writers have dealt with this subject, amongst whom may be mentioned Giraud-Teulon (*Principes de Mécanique Animale*, Paris, 1858) ; Pettigrew (*Animal Locomotion*, London, 1873) ; Marey (*La Machine Animale*, Paris, 1873 ; Engl. Tr., London, 1874 ; *Le Mouvement*, 1894, Paris ; Engl. Tr., London, 1895) ; Du Bois-Raymond (*Specielle Muskelphysiologie, oder Bewegungslehre*, Berlin, 1903) ; Otto Fischer (*Theoretische Grundlagen für eine Mechanik der Lebenden Korper*, Leipzig, 1906 ; *Beitrage zur Muskelstatik und Muskeldynamik*, in *Abhandl d. Sachs. Gesellsch. d. Wiss., Math.-Phys. Cl.*, vols. xxii. and xxiii ; 1895-7). Fischer's work is very good mathematically.

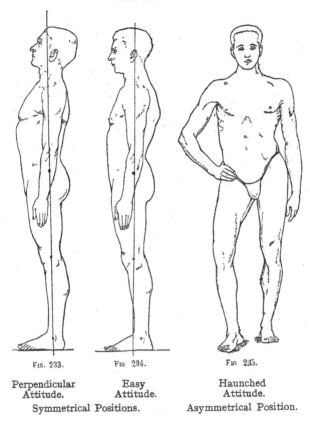

FIG. 233.

FIG. 234.

FIG. 235.

Perpendicular Attitude.

Easy Attitude.

Haunched Attitude.

Symmetrical Positions.

Asymmetrical Position.

wise known as the " haunched position " (station hanchée). In both of the symmetrical positions the weight of the body is equally distributed between the two legs. We can then imagine a " frontal " plane passing through the joints of the hips and at right angles to the " median " plane of the body. Braune and Fischer showed that if all the joints of the foot, the knee, and the thigh lay on the frontal plane, the line of gravity is thrown back, towards the heel. This is the military or " Perpendicular " attitude. If, however, a man stands in an easy pose, the joint of the foot lies behind the frontal plane and the line of gravity passes in front of the heel. The body is more stable in this position than in the former.

In the asymmetrical, or haunched position, the weight of the body is carried on one leg, the other leg serving only to maintain the balance.

The two German savants, above mentioned, investigated ([1]) by photographic means, this question of the centre of gravity of the various members of the human body. The subject of their experiments weighed 58·4 kg. The results of their analysis were as follows :—

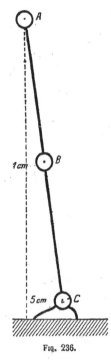

Fig. 236.

In the "easy attitude" (*Bequeme Haltung*) the centre of gravity of the *head* lies 5 mm. in front of the atlanto-occipital joint. The head is therefore somewhat out of balance longitudinally, and, to a slight degree, laterally. This explains the functions of the muscles of the neck in maintaining equilibrium, and also the well-known fact that the head falls forward on the chest during sleep. The *trunk* may be considered as a mass capable of movement around a transverse axis passing through the hip joints. It carries the two arms which hang vertically.

The common centre of gravity of the trunk, arms, and head combined (*vide* § 20) was found to lie at 18 cm. above the axis of the hips, and 8·6 mm. in advance of the frontal plane. For the whole bust the moment of rotation $M = P \times ·0086$.

The weight P totals 36·82 kg. of which the separate items are as follows :—

		WEIGHT IN KG.	PERCENTAGE OF TOTAL WEIGHT OF BODY.	
Head	...	4·140	7·1	
Trunk	...	25·060	42·92	
Arm	...	3·810	6·52	(of which 3·14% is the forearm.)
,,	...	3·810	6·52	
Bust (total)...		36·820	63·06%	

The bust is retained in an erect position by the muscles of the back and the abdomen. Its weight (63% of that of the whole body) is transmitted to the hips. As its centre of gravity lies in front of the axis of the hips the weight tends to thrust back the thighs at their lower extremities (B in fig. 236). These latter transmit the pressure to the knee-joints. These joints stiffen them-

([1]) Braune and Fischer (*Abhandl* . . . vol. xv., No. 7, pp. 631 and 635).

selves so that the knees straighten themselves to resist the pressure and are not bent by the weight. In the " easy " attitude the joint between hip and knee lies 1 cm. behind the frontal plane. The tension caused by the weight of the bust is such that the knees lose their stiffness. If the bone of the *patella* is touched it will be found to be absolutely slack, while, on the other hand, the muscles of the calf and the ligaments of the knee are firmly stretched.([1])

In the same way the joint of the foot, which receives the thrust of the leg, supports at its upper extremity the weight of the bust and the thigh. In the " easy " attitude the joint between the tibia and the foot lies 5 cm. behind the frontal plane, that is 4 cm. behind the plane of the knee-joint. The muscles of the sole of the foot have therefore to balance the moment of rotation of the weights under consideration.

We have, for a lower member, the following :—

	WEIGHT IN KG.	PERCENTAGE OF TOTAL WEIGHT OF BODY.
Thigh ...	6·800	11·64
Leg and foot ...	3·990	6·83
Total for lower member	10·790	18·47%

Therefore the combined weight of both lower members is 21·580 kg., 36·94% of the total weight of the body.

The muscles of the soles of the feet have therefore to balance a moment of rotation produced by a weight of :—

$$36\cdot820 + 2 \times 6\cdot800 = 50\cdot420 \text{ kg.}$$

The arm of the lever is about 4 cm. in length. On the other hand, the *Achilles Tendon* draws up the heel, which causes, in effect, pressure by the front of the foot on the ground, by which the total weight of the body is transmitted, the reaction of the ground on the foot being equal and opposite. As long as the line of gravity of the complete body falls within the base of support constituted by the feet, equilibrium is maintained and the standing position is possible.

261. Economical Attitudes of the Human Body.— In the standing attitude the base of support depends on the position of the feet whether the heels are together or separated. The body is in equilibrium if the line of gravity falls within the base of support. The nearer that line is to the centre of the polygon of support, the more stable is the equilibrium.

When the feet are in the position shown in fig. 237, with the heels touching, the base of support has a greater dimension

([1]) Haycraft *Animal Mechanics* in Schäfer's Text-book of Physiology, Vol. 2, p. 228, 1900.

FIG. 237.

in the sagittal than in the transverse direction. In this position the inherent stability of the body is relatively small. [1] Hence neither of the symmetrical attitudes are really economical.

It is otherwise in regard to the asymmetrical pose (fig. 235). Here the base of support is materially increased by the separation of the feet, and the weight of the body is supported on one leg. This is the real *natural attitude* of man and causes very slight oscillations. The centre of gravity of the body lies almost exactly above the supporting leg, and in the direction of the joint of the foot. Hence the muscles of the calf have but little work to do. The difference of *economy* between the perpendicular attitude of the soldier standing at "attention" and the natural attitude of true repose is as much as 22% as measured by the consumption of oxygen. This subject has therefore practical applications of great importance. [2]

In the *sitting* position the base of support is much larger and the stability of the body is therefore considerably increased. Furthermore the muscles have but little to do. If we measure the relative consumption of oxygen by an adult, first standing in the easy attitude or *Bequeme-Haltung* (fig. 234), and next sitting on a chair, leaning back with all the muscles of the legs relaxed, we shall find that the average economy of the consumption of oxygen is about 6% in favour of the sitting position. [3] The relative expenditure of energy for the positions already considered may be tabulated as follows :—

Sitting position 100
Standing position, "haunched" pose [4] (fig. 235) ... 103
    ,,   ,,   "easy" pose (fig. 234) 106
    ,,   ,,   "upright" pose (fig. 233) ... 125

We see then that the sitting position is that which, under ordinary conditions, is the most restful.

Obviously, however, a *recumbent* attitude provides a far greater base of support for the body when lying on a bed. In this attitude the muscles are fully relaxed, and we find that the expenditure of energy is some 7% or 8% less than in the sitting position. [5]

[1] Leiterstofer, *Das Militarische Training Usw.*, Stuttgart (1897).
[2] Zuntz and Katzenstein (*Pflüger's Arch.*, Vol. xlix, p. 361, (1891).
[3] Jules Amar (*Journ. de Physiol.*, March, 1911, p. 212).
[4] A mean of values lying between 100 and 106.
[5] Emmes and Riche (*Amer. Journ. Physiol.*, vol. xxvii., p. 406, 1911).

But for reasons of mutual benefit and recreation the workman must sit with his friends during his hours of rest.

The attitudes adopted in certain sports, such as boxing and fencing, modify the position of the centre of gravity [1] subject to the principle of the equal distribution of masses (§ 20). Such attitudes also aim at effecting an increase in the area of the base of support. Obviously the person who adopts, or who naturally possesses the largest base of support, will stand the firmest on his feet, and will be able to make the widest movements without losing his balance.

Men carrying heavy loads (*vide* fig. 238), very fat men, hunch-backs, men bent with age, and pregnant women have the centre of gravity of their bodies displaced owing to their additional burdens.

This point of view is seldom overlooked by artists. Harless and Meyer found that the centre of gravity is lower in woman than in man. In pregnancy the whole lumbar region is thrown backwards to counterpoise the weight of the uterus. Obviously the maximum inclination which the body can assume when the heels are together is less than that which is possible when the heels are separated (*vide* fig. 239).

Fig. 238.

In a similar way, in order to maintain balance, the " hunch-back " throws himself slightly backwards, the fat man twists as he walks, and to reduce the amount of this turning he stiffens himself and takes short steps, or the aged man has recourse to a stick. In all these cases the effort made is appreciable and causes comparatively rapid fatigue.

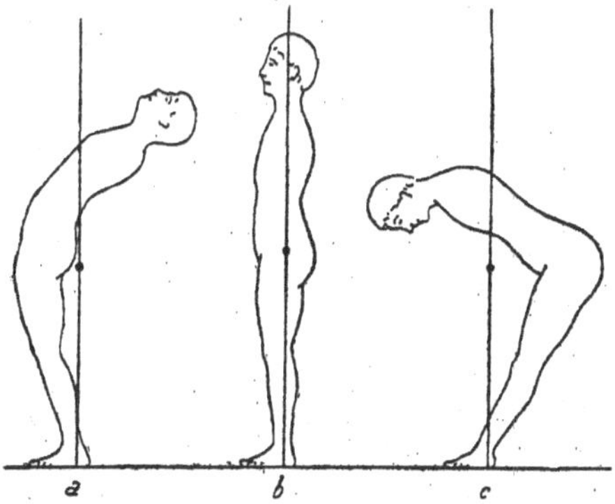

Fig. 239.

Displacements of the line of gravity of the body
(after Braune and Fischer).

[1] Braune and Fischer (*loc. cit.*). Démeny (*Comptes Rendus de Sciences*, October 10th, 1887).

We can observe on every side applications of this principle of equilibrium.. Thus the cyclist (fig. 240) bends over his base of support. The boxer, the fencer, the soldier, with pack and rifle, are ruled by the same principle. In such cases the equilibrium is more or less constrained, and the static expenditure of energy is correspondingly greater than in the state of rest.

FIG. 240.

Equilibrium of a cyclist.

For example, the soldier standing at " attention " with his rifle on his shoulder and his pack on his back, is far from being in a state of rest. The attitude is really most uneconomical. An excess in the opposite direction is exhibited in an asymmetrical attitude, in which the abdomen is allowed to project in front of the chest. This attitude is moderately economical, though less so than the haunched attitude (fig. 235).

262. Summary.—The results obtained by the experiments of Braune and Fischer give a location for the centre of gravity of the whole body, at about $\frac{57}{100}$ of the height. That of the bust alone lies approximately 18 cm. above the transverse axis of the hips. The bust is 63% and the lower members 37% of the total weight of the body. For an adult weighing 65 kg. the bust weighs 41 kg. and the lower members 24 kg. The weight of the lower leg is 6·83% of the total weight of the body. The total length of the lower member of an adult varies from ·87 to ·9 metres or on the average ·88 metres. Its total weight is 12 kg., of which the lower leg claims 4·4 kg.

These measurements and dimensions will be found of considerable use later. It may be remarked that they differ but slightly from the average results obtained by Otto Fischer.[1] The experiments of Atwater (*vide* §103) show that for an adult placed in a chamber at a temperature of 20° C., the expenditure of energy is 2,120 Calories, *i.e.*, $\frac{2120}{65 \times 24} = 1\cdot36$ Calories per kilogram of body weight, per hour. In open-air life, as will be seen later (§ 341), this figure may reach 1·5 Calories, this being due to the lower temperature (14° to 15° C.) and to the general state of

---

[1] Otto Fischer, *Der Gang des Menschen* (vol. xxv., No. 1, p. 16, of the *Abhandl d. Math. Phys Classe d. Sachs. Gesellsch. d. Wiss.*, Leipzig, 1899).

freedom which entails a greater degree of static activity on the part of the muscles.

263. (B) Dynamics of the Human Body.—Whenever the mechanical equilibrium of the body is disturbed movement commences. This movement is the result of forces which may be internal or external, and may be considered as concentrated at the centre of gravity of the body (§ 23).. We know that the interior forces do not affect the position of the centre of gravity. If we imagine a man standing on a perfectly smooth surface and assume that there is no friction between his feet and that surface, he cannot change his position, but can only turn on himself. The only motion possible is that of rotation around a vertical axis on which the centre of gravity remains unchanged (§ 27). Thus if the arms are placed symmetrically and caused to describe two circles having the same direction of rotation, the body will thereby be caused to make a complete revolution in the opposite direction. This cannot be effected in any other manner. If the body is suspended by a rope the extension of an arm in one direction will only cause a corresponding retraction in the opposite direction.[1] The sum of the moments is necessarily always zero.

In regard to external forces, the case is different. Of these the most important, as far as natural bodies are concerned, is that of gravity. Also due attention must be given to friction and air resistance. A man in falling describes a portion of a parabola, this being the trajectory of his centre of gravity.

Fig. 241.

Trajectory of centre of gravity of an animal (cat) thrown horizontally.

Marey ([2]) demonstrated by *chronophotography* that the body of an animal (*e.g.*, a cat) can make a complete rotation under the influence of interior (muscular) forces (fig. 241). Nevertheless the general centre of gravity describes an arc of a parabola just as if the force of gravity was acting on a rigid body.

[1] E. Kohlrauch, *Physik des Turnens*, p. 50, 1887.
[2] *Comptes Rendus Sciences*, vol. cxix., p. 714, (1894).

An acrobat during a leap can, by the use of his arms, turn himself around a transverse axis.[1] However, apart from the slight resistance of the air, it is yet true that the height, the speed, and the duration of the leap are governed and connected by the formulæ :

$$v = \sqrt{2gh}, \ h = \tfrac{1}{2} g t^2, \ t = \frac{v}{g}$$

If the angle of inclination of the initial speed is α the time $t = \dfrac{v \sin \alpha}{g}$. The body reaches its maximum height by a parabolic curve (*vide* fig. 242).

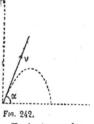

Fig. 242.

Trajectory of a jump.

The laws which govern the movement of projectiles are equally applicable in the case of the human body. Thus to obtain the greatest length of jump the direction of the jumper should be at 45° with the horizontal. The actual distance covered falls short of the calculated distance owing to the resistance of the air (§ 24).

Gravity acts on each component of the human body. Otto Fischer, by a laborious investigation determined the centres of gravity of the various members. But the action of gravity is balanced or overcome by muscular action. The result is motion, *muscular dynamics*. This motion is conditioned, as to its form, by the *degrees of liberty*, and as to its speed by the magnitude of the stresses applied.

264. Remarks on Muscular Movement.—It is of great importance carefully to examine the motions both of the upper limbs (the arms, the fore-arms, and the hands) and of the lower limbs (the thighs, the legs and the feet). When one osseus segment is caused by muscular contraction to approach another (for example, when the elbow or the knee are bent) the motion is denominated *flexion*. Motion in the opposite direction is called *extension*. *Abduction* is the movement of a member in a direction away from the body. *Adduction* is the reverse movement towards the body. When a member turns on a longitudinal axis, the motion is called *supination* if the movement is outwards, and *pronation* if the movement is inwards. Thus the forearm is in *supination* when the back of the hand faces the ground, and in *pronation* when the palm of the hand is downwards.

The joints of the shoulder and of the hip have so great a degree of freedom that these members are able to describe circles, or arcs

[1] E. Kohlrauch (*loc. cit.*, p. 45). This is why good jumpers show highly developed shoulder muscles (Marey, *Exposit. Intern. Univ. de.*, 1900, Sect. 13, Paris, 1901).

of circles. This movement is described as *circumduction*. In this latter connection Leonardo da Vinci, more than four centuries ago, made the following remark : " The movements of the shoulders are infinite. If the arm is caused to sweep out a circle, all the movements which are possible for that shoulder are thereby made.

Furthermore, as any continuous quantity is divisible to infinity, the circle thus swept out is itself a continuous quantity due to the movement of the arm, which latter cannot produce a continuous quantity unless it is itself continuous. Hence the movement of the arm, having passed through every part of a circle, and the circle being divisible to infinity, the variations (of movement) of the shoulders are also infinite." (¹)

The degree of liberty of movement of a limb depends on the nature and form of the joint. For joints of the same type the speed and amplitude of movement are determined by the length of the arm of the lever, the power, and the resistance. We know that the levers of locomotion are almost entirely of the third order (§ 87).

In fig. 243 the planes in which movement takes place are shown : —

(a) The *frontal*, X'ZXZ'.

(b) The *horizontal*, XY'X'Y

(c) The *sagittal* (or anterior-posterior) YZY'Z'.

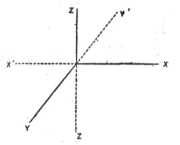

Fɪɢ. 243..

Plan of the orientation of the limbs of man.

Every movement can be referred to these three planes.

Adduction and *Abduction* are, however, referred to the *median* plane of the body which lies in the *sagittal* plane.

265. To simplify the study of the movements of the limbs the following assumptions must be made :

(a) That the longitudinal axes of any limb passes through its centre of gravity, and also through the centre of its joint (Otto Fischer found that this is, actually, approximately correct.)

(b) That any joint may be considered as having one or more definite and fixed axes. (In practice these axes are often subject to slight displacements from their initial positions).

(¹) Leonardo da Vinci (*Trattato della Pittura*, p. 107 (Milan, 1804).

(c) That the muscular "insertions" may be considered as points so that the muscle can be represented as a straight line (a vector force) in the same plane as the longitudinal axis of the limb. (We shall find that this assumption does not affect the validity of the reasoning, although it is not in precise accordance with the physical facts of the case.)

(d) That the movement of any articulated osseus segment can be studied as if the remainder of the body was a solid and invariable mass.[1]

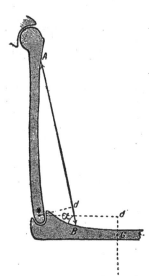

Fig. 244.
Moment of rotation of the forearm.

Let us take, as an example, a movement having only one degree of liberty, e.g., the movement of the forearm in relation to the upper arm. Assume the latter to be rigidly fixed in a vertical position.

In fig. 244 the biceps muscle is represented by the straight line AB. Tension is exerted at the extremities A and B. A is fixed, and B turns round an axis at o, at the elbow. The moment of rotation of the force F (or AB) in reference to the point o is :

$$M = F \times od.$$

The moving segment (the fore-arm and the hand) is however attracted downward by gravitation. If the weight of the segment (the resistance) is P, acting at its centre of gravity G, then this weight has a moment :

$$M' = P \times od'.$$

Flexion can only take place if the "motor" moment M is greater than the "resistant" moment M'.

The muscular effort needed varies inversely as the length of the lever od. Hence in any given position, the shorter the distance from B to the joint, the greater the force which must be developed. Hence : od = oB sin α.

$$M = F \times oB \sin \alpha.$$

[1] Otto Fischer (Abhandlungen . . . vol. xx., 1893 ; xxii., 1895 ; xxiii., 1897).

That is to say, the "motor" moment varies, according to a sinusoidal law, with the inclination of the muscle to the segment which is undergoing displacement. In the course of a complete movement of the forearm the angle α varies from 0° to 180° (from full extension to maximum flexion). When the angle α is zero, sin α = 0 and the moment M is also zero. When α is 30° sin α = $\frac{1}{2}$ (*vide* fig. 245). The position of maximum moment is when the muscle AB is at right angles to the moveable segment.

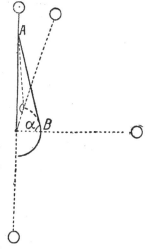

Fig. 245

Different degrees of flexion of the forearm.

In actual fact, since the heads of the joints have projections, and the tendons are attached by surfaces, the "motor" moment is never exactly zero at any given position and instant of time. According to Fischer [1] the residual value is not negligible. Furthermore the muscle, even when reduced to a straight line, does not always lie in the same plane as the member which it is causing to move. If so, the effective component of its force will be its projection on the plane of the member (*vide* fig. 246). The magnitude of this component being proportional to the cosine of the angle α.

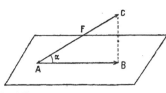

Fig. 246.

AB is the component of the muscular force F in the plane of rotation of the limb.

A movement, having one degree of liberty, may be due to the action of one muscle only or may be effected by several muscles. We only need, however, to consider their *resultant* and we have already seen (*vide* § 15) that any system of forces can be reduced to an equivalent single force and a "couple." This, however, is only true for a single definite position, since the forces change during the displacement.

The movements which have one degree of liberty only are those of certain of the larger joints, joints such as the forearm and the lower leg (§ 75), where no rotational movement is possible,

[1] Braune and Fischer (*loc. cit.*)., vol. xv., No. 3, p. 245).

as the nature of the joint prevents it. Hence the effect of the lateral component BC (*vide* fig. 246) is practically nil, in flexion and extension. It will be seen in fig. 247 that the lower extremity of the *biceps* takes the form of a loop which encircles the *radius*, which carries the hand. Hence the whole osseus segment can rotate in *supination*. At the same time the tendon lengthens slightly to permit of the above movement (*vide* functional adaptations, § 86).

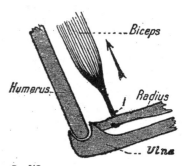

FIG. 247.

Cause of rotation of the forearm.

Generally the forearm can be moved up or down without any rotation taking place. If, however, the hand is supporting a heavy weight, the motions of flexion and rotation may take place simultaneously, the latter causing an unrolling of the ligament of the tendon. A simple analogy is given by R. du Bois-Reymond: [1]

Place a cotton reel on a table and pull the thread in such a direction that would tend to unroll it. If the reel is light it will be drawn forward without rotating. If, on the other hand, it is heavy, it will rotate without moving forward, and the thread will be unwound.

The couple of rotation vanishes when the hand is in *supination*. In this position the muscular movement is exercised in the most simple and efficient manner, especially if a great effort is called for.

The reader will remember that the finger joints are the only articulations which can, with entire accuracy, be described as having a single axis (§ 75). The elbow joint, for example, is an oval articulation and belongs rather to the second degree.

Chauveau [2] has shown that the *flexor* muscles operate more economically than the *extensors*, the consumption of oxygen being less for the same work. He proved this for the muscles of the forearm. Otto Fischer appears to have reached the same conclusion as the result of certain experiments on the movements of the legs.

In the case of joints which are spherical or have three axes, there can, of course, be several simultaneous movements, such as *flexion*, or *extension* (in the *sagittal* plane), *adduction* (in the *frontal*

[1] R. du Bois-Reymond, *Spezielle Muskelphysiologie* (*loc. cit.*)
[2] A. Chauveau (*Comptes Rendus Sciences*, 5th October, 1904).

plane), and *circumduction*; but the motion more often takes
place in a single direction around one determined axis. For
example, the legs generally move in the *sagittal* plane. The result
is an adaptation, an *automatism*, so perfect that the expenditure
of energy is a minimum. We should, therefore, always encourage
those modes of movement which "come naturally" to a man
unless it is clear that such movements are not capable of effecting
useful results.

266. Muscles sometimes control two or more joints. Thus the
extensors which control the fingers are prolonged to the wrist.
This arrangement may be unfavourable for work. For example,
when the wrist is bent, the extensors are already considerably
stretched, and the fingers cannot be strongly flexed. Thus if the
hand is clenched on an object the grip can be relaxed if the wrist
is forcibly bent down.

The same member can call into play in its movements a whole
group of muscles, a group whose constitution varies according
to circumstances. We think of the fore-arm as being necessarily
controlled by the muscles of the upper arm ; but the powerful
muscles of the shoulder make also their contribution. To speak
quite accurately, the elbow joint operates the tractive movement
of the hands ; while the muscles of the shoulder generally operate
the arms. The very mobile wrist joint (§ 75) is hardly subjected
to any effort. It is also very delicate and more adapted to the
exercise of speed than of force. The *supination* and *pronation*
of the hand are effected by the *radius* and not by the bones of the
wrist, although the latter have really several degrees of liberty.

To the action of the muscles which actually produce movement we must, as we have already seen (*vide* § 87) add the action
of their *antagonists*. As Duchenne de Boulogne and Braune
and Fischer have shown, it is by a combination of muscular efforts
that a limb is moved in the direction, and at the speed, required.
Hence, if we wish to estimate the muscular work performed in
flexing the forearm, we must know, not merely the force exerted
by the *biceps*, and the magnitude of the displacement, but also
the work done by the *triceps*, its *antagonist*. The muscular system
functions under the control of co-ordinated nervous excitations.
It is really this co-ordination which governs and regulates human
movement in contra-distinction to the crude idea of muscular
antagonism. The action of the *extensors*, for example, is not
always antagonistic to that of the *flexors*. Thus when a man,
standing, bends forward his head, the *extensor* muscles alone, by
their gradual relaxation, contract, and guide the movement of
the head at the required speed.

Thus muscles act in combination and not in opposition. To
raise the arm, the *abductor*, *adductor* and *levator* muscles come into

action, the first helping to carry the arm forward, or backward. To lower the arm, the *depressor* muscles come into play, not as antagonists of the *levators*, but as moderators of the downward movement. Again, the *brachial biceps* is not exclusively a *flexor* muscle, it is also a *supinator*, for we can perceive that it is distended when we turn a stiff key.

The *rectus femoris*, the straight anterior muscle, is not merely an *extensor* of the lower leg. It is also a *flexor* and *levator* of the thigh and serves to maintain the equilibrium of the hips.

The modes of muscular action are numerous. It is obvious that an exact summation of the energy expended in these various actions is of prime importance in the determination of what is called the " degree of fatigue."

In industry the various movements of the body should be directed towards the attainment of the maximum effect with the minimum expenditure of energy. We shall often find that limbs are moved to an extent which is quite unnecessary. This is to be avoided since muscles, which might otherwise be at rest, are put into action. In various occupations we shall observe that in addition to those movements which are of direct utility there are others which are superfluous, and whose elimination would result in economy. Sports, such as boxing and fencing in particular, are in the same category. Here, however, the useless movements are generally recognized, and are avoided, by the best athletes, who know that such redundant movements are disadvantageous both to professional reputation, and to health.

267. Movements of Parts of the Body. Centres of Gravity. Moments of Inertia.—Otto Fischer determined the position of the centre of gravity for various parts of the body and the proportions of those parts. The upper and lower limbs, the head and the trunk, have centres of gravity which are referable to a common origin, the line of the joints of the shoulders or hips.

It will be obvious that the numerical values thus obtained are to be taken as average results only, and are not applicable to any particular subject.

If we consider the trunk as a cylinder and the limbs as frustra of cones we can calculate, approximately, their moments of inertia.

$I = M\rho^2$, in which M designates the mass $\dfrac{P}{g}$, and ρ, the radius of gyration (see § 31).

Consider first of all the following data for an adult of 65 kilogrammes :

1. *Bust* (trunk and head) ; weight = 50% of the whole or $\dfrac{65}{2}$ = 32·5 kg. Centre of gravity at about 0·32 m. from the line of the hips ; the dimensions of the cylinder are, therefore, : Height, 0·88 m ; radius, 0·13 m. (*vide* fig. 248). The moment of inertia will be :

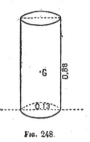

Fig. 248.

$$I = \frac{M}{12}\,(3r^2 + 4h^2) = 0\cdot86.$$

2. *Upper Arm.*—Weight = 2·20 kg. ; centre of gravity at 0·145 m. from the centre of the shoulder joint. Take $h = 0\cdot35$ m ; and compare the segment to a truncated cone.

We obtain $r = 0\cdot047$ m, $r' = 0\cdot04$ m.

Applying the formula for the moment of inertia, we have :

$$I = M\left[\,\frac{h^2}{g}\left(1 + \frac{d}{r + r'}\right) + \frac{(r + r')^2 - 2d^2}{16}\,\right] = 0\cdot0033.$$

3. *Fore-arm* : $M = \dfrac{2\cdot04\ \text{kg.}}{g}$; $h = 0\cdot35$ m ; $r = 0\cdot045$; $r' = 0\cdot027$ m, and the centre of gravity is 0·54 m from the centre of the shoulder joint. Hence :

$$I = 0\cdot0037.$$

4. The moments of interia of the fingers are approximately as follows :—

Little finger.	Ring finger.	Middle finger.	Index finger.	Thumb.
I = 0·000004	0·000012	0·000014	0·000012	0·000006

5. In the whole upper limb the centre of gravity falls at about $\frac{45}{100}$ of the length from the shoulder joint, *i.e.*, 0·32 m. If the fist is closed we have approximately $h = 0\cdot70$ m. As P = 4·20 kg and $r = 0\cdot047$ m, and $r' = \cdot027$ m, we can calculate that I = 0·03 approximately.

6. In the *lower limb* the *lower leg* will be considered separately, and then the whole limb.

Lower Leg.—P = 4·400 kg (foot included) ; $h = 0\cdot44$ m ; $r = 0\cdot062$ m ; $r' = 0\cdot038$ m. From these figures :

$$I = 0\cdot013.$$

For the whole of the leg : P = 12 kilogrammes ; $h = 0\cdot88$ m; $r = 0\cdot086$ m ; $r' = 0\cdot038$ m. Whence

$$I = 0\cdot146.$$

According to the measurements and calculations, the centre of gravity of the lower limb, in the adult, is about 0·38 m. from the centre of the hip joint. The radius of gyration is deduced from the formula $I = M\rho^2$, which gives $\rho = 0\cdot34$ m.

The knowledge of the moments of inertia leads to that of the work of the oscillation, the angular speed being ω, :

$$T = \tfrac{1}{2}I\omega^2.$$

In the above calculations it is assumed that no load is carried by the man. If the various members carry any load, it is obvious that the centres of gravity and the moments of inertia will have different numerical values. The writer's object, in the above calculations has been to show, quite simply, that it is possible to determine the above values in any given case. Of this Braune and Fischer have given ample proof, based both on experiment and on fundamental theory. By *chronophotography* the magnitude and velocity of movements in their various phases can be studied with accuracy. The German scientists, above mentioned, employed Marey's system of *geometrical chronophotography* illuminating the points and lines to be photographed by means of *Geissler tubes.*[1]

268. Human Locomotion.—Locomotion which is the movement of the human body as a whole may be divided into two departments, *terrestial locomotion* and *aquatic locomotion*. Both obey the same laws of muscular action.

The most familiar form of terrestial locomotion is *Walking*. But we have also the motions of *Crawling* (in which the points of contact of the body with the ground are increased) ; *Running* and *Jumping* (in which the amount and duration of such contact is reduced) and *Climbing* (in which the weight of the body is supported by the arms.)

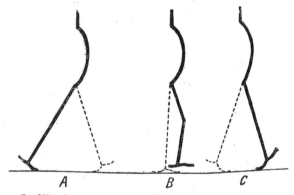

Fig. 240.

Different phases of a simple step; the subject goes from A to C.

[1] Braune and Fischer, *Der Gang des Menschen*, Part I. (*Abhand. d. Math.*, vol. xxii., 1985).

The motions of walking have been specially studied by the brothers Weber, by Marey, and by Braune and Fischer. ([1]) We shall draw most extensively on the two latter authorities, since, while fully utilizing Marey's results, they extended and completed his work. The *technique* of the subject has laid under contribution both *graphic* and *chronophotographic* methods. By these we can determine the relations between the length of the step, the pressure of the foot on the ground, the muscular effort exerted, the nature of the movement, and the speed.

The act of walking is essentially a disturbance of the mechanical equilibrium of the body, producing displacement of the legs, which alternately sustain the total weight of the body. This transference of weight is achieved by a regular oscillation of the general centre of gravity, which is always brought to a position above the leg which is on the ground—the " carrying " leg—while the other leg, the "oscillating" leg, leaves the ground with the point of its foot, swings forward and replaces itself on the ground in advance of the other leg. A " pace " is the distance between the centres of the feet when walking. The " double pace " is the complete cycle after which the legs and feet are in the same relative positions as before.

The double pace has three phases (A.B and C; in fig. 249). The first occupies about $\frac{4}{10}$ of a second during which time the hinder leg leaves the ground by the toe, and swings forward, meeting the ground again with the heel. A period of about $\frac{1}{10}$ of a second then elapses during which both feet are on the ground. There is therefore firstly a period of oscillation and secondly a period of " double support." In ordinary walking (121 paces, 0·75 m. long per minute), the time of a double pace is about one second.

Hence the " oscillating " leg rests on the ground for $\frac{5}{10}$ of a second, acting as a support for the body. Propulsion is attained by the progressive shifting of the point of contact with the ground from the heel to the toe. Fig. 250 exhibits the successive movements in a double pace.

269. Fischer ([2]) analysed the double pace. He took as his subject an adult weighing 58·7 kg. and 1·87 metres in height, the length of his lower limbs being 0·87 m. The average number of double paces per minute was 121 and the average length of pace

---

([1]) E. and W. Weber, *Mécanique de la Locomotion chez l'Homme*, trans. Jourdan, 1843 (a poor translation) ; Marey, *Le Mouvement*, Paris, 1894 ; Engl. tr., London, 1894) ; Braune and Fischer (*Abhandlungen*, vol. xx ., No. 4 ; xxv., No. 1 ; xxvi., Nos. 3 and 7 ; xxviii., Nos. 5 and 7 ; *Der Gang d. Menschen*, 1895 to 1904 ; about 700 quarto pages).

([2]) O. Fischer (*loc. cit.*, vol. xxv., No. 1), Examining 103 soldiers of the 8th Regiment (in Saxony) he found that the size of the step is variable and reaches at least 0.80 m. (*loc. cit.*, vol. xxviii., No. 5, p. 343, 1903).

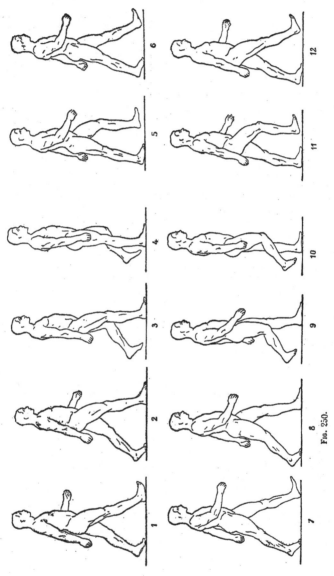

Fig. 250.

The various phases of a double pace in walking.

was 0·75 m. The average time of a single pace was therefore ·495 seconds and the rate of walking 5·445 km. per hour.

Commence at the moment when the right foot leaves the ground and is in the air, the left leg is in front and a pace has been made, the trunk is poised over that leg, and the period of " support " and " propulsion " begins. The right leg, which is lifted, is shortened by flexion of the knee (the angle is 150°), so that it can oscillate. The knee then stiffens, the thigh moves forward to an angle of 25° with the vertical, and the heel of the right foot makes contact with the ground. It should be remembered that this return to the ground is made slowly, without acceleration, the muscles having moderated the pendulum effect that Weber believed to govern the oscillations of the legs. Theoretically, it would be a pendulum of a period :

$$t = \pi \sqrt{\frac{I}{Mgl}}$$

I being the moment of inertia (§ 26) ; this would lead to :

$$t = \pi \sqrt{\frac{0·146}{12 \times 0·38}} = 0·56s.$$

too high a value. There is therefore muscular action which Fischer found to be greater than that of gravity. It is due first of all to the flexors of the lower leg, then to those of the thigh on the pelvis, and finally to the *quadriceps* which contract sharply and throw the leg forward, the sole of the foot bend-

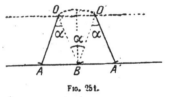

Fig. 251.

ing to soften the shock of contact with the ground. Again, in the period of oscillation, the point of support of the limb, at the hip, is not fixed, but advances by a step which could be represented by the diagram (fig. 251). The hip has moved from O to O′, and the leg OA to O′A′. The duration of the oscillation corresponds to the distance BA′ and the angle of the oscillation is only equal to α, not to 2α. In the example taken by Braune and Fischer $t = \frac{415}{1000}$ of a second, AB = 0·778 m., and OA = 0·870 m. If the triangle AOB is equilateral α would equal 60°, in this case

$$\alpha = \frac{60 \times 778}{870} = 53·60° \text{ approximately,}$$

which leads to an average angular speed of :

$$\frac{53·60 \times 1,000}{415} = 129°,$$

or in radians :

$$\omega = \frac{\pi \times 129}{180} = \frac{43\pi}{60} \text{ (see § 2 and 26)}.$$

When the oscillation of the right leg has finished and the heel is on the ground, and before the left foot has left the ground, there is a moment during which both feet are on the ground. This is the period of "double support." This period is very short. In normal walking it is only ·08 seconds, five times less than that of the oscillation. During this period the weight is transferred to the right leg, which, at this moment, is inclined at about 25° to the vertical, then as the foot comes into full contact with the ground, the leg which was bent straightens at the knee, the lower member takes its full development, and consequently the hip describes a curve of increasing radius. When the upright position of the leg is passed the hip commences to describe a curve in the reverse direction. This curve has some resemblance to the trajectory of a point moving in the interior of a semi-cylinder from the bottom to the edge. Marey made records of the sinuous curves by means of measurements of the movement of the *pubis*.

By certain muscular contractions, especially of the *quadriceps*, the knee is stiffened and the whole weight of the body is supported without flexion of the thigh. The foot " unrolls " (deroule) itself from heel to toe, during which " unrolling " the lower member remains straight owing to muscular contraction of hips and femur. It supports the pressure transmitted to it by the rear leg, which pressure is at its maximum in the vertical position. Fischer found, with a subject weighing 58·4 kg. that the pressure varied from 70 kg to 77 kg, a mean increase of 25%. Marey and Carlet measured the pressure on the feet by means of " exploring shoes " (§ 212), and found that, in walking, the apparent increase of weight never exceeded 20 kg. But there is also in walking, reaction from the ground, a tangential force, represented by a negative value. Fischer found that its value was 7 kg. at the moment when the rear leg was lifting. It increased immediately to 16 kg. and remained at that value during the duration of the period of support. Marey and Démeny used a " dynamographic stage " to measure the vertical and horizontal components of the pressure of the feet. This apparatus consists of a stage resting on coils of small rubber tube. The air which is expelled from them acting

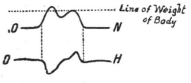

Fɪɢ. 252.｣

N = perpendicular pressure.
H = tangential pressure.
O = zero position of instrument.

on a registering " tambour." From fig. 252 it will be seen that the curve of vertical pressure oscillates from side to side of the line of weight of the body. During the transfer of the weight of the body from one leg to the other the perpendicular oscillation has a negative value. It will also be easily seen that the curve of tangential pressure (H) is negative at the moment when the heel touches the ground and becomes positive at the end of the " unrolling " of the foot. This " unrolling " has been compared by the brothers Weber to the motion of the felloe of a wheel, a somewhat rash comparison seeing that the radius, in this case the lower member, changes in length.

The rear leg is lifted during this " unrolling " and before the other leg becomes vertical. The toe of the hinder foot, as it leaves the ground, transmits a thrust to the trunk by which its weight is thrown forward on to the front leg. If this were not the case the body would fall backwards. The propulsive effort, therefore, takes place during the period of " double support," and produces its whole effect during the support.

In Fischer's experiments, the period of support was $\frac{494}{1,000}$ of a second which added to that of the "double support" gives :—

$$\frac{494}{1,000} + \frac{81}{1,000} = \frac{575}{1,000}.$$

Analysis of phases of a double step in thousandths of a second (after du Bois-Reymond).

Fig. 253 is a diagramatic representation of the periods of activity of the two legs, by R. du Bois-Reymond, expressed in thousandths of a second. As explained above, the angle corresponding to the " unrolling " of the foot averages 53°, and increases with the length of the pace (*vide* fig. 251). The translation of the hip and the impulse given to the trunk must increase in the same proportion, and as, by the separation of the legs, the trunk and the general centre of gravity, is lowered, long paces must cause a more pronounced vertical oscillation than

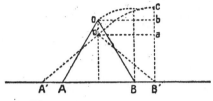

FIG. 254.

Vertical oscillation passes from *bc* to *ac*
when the step is A'B' instead of AB.

small steps (fig. 254) : (*ac* instead of *bc*) and it is also desirable
in lengthening the step, to bend at the same time, the
carrying leg, thus diminishing the radius O'B' and making a
nearly rectilineal movement of the hip. De Raoul ([1]) has a high
opinion of the advantage of marching with bent knees. Agricultural labourers, and others who desire to spare themselves
unnecessary exertion, adopt a similar gait. Furthermore, as
Compte and Regnault ([2]) found by chronophotographic methods,
the vertical oscillations are thereby greatly diminished. On
the other hand, the extra flexion of the knee caused by this
method of walking, entails additional muscular contraction.
Hence, although the practice has much to recommend it, it should
be adopted with caution in the case of infantry marching with
loads.([3])

270. Movements and Oscillations of the Body while Walking.—
The movements which are exhibited in the regular succession of
paces in walking are complicated by oscillatory movements
of various parts of the body besides the lower limbs. Even the
movements of the legs themselves are not exempt from such complications. It can easily be seen that the feet, the knees, and the
hips oscillate from side to side of their *sagittal* planes. Thus the
foot exerts a lateral pressure on the ground besides the vertical
and tangential pressures, and, as will be seen from fig. 253, the
action of the two lower limbs is not absolutely symmetrical.

There would seem to be a real structural difference between
the right and the left sides of the body. · The fact that the great
majority are right-handed may be due to an instinct of protection
in regard to the heart.([4])

([1]) Count de Raoul (*Revue de l'Infanterie*, 15th August, 1896) ; Raoul
and Regnault, *Comment on Marche*, 1897.

([2]) Comte and Regnault (*Arch. de Physiol.*, 1896, p. 180) ; A. Schmidt,
Unser Korper, p. 426, 1899.

([3]) See the criticisms by Paul Richer in the *Traité de Physique Biologique*,
by Marey, d'Arsonval, etc., vol. i., p. 216, 1901, and Regnault's reply in
Journ. de Physiol., 1913, p. 49.

([4]) Aristotle had already made this distinction ; see also Guldberg,
Etudes sur la Dissymétrie chez l'Homme, Christiania, 1897. Chauffard
(*Acad. de Méd.*, 12th November, 1912).

The motion of the legs disturbs the equilibrium of the trunk and causes it to oscillate. The centre line of the hips (the horizontal line joining the *coxo-femoral* joints) rises and falls. The period of this oscillation is the same as that of the step, while its average amplitude is 4 cm. It swings forward towards the leg which is being planted vertically on the ground, and swings back towards the *median* plane of the body when the foot is lifted. It receives, in the anterior-posterior plane, a certain acceleration. All the oscillatory motions described in the preceding paragraphs (§ 269) have the same period.

The line of the shoulders moves in a similar manner. When the body is at rest the lines of the hips and the shoulders are in the same vertical plane. When walking they become out of plane to the extent of 1·5 cm. In other respects these oscillations are similar to those above described.[1]

The arms swing during walking, a motion which is to a great extent involuntary. When the right leg advances the left arm swings forward, being slightly shortened by a small flexion of the elbow. This shortening is augmented in fast walking, resulting in frequent oscillations of short period (§ 2). These motions compensate for the torsion of the trunk, which latter can be readily observed when a man is walking with folded arms.

Marey and Démeny[2] found that the head shares in all these oscillations and that it describes a left-handed curve. The distance of the centre line of the head from the median plane is approximately 2·5 cm. at the moment when the foot is placed on the ground. At the moment of " double support " the above distance is practically zero. The amplitude of the vertical oscillations may be as much as 6 cm., but, as the trunk itself is subject to inclination, this figure is not to be taken as the vertical displacement from the centre of gravity of the body.

This general centre of gravity is subject to oscillations in various planes, and these movements have varying rates of acceleration. We can see, in these facts, a cause of the difficulties which very young children experience in keeping their balance.

The results of the investigations detailed in this chapter may be summarised as follows :—

In the example taken (walking at 121 steps per minute, the average speed being 5·45 km. per hour) ; the centre of gravity has a vertical oscillation of 4 cm. in amplitude, a lateral oscillation of 1·3 cm. and a displacement from front to back of 2·5 cm.[3]

---

(1) Lamy (*Nouvelle Iconogr.* de la Salpétrière, vol. xviii., No. 1, p. 49).
(2) Marey and Démeney (*Comptes Rendus Sciences*, June, 1885, October, 1887)
(3) *i.e.*, the mean *oscillation*, not the *translation* of the body.

271. Marey's method of geometrical chronophotography was as follows :—The subjects of the experiments were clothed in black garments on which white lines were drawn to represent the spinal column, and the lines of shoulders, hips, and other lines whose movements he desired to study. A series of straight lines, representing the positions of the moving limbs as functions of time, were then obtained on one plate, or film, with instantaneous exposures. Braune and Fischer also employed photographic methods in their experiments on the nature of bodily movement, while their determinations of the centres of gravity, the sizes, and weights of the various components of the human body, were the result of experiments with corpses. Thus, having ascertained the distribution of the masses of the body and the laws of its movement, they were able to calculate the forces exerted.

It should be noted that in all such photographs the lower members are never shown in complete extension ; hence the vertical oscillation appears to be less than it really is.

CHAPTER II.

INDUSTRIAL LABOUR AND LOCOMOTION.

(Continued.)

272. The Work of the Muscles in Walking.—The data for the following calculations of the amount of work done by the muscles during each pace have been taken from the experimental results obtained by Marey and Braune and Fischer.

We have, first of all, a vertical rise of the body of 0·04 m., followed by a corresponding fall under restraint (we know that, as far as energy is concerned, the one is 52% of the other). Hence in the case of an adult weighing 65 kg. the corresponding muscular work done is :—

$$T_1 = 65 \times 0.04 \times \frac{152}{100} = 3.952 \text{ kgm.}$$

The oscillation of the lower limb produces work to the amount of

$$T_2 = \tfrac{1}{2} I \omega^2 ;$$

as $I = 0.146$ (§ 267) and

$$\omega = \frac{43\pi}{60} \text{ (see § 269).}$$

The result will be :

$$\tfrac{1}{2} I \omega^2 = \tfrac{1}{2} \times 0.146 \times \frac{\overline{43}^2 \pi^2}{3,600} = 0.370 \text{ kgm.}$$

Taking the restraint into account,

$$T_2 = \frac{0.370}{2} \times \frac{152}{100} = 0.281 \text{ kgm.}$$

Fig. 255.

In the third place, the general centre of gravity is subjected to a variation of *vis viva* in its translation : diagramatically, the speed is a minimum at the summit of the trajectory OCO′ (fig. 255), and it varies by about 0·60 m. according to experimental observations.

Therefore :

$$\tfrac{1}{2} m v^2 = \tfrac{1}{2} \times \frac{65}{9.81} \times \overline{0.60}^2 = 1.192 \text{ kgm.}$$

To include in this evaluation the work of restraint done by the muscles, we have :

$$T_3 = 1.192 \times \frac{152}{100} = 1.812 \text{ kgm.}$$

Small muscular movements due to various other oscillations of the trunk can be disregarded, and finally :

$$T = T_1 + T_2 + T_3 = 3.952 + 0.281 + 1.812 = 6.045 \text{ kgm.}$$

on the average 6 kilogrammetres per step.

It is obvious that the above numerical results are only true for a particular subject walking in a particular manner. Nevertheless the results obtained by the above-mentioned scientists, with subjects of the same weight and walking in the same way, agree fairly well.

For a pace of ·778 metres in length the muscular work *per kilometre covered* will be—

$$\frac{6 \times 1000}{.778} = 7,712 \text{ kilogrammetres.}$$

This result gives an idea of the amount of muscular work done in walking. At the same time the vertical oscillation of the body, which is a preponderating element in the expenditure of muscular energy, is modified by the nature of the ground and the degree of flexion of the legs. Regnault noted that in walking with bent knees the pressure of the feet on the ground was more gentle than in walking with the legs straight.

Although the above computations are based on the results of very careful experiments, they are not to be taken as rigidly accurate. Furthermore, it must not be forgotten that the *static values* of muscular contractions may be considerable. These latter values cannot be registered by the above methods, and are indeed only capable of any exact evaluation by measurements of the consumption of oxygen. As walking is a function to which man is specially adapted, it seems probable that the work done at each step does not much exceed 4 *kilogrammetres*.

273. The Rhythm of Walking.—Marey made some experiments on the effects of *rhythm*, the number of paces in unit time. The apparatus, which he employed consisted of a horizontal track 500 metres in length, provided with electric contacts at intervals of 50 metres.

He measured the variations in the length of the step as functions of the *rhythm* or cadence. Up to 150 paces per minute, the length of the pace increased, but above this it diminished (*vide* fig. 256). In the case of a walker 1·67 metres high (the same height as Fischer's subject) the maximum length of the pace was found to be 0·85 m.

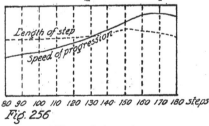

Fig. 256

Effects of the cadence.

Fischer found, as the result of careful experiments with 103 soldiers, that every person's walk has its own individual character. Although his subjects were all very much alike, yet their steps were dissimilar both in length and duration. He came to the conclusion that there is no universal type of walking.

Démeny ([1]) found that the period of *double support* is perceptible up to 200 paces per minute, and that the duration of this period decreased rapidly above 80 paces per minute, being 175 thousandths of a second at this speed, and only 50 thousandths at 200 paces per minute.

The lateral oscillations of the trunk decrease with rapid cadences, because the feet tend to come nearer to the *line of progression*. It must also be pointed out that by reducing the period of movement of the legs, the synchronous oscillation of the bust, which has a relatively long period, is impeded. In the same way the arms bend and reduce their amplitude of oscillation.

It would therefore seem that, as far as the above conditions are concerned, a given distance can be covered more economically by fast walking than by walking slowly. On the other hand, the expenditure of muscular energy increases generally with increase in the number of steps per minute.

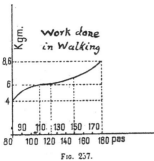

Fig. 257.

Fig. 257 shows the variation of the muscular work with the number of paces per minute. It is based on Marey's results, who found that the work increased up to 110 paces per minute, that from 110 to 130 paces it was practically constant (this is, therefore the best pace), while at over 140 paces the work rises rapidly, as the curve shows. We see, therefore, that beyond a certain point, walking becomes so tiring that it is preferable to run.

274. Conclusion.—From the curve in fig. 257 we can calculate the work expended per *metre-kilogramme* (§ 232). An adult, weighing 65 kg., expends 7,712 kilogrammetres in covering 1 km. at a speed of 5,450 metres per hour. The expenditure is, therefore :

$$\frac{7712}{65 \times 1000} = \cdot119 \text{ kgm. } per \ metre\text{-}kilogramme.$$

([1]) Démeny (*Comptes Rendus Sciences*, 25th June, 1885).

The corresponding expenditures of work *per metre-kilogramme* for 80, 120 and 180 paces per minute are ·088 kgm., ·119 kgm. and ·176 kgm. respectively.

These figures are only useful for the purpose of comparison. From the practical point of view the all-important factor is the expenditure of energy as measured by the consumption of oxygen.

275. Walking with a Load.—The general nature of the step is the same whether walking loaded or unloaded, although the durations of the various movements are altered. The length of the step is decreased while the periods of support, especially those of " double support " are prolonged. The foot is placed flat on the ground, and the contraction of the muscles of the carrying leg is increased.

The vertical oscillations are decreased, both owing to the above reduction in the length of the step and also because the load carried tends to increase the flexion of the knees. Other oscillations are influenced by the manner in which the load is carried. If the load is borne on the head, the Centre of Gravity is thereby raised and the muscles have to contend with an increased instability of the body. Inconvenience on this account is much less if the load is carried by the shoulder or the nape of the neck. In the latter case, the body oscillates in an anterior posterior plane and the muscles have to overcome the inertia of the load. In the former case the effect of this inertia is but little felt since the body adjusts itself to balance, the effect of the load (§ 261) and the Centre of Gravity remains approximately in the same plane as before. It is not, however, possible, by such adjustment, to balance a load exceeding one half, or at most two-thirds, of the weight of the trunk, say from 16 to 22 kg. It would therefore seem that the most economical method of human transport is to carry loads of 20 kg. or so on the shoulder.

For the same reason the soldiers haversack should rest on the *flank* and not on the back. If on the loins, the movement of the limbs are also less restrained. Some labourers carry on their heads loads which, though heavy, are very compact. In such cases the Centre of Gravity is not much raised and the powerful muscles of the neck can maintain the equilibrium of the head.

276. Walking with Displacement of Resistance.—When a man pulls a load or pushes it before him, the periods of support and double support are also increased. The body inclines so as to bring its weight into play, and the Centre of Gravity is thrown forward in the direction of the displacement. Also the lower limbs are slightly bent and the vertical oscillations are reduced (§ 331).

It is obvious that the effort required for propulsion increases in proportion to the resistance. The intensity of the effort can be gauged by the prominence of the *quadriceps* and *sural* muscles.

In this case no certain computation can be made of the work done, as it is dependent, amongst other factors, on the inclination of the body, the manner in which the arms are used, and the parts sustained by various groups of muscles in the operations. Furthermore, familiarity with the work done may result in a reduction in the static effort and an elimination of unnecessary motions which may considerably modify the results. Nevertheless, the variations in the work done can be measured by the corresponding consumptions of oxygen.

277. The Ascending Walk.—We will now consider the operation of walking up a staircase or an inclined plane.

In walking upstairs one of the legs is raised by flexion at the knee, and its foot is placed flat upon the next step of the stair. A contraction of the *quadriceps* muscle permits this elevation and also the previous flexion in regard to the trunk (*vide* fig. 258). The " carrying " leg is now in extension. Next the body is inclined forward and the Centre of Gravity is, thereby, brought over the bent leg. This leg now is gradually straightened, sustaining, the while, the whole weight of the body and the rear leg, by a movement combining oscillation and slight flexion, is brought to the upper step. Generally it does not remain here, but by an increased flexion it is taken on to the next step, the other member becoming in its turn the carrying leg.

If the horizontal distance between the steps is reduced, the oscillation is, likewise, diminished, but the period of "double support " is lengthened.

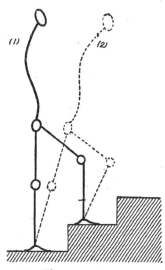

Fig. 258.
Mounting a staircase.

The work done is equal to the weight of the body multiplied by the height ascended. An examination of the curve of ascent will show that the vertical oscillation of the Centre of Gravity, which take place on the level, disappears in this case.

If h is the total height of the stair we have
$$T = P \times h.$$
If the man carries a load Q
$$T' = (P + Q)h.$$

In walking upstairs the lateral swayings of the body are exaggerated. In a rapid ascent there is certainly a slight vertical oscillation. This can be detected by watching the shadow of the climber on the wall of the staircase.

278. In walking up an inclined plane, the conditions are a combination of those found in ascending a stairway and in walking on the level. The front leg B (fig. 259) is necessarily

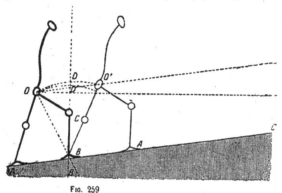

Fig. 259

Walking on an inclined plane.

bent, so that $OCB' = OB$, the body being bent forward to counteract the tangential component of the force of Gravity. As the rear leg becomes vertical it lifts the weight of the body through a distance DD' (*vide* fig. 260) This distance is equal to

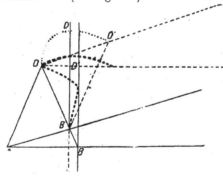

Fig. 260.

the oscillation of the body, plus the inclination corresponding to the step.

Thus walking up an inclined plane is equivalent to walking on a level and up a stair. The period of " double support " is prolonged, the quadriceps, and posterior muscles of the thigh are contracted in the case of the " carrying " leg, and the muscles of the calf cause displacement of the rear leg. But in ascending an inclined plane the inclination of the body calls for a greater *static* effort than would be needed in the ascent of a stair of a height equal to that of the inclined plane. It might therefore be expected that the expenditure of energy in mounting to a given height by an inclined plane would be greater than that required to traverse the corresponding horizontal distance, and then to reach the given height by means of a stair.

279. The Descending Walk.—In descending a stair slowly the body is held upright, the " carrying " leg is bent, while the other leg is moved, fully extended, to the lower step (*vide* fig. 261); the latter, then, in its turn, becomes the " carrying " leg. The legs always bend alternately, while the arms swing but slightly. The force of Gravity is counteracted, and the rate of descent maintained uniform by the action of the *triceps* and *solar* muscles.

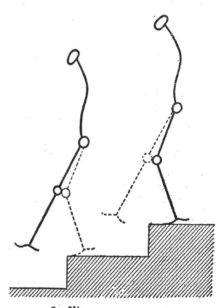

Fig. 261.

Descent of a staircase.

In a rapid descent of a stair the body bends so as to bring forward the centre of Gravity, the flexion of the " carrying " leg is reduced also the work done by it, the oscillation of the arms is almost nil. The carrying leg will, however, be somewhat bent when the lower step is reached so that the shock is reduced, while the tce of the foot alone touches the ground at the first contact, and is not, as in the case of a slow descent, placed flat on the ground. It will be seen that somewhat more work is done by the " carrying " leg. During the transition from one step to another on a stairway the body has to be balanced on one foot only. This explains the difficulty experienced by young children in going up and downstairs. A similar difficulty is experienced when carrying a heavy load. In both cases small steps are taken and large oscillations of the Centre of Gravity are avoided.

A stairway suitable for the use of persons carrying loads should have comparatively low steps. The height of the step should be from 7 to 10 cm. instead of the usual height of from 15 to 20 cm. Especially is this desirable if the persons carrying the loads are of small stature. If this is not done the excessive flexion of the knees induces rapid fatigue.

280. The descent of an inclined plane is not exactly analagous to the foregoing. The body must be inclined in order to maintain the same length of the pace AB' instead of AB" = AB (fig. 262).

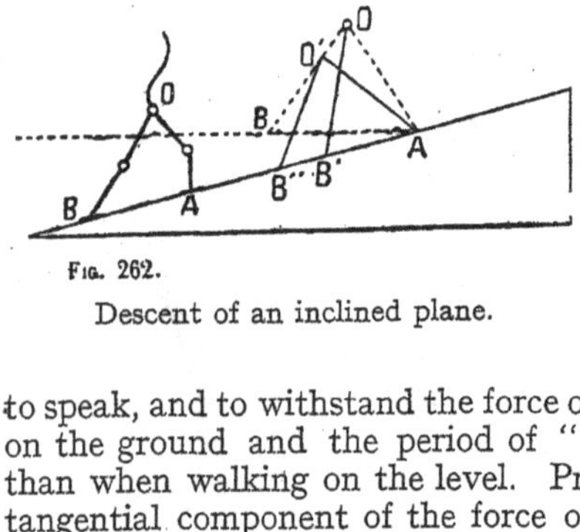

Fig. 262.

Descent of an inclined plane.

The leg OB is in extension, but the leg OA is in flexion and, the steeper the slope of the plane the more is it bent. It is thereby allowed to settle itself, so to speak, and to withstand the force of Gravity. The feet rest flat on the ground and the period of " double support " is longer than when walking on the level. Propulsion is assured by the tangential component of the force of Gravity which is proportional to the slope of the plane (§ 52).

The muscular work is practically the same as that involved in the descent of a stair of the same height as the plane, followed by progress on the level for the corresponding distance, but owing to the bending of the knees the oscillations of the Centre of Gravity appear to be considerably less than when walking on the level. It is also to be noted that this bending appears to increase as the slope is steeper.

This method of walking is very complex in spite of the fact that the muscular activity exerted is comparatively small. Most of the work is done by the *quadriceps* muscle, the important functions of which have been already referred to.

Reaumur and de Mairan have observed that the length of pace in ascent is greater than in descent. They explain this as follows : " In the first case the ' carrying ' leg remains extended, and is not subject to any great fatigue. In the second case it is subject to greater fatigue owing to being bent. The tendency is, therefore, to increase the rate of the change of the weight from one leg to the other. The steps, therefore, become less in length, but more in number, and the descent is carried out with more speed."[1]

281. Running.—The most salient characteristic of the movements of the act of running is not so much its speed, but the fact that the period of " double support " disappears. The legs are, indeed, alternately in single support, but during their alternation there is a moment when the body is completely off the ground, in *suspension*. All the phases of the act of walking are to be found in the act of running, except that the period of " double support " in the former is replaced by the above-mentioned period of "suspension." The lower members, however, remain bent, the degree of flexion depending on the speed of running.

Generally the leg which is on the ground rests on the entire sole of the foot. (In very fast running the toes alone may touch the ground.) Before it is developed by the full extension of the lower limb the flexor muscles — *gastrocnemius* and *soleus*—contract and thrust the limb from the ground sharply. The result is a succession of " bounds " from one leg to the other. As the speed increases the period of the suspension also increases, while the period of support grows less being sometimes no more than a mere touch of the foot on the ground. The resultant impact increases with the speed. Its vertical component V (*vide* fig. 263) is always positive. The tangential component H is first negative and then positive.

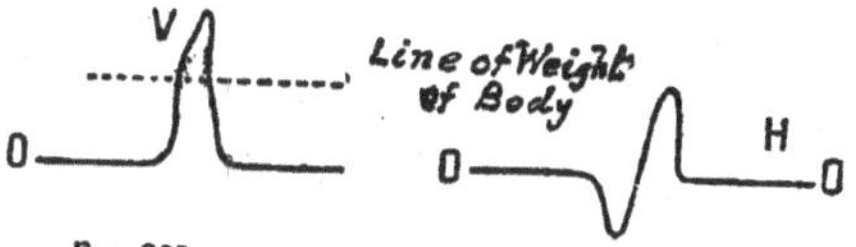

Fig. 263.
Pressures of the feet in running.

The greatest speed which is reached in racing is about 10 metres per second, *i e.*, three or four paces, varying from 2·5 m. to 3 m. in the second. The time of a pace varies from ·20 to ·35 seconds as the length varies from 1·5 m. to 3·4 m. The period of the suspension also increases with increased length of pace. The total period of suspension first for the single leg and then for both together aggregates approximately ·25 seconds, the latter, the " double " suspension lasting for 8 or 9 hundredths of a second (*vide* the curved line in fig. 264).

[1] *Histoire Acad. Roy. des Sciences*, 1721, p. 24.

Various oscillations occur in running. The head describes a curve, of which the lowest point synchronises with the moment when the foot touches the ground. Chrono-photographs prove that the vertical oscillation in running is less than in walking.

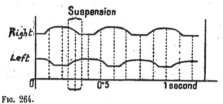

Fig. 264.

Phases of running (Du Bois-Reymond).

The trunk oscillates laterally, and is also subject to a slight torsion, which motions are the more evident if the walker has a broad *pelvis* (as in the case of the female figure) and short legs. As the rhythm and speed increase these various oscillations become less. In effect, the body remains in the " line of progression," which results in economy of movement. Finally, for reasons already stated, the arms oscillate in proportion to the speed.

It will be appreciated, from the above remarks, that in running the principal muscular work is effected by the flexions of the leg. There is also contraction of the muscles of the hip and thigh at the commencement of oscillation, and during the period of suspension. The contraction of other muscles is also requisite to maintain the equilibrium of the trunk. It is essential for quick running that the thorax should be upright so that the runner can inhale deeply. Experience also shows up that the best results are obtained in running long distances by keeping the knees well bent, as thereby the tiring oscillations of the body are reduced.

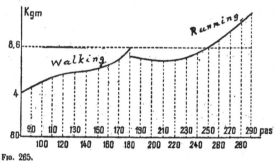

Fig. 265.

Curves connecting expenditure of energy with number of paces per min. (Marey).

282. Muscular Work in Running.—Attempts have been made, by Marey and Démeny, to calculate the muscular work in relation to the number of paces per minute. In fig. 265 are given curves

Fig. 266.

Different phases of a jump (from chronophotographs
by Richer and Londe).

showing the expenditure of energy in walking and running. An inspection of these curves will show that beyond 160 to 170 paces per minute it is more economical to run than to walk, and also that the maximum economy in running is attained at a speed of about 220 paces per minute.

The values shown in fig. 265 are only approximate, but they clearly exhibit the point at which running becomes preferable to walking. In the case of very rapid walking the enforced extension of the legs causes painful sensations. In running, on the other hand, the flexion of the legs renders great speed possible without any such painful sensations.

283. Jumping.—The jump [1] is a muscular movement by which the body is projected upwards and caused to traverse a certain space in the air at a considerable speed.

In jumping, the body follows the same laws as those which govern the movements of projectiles (§ 263). The various phases of the action are as follows :—

There is a first "preparatory" stage in which the trunk is bent forward, the knees are flexed, and the arms are drawn back. Next there is the phase of "impulsion," which is effected by the sharp contraction of the muscles of the calf (triceps), and of the thigh (quadriceps) ; the arms are raised and the body develops a momentum whose amount is MV (§ 27). Next comes the period of "suspension" during which the body is in the air, followed by the "fall." The various phases in the action of jumping are depicted in fig. 266, which is a reproduction of chronophotographs by Richer and Londe. It will be seen that in the act of falling the positions of the muscles are such as to "cushion" the shock of contact with the ground. Were this not done the shock of impact would probably have an injurious effect on the brain.

It will be observed from fig. 267 that the pressure of the feet is much less in the former than in the latter case. The unilateral jump (with one leg) is more advantageous than the bilateral jump, because it

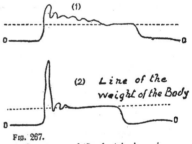

Fig. 267.
Pressures of the feet in jumping
(1) cushioned fall ; (2) uncushioned fall.

[1] Marey (*Comptes Rendus Sciences*, vol. ciii., 1888) ; du Bois-Reymond, *Zur Physiologie des Springens* (*Arch. f. Anat. u. Physiol. Abt.* Suppl., 1905. p. 329).

diminishes the effects of the traction towards the base at the moment of the impulsion and the horizontal speed of the body at that instant, diminishes also, because it gives rise to a vertical speed resulting from that impulsion.

In jumping, the greater part of the work is done by the muscles of the legs and shoulders. We therefore find that these muscles are highly developed in athletes, who devote their attention to jumping. The mass of the body is also an important factor, since the height of the jump must necessarily be inversely proportional to that mass. Also those with long legs can jump higher than those with short ones.

Calculations of the work done in jumping lead to very variable results.

The man is flung like a projectile with an initial speed v; whence the work done :

$$T_1 = \tfrac{1}{2} mv^2 ;$$

then gravity performs work which the muscles can in no way modify, except that they arrange the body so as to deaden the shock. As a whole, the muscular work is difficult to estimate. One can only get an approximate idea of it. For example, a man weighing 65 kilogrammes leaves the ground at a speed of 8 metres per second, whence :—

$$T_1 = \tfrac{1}{2} \times \frac{65}{9\cdot81} \times 8 \times 8 = 212 \text{ kilogrammetres.}$$

We must add to the above amount the work done in the preparatory run necessary to give sufficient speed for the spring. With this addition the total will be some 300 kilogrammetres.

If the angle of the spring is 45° the space covered, at the above speed, will be 6·52 metres (§ 24). We have therefore to compare $6\cdot52 \times 65 = 424$ metre-kilogrammes and 300 kilogrammetres, which gives about ·77 kgm. per metre-kilogram.

284. Climbing.—In this method of progression the body is pulled upwards by the arms, the elbows are more or less bent, but most of the work is done by the powerful muscles of shoulders and the back, and also by the larger *pectoral* muscles. Man is far less favourably adapted for climbing than the *anthropoids*, especially the apes. The big toe is used to prevent the body slipping back, as is particularly noticeable in the case of savage races.

Since the muscles of the arms are less powerful than those of the legs climbing is a most fatiguing operation, and is indeed a form of movement at variance with the anatomical and physiological principles of the human body.

285. Crawling.—This method of locomotion is a progression on hands and knees. Owing to the fact that the inflexions of the vertebral column ([1]) are numerous certain therapeutic applications have been made of it. Crawling is very troublesome, and is not to be recommended either in games or in military exercises, unless absolutely necessary. It gives rise to callous formations on those parts which constantly rub on the ground.

286. Swimming.([2])—As swimming is a mode of progression used principally in sport and recreation, and not in industry, it will not be examined in any detail here. The effect of environment is of the first importance. This environment, the water in which the swimmer is immersed, is of approximately the same specific gravity as the human body. The swimmer floats on his back because the Centre of Gravity of his body is nearer to his back than his front. He maintains his position by movements of the arms from below upwards, as also by inflation of his lungs (§ 178). If he lifts his head entirely out of the water he sinks. His feet touch the bottom and the body remains in an inclined position.

In swimming the legs are alternately bent and straightened, the soles of the feet exerting a thrust against the water. The arms describe lateral circles, the hands acting like paddles.

The muscular energy exerted in swimming is considerable, the more so if there is any current of the water opposing the swimmer's progress (§ 178). The temperature of the water also may cause considerable loss of heat energy and, altogether, the expenditure of energy in swimming is very high.

The famous swimmer, Burgess, crossing the Channel between Cape Gris-Nez and Dover, took 23 hours 40 minutes to cover about 36·200 km., or 1·53 km. an hour. Though, owing to deviations from the straight course, he claims to have attained a speed of 2·800 km. an hour ([3]) and it may be remembered that at Joinville-le-Pont five years before, he covered 44 kilometres in 24 hours, or 1·860 km. an hour.

At an average speed of 1·800 km. and against a current of 2 metres, the work done per hour rises to:

$$73 \times 0.035 \times \overline{2.50}^2 \times 1,800 = 28,734 \text{ kilogrammetres.}$$

a power of about 8 kilogrammetres per second.

([1]) Klapp (*Münsch. Med. Wochensch.*, vol. lii., No. 48, p. 2311, 1905).
([2]) R. Thomas, *Swimming*, London, 1904.
([3]) *Le Matin* of 7th September, 1911, completed by *Le Temps* of the same day. (Burgess consumed on the journey chocolate and soup, but no alcohol).

·287. Expenditure of Energy in Locomotion-Walking.—The expenditure of energy in walking is measured by the consumption of oxygen in calories. The *dynamic* expenditure is the excess of that consumption over that of the subject when at rest.

This study commenced with the striking investigations of Zuntz, whose book ([1]) received the highest approbation from German military authorities.

His experiments were carried out on five subjects of from 1·70 m. to 1·81 m. in height, and weighing from 65 to 80 kilogrammes. As an example one will be chosen from them weighing 65 kilogrammes (the average weight of an adult), his height being 1·69 m., and the length of the lower limb equal to 0·86 m.

When walking at a speed of 4,588 metres per hour, the dynamic expenditure of this subject was ·574 small calories for each kilogramme of his weight per metre covered. We have called this the *metre-kilogramme*, which, in this case, is equivalent to slightly more than half a small calorie.

From the whole of his experiments Zuntz found an average of ·518 small calories per metre-kilogramme. The writer ([2]) obtained, under similar conditions an average of ·506 small calories, which result is confirmed by other investigators. ([3])

The speed profoundly modifies the expenditure of energy, as will be seen from fig. 268. Between 2·9 km. and 8·9 km. per hour, it

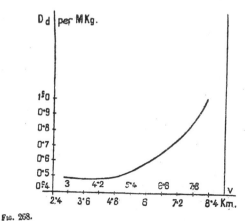

Fig. 268.

Dynamic expenditure per metre-kilogramme
at different speeds.

([1]) Zuntz and Schumburg, *Studien zu einer Physiologie des Marsches*, Berlin, 1901 (361, pp. 8vo).
([2]) Jules Amar (*Journ. de Physiol.*, March 1911, p. 212).
([3]) Leo Zuntz, A. and I. Loewy (*Pflüger's Arch.*, vol. lxvi., p. 477); W. Kolmer and E. Brezina (*Biochemische Zeitsch.*, vol. xxxviii., p. 129, 6th Jan., 1912).

varies from ·4 to ·9 small calories approximately. It will be seen from the curve in fig. 268 that the minimum expenditure is at a speed of 4·5 km. per hour which is therefore the most economical speed of walking.

To take a concrete case. If a man, weighing 65 kg., walks at 5·4 km. per hour, the expenditure per metre-kilogramme is ·56 small calories per kg. of the body's weight.

The expenditure, for a single pace of ·78 metres in length, is therefore

$$·56 \times 65 \times ·78 = 28·392 \text{ small calories.}$$

We have seen (vide § 272) that, in the case of the experiments of Braune and Fischer under similar conditions, the muscular work was found to be 6 kilogramme-metres. If, therefore, we convert the above expenditure of 28·392 small calories into kilogramme-metres we find that the apparent nett efficiency is :

$$\frac{6}{28·392 \times ·425} = 49\% \text{ approximately.}$$

This efficiency is obviously too high. We cannot therefore have much confidence in the accuracy of values obtained by the above method. Reliable results are only to be obtained by measurements of the consumption of oxygen. On this basis we shall find that, for ordinary speeds of walking (without a load) from 4 km. to 6 km. per hour, the consumption is equivalent to from ·5 to ·6 small calories per metre-kilogramme. We shall also see that the most economical speed is 4·5 km. per hour.

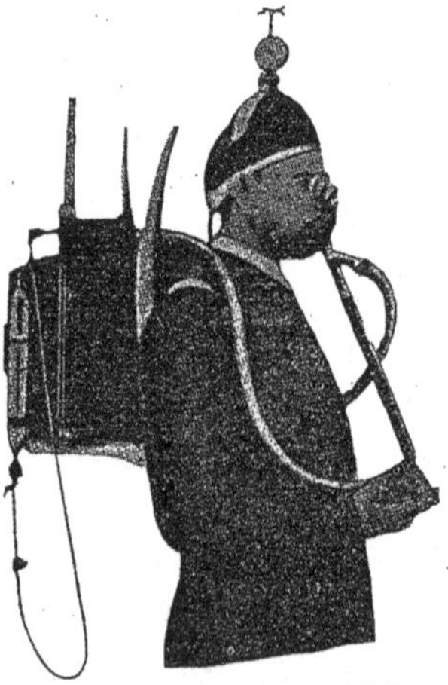

288. The preceding experiments are fairly consistent and reliable. The probable error is not more than 2% plus or minus. Zuntz's experiments were carried out with a portable apparatus for the measurement of the gases mounted on the shoulders of his subject (vide fig. 269). The speed was measured by a tachometer fixed to the head. He caused his subjects to traverse various distances for at least 8 or 10 minutes.

Fig. 269. Zuntz's portable respiratory apparatus.

Fig. 270. Arrangement of apparatus for measuring the consumption of oxygen in walking (Jules Amar).

The writer places his apparatus in a knapsack when the experiment involves a walk of any length. Generally, however, he avoids the necessity of carrying the measuring apparatus by confining the walk to a distance of eleven metres only, which is traversed a sufficient number of times to occupy three minutes.

The general arrangement of the apparatus is shown in fig. 270. On the table is placed the gas meter, together with an apparatus with a two way connection, by means of which alternate samples of the gases evolved, when the subject is at rest or in motion, can be readily obtained (see also fig. 224).

Kolmer and Brezina employed the Zuntz apparatus (fig. 269) with a length of track of about 155 metres.

289. Walking with a Load.—The expenditure of energy naturally increases when the subject carries a load. At a speed of 4·5 km. per hour and with such a comparatively small load as 7·3 kg. the writer found that the total increase was as much as 20%. Expressed in metre-kilogrammes it varies with the magnitude of the load and the speed of walking.

The following table (from the results obtained by Kolmer and Brezina) gives the expenditure of energy per metre-kilogramme for loads from 11 to 53 kilogrammes and speeds from 3 to 6·6 kilometres per hour.

SPEED.	WEIGHT OF SUBJECT + LOAD.					
(METRES per hour).	70 KGM. (unloaded)	70+11	70+21	70+33	70+43	70+53
m.	c.	c.	c.	c.	c.	c.
3,000	0·486	0·463	0·490	0·485	0·542	0·547
3,600	0·508	0·466	0·497	0·484	0·545	,,
4,200	*0·508*	*0·464*	*0·454*	0·506	0·575	0·673
4,800	0·517	0·474	0·498	*0·523*	*0·600*	,,
5,400	0·537	0·531	0·534	0·575	0·690	0·695
6,000	0·566	0·602	0·605	0·651	0·842	,,
6,600	0·653	0·688	0·724	0·773	,,	,,

The Expenditure per metre-kilogramme.

The figures in italics show which are the most economical speeds for the various loads. It will also be seen that the most economical combination of speed and load is 21 kg. and 4·2 km. per hour, for which combination a consumption of ·454 small calories is obtained which is the lowest figure in the above table.

But the industrial problem is to find the maximum production of *daily labour*. In other words, to discover the conditions as to speed and load, by which, in any given time, the maximum output of work can be obtained with a steady minimum of fatigue, which latter is a measure of the energy expended.

The financial aspect must not be overlooked, both because a journey, under load, is generally followed by a return journey unloaded, which unprofitable journeys should be reduced as far as possible, and also because the worker has often no power to modify his speed to suit his load.

The following table exhibits the relations between metre-kilogrammes per minute, for values from 4,000 to 12,000 and different loads, and will be found to lead to some interesting results.

Number of Meter-Kilogrammes per minute.	WEIGHT OF SUBJECT + LOAD					
	70 KGM. (unloaded)	70+11	70+21	70+33	70+43	70+53
m.	c.	c.	c.	c.	c.	
4,000	0·4999	0·4630	0·4332	0·4690	0·4957	,,
5,000	0·4978	0·4323	0·5106	0·5332	0·5331	,,
6,000	0·5093	0·4469	0·4618	0·4440	0·5560	0·5340
7,000	0·5640	0·4990	0·4757	0·4920	0·5465	,,
8,000	0·6901	0·5913	0·5436	0·5485	0·5825	,,
9,000	0·7867	0·6814	0·5576	0·4981	0·5526	0·5665
10,000	0·8652	0·8804	0·7252	0·6060	0·6959	,,
11,000	,,	0·9185	0·8717	0·7012	0·7995	0·6907
12,000	,,	,,	,,	0·8181	,,	0·7105

The Expenditure per metre-kilogramme.

Let us take, as an example of the application of the above table, the transportation of a load of 43 kg.

The maximum economy will be attained with a rate of production equal to 4,000 metre-kilogrammes per minute. The corresponding speed is quite slow, namely :—

$$\frac{4000}{70 + 43} \times 60 = 2\cdot124 \text{ kilometres per hour.}$$

To obtain the maximum power, at a rate of production equal to 10,000 metre-kilogrammes per minute, a load of 33 kg. will be chosen and the speed will be :

$$\frac{10,000}{70 + 33} \times 60 = 5\cdot825 \text{ kilometres per hour.}$$

With a rate of production of 11,000 metre-kilogrammes per minute the heavy load of 53 kg. will be chosen, and the speed will be :—

$$\frac{11,000}{70 + 53} \times 60 = 5\cdot366 \text{ kilometres per hour.}$$

We see, from the above figures, that the development of great power is attained by walking heavily loaded (with a load of 53 kg. at 5·4 kilometres per hour approximately). We also see that a reduction of the load to 33 kg. is compensated for by an increase of speed to 5·8 kilometres per hour. We have, however, to consider the nature of the workman and the difficulty which will be experienced in carrying the heavier load, even with frequent intervals of rest.

290. The above experimental results have one defect, namely, that the expenditure of energy was measured for a very short time only, generally from two to three minutes. They will therefore be supplemented by the data given in the following table. The subjects of the experiments were men of good physique. They walked many kilometres during a working day of from seven to eight hours. No unloaded return journeys were made, but, after each kilometre, there was a period of rest for from two to five minutes, as also a rest of one or two minutes every 600 metres. (The table is taken from the writer's work, *Le Rendement de la Machine Humaine*, p. 72).

Weight of Man and Load.	Speed per hour.	Total journey.	Expenditure per metre-kilogramme.	Dates of observations.
kg.	m.	m.	c.	
67 + 45	4,320	24,300	0·301	August, 1908
67 + 45	4,824	13,568	0·402	August, 1908.
66·2 + 45	4,320	21,430	0·305	December, 1908.
64·7 + 45	4,320	17,850	0·297	January, 1909
69·4 + 45	4,824	18,380	0·329	——
69·0 + 45	5,400	25,930	0·309	September, 1908
71 + 45	4,824	12,060	0·257	May, 1908
71·4 + 45	4,824	29,980	0·289	December, 1908 (excellent walker)
71 + 45	4,824	25,930	0·345	September, 1908
71·5 + 45	4,320	22,311	0·277	——
78 + 45	5,400	21,450	0·302	January, 1909
59 + 45	4,824	18,900	0·285	May, 1908
72·6 + 60	4,824	21,146	0·324	November, 1908
74·5 + 60	4,320	19,055	0·335	August, 1908
75·1 + 60	4,320	16,540	0·310	September, 1908

The average expenditure per metre-kilogramme at speeds between 4 and 5 km. per hour is ·311 small calories for continuous work under the above-mentioned conditions. The subjects of the experiments were shepherds and agriculturalists of Northern Africa. It is interesting to note that these men, who are used to carrying heavy burdens, adopt the walk with bent knees previously referred to.

With the same type of subjects, tested on his experimental bicycle (§ 221) the writer obtained a nett efficiency of $32\frac{1}{2}\%$. The work corresponding to one pace can be calculated from the above figures ·311 small calories. An adult weighing 65 kg. expends $65 \times ·311$ small calories in traversing one metre. The expenditure for a pace of ·78 m. is therefore :

$$65 \times ·311 \times ·78.$$

and the work done is :

$$\mathbf{T} = 65 \times ·311 \times ·78 \times ·325 \times ·425 = 2·18 \text{ kgm.}$$

The speed of walking should not, under any circumstances, exceed 5 km. per hour when carrying heavy loads. As the writer remarks on p. 73 of his above-quoted work : "A man weighing 71 kg. carries a sack on his shoulders weighing 60 kg. and walks a total daily distance of 22·311 km. at a speed of 4·82 kilometres per hour. If he increases the speed of walking to 5·4 km. per hour he will not be able to traverse more than 12·14 km. per day, which is little more than half of the former figure. The maximum result was obtained when the load was 45 kg. and the speed of walking 4·8 kilometres per hour. The experiments were carried out for a period of from eight to ten days with each subject, without fatigue, or any serious complaints.

The maximum of daily activity is represented by

$$(71 + 45)\ 25930 = 3,007,880 \text{ metre-kilogrammes.}$$

This is undoubtedly the maximum result which can be obtained.

291. Coulomb's Observations and Methods.—Coulomb ([1]) was the first to investigate the maximum work done in carrying loads. He noted that, if the normal speed of walking was maintained an increase of load caused a reduction in work, and in the daily output. He took a subject weighing 70 kg. who carried a load of 62·3 kg. for a total distance of 17·32 kilometres and obtained, as a result :

$$17320\ (70 + 62·3) = 2,291,436 \text{ metre-kilogrammes.}$$

It is hardly necessary to point out that the illustrious physicist was in error in this calculation. It is by physiological considerations alone that we can decide with certainty as to the load which causes excessive muscular fatigue. Furthermore, the principles of the science of energy were then unknown, nor had any consideration been given to the waste of energy caused by " static " efforts, or useless movements. Nor was it until M. Chauveau and others of his school, carried out their investigations, that the relations, between speed and load, conducive to the best results were understood.

It was by these principles that the able American engineer, Frederick Taylor, was guided in his experiments as described in the following paragraph.

292. Handling of Pig Iron.—In this elementary form of labour the labourer had to stoop to pick up from the ground a billet of iron weighing 42 kilogrammes, to carry it a few steps, and then to put it down. 80,000 tons of pig iron were piled alongside a railway siding. The labourers took the pigs, one by one from the pile, walked up inclined gangways, and placed them in the railway trucks.

([1]) Coulomb, *loc. cit.* (*vide* § 122).

At the Bethlehem Steel Works, before Mr. Taylor's advent, the output was 12½ tons per man per diem. Taylor increased this to 47 tons per man per day. Since 1881, while works manager of the Midvale Steel Co., he had made an exhaustive study of the relations between speed and time in human labour.[1] His experiments were conducted thus : He selected two of his best labourers, strong, reliable, and intelligent men. He gave them double pay during the period of the experiments, on the condition that they would, throughout, work their hardest. He also warned them that their output would be tested from time to time, and that any deliberate " slacking " would entail dismissal. As a matter of fact, the men did their best throughout the experiments. In fact, Mr. Taylor adopted Coulomb's method as developed by Chauveau.

Under the above conditions the selected labourers carried out various tasks. The time taken in each movement was registered by a stop-watch, and other elements of labour were carefully noted and recorded.

It was found that the men could develop from ⅛ to ½ of a horse-power according to the nature of the task on which they were engaged, i.e., from 34,000 to 140,000 kilogrammetres per diem. There did not appear to be any strict relation between work and fatigue (see above, § 125 and 130).

At a later date M. Barth, a mathematician, took up the same study. As the result of numerous observations he formulated his " law connecting work and fatigue."

It was found that the actual period during which the labourer was sustaining a load should be approximately 43% of the working day and that for the remaining 57% he should have no load. If " half pigs," weighing 22 kg., were carried, the loaded period might be increased to 58%. It was also found that there is a limit to the load which can be carried continuously throughout the day without fatigue.

Chauveau and his pupils, by their experiments on the expenditure of energy, had already arrived at similar conclusions to those of Barth and Taylor. It is clear, however, that Taylor was chiefly influenced by Coulomb. He observed, indeed, that " static effort " caused muscular fatigue and necessitated intervals of rest. He did not, however, frame any general formula for these effects, as Chauveau did at a later date (vide § 113).

---

[1] See Taylor's papers before the American Society of Mechanical Engineers : A piece-rate System and Shop Management, and Scientific Organisation of Workshops (loc. cit.).

By careful observation, and by the elimination of unnecessary motions Taylor obtained important practical results, inasmuch as he increased the daily output per man from $12\frac{1}{2}$ tons to 47 tons.

The work done represented the carrying of 1,156 pigs of 41·4 kg. weight each. The total time under load being 252 minutes out of the working day of 10 hours (600 minutes). The " loaded " time per pig was 13·2 seconds. The labourer walked on the level at ·83 metres per second (3 km. per hour). He covered 11 metres per trip, i.e., 26 kilometres per day.

This result agrees with the author's observations (§ 290) on the carrying of loads of from 45 to 50 kg., by which it was found that willing subjects could cover as much as 30 kilometres at a speed of 1·34 metres.

The short distance of the trip (11 metres) in Taylor's experiments necessarily reduced the speed of walking, although some of the men exceeded the above speed of ·83 metres per second and carried as much as 58 tons per diem.

The maximum number of metre-kilogrammes a day, with workmen of 75 kilogrammes, was therefore:

$(75 + 41·4)\ 13,000 = 1,513,200$ metres-kilogr. in going.

$75 \times \quad 13,000 = \quad\ \ 975,000$ metres kilogr. in returning.

Total, $\quad$ 2,488,200 metre-kilogrammes.

This result has a two-fold interest   On the one hand, it shows that, under certain conditions, a man can increase his output by due regulation of speed and effort, and by taking definite periods of rest. On the other hand, it reveals the inadequacy of empirical methods based, as in the present case, on what might be described as a " standard labourer."

Taylor should have increased the speed of his men to about $4\frac{1}{2}$ km. per hour and also increased the number of periods of rest. It should also be noted that, before the pigs were carried, they had to be lifted to the height of the waist, and that they were loaded into a truck reached by a small inclined plane. Also the unloaded return journeys were numerous. Altogether, the conditions were different from those of simple transportation, broken only by periods of rest, sufficient to restore the vital forces. Also Taylor's method, based on the timing of movements, is open to physiological objections, it is useful, but incomplete (see below).

293. Various Observations.—Amontons ([1]) quotes the case of those who carry baskets (*hottes*). The basket weighed 14·7 kg.,

---

([1]) Amontons (*Hist. Acad. Roy. Sciences*, 1703, p. 104).

the distance covered was 721 metres, and 22 trips were done per diem, which was certainly the most that could be done.

The distance covered under load was therefore :

$$721 \times 22 = 15,862 \text{ metres.}$$

And the same distance unloaded. Hence we get :

$15862 (70 + 14·70) + 15862 \times 70 = 2,453,851$ metre kilogrammes. which is very nearly the same as the result obtained by Taylor, but here also the speed and load are insufficient and badly combined.

Various other observations have given 2,430,000, 2,257,200, and 2,280,000 metre kilogrammes, with loads of 85, 50 and 44 kilogrammes.

Fig. 271.—Marking time (with the body motionless).

Some examples taken from infantry prove that the French soldier can do, normally, 30 kilometres with an average load of 30 kilogrammes, that is :

(70 + 30) 30,000 = 3,000,000 metre kilogrammes.

In certain special cases this result is exceeded. The speed is usually about 5,500 metres. According to the military writer, Végèce, the Roman soldier could cover 36 kilometres with a load of 29 kilogrammes.

294. Marking Time.[1]—In infantry drill "marking time" appears to be often considered as if it was almost equivalent to resting, whereas, in actual fact, it is only the motion of progression that is suspended, the muscular oscillations of the body having practically the same value as in marching.

In the following evaluation of the consumption of energy in "marking time," it is assumed that the lateral oscillations of the body are nil and that the legs alone move.

Let n be the cadence of the motion, the number of flexions and extensions per minute. In the following experiments (*vide* fig. 271) the "respiratory valve" is carried on a fixed support, the subject stands on a thick plank, to which his heels are attached by two straps which limit the lift of the feet to a definite amount. The following table gives the result of one experiment, among many, the subject being an adult weighing 65 kg.

The consumptions of oxygen in cubic centimetres per step for various cadences were as follows :—

Consumption	...	2·25	2·521	2·708	2·911	3·115
Cadence	... ...	76	85	94	103	113

The expenditure is: $d = an + b$

a and b being constants having the following values :—$a = \cdot02$ cubic centimetres and $b = \cdot83$ cubic centimetres.

The equivalent calorific expenditure, for the above cadences can be calculated, and is ·16, ·178, ·191, ·206, ·220 small calories respectively, per step, per kilogramme.

Thus "marking time" consumes about half the energy of ordinary walking, and increases with the speed and the height to which the legs are lifted. In the above experiment this height was ·13 metres.

---

[1] Jules Amar (*Journal de Physiol.* 1911, p. 314).

295. Walking on the Level Summary.—Taylor's results, for the carrying of loads, represent the maximum results obtainable with the average workman—namely, a total distance traversed per working day of 26 km. (13 under load and 13 empty handed) a load of about 42 kg. and an average speed of walking of 3 km. per hour, resulting in an average expenditure of $2\frac{1}{4}$ million metre-kilogrammes per diem equivalent (*vide* the table in para. 289) to a total dynamic expenditure of 1348 great calories. Hence the expenditure per kilogramme of body weight per hour is approximately :

$$\frac{1348}{75 \times 24} = \cdot 75 \text{ great calories.}$$

This figure represents practically the highest co-efficient of utilization of muscular energy.[1] It is important to note that such a muscular output has no injurious effects on the physiological condition of the subjects. Certainly the rate of the pulse increased from 30% to 50% above its normal value, but this is not followed by any abnormal effects unless the subject is predisposed to any functional weakness of the heart. The duration of the *systole* increases by 20% or 25%, while the *diastole* diminishes in duration by one-third or even a half. The ratio between them $\dfrac{D}{S}$ may reach 1·5 (*vide* § 143). The respirations also increase, from the normal rate of 16 per minute in repose to as much as 25 per minute. The " vital capacity " decreases with increase of load, though not in any regular proportion. The temperature of the body also varies slightly by a quarter or half of a degree centigrade. Lastly, as we have previously seen (§ 144), and, as Zuntz has observed, walking exercise strengthens the muscles of the arms, as has been observed by Mosso's *ergograph*, also the " personal equation " is slightly reduced, *i.e.*, the subject responds more quickly to stimuli.

The conditions of normal industrial work are only adequately to be met by increasing the speed of walking, by restricting the load to a maximum of 45 kilogrammes and by providing numerous, though short, intervals of rest. Taylor's selected workmen were able to carry 58 tons per diem with a speed of walking which was probably about 5 kilometres per hour, the total work done being approximately 3 million metre-kilogrammes.[2]

296. The Ascending Walk.—In ascending a stair the work done by the muscles is the product of the weight and the height, and we can, for an approximate result, neglect the horizontal component of the motion.

---

[1] Since the expenditure of energy at rest is $1\frac{1}{2}$ great calories, the total expenditure is $1\cdot5 + \cdot 75 = 2\cdot25$ great calories.
[2] Publication of the *Revue de Métallurgie*, p. 330, 1907.

Katzenstein,[1] who was the first to make any reliable measurements of the expenditure of energy, obtained a result of 8 small calories per kilogrammetre. Chauveau [2] showed that the ascent under load increased the expenditure of energy, while an increased speed of walking decreased the expenditure (§ 115), and that it generally varied between 9 and 12 calories. It is, however, to be observed that Chauveau's experiments were not sufficiently prolonged.

Zuntz and Schumburg [3] obtained, as an average result, 7½ small calories. Frentzel and Reach [4] obtained a similar result. Laulanié, by measuring the expenditure of energy during a period of 75 seconds, obtained results varying from 9·6 to 15 small calories according to the load.[5]

The experiments of the above-quoted authorities were confined to loads of from 10 to 30 kilogrammes and speeds of from ·04 to ·07 metres per second. Also the duration of each trial did not exceed two or three minutes, or less in the experiments of Chauveau and Laulanié.

The writer's investigations have, however, been directed to establishing the conditions for *continuous work*. He took the case of men ascending and descending a stairway of which the steps were a little more than ·16 m. high, while the inclination of the stairway was steep. The loads varied from 40 to 60 kilogrammes, and consisted of sacks of beans, which the bearers carried on their shoulders or necks. The speed was left to the discretion of the bearers, but, when adopted, was kept constant to the end of the trial. The rests were of two or three minutes. The subjects of the experiments were strong and healthy labourers, of ages varying from 20 to 40 years, and they did their best. The average speed varied from ·07 to ·1 metres per second.[6]

A descent followed each ascent. In this case the expenditure of energy is 1·52 times that of a simple ascent (§ 140), hence the expenditure of energy in the ascent alone is $\dfrac{1}{1\cdot52}$ of that of the complete trip, up and down. The following table gives a summary of the writer's observations:

[1] Katzenstein (*Pflüger's Arch.*, vol. xlix., p. 330, 1891).
[2] Chauveau (*Comptes Rendus Sciences*, vol. cxxxii., p. 194, 1901).
[3] Zuntz and Schumburg, *Physiol. des Marsches*, p. 277, 1901.
[4] Frentzel and Reach (*Pflüger's Arch.*, vol. lxxxiii., p. 441, 1901).
[5] Laulanié, *Traité de Physiol.*, p. 792, 1905.
[6] Jules Amar, *Le Rendement*, pp. 68-71.

WEIGHT MAN + LOAD	HEIGHT ASCENDED	TOTAL JOURNEYS	TIME TAKEN		EXPENDITURE PER KGM.
kg.	m.		h.	m.	c.
80·2 + 45	4·25	128	4	00	5·00
74·5 + 45	4·25	131	4	30	5·20
74·5 + 40	4·80	46	1	00	5·70
71·3 + 45	4·25	141	5	00	6·10
56·6 + 40	4·80	45	1	00	6·60
67·7 + 50	3·78	158	4	00	8·30
70·5 + 50	3·78	124	4	30	8·40
61·3 + 40	3·78	52	1	25	9·50
60·4 + 50	4·80	112	4	00	9·50
69·2 + 50	3·78	50	1	30	9·60
68·0 + 50	4·80	100	3	00	10·20
62·7 + 50	3·78	105	3	30	10·30
62·3 + 50	3·78	120	4	00	10·30
Average expenditure per kilogrammetre :					8·05

We see from these experiments that the expenditure of energy per kilogrammetre varies by 100%, averaging about 8 small calories. To account for these variations we must compute the total work done by each subject (the *resistant* work being 52% of the *motive* work) and the speed per second, and relate these to the expenditure of energy. The curves in fig. 272 show that, with very few exceptions, the output per kilogrammetre decreases with increase in the work done and the speed, increase of load having an adverse effect on economy, as is shown in the above table. Lastly, it will be seen that in the cases where the subjects chose their own speeds, the differences observed show the effects of personality in lifting or balancing the loads or in adjusting them from time to time to suit their convenience.

It is to be noted that the best result was 31716 kilogrammetres per hour with a subject weighing 57 kg. and a load of 40 kg., the speed being ·12 metres per second. Hence the maximum output of work per day of eight hours was :

$$31716 \times 8 = 253728 \text{ kilogrammetres.}$$

Hence, under the most favourable conditions, a daily output of about 250,000 kilogrammetres can be attained, which gives a dynamic expenditure of :

$$250,000 \times \cdot008 = 2000 \text{ great calories.}$$

The experiment shows that, with heavy loads, of 50 or 60 kg., a total daily output of 200,000 kilogrammetres cannot conveniently be exceeded.

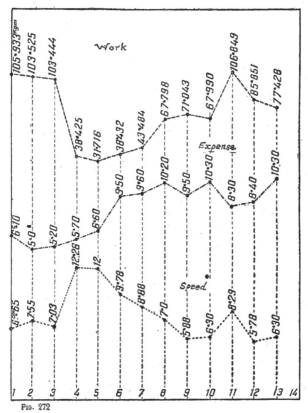

Fig. 272

Relations between output per kilogrammetre, speed,
and amount of work done.

297. Early Observations.—The observations of Borda (at
Teneriffe) of Coulomb, Hachette and Navier have only a historic
interest. Coignet's ([1]) observations, however, merit some attention. When supervising the construction of field works at Vin-
cennes, that officer introduced an arrangement by which the
labourers mounted the banks by ladders, but descended by means
of counterbalanced platforms so that the men's weight in descending drew up loaded barrows. He observed that 310 ascents
were made per diem, the height being 13 metres and the speed
·18 metres. He estimated the maximum daily work done by a
labourer weighing 70 kg., as :

$$70 \times 310 \times 13 = 282,100 \text{ kilogrammetres.}$$

([1]) Coignet (*Memorial de l'Officier de Genie*, No. 12, p. 285, 1835.

By the above system he removed 55,000 cubic metres of earth with an economy of 75%:

The following observations, hitherto unpublished, were made by the writer in the years 1910 and 1911.

1. A labourer weighing 85 kg., 45 years of age, carried 7 bundles of wood, each weighing 50 kg., to a height of 12·71 metres. His speed was ·17 metres, and he made 12 such trips per diem, hence :

$$T := \begin{cases} (50 + 85)\ 12 \cdot 71 \times 12 \times\ 7 = 144{,}131 \text{ kgm. (ascending).} \\ 85 \times 12 \cdot 71 \times 7 \times 12 \times \dfrac{52}{100} =\ 47{,}189 \text{ kgm. (descending).} \end{cases}$$

Total   191,320 kgm.

2. In a single afternoon another labourer carried to the seventh floor of a building, a height of 22 metres, 36 sacks weighing 50 kg., each at a speed of ·12 metres. Here :

$$T = (70 + 50) \times 22 \times 36 \times \frac{152}{100} = 144{,}461 \text{ kgm.}$$

Adding to the above figure three such deliveries, made during the same morning, equivalent to 42,126 kgm. and a walk of about 1½ kilometres, the total reached 200,000 kilogrammetres.

298. The Inclined Plane.—Little attention has been devoted to this subject, although the various relations between height, load, speed and inclination are of interest and importance in our present investigation.

Zuntz and Schumburg [1] confined their investigations to inclinations varying from 0°-6′-30″ to 3°-44′-15″, but their results are vitiated by the fact that they consider walking up an inclined plane as, in all respects, equivalent to walking the equivalent horizontal distance, and then ascending to the height of the plane. This, though true from the point of view of mechanics, is wrong physiologically. Nor did they make any measurements of the expenditure of energy in descending the planes.

Such experiments are not easy satisfactorily to carry out. Special apparatus is necessary for accurate results such as a gangway of considerable length, about 200 metres, of which the slope can be adjusted.

The writer constructed [2] a plane 12 metres long, of which the slope could be varied from 8 to 13 centimetres per metre. He used this apparatus to investigate the effect of steep gradients. The subject walked at a steady pace from the ground on to the plane. The consumption of oxygen was measured in ascent and in descent.

---

[1] Zuntz and Schumburg, *Physiol. des Marsches*, pp. 238, *sqq.*, 1901.
[2] Jules Amar (*Comptes Rendus Acad. Sc.*, 25 May, 1911, p. 1327).

The speed of walking was 3·7 kilometres per hour and 100 paces per minute. The subject weighed 66 kilogrammes. The weight was only 7·3 kilogrammes. The results obtained are given in the following table, and the general arrangement of the apparatus is shown in fig. 273.

SLOPE OF THE PLANE	MAN + LOAD	EXPENDITURE PER METRE-KILOGRAMME		
		ASCENT	DESCENT.	LEVEL
m.	kg.	c.	c.	c.
0·08	66	1·00	0·85	0·41
	66+7·3	1·50	1·13	0·49
0·13	66	1·80	1·00	,,
	66+7·3	2·20	0·84	,,

Fig. 273. Walking on an inclined plane (J. Amar).

We see that, in ascending, the expenditure of energy increases in proportion to the slope of the plane. If we deduct from the total expenditure in the two ascents the ascertained value of the expenditure on the level, we have respectively :

$$1·0 — ·41 = ·59c \text{ and } 1·8 — ·41 = 1·39c.$$

Hence the work done in raising 1 kg. through 8 cm. (*i.e.*, ·08 kilogrammetres) involves an expenditure of energy of ·59c., which is about 7·4 small calories per kilogrammetre. While in the second case, where the slope was 13 cm. per metre, the expenditure of energy was 10·7 small calories per kilogrammetre.

It is clear, therefore, that the relative expenditure of energy for slopes of 8 and 13 centimetres is far from being proportional to the sum of the energy expended in the equivalent horizontal distance and vertical ascent (*vide* para. 278).

The descent of an inclined plane is a somewhat complex phenomenon. The expenditure of energy increases slightly with the declivity. With an inclination of 8 cm. the energy increases with the load, while, with an inclination of 13 cm. it decreases ! If we compute the expenditure of energy in the vertical descent we have : in the first case

$$\frac{\cdot 85 - \cdot 41}{\cdot 08} = 5\cdot 5 \text{ small calories per kilogrammetre.}$$

In the other case,

$$\frac{1 - \cdot 41}{\cdot 13} = 4\cdot 53 \text{ small calories per kilogrammetre.}$$

This reduction is more noticeable if the subject is loaded. Detailed investigation is needed to arrive at the most economical conditions for so complex a form of locomotion. All that we can now say is that if the labourers have to carry loads down a plane and return unloaded up the plane, it is best that the inclination should be fairly steep, about 13 cm. rise per metre.

299. The Descending Walk.—It will be remembered that Chauveau, by a series of very consistent experiments, proved that the expenditure of energy is less in the (resistant) work of descent than in the (motor) work of ascent. The ratio is 52 : 100 at ordinary speeds (*vide* § 140). We have just seen that this ratio is 85 : 100 in the case of unloaded descent down a slope of 8 cm. per metre. With load, on the same slope, the ratio is 75 : 100. If the slope is 13 cm. per metre the ratio is almost the same as that obtained by Chauveau (for no load). With load the ratio is reduced to 38 : 100.

300. Comparison between Horizontal and Vertical Walking.— It has been shown that the expenditure per kilogramme per metre traversed horizontally is ·51 c., and that in ascending a stairway is 8 c. approximately. Hence the ratio between the kilogrammetre and the metre-kilogramme is $\frac{8}{\cdot 51} = 16$ approximately.

However, it was found that one of the subjects of the experiments could, for the same total expenditure of energy per diem, achieve no less than 2,220,738 metre kilogrammes in horizontal walking or 69,027 kilogrammetres in ascending and descending a stair.[1] The ratio in this case was 20. The load carried was 45 kg. and the speed and periods of work and repose were irregular.

---

[1] Jules Amar, *Le Rendement*, p. 74.
[2] Haughton (S.), *Principles of Animal Mechanics*, 1873.

Haughton ([2]) as a result of his researches adopted the same figure while Coulomb calculated the ratio to be 18.

In the great majority of cases a ratio of 16 : 1 is probably the most accurate approximation that can be made.

Adopting this ratio a man weighing 65 kg. does 65 metre-kilogrammes per metre, or $\frac{65}{16} = 4$ kilogrammetres approximately.

Hence a pace ·8 metres long is equivalent to $4 \times ·8 = 3·2$ kilogrammetres, a much lower value than that deduced by the graphical methods of para. 272. By this method the efficiency of ordinary walking would be calculated to be 32%.

CHAPTER III.

301. The relations between the Workman and his Tools—Apprenticeship.—The investigations discussed in the preceding chapters are of a comparatively simple nature. The objects in view were to adjust the efforts and the speed of the " human " motor " so as to give the best results and by careful observations to eliminate those attitudes or motions of the body which are valueless or even detrimental. The factors to be considered are not numerous and can, with comparative ease, be isolated and studied separately.

When, however, we pass on to investigate the use of tools, the opportunities for defective attitudes are far more numerous. We may take as examples of this the stiffness and clumsiness of the apprentice, faulty positions of the body in relation to the work or tool operated, unnecessary oscillations of the body, or irregularity in the movement of the limbs. We have also to decide on the effort, the speed, and the frequency and the intervals of rest, to be adopted, in each particular case.

If, to the above, we add the personality of the individual workman, his figure, his strength, his education, in the full sense of the word, we shall have enumerated nearly all the possible *physiological* variables.

But the useful output of the workman is obviously also greatly affected by his equipment of tools, their arrangement, quality, and selection (*vide* § 192). These points might be described as the *mechanical* variables which must receive careful investigation.

The " science of apprenticeship " comprehends the study of both the physiological and the mechanical variables. This is laboratory research, but the laboratory must be in close and intimate touch with the workshop. To enable the physical and moral qualities and the mental and muscular powers of any man to attain their best results the man must work under the best *internal* and *external* conditions (*vide* Book IV.). In particular, the closest attention must be given to the movements of man and tool, for thereby great economies both in time and effort can be realised. Taylor's comprehensive investigations showed clearly the influences of load and speed on the output of labourers. Such work is, however, of a simple nature, in which but few variables have to be considered. When we pass to the study of a turner at his lathe, other factors have to be reckoned with. The workman's efforts and movements must be carefully observed, with a view to eliminating all that is unnecessary. The speed, the selection of tools, the length and distribution of rest and meal times during the day have also an important bearing on the results obtained.

If there be a " science " of labour, there is also an " art " of working, an art which, properly studied, can confer rich economic benefits. It is to this that Taylor has so insistently directed the attention of the industrial world, both employers and employed. But human labour can never reach its maximum unless the worker is assured of a corresponding maximum of well-being. Let us confine our attention to the technical side of this new study. We have, in effect, to find the laws by which the maximum economical output of work can be obtained from the movements of the human motor and its mechanism. We know, from experience, that rapid movements tend towards the desired result, since by becoming *automatic* they gain in speed and accuracy. But in such cases bad habits of working may be the cause of superfluous movements. All such must be eliminated, and only those retained which conduce to efficiency. As Gilbreth ([1]) says, the new science of management demands that trades be taught in accordance with standardised movements laid down by a central authority. Or, as Taylor cogently remarks, we see the forests disappear, the energy of rivers running to waste, the land destroyed by erosion of the sea, and the approaching exhaustion of our supplies of coal and iron. But the daily waste of *human energy* by unskilfulness, bad management, and incapacity (which the late Mr. Roosevelt considered to be a real loss of national output) is less tangible and less easily observed or understood. Wastage of material can be easily observed, but it is indeed difficult adequately to understand and appreciate the waste of energy due to human incapacity and unskilfulness.([2])

On the average one-third of the available energy of man is wasted. In other words, methodical organization could increase the industrial output in the same proportion. Such increased output from the manual worker would permit a corresponding increase in his wages, and form a powerful inducement towards the maintenance of industrial peace.

The analysis of motions, their classification, in accordance with their utility, the determination of the suitable speeds for such motions and of the best methods in which they can be combined require very special treatment as a department of kinematics. By *graphic* and *chronophotographic* methods we can find the path of any moving body and the laws connecting space, time, speed and acceleration. By these methods we can resolve

---

([1]) F. Gilbreth, *Motion Study*, p. 98.
([2]) F. Taylor, *Scientific Organisation of Workshops*, loc. cit., p. 27.

into elementary motions all the actions of a thoroughly competent workman. Having done this we can observe and eliminate the unnecessary and useless motions which are made by less competent men in carrying out similar work. Such men should be instructed by the exhibition of the results of cinematographic synthesis. In their interests we must co-ordinate science and experiment, figures and facts. For them, instructors must be provided who can intelligently and tactfully combat " rule of thumb " methods, who can enlist the sympathetic co-operation of the workmen, and demonstrate to them the advantages of scientific methods in industry. Instruction charts would be provided for each class of work, summarising the results obtained by competent experimentalists. For the sake of the workmen, be they young apprentices or experienced journeymen, the man of science will forsake the peaceful seclusion of his laboratory and will bring to the realm of industry, to factory and to workshop, the marvellous working tools of science which he alone can use ; tools undreamt of by the first observers, to whom the human machine was a mechanism working in mysterious and unaccountable ways, in no measure referable to the ordinary laws of mechanics.

303. Historical Sketch.—The scientific study of labour is no more than 25 years old (this was written in 1914). In ancient times there were no laws for the regulation of labour other than those of slavery, by which it is unlikely that efficiency was obtained.

Until the laws of general mechanics were formulated, no study of man, " the first prime mover," was possible. We owe the inception of the science of mechanics to Galileo (1564–1642). He established the principles governing the operation of simple machines, such as the lever and the inclined plane, and the laws of the resistance of materials. Out of curiosity he endeavoured to apply these laws to living beings. He noted the phenomenon of fatigue, and thought that it was explained by the fact that all bodies tended to fall downwards. Hence the ascent of a stair caused fatigue because it was an action against the force of Gravity. When, however, he considered that fatigue was also produced by a prolonged descent of a stair, he saw that the above explanation was inadequate, and explained this by stating that the muscles had to move not only their own weight, but that of the skeleton, or even the whole body. This was so with the legs, but he considered that the heart suffered no fatigue because it had only to move its own mass.[1]

---

[1] Galileo, *Opere*, Milan edition, vol. xi., p. 558, 1911. (Leonardo de Vinchi (1452–1519) who preceded Galileo, made some remarkable observations on the attitudes and motions of the human body which should not be overlooked. *Trattato tella Pittura*, Milan, 1804, p. 121, *et seq.*).

At the end of the seventeenth century some illustrious physicists and geometricians, such as Sauveur, Phillippe de la Hire, and Amontons, gave some consideration to the human mechanism. De la Hire showed, by experiment, that the weight of a man is a factor in his physical strength, and may be of actual utility, as in the case of lifting weights by means of a rope and pulley up to a limit of about 65 kg. He also noted that in pulling a rope upwards a man could exert more force standing than sitting. He considered that 75 kg. was the maximum load which could profitably be carried on the shoulders of a man walking slowly on level ground. He concluded that any given height can be most economically reached by mounting to it by an inclined plane, and he also was of opinion that human labour is not profitably employed in traction.[1]

Amontons [2] concerned himself chiefly with measurements of the power developed in executing rapid operations in very short times. His results will be dealt with later. It should be noted that most of these early researches were confined to the evaluation of *static* force, although the above-quoted scientists were aware that the work done in overcoming resistance and producing displacement corresponded to the lifting of a weight to a certain height. The prominence given to the study of hydraulic energy during the seventeenth century led to a consideration of the mechanical work produced by muscular activity. It was during this period that Bernoulli, Bouguer, Deparcieux, Euler, and Schultze carried out the investigations which have been referred to in para. 119. In 1785 the great French philosopher, Coulomb (1736–1806) [3] communicated to the " Institute " his remarkable researches on " the strength of man," although they were not published in the Proceedings of the Institute until the beginning of the year 1799. He proposed to investigate the maximum work which could be done without injury to health in the most arduous occupations. His results are dealt with later.

Lazare Carnot [4] at the same date expressed the same views as Coulomb, although he made no independent experiments. It may be said that up to the year 1850 all the researches in this subject were dominated exclusively by the physical point of view, in spite of the birth of the science of energetics. Nevertheless, the work of these earlier scientists, based as it was on the " degree of fatigue," was not without utility. They measured,

---

[1] De La Hire (*Hist. Acad, Roy. des Sciences*, 1666 to 1686, p. 70 ; *Mémoires Acad. Roy. des Sciences*, 1699, p. 155 and 1702, p. 95).

[2] Amontons (*Mémoires Acad. Roy. Sciences*, 1699, p. 112, and 1703, p. 100).

[3] Coulomb (see his *Théorie des Machines*, Bachelier, 1821).

[4] L. Carnot, *Essai sur les Machines en Général*, 1786.

with fair accuracy, the production of work by man under normal conditions. Coulomb, alone, at that time, and Bouguer ([1]) and S'Gravesande ([2]) at a later date, recognized the important influence of the speed of working, on the daily output. The others paid no attention to this factor.

In the nineteenth century the professors of pure mechanics ceased to hold the field. Navier ([3]), Corioli, Dupin and Poncelet, who did so much for the development of workshop machinery, failed, through want of proper methods and apparatus, to solve the problem of the human machine, although they fully appreciated its importance and the value of the practical results which might spring therefrom.([4]) Whilst Dupin devoted his lectures at the Conservatoire to this matter, Poncelet made it his subject at Metz. The enthusiasm was quickly exhausted, because there was really nothing with which to feed it.

Since 1855, thanks to the work of Chauveau, the evaluation of the expenditure of energy has been carried out by the application of the science of *energetics*. It must not, however, be forgotten that Lavoisier was the first to formulate and apply the principle of measuring the work done by the corresponding consumption of oxygen. He remarked that by this method comparison could be made between forces which, at first sight, appeared to have no inter-relation. Thus it was possible to measure in ordinary physical units, the expenditure of energy of the orator, the musician, the writer, the composer, or even the philosopher immersed in thought. Such actions, generally considered as purely mental, have, then, their physical and material elements, by virtue of which they can be compared with the actions of manual labour. It is therefore not without fitness that the French language includes, under the one word, " travail," the work both of head and hand.([5])

The logical development of this far-reaching generalization was due to the masterly work of Chauveau alone, as far as France was concerned. In America Atwater and his school followed on the same lines. Much data of value in the scientific study of labour was, however, collected in other countries, by Mosso and Treves in Italy, by Zuntz ([6]) du Bois-Reymond, and A. Loewy, and their numerous followers in Germany.

([1]) P. Bouguer, *Traité du Navire*, p. 109, 1746.
([2]) S'Gravesande, *Physices Elem. Math.*, I., No. 1856.
([3]) Navier, *Architecture Hydr.*, Bélidor, 1819, notes, p. 382.
([4]) See especially the Inaugural Lecture of C. Dupin at the Conservatoire Nationale des Arts et Mètiers (Discourse of 25th Jan., 1829).
([5]) Lavoisier *Œuvres Complètes* ii. p. 688 (Edition Officiele).
([6]) Zuntz and Schumburg *Studien zu einer Physiol. des Marsches* Berlin, 1901.

On the other hand Marey [1] and his followers devoted all their attention to graphical methods, for the complete registration of muscular efforts. Braune and Fischer confined their attention to the phenomena of locomotion ; Imbert and Amar dealt with industrial work.

It is now appreciated that the " degree of fatigue " is measured by the expenditure of energy, and that it is intimately connected with the effort, speed, frequency, and duration of the work by which it is caused. The nett output of muscular energy is a measure of the force exercised in the production of mechanical work.

Separate consideration must be given to the work of Taylor,[2] Gantt, and Gilbreth,[3] who studied industrial labour under factory and workshop conditions. Their methods consisted, essentially, in the accurate timing of movements, and careful observation by which they eliminated useless motions. By timing the useful movements of a specially selected workman, they were able to arrive at the maximum possible output. Increased wages stimulate the workman to strive at the attainment of this maximum. The admirable work of these engineers was first made known in France by Henry le Chatelier, who translated and wrote an introduction to Taylor's work. This publication was most successful and evoked much interest.

The reader of these pages will appreciate the important, though hitherto unrecognised part which French scientists have played in laying the foundations of the forthcoming economic revolution, and will regret that their ideas have had to struggle against delay, hesitation and indifference. The work of the French investigators has, indeed been more truly scientific than that of Taylor, for it has given consideration to the physiological aspect of the subject. It was, however, academic rather than practical, and did not then appear to have any useful application in industry. Taylor's methods, however, were eminently practical, being based on actual workshop experience and on long familiarity with the qualities, good and bad, of the average workman.

He endeavoured to improve the good and eliminate the bad. He resolved industrial operations into their elements, so that he might speed up the rate of working. Thus, as described in para. 292 above, in the case of the handling of pig iron, he distinguished the separate elements of the operation, the lifting of the pig from the ground, the walking with the load on the level, and on the

[1] Marey La Méthode Graphique 1878 ; Le Mouvement 1894 Engl. tr., London 1895.
[2] Frederick Winslow Taylor Principles of Scientific Organisation of Workshops.
[3] Frank Gilbreth Motion Study, 1911.

incline, the deposit of the load, and the return empty-handed. He took as his standard the results obtained by timing the very best men. He found that hardly one man in five could attain to such a standard. Hence he emphasised the need for the selection of workmen. The leading features of Taylor's system are therefore time measurement and selection.

304. Classification of Manual Operations.—We shall, provisionally, adopt the following order and sub-division :—

(1) Operations in which the weight of the human body is alone employed.

(2) Operations in which the muscles of the arms are used.

(3) Operations employing the muscles of the legs.

(4) Miscellaneous operations.

If we had full knowledge of all the factors which enter into such operations we might survey the various occupations of industry *seriatim*. We could also draw a distinction between the exercise of force and speed. This being impossible, we are constrained to adopt a classification in accordance with those factors with which we are familiar.

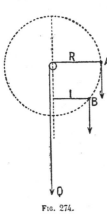

Fig. 274.

Diagram of a treadmill.

(*a.*) *Work done by the Weight of the body.* A form of treadmill, an illustration of which was given in fig. 216, and which is shown, diagramatically, in fig. 274, is still employed in some stone quarries for raising stone from pits (*vide* para. 233). The weight of the man who climbs the wheel is the power P. The leverage is the radius R of the wheel if the power is exerted on the level of the axis at A. If exerted at a point B below that axis the leverage is represented by the distance l. Let the resistance be Q, then the motor moment P × R or P × l = the resistant moment Q × r, r being the radius of the barrel on which the rope is coiled.

Whence :

$$P = Q \times \frac{r}{R} \quad \text{or} \quad P = Q \times \frac{r}{l}.$$

The work done per rotation is $2\pi R \times P$. For n revolutions in a day, the expression will be :—

$$T = 2\pi R n \times P.$$

Replacing P by its value, it will be written :—

$$T = 2\pi R n \times Q \times \frac{r}{l} \quad \text{or} \quad 2\pi r n \times Q.$$

The friction of the wheel increases the resistant work. Generally the speed depends on the point of application of the power. Navier found a speed of 0·15m. for a duration of 8 hours, the man working at the level of the axis. Then his weight of 60 kilogrammes takes its full effect.

Navier calculated that :—

$T = 0·15 \times 60 \times 3,600 \times 8 = 259,200$ kilogrammetres.

The speed was 0·70 m. when the man worked at a point of the wheel at 24° from the base. His effort is then only 12 kilogrammes, which is a total of work done for 8 hours of :

$T = 0·70 \times 3,600 \times 8 \times 12 = 241,920$ kilogrammetres.

Thus, according to Navier, a man can perform 250,000 kilogrammetres per day in climbing a treadmill.

The following results, which were obtained from official sources, show the work done by the treadmill in various English jails :

LOCALITIES	WORK DONE.
Northampton	143,643 kilogrammetres
Nottingham	174,360 ,,
Devonshire	195,625 ,,
Middlesex	212,946 ,,
Cambridge	259,690 ,,
Boston	281,104 ,,
Warwick	205,517 ,,
——	274,022 ,,
——	342,529 ,,
General Average	231,000 ,,

305. (b). *Actions of the Arms.*—The use of the winch and capstan. In both of these machines the work is done by the exercise of the arms. Navier estimated that the efforts of a man working a capstan at a speed of ·6 metres per second, was about 12 kg. This would mean a quantity of work done in 8 hours of $12 \times ·6 \times 3,600 \times 8 = 207,400$ kilogrammetres approximately.

The work done per second is $·6 \times 12 = 7·2$ kgm. Schultze and Langsdorf investigated the work done in turning the crank handle of a winch and obtained results varying from 10 to 11 kilogrammetres per second. The corresponding efforts and speeds were :

WORK PER SECOND KILOGRAMMETRES.	EFFORT IN KILO- GRAMMES.	SPEED METRES PER SECOND.
10	13·7	·76
11	13·3	·757

The production for eight hours of actual labour was therefore :

$13 \cdot 7 \times 0 \cdot 76 \times 3,600 \times 8 = 299,865$ kilogrammetres
$13 \cdot 3 \times 0 \cdot 757 \times 3,600 \times 8 = 287,081$　　　,,

i.e., a quantity of　300,000 kilogrammetres
approximately.

In practice, at a speed of ·75 metres, the maximum period of actual labour is 6 hours.　Hence the real daily output is :

$$\frac{300,000 \times 6}{8} = 225,000 \text{ kilogrammetres.}$$

The most accurate experiments show that the speed·and the effort should not be reduced to less than 0·50 m. and 15 kilogrammes respectively.　Hachette, with a man working quite easily at 3·8 kgm. per second, obtained a daily output of barely 110,000 kilogrammetres of work done.

306. The muscular power, acting on the crank-handle, develops a variable quantity of work.　It is not only the muscles of the arms which furnish the necessary effort.　The horizontal component of the weight of the man has also a certain effect.　As a rule, the workman adopts an attitude making 65° with the direction that the crank handle must take, and he acts by a lever having its fulcrum at the height of the loins, or at about ⅜ of his height. If he weighs 65 kilogrammes, his effort will be :

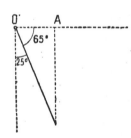

Fɪɢ. 275.

$$\frac{65 \times 3}{5} = 39 \text{ kilogrammes.}$$

The effective component is (fig. 275) :

OA = $39 \times \sin 25°$ (or cos 65°) = $39 \times 0 \cdot 423 = 16 \cdot 500$ kg.

If the body is inclined 45°, the component is :

$39 \times 0 \cdot 707 = 27 \cdot 600$ kg.

but then the equilibrium of the man is upset.

One of the earliest observers, Sauveur, found the values of 12·24 kg. and 0·51 m. for a continuous labour of 8 hours.　This gives for the day's work :

$12 \cdot 24 \times 0 \cdot 51 \times 3,600 \times 8 = 260,000$　kilogrammetres

approximately, and this is a maximum.[1]

---

[1] Bélidor (*Architecture Hydraulique* i. p. 72 quoted above).

In referring to this result Lazare Carnot [1] gives the speed as ·97 metres, which is, of course, an error. Coulomb[2] considered that a continuous effort of 12 kg. was impossible, and that no more than 7 kg. could be expected. The crank handle used in his experiments, described a circle of 2·3 metres in circumference and the speed was 20 revolutions per minute. He found the output for 6 hours to be :

$$7 \times 2{\cdot}30 \times 20 \times 60 \times 6 = 116{,}000 \text{ kilogrammetres,}$$

at the average speed of

$$\frac{2{\cdot}30 \times 20}{60} = 0{\cdot}77 \text{ m. per second.}$$

A workman rarely exceeds a speed of 0·80 m. In regard to the duration Navier was able to extend it to 8 hours. Taking an effort of 8 kilogrammes and a speed of 0·75m., the work done was:

$$8 \times 0{\cdot}75 \times 3{,}600 \times 8 = 172{,}800 \text{ kilogrammetres.}$$

Christian's [3] experiments are more instructive because they lasted three months without interruption.

The speed was ·5 m. per second, the effort 14 kg., and the effective working day was seven hours. The total work done was therefore :

$$14 \times {\cdot}5 \times 3{,}600 \times 7 = 176{,}400 \text{ kilogrammetres,}$$

which is nearly the same as Navier's result.

To the above useful work must be added the energy expended in bending the upper portion of the body. The moment of inertia I., is about ·86. This bending corresponds to an angular displacement of 65° per half turn of the handle, i.e., 130° per revolution, the speed of revolution being 20 turns per minute, i.e., a revolution per 3 seconds. The angular displacement per second is 130° = 43°. By the method of computation described above (§ 272), the work done per revolution of the crank handle would be

$$\tfrac{1}{2} \times 0{\cdot}86 \times \frac{\pi^2 \times 43^2}{180^2} \times \frac{152}{100} = 0{\cdot}368 \text{ kgm.}$$

In 8 hours, the $20 \times 60 \times 8$ revolutions will give muscular work amounting to

$$9{,}600 \times 0{\cdot}368 = 3{,}533 \text{ kilogrammetres approximately.}$$

Certain authorities have given much higher values which are not justified.

307. Vertical Haulage of Ropes.—The Pile Driver. If a force P is applied to one end of a rope, passing over a fixed pulley, in

[1] L. Carnot *Essai sur les Machines*, 1786.
[2] *Loc. cit. —Bull. Soc. Ing. Civ.* Feb., 1885.
[3] Christian, *Mécanique Industrielle*, 1822, vol. i., 114.

order to lift a weight Q attached to the other end of the rope, P has to overcome, not only the resistance of Q, but also the function of rope and pulley. P is, therefore, always greater than Q. This applies to the pile driver (§ 228).

In Coulomb's experiments with a pile-driver, the "monkey" (the head which drives the pile) weighed 350 to 450 kg., and was raised to a height of 1·1 metres. The dynamometer showed an average effort of 19 kg. per man.

Eighty blows were made in succession at a rate of 20 per minute. For an actual working time of three hours, the work done was therefore :

$$19 \times 1\cdot10 \times 20 \times 60 \times 3 = 75{,}200 \text{ kilogrammetres.}$$

A pile-driver, used at the construction of the Jena Bridge in the year 1808, had a "monkey" weighing 587 kg., which was lifted to a height of 1·45 m. by 38 men. The load per man was therefore $\frac{587}{38} = 15\cdot45$ kg. The working day was 10 hours, and 360 blows were given, on the average, per hour. The work done per man, per diem, was therefore :

$$360 \times 15\cdot45 \times 1\cdot45 \times 10 = 80{,}648 \text{ kgm.}$$

The work done per man per diem, therefore, seems to be about 80,000 kilogrammetres.

Coulomb also made some measurements with a "drop stamp" used at the Paris Mint. The punch weighed 38 kg., and was raised to a height of ·4 metres by two men, 5,200 blows were struck per diem. The work done was therefore :

$$38 \times \cdot4 \times 5{,}200 = 79{,}000 \text{ kgm.}$$

Coulomb considered that one man could have done the work.

In the above experiments the effort per man was considerably higher than the economical effort. The latter was shown (*vide* para. 124) to be approximately 13 kg. at a speed of ·75 metres per second. It is therefore not surprising that the pile-driver is not at all an economical apparatus for the utilisation of muscular strength.

308. Some experiments on the drawing of water from a well confirm this conclusion. A man lifted 18 kg. at ·2 metres per second by a rope and pulley.[1] For six working hours the work done was :

$$18 \times \cdot2 \times 3{,}600 \times 6 = 77{,}760 \text{ kilogrammetres.}$$

Coulomb measured the energy expended in drawing water from a well 37 metres in depth. The tractive effort, as measured by

---

[1] Navier's observations (*loc. cit.*).

a spring balance was 16 kg. ; 120 buckets were lifted at a speed of ·2 metres per second. The work done was therefore :

$37 \times 16 \times 120 = 71{,}000$ kilogrammetres approximately.[1]

This leads to an effective duration of six hours. The resistant work due to the descent of the empty buckets, added to the motor work, brings the total to 80,000 kilogrammetres.

If, on the contrary, a man lifts a weight of 6 kilogrammes at a speed of 0·75 m., Navier found that he could work for 10 hours and produce 162,000 kilogrammetres, that is, double the quantity above.

$6 \times 0{\cdot}75 \times 3{,}600 \times 10 = 162{,}000$ kilogrammetres.

Drawing water is a primitive operation which is hardly ever done by hand now, and it is also very troublesome. A man drawing water from a tank by means of buckets or tubs, without using a rope and a pulley, only produces 45,000 to 50,000 kilogrammetres per 8-hour day.[2] By using a scoop, notably the Dutch scoop (see § 228) he will produce in the same time 100,000 to 120,000 kilogrammetres.[3]

A bucket worked by a cord coiled round a windlass will allow work to be done to the amount of 150,000 to 160,000 kilogrammetres.[4]

With an ordinary hand pump, a man can give a useful output of 150,000 kgm. per day for 10 hours. Armand Gautier [5] estimated that the corresponding output of muscular work was 260,000 kgm. Under very favourable conditions the average effort and speed are 13 kg. and ·6 metres respectively.

309. The Use of the Hammer.—Hubert investigated the work done in the use of a hammer at varying speeds and amplitudes of movement.

The hammer used weighed 7·065 kg. When it was swung through a complete circle the workman could strike 1,690 blows per diem, an output of 65,000 kilogrammetres. When the hammer was swung through an arc of a circle only, and at a lesser speed, 2,560 blows could be struck per diem and the corresponding output of work was 67,000 kilogrammetres (see para. 230 for the method of calculation). Unfortunately no accurate observations were made as to the effect of various shapes and weights of hammers and the speeds at which they were swung. Neverthe-

---

[1] *Loc. cit.*
[2] Perronnet.
[3] Various observers (Bélidor, Perronnet, d'Aubuisson).
[4] D'Aubuisson.
[5] See § 136 above.

less Hubert recognised that with a light hammer, such as that used by a nail-maker, a production of work, of as much as 160,000 kilogrammetres per diem might be attained.

Gilbreth noted that the weight of the hammer was an important matter in the work of the stone mason. In splitting blocks of granite a hammer weighing 12 kg. would effect as much in 5 blows as a hammer of 5 kg. could effect in a hundred strokes.

Each trade needs an appropriate weight and shape of hammer. A carpenter's hammer weighs about ·55 kg. and has a handle about half a metre long. The work of the smith necessitates a very heavy implement (§41). The rapidity with which the hammer is used varies also in different trades. For example, a carpenter driving stakes into the ground will deliver about 60 blows per minute, his arm describing a semi-circle at a peripheral speed of about 7·5 metres per second. The corresponding expenditure of energy will be :

$$\tfrac{1}{2}\,mv^2 = \tfrac{1}{2}\,\frac{5\cdot50}{9\cdot81}\,.\,7\cdot5^2 = 15\cdot75 \ \text{kgm.}$$

For double oscillation of the hammer it will be 31·50 kgm.

If a workman drives 350 stakes per diem, he will deliver 350 × 11 blows of the hammer, at 11 strokes per stake. The total work done will be :

31·50 × 11 × 350 = *121,276* kilogrammetres.

If the small accessory operations are added to this, such as the effect of the 350 × 11 = 3,850 oscillations of the arm,[1] the total muscular action will be about 130,000 kilogrammetres a day.

310. The Use of the File.—This operation in metal working has received special attention.[2] The workman must exert both a downward pressure, in order that the teeth of the file may obtain a bite on the metal, and also the horizontal effort needed to traverse the file over the work at the required speed. The general conditions which will be found by an analysis of the operation, are as follows (see fig. 276).

The efforts of both arms have horizontal and vertical components, V V′ and H H′ respectively. The vertical components keep the file down on the work, while the horizontal components drive the file and, properly speaking, do the actual work.

---

[1] The moment of inertia of the upper limb being 0·03, it is calculated that about 0·60 kgm. of work is done at each oscillation, or altogether
3,850 × 0·6 = 2,310 kilogrammetres.

[2] Jules Amar (*Journal de Physiol.*, Jan., 1913, p. 62 ; *Comptes Rendus Acad. Sciences*, Nov., 1912).

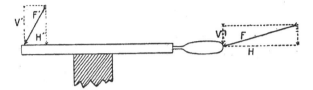

Fig. 276.

If l is the effective travel of the file and n the number of strokes the total work done in the working strokes is

$$(H + H') \times l \times n.$$

As far as the working stroke of the file is concerned the vertical components VV' could be replaced by equivalent weights.

But the return stroke has also to be considered. An effort h is needed for this.

The total work done for both forward and return strokes is, therefore :

$$(H + H' + h) \times l \times n.$$

Since the expenditure of energy by the human organism is proportional to the total of the muscular contractions involved in the carrying out of any operation, and not to the useful work done, we must next calculate the muscular effort both static and dynamic.

311. Experimental Methods.—Flat " bastard " files were used in the experiments. They were, as usual, of constant width, but of a thickness diminishing towards the point giving a slight convexity to the working surfaces. They were cut on two faces and one edge. The length was 34 cm., of which 26 was actually used in working. The width was 3·2 cm. and the thickness tapered from 1 cm. to ·55 cm. The files were of best quality.

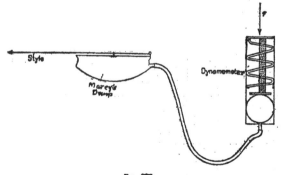

Fig. 277.

Marey's system of graphic registration was employed. The general principle of the experiments consisted in arrangements by which the muscles of the hands acted on springs compressing the same slightly. The pressure of the springs was transmitted to small rubber bulbs, which latter were each connected to a Marey's " tambour " (*vide* fig. 277).

The amplitude of the movement of the stylus is so arranged that legible charts can be obtained. The dynamographic arrangements applied to the tool, and the work are those described in para. 214 above.

By this apparatus both the pressure of the left hand, V', and the combined pressure of both hands, V + V', can be measured; hence the pressure of the right hand V, can be readily deduced.

The horizontal components, H and H', are measured separately.

The total weight of the file, complete with the dynamographic fittings, was 1,850 grammes, which weight must be added to V + V' in our computations.

The material on which the experiments were carried out was a block of brass.

The power needed to draw the file back over the work (*vide* fig. 278) was found to be 550 grammes. The co-efficient of friction was therefore approximately :

$$f = \frac{\cdot 550}{1 \cdot 850} = \cdot 3.$$

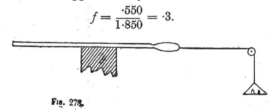

Fig. 278.

Measurement of power on the return stroke of a file.

The workman stands at the vice, on a platform the height of which can be adjusted. As will be seen later, this height, and the consequent attitude of the workman, have an important influence, both on the fatigue and the output of work.

The expenditure of energy is measured by the consumption of oxygen, using the thermal equivalent of a litre of oxygen. By analysing the gases expired, at rest, and at work, respectively, the additional consumption due to the work can be arrived at.

Also the *respiratory quotient* $\frac{CO_2}{O_2}$ gives the calorific value of the additional consumption, in other words, the actual dynamic expenditure. The respirations were recorded, graphically, simultaneously with the other observations. The number of strokes of the file per minute was, in some cases left to the discretion of the workman, and in others kept at a definite rate in accordance with a frequency set by a metronome.

The method of measuring the respiratory exchanges is fully described on para. 239.

Fig. 279.

The general arrangement of the apparatus is shown in fig.[279, the subject of the experiment being an apprentice. The respiratory valve (*vide* fig. 218) is supported by a metal strap fixed to the head.

Calibration of the Apparatus.—In fig. 280 a specimen of the graphical records taken with a journeyman fitter as a subject are given.

The ordinates of the curves represent the pressures. In order that the actual pressures in kilogrammes corresponding thereto can be ascertained, various definite weights are applied either

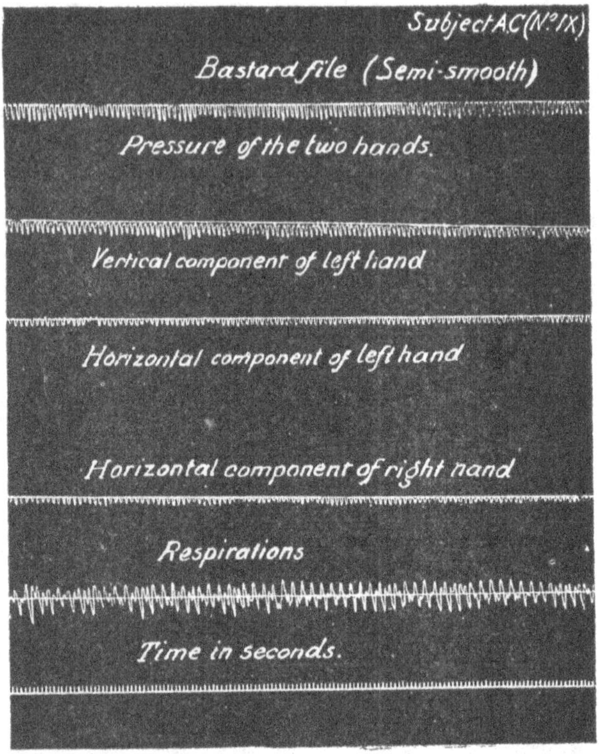

Subject A.C (N.º IX)

Bastard file (Semi-smooth)

Pressure of the two hands.

Vertical component of left hand

Horizontal component of left hand

Horizontal component of right hand

Respirations

Time in seconds.

FIG. 280. -

directly or through a cord, to the portions of the apparatus at which the pressure of the hands is exerted. The value, in kilogrammes, corresponding to any given height of ordinate can thus be obtained. It is essential that the apparatus shall be recalibrated for each series of experiments, as the indications of the receiving tambours do not remain absolutely constant.

Fig. 281 shows the calibration graph for the experiment shown in fig. 280. Here the weights corres-

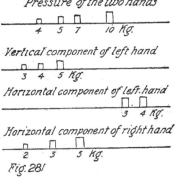

Pressure of the two hands

4   5   7   10 Kg.

Vertical component of left hand

3   4   5 Kg.

Horizontal component of left hand

3   4 Kg.

Horizontal component of right hand

2   3   5 Kg.

Fig. 281

ponding to an ordinate of 1 centimetre are 20, 17, 10 and 11 kg. respectively, for the four graphs, reading from top to bottom.

It should be noted that the effort exerted by the arms of the workman is variable. Hence the ordinates represent the maximum efforts which maximum is very rapidly reached.

Before and after each experiment the block of metal is weighed on a balance reading to 1 milligramme. Hence the weight of metal removed can be very accurately measured.

312. Experiments and Calculations.—The two regular subjects of the experiments were :

A.C.—A journeyman fitter of 20 years' experience and good physique. His age was 38 years. His weight 74 kg. His height 1·72 metres.

XP.—An apprentice, aged 16, agile but not strong, weight 55 kg. Height 1·65 metres. He had served two years of his apprenticeship.

Fifty-seven series of experiments, extending over a period of eight months, were carried out on these two subjects.

Various other persons (J.A., L.M.., H.R., E.A., C.G.), of various professions and trades, but all of them unfamiliar with the use of the file, were from time to time utilised as subjects.

In all the experiments the subject worked at a comfortable rate in an atmosphere maintained at a temperature of, approximately, 17°C. The air breathed was brought from the outside of the room through a large pipe.

The following results were obtained with A.C. as subject. (Experiment No. IX.)

(a) The subject at rest, seated.

Air expired in 3½ minutes........................ 30·25 litres
Respirations per minute 18
Temperature .... 17·5°C
Barometric pressure .... 758 mm.

An analysis of the air expired gave:

$$CO_2 \quad 3·15\%$$
$$O_2 \quad 17·4\%$$

This is an absorption of $21 - 17·4 = 3·6\%$

The " respiratory quotient :"

$$\frac{CO_2}{O_2} = \frac{3·15}{3·6} = ·875$$

The volume of gas (reduced to 0°C and 760 mm. barometric pressure) was 28·41 litres.

The consumption of oxygen in 3½ minutes (reduced to 0°C and 760 mm.) was therefore :

$$\frac{28 \cdot 41 \times 3 \cdot 6}{100} = 1 \cdot 023 \text{ litres.}$$

A consumption per hour of:

$$\frac{1 \cdot 023 \times 60}{3 \cdot 5} = 17 \cdot 53 \text{ litres.}$$

(b) The subject at work, under the following conditions :— The subject chose his own attitude and kept it, as far as possible uniform throughout the experiment. The feet were kept in a definite position. Hence, the height of the vice being fixed, the general attitude of the body might be considered as constant.

The subject (A.C. as before) worked for a period of $3\frac{1}{2}$ minutes and made 54 strokes of the file per minute, (The experiment is depicted in fig. 282.) The results were as follows :—

Air expired in $3\frac{1}{2}$ minutes .... 70 litres
Respirations per minute 28
Temperature .... 17·5°C
Barometric pressure .... 758 mm.

The analysis gave

$$CO_2 \qquad 3 \cdot 7\%$$
$$O_2 \qquad 17 \cdot 2\%$$

An absorption of $21 - 17 \cdot 2 = 3 \cdot 8\%$.

The " respiratory quotient "

$$\frac{CO_2}{O_2} = \frac{3 \cdot 7}{3 \cdot 8} = \cdot 973$$

The volume of gas (reduced to 0°C and 760 mm. barometric pressure) was 66·455 litres.

The consumption of oxygen (at 0°C and 760 mm.) was :

$$\frac{66 \cdot 45 \times 3 \cdot 8}{100} = 2 \cdot 525 \text{ litres.}$$

A consumption per hour of :

$$\frac{2 \cdot 525 \times 60}{3 \cdot 5} = 43 \cdot 921 \text{ litres.}$$

The corresponding equivalents of the above consumptions, in grand calories, as deduced from the " respiratory quotients " are, per litre.

The subject at rest, **4·9 Cal.**

The subject at work, **5·05 Cal.**

Hence the equivalent expenditure per hour in grand calories is :

At rest ....17·53 × 4·9 = 85·91 Calories
At work ....43·29 × 5·05 = 218·62 Calories

Fig. 282. Experiment with journeyman fitter.

The net dynamic expenditure is therefore :

$$218{\cdot}62 - 85{\cdot}91 = 132{\cdot}71 \text{ Calories.}$$

313. We have next to consider the muscular activity. The top curve in fig. 280 represents the downward pressure of both hands. The average for 158 strokes of the file was 10 kg. Hence :

$$V + V' = 10 \text{ kg.}$$

To this has to be added the weight of the file (1·85 kg.). Hence the actual total pressure on the work is 11·85 kg. The horizontal component of the right hand, H. was 2·2 kg.

The efforts of the left hand were :

Horizontal component .... 2·5 kg.
Vertical component .... 6·8 kg.

Hence

$$V = 10 - 6{\cdot}8 = 3{\cdot}2 \text{ kg.}$$

As above stated, the actual length of file utilized was 26 cm., this being fixed by two stop blocks (*vide* fig. 184). The effort of the working stroke,

$$H + H' = 2{\cdot}2 + 2{\cdot}5 = 4{\cdot}7 \text{ kg.}$$

that of the return stroke

$$h = \cdot 55 \text{ kg.}$$

The work done, per complete stroke, is therefore :

$$\cdot 26 \ (4 \cdot 7 + \cdot 55) = 1 \cdot 365 \text{ kgm.}$$

The rate of working being 54 strokes per minute, the hourly production of work is :

$$1 \cdot 365 \times 54 \times 60 = 442 \cdot 6 \text{ kilogrammetres.}$$

The weight of metal removed per hour was 45·57 grammes.

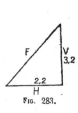

Fig. 283.

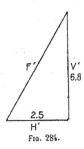

Fig. 284.

If the muscular efforts of the two arms are calculated, we find that they considerably exceed the useful efforts, owing to the fact that they are exerted at an angle to the plane of the file. Fig. 283 shows this in the case of the right arm, and fig. 284 for the left arm. From these figures we can readily see that

$$F = \sqrt{(3 \cdot 2)^2 + (2 \cdot 2)^2} = 3 \cdot 88 \text{ kg.}$$

$$F' = \sqrt{(6 \cdot 8)^2 + (2 \cdot 5)^2} = 7 \cdot 24 \text{ kg.}$$

The effort required for the return stroke of the file is, as above stated, ·55 kg. The total effort is therefore -

$$3 \cdot 88 + 7 \cdot 24 + \cdot 55 = 11 \cdot 67 \text{ kilogrammes.}$$

The useful effort $H + H' + h$ is $4 \cdot 7 + \cdot 55 = 5 \cdot 25$ kg. as shown above. Hence the efficiency is :

$$\frac{5 \cdot 25}{11 \cdot 67} = 44 \cdot 9\%.$$

In other words, 55% of the total muscular effort is expended in maintaining a pressure of the file on the work.

It should also be noted that the efforts of the muscles are consecutive and not concurrent. This can be demonstrated by using three similar tambours whose styles operate on one cylinder revolving at a very high speed, and arranging that the lengths of the connecting tubes, etc., for each tambour are, as far as possible, of equal dimensions. The results of such an experiment are given in fig. 285.

It will be seen from these curves that the combined pressure of the hands is the first effort to come into play. The horizontal effort of the left hand commences $\frac{8}{100}$ seconds later, and that of the right hand at a further interval of $\frac{11}{100}$ seconds. It follows, therefore that the workman does not commence his stroke for a short time after he has placed the file on the work.

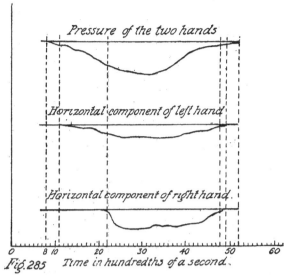

Fig. 285 Time in hundredths of a second.

The net expenditure of energy per hour being 132·71 Cal. and the work done being 4422·6 kilogrammetres. The expenditure per kgm. is

$$\frac{132 \cdot 71}{4422 \cdot 6} = \cdot 03 \text{ grand calories.}$$

A net yield of about 8%.

In this experiment any point of the file travels :

$$54 \times \cdot 26 \times 2 = 28 \cdot 08 \text{ metres per minute, or :}$$

·468 metres per second.

The expenditure per gramme of filings is :

$$\frac{132 \cdot 71}{45 \cdot 57} = 2 \cdot 91 \text{ Cal.}$$

As far as physiological effects are concerned, it will be noted that the respirations increase from 18 to 28 per minute, while, as will be seen from fig. 286, the period of the inspirations is longer than the normal. The pulse also increases from 72 to 89 per minute.

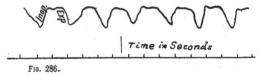

Time in Seconds

Fig. 286.

Respiratory curve during filing.

THE HUMAN MOTOR

WORKMAN—"A. C." BASTARD FILE

Numbers in order		Strokes of the file per minute	Muscular effort per stroke of File.		Useful effort of both arms	Co-efficient of Utility	Work done per hour
			Right arm	Left arm			
1		2	3	4	5	6	7
			kg.	kg.	kg.	%	kgm.
1	IV	33·14	4·87	7·42	4·35	35·4	2,247·33
2	XII	35·14	6·96	5·55	4·44	35·5	2,436.96
3	VIII	36·28	3·72	7·75	4·07	35·4	2,301·23
4	XXIII	36·28	8·23	7·03	5·52	36·2	3,124·63
5	XX	36·85	6·40	8·54	6·65	44·5	3,823·54
6	XV	38·00	5·91	7·89	5·72	41·5	3,390·81
7	XVIII	38·85	6·25	8·42	6·20	42·2	3,757·57
8	V	39·43	4·97	7·26	4·27	34·9	2,625·27
9	XIII	41·43	5·33	7·42	4·56	35·8	2,947·13
10	VI	41·71	5·06	7·51	4·48	35·7	2,916·36
11	XIX	42·28	5·76	6·20	4·30	36·0	2,861·19
12	VII	42·57	3·04	8·05	4·04	36·4	2,679·10
13	III	43·71	5·28	9·72	6·37	42·5	4,317·33
14	XVII	45·71	5·00	8·79	6·11	44·3	3,356·89
15	XXI	46·00	5·60	8·24	5·75	41·50	4,126·20
16	XXIX	48·28	4·95	7·86	5·60	43·70	4,217·74
17	XXII	50·00	4·70	8·17	5·94	46·20	4,633·20
18	I	51·42	5·60	8·85	6·34	43·9	5,085·64
19	XXVIII	53·14	4·03	7·64	5·13	44·00	4,152·68
20	IX	54·00	4·43	7·24	5·25	44·9	4,422·60
21	L	57·14	6·17	9·76	7·08	44·5	5,273·67
22	XXIV	58·00	5·48	8·87	5·68	39·5	5,140·25
23	XXX	60·00	4·90	9·14	5·70	40·6	5,336·13
24	XXV	63·06	5·10	8·17	6·12	46·1	6,018·35
25	XXVI	66·00	4·97	9·34	6·90	48·2	7,109·30
26	II	67·00	5·25	8·92	7·45	52·5	7,786·74
27	X	70·00	7·08	8·99	8·00	50·0	8,736·00
28	XIV	72·00	7·26	8·80	7·55	47·0	8,480·16
29	XI	74·00	7·00	9·15	8·11	50·0	9,362·18
30	XVI	76·00	6·95	9·66	8·05	50·8	9,544·08
31	XXVI	79·00	7·15	9·82	8·01	49·5	9,871·52
32	XXXI	70·00	7·09	8·88	7·98	49·9	8,714·16
33	XXXII	70·00	7·00	8·97	8·13	50·9	8,877·96
34	XXXIII	72·00	7·41	9·84	8·00	46·3	8,985·60
35	XXXIV	72·00	7·19	9·37	7·77	46·9	8,727·26
36	XXXV	75·00	7·12	9·45	8·10	48·9	9,477·00
37	XXVI	80·00	6·88	8·90	7·45	47·2	9,297·60
38	XXXVII	84·00	5·90	8·42	6·01	41·9	7,875·50
39	XXXVIII	88·00	5·26	8·00	4·48	33·7	6,150·14
40	XXXIX	70·00	6·05	8·65	7·78	52·9	8,495·76
41	XL	70·00	8·31	8·59	7·81	52·4	8,611·40
42	XLI	70·00	6·96	7·95	7·92	53·10	8,648·64
43	XLII	70·00	7·71	7·89	8·10	51·9	8,835·20
44	XLIII	70·00	7·00	8·02	7·96	53·0	8,692·32
45	XLIV	70·00	7·56	8·37	8·35	52·4	9,118·20
46	XLV	70·00	7·12	8·49	8·07	51·7	8,812·44
Average of last 5 experiments		70·00	7·27	8·14	8·08	52·4	8,821·3

ON BRASS (DURATION 3½ MINUTES)

Filings per hour	Nett hourly expenditure	Expenditure per Kilogram-metre	Expenditure per gramme of Filings	Rate of increase of		Various remarks
				Respiration	Pulse	
8	9	10	11	12	13	14
gr	Cal	Cal	Cal.	%	%	
20·57	105·04	0·046	5·10	21·4	16·8	
26·57	111·97	0·045	4·21	23·8	19·0	
27·14	112·13	0·048	4·13	20·6	25·1	
30·45	110·04	0·035	3·61	34·2	31·7	
35·53	117·26	0·030	3·30	35·0	30·9	Slight fatigue in the forearm. No trace of pain. The body a little bent. No oscillations.
31·90	115·28	0·034	3·61	29·7	26·1	
34·25	127·75	0·032	3·73	33·1	24·8	
22·28	111·84	0·042	5·01	22·4	19·6	
25·15	123·78	0·042	4·92	28·8	17·4	
25·71	124·77	0·042	4·85	28·8	22·5	
30·68	119·58	0·042	8·89	26·4	20·4	
31·58	117·83	0·043	3·73	20·9	17·3	
50·25	138·15	0·032	2·75	35·4	26·9	
51·14	139·42	0·032	2·72	36·8	25·7	
48·20	136·16	0·033	2·82	34·9	24·8	
49·70	139·18	0·033	2·80	35·0	26·1	
54·04	143·69	0·031	2·66	34·8	29·0	
56·07	167·82	0·033	2·99	38·9	28·9	Fatigue of the whole forearm as far as the elbow. A little pain. Slight oscillation of the body.
56·60	137·04	0·033	2·71	33·6	24·2	
45·57	132·71	0·030	2·91	36·9	27·1	
48·86	151·48	0·028	3·10	45·2	31·7	
48·20	149·07	0·029	3·08	45·0	29·3	
52·93	149·41	0·028	2·82	48·1	29·9	
57·45	178·80	0·029	3·11	46·9	30·7	
68·66	213·28	0·030	3·10	51·3	30·8	
70·25	218·10	0·028	3·10	47·7	31·9	
80·93	218·50	0·025	2·70	36·1	27·7	Fatigue appreciable.
82·30	228·97	0·027	2·78	39·9	32·3	
85·75	252·78	0·027	2·94	40·6	31·4	Fatigue and a little pain.
89·87	248·14	0·026	2·76	48·2	32·2	
93·78	256·70	0·026	2·73	48·7	31·9	
81·25	217·85	0·025	2·68	38·1	29·7	
82·01	221·95	0·025	2·70	33·9	30·1	Fatigue and a little pain.
81·97	233·65	0·026	2·85	37·4	21·9	
78·64	226·10	0·026	2·87	35·9	25·4	
86·08	255·90	0·027	2·97	39·3	29·9	
85·42	251·20	0·027	2·94	43·7	35·2	Pain very acute, stopping the work.
69·18	253·00	0·032	3·80	52·1	36·3	
49·96	211·47	0·034	4·23	54·7	35·9	
77·86	204·01	0·024	2·62	30·1	21·9	
78·40	204·62	0·024	2·61	29·4	22·3	A little fatigue. No trace of pain. No oscillations of the body.
78·63	198·93	0·023	2·53	27·9	19·4	
83·81	212·05	0·024	2·53	25·8	20·8	
78·71	199·93	0·023	2·54	26·4	22·1	
80·56	200·60	0·022	2·49	26·9	20·9	
84·59	211·49	0·024	2·50	25·3	21·4	
81·26	204·60	0·023	2·51	26·4	20·9	

Continuous work for $3\frac{1}{2}$ minutes causes a certain fatigue. At first this is confined to the right brachial triceps, the forearm, and particularly the elbow joint. Next, the fingers of the right hand are affected. Little fatigue is felt in the left arm. After a long period of work the fatigue is less localised, and generally affects, more or less, the whole of the upper portion of the body.

314. Various Conditions affecting the Use of the File.—The writer made a lengthy series of experiments with the object of determining the factors which influence, favourably or unfavourably, the economical use of the file. Apart from the internal factors, alimentation, health, physique, and so forth, there are the even more important " external factors," such as the position of the feet, the general attitude of the body, the manner in which the tool is held and manipulated, and the speed of the various motions.

The table on pages 430 and 431 embodies most of the experimental results obtained by the writer.

The following deductions may be drawn from the foregoing table :—

(a) *Influence of Frequency.*—Up to a frequency of 80 strokes per minute, an increase in the frequency of the strokes causes a corresponding increase in the work done as measured by the weight of filings removed. Such a frequency is about the highest at which the file can be satisfactorily used, and, above this figure, the work done actually diminishes. It is very difficult to work properly at 85 strokes, and almost impossible at 90 strokes per minute, even for two minutes continuously.

Working slowly, at 33 and 35 strokes per minute the hourly production of work is 2,200 and 2,400 kilogrammetres respectively, the weight of filings removed being 20 grammes and 26·5 grammes respectively. At double these speeds, *i.e.*, 66 and 70 strokes per minute, the production is more than trebled, *i.e.*, 7,000 and 8,000 kilogrammetres, and 68 and 81 grammes of metal removed, respectively.

An examination of the experiments Nos. 1 to 39 in the table show that a frequency of 79 strokes per minute gives the best hourly production of work. It will be seen that, within the above-mentioned limit, increase in the number of strokes per minute causes more efficient utilisation of the muscular effort developed. That of both arms together rises from 12 to nearly 18 kg., of which nearly $\frac{2}{3}$ is furnished by the left arm. It will also be seen that the " useful effort " increases from approximately 4 to 8 kg., and, as this latter increases more rapidly than the total muscular effort, the "co-efficient of utility" rises from 35% to 50%.

(b) *Influence of the Inclination of the Arms.*—In some cases variations in the inclination of the arms, relatively to the plane of the surface of the work, may result in different "co-efficients of utility" for the same total effort. Thus in Nos. 2 and 16 of the table the total muscular effort was approximately the same, but the useful efforts were 4·4 kg. and 5·6 kg. and the "co-efficients of utility" 35·5% and 43·7% respectively. Such variations are not, however, generally due to this cause, but result from increase in the total effort and the number of strokes per minute.

Measurement of the consumption of oxygen is the most accurate method by which the influence of other variables, such as the length and number of rest periods, position of feet, attitudes of the body, etc., can be discovered.

(c) *Relations between the Expenditure of Energy and the Rate of Filing.*—Columns 10 and 11 of the table give the expenditure in great calories per kilogrammetre, and per gramme of filings removed respectively. It will be observed that these are a minimum for a rate of 70 strokes per minute when they are ·025 Cal. and 2·7 Cal. respectively. At this rate the weight of filings removed per hour (Column 8) is about 82 grammes, and the hourly output of work (Column 7) 8,800 kgm. The muscular efforts of the right and left arms (Columns 3 and 4) are 7 kg. and 9 kg. respectively, the total useful effort per stroke (forward and return) is 8 kg. approximately, while the "co-efficient of utility" is 50% (*vide* experiments Nos. 27, 32 and 33).

(d) *Influence of the Attitude of the Workman.*—In the experiments Nos. 1 to 39, considered above, the workman leaned over the vice somewhat, the upper part of his body being inclined at an angle of about 20° from the vertical. In experiments Nos. 40 and 41 the body was maintained in an upright, though easy, position, no change being made in the position of the feet. This resulted in a reduction of about 4% in the hourly expenditure of energy (Column 9) and 3½% in the useful effort (Column 5) while the "co-efficient of utility" increased some 2½%. The output remained practically unaltered, hence the economy was somewhat increased. It may also be remarked that an easy upright attitude conduces to increased regularity in working.

The periodic oscillation of the body is another cause of fatigue, though this is but slight in the case of a skilled workman such as the subject "A.C." With other subjects the body is thrown forward during the working stroke and brought back with the return stroke. At high rates of filing a considerable amount of unproductive energy is thus expended. This unnecessary motion is conditioned by the positions of the feet, the distance of the workman from the vice, and the height of the latter in relation to that of the workman.

The following experiment was made in regard to the distance of the man from the vice (*vide* fig. 287).

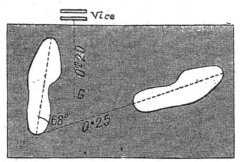

Fig. 287.

Best position for working at the vice.

The feet were placed in the positions shown, and the distance was measured from the umbilicus (G) to the vice. The workman was at rest, but he held the file on the work in the same position as if he was about to commence a stroke. The oxygen consumption for various distances was:

Distance in centimetres	15	20	25	30
Oxygen consumption in litres	1·045	1·03	1·036	1·07

The best distance, from this point of view, was, therefore, 20 cm. (*vide* fig. 287).

The relative positions of the feet shown in the above fig., namely, a distance of 25 cm. between the heels and an angle of 68° between the centre lines of the two feet was found to be the best for the subject " A.C." It must, however, be admitted that most workmen do not adopt such a position. They bring the left foot further forward and place the feet nearer together. They also lean slightly on the vice. It is clear that such an attitude calls for certain static efforts, the cumulative effect of which may be quite appreciable. Thus our experimental observations may be the means of improving the usual methods of working.

315. The Economical Use of the File.—After some little practice the journeyman fitter, A.C., became quite accustomed to this attitude, which the writer considered to be the most favourable.

In this attitude, as previously described, the workman held himself quite upright and placed his feet in the relative positions shown in fig. 287, the weight of the body resting chiefly on the left leg. The hands were applied to the file in the usual way, while care was taken that no pressure was applied during the return strokes. Under these conditions a speed of 70 strokes per minute gives the best economy. At this speed the output of work is steady, the fatigue relatively small, the respirations regular and, in general, the mechanical and physiological conditions favourable. The expenditure of energy per kilogram-metre, and per gramme of metal removed, do not exceed ·023 Cal. and 2·5 Cal. respectively. The results will, of course, be affected by any variations in the weight of the file, the effective length thereof which is actually used, and the shape and nature of the surface operated upon.

316. Effects of the Return Stroke and the Intervals of Rest.— It will be observed that the economical rate, 70 strokes per minute is about one quarter of the maximum " rhythm " of the shoulder joint (§ 91). We have seen that, in the return stroke, the right arm exerts an effort of ·55 kg., an almost negligible amount compared with the total effort. The relative duration of the working and return strokes varies with the speed of working, as is shown by the following table showing the times taken, in seconds, for the working and return strokes for various speeds of working :—

Strokes per minute	32	40	44	48	54	70
Time of working stroke	·72	·59	·58	·51	·36	·44
Time of return stroke	1·15	·91	·78	·74	·77	·42
Percentage of Total Period of Cycle :						
Working stroke	38	39	42	41	32	51
Return stroke	62	61	58	59	68	49

The results are somewhat irregular, but it will be noted that, at the economical working speed of 70 strokes per minute, the duration of the forward and return strokes is approximately equal.

The frequency and duration of the periods of entire rest naturally depend on the speed of working. At the speed of 70 strokes per minute continuous working for 3½ minutes caused fatigue of the right arm that was actually painful. At 54 strokes per minute the fatigue was much less and work could be carried on without inconvenience for continuous periods of as much as 10 minutes, if followed by two or three minutes of complete rest. As a rule, the ratio of rest period to working period should be about 1 to 5. Under this condition no disturbance of the physiological functions of the organism is generally to be observed after an hour's work other than an increase of about 20% above the normal in the rate of respiration and pulse.

Observations at some large Paris workshops show that a man can work at the vice for about 8½ hours per diem. Assuming the above proportion of actual working time to time of repose, this means 7 hours of actual working time and 1½ hours of rest interpolated therewith. Assuming the work per hour to be 8,800 kgm. the work per day is :

$$8,800 \times 7 = 61,600 \text{ kilogrammetres.}$$

The weight of metal removed would be :

$$82 \times 7 = 574 \text{ grammes.}$$

and the approximate expenditure of energy :

$$61,600 \times \cdot023 = 1417 \text{ Calories.}$$

317. The Work of the Apprentice.—The foregoing calculations have dealt with the work of the skilled mechanic. When we consider the work of an apprentice (fig. 279) we find that the mechanical and physiological conditions are less satisfactory.

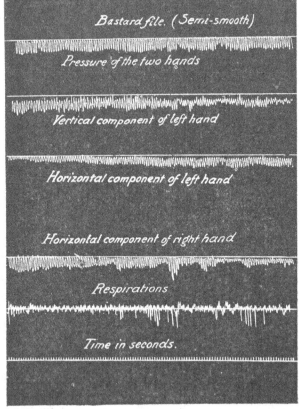

FIG. 288.

Graphical record of efforts and respirations of an apprentice.

The apprentice " X.P." (§ 312) who formed the subject of the writer's experiments was not, however, entirely an untrained worker, as he had had two years' experience. We can see, however, from the graphical record of his efforts (*vide* fig. 288) that these are defective in several respects.

The chief defects are irregular and spasmodic action leading to unduly rapid fatigue and conducing to breathlessness. Thus the pressures exerted by the hands vary very considerably, while the rate of working varied from 71 to 79 strokes per minute, which figure is far too high in view of the fact that the subject was only 16 years of age. If these high rates of working could have been maintained the work done would have been considerable, as much as 12,000 kilogrammetres per hour, and 85 grammes of metal removed in the same period. This was, however, quite impossible, as the subject was exhausted after two minutes work at the above rate. The irregular movements of the spirometer also showed that there was considerable respiratory disturbance. The muscular effort of the arms, 19 or 20 kg., was also excessive and badly distributed. It is clear, therefore, that the attitude and movements of the apprentice were uneconomical and inefficient. The expenditure of energy per kilogrammetre and per gramme of metal removed being on the average ·035 Calories and 4·9 Calories respectively (*vide* the following table), instead of ·025 Calories and 2·5 Calories in the case of the skilled journeyman fitter. In the case of this apprentice it was not possible to carry out the long and varied series of experiments which were made with the journeyman fitter " A.C." A considerable improvement was, however, effected in his attitude and methods by inducing him to assume an upright attitude, to place his feet in the position shown on fig. 287, and to work at a steady rate of 70 strokes per minute. The benefits of these conditions were apparent as soon as the apprentice had become thoroughly familiar with them. The expenditure of energy per kilogrammetre and per gramme of filings was reduced to ·03 Calories and 4·12 Calories respectively, a reduction of about 16%, and, had it been possible continuously to supervise his work and correct his attitudes and movements, it is probable that results would have been obtained not greatly inferior to those of the skilled workman. Fatigue would certainly have been greatly reduced. Thus, when the apprentice worked according to his own ideas, the rates of respiration and pulse were increased 54% and 35% respectively above the normal, after two or three minutes work. When his movements and attitude were regulated these increases were but 30% and 20%.

In the case of the apprentice the ratio of the rest period to the working period appears to be about 1 to 3 ; hence, in a total working day of 8½ hours, 6 hours will be spent in actual work.

"APPRENTICE" X.P.—BASTARD FILE ON

Numbers in order		Strokes of the File per minute	Muscular efforts		Useful effort of 2 arms	Co-efficient of Utility	Work done per hour
			Right arm	Left arm			
1		2	3	4	5	6	7
			kg.	kg.	kg.	%	kgm.
47	XLVI	71·42	8·05	10·90	10·41	54·9	11,598·3
48	XLVII	73·39	7·62	11·00	10·85	58·2	12,422
49	XLVIII	75·10	8·20	10·45	9·37	50·2	9,897·5
50	XLIX	76·20	7·10	12·53	8·95	45·5	10,530·6
51	LI	78·00	8·20	11·45	9·67	49·2	11,766·4
52	LII	78·90	7·81	10·16	9·04	50·4	11,126·8
Averages		75·5	7·83	11·07	9·71	51·6	11,223·6
53	LIII	70·00	8·45	10·85	9·80	50·7	10,702·8
54	LIV	70·00	8·90	10·40	9·15	47·4	9,991·8
55	LV	70·00	8·85	10·20	8·98	47·1	9,806·2
56	LVI	70·00	9·10	9·85	8·88	46·8	9,696·9
57	LVII	70·00	8·74	10·49	9·34	48·5	10,199·2
Averages		70·00	8·81	10·36	9·23	48·1	10,079·4

Taking the average results given in the foregoing table, we have :
11,222 × 6 = 67,322 kilogrammetres per diem.
80·45 × 6 = 482·7 grammes of metal removed per diem.
and the expenditure of energy is :

$$482·7 \times 4·87 = 2{,}356·75 \text{ Calories.}$$

In short, the work done per diem by the apprentice is about 15% less, and the corresponding expenditure of energy about 65% more than in the case of the skilled mechanic.

It need hardly be remembered that conditions of activity, at variance with scientific principles, are unfavourable both to the well-being and output of the workman.

318. Individual Variations.—The experience gained as apprenticeship proceeds is evident in the increasing output for the same expenditure of energy. The numerous graphical records which have been taken show that this is largely due to the adoption of a suitable speed.

These records, however, also show that even under definitely determined conditions, personal variations are exhibited which affect the results obtained. Thus the distribution of the efforts of the two arms during the working stroke, varies considerably. The writer was not able to make any experiments with left-handed

BRASS (DURATION 2 MINUTES.)

Filings per hour	Expenditure per kilogrammetre	Expenditure per gramme	Increases of		Remarks
			Respirations	Pulsations	
8	9	10	11	12	
gr.	Cal.	Cal.	%	%	
80·60	0·034	4·89	46·2	31·4	Accentuated swaying of the
85·12	0.032	4·67	49·8	32·2	body, stooping attitude, fati-
72·27	0·036	4·93	53·0	35·1	gue and a tendency to
81·17	0·038	4·93	51·9	30·8	breathlessness.
84·05	0·035	4·90	65·1	42·0	
79·50	0·035	4·91	59·9	40·0	
80·45	0·035	4·87	54·3	35·2	
77·36	0·030	4·15	36·6	20·1	Slight swaying of the body,
74·63	0·031	4·15	30·9	17·9	but less pronounced fatigue,
72·89	0·031	4·17	24·9	16·8	and regular respiration.
70·10	0·030	4·15	37·9	22·3	
74·44	0·030	4·11	45·6	27·7	
73·88	0·030	4·14	35· 0	21·0	

workmen, but he is inclined to think that such men apply their efforts more symmetrically than right-handed men.

Muscular atrophy and paralysis are shown by a more or less pronounced asymmetry of the efforts. For instance, the subject, E.A., who had hardly any power in his right arm, furnished a graph in which the horizontal component of the effort of this arm was insignificant, whilst that of the left arm was equal to 6 to 8 kilogrammes, and the same with the vertical components. In spite of this, the tracings are regular, E.A. being an experienced workman. In short-sighted people the necessity for bending down to the work results in an excess of fatigue.

Irregularity of muscular action as evinced by spasmodic variations in the heights of the ordinates of the curves is a sure sign of bad work and excessive expenditure of energy, which must tend to undue depreciation of the organism. As has been said above, such defects are only to be remedied by careful study of the respiratory exchanges and close supervision of the attitudes and motions of the workman. Matters which demand the attention of all those who desire the proper organisation of our workshops.

319. General Conclusions.—To determine the conditions of maximum output (with due regard to all physical and physiological variables), is the chief problem of industry. It is to be solved not by theory, but by practical experiment on truly scientific lines.

The above experiments are only true for tools of the specified nature and dimensions. They are, indeed, generally appliable to files of the same general dimensions, but of different cuts, but they are not correct for small files where a much higher speed of working is required which, in the case of a triangular file 17 cm. long, was found to be about 150 strokes per minute.

To recapitulate : With a flat bastard file, total length 34 cm., and effective length used 26 cm., the muscular work expended amounted to 65,000 kgm. in 8½ hours, out of which 7 hours were actually spent in work. The corresponding weight of metal removed was, at most, 600 grammes of brass. The expenditure of energy was ·023 Calories per kilogrammetre. This gives a net yield of

$$\frac{1}{·023 \times 425} = 12·3\%.$$

This small yield shows that filing is not a profitable method of utilising muscular activity.

We have also seen that the workman should hold himself upright but without stiffness, that he should stand at 20 cm. from the vice with his feet in the relative positions shown in fig. 287, that the left arm should be fully extended and should exert somewhat more pressure than the right arm, the respective figures being 8·5 kg. and 7·5 kg., for a total useful effort of 8 kg. We have also seen that no pressure should be exerted during the return stroke and that best economy is attained at a speed of 70 strokes per minute.

If the above conditions are complied with work can be carried out for continuous periods of five minutes followed by periods of complete rest for one minute. The rates of respiration and pulse do not then increase more than 25% and 20% respectively above the normal, the local fatigue of the forearm is bearable, and the general fatigue of the body is but slight.

The above output is at least double that obtained from the majority of workmen. The regularity of the graphical records of the muscular action of skilled workmen has been already pointed out by Imbert.[1] The irregularity and discontinuity exhibited in the work of unskilled apprentices and beginners, has already been referred to.

320. The Use of the Saw.—No definite experiments have been made in regard to the use of saws, on wood, metal or stone. We may, however, infer, from some workshop observations, that a

---

[1] A. Imbert, *Revue Generale de Sciences*, June, 1911, p. 485. *Comptes Rendus Acad. Sciences*, July 10th, 1911, p. 128.

man using a saw developes an effort of from 3 to 6 kg., and generally adopts a speed from ·3 metres to ·6 metres per second. The various factors affecting the use of the saw are at least as numerous as in the case of the use of the file. The daily output for seven effective working hours varies from 30,000 to 100,000 kilogrammetres. Poncelet and some other observers have stated that, in the case of a double-handed saw operated by two men the daily output reaches 160,000 kgm., the best results being obtained at a regular and moderate speed, a travel of ·45 metres, and a speed of 80 strokes per minute. The efforts exerted being 15 kg. on the working stroke and 1·8 kg. on the return stroke. The work per day of 8 hours would therefore be :

$$(15 + 1\cdot8) \ \cdot45 \times 80 \times 60 \times 8 = 290,304 \text{ kgm.}$$

i.e., 145, 152 kgm. per man.

The stooping position, which is necessarily adopted, causes considerable fatigue.

321. The Work of the Machinist.—Taylor carefully studied the various factors affecting output in the use of metal-working machinery, such as speed of cutting, feed, depth of cut, and shape of cutting tools. He found that very considerable improvement in the output could thus be affected. Taylor's experiments included the accurate timing of the various motions of men and machines, and a study of the various speeds, feeds, and cutting edges, suitable for different qualities of materials operated upon.[1] By this investigation of all the mechanical variables he was able to define the conditions needed for maximum output. Carl Barth [2] systematized Taylor's observations and laid down certain general rules resulting therefrom. The results of this work have had a profound influence on American workshop practice.

It must, however, be always remembered that the physiological factors in any industrial occupation must receive due consideration ; factors to which even Taylor seems to have given inadequate attention. During his twenty-six years of investigation he had before him the purely industrial problem of obtaining the maximum output from the best workshop equipment. He concluded that in all operations, where the work or the tool rotated, such as turning, boring and drilling, there were twelve variables to be considered :—(1) The nature of the material ; (2) The working diameter ; (3) The depth of the cut ; (4) the thickness of the shavings ; (5) the elasticity of the work and the tool ; (6) The shape of the cutting edge ; (7) The chemical composition of the tool steel ; (8) the temperature ; (9) the time taken

---

[1] Taylor (*Tran. of Amer. Soc. of Mech. Engin.*, vol. xxviii., 1906).
[2] Carl Barth (*Trans. of Amer. Soc. of Mech. Engin.*, vol. xxv., 1903).

for a complete cut ; (10) the pressure exerted on the edge of the tool ; (11) the speed and feed ; (12) the power needed to drive the machine.

After prolonged experiment it was found possible to devise formulæ to take account of all these mechanical variables.

The author's experiments have been directed chiefly towards the physiological aspect of the problem, to determine the maximum output possible without undue fatigue to the workman ; although it is recognised that these have been unfortunately inadequate for a complete solution.

It is none the less true that the intelligent and tactful application of the principle enunciated by Taylor will produce a remarkable increase in the output of both military and civilian labour if the goodwill and co-operation of the workers can be assured (*vide* § 346).

CHAPTER IV.

INDUSTRIAL WORK (Continued).

322. Work with Pruning Shears.—Imbert ([1]) measured the effort needed in trimming vine shoots with pruning shears (secateur) worked by one hand. This work in the " Midi " is performed by women. He obtained, by the methods already described the following results :—

Thickness of vine shoot, in millimetres	3·5	4·	6·75	10·5
Effort in kilogrammes	2·	3·4	4·4	13·

The average output of a good workwoman was 3,000 cuts, equivalent to an output of muscular effort of, at least, 27,138 kilogrammes. No determination was made of the expenditure of energy.

The variation in output of different women was about 100%. This variation was due to differences in manual skill which resulted in saving time as much as to variations in the thickness of the shoots cut. The experienced woman arranged matters so as to move her body as little as possible and to interupt the motion of the shears for only such a time as was needed to pass from one shoot to another. A graphical record of such work shows great regularity, except in the case of a woman new to the work.

323. Working in Wood.—No investigation has yet been made of the work of the joiner or the wood turner, nor has any scientific study been made of wood-working tools and machinery. It would seem to have been thought that such study would be wanting in practical value. Yet here also scientific organisation might render possible some reduction in the hours of labour, a desirable consummation since the dust of certain woods may have toxic qualities (§ 185).

324. Glass Polishing.—Amontons ([2]) made some measurements of this with a spring balance, and from his data it may be calculated that a glass polisher exerts an average effort of 12·24 kg. at a speed of ·97 metres for an effective working day of 10 hours, the daily production being 205,109 kilogrammetres. This figure must undoubtedly represent the maximum obtainable.

---

[1] A. Imbert (*Revue d'Hygiène*, 1909, p. 749 ; *Rev. Gén. des Sc.*, 1911, p. 481).

[2] Amontons (*Mém. Acad. Roy. Sc.*, 1699, p. 112).

325. Spade Work.—Before considering earlier experiments, Taylor's remarks on the subject should be considered. They are to the following effect :—" It might be thought, at first sight, that a few hours consideration would suffice to discover the essential principles involved in the use of spade or shovel. However, up till now, the writer has never come across any contractor who had any idea that scientific management could be applied to the use of the spade or shovel.

" For any man using a shovel, there is a given load corresponding to his maximum yield. . . . By selecting two or three men and paying them extra wages for doing reliable work and then gradually varying the shovel load and having all the conditions accompanying the work carefully observed for several weeks by men used to experiments, it was found that a first-class man would do his greatest day's work with a shovel load of about 10·250 kg.

Thousands of measurements were made with a stop watch, to find the speed at which a man, provided with a suitable implement, could drive his spade or shovel into the earth and lift it with a proper load. These observations were made on the removal of earth from heaps, the heaps standing on ground of irregular surface, on wooden planks, and on iron plates. The time was also carefully determined for the swing of the shovel in throwing the earth to various distances and heights."

Coulomb made some experiments on the value of the work done in digging. His subject shifted a total of 45¼ cubic metres per diem. He used a shovel weighing 1·7 kg. and the average weight of each spadeful of earth was 6 kg. The total load, spade and earth, was therefore 7·7 kg., which is a smaller load than that recommended by Taylor. Taking the average weight of a cubic metre of earth as 1898 kg., the number of spadefuls was :

$$\frac{45 \cdot 25 \times 1898}{6}$$

As the labourer lifted his spade to a height of ·4 metres the work done in lifting the earth was :

$$\frac{45 \cdot 25 \times 1898}{6} \times 7 \cdot 7 \times \cdot 4 = 43,000 \text{ kilogrammetres.}$$

He drove the spade into the earth to a depth of ·25 m. and exerted a pressure of 15 kg. The work done in this operation was therefore :

$$\frac{45 \cdot 25 \times 1898}{6} \times 15 \times \cdot 25 = 53,600 \text{ kgm.}$$

Coulomb's total was therefore about 100,000 kgm. per diem, or, adding the empty return motions, about 116,000 kgm. This is a relatively small value.

In the construction of embankments, the shovel is swung to a height of nearly 1·6 metres and the load of earth is consequently reduced to between 1½ and 2 kilogrammes. From 15 to 20 cubic metres can thus be shifted in 10 hours. Taking the higher figure in each case, the number of spadefuls was—

$$\frac{20 \times 1898}{2} = 18,980.$$

and the work done :

$$18,980 \times 1·6 \times 3·7 = 112,362 \text{ kgm.}$$

(taking the weight of the spade itself as 1·7 kg. as before.)

In spite of the length of the working day, this result is far from being the maximum obtainable, owing to the same load of earth lifted by each spadeful. Owing to the considerable amplitude of the movements much fatigue is caused to the muscles of the legs and the loins. The value of the muscular work is, therefore, very high, and, in addition, the muscles of the lower limbs are, to some extent, utilised.

326. The Action of the Legs. Use of the Wheelbarrow and Stone Truck.—Imbert investigated these operations from the mechancial and muscular point of view and not from the energetic aspect. His results are most interesting.

The transport of cut stones for the mason's use is often carried out by the stone truck (*cabrouet*) sometimes known as a "devil." In its use the work of the legs is no less important than that of the arms.[1] and the mechanical actions of the labourer consist in loading the truck, pulling or pushing it to its destination and unloading it. The methods given above (§ 210) were employed to register the efforts normally exerted on the handles, in support, loading and unloading, and those exerted in the direction of the handles in pushing.

A load of 60 kg. required an exercise of force by the right leg equivalent to that needed to mount a step 12 cm. high [2] and also called for an expenditure of force, by the extensor muscles of the trunk and upper members, equal to about 30 kg. This last result shows that such work is rather too heavy for youths of 15 or 16. The work is also less fatiguing for the tall than the short.

Imbert found that the work done in conveying 62 loads (of 60 kg. each) per hour over a distance of 24 metres along a smooth horizontal surface of concrete was certainly not less than equivalent to the following.

1. An ascent of a stairway with 62 steps, *i.e.*, an effort of between 25 and 30 kg. repeated 62 times.

[1] Imbert and Mistre, extract from the *Bulletin de l'Inspection du Travail*, 1905, No. 5, pp. 15-32).

[2] This effort is needed to balance the load on the truck. The comparison thereof with the effort in mounting a step is hardly satisfactory.

2. A journey, on the level, of about 3 kilometres.

3. A total effort, by the muscles of the upper limbs, of 1,862 kg. The work done by a subject weighing 70 kg. was :

$$\frac{3,000 \times 70}{16} = 13,125 \text{ kilogrammetres.}[1]$$

This, for a day of 10 hours, is 131,250 kgm.

327. The use of the two-wheeled stone truck (*cabrouet*) requires some attention. If the handles of the truck are held at the proper height, the centre of gravity of the load can be brought to lie vertically above the axis of the wheels. The labourer propelling the truck has then only to overcome the fractional resistances of the ground and the wheels (fig. 289). If, however, this is not the case, the centre of gravity will lie in front of, or behind, the axis of the wheels (*vide* fig. 290). If, for example, the centre of gravity of the load lies behind the axis of the wheels, at G_2 in fig. 291, the force will act partly on the axis O and partly on the arms of the labourer, and the " couple " will

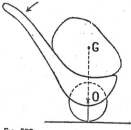

Fig. 289.

Position of the load on a stone truck.

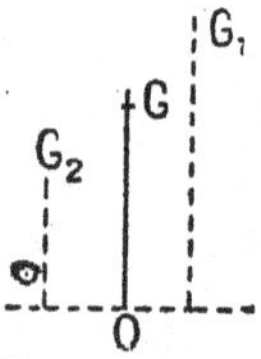

Fig. 290.

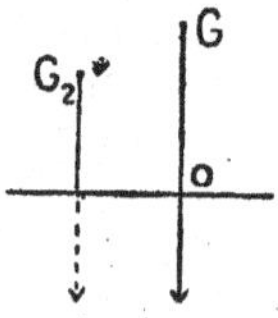

Fig. 291.

tend to turn the truck in the direction of the arrow. If, on the other hand, the centre of gravity of the load is in front of the axis, at G_1 the labourer will have to exert a downward pressure on the handles of the truck.

On sloping ground the conditions will be further modified. In fig. 292 let the centre of gravity G of the load lie vertically above the axis O (the inclined surface of the ground being shown by the shaded line). The force P has a component V at right angles to the surface of ground and producing the friction therewith, which friction

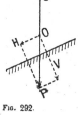

Fig. 292.

[1] The ratio of 1:16 between the metre-kilogramme and the kilogram-metre is here made use of.

will be less than on a horizontal surface. There is also a horizontal component, H, proportional to the inclination of the slope, which acts in opposition to the propulsive force.

Obviously a tall man has an advantage over a short man, since the former can more easily raise the handles of the truck so as to bring the centre of gravity of the load over the axis of the wheels, O.

Imbert made no calculations of the work done in wheeling the stone truck. He stated, however, that, on a smooth level surface, and with the centre of gravity of the load in the same plane as the axis of the wheels, the effort needed for propulsion was 3 or 4 kilogrammes. Taking an average effort of 3·5 kg the muscular work done by the arms in 10 effective hours would be :

$$3·5 \times 3,000 \times 10 = 105,000 \text{ kilogrammetres.}$$

The total daily work would therefore be :

$$131,250 + 105,000 = 236,250 \text{ kgm.}$$

Differences in the nature of the ground, over which the truck is wheeled, cause variations in the friction between the wheels and the soil, and may therefore considerably modify the above values. It is interesting to note that when working under normal conditions the rates of respiration and pulse are increased from 25% to 40% and from 17% to 20%, with various subjects. This is similar to the results observed in the use of the file.

There is not much general fatigue this being chiefly confined to the muscles of the arms, where it persists for a relatively long time. Little fatigue is experienced in the right leg owing to the strength of its muscles.

328. Use of the Wheelbarrow.—This has been investigated by the same general methods.[1] As this vehicle has only one wheel, the efforts needed to support and balance it under load are greater than in the case of a two-wheeled truck, or cart, such as the " *cabrouet.*" Imbert found that, if the load was centrally placed on the barrow, the effort of support was 42% of the total load, P. Taking a barrow weighing 29 kg., the effort of support in wheeling it empty will be :

$$\frac{29 \times 42}{100} = 12 \text{ kg., approximately.}$$

We can readily calculate the value of the net load x, numerically equal to the effort of support, from the equation

$$x = \frac{(29 + x)\ 42.}{100}$$

whence $x = 21$ kilogrammes.

---

[1] A. Imbert (*Bulletin de l'Inspection du Travail*, 1909, Nos. 1 and 2.

Hence it is only for loads exceeding this figure that the wheelbarrow offers any advantage. It is interesting to compare this result with those given in para. 287 above, where it was shown that the maximum economical load which can be carried directly, by a labourer, is also 21 kg.

A person using a wheelbarrow seldom employs muscular effort alone. The bent attitude generally adopted in wheeling a barrow shows that the weight of the body is also utilised. Hence a heavy man can do more work than a light man.

Imbert measured the tractive effort exerted in wheeling a loaded barrow along an ordinary gravel path (see para. 211 for the method of experiment). Under these conditions, the results obtained may be represented by the following formula :—

$$F. \text{ (tractive force)} = \cdot 043 \times P \text{ (load)}.$$

With a total load of 110 kg., wheeled on ground soaked by rain and very heavy, the tractive force rose to more than three times the above figure

$$F' = \cdot 132 \times P.$$

Leaving out of account, for the moment, the question of static forces, we can calculate that the work done by a man weighing 70 kg. in wheeling a barrow weighing 29 kg. loaded with 20 kg., a distance of 1 kilometre is :—

$$(20 + 29) \cdot 043 \times 1,000 + \frac{70 \times 1,000}{16} = 6,482 \text{ kgm.}$$

If, in a working day, the man covers 30 kilometres, the work done per diem would be 194,460 kilogrammetres.

We ought to add to the weight of the labourer a weight numerically equivalent to the downward pressure on the arms. For the same distance covered as above, but with a load of 60 kg, the total daily work would be :

$$(29+60) \cdot 043 \times 30,000 + \frac{(70+26)\,30,000}{16} = 332,310 \text{ kgm. (approx.)}$$

The above assumes that the weight sustained by the arms is 42% of the total load, i.e., 36 kg.

Under similar conditions the transport of loads by a wheelbarrow calls for more effort than by a stone truck (*cabrouet*), and, as Imbert observed, entails a greater increase in the rate of respiration (40%) and an increased, and more persistent, fatigue, especially in the arms.

The above outputs of work are in excess of those obtained from the average labourer, whose working day appears to be generally only 8½ hours.

329. Early Observations.—Coulomb measured, by means of a spring balance, the effort exerted in wheeling a barrow weighing

30 kg., and carrying a load of earth weighing 70 kg., over hard, dry ground. He found that the tractive effort, F, was 2·5 kg., whence we get the equation F = ·025 × P (load). Vauban, in his " Instructions " [1] laid down that a man could transport 14·8 cubic metres of earth a distance of 29·3 metres, making 500 trips in all. A total distance traversed (loaded and empty) of 14·6 kilometres, approximately.

The work done in the loaded trips was therefore :

$$14600 \times 2·5 + \frac{70 \times 14,600}{16} = 97,900 \text{ kgm.}$$

The tractive effort exerted in the return journeys was only :

$$\frac{30 \times 25}{1000} = ·75 \text{ kg.}$$

The work done was :—

$$14,600 \times ·75 + \frac{70 \times 14,600}{16} = 82,300 \text{ kgm.}$$

Coulomb found that the supporting effort was only 19% of the total load, i.e., 19 kg. on the loaded journey and 5·5 kg. on the return journey. (These figures are twice as favourable as those obtained by Imbert.)

The mean effort, per trip, was therefore :—

$$\frac{19 + 5·5}{2} = 12·25 \text{ kg.}$$

Adding the weight of the man, the supplementary work is :

$$\frac{12·25 \times 14,600 \times 2}{16}$$

The summation of all these quantities gives a total daily work of : 202,730 kilogrammetres.

330. The Two-Wheeled Barrow.—Gilbreth [2] observes that the two-wheeled barrow (fig. 293) causes less fatigue than the single-wheeled barrow because the load is better balanced in the former case. He found that the maximum economical load was 490 kg. The author considers, however, that such a heavy load entails excessive fatigue.

Guenyveau [3] found that a tractive effort of 3 kg. was required to transport a load of 70 kg. on a two-wheeled barrow itself weighing 30 kg. A total gross load of 100 kg. The effort needed to propel the same barrow empty was ·9 kg. ; 18 kilometres per day was covered.

---

[1] Vauban, *Instructions*, or the *Directeur General des Fortifications*.
[2] Gilbreth, *Motion Study*, p. 57 (G. Routledge & Sons, 1911).
[3] Guényveau, *Essai sur la Science des Machines*.

FIG. 293.

Neglecting static efforts the work done was :

$$18{,}000 \ (3 + \cdot 9) + \frac{18{,}000 \times 2 \times 70}{16} = 230{,}000 \ \text{kgm.}$$

To sum up the foregoing results : The transportation of loads varying from 60 to 80 kg. and a total distance traversed (loaded

Fig. 294. Subject No. 2 is pulling a heavier load than subject No. 1.

and empty) of 30 kilometres represents about the best attainable
result.

Fig. 295. A youth drawing a light load.

With a two-wheeled barrow the load can vary from 100 to 500
kg. In this case, however, we should introduce a number of
periods of rest.

All two-wheeled hand-carts fall into the same category as the
two-wheeled barrow, although they are generally pulled and not

Fig. 296. Instantaneous photograph shewing flexion of the knees.

pushed like a barrow.   The average co-efficient of traction reaches ·025 (§ 255).

An examination of the instantaneous photographs reproduced in figs. 294, 295 and 296 will show that the labourer makes considerable use of his weight, that the heavier the load the more he bends forward (*vide* figs. 294 and 295).   Often the knees are bent which, as previously pointed out, advantageously diminishes the vertical oscillations of the body (*vide* fig. 296).

331. The Bicycle.—In fig. 297 let P be the pressure exerted on the pedal and p the force transmitted by the chain, then

$$p = P \times \frac{oo'}{oA}$$

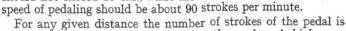

where oo′ is the radius of the crank and oA the radius of the chain wheel, experience shows that to obtain the best results the radius of the crank should not exceed 19 cm., while the

Fig. 297.

speed of pedaling should be about 90 strokes per minute.

For any given distance the number of strokes of the pedal is inversely proportional to the gear of the cycle.   A high gear calls for increased effort. The gear should therefore be proportional to the age and strength of the rider.

Leo Zuntz [1] measured the expenditure of energy during a bicycle ride of 5 or 6 minutes duration. He employed the method described in para. 288, mounting the gas measuring apparatus (which weighed 7·5 kg.) on the handle bars of the machine (*vide* fig. 298). The weight of the rider was 65 kg.   The total weight of rider, plus load, was therefore 72·5 kg.

At a speed of 15 kilometres per hour, the expenditure of energy per

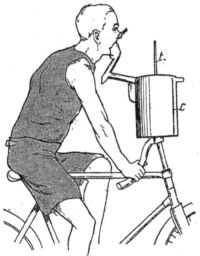

Fig. 298.

[1] Leo Zuntz, *Untersuchungen uber d. Gaswechsel und Energieumsaz des Radfahrers* (Thesis, Berlin, 1899) ;   Atwater, Sherman, and Carpenter (*Bulletin*, No. 98, p. 55, 1901).

metre covered was, on the average, 27 small calories, *i.e.*, a little more than one-third of a small calorie per kilogramme per metre. The expenditure of energy in riding a bicycle is therefore less than in walking. In longer rides at moderate speeds the above expenditure falls to ·26 small calories, but at a speed of 21 km. per hour it rises to ·37 small calories. In general, cycling is about twice as economical as walking. The best results are only to be attained by the use of a machine suited to the rider and the adoption of proper attitudes in riding. Bad attitudes, especially if the rider bends too low over the handle bars, cause rapid fatigue.[1] From his calculations of the work done and the expenditure of energy Leo Zuntz deduced a yield of 33%.

The comparatively high efficiency of the bicycle as a means of locomotion is due to the fact that it enables the powerful muscles of the lower limbs to be adequately utilised, while the frictional resistances of the machine itself are but small.

332. In many industrial machines, such as the grindstone or the foot lathe, the legs are utilised to effect the rotation of the apparatus. The motion of the foot is periodic, and its speed depends on the construction of the machine and the nature of the work being done. It will be observed that a knife grinder varies the speed considerably according to the nature of the work in hand and the pressure which it is necessary to exert on the revolving stone.

333. Miscellaneous Operations.—Typewriting.—Most of the occupations which have been considered above require a considerable expenditure of force. There are, however, others in which the force exerted is but trifling, while the speed is considerable, such as the operation of the sewing machine, the typewriter, the piano or stringed musical instruments. Speed of execution in such professions and occupations is due to both physiological and physical factors. Chief amongst the former is the " personal equation " of the subject, a purely individual characteristic, acquired or hereditary. Amongst the latter the flexibility of the joints of wrists, fingers and toes are important, which joints have several degrees of freedom (§ 75 and 81). These factors vary widely in different individuals. Apart from the stiffness and clumsiness due to inexperience the rate of reaction of the muscles to excitation varies considerably.

A distinction should therefore be made between subjects who are physically and physiologically adapted to occupations entailing rapid movement, and those who are suitable only for com-

---

[1] R. du Bois-Reymond, Berg, and L. Zuntz (*Arch. f. Anat. ü. Physiol.*, Suppl., 1904, p. 21).

paratively slow movement, and their occupations should be arranged in accordance with these characteristics (§ 162).

The use of the typewriter has been specially investigated.[1] Various experiments were made with five different subjects, at speeds varying from 57 to 115 words per minute, the physiological energy increasing from 30% to 70% of that when at rest. The average increase of energy per thousand words averaged 7 Calories, a consumption of 2·5 grammes of oxygen. The expenditure per 1,000 keystrokes was 1·6 Cal. The keys are displaced through a distance of 1·5 cm., and the pressure needed to depress a key is about 90 grammes. At a speed of 7 strokes per second the total mechanical work per hour is :

$$·090 \times ·015 \times 7 \times 3,600 = 34·02 \text{ kgm.}$$

Each stroke necessitates both the flexion and extension of the finger. The total muscular work is therefore about double the above figure, i.e. 68 kgm. or $\frac{1}{8}$ of a Calorie.

At the above rate of 1·6 Cal. per thousand key strokes, the hourly expenditure of energy would be :

$$\frac{1·6 \times 7 \times 3,600}{1000} = 40·32 \text{ Calories.}$$

It will be seen that the expenditure of energy is disproportionate to the useful work done, chiefly because of the intermittent nature of the motions. The typist could, however, do as much as ten hours work per diem without excessive fatigue.

Carpenter showed that economy is effected if the body is held upright, the forearms supported, and the strokes lightly and rapidly made.

The muscular work of the pianist is analogous to that of the typist. The keys are struck at a rate of from 6 to 8 per second (§ 231).

In general, it may be stated that fatigue results from the speed of working, from the concentration of attention needed, and very often from defective attitudes of body and limbs.

334. Sports and Pastimes.—Speed is the essence of success in many sports : hence unnecessary amplitude of movement is avoided. Thus, in fencing, the " parrying " of a thrust with the foil is an operation of great rapidity. The interval of time between the moment when the foil threatens the fencer and the moment when it is parried, is only about $\frac{18}{100}$ seconds. Deducting the time necessary to see the thrust, the " parry " occupies only about $\frac{1}{10}$ of a second. Marey stated that the speed of the foil in a straight thrust was 3·12 metres per second.

---

[1] T. Carpenter (*Journal Biol. Chem.*, vol. ix., p. 231, 1911).

Fencing calls for rapid displacements of the body and is fatiguing. Under normal conditions gymnastic exercises, without apparatus are satisfactory and hygienic. They strengthen the muscles and predispose the subject to better work.

Rowing can cause excessive fatigue. Some dynamo-metric measurements were taken with a boat manned by five rowers. It was found that at a speed of 5 metres per second the work done by each rower amounted to 22 kilogrammetres,[1] *i.e.*, 237,600 kgm. for an effective duration of rowing of 3 hours.

Boxing is a sport which makes severe demands on both strength and speed. The blow of the fist is delivered at a very rapid rate —6 to 8 metres per second ; but its total duration is of the same order as that of a sword thrust.[2]

As a rule, the conditions requisite for best results have been studied with some care in sports and warlike exercises, with the result that substantial progress has been made therein. Far less attention has, up to now, been accorded to similar studies on the arts of peace which are the source of human well-being. The failure adequately to investigate the conditions conducing to economy in human industrial labour is a sign of bad industrial organisation.

335. Nervous Activity.—The effective energy of man is not exclusively muscular. Many occupations call for intellectual activity and cause important " nervous expenditure." Skill is compounded of attention and intelligence. By long practice motions tend to become automatic. But such acquired qualities still demand for their rapid manifestation a certain expenditure of nervous energy.

The careful selection of persons whose qualities fit them for the work which they have to perform results in increasing output in factory and workshop. Taylor gives a simple example of this. Certain girls were employed in the examination of the steel balls for cycle bearings. The operation was as follows :—The balls to be examined were placed on the back of the left hand and rolled along between the closed fingers under a very bright light to detect scratches, dents or similar defects. The rejected balls were removed by means of a small magnet held in the right hand. The work needed the closest attention, the nervous fatigue of the girls was often considerable, although they were comfortably seated.

By careful selection of the workwomen, and by the control and direction of their movements, Taylor was able to reduce the working day to 8½ hours and at the same time increase the daily

---

[1] *Bull. Soc. Ing. Civ.*, Dec., 1888.
[2] Demeny (*La Nature*, Oct. 11th, 1890).

output. He found that the personal equation of the workers was an important factor. He considered that rest periods of 10 minutes duration should be interpolated after 75 minutes of work, and that during the day there should be four breaks during which the girls could walk about and talk to each other.

336. The Organisation of Bricklayer's Work.—The foregoing study of the use of the file has shown that the scientific investigation of the operations of a handicraft can produce economy and augment the yield of work.

Gilbreth[1] studied the work of the bricklayer in the same manner. The results obtained are equally comprehensive and instructive. He also made use of the mathematical method, which consists in studying separately the different variables of the operation under reference. These have been dealt with in Book IV. of the present work as internal and external conditions.

These conditions, as far as bricklayers' work is concerned, are as follows :—

(1) If the workman is left-handed, the usual positions of the bricks and the mortar will be reversed. All obstacles to rapid execution will be eliminated. The staging (*vide* fig. 299) will be

Fig. 299. Suitable staging for bricklayer's work
(after Gilbreth).

arranged to this end. It will be level, and its supports will be so located as to form no obstacle to the movements of the workman.

[1] Gilbreth (*Motion Study*, 1911).

(2) The load of bricks carried should not exceed 40 kg. for the very strongest labourer. Men of average strength should only carry from 27 to 31 kg. per load.

(3) The labourer should place the bricks and mortar within easy reach of the bricklayer (*vide* fig. 300) so that he has only to

Fig. 300. Bricks and mortar properly placed.

attend to the work of building. The top of the brick to be used should be at the height of the hand so that it can be held *vide* " B " of fig. 301, utilising the force of gravity to return the brick

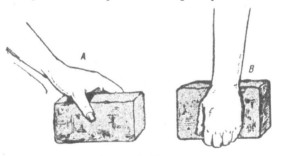

Fiu. 301.

in the hand and avoiding the necessity for a contracted grip, as at " A " in the same figure.

(4) As the height of the wall increases, the pile of bricks should be correspondingly raised, and in no case should it be necessary

for the bricklayer to stoop either to work or to pick up materials as depicted in figs. 302 and 303.   It is obviously absurd to move

Fig. 302.   Bricklayers stooping to pick up bricks.

the whole body to pick up a brick weighing 2 kilogrammes.

As an example of these bad methods we might take the case of labourers unloading paving stone from a cart.   One man picks

Fig. 303   Bricklayers working in a bent position.

up the stones from the ground, passes them to a second man, who throws them to a third man, who deposits them in an enclosure (*vide* fig. 304).

Fig. 304. Labourers handling paving stones, showing defective attitudes (J. Amar).

(5) Rapid work, under the foregoing conditions, only demands short intervals of rest, but this rest must be complete.

(6) The working platform of the scaffolding should be ·65 metres below the top of the wall.

Figs. 205 and 206 show suitable arrangements of scaffolding and building material.

Fig 305 Scientifically arranged scaffolding.

Fig. 306.   Building material scientifically arranged.

(7) The bricklayer will have at hand a support in which to rest his trowel. The mortar will be properly prepared without lumps or stones in it. The trowel should be of a special type, by which the mortar can be spread on several bricks at once. Gilbreth recommends the " Fontain " pattern of trowel, with which 21 bricks at a time can be spread with mortar.

(8) The bricklayer's labourer should use a two-wheeled barrow, since he can thereby transport 216 bricks with the same fatigue as 60 bricks can be transported with a single-wheeled barrow (the ordinary brick measures $22 \times 11 \times 5.5$ centimetres).

(9) The weight of the tools is of some importance ; the hammer used should weigh from 1·8 kg. to 2 kg. The shovel for mixing the mortar should weigh 9·75 kg. A smaller trowel should be used for pressed bricks and a larger one for ordinary bricks.

Enhanced output is not to be attained by improvement in tools and appliances alone. Gilbreth also gave attention to the " internal factors," the nourishment and the mental and bodily health of the worker, and he specially studied the problems of economic movement, and came to the following conclusions :—

(10) The feet of the workman should be so disposed that the bricks can be rapidly laid without any unnecessary movements of the body. The hands should move symmetrically and evenly. The movements should be combined to serve various purposes. Fallen mortar should not be picked up during working. It is cheaper to fill a space less than half a brick in width with good cement than to spend time in cutting a brick to suit or in looking for a suitable piece to fill the space.

(11) The motions of the bricklayer should be restricted to those actually needed for the work he is doing, thus a bag of cement

should not be opened by tearing the paper and separating the pieces, but the paper at the base should be broken by a blow of the shovel and the bag emptied by pulling on one end.

(12) The speed of the various movements is a factor of the greatest importance in attaining the best results. When the defects of the ordinary methods of bricklaying had been fully analysed, an instruction card was prepared which laid down, for the guidance of the workman, the proper arrangements, attitudes and motions to be adopted and the unnecessary movements to be eliminated.

If Gilbreth's methods are faithfully followed it is possible to eliminate no less than 13 movements out of 18 which usually are made in the laying of a brick, indeed by special arrangement it has been found possible to lay a brick with two movements only.

It will be clear from the above that proper organisation and equipment in bricklaying is at least as important as manual skill and the proper utilisation of muscular force.

Gilbreth quotes the following case as a practical example of the advantages of scientific methods. The work was the construction of the walls of a factory. The walls were ·3 metres in thickness. Two kinds of bricks were used, and the joints were pointed on both faces. Under ordinary conditions 120 bricks were laid per man per hour. By the application of the foregoing principle this output was nearly tripled, 350 bricks being laid per man per hour.

337. To sum up, the American engineers to whom the application of the above principle is due, recognise unanimously that there are four main conditions which have to be met to obtain the best output both in quantity and quality from the workman.

1. The correct determination of the laws and circumstances of the work, according to the adequacy of the tools.

2. Education and even elimination of unskillful workmen so as to have only those absolutely fitted for the work.

3. The control by well-informed and sympathetic foremen to encourage good workmen and correct the bad.

4. The equal distribution of labour and responsibility between employers and employed to create between them a unity and an understanding which will benefit all.

The first condition is, assuredly, the most important, but it is no less certain that the workman must be patiently but continuously supervised. Written instructions are insufficient; they soon become part of the routine and their observance is neglected. The management must assure itself that the workman does really understand and apply such instructions and that he realizes that scientific methods in industry are as much to his advantage as to that of his employers.

Finally the endeavour must be made to allocate men to the work for which they are most suited, and to assure that his well-being and interest are not sacrificed to obtain financial results.

We will, in conclusion, quote two cases which exemplify both the general character of these scientific methods and also the care that is needed in their application.

(1) In the office of *Industrial Engineering* some 20,000 letters a day were sent out which had to be folded and stamped. By careful attention the time taken in these simple operations was reduced to one-fourth of the previous time. One of the girls engaged on this work was able to stamp from 100 to 120 envelopes per minute without any abnormal fatigue. The envelopes were set up on edge in a long row, the addressed sides facing the operator. The sheets of postage stamps were torn into horizontal strips. The girl had a small sponge fixed to the index finger of the right hand. Taking a strip of stamps in the same hand she drew them across the sponge to moisten the gum, using the thumb to move the strip and guide the stamps into their proper positions on the corner of the envelopes. With her left hand she drew forward the stamped envelopes from the pile using the left thumb to give the necessary pressure on the stamps and to detach the latter from the strip. Lastly, the finished letters fell by their own weight into a basket.

2. A friend of Gilbreth's, visiting the Anglo-Japanese Exhibition in London, noticed a girl who was putting circulars into boxes of boot polish at a wonderful speed. He led the American there to show him how, by instinct, the girl applied the right method. But Gilbreth had no sooner examined the work than he pulled out his stop watch, noticed the unnecessary movements and took the time necessary to prepare 24 boxes, which was 40 seconds. He then told the girl that she was doing her work badly. The latter, very sure of her skill, made fun of him, but consented to leave out the movements that he considered unnecessary. As she was doing piece-work she was tempted by the idea of a higher wage. In a few days the girl was able to do the 24 boxes, no longer in 40 seconds, but in only 26 seconds. She declared, in addition, that the reduction of the number of movements of her muscles had made the work less tiring.

What more instructive lesson than this of the necessity for scientific organisation of labour ?

Gilbreth also maintained that a handwriting which was characterised by unnecessary flourishes and similar peculiarities was anti-economic.

Taylor's system has gained ground in industry owing to the undoubted value of its practical applications. In effect he put into practice the theoretical conclusions which had already been set forth by Chauveau, although it is not known whether he was at first acquainted with that scientist's work. This application was, however, incomplete, inasmuch as the important question of the degree of fatigue was not dealt with by Taylor.

338. The Expenditure of Energy in Speaking.—A man expends muscular energy in speaking as well as in lifting a weight. The work done in the production of speech is complex in its nature. It comprises *phonation* in the strict meaning of the term which is the emission of a volume of air varying according to the speed of talking and the intensity of the sound. If air of volume V is inspired or expired under a pressure H, the work done in these respiratory movements, $T = V \times H$.

The pressure H should be measured in the treachea, or wind-pipe, of the subject by means of a tube joined to a manometer (*vide* fig. 307). The volume V is measured by a spirometer at the temperature of the lungs and at atmospheric pressure.

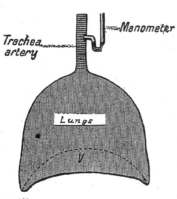

Fig. 307.

Diagram of lungs and broniceal tubes.

Cagniard-Latour ([1]) was the first to make an observation of this kind, on a subject 32 years of age, whose larynx was, as the result of an accident, perforated by a hole of ·8 cm. diameter. The manometer indicated a positive pressure of 4 cm. of water in expiration and a negative pressure of 5 or 6 cm. in inspiration, or an average respiratory pressure of about 5 cm. An adult displaces per hour a volume of air of about 500 litres. Hence the work done $T = 500 \times ·05 \times 2 = 50$ kilogrammetres. "We see, therefore," says Caigniard-Latour, "that the efforts exerted in the motor insufflation of the vibrations of the larynx are not so small as might have been anticipated in view of the apparently effortless manner in which the voice is employed under ordinary conditions."

([1]) Cagniard-Latour (*Comptes Rendus Sciences*, vol. iv., page 201, 1837.

The same scientist observed a pressure of ·3 metres in playing a clarionet. As the gaseous exchanges are considerably increased in this exercise the work expended in phonation rises to about 550 or 600 kilogrammetres.

Marage ([1]), who made certain investigations in the year 1904, describes two interesting cases. The first was that of a man who had undergone the total ablation of his larynx. Marage by means of a flexible tube effected a junction between the patient's trachea and a membraneous rubber reed fixed to an artificial palate. This tube was connected to a manometer which indicated a pressure varying from ·1 m. to ·2 m. during ordinary conversation. The quantity of air expired per hour was 2,070 litres. Hence :

$$T = 2,070 \times 2 \times ·15 = 621 \text{ kilogrammetres.}$$

The second subject ([2]) had a tracheotomy tube enabling H to be measured. The average value was ·13 m. and the volume of air V 300 litres. Hence when at rest :

$$T = 300 \times 2 \times ·13 = 78 \text{ kilogrammetres.}$$

The experiment with the artificial larynx does not represent natural conditions, the efforts are abnormal, and the volume of air expired per hour (2,070 litres) was excessive. Such conditions are fatiguing.

With the second subject, when speaking in a large room, V was 1,440 litres and H varied from 10 to 20 centimetres. Hence T issued from 288 to 576 kgm. An average of 434 kgm. We may infer that with the natural larynx the work done in phonation may vary from 50 to 600 kilogrammetres.

The expenditure of energy is very considerably increased when the speaker has to make himself clearly heard throughout a large hall. The comparative effort, needed with various qualities of voices, to attain equal range and distinctness, has been measured by having the same note sung by three singers, a bass, a baritone, and a tenor. The comparative results were as follows :—

HALLS	TENOR	BARITONE	BASS
Sorbonne (amphitheatre Richelieu)	1·00	0·24 (?)	7·14
Sorbonne (Chapelle)	4·19	5·71	42·38
Academy of Medicine	1·42	4·28	12·38
Trocadero	4·19	5·71	66·66

([1]) Marage (*Journal de Physique*, 1908, p. 298).
([2]) *Id., Ibid.*, and *Physiologie de la Voix*, Paris, 1911).

Thus the tenor expends less energy, for equal range and distinctness of articulation, than the baritone or the bass voice. Generally a speaker will exceed the minimum values given above, since he has to make himself easily heard to all his audience. Careful articulation increases the effective range of the voice.

If men, women and children are compared, it is found that, for the same effect, women tire four times less than men, because their vocal cords are shorter. The advantage is greater still in children, who, as every one knows, talk with an extraordinary volubility.

The limits of the human voice are:

Bass. F_1 to F_3 equivalent to 174 to 696 simple vibrations.
Tenor. C_2 to C_4 ,,   261 to 1,044   ,,
Alto F_2 to F_4 ,,   348 to 1,392   ,,
Soprano C_3 to C_4 ,,   522 to 1,044   ,,

The limits of auditory perception correspond to a *minimum sonorous intensity* acting on a plane at right angles to the path of the sound waves. The ear is most sensible to sounds having a frequency of about 500 vibrations per second. This means an expenditure of energy of about one hundred thousandth of an erg per second per square centimetre. This quantity of energy is so minute that one kilogrammetre would sustain the sound for many thousand years. The sensation of the persistence of a sound sung after it has actually ceased is the more marked the lower the note. The acoustic properties of large halls depend on their cubic contents and the absorption caused by the walls, the furniture and the audience itself. The best results are attained when the period of resonance lies between $\frac{1}{2}$ and $\frac{2}{3}$ of a second. If the capacity of a hall is C, the absorption of the walls A, and N the number of persons present. The duration of the resonance T can be obtained from the following equation:

$$T = \frac{\cdot 17 \ C}{\cdot 44 \ N + A}$$

The fatigue experienced by a speaker depends therefore on several variable qualities, some of which are unknown.

339. The Expenditure of Energy in Speaking.—The expenditure of energy by a speaker or a vocalist can only be measured by a *calorimetric chamber* similar to that of Atwater and Benedict. The respiratory valve which is employed in other cases to measure the consumption cannot be easily employed in this case, as it obstructs free vocalisation. The results of an experiment made with this apparatus, with a valve adjusted to the mouth by a large rubber membrane, may, however, be given.

The subject was 30 years of age, and weighed 69 kg. When at rest the following results were obtained :—

Gaseous exchanges per hour: 565·3 litres, CO_2 2·55%, O_2 3%

$$\frac{CO_2}{O_2} = .855.$$

Consumption of oxygen per hour $\dfrac{565\cdot3 \times 3}{100} = 16\cdot96$ litres.

After a recitation at such a voice as to be clearly audible at a distance of 6 metres from the speaker in a room of 250 cubic metres capacity, the subject reciting at an average speed of 150 syllables per minute while seated motionless in a chair the results obtained were as follows:—

Gaseous exchanges per hour : 799·5 litres CO_2 3·1% O_2 3·6%

$$\frac{CO_2}{O_2} = \cdot86.$$

Consumption of oxygen per hour $\dfrac{799\cdot5 \times 3\cdot6}{100} = 28\cdot78$ litres.

The gaseous exchanges in both cases are reduced to 0°C and 760 mm. barometric pressure

The expenditure of energy in phonation was therefore : 28·78 — 16·96 = 11·82 litres of oxygen, equivalent to 11·82 × 4·9 = 57·92 Great Calories per hour.

It is known that a man who climbs a mountain quickly, expends 4 Calories per 425 kilogrammetres effected (an average yield of 25%). The equivalent in work done in lecturing in a loud voice for an hour, and without other movements will be :

$$\frac{57\cdot92}{4} \times 425 = 6,154 \text{ kilogrammetres.}$$

equivalent to an ascent of a 100 metres up a mountain, at a speed of 100 metres an hour.

It must be pointed out, however, that the orator, the singer, and the actor make numerous muscular movements and gestures whose energetic equivalent must be added to the preceding expenditure. To produce expression the artist brings into play his limbs and muscles, so that the work of phonation is inappreciable in comparison with all this muscular activity.

Speaking causes a perceptible increase both in the frequency of the respirations and also in the depth of the inspirations and expirations, the former are more prolonged than the latter, in a ratio of about 2 to 1 (*vide* fig. 308). It will be observed that respiratory curves are unequal and irregular, and it would seem that during speaking the thoracic enlargement is maintained and diminishes but slightly, the expirations being brief.

340. Intellectual Work.—It has already been stated that Atwater, after numerous experiments, could not find that the

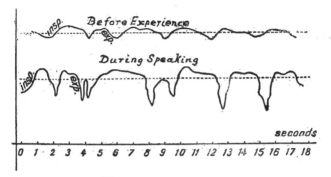

Fig. 308.
Respiratory curves of an orator.

most intense intellectual work gave rise to any expenditure of energy measurable in calories. Thus when a scientist was enclosed for three days in a calorimetric chamber while engaged in heavy intellectual work (the study of a German treatise on physics), no appreciable increase in the static expenditure could be observed.[1] Nevertheless we know that mental activity has definite physical and physiological effects (§ 149). It diminishes muscular power, produces toxic substances in the organism and causes general fatigue. If continued for long periods, ten hours or more, the circulation is retarded, the properties of the nervous matter are modified, the reaction to external stimuli decreases, the personal equation increases, and the senses, in general, become less alert.

Although the expenditure of energy in intellectual work cannot be measured as that expended in muscular labour, yet it is certain that as far as *fatigue* is concerned the difference is one of degree, not of kind. Hence, in all intellectual occupations, a consideration of the fatigue involved must not be neglected.

Mental activity, as muscular exertion, can be organised and directed. Great intellectual power is often dissipated uselessly by confused and unsystematic methods of thought. This is generally the result of unscientific training and the failure to acquire the habit of reasoning logically. The delicate mechanism of the brain must not be overstrained. Such matters, however, belong to the domain of psycho-physiology.

341. Food and Occupation.—Since the expenditure of muscular and nervous energy differs in various occupations, it would be reasonable that the nourishment provided for the body should be arranged with due regard to the exertion which it is called to undergo. Certain investigations have been made on this subject.

[1] *Bulletin*, Nos. 44 and 136 (1897 and 1903).

In the case of a man eating his usual food, and at rest, the writer ([1]) found that the equivalent value of the alimentary ration was 1·57 Calories per kilogramme per hour. Gautier ([2]) gives the value as 1·6 C. Hirn gives 1·53 C., while the American experimenters obtained (in an environment of 20° C. in temperature) 1·32 C. The average seems to be about 1·5 C. under ordinary conditions.

The gross dynamic expenditure includes the expenditure caused by the work done which varies with different subjects. Inquiries have therefore been made as to the consumption of foods by families in various countries. To enable comparisons to be made certain co-efficients have been arrived at in accordance with the following table ([3]) :—

Man	... 1·00	Child of 10 to 13	0·60	Child of 2 years and
Woman	... 0·80	„ 6 to 9	0·50	under ·30
Boy or girl				
(14 to 16)	0·75	„ 2 to 5	0·40	

The consumption of a family composed of husband, wife, and a boy of 15 years would be

$$1 + 0·80 + 0·75 = 2·55 \text{ times that of the man alone.}$$

Ch. Richet, as the result of certain investigations on the food consumed by families in Paris, arrived at the conclusion that the average ration per adult for 24 hours had a value of 3,262 Calories having the following percentage composition by weight :—

Proteids	....	17·5%
Fats	....	11·5%
Carbo-hydrates	....	71· %

Gautier's results agree with the above as far as the composition of the food is concerned. He obtained, however, a lower and probably more correct value of 2,568 Calories. This gives :

$$\frac{2,568}{65 \times 24} = 1·65 \text{ C. per kilogram-hour.}$$

Approximately equal values were obtained by Lapicque ([4]) (on Abyssinians and Malays, 1·6 C), Mori ([5]) and Tahara ([6]), whose results, with Japanese subjects averaged 1·65 C. The rations investigated by the last three authorities consisted chiefly of rice and vegetables. The difference between 1·65 C. and 1·5 C. i.e. ·15 C. represents the dynamic expenditure per kilogram-hour in ordinary

([1]) Jules Amar, Le Rendement de la Machine Humaine, pp. 57 and 72.
([2]) Armand Gautier, L'Alimentation et les Regimes, 3rd edition, 1908.
([3]) Engel (Bull. Inst. Internat. de Stat., vol. ix., p. 5, 1895) ; Atwater (Annual Report of the Office of Exper. Stations, 1903, p. 33).
([4]) L. Lapicque (Comptes Rendus Biol., 1893, pp. 251-8 ; Archives de Physiol., 1894).
([5]) Mori (Arch. f. Hygiene, vol. v., p. 333, 1886).
([6]) Tahara (Bull. Inspect. Sanit. Labor, Tokio, No. 2, 1887).

life. This gives for 10 hours :

·15 × 65 × 10 = 97·5 Calories.

Taking 25% as the average yield the corresponding amount of work done per day of 10 hours is small, namely :

97·5 × ·25 × 425 = 10,400 kilogrammetres.

For work amounting to 70,000 kgm., the writer [1] and Atwater [2] obtained values averaging 1·9 C. per kilogram-hour.

The expenditure of energy, naturally, rises with increased production of work.

The American scientists investigated the diet of nearly 14,000 persons in the northern states of America, taking the consumption of foods from the records of public institutions, schools, factories, etc. They found that the proportion of proteids, which increase bulk rather than give nourishment, was excessive. The average of their observations was as follows :—

SUBSTANCES	PROTEIDS	FATS	CARBO-HYDRATES
Animal foods	72 gr.	118·40 gr.	24·30 gr.
Vegetable foods	51 gr.	14·00 gr.	363·30 gr.
	123 gr.	132·40 gr.	387·60 gr.

342. The *Institut Solvay* carried out inquiries in 1,250 working class homes in Belgium (equivalent to about 6,000 individuals) [3]. Records were taken of the food consumed in a fortnight. The working men in question were of various trades, miners, agricultural labourers, weavers, quarrymen, and others. In spite of the fact that they were engaged in heavy manual labour their daily consumption of proteids did not average more than 90 grammes, being highest in the heaviest trades and best paid occupations and least in the lightest and worst paid occupations.

The heat value of the food consumed in 24 hours was about 50 Calories per kilogramme, chiefly contributed by fats and hydro-carbons, *i.e.*, approximately 2 Calories per kilogramme-hour.

The report of the above enquiry draws attention to the great diversity of the food of the working classes both in quality and

---

[1] Jules Amar, *Le Rendement*, p. 72.
[2] Atwater and Benedict (*Bull.*, 109, p. 140, 1902).
[3] A. Slosse and E. Waxweiler, *Recherches sur le Travail Humain dans L'Industrie*, Bruxelles, 1910.

quantity. The opinion is expressed that it is faulty, badly compounded, and generally not well chosen for the physiological purposes which it is supposed to satisfy, further, it is often insufficient (loc. cit., p. 109).

It should be noted that all the inquiries which have been made as to the food of the working classes have, with few exceptions, led to the same general conclusions as are above set forth.[1]

The results, tabulated below, for various trades, are interesting :—[2]

TRADES	PROTEIDS	FATS	CARBO-HYDRATES	CALORIFIC POWER [3]
	gr.	gr.	gr.	Cal.
Builders	204	264·00	714·00	6,166·20
Sailors	140	145·00	558·00	4,181·30
Barge men	171	171·00	460·00	4,143·20
Mechanics	153	139·00	528·00	4,057·00
Carpenters	151	154·00	459·00	3,902·40
Labourers	142	142·00	444·00	3,694·80
Costermongers	141	164·00	377·00	3,616·20
Agriculturists	139	119·00	345·00	3,067·30
Pedlars	104	129·00	344·00	3,010·70
Jewellers	101	106·00	296·00	2,592·30
Watchmen	87	96·00	296·00	2,443·90
Dyers	72	98·00	314·00	2,474·00
Pensioned Sailors	96	129·00	181·00	2,309·60
Woodcarvers	87	89·00	262·00	2,240·80
Domestic servants	57	41·00	237·00	1,578·50
Averages	123	132·40	387·60	3,298·30

[1] Inquiries on alimentation are numerous. We quote :
In England : Rowntree, Poverty : a Study of Town Life, London, 1902 ; Paton, Dunlop & Inglis, A Study of the Diet of the Labouring Classes in Edinburgh, 1898 : Cameron, Preced. of Roy. Soc. of Edinburgh, 1906.
In Belgium : Slosse & Waxweiler, loc. cit. ; A. Lonay (Revue d'Hygiène Alimentaire, 1906, p. 70) ; Julin (La Réforme Sociale, 1891-2).
In Sweden : Hultgren and Landergren, Untersuchung ü. die Ernahrung Schwedischer Arbeiter, Stockholm, 1891).
In Germany : Ohlmüller (Zeitsch. f. Biol., 1884) ; Voit (Ibid., 1889) ; Stefan, Die Ernahrung des Bauern. Dissertation, Würzburg, 1890.
In France : Maillard (Revue d'Hygiène Alimentaire, 1909) : A. Imbert (Ibid., 1906) ; de Maroussem, la Question Ouvrière. Ebénistes du Faubourg Saint-Antoine, Paris, 1892) ; Landouzy and Labbe (Presse Medicale, 1905) ; O. Piecquet (Revue d'Hygiène Alim., 1906).
In Italy : Albertoni, Sul Bilancio Nutritivodi del Contadino Italiano, Bologne, 1894 ; id., Sul Bilancio Nutritivo di una Familia Borgese Italiano.

Tiegersted ([4]) divided working class diets into seven classes, in accordance with the calorific value of the food.

1. From 2,000 to 2,500 Calories
2. „ 2,500 to 3,000 „
3. „ 3,000 to 3,500 „
4. „ 3,500 to 4,000 „
5. „ 4,000 to 4,500 „
6. „ 4,500 to 5,000 „
7. „ 5,000 and above.

The following table gives the composition and average value of the diet in each of the above classes (the letter *t* denotes Tiegersted's results, and the letter *a* the mean results of the American investigators) :—

CLASSES		CARBO H'DRATES	FATS	PROTEIDS	ENERGY	PER KILO- GRAMME HOUR
		gr.	gr.	gr.	Cal.	Cal.
1	*t*	295	81	86	1921	1·13
	a	362	44	82	2007	1·21
2	*t*	345	108	88	2501	1·50
	a	464	60	104	2600	1·54
3	*t*	409	125	103	2936	1·75
	a	466	85	127	2900	1·71
4	*t*	476	137	125	3364	2·00
	a	556	93	136	3332	2·00
5	*t*	538	158	116	3762	2·25
	a	569	135	162	3827	2·29
6	*t*	557	195	145	4223	2·50
	a	737	106	182	4277	2·54
7	*t*	666	235	145	4954	2·92
	a	952	156	166	5433	3·25

It will be readily seen from the above tables that the proportion of proteids is relatively high in working-class diet. Pflueger, and others of his school, have maintained that this is essential. The experimental results obtained do not, however, conclusively

1897 ; id. and Rossi, *Bilan Nutritif du Paysan des Abruzzes.*, *Arch. Ital. Biol.*, 1908, etc.

In Africa : L. Lapicque (*Arch. de Physiol.*, 1894) ; Jules Amar, *Le Rendement de la Mâchine Humaine*, 1910.

([2]) Atwater and Woods (*Bull.*, No. 46, p. 117) ; Atwater and Bryant *Bull.*, No. 116, pp. 74-75). The figures relating to domestics are doubtful.

([3]) The calorific power is calculated here from our co-efficients 4·10 Cal., 9·10 Cal., and 4·10 Cal. (§ 96). Atwater provisionally adopted Rubner's figures, 4·10 Cal., 9·30 Cal., and 4·10 Cal.

([4]) Tiegerstedt, in *Nagel's Handbuch*, vol. i., p. 549, 550.

support this view. Thus many races (Tyrolese, Africans, Japanese, Chinese, etc.) consume a far higher proportion of carbohydrates than of proteids. The Finns, for example, hardly consume 40 grammes of albumens per diem.([1])

The foregoing inquiries have established two important facts :

(1) The gross dynamic expenditure in the case of heavy work can reach 80 Calories per kilogramme per diem, *i.e.*, 3·33 Calories per kg. per hour. Under normal condtiions it appears that this expenditure cannot be exceeded for several days continuously.

This gives for an adult weighing 65 kg. a total calorific equivalent of 80 × 65 = 5,200 Calories in 24 hours.

The static expenditure in the same period was found to be 1·5 × 24 × 65 = 2,320 Calories.

Hence the greatest daily total of work is equivalent to ·25 (5,200 − 2,320) = 715 Calories = 300,000 kgm., approximately.

(2) The normal diet is generally the most readily assimilated and gives the best yield. It should not be altered, but attention should be directed to improving its quality and assuring that it is adequate in quantity and proportions.([2])

343. Beverages.—The following table gives the total annual consumption of alcoholic drinks in France for the years 1907 and 1908 :—

TOTAL ANNUAL CONSUMPTION (IN HECTOLITRES).

YEAR	VARIOUS WINES	CIDERS, PERRY, HYDROMEL	DRIED GRAPE WINES	BEERS	SPIRITS
1907	69,107,201	3,333,151	2,692	11,349,098	2,514,810
1908	65,158,962	19,956,299	1,207	11,748,796	2,538,030

These quantities are undoubtedly too low since octroi posts do not exist at several towns.

The following table giving the consumption per head of alcoholic beverages has been compiled from the statistics of the Ministry of Finance, based on the customs house records :—

([1]) Sundstrom, *Unters: über d. Ernahrung d. Llandbevolkerung in Finland*, Helsingfors, 1908).

([2]) The traditional ideas in regard to the selection of food stuffs are not to be considered as condemned by the results of scientific research. The latter draws attention to the " psychic influences " which stimulate the digestive secretions (Pawloff).

ALCOHOLIC DRINKS—CONSUMPTION PER HEAD.
(1908).

TOWNS	WINES	CIDER	BEERS	SPIRITS	TOTAL
Paris	235 l.	2 l.	16 l.	4·44 l.	257·44 l.
Marseilles	180	,,	11	4·07	195·09
Lyons	205	,,	11	3·41	219·41
Bordeaux	255	,,	4	3·03	262·03
Lille	·31	1	338	4·42	374·42
Toulouse	265	,,	10	2·81	277·81
Saint-Etienne	318	,,	11	3·45	332·45
Nice	222	,,	16	2·76	240·76
Nantes	222	11	5	2·82	240·82
Le Havre	71	44	18	12·33	145·33
Roubaix	19	1	323	3·97	346·97
Rouen	75	113	13	12·30	213·30
Nancy	202	,,	85	2·87	289·87
Reims	165	6	51	4·72	226·72
Toulon	195	,,	8	4·63	207·63
Amiens	53	17	70	7·84	147·84
Limoges	247	4	7	2·39	260·39
Brest	107	7	17	5·78	136·78
Angers	173	7	4	2·74	186·74
Tourcoing	15	1	278	4·15	298·15
Nimes	308	,,	8	2·63	318·63
Montpellier	439	,,	7	2·82	448·82
Rennes	51	440	23	6·18	520·18
Dijon	174	,,	7	3·04	184·04
Grenoble	224	,,	10	2·90	236·90
Orléans	187	1	5	3·46	196·46
Tours..................	251	3	10	3·12	267·12
Calais	32	1	182	8·03	223·03
Le Mans	47	21	5	5·90	78·90
Saint-Denis	279	4	24	4·67	311·67
Levallois-Perret ...	264	4	16	4·48	288·48
Clermont-Ferrand	266	,,	12	3·35	281·35
Besancon	259	,,	31	3·67	293·67
Versailles	201	8	17	4·52	230·52
Troyes	215	7	20	4·09	246·09
Saint-Quentin ...	51	16	235	6·52	308·52
Béziers	439	,,	7	2·11	448·11
Boulogne-sur-Mer	42	5	177	11·64	235·64
Boulogne-sur-Seine	274	4	21	4·49	303·49
Avignon	196	,,	51	4·24	251·24
Lorient	96	92	6	6·36	200·36

ALCHOLIC DRINKS—CONSUMPTION PER HEAD.—*Continued.*

TOWNS	WINES	CIDER	BEERS	SPIRITS	TOTALS
Caen	66	92	6	11·48	175·48
Boruges...............	114	,,	4	2·68	120·68
Cherbourg............	13	125	4	8·50	150·50
Clichy	275	6	13	4·31	298·31
Neuilly-sur-Seine	194	3	19	3·59	219·59
Poitiers	219	,,	16·	2·20	237·20
Perpignan	340	,,	7	4·49	351·49
Dunkerque	36	1	291	7·05	335·05
Saint-Ouen	287	3	19	4·49	313·49
Angoulême	253	1	7	2·16	263·16
Rocheford............	200	1	5	2·58	208·58
Asnières	228	5	18	4·05	255·05
Montreuil-sous-Bois	269	2	12	4·01	287·01
Saint-Nazaire	277	15	8	5·15	305·15
Roanne	294	,,	5	2·48	301·48
Pau	228	,,	9	3·27	240·27
Belfort	227	,,	66	3·58	296·58
Montlucon	248	,,	8	2·13	258·13
Vincennes	219	3	20	3·60	245·60
Aubervilliers	286	3	20	5·03	314·03
Cette	226	,,	4	5,24	235·24
La Rochelle	246	,,	5	2·22	253·22
Le Creuzot	212	,,	9	4·43	225·43
Douai	46	1	482	5·27	534·27
Ivry-sur-Seine	289	,,	,,	4·34	293·34
Pantin	277	3	18	4·74	302·74
Valenciennes	47	2	476	4·60	529·60
Périgueux	249	2	4	2·31	257·31
Courbevoie	252	6	19	4·37	281·37
Carcassonne	390	,,	14	1·53	405·53

It is interesting to note that, according to M. Jacques Bertillon [1] who has examined the statistics for many years, the consumption of spirits in France has grown steadily less since 1901. The demand for wine has, however, increased. These changes are more noticeable in the case of the larger towns. Cider and beer do not seem to take the place of spirits in the same way that wine does.

[1] Jacques Bertillon (*La Presse Médicale* of 18th Nov., 1911, p. 937).

The explanation of this decrease in the consumption of spirits is to be found in the law passed on December 29th, 1900, by which the tax on spirits was raised from 156·25 francs to 220 francs per hectolitre. Thus legislation introduced, not from motives of national hygiene, but simply as a means of raising revenue, has had the welcome and beneficial result of decreasing the consumption of spirits. The curves in fig. 309 show the variations in consumption of spirits and of wine respectively per head per annum in the City of Troyes from the year 1885 to 1910.

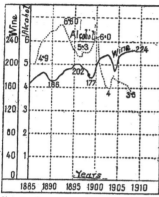

Fig. 309.

Consumption in litres per head per year of wine and spirits in the city of Troyes.

Statistics show that the same result has taken place in many other towns. Also, as will be seen from the tables, the consumption of spirits is smaller in those towns where much wine is drunk, but not in those where beer and cider are the chief beverages (Dunkirk, Rennes, etc.).

Those who are engaged in combating alcoholism can gain useful practical lessons from the above data. Diminution of alcoholic consumption and improvement of food hygiene are vital factors in our national prosperity.

344. Human Strength.—The power which man can exert is necessarily a variable quantity. The manifestations of muscular activity are manifold, and its duration variable, and discontinuous.

Under the most favourable circumstances 300,000 kilogrammetres of work can be effected in a working day of 8 hours. The power per second is therefore :

$$\frac{300,000}{8 \times 3,600} = 10\cdot4 \text{ kgm. per second.}$$

This is about $\frac{1}{7}$ of a horse-power.

Increase in the duration of work leads to reduced power. Atwater found that the above figure could only be attained with the very greatest difficulty over a period of 16 hours, and that the power generally fell to $\frac{1}{10}$ H.P.

In the case of an Alpinist in first-class physical condition Jules Lefèvre [1] calculated that he could exert as much as $\frac{1}{4}$ H.P.

---

[1] Jules Lefèvre, *Bioénergétique* (*loc. cit.*, p. 801).

in climbing. This figure, however, seems to the writer to be altogether excessive.

By reducing the duration of the work the power exerted can be increased. Thus a man lifted a weight of 12·24 kg. to a height of 71·465 metres in 145 seconds by means of a rope and pulley. This gives as the power exerted

$$\frac{12·24 \times 71·465}{145} = \tfrac{1}{7} \text{ H.P.}(^1)$$

A wood sawyer made to 200 working strokes of the saw in 145 seconds. The length of each stroke was ·487 metres and the equivalent effort 12·24 kg. at the end of the time the workman was in a somewhat breathless condition, and certainly could not have continued to work at this rate for more than three minutes without a rest. The power exerted in the working strokes was

$$\frac{·487 \times 12·24 \times 200}{145} = 8·22 \text{ kgm.}$$

Adding the power exerted in the return strokes the total was about 12·5 kgm. equivalent to $\tfrac{1}{8}$ H.P.

A man weighing 65·1 kg. raised himself to a height of 20·15 metres in 34 seconds, and at the end of this time was quite out of breath. The power developed, which can easily be estimated amounted to

$$\frac{55·1 \times 20·15}{34} = 41·16 \text{ kgm.}$$

This is slightly over $\tfrac{1}{2}$ H.P., and is the highest value which has been recorded. The period of time was, however, very short.

M. Lefèvre calculated the power exerted in a climb of two hours up a mountain as ·45 H.P.

Many other calculations of the power of man could be given. They would, however, only prove that the human motor has no intrinsic power, but that its power capacity is the resultant of the numerous factors and variables which must occur in daily work. The power which can be developed for very short periods is a matter of but little practical importance. In the same way the speed of a runner in a sprint race of 100 metres may reach a rate of 33 kilometres per hour (the average of some of the best short distance runners shows that the 100 metres is covered in 11 seconds, which is a speed of 32·73 km. per hour). Long distance races of 40 and 100 kilometres, such as the "Marathon" race are tests of endurance. The best time on record for 40 km. was 9,330 seconds, a speed of 16 km. per hour approximately. (H. Siret at Paris, August 27th, 1911) ; 100 km. has been covered (by Littlewood in 1884 and Jack in 1909) in nine hours, which

---

(^{1}) Amontons (*Mem. Acad. Roy. Sciences*, 1703, p. 100).

gives a speed of 11 km. per hour. In a walking race held in May, 1912, the course being 765 kilometres, with periodical rests of 24 hours, Orphe walked at a mean rate of 10 km. per hour and covered nearly 85 km. per diem.

The speed of the athlete is sometimes very regular. Thus Jean Bouin (age 24, weight 69 kg) covered 9·72 km. in 30 minutes, and the speed 19·44 km. per hour was found by careful measurements at frequent intervals to be practically uniform.

In various athletic exercises the power developed for very short periods is remarkably high. No attention need be paid to feats of strength, real or apparent, as so much depends on skill and experience in the adoption of proper bodily attitudes.

We may conclude this department of the subject by repeating that in prolonged work, a man can at the very most exert $\frac{1}{7}$ H.P., and we may repeat that the power of the human body is greatly conditioned by the proper proportioning of the working periods to the periods of rest.

GENERAL CONCLUSIONS.

345. Comparison of Various Motors.[1]—The human motor is probably an "*electro-capillary*" engine in which nervous excitation modifies the superficial tension and produces contraction (Lippmann & D'Arsonval). The nature of the nervous agent and the origin of human motive power are, however, veiled in obscurity.

The power of man, approximately ¼ H.P., is very small compared with other motors, but the efficiency is good. An input of 8 small calories produces about 1 kilogrammetre of work which is an efficiency of 30%

$$\frac{1}{\cdot 008 \times 425.}$$

The human motor can develop, on the average, 300,000 kgm. per diem. The equivalent dynamic expenditure is $300,000 \times .008 = 2,400$ great calories. Adding the expenditure when at rest, 2,340 Calories, we get a total of 4740 Calories.

A good steam engine would require about 1 kg. of fuel to do the above work, about double the consumption of the human motor.

The life of the human motor is greater than that of any inanimate prime mover, which latter is at most 20 years, unless repairs and renewals have been frequently effected. The human motor, on the other hand, until old age sets in, is capable of continuous self-repair. Also a suspension of nutrition does not cause an immediate stoppage, for it can draw on its "alimentary reserves." Further, within limits, it is capable of improvement, while the efficiency of an inanimate machine is at its best when it is new.

Experience and skill are factors capable of growth and improvement.

Lastly, the control of the human motor is *internal*. It conforms to those unseen needs, generally organic, from which are derived the principles of its conservation. Hence work under natural conditions gives the greatest economy of effort making good the wastage of energy by the more perfect adaptation of bodily motion. which is capable of almost infinite flexibility.

Inanimate motors cannot approach the human motor in this latter quality.

---

[1] *Vide* Reyer's interesting work *Kraft*, 2nd Edition, p. 251, Leipzig, 1909.

The efficiency of the human motor confirms this statement. Its superiority would be decisive were there not other considerations in its applications in industry. such as speed, power, and the work done in a given time, also the high cost of human food and the question of health. This latter consideration, however, introduces no disadvantage if the work is intelligently supervised and properly graduated. (Electric motors, which have efficiencies of over 90% in the larger sizes, are not prime movers, but simply convert one form of energy into another).

Man is indeed a valuable machine, which can be utilised in any position and immediately, so long as his fuel (food) can be supplied, also he can himself win this fuel from the earth on which he lives.

The economical employment of human labour should be the constant care of our captains of industry, the officers of our army, and our Colonists, who exploit the labour of the indigenous natives (the writer's investigations in North Africa showed that the natives of Morocco are stronger than those of other districts).

The maintenance of the human machine is as difficult and important a matter as the maintenance of any inorganic motor, We must do our best to eliminate all internal and external conditions tending to cause depreciation. Especially must physiological discomfort be avoided, and removed, as far as possible. In the due proportion of effort and speed, in industrial labour, lies the key to intensive production and the well-being of the workman.

346. The Organisation of Human Labour.—The knowledge of tne basic principles governing human labour has to-day reached a pitch which was undreamed of twenty years ago. Scientific methods can now replace the " rule of thumb " methods and the " tricks of the trade " which were formerly handed down from one generation to another, and of which the knowledge was jealously confined within the bounds of the various branches of handicraft, and even to families. These scientific principles can be applied to workers of any sex, age, and strength. Further, they give due weight to the intellectual factor in industrial occupations. Man is indeed an automatic engine, but science can improve its working, and can exhibit its beneficent effects in increased wages, and improved bodily health.

The workman cannot, by trial and error, discover for himself the most favourable conditions for the work which he has to do. These are only to be found by painstaking and careful experiment. Thus Taylor's classic researches in the engineering trades involved 25 years' work, and cost a million francs.[1] The best

---

[1] Henry Le Chatelier, Preface to Taylor's *Principles of Workshop Organization*; also *Tech. Mod.*, June 15th, 1913.

results, in any industrial operation, are only to be attained by accurate time records of the various motions involved, and by careful selection of those which are useful, and the elimination of those which are useless.

Taylor's system, however, does not give sufficient weight to the physiological factors. The writer, on the other hand, has endeavoured to emphasise these. The true interest of industry lies, not in the realisation of the maximum output, irrespective of the health of the worker, but to conserve and husband human energy in the interest, both of employer and employed. Therefore a strict observance of the principles laid down by Chauveau must supplement the methods of Taylor.

Organisation on these lines cannot fail to be financially beneficial, and to turn to full account the mental and physical energies of the six million male, and three million female workers in the seventy-one industries of France, who represent 24% of our total population.[1] If we add our soldiers and sailors, our employers and their staffs, we may say that the social efficiency of at least half the population can be improved.[2]

Apprenticeship, as has been shown by the experiments in the use of the file, is particularly susceptible to the benefits of scientific control. Its neglect, in such cases, is almost criminal. Even in the domain of sport the following strong remark has been made by Lieut. Hebert : In some cases the body is required to exert efforts quite beyond its power, which cause rapid depreciation ; in other cases, the efforts called for are so small that its powers are but partially utilised.[3]

The problem of the best utilisation of human strength is of particular importance in the Army. We have only to refer to the results attained in the German Infantry. Mosso made the trenchant remark that " the catastrophe of Sedan represents in history the triumph of German legs." [4]

347. The Universality and Utility of the Science of Work.— We see, therefore, that physiological mechanics, the science of human energetics, has a very wide field. It satisfies Aristotle's aphorism, " every true science is universal," although the general public do not yet appreciate this. When Gilbreth's *Motion Study* was first published, it was thought that its principle were only applicable to Building Construction. It was only at a later date that the applicability of his principles and methods to all branches of industry was recognised. Gilbreth's first article in Robert Kent's publication, *Industrial Engineering,*

[1] Census of March 4th, 1906 (*Ministere du Travail*, 1911, p. 210).
[2] Reyer, *loc. cit.*, p. 400.
[3] G. Hébert, *Le Code de la Force*, p. 11 ; Paris, Laveur, 1911.
[4] A. Mosso, *Les Exercises Physiques*, p. 56 (*loc. cit.*).

passed almost unnoticed. The second article, however, elicited inquiries from boot and shoe manufacturers, printers, bookbinders and several other trades. It was these inquiries, as Kent says, which convinced Gilbreth and himself that the system set forth was of real value and of general application.[1] Taylor, in conjunction with Sanford Thompson, a brilliant mathematician, made an exhaustive analysis of several classes of labour. Stonemasons' work, Bricklaying, Concrete-Construction, Excavation, Stone-quarrying, Carpentry, etc.

The art of working rests, therefore, on a firm basis of scientific fact. It lends itself admirably to industry. It rapidly developes the apprentice into the skilled workman, and has great educational value. It also makes for initiative and co-operation in the workshop.

We must, however, again repeat that the objection to Taylor's system is that it failed to give due weight to the question of fatigue. All that Taylor tells us is that he never had any serious accidents due to over-fatigue amongst the workers under his control. Must not this, however, be attributed to selection?

Taylor also remarked that the demand for manual labour was so great that no man need be out of work for more than a day or two, hence the least efficient workers were no worse off than they were before. On the other hand, the efficient workmen had now the opportunity of drawing big wages and making adequate provision for their families.

In regard to wages, Taylor said that these should exceed the rates current at that time by the following percentages :—

Ordinary unskilled labour, 30% ; labour requiring little intelligence, but considerable muscular strength and exertion, 50% to 60% ; work requiring no great physical exertion, but demanding special intelligence, skill and sustained attention, 70% to 80% ; work requiring the combination of both skill and intelligence and strength, 80% to 100%.

Taylor remarked that men will not do their best unless they are assured of an adequate and continuous wage, and he made the trenchant observation that the limitation of output must tend, in the long run, to reduce wages.

In truth, it is an incredible thing that there should exist a science able to restrain or suppress the waste of human energy, and that its sovereignty is not yet extended to all its domains, that its beneficial power is not employed to the profit of society and to the advantage of the workers. Yet war employs scientific principles in fighting and forces man to produce his maximum

[1] Preface to *Motion Study*, p. 13.

output, and sports (fencing, boxing, gymnastics) are carried out on the same principles.

We must never forget that the battle of life is essential to humanity. Let us, therefore, assure to the worker the largest possible yield for his labour, so that he can both live in comfort and security, and also give value to those who employ him. Let us also watch over his health and organise " social hygiene."

Strong nations do not suffer from the scourges of alcoholism and tuberculosis to the degree that we suffer. They do not trouble about hydropathy or Swedish gymnastics, but find a growing energy in a healthy and active existence. They find a new strength in the work of each day.

Taylor's system, supplemented by due consideration to physiological conditions, and applied patiently, wisely and tactfully, gives a scientific solution of the social problems of industry, the relations between capital and labour. Its principles must be accepted, and its practice applied, because it is, as has been finely put by one of our great writers, the function of science " to throw across the clouds of to-day the rainbow of the peace of to-morrow." [1]

---

[1] Frederic Winslow Taylor was born in 1856 at Germann Town, Pa. He rose from an apprentice to be Chief Engineer to the Midvale Steel Co. The system, which was the result of his experience and observations both as workman and manager, had a long struggle against prejudice and " rule of thumb." He had to meet the opposition of socialists and syndicalists, and even of economists, who had their own systems to further. Thus Admiral John Edwards, while realizing the educational value of Taylor's system, considered it far too complicated (*Journal American Society of Naval Engineers*, May, 1912).

No critic has, however, been able to confute the principles which Taylor laid down (except, in so far as Taylor's neglect of the physiological conditions of labour is concerned): Schuchart (*Technik und Wirtschaft*, January, 1913) has demonstrated the value of Taylor's methods in the evolution of the workman and the development of his individuality and initiative.

THE END.

INDEX.

A.

Acapnie, 246
Acceleration, 2, 5, 31
Acid, Butyric, 148, 219
— Lactic, 205
Acidity, Muscular, 205, 209
Acoustic field, Influence of, 258, 259
Adrenalin, 210
Age, Influences of, 108, 222
— Co-efficients of, 309, 468
Air, Composition of, 227
— Resistance of, 240, 241
— Compressed, 250, 251
Albumenoids, 136–8, 143, 467, 472
Albumen, 146, 158
Alcaloids, Nervine aliments, 147–50, 218, 219
— Toxic, 253
Alcohol, 148, 472–5
— Food-value, 215–7
— Toxic effects, 217, 218
— Consumption of, 456–9
Alimentation, 132 seq.
Aliments, Classification 135–8
— Composition, 139–141
— Calorific equivalents, 143–7
— Nervine, 147–50
— Statistics of, 309, 451–6
Amphiarthroses, 102
Angle of friction, 55
— of torsion, 65
Anisotropic bodies, 66
Anthropometric measurements, 108 seq., 270–6
Apprenticeship, 392, 420–2, 480
Aptitude, natural, 108, 206, 224
Arborization, Terminal, 94
Areas, Measurements of, 289–93
Arms, Action of, 301 seq., 399 seq.
Arterial pressure, 201
Articulation of the body, 23
86 seq., 102–7, 129
Assimilation, 138
Atmosphere, 227, 228
— Pressure of, 245 seq.
Atom, Definition of, 25
Atmosphere, Properties of, 227–32
— Effects of, 241, 245–52
Aviation, Its physiological effects, 247–9
Axis of rotation, 12, 14, 107

B.

Barometer, 244, 319
Base of support, 28, 334–41
Baths, Effects of, 243
Beverages, 215–9, 456–9
Bicycle, Experimental, 155, 189, 190, 294
— Frictional resistance of, 304
— Work of, 452
Body, Human, 85–116
— Composition of, 85–91
— Dimensions of, 107–113
— Strength of, 91–101
— Measurements of, 108–113, 270–276
— Weight of, 113–116, 276
Bones, 86 seq.
— Strength of, 92, 93
Boxing, 340, 439
Brachysoles, 111
Bricklayers' work, 440–5
Bust, Proportions of, 110, 111
Butyric Acid, 148, 219

C.

Cabrouet, see Wheelbarrow
Capstan, 75, 303
Calorimetric Chamber, 150–2, 294, 323
Calorie, 44, 83
Calorimeters, 47, 136
Carbo-hydrates, 135 seq.
Cardiograph, 201, 263, 321
Carnot, Principle of, 47–9
Cartilages, 98, 122
Cellular Excitants, 135
Centre of Gravity, 26–8, 33
— Of the human body, 342 seq.
Chauveau, Formulæ of, 167–174
Chronographs, 266–8
Chronophotography, 11, 169, 341, 350, 358, 369, 370, 393
Chyle, 146 (footnote)
Classification of human beings, 108, 225, 414, 439
Climate, Influence of, 227–31
Clothing, 232–6
— Conductivity of, 324–7
Cocoa, 148, 219
Coffee, 148, 219
Colloids, 85

Combustibles, vital, 132 *seq.*
Combustion, 47–51
— Vital, 132 *seq.*
Compression, 61
Condiments, Effects of, 219
Conduction, Heat, 228, 324
— Nervous, 119
Conservation of energy, 44 *seq.*, 150
Contraction, Muscular, 96, 119–124, 165 *seq.*
Convection, 155, 228
Circulation, Effects of work on, 201, 202
Circulatory action, 321
Cooling of bodies, 241 *seq.*
Corpulence, 114
Corpuscles, Red, 138, 245
Cosine, Definition of, 4
— Directing, 7, 18
Coulomb, Co-efficient of, 65
Couple of Forces, 22
Curare, 96
Cycloid, 14

D.

Darkness, Influence of, 254
Dactylography, 304, 453
Death, 116
Density, Human body, 112 *seq.*
— of sea water, 243
Diaphysis, 87
Diastole, 201
Diathroses, 102
Dicrotism, 201
Digestibility, Co-efficient of, 136, 138
Disassimilation, 138
Dust, Influence of, 252–4
Dutch scoop, 302, 403
Dynamometers, 17, 189 *seq*, 277–282, 293 *seq.*
Dynamic expenditure, 143
Dynamics, Definition of, 1, 42,
— of the human body, 341 *seq.*
Dynamographic gangway, 283, 464
Dyspnœa, 201, 209

E.

Elasticity, 60–9, 101
Electricity, Physiological effects of, 256, 257
Embolism, 251
Energetic value of aliments, 132 *seq.*
Energy, Conservation of, 44 *seq.*, 150
— Measurement of, 308 *seq.*
Energetics, 42 *seq.*
Entropy, 48, 49
Environment, External, 227–60
— Internal, 215–26
Epicycloid, 14

Equilibrium, 19, 28
— Nutritive, 143
— of the human body, 334 *seq.*
Equivalence, Principle of, 44
Erg, 37, 83
Ergograph, 175–7, 192, 293 *seq.*
Ergograms, 175–7, 206–8
Ergometers, 294, 295
Errors in measurement, 261, 262
Esthiometer, 321, 322
Eudiometer, 315–8
Euler, Formulæ of, 181
Exchanges, Respiratory, 310 *seq.*
Excitants, Cellular, 134
Explosives, 133

F.

Falling bodies, Laws of, 2, 9, 31, 32
Fasting, 115, 220
Fats, 135 *seq.*
Fatigue, 79, 118, 171, 206–14
Fencing, 438
Fibres, Nervous, 99
— Muscular, 233
Fick, Experiments of, 157, 192
File, Experimnets with, 187, 284 *seq.* 404 *seq.*
Force, 16 *seq.*, 31 *seq.*
— Elastic, 61, 130
— Muscular, 125 *seq.*
Friction, Co-efficients of, 53–5, 329–331
Functional Adaptation of the muscles, 95, 101, 122, 126, 346
— of the cartilages, 122
— of the bones, 93
— of the respiration, 163

G.

Gasses, expired, Measurement of, 310–314
— Analysis of, 314–8
Gasses, Respiratory, 163, 199, 310 *seq.*
Geophagy, 135
Gilbreth, F., 180, 225, 260, 393, 397, 440 *seq.*
Glucose, 158 *seq.*
Glycerine, 216
Glycogen, 146, 158
Gravity, Centre of, 26–8, 33
— of the human body, 342 *seq.*
Gravitation, 17, 334
Growth of the body, 113–6, 142

H.

Hæmoglobin, 138, 247
Hearing, 222

Heat, 41 *seq.*, 150 *seq.*, 250 *seq.*, 324 *seq.*
— Value of foods, 135 *seq.*
— Effects of, 237, 254
Horse power, Definition of, 79
Human body, 85–116
— Composition of, 85–91
— Dimensions of, 107–13
— Strength of, 91–101
— Measurements of, 108–13, 270–276
— Weight of, 113–6, 276
Humidity, 237 *seq.*
Hunger, 115
Hygrometer, 313, 327 *seq.*
Hygrometric state, 237 *seq.*
Hypertrophy, Functional, 204
Hypocycloid, 14

I.

Inanition, 115, 220
Inertia, 16, 25, 78
— Intellectual, 213
— Moment of, 40, 41, 57, 348 *seq.*
Inclined plane, Ascent of, 364
— Descent of, 366
— Experiments on, 388 *seq.*
Instruction cards, 394, 445
Internal massage, 204
Irritability, 85
Isodynamics, 158 *seq.*
Isogluscosics, 158 *seq.*

J.

Joints, of the body, 90, 91
Jumping, 369–71

K.

Kinematics, 1, 2
Kola, 149, 219

L.

Lactic acid, 205
Laplace, Formula of, 244
Lavoisier, Ratio of, 203
Legs, Work of, 304 *seq.*
Le Chatelier, Law of, 48
Levers, 70 *seq.*, 86, 123
Light, Action of, 254–6
Liver, 140, 211
Loading of labourers, 169 *seq.*, 491 *seq.*
Locomotion, Human, 114, 333 *seq.*

M.

Machines, Inorganic, 70 *seq.*
— Human, 85 *seq.*
Macrosoles, 111
Marey's, Tambour, 10, 263

Marey's Dynamograph, 277, 293
— Experimental shoes, 282
Mason, Work of, 440 *seq.*
Mass of human body, 112, 113, 142
Massage, 204, 223
Mayer, Principle of, 44
Mechanics, General, 1 *seq.*
Meeh, Formulæ of, 113, 275
Metabolism, 133, 204 *seq.*
Metronome, 35, 266
Micella, 94
Microspirometer, 211
Mines, 250
Modulus, of rigidity, 61
— of torsion, 65
— Youngs, 61 *seq.*
Morphology, 225, 226
Mosso, Ergograph of, 175, 296 *seq.*
Myophone, 119
Myotome, 96, 223

N.

Negroes, 234, 256
Nerves, 99 *seq.*
Nervine aliments, 147 *seq.*
Newton, Laws of, 130, 322
Noise, Influence of, 222, 258
Nutritive equilibrium, 144

O.

Obesity, 113
Organisation of work, 463 *seq.*
Oscillometer, Pachon's, 202, 321
Ossein, 87
Oxygen, 138, 227, 245
— Method, 144 *seq.*, 309 *seq.*, 409 *seq.*

P.

Pachon's oscillometer, 202, 321
Parabola, 9, 182, 290, 342
Pedometer, 268
Pendulum, 34, 57, 353
Percussion, 55, 57, 303
Perimeter, Thoracic, 111, 274, 275
Perspiration, 151, 205, 238
Phosphorus, 205, 212
Photography of movements, 11 *seq.*, 359
Plane, Inclined, 364–6, 388
Planimeter, 291, 292
Pneumographs, 199 *seq.*, 263, 321
Poncelet, Formula of, 292
Poisson, Co-efficient of, 66
Poisons, Muscular, 209, 221
— Nervine, 217 *seq.*
Power, Human, 459–63
Proteids, 136–50, 309, 451–6
Protoplasm, 85, 137

R.

Radian, Definition of, 2
Radiant energy, 50
Radiation, 50, 153, 228, 254, 322
Radio-activity, 52
Rations, Alimentary, 185 *seq.*, 308, 451 *seq.*
Reactions, Tactile, visual, and auditory, 120
Reflex actions, 119
Renal force, 125
Resistance of solids, 60 *seq.*
— of liquids, 59, 243 *seq.*, 372
— of the human body, 91 *seq.*, 98 *seq.*
Resolution of movements and forces, 13, 17
Resonance, 465
Respiratory exchanges, 310 *seq.*
Respiration, 143, 163, 310 *seq.*,
— Quotient of, 145 *seq.*, 163, 183
Running, 367, 460

S.

Salts, Mineral, 134, 147, 148
Saw, Use of, 5, 301, 424
Screw jack, 303
Segment, Anthropometric, 114
Senile decay, 110
Senile diminution, 114
Sensibility, 86, 206, 213, 321
Sex, Influence of, 86, 109, 114, 126, 222
Shears, Use of, 283, 287, 288, 300, 301, 427
Shearing, 67
— of bones, 93
Shock, 55 *seq.*, 67-9, 258
Shoes, Experimental (Marey's), 282, 354
Sight, 222, 255
Similitude of machines, 130 *seq.*
Skeleton, 86 *seq.*
Sleep, Influence of, 223
Solar action, 254
Solvay Institute, 309, 453
Speaking, 447 *seq.*
Speed counters, 268, 269
Sphygmograph, 201, 263, 321
Statics of the human body, 334 *seq.*
Stearin, 158
Sun, Action of, 254
Surface of the body, 112, 113, 161, 275
Symphyses, 107

Synovia, 102
Systole, 201, 384

T.

Tambour, Marey's, 10, 263
Taylor, System of, 397, 439, 463 *seq.*
Tea, 147, 148, 218
Temperature, Absolute, 48
— of the human body, 86, 153 *seq.*, 206, 232
— Effects of, 227 *seq.*
Tendons, 98, 122, 337
Tension, Elastic, 68
— Surface, 20
— Vapour, 237, 327
Tetanus, 118, 128
Thermodynamics, 41 *seq.*
Thermogenisis, 80, 147, 215
Thinness, 113
Thoracic coefficient, 111
Time, Measurement of, 266 *seq.*
Timing of motions, 381, 397
Tobacco, Action of, 253
Torsion, 65, 92
Touch, 222
Traction, Co-efficient of, 55, 330, 331

V.

Valve, Respiratory, 144, 310
Vectors, 5 *seq.*
Ventilation, 200, 250
Vibration, Effects of, 259
Viscosity, 61, 67
Vital capacity, 111, 275, 310, 320, 384

W.

Wages, 226, 465
Water, Resistance of, 243
— Thermal properties of, 153 *seq.*, 243
Weight of the body, 113 *seq.*, 275, 336 *seq.*
Wheelbarrow, Use of, 279 *seq.*, 429 *seq.*
Woods, Toxic properties of, 252
— Working in, 427
Work, Measurement of, 294 *seq.*

Y

Yield, 80 *seq.*
— of the human machine, 254 *seq.*
Young, Modulus of, 61 *seq.*

Printed in the United States
by Baker & Taylor Publisher Services